Instructional Technology

Instructional Technology

Past, Present, and Future

2nd EDITION

Edited by
Gary J. Anglin
University of Kentucky

1995
LIBRARIES UNLIMITED, INC.
Englewood, Colorado

Stephen Haenel
Project Editor

Judy Gay Matthews
Production Advisor

Susan Brown
Copy Editor

Pamela J. Getchell
Proofreader

Kay Minnis
Typesetter

Lori Kranz
Proofreader

LIBRARIES UNLIMITED, INC.
P.O. Box 6633
Englewood, CO 80155-6633
1-800-237-6124

Library of Congress Cataloging-in-Publication Data

Instructional technology : past, present, and future / edited by Gary
   J. Anglin. -- 2nd ed.
      xix, 431 p. 19x26 cm.
      Includes bibliographical references and index.
      ISBN 1-56308-251-9
      1. Educational technology--United States.   I. Anglin, Gary J.
LB1028.3.I5652   1995
371-3'078--dc20   94-41385
                                                                CIP

To my daughter Robin,
authentic and lucid

Contents

Part 3
Instructional Development

Part 4
State of the Art, Applications, and Future Prospects

Part 5
Research and Evaluation

Part 6
Certification and Professional Development

Preface

This second edition of *Instructional Technology: Past, Present, and Future* provides a general introduction to the field of instructional design and technology. As was the previous edition, this book is designed to introduce graduate students to significant issues and professionals in the field. Anyone interested in current trends and issues in instructional design and technology will, I hope, find the book informative. Seven new chapters have been added addressing current topics including educational systems development and instructional systems development, postmodernism and instructional technology, interactive technologies, the Internet and higher education, qualitative research, and instructional technology and attitude change. Based on feedback from users of the first edition of the book, many of the chapters included in the first edition are also included in the second edition. There are many major contributors to the field who are not represented in the book. It was not possible to be exhaustive given the economy of book publishing.

ACKNOWLEDGMENTS

I wish to express my appreciation to colleagues who contributed chapters to the first edition and to this volume. The success of any edited book is a function of the quality of the individual authors. The expertise and support offered to me by Dr. David Loertscher and Mr. Stephen Haenel at Libraries Unlimited are also greatly appreciated.

A special note of acknowledgment is given to my daughter Robin, who through her influence and presence offers more than she receives.

Contributors

Dee H. Andrews
Naval Training Equipment Center
Orlando, Florida 32792, USA

Gary J. Anglin
College of Education
University of Kentucky
Lexington, Kentucky 40506-0001, USA

Donna J. Baumbach
Instructional Technology Resource Center
University of Central Florida
Orlando, Florida 32816, USA

Ann K. Bednar
Eastern Michigan University
Ann Arbor, Michigan 48103, USA

Barry Bratton
College of Education
University of Iowa
Iowa City, Iowa 52242, USA

Marjorie A. Cambre
College of Education
The Ohio State University
Columbus, Ohio 43210, USA

Richard E. Clark
University of Southern California
Los Angeles, California 90007, USA

William Coscarelli
College of Education
Southern Illinois University
Carbondale, Illinois 62901, USA

David M. Crossman
School of Education
University of Pittsburgh
Pittsburgh, Pennsylvania 15260, USA

Josephine Csete
College of Education
Michigan State University
East Lansing, Michigan 48824, USA

Donald Cunningham
School of Education
Indiana University
Bloomington, Indiana 47405, USA

Marcy P. Driscoll
College of Education
Florida State University
Tallahassee, Florida 32306, USA

Thomas M. Duffy
School of Education
Indiana University
Bloomington, Indiana 47405, USA

Donald P. Ely
School of Education
Syracuse University
Syracuse, New York 13244-2340, USA

Wellesley R. Foshay
The Roach Organization, Inc.
Schaumburg, Illinois 60173, USA

Keith P. Garland
The Arthur Anderson Worldwide
    Organization
St. Charles, Illinois 60174, USA

Cass G. Gentry
College of Education
Michigan State University
East Lansing, Michigan 48824, USA

Ludwika A. Goodson
L. R. O'Neall and Associates, Ltd.
Tallahassee, Florida 32301, USA

Scott Grabinger
School of Education
University of Colorado at Denver
Denver, Colorado 80204-5300, USA

Barbara L. Grabowski
College of Education
Pennsylvania State University
University Park, Pennsylvania 16802, USA

Stephen J. Guynn
Research, Evaluation and Testing
    Department
Indianapolis Public Schools
Indianapolis, Indiana 46204, USA

Kathleen McDermott Hannafin
Center for Educational Technology
Florida State University
Tallahassee, Florida 32306, USA

Michael J. Hannafin
Center for Instructional Development and
    Services
Florida State University
Tallahassee, Florida 32301-4829, USA

Wallace H. Hannum
University of North Carolina
Chapel Hill, North Carolina 27514, USA

Robert Heinich
2214 Wimbleton Lane
Bloomington, Indiana 47401, USA

Denis Hlynka
Faculty of Education
University of Manitoba
Winnipeg, Manitoba, CANADA R3T 2N2

Robert E. Holloway
Center for Excellence in Education
Northern Arizona University
Flagstaff, Arizona 86011-5774, USA

Joseph A. Hutchinson
Division of Instructional Support and
    Development
Louisiana State University
Baton Rouge, Louisiana 70803, USA

Jane B. Johnsen
College of Education
Ohio University
Lancaster, Ohio 43130, USA

David H. Jonassen
College of Education
Pennsylvania State University
University Park, Pennsylvania 16802, USA

Edward Kifer
Department of Educational Policy Studies
    and Evaluation
University of Kentucky
Lexington, Kentucky, USA

Gary R. Morrison
College of Education
University of Memphis
Memphis, Tennessee 38152, USA

Jacqueline K. O'Dell
College of Education
University of Arkansas
Fayetteville, Arkansas, 72701 USA

Jason Ohler
Educational Technology Program
University of Alaska Southeast
Juneau, Alaska 99801-8671, USA

J. David Perry
Learning Resources
Indiana University
Bloomington, Indiana 47405, USA

Dennis Pett
R. R. 2, Box 120
Brattleboro, Vermont 05301, USA

Pauline M. Rankin
Division of Instructional Support and
    Development,
Louisiana State University
Baton, Rouge, Louisiana 70833, USA

Charles M. Reigeluth
School of Education
Indiana University
Bloomington, Indiana, 47405, USA

Robert A. Reiser
College of Education
Florida State University
Tallahassee, Florida 32306, USA

Rhonda S. Robinson
Leadership and Educational Policy Studies
Northern Illinois University
DeKalb, Illinois 60115-2866, USA

Alexander J. Romiszowski
School of Education
Syracuse University
Syracuse, New York 13244, USA

Steven M. Ross
College of Education
University of Memphis
Memphis, Tennessee 38152, USA

Allison Rossett
College of Education
San Diego State University
San Diego, California 92182, USA

David F. Salisbury
College of Education
Florida State University
Tallahassee, Florida 32306, USA

Harold Scharlatt
Training and Development Associates, Inc.
3608 Burcham Way
Lexington, Kentucky 40515-1207, USA

Shirl S. Schiffman
School of Education
University of Virginia
Charlottesville, Virginia 22903, USA

Richard A. Schwier
College of Education
University of Saskatchewan
Saskatoon, Saskatchewan, CANADA
   S7N0W0

Sharon A. Shrock
College of Education
Southern Illinois University
Carbondale, Illinois 62901, USA

Michael Simonson
College of Education
Iowa State University
Ames, Iowa 50011, USA

Michael J. Streibel
School of Education
University of Wisconsin
Madison, Wisconsin 53706, USA

Brenda M. Sugrue
Information Systems Division
National Institute for Higher Education
Limerick, IRELAND

William D. Taylor
College of Education
The Ohio State University
Columbus Ohio, 43210, USA

1

Educational Technology

A Question of Meaning

Cass G. Gentry

College of Education, Michigan State University
East Lansing, Michigan

Members of the profession recognize that while educational technology is a dynamic emerging field, it is, sadly, still seeking definition. In the relatively short period of its evolution, the field of educational technology has taken on a surprisingly wide range of meanings. This has resulted in some confusion about purposes and boundaries of the field. The writing of this article was motivated by the notion that putting these meanings into a more structured perspective might assist both experienced and novice practitioners in developing a clearer view of educational technology.

The following sections present a sampling of meanings for educational technology and for some related terms. While these meanings have been grouped according to a few basic questions, only brief commentary is offered with the thought that the greater value lies in analysis by individual practitioners. As a target for further speculation, a personal view of what the author has come to think educational technology should mean is presented in the last section. References to the meanings used are provided at the end of the article for the benefit of anyone wishing to study the meanings in their original context.

If the study of these meanings has no more benefit than to help educational technologists explain to their respective spouses, children, relatives, and friends "what it is that we do for a living," then the time taken should be well spent!

Reprinted from *Educational media and technology yearbook 1987*. Littleton, CO: Libraries Unlimited.

WHAT IS TECHNOLOGY?

Technology, the root word of interest, is almost as confused in the public mind as *educational or instructional technology* is in that of the profession. The representative meanings that follow bridge several interpretations, including some from education.

1. "Technology is a rational discipline designed to assure the mastery of man over physical nature, through the application of scientifically determined laws" (Simon, 1983, p. 173).

2. "Technology, in its concrete, empirical meaning, refers fundamentally to systems of rationalized control over large groups of men, events, and machines by small groups of technically skilled men operating through an organized hierarchy" (McDermott, 1981, p. 142).

3. Paul Saettler, a well-known historian of instructional technology, states, "The word technology (the Latin form is 'texere,' to weave or construct) does not necessarily imply the use of machines, as many seem to think, but refers to 'any practical art using scientific knowledge.' This practical art is termed by the French sociologist Jacques Ellul, as 'technique.' He believes that 'it is the machine which is now entirely dependent upon technique, and the machine represents only a small part of technique. Not only is the machine the result of a certain technique, but also its instructional applications are made possible by technique. Consequently, the relation of behavioral science to instructional technology, parallels that of the physical sciences to engineering technology, or the biological sciences to medical technology' " (Saettler, 1968, pp. 5-6).

4. The renowned educational technologist, James Finn, defined technology by saying, "In addition to machinery, technology includes processes, systems, management and control mechanisms both human and non-human, and ... a way of looking at the problems as to their interest and difficulty, the feasibility of technical solutions, and the economic values—broadly considered—of those solutions" (Finn, 1960, p. 10).

5. In contrasting science and technology, Admiral Hyman Rickover, the father of the nuclear submarine and a self-proclaimed critic of education, stressed, as reported by Knezevich and Eye, "that science should not be confused with technology. Science dwells on 'discovering true facts and relationships of observable phenomena in nature, and with established theories that serve to organize masses of verified data concerning those facts and relationships.' In contrast, he declared, 'technology cannot claim the authority of science,' for technology deals with 'tools, techniques, procedures: the artifacts and processes fashioned by modern industrial man to increase his powers of mind and body.' He then added that the 'methods of science require rigorous exclusion of the human factor,' for 'the searcher for truth cannot pay attention to his own or other people's likes or dislikes, or to popular ideas of the fitness of things.' On the other hand, since 'technology is action' rather than the pure thought that is science, technology may be potentially dangerous, if it is allowed to disregard human considerations" (Knezevich & Eye, 1970, p. 17).

WHAT IS THE ROLE OF TECHNOLOGY IN EDUCATION?

If one agrees with the meanings of technology just presented, it is clear that technology by definition is a major component of all human activities. Therefore, it is not a question of "having technology or not having technology," but rather what role it is allowed to play in human activities. That question has been the subject of study for a number of prestigious groups and individuals, as follows.

1. Herbert Simon views technology as man's way of interfacing between the in (natural) and outer (artificial) environments (Simon, 1969, p. 9).

2. The Carnegie Commission concluded that: "technology should be the servant and not the master of instruction. It should not be adopted merely because it exists, or because an institution fears that it will be left behind the parade of progress without it. We also believe that sophisticated technology is not to be equated with saturation. In some courses, the use of technology may be appropriate for a few hours in an entire term. In a few, technology may be constructively used for two-thirds of the hours allotted for a term of instruction; in a very few, it may take over the entire process" (Carnegie Commission on Higher Education, 1972, p. 11).

3. There are a considerable number of writings that discuss technological inventions that affect education. The following examples make the point.

    a) "The alphabet provided the intellectual means for expressing, recording, and preserving the knowledge of mankind. The invention of paper and the refinement of writing instruments reinforced and made more practical the process of recording information with alphabetic symbols. The book [may be defined as] a 'series of paper-based levers of varying sizes which can be bound together, within a hard or soft cover, and organized for the purpose of presenting information in a sequential manner.' In short, the book, like TV and the computer can be viewed from the mechanical aspects as separate from its substantive content. Movable type (Gutenberg) made [it] possible to have the written word within reach of the common man. The blackboard was one of the first joint communication devices that permitted teacher and student to view the same flexible referent at the same time. The school bus influenced the way pupils were organized for learning even in the most isolated areas" (Knezevich & Eye, 1970, pp. 19-22).

    b) Engler views technology as being inextricably related to education. He states, "If we view the ecology of education as the web of relationships between and among learners, teachers, and the environment in which they operate, then it becomes apparent that these relationships are large defined by the prevailing technology of instruction" (Engler, 1972, p. 62).

    c) Professor Robert Heinich of Indiana University raises an interesting question about the relationship of teachers to educational technology, when he says: "Peter Drucker's largely misunderstood quote states that:

'Learning and teaching are going to be more deeply affected by the new availability of information than any other area of human life. There is a great need for a new approach, new methods, and new tools in teaching, man's oldest and most reactionary craft. There is a great need for a rapid increase in learning. There is above all, great need for methods that will make the teacher effective, and multiply his or her efforts and competence. Teaching is in fact, the only traditional craft in which we have not yet fashioned the tools that make an ordinary person capable of superior performance.'

I say misunderstood, because most educators, after reading the Drucker quote, will nod their heads and automatically assume that he is asking for means to increase the effectiveness of the 'classroom' teacher. Not at all. What he is asking for is a technology of instruction that can make an ordinary person capable of superior performance and a means, either printed or electronic, to distribute that instruction" (Heinich, 1970, p. 56).

WHAT IS EDUCATIONAL TECHNOLOGY?

Now that something is known about the roots of educational technology and its role in education, one can ask the more difficult question, What is it? From the following attempts it is possible to see that meaning depends considerably on what part of the elephant is being touched and by whom!

1. The National Academy of Engineering's Instructional Technology Committee on Education defines educational technology as the "body of knowledge resulting from the application of the science of teaching and learning to the real world of the classroom, together with the tools and methodologies developed to assist in these applications" (Dieuzeide, 1971, p. 1).

2. Educational technology "is concerned with the overall methodology and set of techniques employed in the application of instructional principles" (Cleary et al., 1976).

3. Educational technology "involves the applications of systems, techniques, and aids to improve the process of human learning.... It is characterized by four features in particular: the definition of objectives to be achieved by the learner; the application of principles of learning to the analysis and structuring of the subject matter to be learned; the selection and use of appropriate media for presenting material; and the use of the appropriate methods of assessing student performance to evaluate the effectiveness of courses and materials" (Collier et al., 1971, p. 16).

4. Two conceptions of educational technology (ET) presented by Silverman are relative ET, which focuses on both procedures and devices, and constructive ET, which focuses on analyzing instructional problems, constructing and selecting evaluation instruments, and on production techniques and devices, all in terms of reaching desired outcomes (Silverman, 1968, p. 3).

5. Educational technology "is a complex, integrated process involving people, procedures, ideas, devices and organization, for analyzing problems, and devising, implementing, evaluating and managing solutions to those problems, involved in all aspects of human learning" (AECT Task Force, 1977, p. 164).

WHAT IS INSTRUCTIONAL TECHNOLOGY?

A term often used interchangeably with educational technology, instructional technology (IT) presents refinements not found in meanings of educational technology.

1. The Commission on Instructional Technology defines IT in two ways: (1) as "the media born of the communications revolution which can be used for instructional purposes along side the teacher, textbook, and blackboard," and (2) as "a systematic way of designing, carrying out, and evaluating the total process of learning and teaching in terms of specific objectives, based on research in human learning and communications, and employing a combination of human and nonhuman resources to bring about more effective instruction" (Commission on Instructional Technology, 1970, p. 19).

2. David Engler, who has studied meanings of IT, tells us it is defined in two rather different ways, "First, and most commonly, it is defined as hardware—television, motion pictures, audiotapes and discs, textbooks, blackboards, and so on; essentially these are the implements and media of communication. Second, and more significantly, it is defined as a process by means of which we apply the research findings of the behavioral sciences to the problems of instruction. Defined either way, instructional technology is value free. Gutenberg technology, as an example, can produce the *Bible, Mein Kampf,* and *Portnoy's Complaint,* with equal indifference" (Engler, 1972, p. 59).

3. Saettler thinks that the physical science concept of instructional technology "usually means the application of physical science and engineering technology, such as motion picture projectors, tape recorders, television, teaching machines (including the computer), for group (or individual) presentation of instructional materials" (p. 2). The behavioral science concept of instructional technology, on the other hand, suggests that "educational practice should be more dependent on the methods of science as developed by behavioral scientists in the broad areas of psychology, anthropology, sociology, and in the more specialized areas of learning, group processes, language and linguistics, communications, administration, cybernetics, perception, and psychometrics. Moreover, this concept includes the application of engineering research and development (including human factors engineering) and branches of economics and logistics related to the effective utilization of instructional personnel, buildings (learning spaces), and the new computerized machine systems such as data processing and information retrieval" (Saettler, 1968, pp. 4-5).

4. Instructional technology is made up of "the 'things of learning,' the devices and the materials which are used in the processes of learning and teaching" (Armsey & Dahl, 1973, p. vii).

5. Instructional technology is "an effort with or without machines, available or utilized, to manipulate the environment of individuals in the hope of generating a change in behavior or other learning outcome" (Knezevich & Eye, 1970, p. 16).

6. An instructional technologist is a team member who "is a specialist in the learning process. His or her job is to help faculty members define the objectives of courses of instruction, to plot the learning strategies to be employed, and to evaluate results" (Carnegie Commission on Higher Education, 1972, p. 71).

7. A summary by the Commission on Instructional Technology states that the purpose of instructional technology is "to make education more productive and more individual, to give instruction a more scientific base, and to make instruction more powerful, learning more immediate, and access more equal" (Tickton, 1971, p. 32).

WHAT ARE THE APPLICATIONS OF TECHNOLOGY?

In discussing the levels of useful applications and their promise, the commentary runs from the pessimistic to the optimistic: "We pays our money and takes our choices" (or is that chances?).

1. In describing the state of educational technology in 1972, Engler said that "the most accurate statement that one can make about our present (instructional) methods is that they are old technology. The basic media of instruction, such as textbooks, chalkboards, and teachers, have been used for many years. Today, teachers are better prepared, textbooks are better written and better designed, and chalkboards have changed color, but their functions and their relationships to learners have not changed essentially in over one hundred years. Moreover, the process by means of which instruction is carried on has not changed in any fundamental respect during this period. It remains teacher-centered, group-oriented, and textbook-based.... Its prototype was the Lancastrian model of large-group instruction which developed and spread in Britain and the United States in the nineteenth century; and while this model has undergone many modifications over the past century and a half, the general configuration of mass production education remains fundamental to this technology (derived from the impact of an industrial society on the role and methods of education)" (Engler, 1972, p. 61).

2. Clifford H. Block, of the U.S. Agency for International Development, comments on the mammoth experiment with distance education technology by the British government. "By using television, radio, and the post, the production skill of the BBC, the instructional design skill of its superb educational technology group, and the content expertise of a first rate faculty, the British Open University has grown to more than 65,000 students, by all odds the largest university in Britain and one of the larger in the world. Its graduates have acquitted themselves so well, and their intellectual standards are so high, that an Open University degree means a good deal even in status-conscious Britain" (Block, 1981, p. 73).

3. In discussing technology and change, Block further tells us, "It is tempting—very tempting—to speculate about the new world that we see coming into reality in the next few years: whole libraries available on a handful of videodiscs; students of all ages learning at home through microcomputers linked by phone with vast educational data bases; instant access by satellite to an unlimited variety of televised information. But I, like many of the other contributors believe that we have learned that those fundamental changes will come to realization, in most cases, only in a gradual and often evolutionary way—rather than by some instantaneous sea change. Educational institutions, and those within them who learn, and teach, and administer, need time and experience to incorporate these new ways of learning into their individual, social and economic patterns of behavior" (Block, 1981, p. 72).

THE AUTHOR'S VIEW

The remainder of this article synthesizes the major definitions of the past into a current set which might be discussed by the profession at large. To do that, the author presents a proposed definition and provides an analysis for each definition.

Technology

Definition. The systemic and systematic application of behavior and physical sciences concepts and other knowledge to the solution of problems.

Analysis. Important terms in the definition are to be understood as follows:

1. "Systemic application" is included, because of a concurrence with the system's notion that all things have an impact upon and are affected by other things in their environment. The effect of this interaction needs to be considered in constructing any system, if it is to be effective, efficient, and relevant in its purpose.

2. "Systematic application" is included because it is easy to pass over or leave uncontrolled many significant variables in a complex system such as learning.

3. "Application" is the translation and implementation of scientific and other knowledge into a system of strategies and techniques designed to solve a problem. Thus, strategies (designs for action) and techniques (practical or established means for accomplishing something) become the primary units of technology. In other words, the strategies selected for solving a problem are equated with action designs, while the tactics for making the strategy work are equivalent to techniques.

In support of the author's definition, the following points should be considered:

1. Technology is value free; its use or misuse depends on the values of those who employ it.

2. The application of technological solutions to one problem may create other problems which may be more serious than the original problem.

3. Applications of technology should be selected and/or continued only after determination that desirable consequences outweigh undesirable consequences.

4. Fear and hesitancy about using advanced technologies is largely a fear of unknown consequences. To be supportive of appropriate technologies, individuals need to progress through the stages of awareness, interest, trial, and appraisal before either acceptance or adoption will take place (Rogers & Shoemaker, 1971, p. 100).

Instructional Technology

Definition. The systemic and systematic application of strategies and techniques derived from behavior and physical sciences concepts and other knowledge to the solution of instructional problems.

Analysis. Concerns about the definition of instructional technology include:

1. Instructional technology may be divided into more narrow technologies. For example, there are message design, message delivery, and evaluation of message effect as subsets of instructional technology. To communicate effectively, one must clearly state the referent technology on which the broadening or narrowing is based.

2. Instructional technology can be viewed as a subset of a larger technology, that is, educational technology. To illustrate, educational technology might be a combination of instructional, learning, developmental, and managerial technologies. In turn, educational technology could be combined with others to form an even larger or higher order technology.

3. Many of the strategies and techniques of one technology may also be relevant for other technologies.

4. The profession must internalize the idea that the selection of technology depends on both purpose and values. Some strategies and techniques are superior to others and should be chosen on that basis.

Educational Technology

Definition. The toughest construct to define is "educational technology." Consider the following: The combination of instructional, learning, developmental, managerial, and other technologies as applied to the solution of educational problems.

Analysis. Several points to consider in this definition are:

1. The referent for both instructional and educational technology remains the root concept "technology." There is need to provide one other referent, that of "education." John Dewey (1916) defined education as "the enterprise of supplying the conditions which ensure growth, or adequacy of life, irrespective of age" (p. 61).

2. Others differentiate between education and training: "Where the inculcation of skills, habits, attitudes, or beliefs is intended ... the process ... is called training. In contrast ... to increase the student's ability and inclination to employ critical, independent, and creative judgement (is called education)" (Smith, 1965, p. 23).

3. Good defines instruction (under teaching) as "the act of providing activities, materials, and guidance that facilitates learning, in either formal or informal situations" (Good, 1959, p. 552).

WHENCE FROM THENCE?

To plug these meanings for education and instruction into educational and instructional technology can leave one impressed and humble at the idea of being in the business of developing supporting technologies for what is probably mankind's most significant invention.

Regardless of how well this collection of interpretations of educational technology clarifies or confuses matters, it is safe to assume that some time will pass before precise meanings are accepted across the field. It is also safe to assume that educators will continue to chip away at the problems of definition. No doubt many of the efforts will be at the level of a UNESCO study that concluded that whether a project was labelled ET or IT was dependent on the project's size and duration, with ET projects being large-scale and involving long periods of time, whereas IT projects would be those of small size requiring less time for completion (Dieuzeide, 1971). For those searching for substantive answers, this doesn't help.

Fortunately, there are increasing numbers of thinkers who have joined the definitional fray, and a continued refinement of the meanings of educational technology can be expected.

On studying the meanings presented here, including the author's interpretation, one can see both differences and similarities. A closer look often gives the impression that definition depends on the project being focused on or on the point being made at the moment. Thus, no doubt, some of the many meanings can easily be subsumed by others. However, among them are meanings that are clearly at variance with one another. These could well point the direction toward major issues seeking resolution.

At any rate, the range of speculations suggests considerable ferment within the profession, and change theorists state that ferment is a time of opportunity for those with prepared minds!

REFERENCES

AECT Task Force. (1977). *Educational technology: Definition and glossary of terms.* Washington, DC: Association for Educational Communications and Technology.

Armsey, J. W., & Dahl, N. C. (1973). *An inquiry into the uses of instructional technology.* New York: Ford Foundation Report.

Block, C. H. (Ed.). (1981). *Proceedings of the National Conference on Technology and Education.* Washington, DC: Institute for Educational Leadership.

Carnegie Commission on Higher Education. (1972). *The fourth revolution: Instructional technology in higher education.* New York: McGraw-Hill.

Cleary, A. et al. (1976). *Educational technology: Implications for early and special education.* New York: John Wiley.

Collier, K. G. et al. (1971). *Colleges of education learning programmes: A proposal* (Working Paper No. 5). Washington, DC: National Council for Educational Technology.

Commission on Instructional Technology. (1970). *To improve learning. A report to the President and the Congress of the United States.* Washington, DC: Commission on Instructional Technology.

Dewey, J. (1916). *Democracy and education.* New York: Macmillan.

Dieuzeide, H. (1971). *Educational technology: Sophisticated, adapted and rational technology. Series B: Opinions* (No. 30). Paris: International Commission on the Development of Education, UNESCO.

Engler, D. (1972). Instructional technology and the curriculum. In F. J. Pula and R. J. Goff (Eds.), *Technology in education: Challenge and change.* Worthington, OH: Charles A. Jones.

Finn, J. D. (1960). Technology and the instructional process. *Audiovisual Communication Review, 8* (1), 9-10.

Good, C. V. (Ed.). (1959). *Dictionary of education.* New York: McGraw-Hill.

Heinich, R. (1970). *Technology and the management of instruction.* Washington, DC: Association for Educational Communications and Technology.

Knezevich, S. J. (1969). *Administration of public education* (2nd ed.). New York: Harper & Row.

Knezevich, S. J., & Eye, G. G. (Eds.). (1970). *Instructional technology and the school administrator.* Washington, DC: American Association of School Administrators.

McDermott, J. (1981). Technology: The opiate of the intellectuals. In A. H. Teich (Ed.), *Technology and man's future*. New York: St. Martin's Press.

Rogers, E., & Shoemaker, F. (1971). *Communication of innovations* (2nd ed.). New York: Free Press.

Saettler, P. (1968). *A history of instructional technology*. New York: McGraw-Hill.

Silverman, R. E. (1968, January). Two kinds of technology. *Educational Technology*, p. 3.

Simon, H. A. (1969). *The sciences of the artificial*. Cambridge, MA: MIT Press.

Simon, Y. R. (1983). Pursuit of happiness and lust for power in technological society. In C. Mitcham & R. Mackey (Eds.), *Philosophy and technology*. New York: Free Press.

Smith, P. G. (1965). *Philosophy of education*. New York: Harper & Row.

Tickton, S. G. (Ed.). (1971). *To improve learning: An evaluation of instructional technology* (Vol. 1). New York: R. R. Bowker.

2

A Brief History of Instructional Development

Sharon A. Shrock

*Curriculum and Instruction, Southern Illinois
University, Carbondale, Illinois*

Before one sets out to write or read a history of instructional development (ID), it seems there are a few points that should be made to put the endeavor into perspective. First, the history of instructional development is unlike the history of the steam engine or the history of the computer. The reason is the absence of unanimity or even of consensus regarding the definition of instructional development. Some use the terms *instructional development* and *instructional technology* interchangeably. Others use the terms *instructional development* and *instructional design* interchangeably.

The second point is that even if one does distinguish between these terms, it would be hard to argue that the concepts to which they refer are irrelevant to a history of instructional development. In other words, rather than a linear progression of well-documented events, the history of instructional development is the story of a gradual confluence of ideas, which took place over several decades. Many of the composite ideas have been legitimately attributed to several different sources, and many of these ideas have and still do overlap with other concepts and procedures that are not instructional development.

This chapter focuses on the history of instructional development, rather than of instructional media or instructional design. However, given the ambiguity of the concept and the divergent nature of its roots, this chapter necessarily reflects judgments based on my experiences in the field. This is to say that there exist other ways to describe the history of ID that would be no less correct. The chapter begins with a definition of instructional development. The remaining sections are defined by decades, beginning with the years before the 1920s. Because this is largely a history of ideas rather than of events, the separation into decades will at some times seem arbitrary. Ideas are difficult to date with precision; they arise from previous ideas and carry over into ensuing decades. It is hoped that the use of decades as divisions will provide a cognitive scaffolding onto which the reader may attach the major points of progression in the evolution of instructional development.

INSTRUCTIONAL DEVELOPMENT: A DEFINITION

So of what is this chapter a history? A workable definition of instructional development for this chapter might be a self-correcting, systems approach that seeks to apply scientifically derived principles to the planning, design, creation, implementation, and evaluation of effective and efficient instruction. This definition is appropriate for the purposes of this chapter because it is a general one that does not include specific steps in the ID process. The way the steps are portrayed differs from model to model (Andrews & Goodson, 1980), and this is not a history of any particular ID model. Notice that the definition implies instructional design, but makes no explicit reference to instructional media; nevertheless, media professionals have played an important role in the history of instructional development, and the following sections include frequent references to the media field.

BEFORE THE 1920s: BIRTH OF AN EMPIRICAL KNOWLEDGE BASE FOR EDUCATION

One of the fundamental ideas supporting instructional development is the idea of instructional design, that is, the notion that empirically based principles can be applied to generate predictably effective instruction. While it may be difficult to imagine now, in the not too distant past instruction was dominated by the exercise metaphor: the mind was thought to consist of faculties in need of exercise. The study of certain disciplines was thought to improve mental performance in the way that calisthenics improve muscle functioning. Schooling was conducted in accordance with such traditional practices unencumbered by a systematic examination of outcomes. A major ideological breakthrough occurred with the advent of scientific investigation into human and animal learning.

While many contributions could be listed here as important in shifting the prevailing concept of instruction, the work of E. L. Thorndike at Columbia University was perhaps most influential (Baker, 1973; Saettler, 1968) and particularly salient for the field of instructional development. While the details of Thorndike's theories may not appear to be influential in instructional design today, the so called "big picture" of what he was trying to do presaged many of the tenets of ID. Beyond his importance as an early figure in the effort to establish a knowledge base for human learning, two points in particular are noteworthy. First, during his long career Thorndike moved from a strict concern with discovering the laws of learning to an interest in and advocacy of social engineering, the idea that instruction should pursue prespecified, socially useful goals. Second, Thorndike was a strong advocate of educational measurement, a research tool and then a field in itself that became very important in establishing education as a science (Snelbecker, 1974). It is not difficult to see in these ideas the fundamental shift in thinking about education that would ultimately make possible the development of ID.

THE 1920s: OBJECTIVES

The third decade of the century saw the maturation of several ideas that are fundamental to instructional development. Most prominent among these are educational objectives and individualized instruction. Also in this decade appeared the seeds of ideas that would be fully elaborated only decades later.

According to Baker (1973), the waning of the "mind as a muscle" metaphor accelerated the acceptance of the utilitarian or social efficiency movement advocated by Franklin Bobbitt. Bobbitt (1918) believed that schools should provide experiences specifically related to those activities demanded of citizens by their society. Furthermore, he thought that the goals for schooling could be derived from an objective analysis of those skills necessary for successful living. It is not difficult to see here the roots of job and task analysis: the notion of analyzing a complex skill into its component subskills. Even more clearly discernible was endorsement of the connection between outcomes and instruction: specifying desirable outcomes and then planning instructional experiences that would facilitate their acquisition.

Others translated the ideas posited by Bobbitt, Thorndike, and others into actual curricula and instruction that sought to apply the tenets of objectives-driven learning. These were the famous individualized instruction "plans" begun in the late teens but realized and popularized in the 1920s. The first of such plans appears to have been that of Mary Ward and Frederic Burk at the San Francisco State Normal School. The distinctive feature of this plan was its reliance on self-instructional materials that allowed learners to progress at their own pace with a minimum of teacher direction. The endeavor was abruptly curtailed by a California court ruling that only the State Board of Education could publish printed instructional materials (Saettler, 1968). However, two of Burk's associates, Carleton W. Washburne and Helen Parkhurst, went on to develop more elaborate and better known individualized instructional plans.

Washburne created the Winnetka Plan while superintendent of the Winnetka, Illinois, public schools. This plan not only made use of self-paced, self-instructional, self-corrective workbooks, but also incorporated diagnostic placement tests and self-administered tests that students could use to determine if they were ready for testing by the teacher. Only after performing satisfactorily on the teacher administered test could the student undertake new tasks (Saettler, 1968).

The Dalton Plan was originally developed by Parkhurst for use in an ungraded school for crippled children. It was subsequently implemented in Dalton, Massachusetts, and New York City (Saettler, 1968; Tyler, 1975). The plan centered on what we would call today "contract learning." After having agreed to contracts, students were free to complete them at their own pace. However, no new contracts were permitted until the current one was satisfactorily completed.

The Winnetka and Dalton plans thus embodied not only prespecified learning outcomes and self-pacing within school subjects, but mastery learning as well. Of these the concept of prespecified objectives was perhaps the most seminal; the others can be seen as logical consequences of this one remarkable idea. The concept of mastery learning is made possible by goal specification and assessment. Once intended outcomes are made clear and their assessment is sought, the need for self-pacing and other forms of individualization becomes apparent as individual differences in goal attainment are revealed. It is not surprising that instructional development, with its grounding in objectives, has always been firmly linked with advocacy of individualized instruction and mastery learning (Reiser, 1987).

Besides providing impetus to the concepts of objectives, individualized instruction, and mastery learning, these plans provided evidence that there was an alternative to the normal curve of student achievement resulting from traditional instruction. Because they involved so much self- as opposed to teacher-led instruction, the experience of these plans made clear the need for carefully designed materials. Thus the individualized learning plans of the 1920s provided a rationale for continued development of designed as opposed to traditional instruction.

THE 1930s: BEHAVIORAL OBJECTIVES AND FORMATIVE EVALUATION

Progress toward the creation of instructional systems slowed during the 1930s (Baker, 1973; Reiser, 1987). Two reasons typically are identified: the Great Depression and the ascendency of the Progressive Movement in education. The economic depression decreased funds for research and educational experimentation. Progressivists advocated student-initiated activities; taken to excess, this stance resulted in an educational climate inhospitable to prespecified instructional outcomes.

However, it was during the 1930s that Ralph W. Tyler began the work that was to make him famous, work that in retrospect advanced the evolution of instructional development. In 1933 the Eight Year Study was launched from The Ohio State University, where Tyler was a member of the Bureau of Educational Research. According to Guba and Lincoln (1989), the study had been designed in response to postwar pressures to revise the prevailing college preparatory high school curriculum in order to meet the needs of increasing numbers of students who in earlier years would not have gone beyond elementary school. The Eight Year Study sought to determine if students completing alternative high school curricula could succeed in college; an eight-year longitudinal study was required for the students to complete both the high school and the college degree programs. Thirty public and private secondary schools developed alternative curricula as a part of the research. Tyler was recruited to work on the study because he recently had been working with Ohio State faculty to develop tests of intended learning outcomes, which he termed *objectives* (Guba & Lincoln, 1989).

The Eight Year Study is notable as part of the history of instructional development for two reasons. The first is that the study served to refine the procedures for writing instructional objectives. The study confirmed that objectives could be clarified if written in terms of student behaviors, hence the still current term, *behavioral objectives* (Reiser, 1987). Second, it was essential during the Eight Year Study to ensure that the alternative curricula were implemented as planned. Therefore, the objectives and their assessment were used to revise and refine the new curricula until they produced "an appropriate level of achievement" (Guba & Lincoln, 1989, p. 28). Though the term would not be coined for almost thirty-five years, instructional developers recognize this process as *formative evaluation*. It is clear that Tyler well understood the cyclical nature of evaluation within the process of creating instruction designed to produce specific outcomes (Cambre, 1981). Thus in a frequently overlooked decade two definitive aspects of ID became visible.

THE 1940s: INSTRUCTIONAL MEDIA AND RESEARCH AND DEVELOPMENT

World War II created an enormous instructional problem: thousands of military personnel had to be trained rapidly to perform thousands of tasks critical to their own survival and the war effort. The response to this instructional problem had a far-reaching impact on the evolution of instructional development (Olsen & Bass, 1982; Saettler, 1968).

Part of the government's response to this urgent need was the creation and distribution of thousands of training films and other mediated learning materials. According to Saettler (1968), the Division of Visual Aids for War Training within the U.S. Office of Education alone produced 457 sound motion pictures, 432 silent filmstrips, and 457 instructors' manuals between January 1941, when the division was created, and June 1945. Other agencies within the armed services produced materials as well; 16mm projectors and filmstrip projectors were purchased and distributed by the thousands during these years. Still photographs, audio recordings, transparencies, and slides were used for instructional purposes; mediated strategies were even used to create instructional simulations.

While Saettler (1968) states that "instructional technology came of age during World War II" (p. 179), others might reasonably suggest that it was instructional media rather than instructional technology that was nurtured by the war effort. However, this rapid deployment of mediated instruction undoubtedly influenced the evolution of instructional development in several ways. First, the priority and funding accorded to instruction at this time were conducive to experimentation and innovation. Many of the persons hired by the military to work on the wartime training were well-established researchers (Baker, 1973; Reiser, 1987) and the military training became an example of what a well-funded research and development (R&D) effort directed toward education could accomplish. Furthermore, this R&D effort continued after the war, ultimately predisposing the military toward innovative instructional systems concepts.

Looking more closely, another important development can be discerned that was largely the result of the heavy employment of mediated instruction: the emergence of the role of the instructional technologist. During the process of creating military training films, this role emerged as distinct from that of the subject matter expert (SME) and the technical expert in film making (Saettler, 1968). The need for a professional who could contribute expertise in education to the knowledge of the subject matter expert and the technical expertise of producers was clear to the military staffs responsible for creating effective mediated instruction. The basic instructional development team—designer, SME, and producer—had been conceived, and calls for professionals with formal preparation in this new designer role were forthcoming. Hence, the experience provided important impetus for the growth of a new field.

THE 1950s: PROGRAMMED INSTRUCTION AND TASK ANALYSIS

During the 1950s several ideas that had surfaced earlier were refined and popularized. First among these in historical significance for instructional development was probably programmed instruction; in addition, the analytical processes important to instructional design grew more sophisticated during this decade.

Morgan (1978) dates "the origin of educational technology from the work of B. F. Skinner and others on programmed instruction" (p. 143). While Sidney L. Pressey had invented and demonstrated a testing machine as early as 1925 (Olsen & Bass, 1982; Reiser, 1987), it was Skinner's elaboration of the theory of reinforcement and his advocacy of its application to learning that established the Programmed Instruction Movement.

Skinner's research into operant conditioning and animal learning led him to suggest that human learning could be maximized by the careful control of reinforcement for desired behaviors (Skinner, 1953). Hence, programmed instruction was characterized by clearly stated behavioral objectives, small frames of instruction, self-pacing, active learner response to inserted questions, and immediate feedback regarding the correctness of the response. A unit of programmed instruction was, in fact, a small instructional system (Heinich, 1970).

Though the early excitement surrounding programmed instruction was not sustained beyond the following decade, it is not difficult to see how powerful the implications of programmed instruction have been for the field of instructional development. Programmed instruction assisted in shifting education's focus to the outcome behavior of the learner and away from simple concerns with process or the behavior of the teacher. The movement reaffirmed the feasibility of self-pacing and mastery learning, and made apparent the need for carefully constructed materials. As Heinich (1970) and Olsen and Bass (1982) have pointed out, programmed instruction set the stage for the realization that the methods of programmed instruction could be applied to media other than print and on a very large scale to create macro-systems of instruction. The movement drew new professionals and perspectives into the field of education (Morgan, 1978)—the persons and the ideas that would codify instructional systems in the following decade.

At a time when the value of carefully designed, outcome-oriented instruction was being increasingly recognized, advances in the analytical procedures that would be essential to the creation of such instruction were also being made. The term *task analysis* was first used by Air Force personnel in the early 1950s to refer to procedures for anticipating the job requirements of new equipment under development (Miller, 1962). Work that began during World War II on observing and analyzing human behavior was pursued during the 1950s. Most notable was the work of John Flanagan (1954) on the critical incident technique and that of Robert Miller (1962), who developed detailed task analysis procedures initially for military applications.

Any discussion of advances in instructional design analysis would be incomplete without noting that in 1956 Benjamin Bloom and his co-authors published their *Taxonomy of Educational Objectives* for the cognitive domain. Initiated as a support for cognitive assessment, the Taxonomy was to prove extremely valuable in the specification and analysis of instructional outcomes and the design of instruction to attain them.

THE 1960s: INSTRUCTIONAL SYSTEMS DEVELOPMENT

The decade of the 1960s was so explosive for the field of instructional development that only the highlights can be included in a brief history such as this one. However, as the previous discussion illustrates, most of the ideas that coalesced during the 1960s to form an identifiable field of instructional development had been voiced previously. What was distinctive at this time was the articulation of the components of instructional systems and the recognition of their system properties.

Among the earliest authors to discuss systems were Robert Glaser (1962) and Robert Gagne (1962). In 1962 Glaser employed the term *instructional system* and named, elaborated, and diagrammed its components. He clearly described the breach between psychological research on learning and educational practice and the need for professionals actively engaged in developing the science of instructional technology. This discussion appears quaint now because of references to teaching machines and a heavy reliance on behaviorist language when describing the components of instruction, but clearly the essence of instructional development as we know it today was present. In 1965 Robert Gagne published *The Conditions of Learning*, a milestone that elaborated the analysis of learning objectives and went on to relate different classes of learning objectives to appropriate instructional designs.

Evaluation and feedback are essential features of systems. It is perhaps not surprising that the evolving concept of instructional systems was accompanied by refinement of evaluation procedures during the 1960s. It became clear that the available test construction methods that produced norm-referenced tests were inadequate for assessing the effectiveness of instructional systems. Norm-referenced tests define a learner's performance in terms of the scores of other test takers. Because instructional systems were designed to produce achievement of prespecified objectives, their assessment required tests that could be interpreted in terms of the specific competencies mastered. Reiser (1987) credits Robert Glaser with the first use of the term *criterion-referenced measures* to refer to tests of this type. The development of this alternative testing technology began in the 1960s and continues today.

The 1960s were notable for the support instructional development received from the federal government. By the late 1960s the military was rapidly infusing instructional systems development into their standard training procedures (Olsen & Bass, 1982). On the civilian side the instructional systems concept was encouraged by the passage in 1965 of the Elementary and Secondary Education Act (ESEA), which established 20 federally funded R&D laboratories. Many of these labs became advocates of ID. Through ESEA the federal government also mandated evaluation of many federally funded educational projects. While many of the labs did not survive the 1970s, the labs and the large curriculum development projects funded by the federal government in the 1960s provided visibility for instructional development and encouraged educators to accept the idea that instruction could be developed by teams of professionals outside of individual schools. The level of federal support for instructional development at that time was evidenced by the U.S. Office of Education funding of the Instructional Development Institutes, a large-scale attempt to disseminate instructional development procedures to public school teachers across the nation (Schuller, 1986).

Another important trend affecting the evolution of instructional development began in the 1960s. Leaders among education professionals who had considered themselves primarily media specialists began to lobby actively to broaden the field of audiovisual (AV) instruction to embrace the larger concept of instructional development and technology (Schuller, 1986). James Finn, Arthur Lumsdaine, and other leaders of the Department of Audiovisual Instruction (DAVI) within the National Education Association became very vocal about the need to move the AV field beyond a preoccupation with products toward a focus on the design of instructional messages. While many professionals were comfortable with the larger, more process-oriented concept, many others were not. To a certain extent, tension between "media people" and "developers" remains in the field today. Historically, however, the merger of the AV constituency with the advocates of instructional systems has no doubt had a strong impact on instructional development. Many current ID professionals and the graduate programs that produced them had their roots in instructional media. The decade ended with plans to change the name of the DAVI to better reflect the new direction of the field.

THE 1970s: ID MODELS AND MATURATION

Activities of the 1970s were a logical outgrowth of the path-breaking ideas proposed in the 1960s. The 1970s was a decade of consolidation. Instructional development acquired the accoutrements of a profession as ID scholars and practitioners sought to define and describe more thoroughly the processes they advocated. It was a decade wherein the ramifications of instructional development were discovered and recorded; its practitioners grew familiar with it.

One of the hallmarks of the 1970s was a proliferation of ID models. By 1980 Andrews and Goodson (1980) could identify 60 of them. However, experience with instructional development was revealing problems, and important and permanent modifications of the earlier models were made. One of the most important was the addition of needs assessment (Kaufman, 1972) to the collection of steps that defined the process. ID models no longer simply began with a statement of objectives; analysis processes were included to assist in determining what the objectives of an instructional system should be. Along with this greater sophistication came an awareness of the different roles an instructional developer might be required to play. The field reached out to the literature on consulting and change agents for information to assist with its growing complexity. The potential of cognitive psychology for the refinement of instructional design was noted.

Graduate education programs focusing on instructional systems design grew and existing associations of professionals were redefined to accommodate the new spheres of activity. The NEA's Department of Audiovisual Instruction became the independent Association for Educational Communications and Technology; the National Society for Programmed Instruction became the National Society for Performance and Instruction. Near the end of the 1970s AECT's Division for Instructional Development founded the *Journal of Instructional Development.*

THE 1980s: MICROCOMPUTERS AND PERFORMANCE TECHNOLOGY

The historical significance of the 1980s for the field of instructional development is currently difficult to write; only retrospection from the vantage point of later years will reveal what mattered most in our very recent past. It is hard to imagine, however, that two factors will be left out of future histories: the advent of microcomputers and the rapid adoption of instructional systems development by American businesses.

The instructional applications of microcomputers have come to dominate much of the literature of instructional design. There is little consensus regarding the meaning of this powerful technology to instructional development. Positions seem poles apart. Some regard this high technology as an adjunct to instructional design, an ideal vehicle for researching human learning. Others seem willing to subvert the entire instructional development field to the demands of creating computerized instruction. The possibilities opened by microcomputers seem clearly to have hastened the field's utilization of cognitive psychology and knowledge engineering strategies, thus broadening its theoretical and analytical bases.

The 1980s have witnessed tremendous growth in the utilization of instructional development by businesses and other non-school agencies. These environments have fostered yet another expansion of the systems concept, performance technology. Performance technology comprises instructional technology, yet incorporates the design of non-instructional solutions to human performance problems as well. Just as the military often took the lead during the history of instructional development, the cutting edge of elaboration and applications of performance technology seems to be well outside the realm of schools and even of universities. The significance of this expanded systems concept for the future of instructional development remains to be seen.

IN CONCLUSION

The history of instructional development is about the confluence of research, technology, and systems. The beginning of the 1990s finds instructional development with these major themes still very much in evidence, albeit in much more complex and sophisticated forms. Unfortunately, the breach between educational research and educational practice described by Glaser almost 30 years ago is also still very much in evidence. The power and the promise of instructional development were and are one of the few bridges across the chasm.

REFERENCES

Andrews, D. H., & Goodson, L. A. (1980). A comparative analysis of models of instructional design. *Journal of Instructional Development, 3*(4), 2-16.

Baker, E. L. (1973). The technology of instructional development. In R. M. W. Travers (Ed.), *Second handbook of research on teaching.* Chicago: Rand McNally.

Bloom, B. S., Engelhart, M. D., Furst, E. J., Hill, W. H., & Krathwohl, D. R. (1956). *Taxonomy of educational objectives: The classification of educational goals. Handbook I: Cognitive domain.* New York: David McKay.

Bobbitt, J. F. (1918). *The curriculum.* Boston: Houghton Mifflin.

Cambre, M. A. (1981). Historical overview of formative evaluation of instructional media products. *Educational Communication and Technology Journal, 29*, 3-25.

Flanagan, J. C. (1954). The critical incident technique. *Psychological Bulletin, 51*, 327-358.

Gagne, R. M. (1962). Introduction. In R. M. Gagne (Ed.), *Psychological principles in system development.* New York: Holt, Rinehart & Winston.

———. (1965). *The conditions of learning* (1st ed.). New York: Holt, Rinehart & Winston.

Glaser, R. (1962). Psychology and instructional technology. In R. Glaser (Ed.), *Training research and education.* Pittsburgh: University of Pittsburgh Press.

Guba, E. G., & Lincoln, Y. S. (1989). *Fourth generation evaluation.* Newbury Park, CA: Sage.

Heinich, R. M. (1970). *Technology and the management of instruction* (Association for Educational Communications and Technology Monograph No. 4). Washington, DC: Association for Educational Communications and Technology.

Kaufman, R. A. (1972). *Educational systems planning*. Englewood Cliffs, NJ: Prentice-Hall.

Miller, R. B. (1962). Analysis and specification of behavior for training. In R. Glaser (Ed.), *Training research and education*. Pittsburgh: University of Pittsburgh Press.

Morgan, R. M. (1978). Educational technology—adolescence to adulthood. *Educational Communication and Technology Journal, 26*, 142-152.

Olsen, J. R., & Bass, V. B. (1982). The application of performance technology in the military: 1960-1980. *Performance and Instruction, 21*(6), 32-36.

Reiser, R. A. (1987). Instructional technology: A history. In R. M. Gagne (Ed.), *Instructional technology: Foundations*. Hillsdale, NJ: Lawrence Erlbaum.

Saettler, P. (1968). *A history of instructional technology*. New York: McGraw-Hill.

Schuller, C. F. (1986). Some historical perspectives on the instructional technology field. *Journal of Instructional Development, 8*(3), 3-6.

Skinner, B. F. (1953). *Science and human behavior*. New York: Macmillan.

Snelbecker, G. E. (1974). *Learning theory, instructional theory, and psychoeducational design*. New York: McGraw-Hill.

Tyler, R. W. (1975). Educational benchmarks in retrospect: Educational change since 1915. *Viewpoints, 51*(2), 11-31.

3

Educational Technology in the 1990s

Cass G. Gentry
College of Education, Michigan State University
East Lansing, Michigan

and

Josephine Csete
College of Education, Michigan State University
East Lansing, Michigan

Predicting the future is a risky business, but there are advantages that make the risks worthwhile. First, reasoned predictions about the field of educational technology provide targets against which others may compare their thoughts. Second, such predictions may stimulate efforts on the part of members to either facilitate or inhibit possible futures implied by the predictions. In this chapter issues that seem less likely to be resolved in the next decade are labeled "problems," and promising challenges are labeled "possibilities." There is no intent to imply either exhaustivity or priority for these problems and possibilities. First the predicted effects of ten problems that have an impact on the field are discussed.

PROBLEMS

One—The Boundaries of the Educational Technology Field Will Remain Poorly Drawn

While staunchly defending educational technology as a discipline, its members still wrestle with identifying the distinguishing characteristics of the field. A definition of technology, still popular today, was coined over 20 years ago by John Kenneth Galbraith (1967): "The systematic application of scientific or other organized knowledge to practical tasks." Extending that definition, *educational* technology would become "the systematic application of scientific or other organized knowledge to practical *educational* tasks." At face value, this could mean that almost everyone in education is an educational technologist. What educator is not busy applying scientific or *other* organized knowledge to practical educational tasks? Many are even applying knowledge systematically. What, precisely, is the territory staked out by our field, and what is the rationale for our claim to be technologists? The answers do not appear to be clear to other educators, nor consistently clear among educational technologists themselves.

There is little concerted effort on the part of the field of educational technology to overcome its definitional ambiguity. As Reigeluth (1989) has pointed out, "the field is undergoing an identity crisis like none in its history." Even so basic a task as standardizing terminology across the field has been haphazard and inadequate. The most significant attempt at standardizing terminology was made in 1977, with the publication of a definition and glossary of terms by a task force of the Association of Educational Communications and Technology (AECT). More recently, Ellington and Harris (1986) have compiled a small book of terms relevant to the field. None of the works examined by the author can make any claim to being comprehensive.

To this point in time, educational technologists have had very limited success in selling their wares to the formal educational establishment. A report by the Alberta Department of Education (1987) noted that:

> Historically, the role of technology in education has been incremental and peripheral, with new technologies being added to the traditional teacher-centered model of instruction. This process has resulted in large expenditures and increases in teacher workload with no significant improvements to the performance of the education system (p. 26).

The formal education establishment's focus on the live, certified teacher as central in the classroom is in contrast with educational technology, which, without denying the value of the teacher, puts the learner in the central position. Numerous attempts get our field recognized, including gaining sanctions and requirements of teacher education programs by state and national certifying bodies, have had little impact on the educational establishment. Efforts to set up prototype educational systems that can demonstrate the power of restructured educational environments in concert with the best of educational technology have not been successful, despite schemes proposed by many authors (Skinner, 1948; Heinich, 1984; and Reigeluth, 1988). The problem remains of how educational technologists may define their field beyond these broad, indiscriminant meanings, so that boundaries of the field are clear to its members and to other disciplines. We suspect the definitional problem will continue through the 1990s.

Two—The Curricular Core of Academic and Other Programs Designed to Prepare Educational Technologists Will Remain Ill Defined and Inconsistent

During the 1950s and 1960s, ferment among educational technology academic programs was considered a healthy condition, but hopes of adopting a set of common core experiences were disappointed in the 1970s and 1980s. Diversity among our programs is still very great (Schiffman & Gansneder, 1987), and there is little reason to think that condition will change in the 1990s. Reasons for much of this diversity are clear. Academic programs in educational technology have grown out of several different conditions, with their genesis primarily out of media, curriculum, and design. Silber (1982) set a general model for comparing educational technology academic programs. Efforts like those of Redfield and Dick (1984) to share analyses of their academic program, while commendable, are not sufficient in themselves. Inclusion in the standards of certifying agencies like The National Council for Accreditation of Teacher Education (NCATE) will eventually help. The AECT/NSPI Task Force on ID Certification, led by Barry Bratton (1984), has attempted to provide direction toward a national curriculum through agreement on 16 core objectives. Others, like Hutchison (1989), believe the profession is moving toward a broader perspective that includes organization, design and development, ergonomics, business management, and strategic planning, and advocate a name change from "instructional technology" to "performance technology" to reflect this shift in focus. In contrast, Mager (1988) sees instructional technology and performance technology as separate sets, with both being necessary to the educational technologist. Perhaps it is time to carry out a truly comprehensive needs analysis for the field.

Three—The Bulk of Research in the Field Will Continue to Be Sporadic and Diffuse

While some excellent research has been carried forward by members of the field, "the field appears to lack pervasive research activity and interest" (Hannafin, 1986, p. 25). Most educational technology research can be characterized by a lack of planned, concerted action to firmly ground our discipline in research. Clark (1989) asserts that many literature reviews in support of hypotheses are "scandalously narrow and superficial" (p. 59), and also that researchers have made few attempts to compare models or theories. Ideally, professors of educational technology should draw candidates based on their areas of research expertise. Thus, the professor is the constant that manages the research direction and the contributions of generations of students. Similarly, at the academic program level, it is desirable that professors of that program establish clear and coordinated research goals. In turn, research in the field of educational technology requires some coordination across academic institutions, supposedly through national organizations. This happens more by chance than by design. Constraints of resources, time, and difficulty of task appear to have greater impact on the choice and delineation of research than do the needs of the field. The large majority of educational technologists employed by business and industry, government, and instructional development houses are rewarded for keeping their eye on productivity rather than on research. At any rate, only a small percentage of educational technology professionals do research. There seems little likelihood that this condition will change in the coming decade.

Four—There Will Continue to Be Only Limited Use of Primary Criteria for Evaluating Instructional Development Process, Product, or Implementation

Accountability is a continuing issue with education establishments, but to paraphrase Mark Twain's comment on the weather, "everyone talks about it, but nobody does anything about it." Similarly, beyond the efforts of a small segment of business and industry attempting to turn their training programs into cost centers, there is little valid accountability of instructional effectiveness in that sector. Cost and time pressures placed on instructional developers to get projects up and running make it difficult to carry out activities that would demonstrate the validity of their work. For example, systematic needs analysis is still not the norm for determining what instruction should be developed, and like it or not, too little formative or summative evaluation of ID projects is being carried out in either education or training settings. It is equally rare for concomitant cost-effectiveness and cost-benefit analyses to be done. A number of satisfactory guides to doing cost-effectiveness and cost-benefit analyses are available (e.g., Kearsley's series of articles in NSPI's journal, *Performance and Instruction*, beginning with the February 1986 issue). Application of these various techniques makes sense, but apparently does not seem "practical," since so few apply them. We do not foresee a change in conditions that will make common the use of evaluation and validation techniques by educational technologists in the 1990s.

Five—Undesirable Side-Effects of the Entrepreneurial Practices of Individual Practitioners of Educational Technology Will Continue Negatively to Affect Credibility and Effectiveness

Many educational technologists in their respective settings have developed a strong sense for "targets of opportunity." Too often, high dependence on resources from clients in business, industry, and education, and priorities established for grants from public agencies and private foundations, have caused the adjustment of the objectives of the field to fit external views. Educational technologists have attached themselves to new waves in hopes of syphoning off energy to carry on their own activities. Unfortunately, this has resulted in a short-term gain mentality, rather than one of long-term planning, necessary to building a discipline.

Technologists, like many innovators, have a long history of promising more than they can deliver. Thomas Alva Edison (Church, 1926, p. 59), who knew more about technology than many, is purported to have said that "the radio will supplant the teacher. Already one may learn languages by means of Victrola records. The moving picture will visualize what the radio fails to get across. Teachers will be relegated to the backwoods." Clearly, credibility suffers when expectations are raised only to be dashed, when they go unfulfilled. The side-effects of "technological fixes" may be greater problems than the ones solved. It is unlikely that these conditions will change during the 1990s.

Six—There Will Continue to Be Inconsistent Support for Educational Technology from Administrators, Educators, and Trainers

An indication of status for a program or project is how it is recognized in the parent organization's budget. In many cases, the operations of educational technology fall under the less than desirable budget type known as "no budget budget." This budget type is put into operation usually after major allocations are complete. No budget budget funds come from little pockets of money, including administrative contingency funds. Spending decisions are usually made on the basis of emotional appeals and subjective value judgments. Even with more traditional budget support, educational technology activities are often subsumed under a "projects" category which, like the no budget budget, is prime for cutting. The view of technology as peripheral is stronger in education than in training, but not by much. Certainly, business and industry are much more willing to support educational technology than is the educational establishment. But for the most part this support is inconsistent, and dealt with differently from other organizational activities.

Most education and training programs are locked into a Lancastrian structure of educating, which was excellent at incorporating technology of the industrial revolution (e.g., mass production, replaceable parts), but poor at incorporating more modern technology (e.g., individualized instruction, distance education). Perelman (1987) believes that the schools are beyond reform, and advocates taking a systems approach to radically transforming education. He believes that educational technology could be an important integral part of a new system of education whose goal is productivity. As long as educational technology is considered peripheral, the support of its activities will remain circumspect.

Seven—There Will Continue to Be a Division Between Educational Technologists and Other Educators over the Theories of Learning to Which They Adhere

Although there is good verbal support for an educational technologist's need of a sound learning theory base to guide instructional design, more often than not, students in courses are taught to design instruction using a "cookbook" approach. Winn (1989) points out that while this method may work in test cases developed for the course, this kind of training is insufficient to deal with unexpected constraints that inevitably arise in real situations. Educational technologists need a sound understanding of the learning theory base from which they work, so that they can make creative decisions that take the constraints and assets of a particular situation into account.

Like other beliefs, specific theories, once accepted by an individual or a group, may be clung to tenaciously and passed on to disciples as the *only* legitimate theories for the profession. Many of the good aspects of a prolonged period of detailed research by behaviorists are being ignored by some, while others refuse to consider the contributions that cognitive field theories can make. Skinner's paper in the *American Psychologist* (1984) takes educators to task for their failure to effectively use the findings of behavioral research. Currently, information processing or cognitive field theories are in the ascendancy among academicians. It is not our intention to argue here that one theory is inherently better than another, but rather to suggest that educational technologists be more involved in a mutually beneficial relationship in which they grow by applying diverse learning theories and in turn provide a testing ground for theories. Educational technologists need to increase their involvement in implementing and testing theories such as those relevant to learning transfer (Pea, 1988), learning in and out of the school context (Resnick, 1987), and expert/novice differences (Lovell, 1987). This division among practitioners over the suitability of competing learning theories is closely related to the previously mentioned problem of the inadequacies of current research. To compound the problem, little is being done to relate theories of learning to other important theoretical areas, such as system, instruction, design, evaluation, communication, and change theory.

Eight—There Will Continue to Be Inadequate Response to the Critics of Educational Technology

Much of the criticism of technology is concerned with the use of economic impact as a criterion of "goodness," without much concern for other social effects. One of the leading critics of technology has been Lewis Mumford. In one of his earliest works, *Technics and Civilization* (1934), he examines technological landmarks that were responsible for transforming society. Major among these have been the adoption of the clock by the Benedictine monasteries to provide order among their members. His point is that "the clock is not merely a means of keeping track of the hours, but of synchronizing the actions of men" (p. 14). This imposition of machine-like order upon humankind is contrary to our nature, and has reduced us to a system. Jacques Ellul (1967) is another who points out that the technization of human activities has diminished human beings. He explains his views in terms of technique:

> Technique integrates the machine into society. It constructs the kind of world the machine needs and introduces order where the incoherent banging of machinery heaped up ruins. It clarifies, arranges, and rationalizes; it does in the domain of the abstract what the machine did in the domain of labor. It is efficient and brings efficiency to everything (p. 5).

One of Ellul's major concerns is that the primary role of education has become that of preparing society's members to "conform to the structure and the needs of the technical group" (p. 349).

Having a greater immediate impact are criticisms of specific applications of technology. Computer applications in instruction have received a fair share of criticism. Oettinger (1969) criticizes contemporary instructional technology because in his view it is being force-fed, oversold, and prematurely applied as a quick fix by funding agencies, learning corporations, and technical leaders in the field. Educators are not distinguishing "between the long-range promise of educational technology and the technology that is ready for immediate delivery" (p. 39).

More recently, criticism has focused on unequal distribution of educational technology across society. Malcom (1988) describes our "moral obligation" to research and find ways of closing the gap between the advantaged and disadvantaged portions of our population, which technology threatens to make even wider. In addition to the concern that richer districts will more readily be able to purchase and use newer technologies such as the computer, Malcom also draws our attention to the widely divergent ways in which this technology may be used. She describes two scenarios, one in which the computer is used to present an endless series of mind-numbing drills, and another in which the computer is used as a tool to make education "more meaningful and more accessible."

Nine—Confusion over the Definition of and the Need for Technological Literacy Will Continue

Few would argue with the statement that the growing pervasiveness of technology is fundamentally changing the nature of work. Yet educators are slow to recognize the need to develop a curriculum that will prepare the workforce for the new demands they will face. The general level of our citizens' technological literacy is considered too low to meet the demands of the workplace and of general use of technology. As an example, Toshi (1984) maintains that there is a significant difference in the level of technological literacy between American and Japanese executives. Crohn (1983) culled the views of leading northwestern U.S. business executives on the workforce's need for technological literacy. According to these executives, technological literacy is not composed only of the worker's ability to interact with machines and electronic terminals, which requires a level of math and science expertise as well as computer literacy, the work environment will continue to change so swiftly that workers will also need the analytical reasoning, logic, and communications skills to adjust to changes as they arise.

Devore (1985, p. 23) cautions designers of technological literacy programs against confusing science and technology, which grow out of different traditions and have different goals. He distinguishes technology as dealing with "the *creation, utilization* and *behavior* of adaptive systems including tools, machines, materials, techniques and technical means and the behavior of these elements and systems in relation to human beings, society and the environment," and states that technological literacy is understanding "the primary elements stated in the definition." Scientific, technological, and computer literacy are not the only "literacies" vying for attention. For example, the right brain/left brain controversy has brought forward (again) the need for visual literacy and it's affects on learning and performance. Given the absence of a clear and accepted meaning for technological literacy, it is unlikely that practitioners will reach agreement on a common curriculum to *teach* technological literacy in the near future.

Ten—The Predilection of Educational Technologists and Other Educators to Reinvent the Wheel Will Not Significantly Lessen

A tremendous amount of resources is lost to educational technologists and their clients because they are not aware of such resources. Even in cases where the materials are known to exist, they may be rejected out of hand because of the "it wasn't invented here" rule. A more legitimate reason for not adopting existing materials is the difficulties and expense of revising materials to fit the needs of a different set of learners. Of interest is whether the greater ease of revising electronically coded computerized instruction will affect willingness to adopt or adapt programs in that medium. Another major reason limiting the adoption of existing materials is the general lack of validation data. As far back as 1972, Wall was addressing the need to rigorously field test and validate materials and programs. He argued that without such evidence, those responsible for selecting materials could not make sound adoption decisions.

Beyond the fitting of extant materials to local learning conditions is the attempt to adapt materials to cultural differences. As an example, Rojas (1985) evaluated the effectiveness of adapting instruction created for an American audience to a similar Brazilian audience, and proposed translation and evaluation procedures. Instances of successful adaptation are relatively rare in the literature. The trend of continually reinventing the wheel is likely to continue.

POSSIBILITIES

One—The Growing Diversity of the Student Population Will Encourage the Development of Alternative Instructional Delivery Programs

Higher education has not yet moved to accommodate the significant shift in the characteristics of its student populations. Increasing numbers of older students are entering higher education, who in many cases would like to acquire their education on a part-time basis because of family and job responsibilities. This pressure will require development of instructional systems that can certify their students and deliver instruction that fits the working person's schedule in the coming decade. In addition to the part-time and older students mentioned above, there are other non-traditional students who require special conditions, including growing numbers of women, minorities, the disabled, and low-income groups.

Technology systems able effectively to serve some of these divergent student groups have been in place for several years. One such system is the prestigious British Open University, a model of distance education. It has successfully catered to non-traditional student needs for about 20 years. Other countries, like Australia, have developed similar part-time undergraduate degree programs (Noad & MacFarlane, 1984). Efforts in the United States include the National University Teleconference Network, begun in 1982. The technologies and economies of scale are combining with markedly increased recognition of non-traditional students to create an environment that encourages proliferation of such systems in the 1990s.

Two—Pressure from Business, Industry, and the Government Will Force the Educational Establishment to Better Prepare Graduates for the Workplace

Business is finding it more and more difficult to find employees who can take on the new information services type jobs that are surfacing as other tasks are increasingly being automated. Despite a concern over this last decade (Mikulecky & Cousin, 1982) about the increased number of individuals with insufficient writing and reading skills, little has been done to reduce that number. The private sector is spending billions of dollars to train its workers (Toffler, 1980, p. 230). It is estimated that in the United States there are over 20 million functionally illiterate adults who read below the fourth grade level, and another 30 million reading below the ninth grade level. Of the students entering high school, 30 percent do not graduate, and 75 percent of the workforce that will be available in the year 2000 is already out of school (Galagan, 1988). In response to this situation the private sector has felt compelled to set up its own classes to teach remedial skills. However, it will continue to press the schools to deal with the problem. The government, because of its responsibility to see that the United States remains economically competitive with other nations, will also increase pressure on schools to better prepare graduates. Educational technologists can play a major role in the development of this instruction.

Three—Business and Industry Will Recruit Increasing Numbers from Among Their Current Employees and Will Subsidize Their Degrees in Educational Technology

Companies who have overseas subsidiaries have generally filled any educational technology positions with Americans trained in America. There is a question about how their level of fluency in the language and understanding of the culture of the country affect productivity. Foreign nationals completing academic programs in the United States in educational technology are usually absorbed by the academic institutions and businesses of their respective countries. American companies are beginning to see the advantages of hiring foreign nationals, trained in this country, to work in their overseas subsidiaries. These foreign nationals not only have the required professional knowledge, but also are versed in the country's language and culture. Currently they constitute a relatively small pool from which to draw. A means of increasing that pool is for American companies to recruit promising nationals from among their foreign national employees, and to subsidize their education in educational technology programs, here and elsewhere.

A similar solution may prove valuable to meet the shortage of qualified educational technologists in this country. The rate of change in American industries and businesses requires continual upgrading of personnel, and the common practice for doing this is by instituting training programs. The demand for qualified educational technologists in these training programs exceeds the number of candidates applying to and graduating from academic programs in educational technology. This is partly because of the university's limited resources for support of graduate students. A partial solution to the shortage of candidates is for companies to subsidize the education of selected employees at the master's and doctoral levels.

Four—Increasing Access to Electronically Delivered Instruction and Other Services Will Provide Channels for Delivery of Instruction Developed Independently of Traditional Education Systems

As Naisbitt has noted (1982, p. 18), our society is in transition from an industrial focus to an information focus: "While the shift from an agricultural to an industrial society took 100 years, the present restructuring from an industrial to an information society took only two decades. Change is occurring so rapidly that there is no time to react; instead we must anticipate the future." Because most of the new jobs being formed today are based on information services of some kind, it is important that people be trained in such services. Cleveland (1985, p. 13), predicts that "people who do not educate themselves—and keep reeducating themselves—to participate in the new knowledge environment will be the peasants of the information society."

To paraphrase Naisbitt, *Sputnik* did not so much usher in space exploration, as it did a revolution in communications through a system of satellites. As long ago as 1973, Neben predicted that two-way satellite systems would be within the reach of schools and many homes by the year 2000. The new fiber optic communication systems with their increased ability to carry information will complement satellite systems. Increasing numbers of vendors (e.g., Bibliographic Research Service, CompuServe) can each make as many as 100 to 300 commercial, online databases available to their respective subscribers. Sadly, few of the schools have yet subscribed to these databases, or even developed formal means for teaching students how to access and use them. There have been grand visions such as Jack Taub's Education Utility

(Gooler, 1986), which proposed to put everything relevant to public schooling into a giant database and to make it accessible to the students and teachers for a nominal fee. More likely, the distribution of databases among schools and homes will come through programs stored on fixed technologies such as CD-ROM.

Decreasing costs and increasing sophistication of computers and related technologies will soon enable independent designers to compete with larger companies in design and production of instruction. These powerful instructional design tools include user-friendly, computer-driven expert systems, coupled with CD-ROM and other laser technology for storing a wide range of text, pictorial, and auditory information. Instructional development will become an important cottage industry for the production of instructional programs that will provide cost-effective solutions for both training and education.

Five—Sophisticated Expert Systems and Other Forms of Artificial Intelligence Will Find Increasing Application in Education and Training Establishments

Heinich (1970, p. 56) quotes Paul Drucker as saying that "teaching is, in fact, the only traditional craft in which educational technologists have not yet fashioned the tools that make an ordinary person capable of superior performance." Bloom (1984) found that students who were taught the same content in a traditional manner, with the only difference between experimental and control groups being a tutoring component, resulted in the average tutored student being 2 Sigma above the average student in the control group. Because of the prohibitive costs of tutoring, he does not see this as a solution to raising the performance level in schools. He terms this the "2 Sigma" problem, which he states as the question: "Can researchers and teachers devise teaching-learning conditions that will enable the majority of students under *group instruction* to attain levels of achievement that can presently be reached only under good tutoring conditions?" (pp. 4-5). Whether this can be accomplished through improving group instruction is not certain, but perhaps educational technologists should be asking instead: "Are there other economically feasible ways of meeting the standard set by the combination of tutoring with traditional instruction?" Advances in expert systems and related technologies during the coming decade may go a long way toward making an ordinary person capable of superior performance in designing and delivering instruction. Interactive video, CD-ROM, and other storage systems, with instructional programs driven by expert systems, will become increasingly sophisticated in their adaptation to the idiosyncrasies of individual learners. Such systems will become commonplace in training programs of the 1990s. The strongest trickle-down effect is expected to be to community colleges and trade schools, with little effect on institutions of higher education, or on elementary and secondary schools.

Six—As Applications of Educational Technology Become More User Friendly, Many Educators Who Are Easily Frustrated by Instructional Technology Will Become Adopters

In the past, man-machine interfaces have seldom been comfortable even for those who were technically adept. Some of the same people who expertly handle a $20,000 automobile cannot handle the thought of using far less expensive educational technology. While no doubt there are instances of true technophobia, most resistance to technology is not because of fear but because of (1) a limited technical aptitude, (2) not wanting to contribute the time necessary to learn how to use the technology, or (3) past hardware or software breakdowns (and accompanying embarrassment). The science of ergonomics is being applied to reduce the discomfort of users in some industries. For example, the automobile industry takes great care to ensure the comfort and ease of operators in interacting with the controls of their vehicles. Further, it is not necessary for a driver to have the knowledge of an engineer in order to effectively operate a car. Similarly, computer applications are being developed that focus on ease of operation, with less technical knowledge required of the user. Menu and macro concepts have been applied to computer programs so that users need to know less and less about technicalities of programming or of complex routines in order to successfully design or use computer-assisted instruction. Unlike many of the other instructional media, computers are relatively trouble free. These changes should encourage increased client adoption of technology, and thereby expand the need for the services of educational technologists.

Seven—Pressure for Adoption of High-Tech Instructional Delivery Systems Will Come from a More Knowledgeable Student Body

Earlier I mentioned that the college population is becoming older and more part-time in their attendance. Because of family and job responsibilities, these individuals are much more critical of demands on their time. Given the educational establishment's control over certification, these students have had to adjust to universities and colleges designed for younger, full-time students. But increasing numbers are opting for educational systems (when available) that are more flexible in terms of when, where, and how they learn. As non-traditional students become aware of more flexible alternative educational programs, they will pressure existing institutions and newly formed ones to bend in that direction. Flexibility in terms of curriculum content and scheduling of courses probably has been a major factor in the rapid expansion of community colleges. Community colleges should be prime targets for educational technologists in this decade. One important opportunity for expanding educational technology in more traditional four-year colleges and universities will be in off-campus courses, where novel instructional delivery systems are not as threatening to on-campus gatekeepers. Again, both of these structures tend to serve the part-time or non-traditional student. Given the steady increase in the number of non-traditional students, the market should move to meet their needs.

Eight—Independent Learning Skills Will Become Increasingly Important to Students and to Society

This possibility is closely related to the preceding one. Everywhere, the increasing rate of job obsolescence and of regular changes in job descriptions makes it necessary to learn new skills and update old ones. These changes have precipitated the need for lifelong learning of all workers to be successful in a rapidly changing workplace. As it becomes less and less convenient to interact with live teachers or trainers because of conflicting responsibilities, many workers and their employers will find independent learning systems attractive. The independent learning skills of decision making, problem solving, and self-management are among the entering behaviors essential to effective use of alternative self-learning systems. An interesting corollary to the development of such instructional systems is that the need for some independent learning skills may be reduced by the application of artificial intelligence (AI) technology. For example, many of the library and other search skills now required of independent learners may be carried out by such AI-enhanced instructional systems through nontechnical commands, given by the user. We anticipate that the development of such validated self-learning systems, in almost every content area, will be a major challenge for educational technologists during the coming decade.

Nine—The Natural Desire of Individuals to Control
Their Environments Can Be Aided by Technology

Traditional systems of education pretty much place control of the learning environment in the hands of teachers, administrators, and other educational specialists, thus requiring close conformity of the learner. An alternative to the traditional system is learner-controlled instruction. Wydra (1980, p. 3) describes learner-controlled instruction as "a mode of instruction in which one or more key instructional decisions are delegated to the learner. Some of these decisions include pacing, sequencing, resource accessing, and even evaluation." The idea that people must conform to technology comes out of the industrial revolution. The view that "every system design should be made to fit the diversity of people using it, rather than standardize the people to assume conformity" (Strassman, 1985, p. 244) more closely fits the concept of an information society. Research has demonstrated that learner control is a variable that has a significant effect on learning (Carrier & Williams, 1988). Computer and related technology, when coupled with instructional design, has promise of maximizing learner control for pacing, sequencing, resource accessing, and evaluation. The popularity of such systems should provide increased instructional development work for educational technologists.

Ten—Educational Technology Will Assist Education Institutions
in Their Response to Changing Societal Needs

Coleman (1987) describes how changes in the traditional American family are placing greater expectations upon education. As the number of two-income and single-parent households increases, there is a corresponding demand for services. An example of this is a growing societal expectation that schools will provide after-school and summer activities, as well as educate in the realms of socialization previously assumed by parents; an example is sex education. Keough (1986) argues that schools also need to respond to the increasing dropout rate, levels of drug and alcohol abuse, and even teen suicide. Many of these topics can be dealt with effectively through solutions found in educational technology. In other cases, technology can take on the more routine instructional tasks, so that administrators, teachers, and counselors may be free to concentrate on the "uniquely human" aspects of education.

CONCLUSION

Concept and space limitations prevent a more balanced perspective in this chapter, which could have included the many positive efforts being expended by colleagues in the field. At any rate, the purpose here is neither to praise *nor* to bury educational technology, but rather to look at part of its soft underside, and at some of the factors that show promise for its improvement. The relationships among many of these problems and possibilities are obvious, but it is likely that many other relationships, perhaps more important than these, are not obvious. An example would be the growing numbers of students who bring with them to the classroom technological expertise resulting from exposure to home computer games, arcades, and other non-formal uses of computers. What impact does that experience have on the process of "technocizing" the classroom? Another important factor is the effect that the continuing lack of standardization across hardware and software systems may have on the adoption and use of technology. Again, it is not inevitable that these problems will remain unsolved during the decade to come, or necessarily that the field will take advantage of the possibilities. The value of predictions like these depends on members of the field sifting through them so that greater truth may be determined, and on their taking action that will be beneficial to the field of educational technology.

REFERENCES

AECT Task Force on Definition and Terminology. (1977). *Educational technology: Definition and glossary of terms* (Vol. 1). Washington, DC: Association for Educational Communications and Technology.

Alberta Department of Education. (1987). *Visions 2000: A vision of educational technology in Alberta by the year 2000.* Alberta, Canada: Technology and Education Committee. (ERIC Document Reproduction Service No. ED 291 364).

Bloom, B. (1984). The 2 sigma problem: The search for methods of group instruction as effective as one-to-one tutoring. *Educational Researcher, 13*(6), 4-16.

Bratton, B. (1984). Professional certification: Will it become a reality? *Performance and Instruction, 23*(1), 4-7.

Carrier, C., & Williams, M. (1988). A test of one learner-control strategy with students of differing levels of task persistence. *American Educational Research Journal, 25*(2), 285-306.

Church, V. (1926). *Teachers are people, Being the lyrics of Agatha Brown, Sometime teacher of English in the Hilldale High School.* Hollywood, CA: David Graham Fischer.

Clark, R. E. (1989). Current progress and future directions for research in instructional technology. *Educational Technology Research and Development, 37*(1), 57-66.

Cleveland, H. (1985). Educating for the information society. *Change, 17*(4), 13-21.

Coleman, J. S. (1987). Families and schools. *Educational Researcher, 16*(6), 32-38.

Crohn, L. (1983). Technological literacy in the workplace. Portland, OR: Northwest Regional Educational Laboratory. (ERIC Document Reproduction Service No. ED 270 599).

Devore, P. W. (1985). *Differentiating between science and technology.* Paper presented at the International Technology Education Association Annual Conference, San Diego, California. (ERIC Document Reproduction Service No. ED 265 407).

Ellington, H., & Harris D. (1986). *Dictionary of instructional technology.* New York: Kogan Page; London: Nichols.

Ellul, J. (1967). *The technological society.* New York: Vintage Books.

Galagan, P. (1988). Joining forces: Business and education take on competitiveness. *Training and Development Journal, 42*(7), 26-29.

Galbraith, J. (1967). *The new industrial state.* Boston: Houghton Mifflin.

Gooler, D. (1986). *The education utility: The power to revolutionize education and society.* Englewood Cliffs, NJ: Educational Technology Publications.

Hannafin, M. (1986). The status and future of research in instructional design and technology. *Journal of Instructional Development, 8*(3), 25.

Heinich, R. (1970). *Technology and the management of instruction.* Washington, DC: Association for Educational Communications and Technology.

———. (1984). The proper study of instructional technology. *Educational Communication and Technology Journal, 32*(2), 67-88.

Hutchison, C. (1989). Moving from instructional technologist to performance technologist. *Performance and Instruction, 28*(9), 5-8.

Kearsley, G. (1986). Analyzing the cost and benefits of training: Part I—An introduction. *Performance and Instruction, 25*(1), 30-32.

Keough, K. E. (1986). *Scenario 2000: Intercepting the future.* Alexandria, VA: National Association of the State Boards of Education. (ERIC Document Reproduction Service No. ED 291 161).

Lovell, P. (1987). *Expert and novice instructional developers: A study in how organization of knowledge/experience is displayed in problem-solving performance.* Unpublished doctoral dissertation, Michigan State University, East Lansing.

Mager, R. F. (1988). *Making instruction work.* Belmont, CA: David S. Lake.

Malcom, S. M. (1988). Technology in 2020: Educating a diverse population. In R. S. Nickerson & P. P. Zodhiates (Eds.), *Technology in education: Looking toward 2020* (pp. 213-230). Hillsdale, NJ: Lawrence Erlbaum.

Mikulecky, L., & Cousin, P. (1982). Literacy training in business: A survey of fortune 500 training programs. *Performance and Instruction, 21*(8), 29-30.

Mumford, L. (1934). *Technics and civilization.* New York: Harcourt, Brace & World.

Naisbitt, J. (1982). *Megatrends: Ten new directions transforming our lives.* New York: Warner Books.

Neben, M. D. (1973). *The future of educational technology.* Washington, DC: Office of Education (DHEW). (ERIC Document Reproduction Service No. ED 086 246).

Noad, P., & MacFarlane, P. (1984). The planning and management of an innovative part-time BA degree: The Griffith programme. *Journal of Tertiary Educational Administration, 6*(1), 47-54.

Oettinger, A. (1969). *Run, computer, run.* Cambridge: Harvard University Press.

Pea, R. D. (1988). Putting knowledge to use. In R. S. Nickerson & P. P. Zodhiates (Eds.), *Technology in education: Looking toward 2020* (pp. 169-211). Hillsdale, NJ: Lawrence Erlbaum.

Perelman, L. J. (1987). *Technology and transformation of schools.* Alexandria, VA: Technology Leadership Network.

Redfield, D., & Dick, W. (1984). An alumni-practitioner review of doctoral level competencies in instructional systems. *Journal of Instructional Development, 7*(1), 10-13.

Reigeluth, C. M. (1988). The search for meaningful reform: A third wave educational system. *Journal of Instructional Development, 10*(4), 3-14.

————. (1989). Educational technology at the crossroads: New mindsets and new directions. *Educational Technology Research and Development, 37*(1), 67-80.

Resnick, L. (1987). Learning in school and out: The 1987 presidential address. *Educational Researcher, 6*(9), 13-19.

Rojas, A. M. (1985, April). *When to adapt materials and when to initiate fresh instructional development.* Paper presented at the Annual Meeting for the National Society for Performance and Instruction, Chicago, Illinois. (ERIC Document Reproduction Service No. ED 263 908).

Schiffman, S., & Gansneder, B. (1987). Graduate programs in instructional technology: Their characteristics and involvement in public education. *Journal of Instructional Development, 10*(3), 22-28.

Silber, K. (1982). An analysis of university training programs for instructional developers. *Journal of Instructional Development, 6*(1), 15-28.

Skinner, B. (1948). *Walden two.* New York: Macmillan.

————. (1984). The shame of American education. *American Psychologist, 39*(9), 947-954.

Strassman, P. (1985). *Information payoff: The transformation of work in the electronic age.* New York: Free Press.

Toffler, A. (1980). *The third wave.* New York: Bantam Books.

Toshi, T. (1984). Too many managers are technologically illiterate. *High Technology, 4*(4), 14-16.

Wall, J. E. (1972, October). *Adapting curriculums to local needs.* Presentation at a Training Institute for Curriculum Personnel Development, Ft. Collins, Colorado. (ERIC Document Reproduction Service No. ED 070 867).

Winn, W. (1989). Toward a rational and theoretical basis for educational technology. *Educational Technology Research and Development, 37*(1), 35-46.

Wydra, F. (1980). *Learner controlled instruction.* Englewood Cliffs, NJ: Educational Technology Publications.

4

Trends in Educational Technology 1991

Donald P. Ely

Professor, Instructional Design, Development, and Evaluation
Associate Director, ERIC Clearinghouse on Information Resources
School of Education, Syracuse University
Syracuse, New York

with

Anne Foley

Graduate Student, Instructional Design, Development, and Evaluation
Syracuse University
Syracuse, New York

Wendy Freeman

Graduate Student, Instructional Design, Development, and Evaluation
Syracuse University
Syracuse, New York

Nancy Scheel

Graduate Student, Instructional Design, Development, and Evaluation
Syracuse University
Syracuse, New York

INTRODUCTION

There are many ways in which trends could be identified: expert opinion, panels of specialists, or informed observation. This study chose content analysis as the primary vehicle for determining trends, based on earlier works of Naisbitt (1982) and his model (Janowitz, 1976). The basic premise of these works is that current trends can best be determined by what people are saying publicly, through newspapers and magazines. Naisbitt used actual counts of linear inches in key periodicals to determine trends. This study, and the two that preceded it,

Reprinted from *Educational media and technology yearbook 1992*. Englewood, CO: Libraries Unlimited.

used the same basic procedure: the identification of emerging topics in key publications over a period of one year. The rationale seems sound; it is possible to determine trends by considering what people are saying publicly about matters within the field. There may be other trends that can be determined by such methods as counting sales of products or discovering where professionals are being placed and analyzing what they are doing. We chose to use the literature of the field as the best comprehensive coverage of current thinking and events in the field. We carefully reviewed a selected body of literature using a team of educational technology specialists to help determine the status of the field today and, perhaps, to indicate where it might be headed in the future.

A consistent methodology has been used from year to year. Basically, it has followed the general principles of content analysis, using a group of trained coders who made independent judgments about the literature being reviewed. Group discussion about findings had to reach a high interrater reliability for each item before it was placed in an agreed-upon category. The recording units remained constant (for the most part) each year. Some additional subcategories were required to reach a higher level of specificity.

While reading this study, one must be careful not to extrapolate the trends too far into the future. It is often tempting to use trends as predictors of future developments. Actually, they are more like indicators that foreshadow the future. They are statements of current happenings in the field and, as such, must be considered tentative movements that will bear watching as time goes on. They are useful because they represent current public statements of many professionals that have been systematically analyzed and reported.

LITERATURE SOURCES

To maintain consistency from year to year, the same sources of information were used as in the 1988 and 1989 studies, with a few exceptions. To aid in the selection of sources, the Moore and Braden (1988) report, "Prestige and Influence in the Field of Educational Technology," was used. This source reported the people, publications, and institutions of "high prestige" that were identified by a survey of personnel in the field. The highest ranking journals and the dissertations produced by the universities that ranked the highest served as two major sources of literature. Additional sources of data were the papers given at major national and international conferences and the input to the ERIC database in the field of educational technology. Conferences are one of the most visible ways of presenting new ideas and findings to colleagues and therefore contribute to the trends. The ERIC system solicits unpublished materials such as reports, evaluations, studies, and papers for review and, following evaluative criteria, selects the best for inclusion in the database. The Clearinghouse on Information Resources is responsible for the field of educational technology; therefore, documents selected from that source are likely to represent current developments in the field. The sources are presented in figure 4.1.

Journals

British Journal of Educational Technology (United Kingdom)
Education and Training Technology International (United Kingdom)
   [Note: a replacement for the *Journal of Instructional Development*, which ceased publication in 1989]
Educational Technology
Educational Technology Research and Development
   [Note: a merger of the *Journal of Instructional Development* and *Educational Communication and Technology Journal*, both of which were analyzed separately in 1988]
TechTrends

(Fig. 4.1 continues on page 36.)

Dissertation Sources

Arizona State University
Florida State University
Indiana University
Syracuse University
University of Southern California

Conferences

Association for Educational Communications and Technology
Educational Technology International Conference (United Kingdom)
National Society for Performance and Instruction

ERIC Input

All documents in the field of Educational Technology entered into the ERIC system

Fig. 4.1. Content sources.

The journal *Education and Training Technology International* was chosen to replace the *Journal of Instructional Development* and to provide a greater international perspective on the literature. All journals were published between October 1990 and September 1991. The conferences were held in 1991. The ERIC documents were entered into the system between October 1, 1990, and September 30, 1991.

LEADING TOPICS

From the reviews of four coders, who discussed more than 1,300 items, came a list of "topics" that were most frequently presented in the literature. That list, together with the 1988 and 1989 numbers, is presented as table 4.1.

Table 4.1.
Rank Order of Content Analysis Categories

	1991	1989	1988
Instructional processes	1	1	1
Management	2	3	4
Technological developments	3	2	3
Research/theory	4	8	8
The field	5	4	5
Services	6	5	6
Society and culture	7	7	7
Personnel	8	6	2

Each of the categories has a series of subtopics (or recording units) that attempt to identify content more specifically. These subcategories help develop the themes that eventually get translated into trends. Table 4.2 shows the top 13 recording units, with subcategories as appropriate.

Table 4.2.
Rank Order of Top 13 Recording Units

	1991	1989	1988
Design and development (includes message design, product development, individual differences)	203	259	448
Implementation	146	98	24
Evaluation (includes process evaluation, product evaluation, cost/benefit)	144	99	97
Research/theory	91	38	51
Distance education	88	81	61
Status	80	95	61
Computer-related	65	90	82
Telecommunications	59	71	14
Curriculum support	51	79	25
Society and culture	45	71	72
Interactive learning	41	83	29
Artificial intelligence/expert systems	35	46	31
Logistics	3	32	43
Others	265	387	228
TOTAL	1,316	1,514	1,338

The recording units offered a first indicator of trends. Further analysis of each category and subcategory revealed sharper distinctions. At this point the key literature was added to the mix. *Key literature* included policy papers, reports, and statistical data for each topic area that were published during the time period of the study. This literature came from professional associations representing large numbers of people within and outside the field of educational technology, state and national governmental agencies that speak with some authority, organizations of policymakers, and business/industry sources. This information, together with the content of the literature reviewed, was studied by the author of this article, who, using personal observations (probably with some personal biases), drafted the trends and sent them for further discussion to the individuals who reviewed and categorized the literature. A copy of the draft was sent for review to a recognized professional in the field and to a reviewer in the Office of Educational Research and Improvement of the U.S. Department of Education. Changes were made when compelling arguments were presented.

CONCERNS ABOUT PREVIOUS STUDIES

As past editions of the *Trends and Issues* publications have been read and critiqued, four concerns have been expressed. These were addressed before the 1991 version was prepared. The first, whether content analysis is effective for large bodies of text; the second, the validity and reliability of coding; the third, the selection of the documents reviewed; and the fourth, the translation of quantitative content data into descriptive trends. Each of these concerns is addressed here.

Content Analysis of Large Bodies of Data

Conventional content analysis looks at words and phrases in an effort to "tease out" substantive meanings. The approach followed here uses complete journal articles, doctoral dissertation abstracts, conference program descriptions, and ERIC document input. Weber, in a new monograph on content analysis, says:

> Large portions of text, such as paragraphs and complete texts, usually are more difficult to code as a unit than smaller portions, such as words and phrases, because large units typically contain more information and a greater diversity of topics. Hence they are more likely to present coders with conflicting cues (Weber, 1990, 16).

In following the "large portions of text" approach, the findings of this study must be tempered by Weber's caution. He also points out that "[t]here is no simple *right* way to do content analysis. Instead, investigators must judge what methods are most appropriate for their substantive problems" (1990, 13). If there is some flaw in the approach used here, it has been consistent from year to year. Analyzing the periodical and document literature for a specified period of time still seems to be a useful procedure to identify the general trends or emphases that come from the literature of that period. Much of the value comes from the consistency of recording thematic units that have been used over the past four years.

The Validity and Reliability of Coding

The concern here is the stability, reproducibility, and accuracy of the coding process (Krippendorff, 1980, 130-154). Weber (1990, 15) says: "Classification by multiple human coders permits the quantitative assessment of achieved reliability." Each year graduate students in educational technology are trained as coders. Definitions of categories are given together with practice items for each document type. The author provides consistency in reviewing by serving as an additional coder each year. The criteria level for intercoder reliability in 1991 was .75; that is, three of the four coders had to agree upon a category for placement of each item.

Content Selection

Journals, conference programs, doctoral dissertations, and ERIC documents constitute a broad range of the literature generated by the field each year. There seems to be no stronger argument than that the content appearing during any given year is what professionals in the field are saying; hence, content units that can be counted provide a reasonable representation of the topics or themes that are emerging. One must be careful not to use these topics as *projections*, since they represent what *has* already happened.

In selecting the journals, conferences, and universities, questions may arise such as, "Why these and not others?" The decision was based on the survey by Moore and Braden (1988) that reported the most prestigious journals and university programs. Beyond this criterion was another that eliminated journals or conferences devoted to a specific medium, such as computers in education. If articles about computing were found in the general literature, they were counted. However, a journal or conference devoted entirely to a subfield within educational technology would skew the findings toward one medium.

Translation of Data into Trends

This is a subjective step and probably the most difficult to defend, as it ultimately relies on the judgment of one person. The numbers of articles, conference papers, dissertations, and ERIC documents report the volume of information about specific topics by category. These numbers are then the basis for identification of the most frequent topics. The topics are the basis for selecting confirming topics in the policy literature. *Policy literature* includes statements, reports, "white" papers, and other official publications of professional organizations, government agencies, and influential bodies such as foundations and think tanks. For each of the leading trends, the policy literature is searched for supporting statements to support the dominant trends. For example, in the past the study team has used publications of the Office of Technology Assessment of the U.S. Congress, the National Governors' Association publications about education, publications of the U.S. Department of Education's Office of Educational Research and Improvement (OERI), and publications of the various educational laboratories and research and development centers funded by OERI. Public statements and reports of the National Education Association and the American Federation of Teachers are used, as are the publications of the Association for Educational Communications and Technology. Quantitative data from Quality Education Data and Market Data Retrieval provide consistent, reliable trend information on hardware and software. When the dominant themes from the primary literature sources are verified by policy statements from responsible organizations, trends are confirmed and provide a reasonable rationale.

Summary

Trends do not flow fully developed from the literature. Using a content analysis procedure that goes beyond the conventional word-and-phrase approach, the magnitudes of general themes in the annual literature of educational technology are identified, counted, and verified by the policy literature. The translation from quantitative summaries to qualitative trend statements is mostly subjective in nature.

CONTEXT

This publication should answer the question, "Where is educational technology headed?" Technology does not move alone, apart from the society in which it exists. Information and communication technologies are being used in the home and workplace at all levels—local, state, regional, national, and international. To separate them from the context is to highlight the products rather than their uses and impact. Therefore, much of the discussion in this article involves the total fabric of technology in society rather than technology as an entity in itself. Technology is often referred to as a "tool" that incorporates the "media" of communication. The hardware and systems that carry information are often the primary focus, with little attention paid to the audience, purpose, and consequences of their use. Design, development, evaluation, and diffusion are lost by the overpowering influence of hardware and software.

It is clear that educational technology is frequently used in the local school and, increasingly, in the home. Within the school, college, or university, the individual teacher or professor is the single most important factor leading to appropriate implementation of media and technology for learning. That key individual is usually part of a system which, in turn, is connected to a larger unit—a state department of education or a university. National programs and initiatives are somewhat remote. International efforts seem even more distant.

Since the last study of *Trends and Issues*, there have been major national and international efforts to explore and promote the use of educational technology in the schools. In the United States, *America 2000* has been launched to focus attention on educational goals for the nation's schools. The New American Schools Development Corporation has been established as a further effort to build schools in visible locations where citizens can see educational restructuring, much of it enhanced by technology. The National Governors' Association continues to monitor programs in all the states, with technology in the schools as one major focus.

A report of the International Association for the Evaluation of Educational Achievement, *The Use of Computers in Education Worldwide* (Pelgrum and Plomp, 1991), contains findings from a major survey of 19 countries worldwide. The ministers of education from 27 European states met to discuss *Education and the Information Society: A Challenge for European Policy* (Eraut, 1991). This meeting was "the response of European education systems to the development of an 'information society' " (p. ix). The World Conference on Distance Education, held in Caracas, Venezuela, in October 1990, attracted the largest number of participants ever. Much of distance education is dependent upon educational technology applications. Educational technology has become more global than ever before.

One of the major outcomes of these efforts is linkage, between the schools and other entities, that has not been evident in previous times. *Networking* is being used as the code word for the many connections that are being made, most of them new. Networking by definition is the linkage made between and among people held together by a common theme or connection. The means for networking use both new and existing systems that permit real-time, live interaction between individuals and groups: telephone, fax, E-mail, computers, and cable and satellite television, as well as face-to-face and traditional correspondence approaches. Other systems store information for use at a chosen time: videotape recordings, videodiscs, CD-ROM discs, floppy discs, and audiocassettes. It is easy to be enthusiastic about these new media (and they dominate the literature), but voices of concern about cost, equity of access, skills required, and purpose still are heard and will have to be heeded.

Networks exist within a school; within a school system; within a region; within a state; and among the states. Networks exist between schools and business; schools and government agencies (state and federal); schools and universities; schools and public libraries; schools and professional associations; schools and broadcasting sources; and schools and homes. There appears to be a movement to create networks where none exist and to connect networks that already exist. Passage of the High Performance Computing Act of 1991, which authorizes the creation of the National Research and Education Network (NREN), is a significant move in this direction.

With all these contexts impinging upon educational technology, it must be remembered that the trends discussed in this article are more internal to the field than external to the settings in which they happen to reside. The literature reviewed is authored by people inside the field and the intended audience is mostly people inside the field. These are often practitioner-advocates who have agendas to promote educational technology and use publications and conferences to do so.

At the same time, there appear to be stronger calls for technology in education by groups outside education, such as state governors, business and industry executives, and newspaper education writers. The target of both the educational technologists and the influential critics seems to be mainline schools—the "establishment" that tends to perpetuate the status quo. Until there is openness to using technology among educators in general, the calls for technology in the schools will be unheeded or accepted only in marginal ways.

This study focuses primarily on the K-12 schools in the United States, although some information addresses higher and adult education. Information from other technologically advanced nations is used when appropriate. Attempts are made, whenever possible, to relate the trends to the educational goals set by the president and the nation's governors.

It should be noted that many trends in the field of educational technology are found outside the educational settings that are featured in this study. New professionals graduating from the many graduate programs in the field are being placed in business and industrial training environments. There is another body of literature, not covered in this study, that reflects the many new developments in nonschool settings. That fact is, in itself, a trend.

TRENDS 1991

Using a content analysis of the 1991 educational technology literature, the following trends have emerged.

Trend 1

The creation of technology-based teaching/learning products is based largely upon instructional design and development principles.

There appears to be more evidence that materials developed for the purpose of teaching and learning use design principles that have their roots in cognitive psychology and instructional science. More than 15 percent of the items reviewed for this year's study were devoted to design and development. Major subheadings included message design, product development, individual differences, and course development. Less prominent were needs assessment and task analysis. Further, models and theories in support of specific design and development approaches are being proposed and hold a substantial place in the literature.

The term *constructivism* appears with increasing frequency. At least two major sessions as the 1991 conference of the American Educational Research Association were devoted to the topic, and two special issues of *Educational Technology* focused on constructivism. The concept of constructionism (now called constructivism) was first proposed by Bruner in the mid-1960s and builds on earlier ideas of Piaget. Basically, it holds that the learner rather than the teacher develops (or "constructs") knowledge and that opportunities created for such "construction" are more important than instruction that originates from the teacher. This line of reasoning supports the work of Papert and other Logo advocates. It is fully explained in a new work, *Constructionism*, edited by Idit Harel and Seymour Papert (1991). The debate, which focuses on constructivism and educational technology, is thoroughly discussed in the special issue of *Educational Technology*, which was edited by Tom Duffy and David Jonassen (1991). The authors take sides for or against constructivism; those who are more negative toward the concept seem to emphasize the design element of instruction as a more appropriate position. Some authors would like to choose sides based on specific goals rather than on firmly held positions regarding constructivism or instructionism.

As more research on screen design is reported, designers and developers are beginning to incorporate findings into teaching/learning products. The traditional concepts of message design, which follow earlier research in perception psychology, are being enhanced by new efforts aimed at the individual learner using a display surface, usually a computer monitor (visual display unit).

Trend 2

Evaluation has taken on greater importance as the concept of performance technology has been further developed.

More than 10 percent of the 1991 literature was concerned with some aspect of evaluation: process evaluation, product evaluation, cost-effectiveness assessments, and formative evaluation.

Performance technology is appearing more frequently in the literature as a descriptor for instructional design and delivery that works. It is being used more in business-industry-government settings than in school and college environments. It is based on the conviction that training does not necessarily solve all performance problems in an organization. Rather, personnel selection, assignment, motivation, and environmental characteristics are as likely to be critical factors, as is a need for more information.

Other contributions from the 1991 educational technology literature that feature evaluation seem to stress outcomes for decision making rather than for information alone—the evaluation versus research question. Topics that once would have been studied using a research approach are now being evaluated. Evaluation is becoming a more important aspect of educational technology than ever before.

Another dimension of evaluation is *product evaluation*, the assessment of instructional materials that have been recently produced and have some potential use in other settings. As more software for microcomputers has been created, evaluations have been published in journals and by organizations that recommend instructional resources to schools, such as the Educational Products Information Exchange (EPIE). *Only the Best: The Annual Guide to Highest-Rated Education Software, Preschool-Grade 12* (Neill and Neill, 1990) uses 37 "respected" education evaluation services in the United States and Canada and requires software to receive two "excellent" grades or one "excellent" and three "good/favorable" grades to be published in this annual sourcebook.

Typically, evaluation has been an add-on or afterthought in the field of educational technology. As more emphasis is placed on instructional design, it is becoming an integral part of the process and, as such, is often an ongoing part of the larger process.

Trend 3

The number of educational technology case studies is growing and provides general guidance for potential users.

More than 11 percent of the literature reported on specific use of media and technology in teaching/learning settings. Almost all the case studies were "successful" and many could serve as models for potential users. Very few reported failure or negative outcomes. About one-half of all the case studies related to computer use in teaching and learning. Less than one-half reported on the use of telecommunications. There were almost no cases of traditional media use or instructional procedures that have been proven in the past.

In making the content analysis, the key words were *diffusion* and *implementation*. Almost all the case studies in this category emphasized implementation. Implementation not only means that educational technology ideas have been diffused and accepted, but that there has been actual use of new media or technology in an educational setting.

The results of case studies are not always fully documented. Most of them are not experimental in nature. Therefore, it is difficult to generalize about the outcomes, because they vary in substance and in presentation. However, a closer analysis of these items could create some general principles for others in similar circumstances to follow.

Trend 4

Distance education is evident at almost every educational level in almost every sector.

Distance education (or distance learning) has become a major instructional force in American education. A recent estimate is that 25 to 50 percent of the nation's students are reached by distance learning technology ("Wade right in," 1991). The National Governors'

Association reported that "virtually all states" use distance learning (National Governors' Association, 1991). Distance education provides systematic instruction to individual learners who are physically separated from teachers. The delivery of instruction is usually by telecommunications and computer hardware and software, although not always. Learners sometimes work independently and sometimes in small groups.

A database of distance learning projects compiled by the U.S. Department of Education (Garnette and Withrow, 1990) reveals more than 100 projects that involve "live, real-time interactivity between student(s) and their teacher ... in elementary and secondary school." The authors state that "specific projects were noted in 37 states [and] there appear[s] to be distance learning activities under way in every state with the exception of three states" (p. 520). Over 1,500 school districts are participating in some form of distance education, with some states sparsely represented and others including virtually every district. Specific numbers from the database help to illustrate the extent of impact.

- Technologies used:

Satellite	56	Coaxial cable	21
Audiographics	15	Computer-based	13
Microwave	17	Fiber optics	11

- Of those projects that offer courses for students, half offer foreign languages, one-third of the projects offer advanced mathematics, and a quarter offer at least one science course.

- Half the projects offer teacher training or staff development as one component of the project.

- Less than 25 percent of the projects have had any kind of formal evaluation.

- 40 percent of the projects were initially funded by the states.

- 20 percent of the projects involved collaboration between the school district and an outside agency such as the local telephone or cable company.

- 60 percent of the projects have been in operation since 1986.

A final note regarding the breadth and variety of projects helps to confirm the magnitude of distance education efforts. The range of participation is "from one school producing and developing its own courses using telecommunications to the 780 sites in 32 states served by the Texas Interactive Instructional Network (TI-IN)" (Garnette and Withrow, 1990, 517).

State policies regarding distance education are evolving. Of particular note are the state programs in Kentucky, Oklahoma, Michigan, Minnesota, Texas, and Virginia. Also, Iowa is investing $50 million in statewide telecommunications infrastructure. Missouri is taxing videotape rentals to subsidize distance learning. Minnesota has about 30 distance learning networks with over 150 schools participating. About 40 percent of the state's low enrollment courses share the networks ("Distance learning," 1990). The University of Texas at Austin is using two-way audio communication as a cost-effective delivery system for rural school districts. Telelearning classes are "live," as teachers and students talk with each other via telephone equipment that uses multiple source input and reception, connecting all participants in a manner similar to a telephone conference call. The cost of the courses ranges from $200 to $400 per student per semester.

Many distance learning programs are course-based; that is, they offer complete courses with the teacher in a remote location. However, some users of distance learning are using this approach as a supplement to classroom instruction to enrich learning. The Northwest Regional Educational Laboratory's *Enhancing Instruction Through Telecommunications* (1991) describes federal resources in telecommunications (such as NASA's Spacelink bulletin board and satellite teleconferences); news by telecommunications (such as CNN Newsroom); and student/teacher connections by telecommunications (such as the AT&T Learning Network). Course-based distance education dominates higher education efforts.

There is probably no other single trend that encompasses the theory and practice of educational technology better than distance education. Its frequency in the literature confirms this observation.

Trend 5

The field of educational technology has more and better information about itself than ever before.

Eighty surveys about various aspects of the field were reported during the timeframe of this study. For example, studies of the most frequently published textbook authors, a list of current dissertations, the extent of microcomputer penetration in the schools, and other such reports help to paint a quantitative picture of the profession. They are found most frequently in documents entered into the ERIC system, but also in journals and in conference presentations. Only one dissertation in 1991 was devoted to status.

These are reports of studies in which professionals are looking at themselves and the activities or facilities they administer. They tend to count things, people, and activities. They survey the state of the art in reference to a specific topic, as in Gustafson's *Survey of Instructional Development Models* (1991).

This trend also includes special publications about the field itself, usually by organizations with specialized interest in development and advancement of the field. Paul Saettler's *Evolution of American Educational Technology* (1991) is one such publication. This volume is the most comprehensive history of the field ever written. It goes beyond the events of the past and looks into the 1990s and beyond. The final chapter in this nearly 600-page volume covers state-of-the-art sections on instructional television, computer-assisted instruction (CAI), CAI software, instructional theory and design, interactive multimedia systems, and intelligent tutoring systems, and offers future prospects for the field. The International Society for Technology in Education (ISTE) published *Vision:TEST (Technologically Enriched Schools of Tomorrow)* (Braun, 1990) as a set of recommendations to the profession and to other professional educators regarding the future of education in America and the potential role of technology in that future. The staff for the study consulted some 200 experts and visited 45 schools nationwide to find examples of teachers producing dramatic educational improvements through technology. The *Educational Media and Technology Yearbook* (Branyan-Broadbent and Wood, 1991), published in cooperation with the Association for Educational Communications and Technology (AECT), reviews events of the year, reports on educational technology activities in the states, lists organizations and associations in the field within North America, and provides an updated list of graduate programs in the field.

Even with all the information published in 1991, there is still some uncertainty about the definition of the field of educational technology—what is included and what is not—and what constitute appropriate roles for personnel serving in the field. The Definition and Terminology Committee of the Association for Educational Communications and Technology will issue a report in 1992. Perhaps some of these questions will be answered at that time.

Trend 6

Computers are pervasive in the schools. Virtually every school in the United States has microcomputers.

Computer applications permeated the literature of educational technology in 1991. Purposely omitted from the analysis of trends and issues were 14 journals associated with computer-assisted instruction and conferences that focused on the computer as an instructional medium. Inclusion of such works would have skewed the data sufficiently to overshadow all the other trends. Even with this omission, computers frequently emerged in the general literature, dissertations, conference programs, and ERIC input. Sometimes the items were directly focused on the use of computers in the classroom for direct subject-matter instruction, but most referred to learning about the computer as a tool. Many items discussed the resistance or "roadblocks" to the use of computers in schools.

Two organizations surveyed the schools in 1990 and 1991 to determine the quantitative state of computers (and other technologies) in the schools. Quality Education Data, Inc., Denver, Colorado, has conducted annual surveys since 1981 and includes in its most recent report (Quality Education Data, 1991b) results from 83,283 elementary and secondary public schools in the United States. Market Data Retrieval's first-ever examination of emerging technologies in the education market used responses from 40,000 schools representing nearly 50 percent of the total K-12 enrollment in U.S. public schools (Market Data Retrieval, 1991). The findings are not always comparable and often vary significantly. Therefore, in reporting the findings here, basic numbers, rather than percentages, are used. Since Quality Education Data (QED) reports annually and comprehensively on computers in schools, their data are used.

Microcomputer density (students per computer) has been reduced from 125:1 in 1983-1984 to 20:1 in 1990-1991. The range is from 8,858 schools with less than 9 students per computer to 7,082 schools with more than 90 students per computer. The percentage of schools with microcomputers in the United States has steadily increased for the past 10 years until it reached 98 percent in 1990-1991. QED also reports "market share" for each company: Apple (including Macintosh)—65.7 percent; IBM—14.1 percent; other MS-DOS—4.5 percent; Radio Shack—6.2 percent; Commodore—5.4 percent; other—4.2 percent. Of the 81,203 schools that have microcomputers, 34,662 have 21 or more units.

In 1991, the National Education Association embarked upon a campaign to make microcomputers available to its members (Merina, 1991). The NEA EdStar computer was jointly developed by NEA and IBM. It is a special-edition IBM PS/1 with a VGA color monitor, a 30-megabyte hard disc preloaded with a computer-based grade book, a desktop publishing program, Microsoft Works, and IBM Linkway. A modem and printer are also part of the package. To make the computer package attractive to potential users, a price under $2,000 was established, with the possibility of financing for under $50 a month with no down payment. The director of NEA's Center for Innovation said, "We're not going to have computer-using teachers until teachers become computer-using people" (Merina, 1991).

Universities have also been studied. The National Survey of Desktop Computing conducted by the Center for Scholarly Technology at the University of Southern California determined "that the *placement* of computers, rather than the total number, is perhaps the key variable in defining access and assessing the deployment of institutional computing resources" (Green & Eastman, 1991). Access, or microcomputer density, in higher education institutions in general averages about 47:1 across all types of institutions.

A major comparative study, *The Use of Computers in Education Worldwide*, was published in 1991 by the International Association for the Evaluation of Educational Achievement (IEA). It summarizes the results of a survey of computer use in education in 19 countries (Pelgrum & Plomp, 1991). Major topics in the report, too complex to present here, involve the availability of computer hardware and software, the purposes for which computers are used, staff development, attitudes of principals and teachers toward computers, and gender equity in relation to computers.

The U.S. Department of Commerce, Bureau of the Census, studied computer use in the United States in 1989 and published its report in 1991 (Kominski, 1991). From the highlights of the findings, it is reported that 15 percent of all U.S. households had a computer, an increase from 8.2 percent in 1984. Among children 3 to 17 years of age, 46 percent used a computer at home or at school (or both), a rise from 30 percent in 1982. Of over 115 million employed adults, 36.8 percent said that they use a computer at work, compared with 24.6 percent in 1984. By the fall of 1989, about a third of the U.S. population (74,884,000 people) used a computer in some way (Kominski, 1991).

All the surveys and statistics do not point to the *purpose* of computer use. In a preliminary paper for the IEA study, Plomp and Pelgrum (1990) discovered that the types of software programs most commonly used by teachers in the United States were: (1) word processing (93 percent); (2) drill and practice (92 percent); (3) educational games (91 percent); and (4) tutorial programs (81 percent). A study of computer-using teachers who have integrated computers into classroom practice discovered that software was used in the following manner: (1) text processing tools (95 percent); (2) instructional software (89 percent); (3) analytic and information tools (87 percent); (4) programming and operating systems (84 percent); (5) games and simulations (81 percent); and (6) graphics and operating tools (81 percent) (Sheingold & Hadley, 1990).

As these data are considered, it would be well to recall the four major reasons for computer use in schools proposed by Hawkridge, Jaworski, and McMahon (1990):

1. *The social rationale.* Policymakers want to be sure that all children are "aware and unafraid of how computers work." Because "computers are pervading industrial societies and are likely to be important in all countries," learners should be prepared to understand computers and be aware of their role in society.

2. *The vocational rationale.* Learning to operate computers is an important competency. There will be employment opportunities for individuals who have the proper computer skills.

3. *The pedagogic rationale.* Students can learn from computers: "computers can teach." There are advantages over other traditional methods in using computers to learn.

4. *The catalytic rationale.* "Schools can be changed for the better by the introduction of computers." Computers facilitate change. They are symbols of progress. They encourage learning. "Computers are seen as catalysts, enabling desired change in education to occur."

One of the next steps in studying the role of the computer in education is to discover the extent and role of computers in the teaching and learning process according to the social, vocational, and pedagogic rationales. There is still very little evidence in the literature to support computer contributions to learning.

Trend 7

Telecommunications is the link that is connecting education to the world.

Telecommunications is an overarching term that describes electronic point-to-point connections between individuals and groups. Translated into electronic delivery terms, telecommunications technology includes connections that utilize existing telephone lines, dedicated lines, and cable and satellite transmission. Some messages are intended to be *interactive*, such as electronic mail (E-mail), computer conferences, and two-way audio and video conferences. Some are intended to be *one-way*, such as television directed to classrooms through cable and satellite systems. Usually broadcast radio and television are not included in the term, nor are prerecorded audio- and videotapes distributed through nonbroadcast channels.

It is clear from the 1991 literature that the term *interactive* is rapidly becoming popular, especially in relation to telecommunications. Much of the interest stems from distance education applications when computers are used to establish networks between an instructor and students or satellite television beamed to schools in a widely dispersed area. (Interactive video, another rapidly growing area, is usually not considered to be within the ambit of telecommunications, since it is usually delivered by self-standing, independent equipment.

The dominant trend within telecommunications is *networking*, the electronic connection of individuals who have common interests. Basically, networking is conducted by electronic mail (E-mail) between one person with a computer terminal and another person with a computer terminal. Both individuals are participants in the same electronic mail system. Ehrmann (1990) describes four conversational models for networking: (1) direct instruction; (2) real-time conversation; (3) time-delayed conversation; and (4) learning by doing. Kurshaw and Harrington (1991) summarize the state of networks today:

> Technological innovations have paved the way for new communities and collabora-tions to develop. While the modes of conversation have remained the same, the means by which these modes of conversation are carried out have not. Today, electronically networked communities employ all of these modes of conversation with varying technological sophistication (p. 5).

Kurshaw and Harrington (1991) also list the varied purposes for networking:

- Professional collaboration

- Student collaborative investigations

- Access to experts

- Information access

- Access to resources

- Collaborative development (electronic publishing)

- Teacher enhancement

- Online courses

- Networked community support.

All these applications are visible in the current literature. Each one is usually tied to a specific network. Some use commercial information utilities, such as CompuServe and Prodigy. Others are part of education-specific networks such as AT&T Learning Network and the National Geographic Society (NGS) Kids Network. Bulletin board systems, such as FrEdMail and FIDOnet, offer message-sending and receiving capabilities at little or no cost for participation. State networks in New York (NYSERNET), Texas (TENET), and Virginia (VA.PEN) are further indicators of the rapid spread of networking within education.

At the federal level, congressional passage and presidential approval of the High-Performance Computing Act of 1991 authorizes the creation of a National Research and Education Network (NREN). The network, which has been designated America's "information superhighway," is expected to provide access to electronic information resources maintained by libraries, research facilities, publishers, schools, universities, and affiliated organizations. The intent is to improve the information, computing, and communications infrastructure for the country's researchers and educators.

The other principal dimension of telecommunications is the use of television for teaching in a variety of settings. Whether the television image in the classroom comes from a cable outlet, a satellite dish, or a videotape recording, the quality of the program is the ultimate value for teaching and learning. Much of the literature speaks of the delivery systems that are being put in place and the applications of these systems for such uses as distance education. One must remember that it is possible to record on videotape any program that comes into the school, taking into account copyright restrictions and permissions. The recording provides flexibility in use and the possibility of reuse. Most of the 1991 literature was more concerned with getting the signal to the school than with its ultimate use.

Teachers are using television. In a study by Mann (1991), 96 percent of teachers in grades 6 to 12 expressed enthusiasm for television in instruction and three out of four plan to use it more next year. About 60 percent of the schools had access to cable television, but about 45 percent of the teachers said that they had trouble getting equipment to use in the classroom. Some 56 percent of the teachers in the survey listed PBS as their prime source of programming, but there was also considerable use of CNN Newsroom (12 percent use—the most frequently used cable program), followed by A&E Classroom, Assignment Discovery, and C-Span. The subject-matter area ranked first in use was current affairs (56 percent), followed by literature (38 percent), performing arts (37 percent), and history (33 percent). One surprising finding was that one out of eight classrooms did not have an electrical outlet!

Cable and satellite delivery systems reached new heights in 1991. The cable industry established Cable in the Classroom as a national project aimed at providing all junior and senior high schools with free cable service and at least one VCR and one monitor. Through cable access, many programs are entering the classroom. A&E Classroom is a one-hour block of programming airing Monday to Friday from 7 to 8 a.m. EST. The program is divided into subject areas focusing on history, drama and novels, performing arts, biographies, and anthropology and archaeology. Assignment Discovery is delivered through the Discovery Channel from 9 to 10 a.m. every day. They report use by 438,000 teachers and viewing by over 8 million students. CNN Newsroom is a daily 15-minute news program specifically designed for school use. The Learning Channel, a 24-hour television service, offers more than 20 programs for in-school use by teachers.

Channel One remains a controversial cable service because of the commercials that accompany the daily program. In 1991, the network reached over 10,000 schools (Skelly, 1991). Whittle Communications, the sponsoring organization, provides a satellite dish, two VCRs, and television monitors for each classroom. The news program is 12 minutes daily and includes 2 minutes of commercials. Various states have taken legal action to prohibit schools from signing on to the service. New York passed a law prohibiting use of Channel One in the schools. North Carolina judges ruled that the programs are supplementary and that local school boards do have the authority to accept the program. California tried, but failed twice, "to impose an overall statewide ban on 'electronic advertising' " ("Free to Watch TV," 1991).

The Monitor Channel produces Monitor World Classroom in English and Spanish, Monday through Friday, and airs it at 4 a.m. for recording. Printed support materials for classes in geography, social studies, global issues, and international affairs are available along with complimentary copies of The Christian Science Monitor.

Satellite transmission is a vital link in telecommunications. A recent study of satellite dish uses in public schools (Quality Education Data, 1992) reported that 33 percent of the schools in the United States have satellite dishes (27,582 out of 83,281 schools). Hawaii, Kentucky, and the District of Columbia report that all schools have satellite dishes. More than 20 states have joined the Satellite Educational Resource Consortium (SERC). The purpose of SERC is to provide credit courses that would otherwise be unavailable via satellite, microwave, or cable technology. SERC also offers inservice and graduate courses for teachers.

States seem to be the organizing units for the delivery of telecommunications technology. For example, the Massachusetts Corporation for Educational Telecommunications (MCET) operates the Mass LearnPike, a satellite and computer-based network dedicated to improving the quality of learning in the state. The Kentucky Educational Network is linked by satellite to all of its 1,300 public elementary, middle, and high schools. One person in the United States is monitoring state policy issues for telecommunications. Richard Hezel, author of two previous reports on state coordination of telecommunications for the Annenberg/CPB Project, outlines current issues in part of an excellent 1991 publication, *Education Policy and Communication Technologies* (Sheekey, 1991).

Programming for telecommunications was enhanced by this year's announcement of a $60 million grant by the Annenberg Foundation to the Corporation for Public Broadcasting for a new national project designed to improve mathematics and science instruction at the elementary and secondary school levels. The project includes an array of technology-based media: computers, interactive video, laser discs, and electronic networks.

The present trends study emphasizes the use of technology in elementary and secondary education. Higher education is also active in its application of technology to education. PBS Adult Learning Service indicates that 59 percent of all colleges and universities in the United States are using telecourses. Much of the activity is based in the two-year, postsecondary institutions. The International Telecommunications Consortium, an affiliate of the American Association of Community and Junior Colleges, represents more than 400 educational institutions from the United States and Canada and sponsors professional development meetings, supports telecommunications research, and provides a forum for its members to share expertise and materials.

The many telecommunications subtrends will have to be followed individually to keep up to date with the rapidly changing technologies. The technological developments outstrip the schools' readiness to adopt them. But, as this year's report shows, much progress is being made. In light of the restructuring movement that is inherent in the *America 2000* plan, it is likely that technology will have an active role to play.

Trend 8

The teacher's role in the teaching and learning process is changing as new technologies are introduced into the classroom.

"Teachers cannot be replaced by machines!" The cry has been heard since the invention of the printing press. The implicit threat of technology overtaking the teaching function has been ever-present in the generally conservative education community. However, there have been several indicators that the tone of the protest has calmed. One major factor is the growth of distance education programs in the schools and in higher education. In many distance education programs, instruction is delivered by a medium—a teacher surrogate—that is responsible for the major portion of information presentation. Through videotapes, audiotapes, computer programs, programmed textbooks, and combinations of media, subject matter is systematically presented to the learner. Even when the teacher is remote, as in "live" telecourses, the local teacher has been replaced by the teacher at the end of the line, wherever that may be. In reality, teachers are not replaced in the literal sense; they change their role from that of a presenter of information to a coordinator of learning resources. Such a role frees the teacher to work more independently with individuals and small groups while leaving the formal presentations to another medium. When materials are designed for distance learners, the teacher subject-matter specialist is the source of the information and often the designer of the presentation.

The dream of many technologists, and those who would change the role of the teacher, has been *integrated learning systems* (ILS). Known by such trade names as Computer Curriculum Corporation and Jostens and Wicat Systems, ILSs offer comprehensive coverage in terms of lesson plans and integration of electronic media. They generally make fewer demands on the teacher than do individual programs that treat small sections of the curriculum. According to *Inventing Tomorrow's Schools*, a newsletter published by the Mecklenburger Group: "ILSs are the fastest growing segment of the educational software industry.... There are more ILS vendors now than a few years ago—and most are financially healthy—to the point that they are an 'industry' that is among the formidable forces that will shape the future of education" (Sherry, 1991).

The Educational Products Information Exchange (EPIE Institute, 1990) has compiled a detailed report on ILSs that includes information on vendors, program descriptions, courseware evaluation, and visits to implementing sites. Market Data Retrieval (1991) reports that ILSs are in use at more than 4,200 schools, 11 percent of the respondents in their 1991 study.

Much of the value stemming from the ILS and other technologically based learning resources is not possible until teachers are thoroughly prepared to use the new systems. Sherry (1991) ends his ILS report by saying, "ILSs have a bright future, especially as vendors and schools alike pay the necessary attention to pre-service and in-service teacher training that encourages the full use of these ever-more-sophisticated resources." Some of the same issues are addressed by the Southwest Educational Development Laboratory in its newsletter, *New Things Considered*. In the August 1990 issue, pertinent questions and concerns are raised about the new requirements for teachers. For example:

- How do we prepare teachers if the traditional capabilities and applications will no longer be necessary, and we do not know which types of knowledge will be needed instead?

- The changes have happened so fast that relatively few teachers and teacher educators have had an opportunity to become comfortable with using computers, much less other technologies. Consequently, there are few effective staff development programs to help teachers create ways to integrate technology into the curriculum ("What curriculum," 1990).

The need for teacher involvement in technology is being recognized by one of the largest teacher unions in the United States, the National Education Association. Among its adopted resolutions for 1991-1992 was a key resolution related to educational technology.

Technology in the Educational Process

The National Education Association recognizes the advancement and application of instructional technology and high-technology devices and materials that provide new opportunities for developing skills, furthering research, and expanding knowledge in our society.

The Association believes that—

a. All education employees must be afforded the opportunity to explore the potential of emerging technology.

b. Education employees should have access to necessary technology for managing and advancing instruction. Further, they should be provided encouragement, time, and resources to experiment with and to research applications of technology in order to integrate technology into the curriculum.

c. Teachers must be involved in all aspects of technology utilization including planning, implementation and evaluation.

d. Teacher preparation in instructional technology must begin in college and university programs and extend through continuing opportunities for professional development.

e. Students must become aware of the social and economic impact of technology and must be provided with access to and instruction in the use of such technology. Further, technological education programs must provide equity in training, funding, and participation for all students, regardless of age, race, gender, socioeconomic level or geographic location.

f. All students and staff should have an understanding of copyright law and the responsible use of technological materials.

g. Effective use of technology requires a licensed teacher in every classroom. Instructional technology should be used to support instruction, but not to supplant education employees (NEA, 1991).

Voices from diverse sources are calling for more active roles in the use of technology in the classroom. Terrel H. Bell, Secretary of Education from 1981 to 1985, in a 1991 book, *How to Shape Up Our Nation's Schools*, makes an urgent appeal for technology in schools, according to *Washington Post* writer Brent Mitchell. He says in a September 24, 1991, article about the book: "Schools are often the only places that children do not deal with phones, computers and video players, and the book suggests these innovations could occupy one-third of a student's day and free the teacher to give other children more individualized attention." Quoting Bell, "Look at the supermarket and high tech behind the checker today.... Now look at what we are providing teachers." Such a call naturally leads to the next trend.

Trend 9

There is increasing pressure for the schools to consider the adoption of technology while, at the same time, concern is expressed for the impact of technology on children in the society at large.

This trend is a two-edged sword. Pleas for the use of technology in the schools, such as those of Dr. Bell, are increasing in frequency. Simultaneously, there are cries of concern over the impact of technology, especially television, on children and youth. Each matter must be considered separately.

Continued monitoring of the National Governors' Association project, *Results in Education*, reflects progress on one of the seven major themes: technology. The 1990 report shows very little progress in the implementation of technology to bring about major changes in the schools.

Despite the gains, technology's potential to transform and customize American classrooms remains largely unrealized. Most school districts still do not turn to technology to expand and diversify; nor has technology been integrated into the instructional practices of most classrooms. In short, little progress has been made toward the central recommendation of the task force—to use state powers to help schools reorganize, using technology and other means, so that they become more efficient and effective (p. 35).

With the numerical growth of computer and video-based technology in the schools, this observation may seem contradictory. The discrepancy is probably focused on the use of the technologies in ways that bring about dramatic and visible transformations in the schools. Use of media and technology as supplementary aids for enrichment does not improve efficiency and may have minimal impact on effectiveness.

The International Society for Technology in Education (ISTE) received a substantial grant to carry out a study of the potential that technology offers to education. One of the key purposes of the study was "to help educational decision makers identify steps they must take to create educational change in response to the charge given to them by the President and the governors" (Braun, 1990, 5). The complete report, which involved more than 150 educators from all levels of education, is called *Vision:TEST (Technologically Enriched Schools of Tomorrow)*. It spells out five major recommendations, global in nature, that involve the use of technology:

1. As a nation, the United States must recognize the need for improvement in its educational system and seize the opportunities offered by technology.

2. As a nation, the United States must provide every student with the opportunity to become what each is capable of becoming. It must provide each student with an environment that is conducive to learning.

3. As a nation, the United States must empower all teachers to provide the best education for every student in their classes.

4. As a nation, the United States must redesign its school systems to prepare its students for the twenty-first century.

5. As a nation, the United States must ensure that schools are managed effectively (Braun, 1990).

Another perspective, removed from the K-12 focus of this study of trends, is the use of technology for adults. Nell Eurich's book, *The Learning Society: Education for Adult Workers*, is based largely upon the use of technology to train and retrain adult workers. It reports a variety of current activities in which technology is used to make learning more efficient and effective with this special audience. She concludes that "about one-third of the work force is getting trained. That leaves the majority of workers still to be reached, but at least many adults are learning under their employers' auspices" (p. 18). In a case-study-based chapter, Eurich provides rich rationale for the use of media and technology, concluding that "the potential gain could be enormous *if* we supply content of quality for the media and select the technological means wisely for the goal" (p. 38). It is curious that technology has made more impressive gains in business and industry than in the schools.

The National Engineering Consortium released the findings of a study on the usage, value, and needs of technology in education in *Educational Technology in Kindergarten Through Twelfth Grades* (Janowiak, 1990). This highly media-specific study found that videodisc and interactive multimedia systems were the most promising new technologies, while more "traditional" technologies like microcomputers and video recorders had growth potential. An emerging trend seemed to be integrated multimedia systems combining video, data, and sound to provide information on demand.

Turning to the impact of technology on children, continuing concerns have been expressed about the influence of television on children's behavior. One direct outcome of this concern was the passage of the Children's Television Act of 1990. The new legislation limits advertising on children's programs to $10\frac{1}{2}$ minutes an hour on weekends and 12 minutes per hour on weekdays. The Federal Communications Commission is instructed to carefully review the practices of each station up for license renewal to determine compliance and whether its overall programming "has served the educational and informational needs of children." The Act also establishes the National Endowment for Children's Educational Television, which is intended to stimulate the creation and production of educational programs for children. There continues to be an undercurrent of dissatisfaction about the nature and quality of many commercial television programs, even though many studies do not support the notion of gross negative influence of television on children.

To review the comprehensive research conducted by behavioral scientists over the last 40 years on the influence of television on the lives of American children and adolescents, George

Comstock (1991) wrote *Television and the American Child*. The book identifies major topics that have been investigated and focuses on recent research that confirms or rejects the conventional wisdom about the effect of television on youth. There continues to be ambiguity in the findings of dozens of studies, but Comstock is able to put the findings into a perspective that permits the reader to apply the conclusions to specific conditions with specific types of young people.

Trend 10

Professional education of educational technologists has stabilized in size and scope.

There may not be much uniformity in the titles of academic programs that prepare individuals to serve in the field of educational technology (instructional technology, educational systems, instructional design, etc.), and the academic "homes" are not consistent from university to university but, in general, the field is holding its own. Programs tend to include similar content, are primarily offered at the graduate level, and prepare students for similar positions.

Educational Media and Technology Yearbook 1991 (Branyan-Broadbent and Wood, 1991) lists 63 doctoral programs in the United States. No new doctoral programs were instituted in 1991, but the East Texas State University program was eliminated because of economic cutbacks and the University of Northern Colorado program was substantially revised. The *EMTY 1991* lists 195 master's and six-year degree programs, some of which are located at the institutions offering doctoral degrees. Programs were eliminated (or combined with other programs) at four universities in 1991. A third listing in the *EMTY 1991* includes 82 programs in educational computing, 32 more programs than in 1986 when the listing first appeared. Like the master's degrees in educational technology, some of the master's degrees in education and computing are also located at institutions offering doctoral degrees.

New and revised programs reflect emerging trends in the field at large. At Northwestern University, a Ph.D. program in the Learning Sciences has as its purpose, "to advance the research and development of innovative educational structures and technologies." At the University of New Mexico, the Department of Training and Learning Technologies incorporates the areas of training and development, adult learning, and instructional technologies. The revised doctoral curriculum at the University of Northern Colorado is future-oriented, with emphasis areas in instructional design/development, interactive technologies, and technology integration.

More professional conferences, conventions, and workshops feature specific media and technology applications to education and training. The largest is Commtex, which was held in Orlando, Florida, in February 1991 and attracted the largest number of participants in recent years. Other meetings tended to feature computer and telecommunications applications.

BEYOND THE TRENDS 1988-1991—
THE LONGER VIEW

With baseline data from 1988 and 1989, it is possible, using data from 1991, to begin to consider the trends over time. Five or ten years would be a better timespan, but analysis can begin at this point and be adjusted in the years to come. A starting point is with the frequency of items in the literature, dissertations, conference programs, and ERIC input. Tables 4.1 and 4.2 (see pages 35-36 and 37) reveal a relative consistency of content categories and recording units used in this study. Although there are several aberrations from year to year, they do not seem to alter the trends significantly. For all intents and purposes, the sequence of 10 trends uncovered this year is as viable as the 1988 and 1989 lists. Therefore, this longer range view should go beyond the data and attempt to identify the more subtle trends that do not reveal themselves after following the replicable methodology that has been used in the three editions of this report.

This analysis of trends comes from the more personal views of the author, who has lived with this process over the past four years. It includes subjective data gathered while serving as Director (and later, Associate Director) of the ERIC Clearinghouse on Information Resources. As a participant in the document selection process for *Resources in Education* and journal article selection for the *Current Index to Journals in Education* (CIJE), hundreds of items pass his eyes each year and a substantive judgment must be made about each one. As professor and chair of an academic department that prepares professionals for the field of educational technology, he also discusses many substantive issues about new developments in the field with faculty and students. Opportunities to serve as a consultant in other states and other parts of the world generate information about developments in the field that would not ordinarily come through the literature. In 1990, the author was a Visiting Professor for three months at the University of Twente in The Netherlands, and a consultant for the Open University in Indonesia for two months in 1991. Also in 1991, the role of facilitator for the California Educational Technology Summit (Cradler, 1991) provided an opportunity to verify some of the trends that were being held as tentative.

Other signals also add to the mix of inputs that help to articulate the longer view of trends. As the team reviewed the literature of 1991, using the same recording units as past efforts, it was clear that many new concepts were emerging that could not comfortably fit the existing categories. When some of these concepts, now translated into specific terms, continued to emerge, it became apparent that new categories would have to be created. In part, identification of new concepts may reflect a limitation in the old schema, but the fact that so many new terms were independently assigned to items in the literature seemed to indicate that there were emerging ideas that had not been accounted for in the previous rounds. Likewise, some existing terms in the recording units were hardly used at all. They had fallen into disuse, even though they had appeared more frequently in earlier efforts. For example, the following terms grew out of this year's review:

Integrated Learning Systems	Gender
Multimedia	Authoring Systems
Presentation	Constructivism
Cross-cultural	Diversity
Cognitive Science	Instructional Strategies
Program Evaluation	Impact
Educational Technology Competencies for Teacher Education	Networking
	Hypermedia

Other indicators of movement within the field come from placement records. Where are educational technology graduates going? What are they doing on the job? What is the demand for such people? Currently there is no systematic collection of data to answer those questions, but if someone is engaged in the process of helping master's and doctoral graduates find positions, it is likely that some feeling for employer needs is gained. Thus, another ingredient is added to the mixture.

Recognizing these idiosyncratic sources, and the admission of subjectivity by the author, a list of trends that takes a longer view than the year-to-year reports is presented for the reader's consideration. These personal opinions may serve as a basis for further discussion among colleagues in the educational technology community.

- Educational technology is being shaped more by external forces than by the internal influence of its own professionals.

Calls for using technology to solve some of the problems facing schools come more from the business and industry community than from the schools themselves. The National Governors' Association has been advocating and monitoring the use of technology in education for the past five years. The New American Schools Development Corporation expects technology to lead the way in creating "break-the-mold" schools. A relatively small number of professionals within the schools and universities try to reach the vast number of teachers and professors in attempts to encourage the reluctant ones to try technology. There has been little impact. Some partnership ventures between computer companies and schools and cable companies and schools have led the way to greater infusion of technology. Most of these events are isolated in local settings and do not have the impact that technology advocates claim. The potential for contributions to teaching and learning through technology are still waiting for breakthroughs that will reach each teacher in each school in the country.

- The use of traditional media resources has become routine in most elementary and secondary classrooms.

Not many classrooms lack permanent overhead projectors available at all times. They have become as ubiquitous as the chalkboards that they often replace. Audiocassette recorders are easily available to most teachers, whether to introduce a story to preschoolers or to practice foreign language skills. Ninety-four percent of the nation's elementary and secondary schools have videotape recorders (Quality Education Data, 1991b) and that means there are television monitors available as well, for incoming programs on cable or from broadcast sources. Availability of equipment does not seem to be a major problem in most schools. Schools have gradually built up a reservoir of equipment over the past 30 years. Its use is probably uneven, just as the quality of teaching is uneven in the more than 80,000 schools in the land. It appears that teachers could use help in using even the basic hardware that is already available to them.

- There is little evidence to show that the computer has made major contributions to learning in the classroom other than to help learners know how to use it.

The novelty wears off. What starts as a new, exciting teaching/learning medium gradually becomes commonplace and, unless new software is acquired, the extent of computer use seems to be computer literacy and word processing. The studies of computer use in the schools continue, but there is very little solid evidence that computers in the classroom make a difference in learning. Perhaps this is still the era of introduction, when teachers and students are fascinated with the novelty and really do not learn much more than how to use the machine. It may be a function of software quality. Much has been written about the poor quality of software for teaching and learning, although it seems to be getting better. Some commercial organizations are known for having higher quality software than others. There is also some doubt as to where the computers belong in the school. Some classrooms have several units, but rarely enough for the entire class. Some schools have computer classrooms: an entire class comes to one room where two students can work together on one machine. Still other schools use the school library media center as the place where computers can be used or borrowed by teachers to take to the classroom. There appear to be no patterns regarding locale of use. There appears to be little integration of computer-based instruction with regular curricular efforts. It may be too early to demonstrate contributions of the computer to learning, but researchers are still trying and the findings may be near.

- The self-contained classroom is the greatest single barrier to use of educational technology principles and practices.

The self-contained classroom, where most students follow their course of study, is usually the basic unit in most schools. One of the most popular statistics for most schools is the teacher:student ratio, usually expressed as 25:1 or 30:1 or some such figure. The understanding is that one teacher is responsible for a certain number of students. It is the teacher's responsibility to engage the students in learning activities during a specified period of time, perhaps 35 to 45 minutes as most periods are defined. The teacher is autonomous—alone with a syllabus and, hopefully, a repertoire of teaching techniques that will attract and hold attention so that learning will occur. Audiovisual media have been used for the past 40 years as one technique to attract and hold attention. Most media are group-paced; that is, when something is shown, the entire class is involved. If a teacher wants to help an individual learner, or a small group, other activities must be created to engage the rest of the class. Very often such variations on the entire-class theme are a logistical nightmare. Educational technology, properly used, can help to engage students individually or in small groups. Use of teacher aides or teaching teams can open new possibilities beyond the self-contained classroom. Until differentiated staffing arrangements are put in place and resource stations are installed and monitored, educational technology will not make the contributions that its advocates claim. Change begins in the individual classroom with the teacher.

- The field is shifting from the use of media and technology for enrichment to technology for replacement.

Ever since the post-World War II era, the use of media has been encouraged by contemporary educational change agents. The first term to be used was *audiovisual aids*—media for enrichment. The motto "Bring the world to the classroom" indicates the role of media during the early days. Some teachers used media to fill time, while others tried to integrate the use of media with the curriculum. In almost every case, the medium was used for *enrichment*, to improve the quality of teaching. Although this approach was admirable, it did not necessarily guarantee learning. Faint whispers of "replacing the teacher" were heard as each new medium was introduced: radio, motion pictures, and television. However, there were no documented cases of any teacher being replaced by any medium.

In recent times, the distance education movement has in fact replaced teachers. The replacement is actually a television or radio program, a computer disc, printed material, a laboratory kit, or a combination of several media. Teachers have put themselves and their ideas in a medium that replaces the face-to-face instruction that historically characterized most education. For example, when rural schools cannot find a teacher to teach a specialized subject, they can turn to one of the distance education organizations delivering television courses by satellite. When postsecondary students want to pursue a college degree, but must also maintain a full-time job, they seek open university courses offered at a distance. Teachers in their traditional roles in front of a class are replaced by teachers on tape, on film, or in written materials. This is truly an appropriate role for technology in education.

- Instructional development is being practiced more in nonschool settings than in schools.

Instructional development is the process of systematically designing materials and procedures for learning, using a variety of media for delivery. The process is an outgrowth of earlier efforts to create replicable learning packages or modules that guaranteed results. One of its earliest examples is programmed instruction. As business, industry, government, military, and medical communities discovered the cost-effective results of instructional development, they moved to create training packages and programs for their employees. Principles from the field of educational technology worked well in these training environments and soon many nonschool organizations were deeply involved in using these principles. However, schools and universities continued to be reluctant clients and users of media for enrichment, if they used media at all. The graduates of professional graduate programs in educational technology currently obtain employment more in the business and industry sector than in education. This trend began over a decade ago, and there are prospects of it not only continuing but growing, despite the pleas of both educational technology professionals and advocates from business (Bowsher, 1989).

• Distance education has become an operation analog of educational technology.

Distance education and educational technology are congruent concepts. Distance education encompasses virtually every aspect of educational technology. From a basic concern for the individual learner to a complete treatment of instructional design and development procedures, educational technology is apparent. The use of multimedia delivery systems in a variety of dispersed settings requires replicable materials that will ensure attainment of learning objectives by every learner. Evaluation is central, as is feedback to the student. The entire system must be managed well to facilitate learning and to ensure proper recordkeeping.

• Cognitive science provides the best source of theoretical principles that underlie instructional design.

There is a trend toward the use of cognitive science as a basic underpinning for the process of instructional design and development. Even though the remnants of behavioral psychology still dot the landscape, especially in training programs, cognitive psychology seems to be the theoretical direction in which the field is moving. There is some controversy regarding its application among the constructivists and non-constructivists. The concepts and empirical findings are helping to guide instructional design toward new understandings of how people learn and how to design instruction for optimal results.

• Evaluation is valued but infrequently used.

Almost every instructional development model includes evaluation, yet there is not much evidence that it is widely used in practice. Evaluations of products, such as computer software, are published regularly, but evaluations of the instructional development process seem to get lost in the rush to implement a newly developed course. It seems that the "trouble" of evaluation provides an excuse for moving ahead without much data regarding the products and processes developed. Most professional education programs preparing educational technologists do not offer a separate course in evaluation. The concept and procedures are incorporated into other courses, but they tend to have a minor place in the entire professional education curriculum.

• Educational technology continues to be perceived as a field concerned more with hardware and software than with its applications for teaching and learning.

No matter how much is written about the process of instructional design, development, and evaluation, people working within the field of educational technology are perceived to be primarily concerned with the hardware and software used to deliver instruction. References are made to "the technology" when describing hardware/software systems. Most people who use the term, including many in the profession itself, do not fully understand the comprehensive meaning of the word *technology*. Technology is the application of scientific principles to solve practical problems. It is a process; it deals with problem solving. It is *not* machines; it is *not* software. It is a systematic blend of people, materials, methods, and machines to solve problems.

The profession has tried to explain itself. The Association for Educational Communications and Technology (AECT), the national professional association for the field, published *The Definition of Educational Technology* in 1977. It was widely distributed. The Association finds it necessary to create an entirely new volume in 1992 based on reinterpretations of the field and its definition. Perhaps the field will have to continue to explain itself through its actions rather than through its publications.

REFERENCES

Association for Educational Communications and Technology. (1977). *The definition of educational technology.* Washington, DC: Author.

Bell, T. H., & Elmquist, D. L. (1991). *How to shape up our nation's schools: Three critical steps.* Salt Lake City, UT: Terrel Bell.

Bowsher, J. E. (1989). *Educating America: Lessons learned in the nation's corporations.* New York: John Wiley.

Branyan-Broadbent, B., & Wood, K. (1991). *Educational media and technology yearbook.* Englewood, CO: Libraries Unlimited.

Braun, L. (1990). *Vision:TEST (Technologically Enriched Schools of Tomorrow).* Eugene, OR: International Society for Technology in Education. ED 327 173.

Comstock, G., with Paik, H. (1991). *Television and the American child.* San Diego, CA: Academic Press.

Cradler, J. (1991). *California Educational Technology Summit Proceedings.* Sacramento, CA: California Planning Commission for Educational Technology. ED 338 215.

Distance learning usage climbs in Minnesota. (1990, July). *The Heller Report 1*(10): 8-9.

Duffy, T. M., & Jonassen, D. H. (Eds.). (1991, September). Continuing the dialogue on the implications of constructivism for educational technology. [Theme issue]. *Educational Technology 31*(9).

Education and the information society: A challenge for European policy. (1991).

Ehrmann, Stephen C. (1990). Reaching students, reaching resources: Using technologies to open the college. Washington, DC: Annenberg/CPB Project. ED 327 171. Also: (1990, April). *Academic Computing 4*(7): 10-14, 32-34.

Eisenberg, M. B. (1991). *Trends and issues in library and information science.* Syracuse, NY: ERIC Clearinghouse on Information Resources. ED 335 061.

Ely, D. P. (1989). *Trends and issues in educational technology 1988.* Syracuse, NY: ERIC Clearinghouse on Information Resources. ED 308 859.

———. (1990). *Trends and issues in educational technology 1989.* Syracuse, NY: ERIC Clearinghouse on Information Resources. ED 326 212.

EPIE Institute. (1990, February). *The integrated instructional systems report.* Hampton Bays, NY: Author.

Eraut, Michael (Ed.). (1991). *Education and the information society.* London: Cassell PLC.

Eurich, N. (1990). *The learning society: Education for adult workers.* Lawrenceville, NJ: Princeton University Press.

Free to watch TV. (1991, November 20). [Editorial]. *Washington Post.*

Garnette, C. P., Withrow, F. B. (1990). Analysis of the U.S. Department of Education's database of distance learning projects. *Journal of Educational Computing Research 6*(4): 515-522.

Green, K. C., & Eastman, S. (1991, Summer). Access to computing: How many computers and where do we put them? *EDUCOM Review*, 59-61.

Gustafson, K. (1991). *A survey of instructional development models*, 2nd ed. Syracuse, NY: ERIC Clearinghouse on Information Resources. ED 335 027.

Harel, I., & Papert, S. (Eds.). (1991). *Constructionism*. Norwood, NJ: Ablex Publishing.

Hawkridge, D., Jaworski, J., & McMahon, H. (1990). *Computers in third world schools*. London: Macmillan.

High-Performance Computing Act of 1991 (P.L. 102-194, 9 December, 1991).

Janowiak, R. M. (1990). *Educational technology in kindergarten through twelfth grades*. Chicago: National Engineering Consortium.

Janowitz, M. (1976). Content analysis and the study of sociopolitical change. *Journal of Communication* *26*(4): 20-21.

Kominski, R. (1991). *Computer use in the United States: 1989*. Current Population Reports, Special Studies, Series P-23, No. 171. Washington, DC: U.S. Department of Commerce. ED 338 210.

Krippendorff, K. (1980). *Content analysis: An introduction to its methodology*. Beverly Hills, CA: Sage Publications.

Kurshaw, D., & Harrington, M. (1991). *Creating communities: An educator's guide to electronic networks*. Washington, DC: National Science Foundation.

Mann, D. (1991). *How teachers and media specialists grade cable TV*. New York: Teachers College, Columbia University.

Market Data Retrieval. (1991). *Education and technology*. Shelton, CT: Author.

Merina, A. (1991, February). Introducing NEA EdStar. *NEA Today 9*(6): 25.

Mitchell, Brent. (1991, September 24). Educator urges speed in revitalizing schools; Standardized tests, high technology backed. *Washington Post*.

Moore, D. M., & Braden, R. A. (1988, March). Prestige and influence in the field of educational technology. *Performance & Instruction 21*(2): 15-23.

Naisbitt, J. (1982). *Megatrends*. New York: Warner Books.

National Education Association. (1991, September). The 1991-92 resolutions of the National Education Association. *NEA Today 10*(1): 15-25.

National Governors' Association. (1990). *Results in education: 1990. The governors' 1991 report on education*. Washington, DC: Author. ED 327 969.

Neill, S. B., & Neill, G. W. (1990). *Only the best, 1991. The annual guide to highest rated educational software, preschool-grade 12*. New York: R. R. Bowker.

Northwest Regional Educational Laboratory. (1991). *Enhancing instruction through telecommunications*. Portland, OR: Author.

Pelgrum, W. J., & Plomp, T. (1991). *The use of computers in education worldwide*. Oxford: Pergamon Press. Also: Pelgrum, W. J., & Plomp, T. (1991, April). *The use of computers in education worldwide*. Paper presented at the 1991 annual conference of the American Educational Research Association, Chicago. ED 337 157.

Plomp, T., & Pelgrum, W. J. (1990). Introduction of computers in education: State of the art in eight countries. Paper presented at EURIT (Herning, Denmark, April 1990).

Quality Education Data, Inc. (1991a). *Satellite dish usage public school districts 1990-91 school year*. Denver, CO: Author.

————. (1991b). *Technology in schools 1990-91 school year.* Denver, CO: Author.

Saettler, P. (1991). *The evolution of American educational technology.* Englewood, CO: Libraries Unlimited.

Sheekey, A. A. (1991). *Education policy and telecommunications technologies.* Washington, DC: U.S. Department of Education, Office of Educational Research and Improvement.

Sheingold, K., & Hadley, M. (1990). *Accomplished teachers: Integrating computers into classroom practice.* New York: Center for Technology in Education, Bank Street College of Education.

Sherry, M. (1991, November). The future of integrated learning systems. *Inventing Tomorrow's Schools* *1*(1): 6.

Skelly, M. S. (1991, August). Classroom television: Should schools tune in? *School and College*, 22-27.

"Wade right in," manager tells educators. (1991, November). *School Technology News 8*(9): 1.

Weber, R. P. (1990). *Basic content analysis*, 2nd ed. Beverly Hills, CA: Sage Publications.

"What curriculum for the 21st century?" (1990, August). *New Things Considered 6*, 1.

5

The Proper Study of Instructional Technology

Robert Heinich

School of Education, Indiana University
Bloomington, Indiana

The origin of this article was in a request to update my monograph, *Technology and the Management of Instruction* (Heinich, 1970). Since its publication, I have explored and extended the basic premises of the monograph in a series of fugitive and quasi-fugitive papers. I welcomed the opportunity to pull together the main ideas of those papers and present them under a unifying conceptual framework. Prior reading of the monograph will be helpful but not essential.

To be radical is to grasp the root. The root of instructional technology is technology itself. Instructional technology as a field of study is better considered as a subset of technology in general rather than as a subset of Education* (or, in the orientation of some members of the field, psychology). Because technologies of instruction[1] have developed to the point of being able to range from helping an instructor improve a lesson to serving as the modus operandi of an entire institution such as the Open University, the field of instructional technology, and therefore its study, has grown beyond the restrictive boundaries of Education as exemplified in Schools and Departments of Education in colleges and universities.

The vast majority of academic departments of instructional technology emerged from media (occasionally educational psychology) departments or programs in Schools of Education.[2] As implied above, the reason was the historical use of media as tools to improve teacher performance. This relationship not only set organizational and institutional patterns but also shaped the directions of scholarly activity. The consequences were and are limitations on the development of theory, research, and practice.

Reprinted from *Educational Communication and Technology Journal* by permission of the Association for Educational Communications and Technology. Copyright 1984 by AECT. For an extension of this discussion, refer to Instructional technology and the structure of education, *Educational Communication and Technology Journal, 33*(1), 9-15.

This is the 10th ERIC/ECTJ Annual Review Paper, preparation of which was supported by the ERIC (Educational Resources Information Center) Clearinghouse on Information Resources, Syracuse University. The material in this article was prepared pursuant to a contract with the National Institute of Education, U.S. Department of Education. Contractors undertaking such projects under government sponsorship are encouraged to express freely their judgment in professional and technical matters. Points of view or opinions do not necessarily represent the official view or opinion of the NIE.—Ed.

*For purposes of clarity, Education as a discipline will be capitalized; education as a general activity will be in lowercase.

Concomitantly, media service units operating within school systems, colleges, and universities find themselves in institutional settings that assign total curricular and instructional authority to individual faculty. As these service groups struggle to evolve into instructional technology units, they eventually face a decision-making structure that neither encourages nor facilitates the full application of the technology at their command, and that makes the use of the products of their efforts subject to the vagaries of temporary casts of characters. In formal education, the assignment of instructional authority to faculty is taken for granted. Rarely does a counterpart authority exist to institutionalize technologically-based instruction. The consequences are the same limitations on the development of theory, research, and practice.[3]

LIMITATIONS

Because training teachers is the main business of Schools of Education, preparing teachers to use media effectively and preparing service personnel to help teachers select media are assumed by both the Schools and the programs to be the main functions and the primary intellectual interests of media programs. As a result, the energies of faculties are directed toward service courses rather than toward building the knowledge base of instructional technology. The basic assumption of teacher education is that final instructional decisions, whether based on careful planning or spontaneity, are made at the moment of interaction between teacher and students. Consequently, media faculty find themselves accepting the priority of their administrative home: improving the performance of teachers in classrooms by providing stimulus materials and showing teachers how to use them. My complaint is that, while improving teacher performance is a good thing, accepting that function as a primary basis for theory building, research, and practice imposes severe limitations on the intellectual growth and professional development of the field of instructional technology. Before I elaborate on this point, I need to state the foundation of instructional technology.

In contrast to the underlying assumption of teacher education, the basic premise of instructional technology is that all instructional contingencies can be managed through space and time (i.e., they can be incorporated into the interface between student and material and/or device). Our inability to do so in any given situation is viewed as a temporary deficiency in our knowledge base. Primary emphasis is given to the development of more powerful technologies of instruction along with the development of organizational structures that facilitate their use; secondary emphasis is given to improvement of teacher performance. (As we shall see later, this order of priority raises the question of the level of competence required of the individual in direct contact with learners.) As a *strategy*, as an *approach to solving problems*, this basic premise of instructional technology expands theory, research, and development, redirects our efforts to different client systems, and leads to lines of inquiry in direct opposition to the assumptions of teacher education. The following are offered in illustration.

In traditional education, curriculum and instruction are regarded as related but separable processes: Instruction is the responsibility of individual faculty assigned to courses. In other words, curriculum is planned independently of its implementation. When instructors are responsible for both curriculum and instruction, they regard each as separate activities. Providing stimulus materials for this paradigm is what was expected of us.[4] The cause and effect relationship in specific instructional situations, therefore, was not under our control. But as our technologies of instruction became more sophisticated, more reliable, and more powerful, we realized that curriculum and instruction can be (and in certain cases must be) developed at the same time. For example, if a course is to be designed as programmed instruction, or CAI, or video, etc., instruction is designed into the delivery system. Cause and effect relationships can be identified, studied, and managed.[5] Research and development based on a theoretical construct that requires manipulation of all variables, including instructors, can lead us to an instructional science and technology capable of radically altering the institution of education.[6]

However, our colleagues in Education, and other faculty, are extremely reluctant to accept instructional technology as an alternative method of structuring education; they are also less than eager to view us in any other than the service role of provider or designer of stimulus materials. They do not want the craft nature of instruction disturbed by technology. I would like to draw on an example from general technology and a parallel from education to illustrate this crucial point.

Suppose a sales representative from a machine tool maker demonstrates to the manager of a plant that manufactures machine screws a new tool to cut threads. The new tool permits a faster cut, doesn't wear out as quickly, and is easier to mount in the lathe. The foreman wastes no time in showing the new tool to the lathe operators who are delighted to try it out. Here is obviously an innovation that has a high probability of being accepted by the work force.

The following year, the sales representative demonstrates to the manager of the plant a new lathe that *automatically* fashions machine screws. Fewer operators are needed to produce the same volume of screws. The plant manager immediately recognizes an innovation that will have an impact drastically different from the tool that was adopted the previous year. Here now is a device that will appeal to the owner of the plant because it will make the company more cost effective. The consumer benefits also because the unit price of machine screws will drop. In the long run, the work force benefits from the expanded job markets that result. But in the short run, the manager knows that the lathe operators will not look kindly on a machine that will do their job.[7]

(This should go without saying, but I am *not* suggesting by this analogy that learners can be treated like machine screws. The point is that perspective and insight can be gained by studying how similar problems have been resolved in other areas of technology.)

In contrast, consider the place of the textbook in the instructional scheme of things. The textbook is worth examining because it has been around so long and has become so much a part of the system that we tend not to think of it as a product of technology. The textbook endures to a great extent because of the symbiotic relationship that has developed over a long period of time between it and the teacher. Publishers have found that the symbiotic relationship is disturbed if the book takes over too much of the instructional burden. A text is essentially a course of study (a curriculum) between hard covers. It requires the teacher to translate it into instruction. If the text translates itself into instruction, as in a programmed book, the symbiotic relationship is disturbed and the text is rejected. The more "pedagogical aids" (in publishers' parlance) provided with the text the better, but there is a very important difference between pedagogical aids and self-instruction: The former underscores the need for the teacher. The point is that text adopters are telling publishers that the text should be supportive, not threatening. For basically the same reason, producers find it easier to sell individual film titles than a course on film (or video). Producers of CAI will find a readier market for individual lessons than for complete courses.

To generalize, the development of instructional technology has disturbed the symbiotic relationship between instructional materials and teachers. I see why, and I can readily under-stand teachers' reactions. They reject the implied change in the power structure. Correlatively, curriculum personnel and teachers resist instructional technologists when we move toward the union of curriculum and instruction in designing mediated instruction.

We as a field have failed to learn important lessons from our experiences in introducing new technologies of instruction. Reflection on those experiences and on the two examples given above should give us more insight into why we need to look elsewhere for intellectual kinship. Consider the following:

Misunderstanding of Client Systems. If the manager of the plant had tried to convince the lathe operators to adopt the automatic screw machine, we know what the answer would have been. Yet this is precisely what we have done and continue to do in the institutions we serve. We have tended to treat all technological innovations the same in reference to client systems: Introduction of television systems is seen as little different from the introduction of an overhead projector. We have failed to understand that the overhead projector (and other devices) does not disturb power relationships (it is a "better tool"), but that a television system can disturb power relationships. Faculty, like lathe operators, prefer the power relationships the way they are and maintain them by reducing all technologies to the status of "tools." Doing so keeps everything in place.

Analysis and recognition of the differential effects of technology on power relationships can lead us away from butting our heads against a stone wall toward gaining an understanding of why the system reacts the way it does and what needs to happen to change the performance of the cast of characters.

It follows that the same holds true for our research efforts. We act as though faculty are the clients of our research when, in reality, inquiry into most of the systematic aspects of instructional technology is most pertinent to clients other than faculty: Administrators, school boards, boards of trustees, legislators, etc. It is up to us to demonstrate to those clients the policy issues implicit in technology. Even in our traditional areas of research, such as message design, we frequently assume faculty to be our clients rather than the producers of materials who really are: Faculty are not normally in a position to incorporate research findings into the *design* of materials.

Instructional Development Into Faculty Development. Instructional development departments in higher education frequently find themselves pushed more and more into faculty development with less and less effort expended on instructional development. Faculty development and instructional development are not the same. Faculty development is concerned with improving the performance of individual instructors with little regard for instructional development as we define it. Sometimes the fond hope is that faculty can be trained to do instructional development. The problem is that the institution rewards the performance of the individual, *not* of the instructional system.

The original concept of instructional development as being able to account for *all* variables, including instructors, has eroded under institutional pressure. The system does not permit this general accountability to occur. Again, inquiry into the infrastructure that supports the basic assumption of instructional authority in the present system would help us understand why and lead us to how the rules of the game need to be changed.

I conclude this section with the observation that the more successful the instructional development department and the more capable its personnel, the more it will be pushed into faculty development: The instructional development department thus becomes a victim of its own success. The purpose of this observation is not to denigrate these and other activities that serve the purposes of the institution and reward those who perform them. The point is that instructional technologists need to recognize when they are performing functions that do not further their conceptual framework and that delude them into misconceptions of what they are about.

From Leadership to Consultation. To me, a consequence of the erosion of the concept of instructional development is the gradual shift from leadership to consultation. After all, it's hard to remain a revolutionary when your cause is rejected but *you* prevail! Many still espouse the cause, but the lure of profit from the current system softens the protest. It's sort of like being a Norman Thomas socialist (for those of you who remember)—and the system rather enjoys its "safe" rebels!

Seriously, we need to understand what is happening to us when our role changes as the system modifies our intellectual concepts. To prevent any misunderstanding, I am neither belittling the acquisition of consulting skills nor criticizing people for doing their jobs as best they can. It *is* important to learn to work well with clients. But the consulting skills needed in anticipation of leading a design team are different from those needed to advise about "better tools." The latter implies acceptance of the status quo.

Acceptance of Institutional Relationships. Perhaps the most serious consequence of our academic origins is our acceptance of the institutional relationships and governing structure of formal education. This applies to a good extent to training programs because of their tendency to look to education for models. By accepting the underlying assumptions of traditional educational practice, we automatically accept the infrastructure of those assumptions. We grew up academically supporting faculty and are uncomfortable when shaking off that encumbering intellectual heritage. We project the same attitudes into our service roles and back off from the logical consequences of our technology.

A number of reasons for the discomfort come to mind:

1. *A disturbing sense of disloyalty to our "upbringing" in Education and to our colleagues among the faculty.* Typical of this state of mind are frequent reassurances we utter about not replacing teachers with technology; our unease over our presumption that we *could* replace much of what goes on in education; the legacy of our training in Education that instruction is best when created ad hoc or when "the teachable moment" is at hand (one of the hoariest myths of Education); etc.

Even some of our most advanced prophets in instructional technology suffered from this syndrome. For example, James D. Finn, who along with Charles F. Hoban did the most to lead us into a brave new world of technology, balked at the changes in client systems and personnel behavior implied by the consequences of his work. He could deal with it in the abstract, as he did in "Technology and the Instructional Process" (Finn, 1960), but not on the personal level. He received his training during the height of the progressive education movement and could not bring himself to break away by challenging its precepts from the point of view of technology. Ironically, his John Dewey Society lecture, "A Walk on the Altered Side," is his finest attempt to drag Education into the world of technology (Finn, 1962).

To a considerable degree, those parts of the field that came up through programmed instruction and television escaped this syndrome—at least in terms of academic orientation. Unhampered by educationists, the programmed instruction enthusiasts quickly saw the revolutionary nature of what they wrought. The realities of institutional restraints brought them crashing back to earth. Unfortunately, the television people got caught up in the delivery system and thought all one needed was a dynamic personality and a camera. Organizations such as the Agency for Instructional Television and the Children's Television Workshop have been correcting that mistake. Those entering the field from the computer area are repeating the television mistake. They don't realize that programmed instruction, not the machine itself, is their intellectual fountainhead.

2. *Cognitive dissonance caused by the discrepancy between what we* can *do and what the "establishment" permits us to do.* This is related to my previous statement about being a revolutionary whose cause is rejected; or if you can't lick 'em, join 'em. Cognitive dissonance is reduced (even eliminated) by convincing oneself that change can only come about by personal persuasion, better research evidence, and improved courseware: comforting but false.

3. *The necessity to change from a nurturing to a commanding role (and from a support to a design role).* This is a particularly important problem that *may* solve itself in the long run but causes difficulties in the short run. It is a problem that plagues any profession or trade in fundamental transition. One aspect of the problem is a personality dimension: If people have chosen a profession because it is primarily supportive or nurturing, can they take charge if changes in the profession demand it? Obviously some can, but the question is addressed to the average professional. Is denial of the potential of instructional technology by individual professionals an implicit refusal to accept an unanticipated level of responsibility? For example, can a media specialist in a school become an instructional technologist? Can a person who is trained to expect someone else to make curricular decisions and another someone else to make instructional decisions move into a truly collaborative design role as an instructional technologist? Another aspect is a question of different talents as well as different personality. Is the talent for curricular and instructional design qualitatively different from the talent required to perform traditional service functions? Do we need to tap another labor pool, or is a drastic change in

training enough? (And where do those training programs come from?) The same is true of media service roles in higher education. Kerr's (1977) study of the perceptions of media personnel in the schools underscores the need for more work in this area.

Educationists, almost as a professional posture, assume that all of the education professions should emerge from the basic teaching pool and, further, that all education professionals should first be trained as teachers. I would challenge this position by returning to the lathe example. The talent that *designed* the automatic lathe is fundamentally different—by initial selection and by training—from the talent that *operated* the lathe. Was it necessary for the *designers* of automatic lathes to be *operators* of lathes before exercising their design skills?

The legacy of a nurturing role also haunts the professional association with the longest history in the field—the Association for Educational Communications and Technology (AECT). Because AECT originated as a department of the National Education Association and remained so for almost half a century, it looked to the parent association to deal with major policy issues and generally accepted the paternalism implied. AECT has not as yet succeeded in developing a strong, independent, and commanding voice of its own.

4. *The difficulty of analyzing our own profession.* First let me hasten to state that blame for this item cannot be laid at the door of Education but is, rather, inherent in our academic jobs. Allow me to illustrate with an anecdote. A few years ago, I was working with an economist on cost effectiveness of technologically based instructional systems. As it became apparent that, under certain circumstances, cost effectiveness could be improved by reducing the labor intensiveness of instruction, he suddenly exclaimed, "Bob, do you realize we're talking about our jobs?" Our own vested interests as faculty can interfere with our scholarly inquiry into the impact of technology on education institutions. We need to discipline ourselves to separate our jobs from our intellectual study.

We also need to deal with our own cognitive dissonance that arises from the discrepancy between what we profess about the design of instruction and how we ourselves instruct. There is a collective and an individual response to this dilemma. The collective response is that our performance is under the same pressures and forces that shape the performance of our colleagues in other schools and departments. In other words, if the rules of the game shape the performance of the players, we are playing by the same rules. The individual response has to do with our capabilities as instructors.

Different Solutions to Educational Problems. We tend to seek solutions to education problems through technology; Education through teaching personnel. The two are often in direct conflict. At present, the U.S. is lamenting the sad state of instruction in the schools. The National Commission on Excellence in Education reminds us that the gains of the education reforms of the '50s and '60s have been dissipated and the support systems that evolved during that period have been allowed to fall apart. The nation is where it was 25 years ago: in desperate need of quality education in the schools, particularly in science and math. Education's response is to train more teachers, retrain teachers now in service, and pay them more.

What is our response? What have we learned form the experience of the '50s and '60s? For our purpose here, two lessons we should have learned are:

- We do not need *more* teachers in order to improve science and math instruction.

- The reliance then placed on technologies of instruction to carry the burden of reform was appropriate and is even more so today because of our vastly improved capabilities in design and delivery of instruction.[8]

The large scale experiment in Wisconsin using the Harvey White filmed course in physics (Wittich, Pella, & Wedemeyer, 1960), the successful use of filmed courses by the Rocky Mountain Area Project for Small High Schools (Anderson, 1969), the rationale behind, and the experience of the Physical Science Study Committee (Marsh, 1964), the Individually Prescribed

Instruction Program and other technologically based programs should reinforce us in the belief that comprehensive use of technology can result in better instruction in schools more quickly than can be achieved solely by training teachers. But in these days of falling enrollments in Schools of Education, how far would we get advocating an approach to the crisis in the schools that does not hold out much hope for increasing credit-hour production and filling summer session classes once again?

I must stress that I haven't been setting up a good guys versus bad guys conflict. There is nothing inherently "bad" about them and "good" about us. Churchill has been credited with the observation, "First we shape our buildings and then our buildings shape us." Education institutions evolved from basic assumptions about how instruction should be managed. Those institutions now reinforce the assumptions that created them by shaping the behaviors of the faculties and administrators who work in them. Our assumptions about the management of instruction (if you agree with me) are fundamentally different. We need to understand that. Survival depends on establishing our own intellectual identity. Capitulation makes us vulnerable because then we can be easily co-opted. This is contrary to what many of us currently think. We must make a distinction between our administrative "home" and our intellectual foundations.

By establishing our own identity, we stand a much better chance of demonstrating that the future of Education can be enhanced by broadening its mission to include all approaches to designing, delivering, and managing instruction. For example, curriculum faculty tend to restrict themselves to curriculum building within one institutional framework: the schools. Our recent moves into the human resources development area can lead curriculum faculty into an institution-free concept of curriculum building. In this way, we can help other departments increase their survival abilities.

In respect to our service functions, establishing our own intellectual identity would put us in a much stronger position to demonstrate the cost effectiveness of our approach to curricular and instructional tasks. As technology becomes more comprehensive, more sophisticated, more pervasive, its consideration and use move to higher and higher levels of decision making: selecting instructional materials to supplement a lesson affects only one instructor; using telecommunications and information technology to create an autonomous institution involves the legislature and a governing board. Are we intellectually ready to address both levels and all others in between?

THE HOPE OF THE '60s

Do you have a feeling of déjà vu about the current situation in education? If so, then you were around during the latter part of the '50s and the decade of the '60s. Public criticism and Soviet scientific success combined to put pressure on the schools to improve instructional effectiveness and academic standards. We in instructional technology knew we had methods and techniques needed to do the job. The '50s saw the teaching of entire courses by television and then by film. The emergence of the programmed instruction movement gave us great confidence in our ability to design effective and replicable instruction—and isn't that what America needed even more than a good 5-cent cigar? Extensive national curriculum projects were mounted resulting in courses with appropriate academic rigor and backed up by well-developed packages of materials. We discovered systems theory, and instructional development emerged as a process and a method to operationalize a systems approach to instruction.

Business and industry caught the fever. Mergers of electronics and publishing firms became commonplace. They saw the real need for comprehensive, complex packages of instruction. Much money was invested. Many good products were developed. Few were bought and fewer were used. Hardware manufacturers also saw a vast market for their equipment. Federal money made purchase of equipment easier. But much of it wound up on shelves in closets: technological tools whose use was vitiated by an absence of a commitment to technology as process.

A funny thing happened on our way to the systems approach and instructional develop-ment. We stumbled over the rigidity of educational governance and the craft structure of education institutions. We completely misread the institutional framework of which we are a part. A. Rupert Hall, a historian of technology, once commented that "Scientific knowledge is of little material value if the object of technological proficiency is the manufacture of objects of luxury; hence, in backward contemporary societies, the arbitrary installation of a few modern industrial plants, without modification of the basic economy, has little more result than to allow the rich to adopt Cadillacs and television in place of more barbarous means of ostentation" (Hall, 1963). This is precisely what happened in education—except the part about "barbarous means of ostentation"! We must study our institutions from the viewpoint of general technology to understand how the "basic economy" can be changed to make our processes and products central rather than "objects of luxury."

TECHNOLOGY IS THE BASE

Definition and Characteristics of Technology

By asserting an intellectual position independent of Education and education institutions, we can examine what we are about in terms of theory, research, and practice from a different perspective. But what perspective? As I stated in the lead paragraph, I propose that instructional technology be regarded as a subset of technology in general. A definition of technology, then, would be helpful.

Agreeing on a definition of technology that can be applied to all stages of history may be impossible. Early technology evolved primarily through accident and trial and error. While the fortuitous discovery is still important, contemporary technology is mainly the result of a constantly expanding knowledge base. A definition that fits early technology does not apply to advanced technology, and vice versa. Unfortunately for our use, the word was coined during a period of time that used it to describe what artisans do. For a long time, therefore, dictionaries defined technology as "the systematic treatment of an art." New dictionaries and recent revisions of older ones are using definitions that better fit contemporary technology. *Webster's New Collegiate Dictionary* defines technology as "...the totality of the means employed to provide objects necessary for human sustenance and comfort" and "a technical method of achieving a practical purpose."

Nor is it useful to define technology too broadly. Perhaps in reaction to the conventional view of technology as machines, it has become fashionable in certain circles to represent just about anything that uses organized thought as technology. In responding to one such definition, Peter Drucker dryly remarked that, according to the speaker, a fox that has learned to cross a highway without getting killed has acquired technology.

Neither technique nor method, in itself, is technology. A teaching technique is not technology. Neither is my method of organizing a manuscript. I have read prestigious reports that represented a seating chart as technology in the classroom. This trivializes technology. (For example, see Goodlad, 1983, p. 469.)

In 1967, I used Galbraith's definition: "Technology means the systematic application of scientific and other organized knowledge to practical tasks" (Galbraith, 1967). It is still useful. Daniel Bell, the eminent sociologist, defines technology as "the instrumental ordering of human experience within a logic of efficient means, and the direction of nature to use its power for material gain" (Bell, 1973). These two definitions fit our field particularly well.

Valuable as they are, definitions are still abstract. In order to better understand how instructional technology benefits by considering it a subset of technology, we need to look at characteristics and principles of technology that extend into our field. Consider the following:

1. *Replicability.* Certainly the most obvious characteristic of technology is doing things in a reproducible manner. It is this characteristic that changes the goal of technology from serving the few to enriching the lives of everyone. The technological (*not* scientific) developments and inventions that led to the industrial revolution shifted control of technology from the artisan to the skilled tool designer and maker, thereby forever changing the primary purpose of technology from the production of luxury items to mass production of items of necessity. Some historians of technology claim that technology began with the industrial revolution. Before that, all production was craft based.

A hallmark of technology, which makes it into a producer of plenty, is that reproduction is much cheaper than invention and development. The general economy is geared to make that possible. The economy of education does not facilitate the kind of distribution that can amortize the costs of invention and development over large enough units to realize the benefits of large scale production. The economy of education is based on the reinvention of instruction each year. Each instructional act is viewed as the work of an artisan.

2. *Reliability.* As Hoban (1962) put it, "In forty years, this concept of newer media in education has grown from one of a device for a lesson presentation to one of a complete system of remotely controlled instruction covering an entire course." I have addressed this point earlier, but some of you may be thinking that the reliability of our technology is still not very high. Perhaps, but remember, it doesn't take much to be more reliable than what's currently in the classroom. The other point we must remember is that the potential for improving a technology is far greater than that of improving a craft, and the benefits of an improved technology can be realized more quickly than those of an improved craft.

3. *Algorithmic decision making.* As Bell (1973) put it:

Technology is clearly more than the physical manipulation of nature. There is an "intellectual technology" as well. An algorithm is a "decision rule," a judgment of one or another alternative course to be taken, under varying conditions, to solve a problem. In this sense we have technology whenever we can substitute algorithms for human judgment. (p. 52)

He goes on to state that new intellectual technology, while on a "continuum with classical technology," transposes it to a higher qualitative level. Algorithmic decision making in design of instruction, based on our improved knowledge of human learning, raises *our* technology to a new qualitative level. Any process that lends itself to algorithmic treatment can be replicated reliably.

Bell concludes his discussion of algorithms with this grand statement:

Beyond this is a larger dream, the formalization of a theory of choice through stochastic, probabilistic, and deterministic methods.... If the computer is the "tool," then decision theory is its master. Just as Pascal sought to throw dice with God, or the physiocrats to draw a perfect grid to array all economic exchanges among men, so the decision theorists, and the new intellectual technology, seek their own *tableau entier*—the compass of rationality itself. (pp. 52-53)

Isn't this the dream implied by the Hoban quote and implied by the assumption that I earlier asserted as underlying instructional technology?

4. *Communication and control.* There is little need to elaborate on this point—it is the one with which we are most familiar. McLuhan and his global village, Edmund Carpenter, and a host of others have made us aware that we are all within "earshot" of each other. What we have not grasped in education is that our notion of narrow institutional authority is completely dissonant with our ability to deliver instruction wherever the students are in whatever social

groups they choose to form. We can learn from general technology how social institutions can be reshaped by changes in communication systems.

5. *The effect of scale.* Implied in the first four items is the effect of changes in scale caused by an ever-improving technology. As a number of people have pointed out, a sufficient quantitative change causes a qualitative change—a change in scale can mean a change in institutional form. Using a television camera as an image magnifier is a vastly different concept of scale than using television systems to create an institution. The printing press created a totally different scale in the distribution of knowledge thereby changing the social fabric of western Europe. Finn (1960) once commented that instructional technology has developed to the point where it is now possible not only to replace the teacher but also the entire school system, a logical extension of the Hoban quote—increasing the scale increases the range of control. When the linear extension of a technological form reaches its limits, an increase in scale can only occur when the form itself is abandoned. For example, when the limits of piston-driven aircraft engines were reached, the industry shifted to the jet engine. When the limits of an institution to accommodate technological developments are reached, either the institution changes under the pressure to increase scale, or the technology is artificially restrained to fit the institution. As I will point out later, our situation in education begs the question: Have we reached the limits of our institutional frameworks to facilitate the scale of our present and potential instructional technology? The above are not intended to be exhaustive, just illustrative of the kinship between our field and technology.

The beginnings of exploring their relationship have been made. Finn and Hoban in the same year, 1956, separately but not independently, drew parallels between certain problems in instruction and the systems approach to organizational efforts in industry and the military—Hoban in his keynote address to the second Lake Okoboji conference and Finn in a series of editorials in a long-defunct journal called *Teaching Tools.*

Finn later borrowed a principle of thermodynamics, negative entropy, to explain a phenomenon he observed in using technology in education. He maintained that injecting technology into an instructional system has the same organizing effect as introducing additional energy into a thermodynamic system (Finn, 1959). One of the most frequent observations made by television instructors in the 1950s had to do with how much more tightly organized the TV lesson was compared to the same lesson taught in class. Any of us in this field, regardless of the medium in which we work, can easily find examples of how the introduction of technology has caused a higher level of organization.

The concept of negative entropy lends itself to experimental verification, but, unfortunately, our fixation on learning gains as a dependent variable obscures opportunities to explore *system* effects of technology. Cabeceiras (1972) did take note of Finn's interpretation of negative entropy in a study on the effect of use of an overhead projector on the verbal behavior of teachers. However, he mentioned it only in the conclusion of his article; it was not part of the theoretical framework that generated his hypotheses. Many of the studies in programmed instruction reported achievement of specified behaviors in less time when the material was programmed. However, I know of none that attempted to attribute the effect to the process of programming itself—nor were the findings related to negative entropy. The Nebraska studies of film in social studies reported that with film, a year of U.S. history could be taught in a much shorter period. An example of negative entropy? A secondary analysis of studies in various media where time or any other manifestation of negative entropy was a factor could verify the construct. We may even find that learning gains are more accurately attributable to negative entropy than to the medium used.

A study of technology would turn up other principles, laws, and postulates that have some counterpart in instructional technology. Pursuing them can give us important insights into the system aspects of instructional technology.

TECHNOLOGY AND INSTITUTIONAL RELATIONSHIPS

A goodly part of our intellectual difficulty is the limited way in which we think of technology in the context of institutional and societal relationships. I have mentioned that as technology becomes more sophisticated and more pervasive in effect, consideration of its use must be raised to higher and higher levels of decision making. Review the machine screw example I used earlier. The decision to replace the entire lathe is of a totally different order than replacing the cutting tool. The quote from Hoban that I used in discussing *Reliability* can be paraphrased as follows:

> In forty years, this concept of newer media in education has grown from the concern of an instructor choosing a device for a lesson presentation to the concern of a state legislature considering the establishment of a university based on instructional technology.

This is the societal reality of the change in scale noted by Hoban. But, for reasons cited earlier, we have difficulties grasping the full implications of this type of policy shift. My contention is that we can find better guidance in how to deal successfully with these issues in the history of technology than we can from our historic roots in Education.

FROM CRAFT TO TECHNOLOGY

Many of the issues we now face have been dealt with previously—often quite previously— in other sectors of society. For example, one of the main, if not *the* main, conceptual issues we face is the change in instruction from a craft to a technological culture. There are many facets to this issue. I will touch on several for purposes of illustration. How do institutions respond when threatened by technology? If they survive, why do they survive and in what changed form? The medieval guilds dominated the production of goods in Europe. Today's teaching profession has certain characteristics of the craft guilds. As the merchant guilds gradually took over the production of goods they had traditionally only marketed, conflicts between the two types of guilds became frequent and often violent. The craft guilds eventually lost out not only because of the gradual development of manufacturing but also because of improved transportation and communication. What lessons might we learn by knowing more about this early encounter between craft and budding technology?

In our own time, the labor-management technology relationship can best be understood by reviewing the history of craft unionism during the first half of this century. Some of you may be uncomfortable with this, but regardless of the stand of individual teachers, there is little question that the organized teaching profession is far closer to unionism than professionalism. The main questions are: At what stage of unionism are they, and by studying the labor movement in general, what future developments might we expect? What should our relationship be to both management and labor?

We have very little research on how the growth of teacher militancy and unionism can affect our freedom to apply the full range of our technological capabilities to large-scale instructional problems. Yet, the research we do have indicates that we should be paying closer attention to these matters. Dawson's (1971) study of attitudes of members of the education profession toward media, and Schaefer's (1974) study of the implications of negotiated contracts on instructional technology are good but old. Schaefer's, in particular, needs to be updated because it documented a movement in its early stages.

The evidence we have seems to indicate that organized teacher activity parallels the craft union movement in industry. The ways in which the labor movement tried to protect its members from the encroachment of technology are very similar to how teacher groups seek to maintain the labor-intensive character of instruction. How and under what circumstances certain craft unions have accommodated (and are accommodating) technological change could help us analyze our own problems with the clash between the craft and technology of instruction.

Study of the evolution of the specialization of labor in the history of technology could give us important insights into how the craft-to-technology issue might manifest itself in the organization of instructional systems. Specialization of labor can be exploited fully only in a technologically based system. By studying the nature of work as technology changed crafts and industries, we can get a more objective viewpoint of how instructional relationships might become more specialized and how instructional responsibilities could be assigned to those specialties. In presentations on this topic, I often use three film clips to demonstrate how technology changes the nature of work.[9] One of the clips contrasts the cutting out of an aircraft stabilizer by a craft method—use of a template to scribe the outline of the stabilizer and to manually guide the cutting blade—to the same job performed by a machine controlled by a magnetic tape. The crew of workers cutting out the stabilizer is subtly contrasted with the technical knowledge of the designers of the machine and programmers of the control tape. The second clip shows the hand crafting of glass objects contrasted with the manufacture of glass products. The important questions raised by the film clip are these: Under what circumstances of societal need do we call upon the labor intensive, emotionally satisfying hand crafting of glass, and when should we rely on the efficiency of the manufacturing process? Certainly both are necessary. If technology had not entered the glass-making business, most of us would still be drinking out of gourds. The marketplace makes the decision in industry. But what are the mechanisms in a subculture where the marketplace does not make the decisions? How do we reap the benefits of the specialization of labor in instruction? The third clip documents the development of the Pap test. A scanning device analyzes cells from a smear and sends the information to a computer. Normal cells are ignored by the computer, but suspect ones are called to the attention of cytotechnicians for careful examination. It would be impossible for cytotechnicians to handle the volume of smears without the computer. Here for our study is another model of how labor can be deployed more effectively. All three film clips are examples of how the nature of work is changed when technological processes are applied to complex tasks.

It should be clear by now that instructional technology is aligned much more closely with management than with labor, despite what our sympathies may be at any given time. Those of us employed in higher education are more likely to romanticize our relationship with the teaching profession, partly because we are not normally on the firing line of militancy and partly because most of us are both instructional technologists *and* teachers. But make no mistake about it, when we moved as a field from "a device to support a lesson" to the design of instructional systems, we also moved from the side of labor to that of management. I am not suggesting any open hostility to the teaching profession—far from it. What I am saying is that the very nature of our capabilities makes us an instrument of management. Suppose, as an extreme example, teachers in a school system or institution plan to go on strike. Under pressure from public and governing boards, the chief administrator calls you into his or her office and asks you to draw up and prepare to execute a plan to use technology to keep instruction going. Choose your response: "Yes, Sir or Madam," or "I'd rather work somewhere else."

Those instructional technologists working in business and industry are far more likely to know where loyalty lies. Training is more easily identified with management goals. Regardless of whether management supports effective or ineffective instruction (and management often does both), we are hired to implement management decisions. As more and more instructional technologists take positions in nonformal education settings, the weight of their experiences will influence the labor-management perspective of the programs from which they graduated.

The reorientation of instructional technology from its craft origins to its technology present and future is critical to the continued well-being of the field. Depending on a craft orientation makes instructional technology dispensable—like items of luxury in a period of retrenchment. Technology builds systems that collapse if the technological support—men, machines, methods—is removed (e.g., the importance of the telephone to the conduct of business or the importance of the school bus to consolidation of schools). Except in rare instances such as the British Open University, we are not even close to that kind of dependency.

TECHNOLOGY AND THE
EDUCATION PROFESSIONS

One of the aspects of technology least understood by the education professions is the way in which technology changes institutional and professional relationships. Even that part of the academic community whose job it is to study the impact of technology on society generally takes an "it-can't-happen-here" attitude toward the subject of its study and its own profession. Although it is a function of higher education to analyze the problems of society, the difficulty here is that the problem of society to be analyzed happens to be one's own professional function. Many people have pointed out that it is almost impossible for someone to analyze critically an activity in which he or she is presently engaged. Perhaps the best and most objective research on the education professions can be done only by those without an occupational vested interest.

To get a better feel for how technology might affect the education professions, it might help to look at selected examples of how other professions have been changed by technology, not to look for isomorphic models but, rather, to see how technology affects professions uniquely. Technology does not change all professions in the same way. The extent to which technology can subsume certain kinds of professional tasks and how the profession (or craft) responds determine how technology changes a profession.

Of the various professions connected to the health sciences, perhaps pharmacy has been affected the most by industrial (rather than professional) technology. The traditional professional skills of the pharmacist in compounding drugs have been incorporated into the manufacturing process by the drug industry. Rapid advancements in pharmacology made the manufacture of drugs imperative. Pharmacists couldn't possibly keep up with the chemistry. All of this changed the role of the pharmacist from pill roller to pill dispenser. The result is a crisis in the training of pharmacists. Some schools of pharmacy want to shift the emphasis of their curriculum to how to run a small business. In other words, they are willing to acknowledge that the drug industry has made it unnecessary to teach the prospective pharmacist the intricacies of chemistry. Other schools of pharmacy want to create a higher role for certain pharmacists as an intermediary between physician and patient, particularly in states where prescriptions must be written in generic terms. In at least one state, California, hospitals are required to retain a registered pharmacist as an advisor to the patient on medication.

It should be mentioned that the faculties of schools of pharmacy are neither prepared nor interested in teaching their students how to run a small business. They are prepared to teach chemistry and want to teach chemistry, necessary or not. This reminds me of the account by Morison (1966) of the change by necessity from sail to steam power in naval vessels during the Civil War. The admirals had resisted the introduction of steam prior to the war but were forced to accept it because of the tactical advantages it gave them. However, after the war, the admirals went back to rejecting steam because commanding a sailing vessel projected the image of what a naval officer should be, and it was certainly *not* standing on a bridge against a backdrop of black smoke! What is the proper image of the professor?

The main parallel to the education professions of the pharmacy example is the incorporation of professional expertise into a technological process. A little over two decades ago, when the academic disciplines first initiated large-scale curriculum revision projects, one of the main arguments advanced for doing so was that teachers in the public schools did not have the opportunity to maintain expertise in their respective disciplines. For example, the Physical Science Study Committee (PSSC) pointed out that many of the developments in physics had not found their way into the classrooms of the public schools. They felt it was necessary to re-establish the link between the members of the discipline and students in high school. The new developments in physics, of course, would be incorporated into the PSSC materials. When

Jerome Bruner initiated the curriculum innovation that became known as Man—A Course of Study, he not only mentioned the difficulties of public school teachers in keeping abreast of developments in academic areas, but he also stressed that teachers did not know how to develop problem-solving materials for children. In other words, he felt that methodological as well as substantive developments needed to be incorporated into the materials developed by the project. The Individually-Prescribed Instruction (IPI) program developed at the University of Pittsburgh is another example of how the instructional expertise of the professional has been built into the materials. The professional role of the teacher has been limited to determining whether each student is ready to go on to the next unit. Obviously, that function could have also been built into the materials, but politically it was necessary for the IPI program to maintain a professional role for the teachers in those classrooms. The parallel to pharmacy is made even more striking by the use of the word "prescribed" in the title of the program.

On the other hand, the physician and dentist have been able to remain on top of technological developments in their professions. Physicians (and dentists to a lesser degree) have been able to delegate lower skill, lower return tasks to especially created technical specialties, thereby reserving high skill, high return tasks for themselves. Much of the technology of medicine is designed to increase the patient flow through the doctor's office even at the price of passing on those costs to the patients. The use of both cheap, disposable materials (such as disposable hypodermic needles) and elaborate machinery (body X-ray machinery, for example) fits this pattern. The important point is that physicians have realized that increasing the number of patients handled raises income. They have also realized that their long-range interests are in differentiation of staff.

While dentists have generally moved in the same direction as physicians, they seem to be on a plateau. However, in at least one area, the dentist is in danger of losing control of a lucrative professional task because of dental technology. Until recently, all states stipulated that only a dentist can actually place a denture in the mouth. The manufacturers of dentures claim that those regulations are now obsolete. They maintain that the technology of both fitting and manufacturing dentures has advanced to the point where the professional care of the dentist is not necessary and that technicians can handle the entire process from the initial impression to the placement of the denture in the patient's mouth. Oregon became the first state to allow someone other than a dentist to fit and place dentures.

Both physicians and dentists long ago abandoned the notion that the individual in most frequent contact with patients is in the best position to know what is best for them. In Education, we continue to cling to that myth. We are reluctant to move to an organizational structure that permits subprofessionals to be in most frequent contact with students, reserving professional contact for specific instructionally oriented purposes.

Until recently, the law was a profession about as unaffected by technology as education. As with education, it is difficult to see how the actual work of a lawyer might be affected by the introduction of technology. However, as mentioned at the beginning of this section, technology influences professions in different ways. Technology is about to change the profession of law, not by altering what a lawyer does when representing a client but rather by changing the way in which the accumulated wisdom of the profession is made available and to whom. Both identification of pertinent provisions of the law and precedents relied on for interpretation of the law are basically problems of information codification, storage, and retrieval. As we all know, those problems are very amenable to computer technology. In the past, companies specializing in gathering and selling information in the form of monthly or annual compilations in print form sold their products primarily to law firms and law libraries. Processing this information in relation to a specific case was still the job of the lawyer. Computer processing of information, however, makes it possible to change that. To the chagrin of lawyers, some of these legal information companies are now making their services available to anyone willing to pay the fee. The most immediate clients for such services are small companies and businesses that cannot afford expensive legal services in connection with minor legal problems. However, it is not too difficult to see that certain classes of legal problems, regardless of the size of the company, could be handled by a legal information processing firm. It is easy to foresee a time when individuals with problems such as divorce, real estate sales, leases, adoption procedures, etc., could take advantage of legal services provided at the end of a computer terminal. How the American Bar Association reacts to these developments will be interesting.

A final example examines a case where the power relationship between two occupations has reversed due to technological developments. The newspaper and magazine business has for a long time been in the position of being dictated to by the International Typographical Union (ITU). This Union has traditionally looked at the American Newspaper Guild (made up of reporters, editors, etc.) as a strange mixture of union and professional association. The American Newspaper Guild has never exercised the same kind of control as the ITU. However, computer-controlled typesetting has made it possible for reporters to compose and set final copy without manual typesetting. Suddenly, the members of the newspaper guild are in a position to cooperate in the elimination of many typographical union jobs.

These are a few examples of how technology has changed professions and, of course, the institutions of which those professions are a part. While literal translation from these examples to the education professions cannot be made, there are certainly lessons that can be learned from each.

The educational professional most directly affected by instructional technology is the teacher. However, many other education professions are affected directly and indirectly.

Instructional technology can take over much of what teachers traditionally do. The extent of the takeover is a function of subject, grade level, nature of the students (for example, normal, handicapped), etc. There is no question that the ratio of professional and paraprofessional personnel to students can be changed drastically. For example, the ratio of professional to paraprofessional in Banneker School (Gary, Indiana) during the performance contract changed significantly. Douglas Ellson of Indiana University has developed programmed reading for inner-city children in which all of the instruction is incorporated into the program, with adult supervision limited to motivation and the tender loving care that children need constantly. He has successfully used mothers from the neighborhood to perform that function. In this particular situation, the paraprofessional is the only one in direct, constant contact with the student.

In the 1950s, when Alexander Stoddard and Lloyd Trump were developing a model of school organization often referred to as the Trump Plan, reliance was placed on differentiation of staff, with an emphasis on paraprofessionals taking over much of the routine work of the classroom teacher. As an expression of the impact of technology on the profession, this model most closely resembles that of the physician and dentist. Lower skill tasks are delegated to someone else, reserving the higher tasks to professional attention. Stoddard and Trump were wise in realizing that the organizational pattern of the school would need to be changed along with professional roles; otherwise, just the very structure of organization would continue to force teachers to perform much as they had before. This is very clearly revealed in the study conducted by Eaton H. Conant (1973) in the Portland (Oregon) Public Schools. The Conant study was probably the most extensive work productivity analysis of the classroom ever undertaken. It should be required reading. We need more studies of that kind.

Administrators as well as teachers will be affected by the shift to technology. During the Banneker performance contract, Behavioral Research Laboratories found it necessary to hire a second principal to supervise the instructional program, leaving the officially appointed principal to continue doing what principals do. The image that the principal had of himself was not as an implementer of curricular and instructional change nor as disturber of the personnel status quo (Wilson, 1973).

The purpose of this section is not to predict what the education professions will become in the future but to point out that study of how professions and trades in other areas are affected by technology can help us to plan for a much more variegated profession than we have at present.

RESEARCH AND DEVELOPMENT

About 10 years ago, I participated in a Delphi study on trends in instructional technology. One of the statements asked about the future importance of research "to conduct studies to establish the validity of instructional technology." When the results of the first round came back, I was not surprised to find my response to that item at complete variance with the other participants. I rated the item as of no importance while the others deemed it very important. My reply did not mean that I think research unimportant but, rather, that the *stated purpose* of research is unimportant. The implied wishful thought in the item is that success would crown our efforts if only we could "prove" unequivocally the effectiveness of technologically-based instruction.*

First, we already have more research than we need for that purpose; second, the primary purpose of research in any applied field is to *im*prove, not prove, the technology; third, at this stage of our development, research on the specific instruments of instruction is far less important than research on the systems for which they are intended. The first I will ignore. I want to address the second and third.

A technology is not accepted or rejected on the basis of comparative performance in its beginning stages. If this were so, railroads would not have been built because the early locomotive lost a race to a horse, and the automobile would never have survived the derisive taunt, "Get a horse!" If education researchers had been around at the time of Gutenberg, they would have immediately conducted research to determine if people would learn from the printed page as well or better than from hand-lettered manuscripts. They would have found no significant difference, urged the abandonment of the new-fangled device, thereby completely missing the significance of movable type.[10] A technology survives because of faith, continuing internal improvement, an institutional structure that encourages and facilitates continued development, and an environment that permits a new technology to seek the best avenues for its contribution. For example, as of now, technologically-based instruction is finding its most ready acceptance in distance education and in underdeveloped countries where highly structured low-cost learning systems are making instruction cost effective, as in Project Impact in the Philippines (Wooten, Jansen, & Warren, 1982). Study of the history of technological innovations would throw considerable light on the survival features of inventions.

By the way, the obverse of the above is that educators do not need research to adopt an innovation that they favor or to continue what they now do. We are all familiar with the challenge, "What evidence do you have that (any medium) really teaches?" Pick up the other end of the stick. Suppose we stood in every classroom doorway in the country and asked the instructors about to enter, "What evidence do you have that what you are about to do the next 50 minutes will be effective—or that it is the best way to present the material?" The difference is that they don't have to answer because they possess something far more important than research: authority. The moral is that lack of research evidence can be used to stalemate an innovation, but it is of no importance when people want to do what they have the authority to do.

I stated that technology needs to improve constantly to survive. Usually, this type of improvement is development rather than research: how to design CAI courseware, how to develop more effective instructional television, how to develop reliable low-cost learning systems, etc. At this time, it is more important to develop and refine techniques and methods of instructional design than to pursue, for example, the "attributes" of media in experimental settings. Basic or conclusion-oriented research is important, but we are woefully behind on applied or decision-oriented research, and our ultimate survival lies there. However, my fear is that our researchers who are disenchanted with research on and with media will move in the direction of doing conclusion-oriented research in constructs in psychology rather than move

---

*By now you, too, should be asking, "If you build a better mousetrap, is it the mice who rush to buy it?"

the other direction into decision-oriented development in design of instructional systems. This is the implication of a review of research by Clark (1983). It is difficult not to conclude that researchers committed to experimental methods and laboratory settings find it more difficult to change methods and settings than they do the field of inquiry. I would much prefer that our capable researchers get involved in developmental problems of instructional systems. Applied fields don't hesitate to use methods and materials that work even though explanations as to why they work aren't available. Medicine, for example, has many remedies and techniques that are effective but for which there are no explanations. Similarly, our researchers should not be hesitant about exploring complex systems problems even though the exact nature of individual elements is not known.

At the last annual meeting of the Society for the History of Technology, one of the presenters discussed this issue in relation to chemical engineering. His point was that chemical engineers are not chemists but managers of chemical processes. They need to know as much (or more) physics and math as chemistry. By definition, any applied field is concerned with means and ends as opposed to a "pure" field of inquiry, which is concerned with cause-and-effect relationships. This is also a classic distinction between theory and practice: Theory is concerned with cause and effect, practice with means and ends. This is not to say that there are no theoretical constructs in an applied field but that the means-ends relationship is paramount. This also means that an applied field can have an existence independent of the theoretical concerns of contributing disciplines. For example, the shift from Newtonian to Einsteinian physics had virtually no effect on mechanical engineering, even though physics is the main contributing discipline. We need to remember this when we attempt to make literal translations from contributing disciplines (e.g., learning psychology) to the applied field of instructional technology.

Hoban (1965) once commented that "the central problem of education is *not* learning but the management of learning, and that the teaching-learning relationship is subsumed under the management of learning" (p. 124). Instruction is the management of learning, and instructional management, like engineering, is a class of its own made up of a complex organization of men, machines, and processes. A large-scale instructional problem may not be best analyzed in terms of individual personalogical variables or isolated media attributes but by a consideration of demographics of students, organizational relationships, the sociology of the instructional environment, delivery systems, etc. The laboratory approach of many of our researchers frequently is not compatible with instructional management realities. For example, elegant algorithmic decision charts idealizing selection of media are meaningless when real-life decisions are based on totally different factors: accessibility of materials, level of supervision required, display requirements, delivery system capability, etc. We spend too much time telling practitioners what they *should* be doing and not enough in finding out what the conditions are that shape their decisions. Pursuing the latter would take us out into the field to engage us in more "naturalistic" inquiry. The current interest in naturalistic methods came out of the evaluation movement—a decision-oriented, situation-specific line of inquiry. Through the use of naturalistic inquiry, I am sure we will discover important factors in instructional management that have been ignored too long, such as the earlier discussion of negative entropy. Latham (1974), Taylor (1981), and Kerr (1977) have asked the type of questions that can lead to important system-related findings. Siegel and Corkland (1964) proposed a conceptual framework for investigating the "instructional gestalt," as they termed it, that bears reexamination, particularly because of their inclusion of the teacher as a variable. Their framework allows for a combination of quantitative and naturalistic methods.

Our obsession with learning gains as *the* dependent variable, and our acceptance of teacher appraisals of treatments have obscured very important aspects of what I refer to as the sociology of instruction—more critical in instructional management than comparative learning gains. For example, the Wisconsin experiment in the use of the Harvey White physics course on film was undertaken to show what we already knew: Films can teach as well as classroom teachers. The *important* findings of the study, reported in an almost off-hand manner, should have told us much about the effects of teacher hostility to the filmed course (Scott, 1960). The major conclusion of the study should have dealt with how to design an instructional environment that would be conducive to the use of mediated courses. Unfortunately, the NSD finding on learning gains relegated the study to the ho-hum category. Qualitative methods used as an integral part of the experiment could have forced the important issues to the forefront. Such methods would even lead to different interpretations of learning gains. The Scott report and the Anaheim ITV studies led me to postulate the John Henry effect: One of the causes of NSD results is that the teachers of the *control* groups perform at maximum rather than typical levels (Heinich, 1970).

We need to remember that research techniques designed to establish cause-and-effect relationships may not be suitable for means-ends problems. Research designs and statistical techniques most appropriate for conclusion-oriented research may impose artificial and unrealistic constraints on decision-oriented (situation-specific) questions. The inappropriateness of using techniques based on normative testing in criterion-referenced situations is one example that has gained recognition. Even more critical is that conclusion-oriented research designs elegantly *isolate* treatment effects, when what is often sought in decision-oriented research is a methodology that shows how treatments can *reinforce* each other. The techniques of operations research in engineering and business administration are more "sympatico" with decision-oriented problems in instructional systems.

We have emulated science in our research for too long. There are many reasons for this, a few implied earlier, but surely the higher status accorded science over technology in higher education and the virtual adoration of SCIENCE by the public are important factors. History of science departments abound in higher education, but history of technology departments are much scarcer. "Science" in a department title is prestigious, even if misleading. A friend of mine agreed with me that his department was far more concerned with technology than with science, but his department is called "Computer Science." Where is the science in "Library Science" or "Information Science"? "Techniques" would be a better label at the rudimentary level; at the more complex level, "technology" is far more appropriate. (Then there's "Political Science"—but I wouldn't want it as a "technology" either!) The space shuttle completes a mission, and it's a great "scientific" achievement. Technology was more responsible than science. Anyone connected with the space program is a scientist, even the engineers! Our field has had fair success with getting "technology" in department titles but very little success in getting acknowledgment of the technological nature of our major research questions and problems.

We need to reexamine our posture toward the science-technology relationship. We, along with many others, tend to believe that basic research lays the groundwork for invention in a fairly direct way. Because of this general belief, the Department of Defense (DOD) invested about 10 billion dollars from 1945 to 1966 in scientific research with about 25 percent going to undirected, basic research. Growing doubt about the relationship between research and invention led the DOD to mount Project Hindsight, an 8-year study of the key contributions to the development of the weapons systems then the backbone of U.S. defense. The 13 teams of scientists and engineers isolated some 700 developments. They concluded that 91 percent were technological and 9 percent were classifiable as science. Of the latter category, only two events, or three-tenths of one percent, were due to undirected, basic research. Needless to say, the scientific community reacted with shock. In an attempt to redress Project Hindsight, a subsequent study, TRACES, cited five recent innovations as dependent on scientific research (Layton, 1971). As Layton points out, "The question, therefore, is not whether science has influenced technology but rather the precise nature of the interaction" (p. 564). We would do well to ponder the relationship between science and technology, and between research and development, in our own field. As a backdrop for such a study I suggest another article by Layton (1974), "Technology as Knowledge."

WHERE DO WE GO FROM HERE?

I hope by now I have established sufficient cause to consider shifting the intellectual base of instructional technology from education to technology. By doing so, we can more freely explore the consequences of the techniques, methods, instruments, and processes inherent in our continuously developing field. The opportunities for unfettered scholarly inquiry become far more extensive. As Hoban (1965) pointed out, "The term *educational media* does not, in itself, suggest the ramifications for research, educational policy, and operating procedures which are inherent in the term *technology of education*" (p. 124). But as I mentioned, dependence on Education on the part of many of our academic programs and on the institutions within which our service units function can inhibit intellectual freedom. If the basic position of this article is to be furthered, I would expect those programs not dependent on undergraduate or graduate certification of education professionals to take the lead. It helps greatly if the academic program is not too intimately linked to a service unit within the same institution. Within those programs, leadership will have to come from individuals who do scholarly inquiry for its own sake, who do not have one eye (or both) constantly on the alert for the next consulting opportunity—too many of our people are intellectually "bought" by consulting arrangements.

There was much more scholarly activity along the lines of this article during the 1960s than there is now. Skinner (and his followers), Finn, and Hoban made us aware that our technologies of instruction could lead to redesign of the system. Indiana, Michigan State, Syracuse, and the University of Southern California were particularly productive in generating conferences, papers, and dissertations that explored the potential of the "systems approach." Florida State's excellent program was born as a direct result of the ferment of that period. With good intellectual leadership, it quickly established itself as a leading program. The impetus of the scholarly thrust of the '60s must be recaptured, and not necessarily by the same institutions. I must make the observation that much of the leadership that does exist is directed to ventures in developing countries. It's time to bring it home.

While iconoclastic scholarly activity may best be done in the kind of programs I have specified, certainly all programs can move in the direction of pertinent research and development. Surely they can start moving away from experimental to field-based studies that can add so much to the development of informed practice. A climate of acceptance for dissertations based on naturalistic methods should be generated. I hasten to add that I am not implying less rigorous study. In my view, a naturalistic study must be more disciplined, more perceptive, if less mathematical, than an experimental study. Those in our academic programs who claim administration as their specialty must carry their interest into the realm of policy and governance and begin to study education institutions not as givens but as complex organizations whose governing rules are amenable to inquiry and eventual change. The results of these studies should find their way into the important journals not only of the field but also of education and training. Convention programs should provide forums for work in progress as well as completed studies.

It should be clear that we are in dire need of scholars. One of the inevitable characteristics of professional schools is that they turn out too many practitioners and not enough scholars. By scholar I mean someone prepared to examine his or her own field in terms of its basic premises, its status, and its place in the general scheme of things—a reflective, thinking individual. We need skilled practitioners but we also need scholars to study and guide what the practitioners do. We are fortunate indeed when we find someone who is both practitioner and scholar.

About 20 years ago, I was sitting in a bar in the Los Angeles airport with a friend whom I had roomed with as an undergraduate. We had not seen each other for about 15 years. As we talked about our respective fields—he is on the English faculty of one of the University of California campuses—I made the comment that there are many capable people in my field, but few scholars. He was gracious enough to turn my comment around by saying that in his field, there were many scholars but few capable people. When we meet again, I hope to be able to tell him that the balance in my field has shifted.

NOTES

1.   I am using the definition of "technology of instruction" as it appears in the Association for Educational Communications and Technology (1977) Glossary (p. 177): The specific process used to design a specific type of reliable and validated instructional product/instructional systems component (e.g., the process used to develop programmed instructional materials is a technology of instruction).

2.   The reader needs to keep in mind that I am discussing academic programs that prepare professionals for the field, not individuals who are practicing in the field. We can all think of individuals who emerged from a variety of backgrounds, primarily psychology, but if they are part of an academic program that prepares instructional technologists, that program is highly likely to be in a School of Education. The programs at the Rochester Institute of Technology, the New York Institute of Technology, and the Twente University of Technology (See *ECTJ*, 1983, *31*, 239-245) are exceptions worth watching. All are relatively new and based in technology not Education. Are they aberrations or a trend?

3.   Suppose a programmed text (or a CAI course) enables students to reach the same (or better) level of performance as a traditional course. There is no office in the university that can say, "Any student who goes through the programmed text and passes the exam automatically receives credit for that course and the credit counts toward the degree." Isn't that what happens when a faculty member is assigned a course? The ramifications of institutionalization are complex. I hope to deal with them in the near future.

4.   It should not be surprising then that this field began in exhortation and advocacy. These are dead ends. If this is all one has, what does one do when advocacy is either no longer necessary or hits a plateau? Without content, one is left with teaching little more than technique and mechanics, and with service programs with little more than service functions.

5.   I have expressed this principle as a law: Technology makes instruction visible (Heinich, 1970). Its corollary is: Research on teacher behavior is unreliable—replication is uncertain.

6.   I found a slender volume by Dewey (1929) to be extremely helpful in reinforcing my ideas on this subject. I urge all of you to seek it out. The following excerpts are from pages 8-15. Note that I would often use "technology" where Dewey uses "science."

> The important thing is to discover those traits in virtue of which various fields are called scientific. When we raise the question in this way, we are led to put emphasis upon methods of dealing with subject-matter rather than to look for uniform objective traits in subject-matter. From this point of view, science signifies, I take it, the existence of systematic methods of inquiry, which, when they are brought to bear on a range of facts, enable us to understand them better and to control them more intelligently, less haphazardly and with less routine.
>
> There is an intellectual technique by which discovery and organization of material go on cumulatively, and by means of which one inquirer can repeat the researches of another, confirm or discredit them, and add still more to the capital stock of knowledge. Moreover, the methods when they are used tend to perfect themselves, to suggest new problems, new investigations, which refine old procedures and create new and better ones.
>
> The question as to the sources of a science of education is, then, to be taken in this sense. What are the ways by means of which the function of education in all its branches and phases—selection of material for the curriculum, methods of instruction and discipline, organization and administration of schools—can be conducted with systematic increase of intelligent control and understanding? What are the materials upon which we may—and should—draw in order that educational activities may become in a less degree products of routine, tradition, accident and transitory accidental influences? From what sources shall we draw so that there shall be steady and cumulative growth of intelligent, communicable insight and power of direction?
>
> This digression seems to be justified not merely because those who object to the idea of a science put personality and its unique gifts in opposition to science, but also because those who recommend science sometimes urge that uniformity of procedure will be its consequence. So it seems worthwhile to dwell on the fact that in the subjects best developed from the scientific point of view, the opposite is the case. Command of scientific methods and systematized subject-matter liberates individuals; it enables them to see new problems, devise

new procedures, and, in general, makes for diversification rather than for set uniformity. But at the same time these diversifications have a cumulative effect in an advance shared by all workers in the field.

Engineering is, in actual practice, an art. But it is an art that progressively incorporates more and more of science into itself, more of mathematics, physics and chemistry. It is the kind of art it is precisely because of a content of scientific subject-matter which guides it as a practical operation. There is room for the original and daring projects of exceptional individuals. But their distinction lies not in the fact that they turn their backs upon science, but in the fact that they make new integrations of scientific material and turn it to new and previously unfamiliar and unforeseen uses. When, in education, the psychologist or observer and experimentalist in any field reduces his findings to a rule which is to be uniformly adopted, then, only, is there a result which is objectionable and destructive of the free play of education as an art.

But this happens not because of scientific method but because of departure from it. It is not the capable engineer who treats scientific findings as imposing upon him a certain course which is to be rigidly adhered to: it is the third- or fourth-rate man who adopts this course. Even more, it is the unskilled day laborer who follows it. For even if the practice adopted is one that follows from science and could not have been discovered or employed except for science, when it is converted into a uniform rule of procedure it becomes an empirical rule-of-thumb procedure—just as a person may use a table of logarithms mechanically without knowing anything about mathematics.

At the risk of putting words in Dewey's mouth, I believe he is urging a transition from a craft to a technology.

7. This example originally appeared in Heinich, 1983a.

8. This argument originally appeared in Heinich, 1983b.

9. The film clips on the aircraft stabilizer and the Pap test are from the Edward R. Murrow See It Now program "Automation" that appeared on CBS in June 1957. The film is still available. The clip on the glass industry is from the film "Glass" by Bert Haanstra.

10. In case you think this farfetched, an abstract of a funded research project came to my attention about 10 years ago that is as absurd. The study in question sought to determine if students would learn from microfiche as well as from the printed page. Surprise—no significant difference! The future of microfiche hardly hangs on the outcome of such research.

REFERENCES

Anderson, F. A. (1969). The responsibilities of state education agencies for education. In E. L. Morphet and D. L. Jesser (Eds.), *Planning for effective utilization of technology in education*. New York: Citation Press.

Bell, D. (1973). Technology, nature and society. In *Technology and the frontier of knowledge*. Garden City, NY: Doubleday.

Cabeceiras, J. (1972). Observed differences in teacher verbal behavior when using and not using the overhead projector. *AV Communication Review, 20*, 271-280.

Clark, R. E. (1983). Reconsidering research on learning from media. *Review of Educational Research, 53*, 445-459.

Conant, E. H. (1973). *Teacher and paraprofessional work productivity*. Lexington, MA: D. C. Heath.

Dawson, P. (1971). Teacher militancy and instructional media. *AV Communication Review, 19*, 184-197.

Dewey, J. (1929). *The sources of a science of education*. New York: Horace Liveright.

Finn, J. D. (1959). Directions for theory in audiovisual communications. In J. V. Edling (Ed.), *The new media in education*. Sacramento, CA: Sacramento State College.

———. (1960). Technology and the instructional process. *AV Communication Review, 8*, 5-26.

———. (1972). A walk on the altered side. *Phi Delta Kappan*, October 1962, *44*, 29-34. (Reprinted in R. McBeath [Ed.], *Extending education through technology*. Washington, DC: Association for Educational Communications and Technology).

Galbraith, J. K. (1967). *The new industrial state*. Boston: Houghton Mifflin.

Goodlad, J. I. (1983, March). A study of schooling: Some findings and hypotheses, *Phi Delta Kappan, 64*, 465-470.

Hall, A. R. (1963). The changing technical act. In C. F. Stover (Ed.), *The technological order*. Detroit: Wayne State University Press.

Heinich, R. (1970). *Technology and the management of instruction*. Washington, DC: Association for Educational Communications and Technology.

———. (1983a,. Spring). Instructional technology and decision making. *Educational Considerations, 10*, 25-26. (a)

———. (1983b, May 31). Legal aspects of alternative staffing patterns and educational technology. *Synthesis* (Newsletter of the Southwest Educational Development Laboratory, Austin, Tex.), *6*, 1-6. (b)

Heinich, R., & Ebert, K. (1976). *Legal barriers to educational technology and instructional productivity* (NIE Grant No. NIG-G-74-0036). Washington, DC: National Institute of Education. (ERIC Document Reproduction Service No. ED 124 118).

Hoban, C. F. (1962). *Research in new media in education*. Paper presented to the American Association of Colleges for Teacher Education, Washington, DC.

———. (1965). From theory to policy decisions. *AV Communication Review, 13*, 121-139.

Kerr, S. T. (1977). Are there instructional developers in the schools? *AV Communication Review, 25*, 243-267.

Latham, G. (1974). Measuring teacher responses to instructional materials. Research Paper No. 6, Exceptional Child Center, Utah State University.

Layton, E. (1971). Mirror-image twins: The communities of science and technology in 19th century America. *Technology and Culture, 12*, 562-580.

———. (1974). Technology as knowledge. *Technology and Culture, 15*, 31-41.

Marsh, P. E. (1964). Wellsprings of strategy: Considerations affecting innovations by the PSSC. In M. B. Miles (Ed.), *Innovations in education*. New York: Columbia University, Teachers College.

Morison, E. E. (1966). *Men, machines and modern times*. Cambridge, MA: MIT Press.

Schaefer, W. J. (1974). *A study of negotiated contracts and their actual and perceived effects on school district media programs*. Unpublished doctoral dissertation, Indiana University.

Scott, D. T. (1960). Teaching high school physics through the use of films. *AV Communication Review, 8*, 220-221.

Siegel, L., & Corkland, L. (1964). Instructional gestalt: A conceptual framework and design for educational research. *AV Communication Review, 12*, 16-45.

Taylor, W. D. (1981). Teachers and materials: The selection process. In *Secondary school video: A facilitator's guide*. Bloomington, IN: Agency for Instructional Television.

Wilson, J. A. (1973). *Banneker: A case study of educational change*. Homewood, IL: ETC Publications. (Based on *Some effects of performance contracting on the school organization: A case study of educational change*. Unpublished doctoral dissertation, Indiana University, 1973.)

Wittich, W. A., Pella, M. O., & Wedemeyer, C. A. (1960). The Wisconsin physics film evaluation project. *AV Communication Review, 8*, 156-157.

Wooten, J., Jansen, W., & Warren, M. K. (1982). *Project impact: A low-cost alternative for universal primary education in the Philippines*. Washington, DC: Agency for International Development.

6

Educational Systems Development and Its Relationship to ISD

Charles M. Reigeluth
Indiana University

Banathy (1987) has identified four subsystems in any educational enterprise:

1. the **learning experience** subsystem, in which the learner processes information from the environment to produce new or modified cognitive structures,

2. the **instructional** subsystem, in which instructional designers and teachers use information about learning needs (gained through analysis activities), as well as administrative and governance input, to produce environments or opportunities for learners to learn,

3. the **administrative** subsystem, in which administrators use information about instructional needs, as well as governance input, to make decisions about resource allocation, including use of leadership, and

4. the **governance** subsystem, in which "owners" use their goals and values to produce policies and in other ways provide direction and resources for the educational enterprise in order to meet their needs (which usually include those of their learners, teachers, and administrators).

These four subsystems exist in all educational enterprises, regardless of context (e.g., public education, corporate training, health education, military training, higher education).

Instructional Systems Development (ISD) is the knowledge base about the instructional subsystem, whereas Educational Systems Development (ESD) is the knowledge base about the complete educational enterprise. Given that most of this book deals with ISD, this chapter first focuses on describing what ESD is and why it is needed, and then addresses the interdependencies between ISD and ESD.

Note: Excerpts of this chapter have been taken from Reigeluth, C. M. (1994). *Systemic Change in Education.* Englewood Cliffs, NJ: Educational Technology Publications, with permission of the publisher.

WHAT IS ESD?

ESD is like ISD in several ways. First, both encompass knowledge bases for "process" and "product" (means and ends). (See table 6.1.) Regarding the *products* knowledge base, ISD instructional theory (see, e.g., Reigeluth, 1983; 1987) offers guidance as to what the instruction (the product of an ISD effort) should be like to be most effective, efficient, and appealing, for different situations (e.g., kinds of learning, learners, and learning contexts). In a similar way, ESD offers guidance as to what a new educational system (the product of an ESD effort) should be like for different kinds of needs and conditions in its suprasystem (e.g., in a community, for a K-12 educational system; or in a corporation, for a corporate training operation). This design is often referred to as a *vision* of a different paradigm of education, and includes a description of the features the new system should have to meet specific needs under given conditions (see, e.g., Reigeluth, 1994). Regarding the *processes* knowledge base, in ISD the numerous ISD models (see Gustafson, 1991, for a review; and see Dick & Carey, 1990, for an example) offer guidance as to what process an instructional development team should engage in to create a product of high quality. In a similar way, ESD offers guidance as to what process a systemic restructuring team should engage in for creating a new educational system of high quality.

Table 6.1.
The Knowledge Bases of ISD and ESD

	Process	**Product**
ISD	ISD Models	Instructional Theories
ESD	ESD Models	Visions (features)

A second similarity between ESD and ISD is their links to systems theory (Ackoff, 1981; Checkland, 1981) and design theory (Cross, 1984; Nadler, 1981). Both use *systems thinking* to understand and take into account the mutually interdependent relationships (1) between the new system (instructional or educational) and its suprasystem, (2) between the new system and its peer systems (other systems that are parts of the same suprasystem), and (3) among the many functions and components that compose the new system. Both ESD and ISD use *design theory* to inform the process. The fundamental elements of analysis, synthesis, and evaluation and the basic activities of design, development, and implementation are but the tip of the iceberg of design theory that is relevant to both endeavors. Furthermore, in the melding of systems theory and design theory, we understand that the ISD process is not linear—that there is much need for simultaneity and recursion during the process. The same is true for ESD.

Aside from these similarities between ESD and ISD, what really is ESD and why is it needed? ESD is concerned with creating a *new paradigm* of education, as opposed to making changes within the existing paradigm. It entails fundamental change and recognizes that a fundamental change in one aspect of a system requires fundamental changes in other aspects for it to be successful. In public education, it must pervade all levels of the system: classroom, building, district, community, state government, and federal government. Similarly, in corporate training, it must pervade all levels of the corporation. In this way, it can encompass not only the nature of the learning experiences and the instructional system, but also the administrative and governance systems. Such an approach to change is indeed radical, not to mention difficult and risky. So it is important to ask if we really need such a radical change.

WHY IS A NEW PARADIGM NEEDED IN EDUCATION?

Daniel Bell (1973), Alvin Toffler (1980), Robert Reich (1991), and others have identified several massive changes that our society has undergone: from the agrarian age to the industrial age, and now entering into what some call the information age.

The dawn of the industrial age brought with it massive changes in *all* of society's systems, including the family, business, and education. In fact, that is the only time in the history of the United States that education has undergone a paradigm change—from the one-room schoolhouse to the industrial, assembly-line model we have today. The current system is substantially the same as it was when we became an industrial society. The reforms that have been made since then have all been piecemeal changes.

Now that we are entering the information age, we find that paradigm shifts are occurring or will likely soon occur in *all* of our societal systems, from communications and transportation to the family and the workplace. It is little wonder that we again find the need for a paradigm shift in education. Society is changing in sweeping ways that make our current educational system obsolete, in all contexts—K-12, higher education, corporate education, health education, and so forth.

Changes in Society

Let's begin with a look at the family. The extended family in the agrarian age entailed the parents and children living together with grandparents and even aunts, uncles, and cousins. This form gave way to the nuclear family in the industrial age. In turn, the information age has given rise to a diversity of forms, including the single-parent family and the dual-income family. This societal change has important implications for the kinds of changes needed in education.

As a second case in point, businesses in the agrarian age were organized around the family: the family farm or the family trade (e.g., bakery, carpentry). The family represented the organizational structure and determined the lines of authority. This structure gave way to the bureaucratic form of organization in the industrial age. Today, corporations are restructuring to create horizontal "enterprise webs" in place of vertical layers of middle managers (Reich, 1991). Transformations based on team approaches, total quality management, process orientation, and technological imperatives are rapidly changing the structure of businesses worldwide.

Of all our societal systems, business is the most user-driven (client-driven), so it has naturally been among the first to systemically transform itself (Ackoff, 1981). However, *all* our other societal systems, including education, health, legal, and political, are also becoming increasingly dysfunctional as we evolve deeper into the information age; systemic transformation will be needed—and is inevitable—in all these areas, including education.

Educational systems are like transportation systems in some important ways. Like the one-room schoolhouse, the horse was ideally suited to the agrarian age. It was highly flexible and individualized. But as we evolved into the industrial age, the transportation needs of society began to change. It became necessary to transport large quantities of raw materials and finished goods to and from factories. Rather than (or in addition to) trying to improve the prevailing system, an alternative paradigm was developed—the railroad. Like our current educational system, it offered a quantum improvement in meeting the new needs of the industrial age, but everyone had to leave from the same place at the same time and travel at the same rate to the same destination (or be dropped off somewhere along the way).

Since the dawn of the information age in the 1950s, America's transportation needs have again been changing in dramatic ways. Again we have turned to a new paradigm, a combination of the automobile and the airplane. Similarly, society has been changing in such dramatic ways (see table 6.2) that we need a new educational system that is as different from our current system as the automobile and airplane are from the railroad. Like the new transportation system, the new educational system may develop in parallel with the current system, be separate from but coexist with it, and slowly grow while the current system slowly declines. New roles will require new skills, and new resources and facilities will also be required, so it is simply not logistically possible to change the current system everywhere at once.

Table 6.2.
Major Paradigm Shifts in Society

Society:	Agrarian	Industrial	Information
Transportation:	Horse	Train	Plane & car
Family:	Extended family	Nuclear family	Single-parent family
Business:	Family	Bureaucracy	Team
Education:	One-room schoolhouse	Current system	?

Clearly, paradigm shifts in society cause (or require) paradigm shifts in *all* societal systems. This explains why educational performance has generally declined in the United States since the 1960s while educational costs have dramatically increased. Furthermore, it indicates that the situation will continue to get worse no matter what piecemeal changes we make and no matter how much money we pour into the current system—unless we change the paradigm.

Relationships Between Society and Education

The need for a new paradigm of education is based on massive changes in both the conditions and educational needs of an information society. Therefore, we must look at those changes in order to figure out what features the new system should have. Table 6.3, page 88, shows some of the major differences between the industrial age and the emerging information age. These differences have important implications for the features of the new educational system: how it should be structured, what should be taught, and how it should be taught.

Although we can see it beginning to change, our current system has been characterized by adversarial relationships not only between teachers and administrators, but also between teachers and students and often between teachers and parents. Consolidated districts have been highly bureaucratic, centrally controlled autocracies in which students get no preparation for participating in a democratic society. Leadership has been vested in individuals according to a hierarchical management structure, and all those lower in the hierarchy have been expected to obey the leader. Learning has been highly compartmentalized into subject areas. Students have typically been treated as if they are all the same and have all been expected to do the same things at the same time. They have also been forced to be passive learners and passive members of their school community. These features of our current system must all change (and have indeed begun to change), for they are counterproductive—harmful to our citizens and our society—in the information age.

Table 6.3.
Major Differences Between the Industrial Age and the
Information Age That Affect Education

Industrial Age	Information Age
Adversarial relationships	Cooperative relationships
Bureaucratic organization	Team organization
Autocratic leadership	Shared leadership
Centralized control	Autonomy with accountability
Autocracy	Democracy
Conformity	Diversity
Compliance	Initiative
One-way communications	Networking
Compartmentalization (Division of labor)	Holism (Integration of tasks)

In the industrial age we needed minimally educated people who would be willing and able to put up with the tedium of work on the assembly lines. However, those assembly-line jobs are rapidly becoming an endangered species. Just as the percentage of the work force in agriculture dropped dramatically in the early stages of the industrial age, so the percentage in manufacturing has been declining dramatically over the past few decades. As Reich (1991) points out, even in manufacturing companies, a majority of the jobs today entail manipulating information rather than materials. Just as the industrial age represented a focus on, and extension of, our physical capabilities (mechanical technology), so the information age represents a focus on, and extension of, our mental capabilities (intellectual technology). This makes effective learning paramount. Surprisingly, our current system is not designed for learning!

Systems Thinking Applied to Learning

Two things educators know for certain are that different people learn at different rates and different people have different learning needs, even from their first day at school. Yet our industrial-age educational systems present a fixed amount of content to a group of learners in a fixed amount of time, so it is like a race to see who receives the A's and who flunks out. Our current systems are typically *not* designed for learning; they are designed for selection. Again, this is true in corporate and other contexts, not just K-12 education.

To emphasize learning, the new system must no longer hold time constant and allow achievement to vary. It must hold achievement constant at a competency level and allow learners as much time as they need to attain competence. There is no other way to accommodate the facts that different people learn at different rates and have different learning needs. However, to have an *attainment-based* rather than time-based system, we must in turn have *person-based progress* rather than group-based progress. That in turn requires changing the role of the teacher to that of a *coach* or facilitator/manager, rather than that of dispenser of knowledge to groups of learners who pass by at the ring of a bell like so many little widgets on an assembly line.

If the teacher is to be a facilitator and educational manager, learning must occur primarily from sources other than the teacher or trainer. Hence, the system must be *resource-based*, utilizing powerful new tools offered by advanced technology, rather than teacher-based. In addition, it requires much more collaboration and teamwork among students, including *cooperative learning* and cross-age tutoring, rather than our industrial-age view that collaboration among students equates with cheating.

Interestingly, the industrial age not only made a new system of transportation—the railroad—necessary (to ship large quantities of raw materials and finished goods to and from factories), but it also made the railroad possible (with its manufacturing technology). In a similar way, the information age has not only made a new educational system necessary, but has also made a new system possible (with its information technologies). We now have powerful tools to facilitate learning that we did not have a few years ago. And the power of those tools continues to increase, while their cost continues to decline dramatically.

Hence, based on changes in the workplace, the emerging picture of the new educational system includes the changes shown in table 6.4.

Table 6.4.
Emerging Picture of Features for an Information-Age Educational System Based on Changes in the Workplace

Industrial Age	Information Age
Grade levels	Continuous progress
Covering the content	Attainment-based learning
Norm-referenced testing	Individualized testing
Nonauthentic assessment	Performance-based assessment
Group-based content delivery	Personal learning plans
Adversarial learning	Cooperative learning
Classrooms	Learning centers
Teacher as dispenser of knowledge	Teacher as coach or facilitator of learning
Memorization of meaningless facts	Thinking, problem-solving skills, and meaning making
Isolated reading, writing skills	Communication skills
Books as tools	Advanced technologies as tools

Education and Systemic Changes in the Family

The information-age family also has important implications for the new K-12 educational system. Given the predominance of single-parent families and dual-income two-parent families in advanced countries, parenting is not occurring today as it did in the industrial age. Latch-key children are just the "tip of the iceberg" regarding the shortage of communication, caring, and structure that students receive in the home. Add to that the increasing incidence of mental and physical child abuse and the alarming increase in the number of "crack babies" and children born with other chemical-abuse problems, and we can see that our society will face very severe social problems 20 years from now if our educational system does not team up with other social service agencies to become a system of learning and human development—a system that is concerned with the development of the whole child, not just the child's mental development.

In the new K-12 educational system, the "school" needs to become a caring environment, just as the information-age workplace is becoming a caring environment. Our current K-12 system seems to have been designed to be just the opposite. Not only do we require students to change teachers every year, but we require them to change every 45 minutes! And teachers only see students in large groups, as if to minimize personal interaction. Schools are often so large that an atmosphere of impersonality, bureaucratic control, and helplessness results in feelings of anonymity and behavioral problems. We need to create smaller "schools within the school" that operate independently of one another, and each child needs a mentor who will stay with her for a number of years, perhaps a developmental stage of her life. The mentor should be concerned with the development of the whole child, including all of Gardner's (1987) "seven intelligences" and more: mental, physical, emotional, creative, social, psychological, and ethical (see table 6.5).

Table 6.5.
Emerging Picture of Features for an Information-Age
Educational System Based on Changes in the Family

- A "teacher" is responsible for a child for a period of about 4 years.

- That teacher is responsible for educating the *whole* child.

- Each school has no more than 10 teachers, to create a smaller, caring environment (the notion of schools-within-a-school).

- Each student develops a quarterly contract with the teacher and parents.

INTERDEPENDENCIES BETWEEN ISD AND ESD

ESD and ISD are interdependent in that each relies on the other to some degree for its success.

ESD Needs ISD

There are at least two major ways in which ESD is dependent on ISD. First, because ESD is a new knowledge domain and ISD is more fully developed, ESD can benefit from *building on what we know* about ISD. The ISD process can contribute many insights as to what a successful ESD process might be like, including knowledge about analysis, design, development, implementation, and evaluation. In addition, ISD professionals have design skills and a systems perspective that are both much needed in ESD. Therefore, ESD should actively recruit ISD professionals and build on what they have learned about the systems design process.

Second, the new paradigm of education requires *well-designed resources*. Without high-quality resources, the new system will not come anywhere near reaching its potential to improve education. ISD is needed (both the ISD process and instructional theory) to create such quality resources.

ISD Needs ESD

There are at least three major ways in which ISD is dependent on ESD. First, ISD professionals understand that they can better meet learners' needs by personalizing their instructional systems. However, doing so usually *requires significant changes in the larger organization* (administrative and governance systems) for their success. All too often ISD professionals have had to settle for second-rate instructional designs because of organizational constraints. ESD can provide insights and assistance to ISDers to bring about the necessary organizational changes that make higher-quality instructional systems workable.

Second, ESD will open a whole *new clientele* to ISDers. K-12 schools currently have little incentive for using ISD to improve the quality of instruction. However, in the new paradigm, the greater emphasis on well-designed resources will create a higher demand for ISD expertise. Most public schools that are restructuring are placing greater emphasis on teacher-made materials to replace textbooks, and school districts are increasingly establishing the position of curriculum specialist (also referred to as educational technologist or instructional consultant) to support such teacher efforts (see, e.g., Kemp, in press).

Third, ESD helps ISD to see the need for *new directions in instructional theory*. More constructivist approaches, such as problem-based learning (Albanese & Mitchell, 1993; Barrows & Tamblyn, 1980; West, 1992), offer great potential to help learners acquire such qualities demanded by the information age as initiative, responsibility, problem-solving competence, team-building and group-process skills, and communication skills. Instructional theory must be developed to help ISDers create instructional systems that support such learning experiences. In particular, instructional theory is needed to provide guidance on creating an engaging problem space/scenario, on designing personalized, interactive skill-builders, and on creating powerful tools to help learners build causal models (e.g., through multimedia simulations).

SUMMARY

When we look at the ways society is changing as we evolve deeper into the information age, we can see definite paradigm shifts in the workplace and the family, and a growing need for paradigm shifts in virtually all other societal systems. From those changes, we can see that a new paradigm of education is essential to meet the new educational needs of both learners and the suprasystems that sponsor the educational systems. Furthermore, we can identify some general features that an information-age educational system should have to meet the new needs: continuous progress, attainment-based learning, individualized testing, performance-based assessment, personal learning plans, cooperative learning, learning centers, teacher as coach or facilitator of learning, thinking and problem-solving skills and meaning making, communication skills, and advanced technologies as tools.

To foster the advent of this new paradigm of education, an ESD knowledge base is under development and is similar in many ways to the ISD knowledge base: It has process and product components, and it is based on systems theory and design theory. Furthermore, there are strong interdependencies between ESD and ISD. ESD needs ISD to build on what it has learned about the systems design process and to recruit people who have expertise in systems thinking and the design process. ISD needs ESD because it often requires significant changes in the larger organization, it opens up a whole new clientele, and it offers insights into new directions for instructional theory.

Educators must begin to use ESD's needs-based, systems-design approach to improving education in all contexts. Without such an approach, we will almost certainly be condemned to a system that no longer meets our educational needs.

REFERENCES

Ackoff, R. L. (1981). *Creating the corporate future.* New York: John Wiley.

Albanese, M. A., & Mitchell, S. (1993). Problem-based learning: A review of literature on its outcomes and implementation issues. *Academic Medicine, 68(1),* 52-81.

Banathy, B. H. (1987). Instructional systems design. In R. M. Gagné (Ed.), *Instructional technology: Foundations.* Hillsdale, NJ: Lawrence Erlbaum.

———. (1991). *Educational systems design: A journey to create the future.* Englewood Cliffs, NJ: Educational Technology Publications.

Barrows, H. S., & Tamblyn, R. M. (1980). *Problem-based learning.* New York: Springer.

Bell, D. (1973). *The coming of post-industrial society: A venture in social forecasting.* New York: Basic Books.

Boyer, E. (1983). *High school: A report on secondary education in America.* New York: Harper & Row.

Checkland, P. (1981). *Systems thinking, systems practice.* New York: John Wiley.

Cross, N. (1984). *Development in design methodology.* New York: John Wiley.

Dick, W., & Carey, L. (1990). *The systematic design of instruction* (3rd ed.). New York: HarperCollins.

Gardner, H. (1987). Beyond the IQ: Educational and human development. *Harvard Educational Review, 57(2),* 187-195.

Goodlad, J. I. (1984). *A place called school.* New York: McGraw-Hill.

Gustafson, K. (1991). *Survey of instructional development models.* Syracuse, NY: ERIC Clearinghouse on Information Resources.

Kemp, J. (in press). *A practical guide to school change.* Washington, DC: Association for Educational Communications and Technology.

Lieberman, A., & Miller, L. (1990). Restructuring schools: What matters and what works. *Phi Delta Kappan, 71(10),* 759-764.

Nadler, G. (1981). *The planning and design approach.* New York: John Wiley.

Perelman, L. J. (1987). *Technology and transformation of schools.* Alexandria, VA: National School Boards Assoc.

Reich, R. B. (1991). *The work of nations.* New York: Alfred A. Knopf.

Reigeluth, C. M. (Ed.) (1983). *Instructional-design theories and models: An overview of their current status.* Hillsdale, NJ: Lawrence Erlbaum.

———. (Ed.) (1987). *Instructional theories in action: Lessons illustrating selected theories and models.* Hillsdale, NJ: Lawrence Erlbaum.

———. (1994). The imperative for systemic change. In C.M. Reigeluth (Ed.), *Systemic change in education.* Englewood Cliffs, NJ: Educational Technology Publications.

Shanker, A. (1990). Staff development and the restructured school. In B. Joyce (Ed.), *Changing school culture through staff development: 1990 yearbook of the Association for Supervision and Curriculum Development.* Alexandria, VA: ASCD.

Sizer, T. R. (1984). *Horace's compromise.* Boston: Houghton Mifflin.

Toffler, A. (1980). *The third wave.* New York: Bantam Books.

West, S. A. (1992). Problem-based learning: A viable addition for secondary school science. *School Science Review, 73*(265), 47-55.

7

Instructional Technology and Unforeseen Value Conflicts
Toward a Critique

Jane B. Johnsen
College of Education, Ohio University
Lancaster, Ohio

and

William D. Taylor
College of Education, The Ohio State University
Columbus, Ohio

INTRODUCTION

Instruction is not a naturally occurring phenomenon in the physical world; not something that has always been "out there" waiting for an auspicious moment of discovery. Instruction is a human creation and the addition of technology to instruction is also a human activity. Instruction and instructional technology are human inventions that spring from human values and human designs. They are value saturated and operate in the social world quite unlike phenomena in the physical world. Social inventions such as instruction and instructional technology, both in their inception and subsequent histories, are never value-free or value-neutral. They resonate with the values of their human creators, who themselves are situated in a particular culture in a specific time and place. As the culture evolves, old social inventions may be seen as having fortuitous carryover qualities or, at the other end of the continuum, they may be seen as deeply flawed for this time and place. But we can only know or hope to act on this knowledge if we engage in social interpretation and articulate a sense of professional responsibility for open-ended criticism within our own field of instructional technology.

People everywhere are coming to realize that we can ill afford to suspend judgment on our human inventions and technologies. We have done so in the past at a mounting cost to the delicate fabric that sustains our physical and social existence. We continue to read George Orwell's *1984* because it vividly reminds us that technology can be used to eliminate all human freedom, even the freedom to think private thoughts. A recent survey conducted by the U.S. Office of Technology Assessment found that 42 percent of the public believes technological development must be restrained to "protect the overall safety of our society" (Grossman, 1990, p. 44). We are coming to realize that the unforeseen side effects of our technologies are in the long run more important than the presumed advantages that were hoped for at the time the technology was originally invented and installed. It can be argued that nuclear fallout from Chernobyl is more important than the electricity the plant generated. Toxic groundwater has greater consequences for us than the original boost to farm yields that resulted from the use of herbicides and pesticides. The destruction of the ozone layer will hurt us more than a pesky underarm odor. The unintended impact of a technology is part of the reality of technological development regardless of the setting into which the technology is introduced. This chapter explores an unforeseen side effect of technology and, specific to the application of instructional technology, begins to pose the question whether we might not be giving up more than we have gained.

ORIGINS OF INSTRUCTION

The development of instructional technology over the last quarter century can be viewed as a continuation but also a transformation of the 300-year rise of instruction in the West. Instructional technologists have forced to the fore a number of questions present but historically left indeterminate in the growth of instruction. One question, and the one we are concerned with here, is the question of responsibility: Who is responsible for a person's education? Instructional technologists depart from traditional views of responsibility in instruction by assuming singular responsibility for delivering tightly structured programs that theoretically compel student achievement. Consequently, over the past 25 years, responsibility for education has moved away from an indefinite concept shared within a community web to an exact, particularized notion of an individuated possession. Further, instructional technologists claim this possession for themselves, removing the possibility of exercising responsibility from the student, or any other agent in the community.

This current status of responsibility within instruction is troubling to many, even to a few of us who have observed these changes from within the instructional technology field. Admittedly, posing questions about responsibility is a complex task with implications that extend to the limits of the culture. This chapter attempts to examine the notion of responsibility in light of how that concept has been shaped in recent decades in the tradition of instruction. As we discuss responsibility we will have in mind a definition of that concept that presumes that humans have the potential to act as free moral agents in choosing their acts in light of the consequences—choices that are guided by deliberation and internal sanctions (Craig, 1982).

What would happen if students were asked whether they thought they were *responsible for* their education, or that education was something that happens *to* them? Or, to put the question another way: Do they think education is something they do or something that is done to them? Studies conducted by Swedish psychologist Ference Marton helps us speculate about how this question might be answered by students. During the 1970s Marton sought to look at the different ways students experience the notion of responsibility within the learning process. Early in his work he began to identify at least two different orientations to that process.

Marton found that the college students he studied differed in the way they approached academic work. One group defined the content of academic work in terms that connected that work to their lives and world. The second group spoke of academic work in terms of the books that constituted the literature for a specific course, almost as if each course were inclusive and self-referential. "In the first case, they seemed to experience knowledge as a part of themselves or as a change in the way of conceptualizing certain phenomena in the world around them. In the latter case, academic knowledge was experienced as something external, something that existed independent of the person." For Marton, "these two attitudes appeared to be connected with two different conceptions of learning: learning as being something you *do* and learning as being something that *happens* to you" (Marton, 1979, p. 604). Marton sensed that this latter group is growing in number.

When working with our own undergraduate students we continually encounter this latter attitude: that learning is something that happens to someone. For example, we sense that many, if not most, of our students feel that teachers are primarily responsible for their education. They come to class with the expectation that the teacher will provide a clear explication of the course in terms of a list of objectives. These objectives should communicate, as precisely as possible, the exact content of the hours they will spend in class throughout the term. Commonly the objectives represent an organized checklist of skill-based, convergent outcomes. A syllabus becomes the packaging, so to speak, for a product that teachers are responsible for delivering. Through the syllabus they will understand what is expected of them. That is, the total realm of expectations they have for themselves rests on the clarification of that checklist of objectives. Typically, such a checklist is a superficial expression of educational possibilities. Often our efforts to diverge from that checklist and challenge them to think for themselves, ponder, exercise their curiosity, stretch themselves beyond the explicit structure of the course, are met with surprise or even resentment. Evidently, once they have the course in hand, as elaborated in the form of the syllabus—this external, decontextualized document—any hint that they might create internally an extension of the stated curriculum presents an expectation for which they believe they are not responsible.

The notion of responsibility in education and instruction in our society has traditionally been left relatively unsettled. Other societies have been more definite. For instance, the God of Deuteronomy held all Israel's adults responsible for the child's knowledge of God's law. Moses admonished his people that "these words, which I command thee this day, shall be in thine heart: and thou shalt teach them diligently unto thy children" (Deuteronomy 6:6 & 7). Failure to do so, Moses warned in graphic terms, meant the destruction of Israel.

As a modern example of a very specific sense of responsibility, George De Vos (April 1987), a Berkeley anthropologist, states: "The Japanese mother is a very important influence on the education of her children—she takes it upon herself to be the responsible agent, reinforcing the educational process instituted in the schools."

In our culture, various notions of responsibility as it relates to education have lived side-by-side. Ours has been a pluralistic concept, at times emphasizing the role of the community, at other times singling out parents or teachers or children for special treatment. For example, in decades past it was not uncommon to hear a statement such as "education is self-achieved": a statement establishing student responsibility. Other views make responsibility external to the student and leave the primary locus with another agent, such as the teacher. Today, in our view, educational responsibility has been externalized to the point where it no longer resides in traditional agents but in a newcomer on the educational scene: the instructional technologist with systematically designed courseware.

To understand the externalization of responsibility as influenced by instructional technology, we need to look for a moment at the historical conceptions of a particularized mode of teaching called instruction. The modern notion of instruction in the West is an invention, so to speak, of the seventeenth century. In its historical sense, modern instruction began to shift responsibility for education from the student to the teacher. Modern instruction assumes that I, as the teacher, have the critical knowledge you need and I will give it to you. Instruction means, therefore, that through its directing power, students will converge upon the teacher's truth.

This notion of receiving instruction as the legitimate method for becoming educated was first put forward in the mid-1600s by Johann Comenius. Prior to the advent of *instruction*, students engaged in *study*. Education was seen as a student responsibility. Education was a process of self-formation, a personal transformation. One studied, one remade oneself for the glory of God. The function of teaching was primarily hortatory—to encourage study—and teachers provided instruction on the heuristics of study. No one dreamed that a student could be instructed into an educated person, for that involved personal self-formation. But Comenius, who incidentally turned down the presidency of Harvard in 1640, struggled to articulate a sharp departure from the traditional conception of study. His idea of instruction is best expressed by the title of his book on the subject: *The Great Didactic Setting Forth the Whole Art of Teaching All Things to All Men or A Certain Inducement to Found Such Schools in All the Parishes, Towns, and Villages of Every Christian Kingdom, That the Entire Youth of Both Sexes, None Being Excepted, Shall Quickly, Pleasantly, and Thoroughly Become Learned in the Sciences, Pure in Morals, Trained in Piety, and in This Manner Instructed in All Things Necessary for the Present and the Future Life* (Keatings, 1896).

In the title of his text Comenius claimed in effect that he was privy to a specialized knowledge, an expert knowledge that could guide his students into the next life. Comenius claimed to have knowledge that others did not. Correct knowledge is scarce knowledge. Scholars such as Robert McClintock (1971) and Ivan Illich have noted that instruction—the idea that I have it and I have all that you need and I will transfer it to you—has the effect of denying the possibility of student creativity and curiosity. As Illich asserts, "In both traditional and modern societies ... instruction deadened self-confident curiosity" (Illich, 1978, p. 71).

The rise of instruction since Comenius has not been a steady upward progression. In its modern construction, instruction has been subject to a number of detours and elaborations. However, the value base that ultimately supports the notion of instruction—the mechanism of transfer and convergence—can be traced, in our culture, as a straight uphill path.

In the 300 years following Comenius, his central conception of instruction gradually spread throughout Europe and North America. In the mid-twentieth century instruction entered an era of rapid expansion by virtually colonizing all expressions of study. In the 1950s, Ralph Tyler fitted instruction to a technical model. By pre-establishing objectives and determining the achievement of those objectives through evaluation procedures, Tyler provided instruction with a mechanistic teleology: each classroom activity has measurable purpose. His basic formulation of the constitutive acts of instruction has not changed since. Tyler's technical rationality was augmented a few years later by B. F. Skinner and the instructional technology movement. Tyler's operationalized model of instruction laid the groundwork for what Skinner and instructional technologists were to call a *science of learning* and a *technology of instruction*.

INSTRUCTIONAL TECHNOLOGY AND RESPONSIBILITY

Instructional technology, in a sense, was launched with *Sputnik*. Within months of the satellite, B. F. Skinner (1958) had published in *Science* his now famous essay on teaching machines. From a soon to be celebrated laboratory off Harvard Yard, Professor Skinner offered up his prototype machine—an apparatus to implement the programming of instruction—and promised to set it down in every classroom in the land. The assumption was that educators were on the verge of a true science and technology of instruction.

Instructional technology integrates the determination of curriculum, as well as its delivery, within one interdependent and convergent instructional system. The instructional technologists' assumption is that the infinitely patient technology allows the students to go through the program at their own pace and as many times as necessary to achieve the mastery level prespecified in the courseware. Recall that instruction began the shift of responsibility away from the student to the teacher. The new formulation presented by instructional technology shifts the locus of responsibility further away from the student. This time the shift is not to the teacher but to the instructional technologist. To understand this move it is useful to introduce the notion of the Carnegie unit.

In 1905, Andrew Carnegie provided 10 million dollars to establish the Carnegie Endowment for the Advancement of Teaching. Carnegie meant the endowment to be a pension fund for college professors; what eventually became known as the Teachers Insurance and Annuity Association (TIAA). Carnegie established a board to run the endowment made up of college presidents and bankers. The board immediately found there was no agreement as to what defined a college professor because there was no agreed upon definition of what constituted a college in this country. By 1909 the board had defined a college as an institution that matriculated students from a particular kind of high school, which the board members also defined. Their definition was based on the establishment of a unit of academic work based on time (The Carnegie Foundation for the Advancement of Teaching, 1909). In short, a student earned one unit of high school credit in a subject in a class that met five times a week for one school year. The Carnegie board decreed that an official high school was a place that provided its students with 14 Carnegie units spread over four years. An official college was a place with at least six professors and a four-year program providing a specified number of Carnegie units. An official professor eligible for Carnegie's benefaction was one who retired from an official college (Tompkins & Gaumnitz, 1954).

In retrospect, Carnegie's 10 million dollars not only provided the beginning of a retirement fund for college professors, but much more important, the Carnegie board consciously defined and standardized the high schools and colleges of this country both in their structure and their curriculum. "The Carnegie unit became a convenient mechanized way to measure academic progress throughout the country" (Boyer, 1987).

The precise definition of what constituted a Carnegie unit has been enlarged and redefined several times since its establishment. The unit that came to measure academic progress at the collegiate level eventually incorporated several elements. Fifteen hours of student contact spread over 15 weeks with a qualified professor remained the basic element. (What we call today, following the Carnegie unit, one semester credit hour.) Other provisions spoke to the currency of the text materials, the breadth of the library, the number of hours spent studying out of class for each contact hour in class, and so forth.

By the mid-1960s instructional technologists were pointing out that the Carnegie unit was inappropriate to the newly defined realities of instruction. The problem they identified was that the Carnegie unit was concerned with the resources used for instruction, the input, leaving uncertain the outcome, or output, of instruction, that is, what people learned. Generally, for instructional technologists, the output of instruction, or education for that matter, is equated to measurable learning gains. They argued that the important thing in instruction was not the resources put into it (or the number of hours spent in class) but the yield, that is, the amount learned by the student. Recall that with technologically delivered instruction a student can repeat the program endlessly to meet the prespecified criterion level, or yield. Instructional technologists summed this up, as Robert Heinich explains, by stating that under the Carnegie unit time is the constant and learning is the variable, while under the new unit learning is the constant and time is the variable (Heinich & Ebert, 1976).

The technological unit, as we might call it, challenges the notions of instructional time and instructional input, the very core of the Carnegie unit, but it does something more consequential to the concept of responsibility. The Carnegie unit assumes a shared sense of responsibility for the process of becoming educated. A number of people are responsible for providing the resources of education, but the students must assume responsibility for transforming those resources and making connections with their lives and world. With the technological unit, instructional technologists define responsibility operationally in the context of a means/ends rationality. The singular responsibility for a student's education becomes identified with the success of the program. The motto that emerged in the early 1960s, which expressed this conception of responsibility was: "Students don't fail, programs fail." If, after an appropriate number of attempts through the courseware, the student does not achieve the prespecified level, the instructional technologist redesigns the stimulus material. That is, the designers gather responsibility unto themselves for altering the courseware to ensure that the student eventually will achieve.

The emphasis on yield and the altered locus of responsibility represented by the systematic programs of instructional technology and embedded in the assumptions of the new technological unit pervaded schooling beyond those programs. These important ideas gave rise to a set of institutions in education including criterion-referenced instruction (such as mastery systems) and competency-based testing. Another example is seen in teacher accountability systems, which are premised on holding the teacher responsible for the yield of instruction. The assumption might be stated this way: Students don't fail, teachers fail.

Who is responsible for a person's education? We implied earlier that the majority of our students seem to think that education is something that happens to them. Considering the history of instruction and particularly the rationales which have driven instructional technology over the past 25 years, perhaps the more relevant question is: How could they think otherwise?

REFERENCES

Boyer, E. L. (1987). *College: The undergraduate experience in America*. New York: Harper & Row.

The Carnegie Foundation for the Advancement of Teaching. (1909). *Fourth annual report of the president and of the treasurer*. New York: The Carnegie Foundation for the Advancement of Teaching.

Craig, R. P. (1982, November). *Accountability and responsibility: Some fundamental differences*. Paper presented at the meeting of the Midwest Philosophy of Education Society, Detroit, Michigan.

De Vos, G. (1987, April). Personal communication to author.

Grossman, D. (1990, March/April). Neo-luddites: Don't just say yes to technology. *Utne Reader*, 44-49.

Heinich, R., & Ebert, K. (1976). Legal barriers to educational technology and instructional productivity. (ERIC Document Reproduction Service No. ED 124 118).

Illich, I. (1978). *Towards a history of needs*. New York: Pantheon.

Keatings, M. W. (1896). *The great didactic of John Amos Comenius*. London: Adam and Charles Black.

Marton, F. (1979). Skill as an aspect of knowledge. *Journal of Higher Education, 50*, 602-614.

McClintock, R. (1971). Toward a place for study in a world of instruction. *Teachers College Record, 73*, 161-205.

Skinner, B. F. (1958). Teaching machines. *Science, 128*, 969-977.

Tompkins, E., & Gaumnitz, W. (1954). *The Carnegie unit: Its origins, status, and trends*. (U.S. Office of Education Bulletin 1954, No. 7). Washington, DC: U.S. Government Printing Office.

8

Theory into Practice
How Do We Link?

Anne K. Bednar
Instructional Resources, Indiana University
Bloomington, Indiana

Donald Cunningham
School of Education, Indiana University
Bloomington, Indiana

Thomas M. Duffy
Instructional Resources, Indiana University
Bloomington, Indiana

J. David Perry
Learning Resources, Indiana University
Bloomington, Indiana

INTRODUCTION

The field of instructional systems technology (IST) prides itself on being an eclectic field, Dewey's proverbial "linking science" between theories of the behavioral and cognitive sciences and instructional practice. This view of the relationship between theory and the field of IST takes the perspective that it is appropriate to select principles and techniques from the many theoretical approaches in much the same way we might select international dishes from a smorgasbord, choosing those we like best and ending up with a meal that represents no nationality exclusively and a design technology based on no single theoretical base.

The primary strategy for providing this "link" between theory and practice has been to collect concepts and strategies suggested by the theories and make them available to the practitioners. The concepts and strategies are abstracted out of their theoretical framework, placed within a practitioner's framework, and grouped based on their relevance to a particular instructional design task (i.e., positioned in some form of a general systems model). Instructional concepts and strategies are grouped based on their relevance to the particular learning goal, category of learning, or performance objective.

This work was funded in part by AT&T through a grant to the Center for Excellence in Education, Indiana University.

An eclectic approach is clearly preferred by the field of IST. Practitioners, it is argued, need the best guidance possible for their design and development efforts, and that guidance should be sought from the widest array of research and theory on human learning and cognition (Fleming & Levie, 1978). It seems unreasonable to presume that each individual could continually maintain an awareness of all of the research (empirical and theoretical) that is potentially relevant and synthesize that research to arrive at its practical implications. Thus, abstracting the techniques from the theories is a practical mechanism for providing the guidance that practitioners require. While one might be concerned with mixing techniques from different theoretical perspectives, advocates of this strategy simply point to the fact that the instructional moves derived from one learning theory are often very similar to those derived from another learning theory even when the theoretical explanations of those moves may differ (Bonner, 1988; Fleming & Levie, 1978; and Reigeluth, 1987). The techniques that lead to instruction seem separable from their theoretical framework.

The field of instructional systems technology currently draws principles of instructional design and development from empirical studies conducted within the traditions of a variety of paradigms and disciplines: behavioral learning theory, cybernetics, information processing, cognitive theory, media design/production, adult learning, systems theory, and so forth. As we acquire more and more tools with which to work, interesting mixtures of theories and practice emerge. A striking example is Keller's (1987) ARC theory, which draws on theories based on a premise of free will as well as behavioral theories based on the premise of determinism. However, even more unified approaches, such as elaboration theory (Reigeluth & Stein, 1983), reflect this eclecticism in that while they may draw from theories that share common epistemological assumptions, they borrow also from the wide array of alternative, and sometimes significantly different, theoretical representations.

Until recently the field of IST has tended to rely for a theory of learning most heavily on the field of behavioral learning theory. The overwhelming focus of IST on behavioral learning outcomes and on the design of maximally effective and efficient learning environments is incontrovertible evidence of this influence. But as cognitive theory has moved to the forefront of learning theories, the question arises more frequently of whether and how instructional systems designers can add to their arsenal of concepts and strategies by integrating the ideas basic to current cognitive theory into professional practice (Bonner, 1988; DiVesta & Rieber, 1987; Gagne & Dick, 1983; and Low, 1981). The perspectives expressed so far on this question suggest that theories and research on cognitive information processing (currently the most popular version of cognitive psychology), while not currently included as part of instructional design models, could be incorporated into those existing systems to improve their effectiveness. And so instructional designers are encouraged to learn techniques of protocol analysis and knowledge representation, to examine the literatures on expert/novice problem solving, metacognition, imagery processes, etc., as they consider instructional problems within the context of a traditional instructional design model.

In this chapter we challenge the concept that the eclectic nature of the field of IST is necessarily a strength. We illustrate our argument by reference to the implications of various versions of cognitive science for the field of IST, but also emphasize that our argument applies to theories of all varieties which have been assumed to inform instructional design and development.

In brief, abstracting concepts and strategies from the theoretical position that spawned them strips them of their meaning. Theoretical concepts emerge in the context of certain epistemological assumptions that underlie the theory. To use a concept such as knowledge of results apart from the assumption that learning is the strengthening of S-R bonds strips the concept of its fundamental basis. We propose that:

> Instructional design and development must be based upon some theory of learning and/or cognition; effective design is possible only if the developer has reflexive awareness of the theoretical basis underlying the design.

In other words, effective instructional design emerges from the deliberate application of some particular theory of learning. While we certainly have our preferences for some theories as opposed to others, in this chapter we simply promote the idea that developers need to be aware of their personal beliefs about the nature of learning and select concepts and strategies from those theories that are consistent with those beliefs.

We begin by presenting the basic characteristics of the information processing and constructivist viewpoints within cognitive psychology. We then contrast the implications of these views for instruction and the instructional design process. Finally, we reflect on the implications of the discussion for the future directions of the field. In general, our conclusion is that our instructional methods and our methods of analysis reflect a theory of learning and, more fundamentally, an epistemology. The theory and methods simply cannot be separated. The epistemology gives meaning to the methods both globally and in any detailed implementation:

- Globally, theory reflects epistemology. Any theory must of necessity embody a perspective on what we mean by knowing. As we shall see, adoption of a particular epistemological view has far-ranging implications. We think it is essential that designers be aware of the epistemology their instruction embodies. We also think that it is inconceivable to mix epistemologies in an instructional program.

- In detailed implementation, the way in which a technique or concept is realized in its application is a reflection of the theoretical interpretation of that technique or concept. The theoretical framework from which that method or concept was abstracted is essential for guiding the designer in decision making.

THE COGNITIVE SCIENCES

There are many approaches to the study of cognition; we limit our discussion to two general ones: traditional (often referred to as the Turing, symbol manipulation, or information processing view) and constructivist (experiential, semiotic, etc.).

Traditional Cognitive Science

Howard Gardner (1987, p. 6) defines cognitive science as "a contemporary, empirically based effort to answer long-standing epistemological questions—particularly those concerned with the nature of knowledge, its components, its sources, its development, and its deployment." Gardner lists five features generally associated with cognitive science, three of which are relevant to our purposes here. First, cognitive science is explicitly multidisciplinary, drawing especially upon the disciplines of psychology, linguistics, anthropology, philosophy, neuroscience, and artificial intelligence. Second, a central issue for this discipline is cognitive representation, its form, structure, and embodiment at various levels (neurological, linguistic, sociological, etc.). And third is the faith that the electronic computer will prove central to the solution of problems of cognitive science, both in the conduct of research to investigate various cognitive representations and in providing viable models of the thought process itself.

While certainly interdisciplinary, it should be obvious that cognitive science as described above is unanimous in its agreement on certain fundamental assumptions underlying the discipline. We would argue that in spite of the many differences, this version of cognitive science shares many of these assumptions with behaviorism, making its uneasy alliance as a linking science for IST possible. The most crucial of these fundamental assumptions is labeled *objectivism* by George Lakoff (1987).

Objectivism is a view of the nature of knowledge and what it means to know something. In this view, the mind is an instantiation of a computer, manipulating symbols in the same way (or analogously, at least) as a computer. These symbols acquire meaning when an external and independent reality is "mapped" onto them in our interactions in the world. Knowledge, therefore, is some entity existing independent of the mind of individuals, and is transferred "inside." Cognition is the rule-based manipulation of these symbols via processes that will be ultimately describable through the language of mathematics and/or logic. Thus, this school of thought believes that the external world is mind independent (i.e., the same for everyone) and we can say things about it that are objectively, absolutely, and unconditionally true or false. Of course, since we are human, we are subject to error (illusion, errors of perception, errors of judgment, emotions, and personal and cultural biases). These subjective judgments can be avoided, however, if we rely on the methodologies of science and logical reasoning. The use of these will allow us to rise above such limitations so that we will eventually be able to achieve understanding from a universally valid and unbiased point of view. Science can ultimately give a correct, definitive, and general account of reality, and, through its methodology, it is progressing toward that goal. Objectivity is a goal we must constantly strive toward.

Consistent with this view of knowledge, the goal of instruction, from both the behavioral and cognitive information processing perspectives, is to communicate or transfer knowledge to learners in the most efficient, effective manner possible. Knowledge can be completely characterized using the techniques of semantic analysis (or its second cousin, task analysis). One key to efficiency and effectiveness is simplification and regularization: thought is atomistic in that it can be completely broken down into simple building blocks, which form the basis for instruction. Thus, this transfer of knowledge is most efficient if the excess baggage of irrelevant content and context can be eliminated.

Because behaviorism and cognitive information processing share this objectivist epistemology, they can and should both be the source of insights for those in the field of IST who share this assumption. Behaviorist applications will focus on the design of learning environments that optimize knowledge transfer, while cognitive information processing stresses efficient processing strategies.

In a process somewhat akin to religious conversion, we have come to question objectivist epistemology. We have adopted what we will call a constructivist view and have begun to explore the implications of such a view for the field of IST. While we are still in the early stages in this process, one thing is very clear: constructivism is completely incompatible with objectivism. We cannot simply add constructivist theory to our smorgasbord of behaviorism and cognitive information processing.

Constructivist Cognitive Science

The constructivist view of cognition is not new, but it is receiving increasing attention because of an amazing convergence of disciplines that are coming to recognize it: connectionist approaches to cognitive science (Rummelhart & McClelland, 1986), semiotics (Cunningham, 1987), experientialism (Lakoff, 1987), intertextuality (Morgan, 1985), relativism (Perry, 1970), etc.

In this view, learning is a constructive process in which the learner is building an internal representation of knowledge, a personal interpretation of experience. This representation is constantly open to change, its structure and linkages forming the foundation to which other knowledge structures are appended. Learning is an active process in which meaning is developed on the basis of experience. This view of knowledge does not necessarily deny the existence of the real world, and agrees that reality places constraints on the concepts that are knowable, but contends that all we know of the world are human interpretations of our experience of the world. Conceptual growth comes from the sharing of multiple perspectives and the simultaneous changing of our internal representations in response to those perspectives as well as through cumulative experience.

Consistent with this view of knowledge, learning must be situated in a rich context, reflective of real world contexts, for this constructive process to occur and transfer to environments beyond the school or training classroom. Learning through cognitive apprenticeship, reflecting the collaboration of real world problem solving, and using the tools available in problem solving situations are key (Brown, Collins, & Duguid, 1989a; 1989b). How effective or instrumental the learner's knowledge structure is in facilitating thinking in the content field is the measure of learning.

IMPLICATIONS FOR THE INSTRUCTIONAL DESIGN PROCESS

Traditional behavioral theory and cognitive science contrast dramatically to the constructivist theories in terms of the underlying epistemological assumptions. As should be clear from the discussion thus far, these epistemological differences have significant consequences for our goals and strategies in the instructional design process. The objectivist approach to instructional design is well documented, and we will not dwell on it here. The interested reader may see Dick and Carey (1985), Gagne and Briggs (1979), and Romiszowski (1981) for views of instructional design which emerge from the behaviorist tradition. The cognitive objectivist view is perhaps best described in Polson and Richardson (1988), Mumaw and Means (1988), Schlager, Means, and Roth (1988), and Lesgold, LaJoie, Bunzo, and Eggan (1991).

We focus here on the implications for instructional design derived from a constructivist view. The view of learning as a constructive process has wide-ranging implications for virtually all aspects of the design process: the concept of the learning objective; the specification of goals outcomes; and methodologies for analysis, synthesis, and evaluation. Indeed, it even calls into question the traditional separation of method from content.

Analysis

In the traditional approach to instructional design, the developer analyzes the conditions that bear on the instructional system, such as content and the learner, in preparation for the specification of intended learning outcomes.

Analysis of Content

The traditional approach to content analysis has two goals. First is the attempt to simplify and regularize, or systematize, the components to be learned, to translate them into process or method. This is done by identifying content components and classifying the components based on the nature of the content and the goals of the learner. For example, one system would see components as facts, principles, concepts, and procedures, while the goals would be to remember, use, or find. Second, the analysis specifies prerequisite learning. In essence the analysis prespecifies all of the relevant content and the logical dependencies between the components of the content.

The constructivist view is very different. Since the learner must construct an understanding or viewpoint, the content cannot be prespecified. Indeed, while a core knowledge domain may be specified, the student is encouraged to search for other relevant knowledge domains that may be relevant to the issue. It is clear that knowledge domains are not readily separated in the world; information from many sources bears on the analysis of any issue. Further, it is often the case that the most successful individual in non-school related environments is the one who can bring a new perspective, new data, to bear on an issue. We must encourage students also to seek new points of view, to consider alternative data sources. Please note that we are not arguing that there can be no specification of relevant domains of information. We can and must define a central or core body of information; we simply cannot define the boundaries of what may be relevant (Lakoff, 1987; Wittgenstein, 1953). Indeed, we would argue strenuously that the traditional segregation of knowledge domains contributes to the development of much "inert" knowledge. Students simply do not see the use of information outside of the traditional limits of the domain or the setting in which it was learned (e.g., school).

The constructivist view also does not accept the assumption that types of learning can be identified independent of the content and the context of learning. Indeed, from a constructivist viewpoint it is not possible to isolate units of information or make a priori assumptions of how the information will be used. Facts are not simply facts to be remembered in isolation. Surely there is no reason to learn a fact by itself. Instead of dividing up the knowledge domain based on a logical analysis of dependencies, the constructivist view turns toward a consideration of what real people in a particular knowledge domain and real life context typically do (Resnick, 1987; Brown, Collins, & Duguid, 1989a). The overarching goal of such an approach is to move the learner into thinking in the knowledge domain as an expert user of that domain might think. Hence, designers operating under these assumptions must identify the variety of expert users and the tasks they do. For example, our goal should not be to teach students geography principles or geography facts, but to teach students to use the domain of geographic information as a geographer, navigator, cartographer, etc., might do.

Of course, we may not be able to start the student with an authentic task. In some way, we must simplify the task while still maintaining the essence. Reigeluth and Stein's (1983) notion of an epitome seems to fit well here as a means of task definition. However, and most important, the goal is to portray tasks, not to define the structure of learning required to achieve a task. Just as the cartographer or geographer must bring new perspectives to bear and construct a particular understanding or an interpretation of a situation, so too must the student. And just as different geographers identify different relevant information and come to different conclusions, so too must we leave the identification of relevant information and "correct" solutions open in the instructional situation. It is the process of constructing a perspective or understanding that is essential to learning; no meaningful construction (nor authentic activity) is possible if all relevant information is prespecified.

Analysis of Learners

When designing instructional systems from a traditional instructional design perspective, the "learner" is most often the pool of learners, the average conditions, and range under which the system must function. Certainly some adaptive models for instructional design measure individual progress toward learning goals as part of the system; however, those models are not the norm in instructional design. Further, even in adaptive models there is a concept of the general learner that guides the original design of the materials. Then the placement of individuals within the materials is accomplished through pretest.

The constructivist approach will also identify the skills of the learner. However, just as we did not identify content units in the domain, we also do not seek a detailed accounting of deficiencies. The focus is on skills of reflexivity, not remembering. Traditional approaches to learning skills stress the efficient processing of information: the accurate storage and retrieval of externally defined information. Constructivists focus on the process of knowledge construction and the development of reflexive awareness of that process: the possibility of alternative sign systems, the imaginative (e.g., metaphorical) aspects of much of our knowledge, the development of self-conscious manipulation of the constructive process, etc. Since every learner will have a unique perspective entering the learning experience and leaving the experience, the concept of global learner is not part of the constructivist perspective.

Specification of Objectives

In the traditional instructional design approach, the product of the analysis phase is the specification of intended learning outcomes. Throughout the analysis phase the developer classifies the characteristics of the content and learner so as to facilitate their translation in the synthesis phase to instructional method. The categories used by the developer are applied across contents, regardless of the nature of the domain. Similarly, in the synthesis phase the instructional process or methods which are drawn from to comprise the design are considered applicable across domains.

From the constructivist perspective, every field has its unique ways of knowing, and the function of analysis is to try to characterize this. If the field is history, for example, we are trying to discover ways that historians think about their world and provide means to promote such thinking in the learner. Our goal is to teach how to think like a historian, not to teach any particular version of history. Thus constructivists do not have learning and performance objectives that are internal to the content domain (e.g., apply the principle), but rather we search for authentic tasks and let the more specific objectives emerge and be realized as they are appropriate to the individual learner in solving the real world task.

Synthesis

Traditionally, the design (or synthesis) phase of the instructional design process applies principles derived from psychology and media research to design an instructional sequence (macro level) and message (micro level), which are optimal treatments to achieve a specified performance objective. The design principles are considered to be generally applicable across content and across context. The sequence of instruction is specified based on logical dependencies in the knowledge domain and on the hierarchy of learning objectives.

Examined from a perspective which views knowing as a constructive process, these design principles are called into question. Indeed, the approach is simply antithetical to the constructivist viewpoint. What is central, in our view, is the development of learning environments that encourage construction of understanding from multiple perspectives. "Effective" sequencing of the information or rigorous external control of instructional events simply precludes that constructive activity. Also precluded is the possibility of developing alternative perspectives, since the relevant information and the proper conclusion are predefined in traditional instruction.

In the same way that macro design strategies are inappropriate, so too are design strategies at the micro level. For example, it is inappropriate to control or focus the attention of the learner in a manner distinct from a real world context. Instead, the instruction is based on techniques drawn from the constructivist's epistemological assumptions and which are consistent with that theory of learning, e.g., situating cognition in real world contexts, teaching through cognitive apprenticeship, and construction of multiple perspectives.

Situating Cognition

There is a need for the learning experience to be situated in real world contexts (Brown, Collins, & Duguid, 1989a; Resnick, 1987; and Rogoff & Lave, 1984). By "real world contexts" we mean that:

- The task is not isolated, but rather is part of a larger context (Bransford, Sherwood, Hasselbring, Kinzer, & Williams, 1990). We do not simply ask students to do word problems in the book. Rather we create projects, or create environments, that capture a larger context in which that problem is relevant.

- The "real worldness" of the context refers as much to the task of the learner as it does to the surrounding environment or information base (Brown, Collins, & Duguid, 1989a; Resnick, 1987). We are not simply talking about critical and incidental attributes of the environment. We also argue that the reason for solving the problem must be authentic to the context in which the learning is to be applied. Thus we do not have learning and performance objectives that are internal to the content domain (e.g., apply the principle), but rather we search for authentic tasks and let the more specific objectives be realized as they are appropriate to that task.

- The environmental context is critical. An essential concept in the constructivist view is that the information cannot be remembered as independent, abstract entities. Learning always takes place in a context and the context forms an inexorable link with the knowledge embedded within it. Most simply stated, an abstract, simplified environment (school learning) is not just quantitatively different from the real world environment but is also qualitatively different. The reason that so much of what is learned in school fails to transfer to non-school environments or even from one subject matter to another is attributable, in part, to the fact that the school context is so different from the non-school environment. Hence, Spiro (1988) argues that we must not simplify environments as we typically do in school settings, but rather we must *maintain* the complexity of the environment and help the student to understand the concept embedded in the multiple complex environments in which it is found. Salomon and Perkins (1989) make a similar point in their discussion of high-level transfer.

  Authentic learning environments may be expected to vary in complexity with the expertise of the learner. That is, the child would not be confronted with the complexity of the adult's world—indeed, the child's world is not that complex. Similarly, the economic world seen by the average citizen is far less complex than the world seen by the economist. Hence, when we propose an authentic environment and a complex environment, we are referring to authenticity and complexity within a proximal range of the learner's knowledge and prior experience.

A related issue is the tendency in traditional instructional design to separate the content from the use of the content. Hence we learn about something so that we can use that knowledge later. We believe, however, that the learning of content must be embedded in the use of that content. Sticht and Hickey (1988) have nicely demonstrated this approach in their design of basic electricity training. The traditional approach to this particular course was to prepare an electricity curriculum based on an analysis of the facts, procedures, concepts, and procedures in the knowledge domain and taught in a traditional textbook fashion. Once this was learned, the thinking went, the students could go off to their particular specialties and apply the knowledge. This approach was taken by numerous experts in instructional design, in numerous revisions of this particular course.

Sticht and Hickey (1988), in contrast, focused on the functional context of the electricity knowledge. They identified authentic tasks and provided instruction in the context of those tasks. For example, students were asked to diagnose why a flashlight would not light. Then the class discussed how the various diagnoses might be represented in an overall picture (i.e., a functional analysis). From context to context, they moved the students to more complex and less familiar systems, but always maintaining the functional context of the task.

In a similar fashion, adult reading instruction has always been seen as a skill one acquires before using it. Thus, the reading curriculum for a job precedes job training and the content of that reading curriculum is seen as independent of the use of reading on the job. Duffy (1985; 1990), Sticht (1975), and Mikulecky (1982), among others, have argued, consistent with the constructivist view, that the reading instruction, as well as the job knowledge, must be taught in the context of job tasks. The tasks and content combine qualitatively to provide an authentic context in which the learner can develop integrated skills.

Cognitive Apprenticeship

The constructivist teacher must model the process for students and coach the students toward expert performance. Collins, Brown, and Newman (1988) provide an excellent discussion of cognitive apprenticeship and summarize three approaches that are well documented in the literature. A critical feature of these approaches is that the teachers' responses are not scripted. The teachers cannot serve as effective models if they have prepared responses and strategies ahead of time and only reveal an idealized path to the correct solution. Rather, students must come to understand the authentic ways in which a teacher (expert) attempts to represent an issue. For example, Schoenfeld (1985), when teaching university-level mathematics, invites students to bring him word problems (brain teasers). The problems are given to him in class, and he thinks aloud as he searches for a solution. Of course there are numerous blind alleys and errors in thinking. The class discussion afterwards focuses on the strategies that were used, the ways in which the problem was represented, how various sources of information were called upon, and how errors were a natural occurrence of trying alternative representations or strategies.

Multiple Perspectives

The constructivist view emphasizes that students should learn to construct multiple perspectives on an issue. They must attempt to see an issue from different vantage points. It is essential that students make the best case possible from each perspective; that is, that they truly try to understand the alternative views. If we focus on constructing an understanding and if we are providing authentic contexts, then these multiple perspectives can even be applied to content domains that seem very well structured, such as arithmetic (Schoenfeld, 1985; Bransford, Sherwood, Hasselbring, Kinzer, & Williams, 1990). Of course, the students must also evaluate those perspectives, identifying the shortcomings as well as the strengths. Finally, they adopt the perspective that is most useful, meaningful, or relevant to them in the particular context.

A central strategy for achieving these perspectives is to create a collaborative learning environment. Note that while cooperative learning has a long history, the focus in that literature has been on the behavioral principles of learning that can be realized in the group environment. We wish to emphasize instead the use of collaboration to develop and share alternative views. It is from the views of other group members that alternative perspectives most often are to be realized. Thus, sharing a workload or coming to a consensus is not the goal of collaboration; rather, it is to develop, compare, and understand multiple perspectives on an issue. This is not meant to be simply a "sharing" experience, though respect for other views is important. Rather, the goal is to search for and evaluate the evidence for the viewpoint. Different sorts of evidence and different arguments will support the differing views. It is the rigorous process of developing and evaluating the arguments that is the goal. Further, this is not a competitive endeavor, in which groups debate each other to see who is "right." Rather, it is a cooperative effort in which each student is seen as coming to understand each perspective and even contributing to the development of each perspective.

A second important strategy for achieving multiple perspectives and a rich understanding has to do with the use of examples. In traditional instructional approaches the examples are carefully chosen to highlight critical attributes and systematically manipulate the complex of irrelevant attributes. Like word problems at the end of a chapter, there is little that is authentic about the examples: there is a clear correct answer and it is the student's job to find that answer. Of course that is not the nature of the real world: there is little in real life in the way of clear-cut examples with only one correct solution. As an alternative to that approach, we would explore the use of real "slices of life." For example, to support teacher education, we would consider recording entire class periods to provide rich contexts for developing perspectives on teaching. The traditional approach to instructional design might instead select clips that represented correct or incorrect examples of a particular concept or principle. We prefer, as students are exposed to the perspectives of experts and peers, to permit the students to select particular instances and bring to bear whatever perspective is useful rather than learn to classify according to some archetypal, decontextualized categories. Our goal then is to have students see the alternative views of how a concept is seen in actual instruction. Most important, students must learn to develop and evaluate the evidence to support each contention. Note that this task supports a construction of understanding and provides authenticity to the instruction as well as supporting the development of multiple perspectives.

From the traditional instructional design perspective it may be tempting to equate learning in a constructivist sense as pure discovery learning and criticize that approach for its lack of efficiency. It should be apparent, however, from the previous discussions of situated cognition and cognitive apprenticeship that we are not espousing an unstructured discovery environment devoid of learning goals or learning events. In contrast to discovery learning, there is considerable guidance. It is simply not guidance on mastering a particular content element.

Evaluation

In traditional instructional design, evaluation assumes a universal goal or objective for the instruction. An exam measures progress toward the goal, and the data gathered about many students indicate the relative effectiveness of the system in terms of achievement of the goal. With a constructive view of knowledge, the goal is to improve the ability to use the content domain in authentic tasks (Brown, Collins, & Duguid, 1989a). Instruction is the act of providing students with these tasks and providing them with the tools needed to develop the skills of constructing an informed response and for evaluating alternative responses.

Evaluation in the constructivist perspective must examine the thinking process. This is not to suggest, however, that the issue of thinking is independent of the content domain. Quite the contrary—as the extensive research on expert and novice strategies indicates, effective problem solving strategies are intimately tied to the content domain. Experts are experts because of their understanding of the content domain.

One possible type of student evaluation activity would ask learners to address a problem in the field of content and then defend their decisions. Another might ask the learners to reflect on their own learning and document the process through which they have constructed their view of the content. The strategies common to the problem solving approach in writing (Hayes & Flower, 1986) clearly reflect this constructivist view and the important blending of content and process.

Two elements seem to be important: that the perspectives that students develop in the content area are effective in working in that area and that the students can defend their judgments. The first element might be referred to as instrumentality: to what degree does learners' constructed knowledge of the field permit them to function effectively in the discipline? The most obvious application of the concept of instrumentality might be in problem solving. Can learners arrive at reasoned solutions to problems in the field? But the concept equally applies to contents that are not traditionally considered to be problem solving fields, such as literature students analyzing a body of literature or art students critiquing a painting or elementary school students learning how different cultures in the world share universal concerns from differing perspectives.

The second element, the ability to explain and defend decisions, is related to the development of metacognitive skills, thinking about thinking. Reflexive awareness of one's own thinking implies monitoring both the development of the structure of knowledge being studied and the process of constructing that knowledge representation.

While either of these student evaluation mechanisms might suggest a viable system evaluation method, that method would certainly contrast with instructional design's traditional mastery model. One of the issues would be how to operationalize the concept of instrumentality given that no two students would be expected to make the same interpretations of learning experiences nor to apply their learning in exactly the same way to real world problems that do not have one best answer.

CONCLUSION

It appears that the implications of constructivism for instructional design are revolutionary rather than evolutionary. Viewed from contrasting epistemologies, the findings of constructivism replace rather than add to our current understanding of learning. With a new view of what it means to know, it is imperative to reexamine all of the assumptions of any field and particularly one that purports to improve the human condition.

One of the basic assumptions underlying the professional practice of instructional design is the separation of instructional process from content, a belief that general principles of learning apply across contents to a significant enough degree that basic principles of instruction can be successfully applied regardless of content. From a view of knowledge as constructed, the process emerges from the content. In-depth understanding of the content arises from, and is essential to, understanding disciplinary thinking. Since influencing how learners think in a content domain is the goal of instruction, the learning process must reflect those thought processes.

One of the most far-reaching implications of constructivism for instructional design is that designers must attach themselves to content domains in much the same way secondary teachers specialize in a content area or the way faculty at the university refer to pedagogy in their discipline. The next generation of instructional designers may be specialists in the design of instruction for teaching reading or language or biology. Certainly the relationship between instructional consultant and subject matter expert must be reexamined.

Many issues remain. Is critical thinking the goal of all learning? Do the contexts in which learning is to be applied relate to the nature of the learning experience? Are there contexts in which it is appropriate to apply traditional instructional development models and others in which it is not? Does a distinction exist between training and education such that a training environment is more appropriate than a school for instruction based on traditional instructional design principles? At what level of schooling is critical thinking a reasonable goal? Is it reasonable to differentiate levels of learning, for example, introductory learning from advanced knowledge acquisition (Spiro, 1988) or memory from problem solving, and to apply different instructional techniques based on different theories, or does that imply that one must believe that the nature of knowing, what it means to know, changes between introductory and advanced levels?

Where must we go now as a field? First, we must examine the assumptions that underlie the theories upon which our field is based. Turning toward a view of knowledge as constructed requires a major reconceptualization of our assumptions and practices. But even if such a view is ultimately rejected, we must not delay a full analysis of the assumptions that support our field. In those situations where the assumptions lack consistency, we must adopt a consistent set of assumptions and reject the findings of research and the development of theory based on different assumptions. We must constantly reexamine our assumptions in light of new findings about learning.

As a field we must ground ourselves in theory. One of the practices that requires scrutiny is the practice of drawing from fields with different theoretical bases without examining the conflict between the basic assumptions of those theories. Optimally, we would tie our prescriptions for learning to a specific theoretical position—the prescriptions would be the realization of a particular understanding of how people learn. Minimally, we must be aware of the epistemological underpinnings of our instructional design and we must be aware of the consequences of that epistemology on our goals for instruction, our design of instruction, and the very process of design.

REFERENCES

Bonner, J. (1988). Implications of cognitive theory for instructional design: Revisited. *Educational Communication and Technology Journal, 36*, 3-14.

Bransford, J. D., Sherwood, R. D., Hasselbring, T. S., Kinzer, C. K., & Williams, S. M. (1990). Anchored instruction: Why we need it and how technology can help. In D. Nix & R. Spiro (Eds.), *Cognition, education, and multimedia: Exploring ideas in high technology*. Hillsdale, NJ: Lawrence Erlbaum.

Brown, J. S., Collins, A., & Duguid, P. (1989a). Situated cognition and the culture of learning. *Educational Researcher, 18*, 32-42.

———. (1989b). Debating the situation: A rejoinder to Palincsar and Wineburg. *Educational Researcher, 18*, 10-12.

Collins, A., Brown, J. S., & Newman, S. E. (1988). Cognitive apprenticeship: Teaching the craft of reading, writing, and mathematics. In L. B. Resnick (Ed.), *Cognition and instruction: Issues and agendas*. Hillsdale, NJ: Lawrence Erlbaum.

Cunningham, D. (1987). Outline of an educational semiotic. *The American Journal of Semiotics, 5*, 201-216.

Dick, W., & Carey, L. (1985). *The systematic design of instruction*. Glenview, IL: Scott, Foresman.

DiVesta, F. J., & Rieber, L. P. (1987). The next generation of instructional systems. *Educational Communication and Technology Journal, 35*, 213-230.

Duffy, T. M. (1985). Literacy instruction in the Armed Forces. *Armed Forces and Society, 11*, 437-467.

———. (1990). What makes a difference in instruction? In T. G. Sticht, B. McDonald, & M. Beeler (Eds.), *The intergenerational transfer of cognitive skills*. Norwood, NJ: Ablex.

Fleming, M., & Levie, W. H. (1978). *Instructional design: Principles from the behavioral sciences*. Englewood Cliffs, NJ: Educational Technology Publications.

Gagne, R. M., & Briggs, L. J. (1979). *Principles of instructional design*. New York: Holt, Rinehart & Winston.

Gagne, R. M., & Dick, W. (1983). Instructional psychology. *Annual Review of Psychology, 34*, 261-295.

Gardner, Howard. (1987). *The mind's new science*. New York: Basic Books.

Hayes, J. R., & Flower, L. S. (1986). Writing research and the writer. *American Psychologist, 41*, 1106-1103.

Keller, J. M. (1987). Development and use of the ARCS model of motivational design. *Journal of Instructional Development, 10*, 2-10.

Lakoff, G. (1987). *Women, fire and dangerous things*. Chicago: University of Chicago Press.

Lesgold, A., LaJoie, S., Bunzo, M., & Eggan, G. (1991). Sherlock: A coached practice environment for an electronics troubleshooting job. In J. Larkin, R. Chebay, & C. Scheftic (Eds.), *Computer assisted instruction and intelligent tutoring systems: Establishing communications and collaboration*. Englewood, NJ: Lawrence Erlbaum.

Low, W. C. (1981). Changes in instructional development: The aftermath of an information processing takeover in psychology. *Journal of Instructional Development, 4*(2), 10-18.

Mikulecky, L. (1982). Job literacy: The relationship between school preparation and workplace actuality. *Reading Research Quarterly, 17*, 400-419.

Morgan, T. (1985). Is there an intertext in this text?: Literary and interdisciplinary approaches to intertextuality. *The American Journal of Semiotics, 3*, 1-40.

Mumaw, R., & Means, B. (1988). *Cognitive analysis of expert knowledge: Input to test design.* Paper presented at the annual meeting of the American Educational Research Association, New Orleans, Louisiana.

Perry, W. (1970). *Forms of intellectual and ethical development in the college years: A scheme.* New York: Holt, Rinehart & Winston.

Polson, M. C., & Richardson, J. J. (Eds.). (1988). *Foundations of intelligent tutoring systems.* Hillsdale, NJ: Lawrence Erlbaum.

Reigeluth, C. M. (1984). The evolution of instructional science: Toward a common knowledge base. *Educational Technology*, 20-26.

———. (1987). Educational technology at the crossroads. New mindsets and new directions. *Educational Technology Research and Development, 37*, 67-80.

Reigeluth, C. M., & Stein, F. S. (1983). The elaboration theory of instruction. In C. Reigeluth (Ed.), *Instructional design: Theories and models.* Hillsdale, NJ: Lawrence Erlbaum.

Resnick, L. (1987). Learning in school and out. *Educational Researcher, 16*, 13-20.

Rogoff, B., & Lave, J. (Eds.). (1984). *Everyday cognition: Its development in social context.* Cambridge, MA: Harvard University Press.

Romiszowski, A. J. (1981). *Designing instructional systems.* New York: Nichols.

Rummelhart, D., & McClelland, J. (1986). *Parallel distributed processing.* Cambridge, MA: MIT Press.

Salomon, G., & Perkins, D. (1989). Rocky road to transfer: Rethinking mechanisms of a neglected phenomenon. *Educational Psychologist, 24*, 113-142.

Schlager, M., Means, B., & Roth, C. (1988). *Cognitive analysis of expert knowledge: Input into design of training.* Paper presented at the annual meeting of the American Educational Research Association, New Orleans, Louisiana.

Schoenfeld, A. H. (1985). *Mathematical problem solving.* New York: Academic Press.

Spiro, R. (1988). *Cognitive flexibility theory: Advanced knowledge acquisition in ill-structured domains.* (Technical Rep. No. 441). Champaign, IL: Center for the Study of Reading.

Sticht, T. G. (1975). *Reading for working: A functional literacy anthology.* Alexandria, VA: Human Resources Research Organization.

Sticht, T. G., & Hickey, D. T. (1988). Functional context theory, literacy, and electronics training. In R. Dillon & J. Pellegrino (Eds.), *Instruction: Theoretical and applied perspectives.* New York: Praeger.

Wittgenstein, L. (1953). *Philosophical investigations.* New York: Macmillan.

9

Six Postmodernisms in Search of an Author

Denis Hlynka
University of Manitoba

There are those who instantly reject the concept of postmodernism. Some claim that it is anarchistic. Some claim that it is counterproductive. Some claim that postmodernism destroys the logical, scientific mind-set of contemporary society and replaces it with a vision of chaos. Some claim that it is philosophically unsound, because it revels in relativism. Thus a recent article in the prestigious *Encyclopedia of Educational Research* (sixth edition) says boldly:

> A final group of philosophers of education and educational theorists, categorized as postmodernists, have reacted strongly to the foundationalist urge and reject it with varying degrees of ferocity.... From the fact that observation is theory laden—that foundationalism is false—they draw the extraordinary inference that subjectivism is true and that knowledge is relative to time, place, and culture. (Erickson, 1992, v.4, p. 1006.)

The quotation above is remarkable in several ways. First, the reliance on rhetoric clearly gets in the way of an objective comment. Words like "reacted strongly," "ferocity," and "extraordinary" provide a curious and obvious bias to the text. Second, if one extracts phrases from the rhetoric, one can question the truth of the statements. The author in a throw-away phrase argues vigorously against the statement that "subjectivism is true." Yet, surely humans are subjective and this subjectivity has a powerful effect on how we read a text. "Knowledge is relative to time, place, and culture." Again the author tries to belittle such thinking. But is it often not so? Surely, the value of a subject varies depending upon context. Knowledge *is* relative to time, place, and culture.

What is important here is to illustrate the vehemence of the typical argument against postmodernism. The critics wish nothing less than to discredit postmodernism as the root problem of the end of the twentieth century. The final blow, when the above arguments fail to convince, is to argue that postmodernism is nothing more than a neo-Nazi philosophy or radical feminism in disguise.

Yet, the critics need not worry. Postmodernism is not an ideology that one buys into, such as Marxism or even behaviorism. Postmodernism is described by Jean Francois Lyotard as "a condition." It is a condition of contemporary society, and it is a condition that many now think has been caused by technology. If that is so, then educational technologists are part of that condition. Charles Newman writes that "post-modern means the first culture in history totally under the control of twentieth century technology" (1985, p. 187). The significance of that statement must have implications for educational technologists and what we do.

You do not have to like postmodernism, but you do have to know it exists. Quite simply, if you think that the world is troubled by chaos, multiple meanings, lack of direction, uncertainty, irony, and confusion, then you have encountered the postmodern condition. Fortunately, there probably is a remedy for this condition. The first step comes in recognizing the symptoms. This chapter will identify six postmodernisms, or six symptoms of the postmodern condition. You can recognize many of them—perhaps all of them—operative in the domain of educational technology.

Two additional caveats are necessary before we look at the six symptoms. First, our focus will be on the last 50 years, which shall be, for convenience, divided into modernism and postmodernism. Second, the examples are blatantly Canadian. American readers may not empathize with these examples, may not recognize the depth of concern underscoring the examples, or in some cases may not even understand the examples. If that happens, you are experiencing precisely the powerlessness of a displaced minority voice, struggling to be heard. In other words, the examples have been intentionally chosen for that purpose.

Here now are six postmodernisms looking for an author.

1. MULTIPLE VOICING

The modernist classroom was given voice from two major sources: the voice of the teacher and the voice of the textbook. Most often, there was nothing else. The role of the student was to absorb both voices. Usually, the voice of greater authority was that of the textbook, with the teacher in the hermeneutic role of interpreter. (The last four sentences might equally be written in the present tense, because, arguably, many teachers and many classrooms are still modernist. Modernity in this case implies a search for one best way and a belief in the inevitability of progress. Let's try: The modernist classroom *is* given voice from two major sources: the voice of the teacher and the voice of the textbook. Most often, there *is* nothing else. The role of the student *is* to absorb both voices. Usually, the voice of greater authority *is* that of the textbook, with the teacher in the hermeneutic role of interpreter.)

In the postmodern classroom, the myth of the text as authority has been exploded. Knowledge is appearing so fast that often there is no text. Teachers elect to use readings, or parts of selected texts, or even the daily newspaper. However, this practice also presents a dichotomy. On the one hand, when this technique is properly used, students are exposed to the most current information and thinking available. On the other hand, the use of no text decenters structure and places it in the hands of the teachers or students. This may be quite unreasonable in a course with a fixed content focus.

Although once, back at the turn of the century, only the teacher and preacher in a community were literate, now parents and friends and even the students themselves are literate (albeit differently). That means that the teacher is no longer the sole interpreter of a text. At the very least, a student can say "But I saw it on TV." Parents can have as much or more education than their children's teacher. The mass media only add conflicting voices. Television, radio, popular music all have something to say on almost every topic.

Educational technology may merely support the status quo and provide a voice that echoes the voice of the powerful. More likely, educational technology can and does provide new voices, new ways, new methods. Edgar Dale's famous Cone of Experience (1945) was, in retrospect, a postmodern mapping of the different ways educational technologies could speak to the learner. The cone was postmodern precisely because it recognized that each technology on Dale's cone had a unique place and a unique potential contribution to teaching and learning. Dale did not advocate a best medium.

There are indeed problems when multiple voicing takes over. Some voices are inevitably empowered while others are silenced. Society develops a dangerous *selective conscience*, in which it becomes *politically correct* to empower only certain voices. Teachers themselves can become sources of misconceptions. Honest attempts at encouraging multiple voicing can backfire and result in new and unanticipated stereotyping.

Yet, the postmodernist knows that we can never again ask either explicitly or implicitly that chilling modernist question: "Which voices should we silence?"

2. BREAKUP OF THE CANON

When things were simpler (if they ever were) there was a single canon, a single list of "great books" to which the educated and cultured person should be exposed. Modernity taught that we learned certain Shakespeare plays (*Hamlet, Romeo and Juliet, Macbeth*); we learned the standard quota of Charles Dickens (*Great Expectations, A Tale of Two Cities*); and we studied a particular view of history produced for and by the dominant ruling class. Many still believe in a single canon even in a postmodern world. I am writing the first draft of this paper on a Northwest flight on my way to a Professors in Instructional Design and Technology (PIDT) conference in Bloomington, Indiana. Beside me is the latest issue of the Northwest magazine *World Traveler,* in which I read an advertisement for the world's 100 greatest books on audio tape. There is no argument here, just a statement treated as a "fact": There are precisely 100 greatest books. You can almost guess which titles are included, and you can probably guess another hundred that are equally great but have been excluded.

Yet the multiple voicing argument has resulted in challenges to the canon. Should we not teach Canadian authors in Canadian schools? Should not Margaret Lawrence, George Ryga, and Stephen W. O. Mitchell be on the curriculum? My children live and go to school in western Canada. They learned about the Oklahoma drought depicted in *The Grapes of Wrath,* but never studied about the Canadian drought of *The Drylanders.* They learned about racism in the southern United States from *In the Heat of the Night,* but never about Canadian racism illustrated in *The Ecstasy of Rite Joe* by George Ryga. They studied American history and literature, but never read about the French and Ukrainians in the western Canada of Gabrielle Roy.

But to make these changes, something has to go. Will it be Shakespeare? Dickens? Hemmingway? Steinbeck? Modernists immediately sense a danger in this sort of argument. It advocates the destruction of the traditional canon, "the best that is known and thought in the world," as Matthew Arnold (1865, p. 19) has described the elite culture.

When the traditional canon disappears, what if it is replaced with nothing? I recall working with two third-year university students in using ftp to access novels in a hypertext format for the purposes of illustration. I asked them as we scanned a list whether they wanted me to download Joseph Conrad's *Heart of Darkness* or Virgil's *Aeneid.* Their answer: "It doesn't matter. We've never heard of either of them." Yet only 20 years ago, every Canadian high school student about to enter a university would have known about these works.

One role of educational technology clearly is to challenge the existing canon. First and foremost, technologists want to add television to the canon as several decades ago they attempted to add cinema. To the detractors of postmodernism, the argument here is easy. How, they ask, can we take seriously a curriculum that would teach *The Simpsons, Cheers,* Jay Leno, and David Letterman? The postmodernist response is: "We must." The Canadian postmodernist will add a postscript: Notice that each of those four television shows, just as popular on Canadian television as anywhere else in the world, are in fact not Canadian. Or, in fact, are they Canadian after all? *The Simpsons* is shown on Canadian television channels, with all U.S. commercials carefully replaced by Canadian counterparts. Perhaps that is enough to be Canadian?

Once again, postmodernists soon realize that there is another chilling question we can never ask again: "Whose culture should we marginalize now?"

3. SUPPLEMENT

Jacques Derrida writes of the supplementary nature of the postmodern condition. The supplement, he argues, has two functions: It adds on, and it eventually replaces. Educational media has long been called a supplement to teaching, but this was said in a derogatory way. Those who saw technology as supplementary believed that media was an add-on, an extra. First you taught what you had to. Then, if you had time, you could show a movie. As an extra. On Friday afternoons. Heinich (1970) wrote a major monograph documenting just that phenomenon. He argued that educational technology as an add-on would never have any lasting effect. Educational technology must be an integral part of the curriculum process from the beginning. What Heinich was advocating showed that educational technology was "always already" characterized by postmodern "decentering."

Contemporary deconstruction reverses the discussion of supplementarity. A supplement in fact takes over from the original and becomes the new content. Consider the famous multiple volume *Oxford English Dictionary*. When it is time for revision, the entire dictionary is not reissued. Rather, a supplement is produced. The supplement is meant to do more than add new words; old words perceived in new ways are also included. The reader must know enough to look up some words in *both* the original dictionary and in the supplementary volume. Eventually, of course, the supplement will supersede the original.

Postmodern educational technologists know that the single textbook is no longer enough and must be supplemented with others. Yet they are also cognizant of the very real problems that arise from teaching without a text or from contradictory texts. Which texts ultimately get chosen? In the schools I have examined the rule is simple and straightforward: The text you will use is the text that is located in enough quantity in the textbook storage room.

Educational technology, as never before, is providing a Derridian supplement to information. Textual information is often considered dated, so it is replaced by newer information via handouts and readings. These in turn are replaced by the latest, most up-to-date sources via the information databases of the Internet or through other information and educational technologies.

4. NONLINEARITY

Modern education is linear education. Linear models abound. Textbooks are linear and proceed chapter by chapter. Classes are linear, following an exact number, an exact timeline, and an exact schedule. A lecture is linear. Linear teaching is comfortable, effective, and efficient. Give the students a statement of objectives and teach to the objectives. The student learns. Modernist theorists argue that this model is necessary if we are to have order. Consider these three comments by Stephen Covey (1990):

1. Principles are guidelines for human conduct that are proven to have enduring, permanent value. (p. 35)

2. Begin with the end in mind. (p. 99)

All of these are modernist statements advocating one best way.

If only teaching and learning were really like that! Postmodern education, trying to come to grips with the information explosion, finds content everywhere and all at once. Of course, it would be just fine if first things came first, but, in fact, things come as they come.

Educational technology is unique in its ability to deliver content in nonlinear, postmodern ways. The power of hypertext is only beginning to affect the classroom, but already researchers are recognizing hypertext as the first concrete phenomenon completely grounded in postmodern literary theory. To study the meanings of hypertext, one needs to follow the leads of Landow, Heim, and similar researchers.

5. SLIPPERY SIGNIFIEDS

In a postmodern world, meanings do not stay put. In a postmodern classroom meanings get tangled with local contexts. Meanings (signifieds) are slippery and changing. Something means one thing to me, but something else to you. The following question has deep intellectual and philosophic meaning for Canadians, but much less for Americans:

What does Meech Lake signify? 1) nothing, 2) the downfall of the Conservative Party in Canada under Brian Mulroney, 3) an attempt to unify Canada constitutionally from coast to coast, 4) an attempt by "big government" to enact a bill that nobody wanted, or 5) a sleepy summer resort.

The correct answer is: all of the above. Different audiences can empathize with different responses. Each of the above choices is right . . . to certain *interpretive communities*. Option 2 is correct to the interpretive community with a historical sense. Option 3 is a political response. Option 4 is a populist answer. Option 5 is a tourist perspective. All are "correct."

Technology provides us with more options and more choices and ultimately not one answer, but more potential answers, each of which is right to someone. That is a major postmodern perspective. It may indeed appear to lead to a chaotic universe, but no one said that postmodernism had to be fun, or simple, or easy.

6. IRONIC JUXTAPOSITION

In quick terms, this point, "ironic juxtaposition," contradicts the last one, arguing now that as irony, postmodernism is indeed fun. The irony stems from postmodernism's self-referential and self-reflective qualities. It juxtaposes and accepts ironic situations not as being right or wrong, but simply, and existentially, as being. The results are indeed full of irony. Some examples follow:

A local Winnipeg restaurant has two signs in its window. One says "Present coupons before ordering," whereas the other gives the daily U.S. exchange rate on the Canadian dollar. Because this restaurant is in Canada, the proprietor takes care to be bilingual, at least in spirit. So one of the two signs is in French and English. The irony is that they have translated the wrong sign! If indeed the Winnipeg population needs to be served by a bilingual sign, the one that should be translated is the one aimed at the French-Canadian clientele: "Present coupons before ordering." However, it is the other sign, the one aimed at a U.S. clientele, that has a French version.

As a second ironic example, the ubiquitous *Sesame Street* has replaced certain sections of the show with "Canadian content," which is easy to do in a nonlinear program such as *Sesame Street*. Unfortunately, remote communities, especially in the Far North, get their television by satellite . . . direct from the United States. Their *Sesame Street* does not include Canadian aboriginal elements. Instead, these Canadian aboriginal communities get to learn a little Spanish!

A third example deals with multiculturalism. Some time ago, the United States declared February "Black History Month." At first, Canada went its own way. Then, Canadian teachers, perhaps from hearing on American television that February was "Black History Month," began to tailor their curriculum to meet the occasion. Now, it seems that in Canada, too, February is "Black History Month." Nothing is directly wrong with such a designation, unless it is that in Canada, there is no "Aboriginal History Month," no "German History Month," no "Ukrainian History Month," nor even a "French History Month!"

In short, multiple truths and multiple juxtapositions inevitably will result in ironic situations that need to be noted and addressed appropriately.

CONCLUSION

Technology is an integral part of the postmodern dilemma. For this reason, it is unwise to reject the concept of postmodernity out of hand. Rather, educational technology should be reconstructed with respect to the philosophical implications to which postmodernism points. Postmodernism provides an important philosophical underpinning for educational technology for at least two reasons.

First, technology has too long been associated with a technical mode of operation. However, it is *not* a given that technology should be examined only within a technical, systematic, and positivist paradigm.

Second, to be postmodern does not imply the antithesis of educational technology. Educational technology can help us communicate within a very complex worldview. Contemporary educational technology provides a platform for multiple voices. Educational technology, by providing more, better, and faster access to information, is leading to serious questionings of the traditional canon. Educational technology as supplement is providing a new sense of authority from media that have never been so significant before. Educational technology operates within a nonlinear mode. Educational technology, by its very encouragement of nonlinearity, noncanonical texts, and multiple voicing, results in "slippery signifieds" where meaning shifts. Educational technology shows that meaning can be relative to time and place. Finally, educational technologies, by conveying the sheer amounts of information available, inevitably stumble across and even showcase the ironic juxtaposition of ideas, concepts, facts, and theories.

Educational technology research stumbled upon the postmodern dilemma in the very beginnings of its research efforts. In those early days, when researchers hoped to find clear empirical evidence of the superiority of teaching by film or television or programmed instruction, it was at first disappointing when the results came out NSD, or no significant differences. However, educational technology researchers and theorists quickly recovered and put away their comparative studies. It became clear that educational technology *as vehicle* could not claim its products were the one best way. Instead, educational technology *as process* was important because it allowed for alternative presentation modes and alternative learning styles. In the jargon of the deconstructionists, educational technology was "always already" postmodern.

REFERENCES

Arnold, M. (1865). The function of criticism at the present time. In *Essays in criticism.* London and Cambridge: Macmillan.

Covey, S. (1990). *The seven habits of highly effective people.* New York: Simon & Schuster.

Dale, E. (1945). *Audio-visual methods in teaching.* New York: Dryden Press.

Erickson, D. (1992). Philosophic issues in education. In M. Alkin (Ed.), *Encyclopedia of educational research* (6th ed.). New York: Macmillan.

Hein, M. (1993). *The metaphysics of virtual reality.* New York: Oxford University Press.

Heinich, R. (1970). *Technology and the management of instruction.* Washington, DC: Association for Educational Communications and Technology.

Landow, G. (1992). *Hypertext: The convergence of contemporary critical theory and technology.* Baltimore: Johns Hopkins University Press.

Newman, C. (1985). *The post-modern aura.* Evanston, IL: Northwestern University Press.

10

Issues in Emerging Interactive Technologies

Richard A. Schwier

College of Education, University of Saskatchewan
Saskatoon, Saskatchewan

This chapter discusses philosophical stances toward designing interactive multimedia learning environments, considers recent instructional design research in interactive multimedia, and speculates about emerging trends interactive multimedia may follow.

PHILOSOPHICAL ISSUES IN INTERACTIVE MULTIMEDIA LEARNING

Objectivist and Constructivist Orientations

Multimedia developers' products almost always betray a philosophical posture. One way to divide the philosophical pie is between *objectivist* and *constructivist* orientations. Those who view multimedia design from an objectivist stance believe that the role of education is to help learners acquire understanding about a real and objective world (Jonassen, 1991). Content is externally defined, and the role of the multimedia designer is to marry the learner with what is to be learned. By contrast, Merrill (1991, p. 46) summarized constructivism as based on the assumptions that knowledge is constructed by the learner; learning is a personal interpretation of experience; learning is active, collaborative, and situated in real-world contexts; and assessment of learning is integrated within the learning context itself.

Although educational technology has traditionally been firmly rooted in objectivism, each of these orientations has a long and distinguished history in instructional design and development. Few instructional designers feel that one approach is *right* and the other *wrong*; rather that the circumstances surrounding learning dictate which approaches to learning problems are appropriate (*cf.* Shank, 1993; Wilson, 1993). Most acknowledge that some learning problems require highly prescriptive solutions, whereas others benefit from giving the learner control of the learning environment. Therefore, philosophical orientations are dramatically expressed in the multimedia environment created to address a particular learning problem.

Prescriptive, Democratic, and Cybernetic
Multimedia Environments

Interactive multimedia learning environments can be categorized as prescriptive, democratic, or cybernetic (Schwier, 1993a, 1993b; Schwier & Misanchuk, 1993; Shore, 1993). Prescriptive environments emphasize the achievement of externally defined objectives, interaction in which the learner reacts to highly structured and defined opportunities (e.g. embedded questions, menus), and prescribed sequences of exposure to instruction. Democratic environments emphasize proactive learner control over the learning process, including self-generated learning goals and learner control over the sequence, the nature of experiences, and the depth of exposure to learning materials. Cybernetic learning environments emphasize mutual interaction between the learning system and the learner—interaction in which the learner negotiates control of the learning experience with the system and the system attempts to respond intelligently to the explicit and implicit needs of the learner by adjusting to a changing, "multidimensional portrait" (Shore, 1993, p. 4) of the learner.

INSTRUCTIONAL DESIGN ISSUES IN
INTERACTIVE MULTIMEDIA

Learner Practice and Control in Multimedia

Practice and control have been the subject of much research and conjecture over the past few years. The following discussion has implications for the design of interactive multimedia instruction, and it particularly illuminates when it might be appropriate to move from prescriptive (objectivist) environments to democratic (constructivist) environments. Generally speaking, the decision to relinquish control of instruction to the learner carries with it the assumption that the learner will be empowered by that decision. Most research addresses when learners might be empowered by being given more control over instruction and when learners might be hampered by having such control. As a general observation, most studies have emphasized a logical-positive orientation—one in which the measures of learning and performance were externally defined. However, a constructivist might argue that learners construct multiple—and equally valuable—realities from their unique interactions with multimedia, thereby challenging external definitions of "effective" performance.

In democratic and cybernetic environments, practice during multimedia instruction should be varied and available to the learner at any time and in several forms to satisfy self-determined needs. In prescriptive environments, practice should be imposed often during early stages of learning and less often as time with a particular topic progresses (Salisbury, Richards, & Klein, 1985). As facility and familiarity with the learning task increase, so should the difficulty of practice. In prescriptive multimedia environments, the difficulty level would be managed externally by giving the learners access to progressively more difficult tasks as they progress through material. In democratic and cybernetic multimedia environments the learner may be advised about difficulty levels and productive choices, but their selection will be left in the hands of the learner.

Practice events in multimedia instruction should require learners to use information and discover and derive new relationships in information. Practice should also offer strategies for learning, not just specific content or skills. Learners can benefit from memory and organizational strategies to make information more meaningful. Metacognitive strategies can promote learning and can be generalized across learning situations, but they must be learned and practiced (Osman & Hannafin, 1992). Multimedia instruction should give learners opportunities to use higher-order cognitive strategies, such as metacognitive procedures and mental modelling to promote complex learning and transfer (Jih & Reeves, 1992; Osman & Hannafin, 1992).

In multimedia instruction, control refers to the selection of content and sequence, but may also include the full range of learner preferences, strategies, and processes used by the learner. Giving the learner control may increase motivation to learn (Santiago & Okey, 1990; Steinberg, 1977), but it does not necessarily increase achievement and may increase time spent learning (Santiago & Okey, 1990). One problem may be that giving the learners control over instruction may permit them to make poor decisions about which content is important and how much practice is required, which may in turn be reflected in decremented performance (Ross, 1984; Coldevin, Tovar, & Brauer, 1993).

Conversely, metacognitive strategies can be learned that will help the learner make more productive decisions (Osman & Hannafin, 1992). Multimedia designers cannot assume that learners can be self-directed without learning *how* to take control and make productive decisions. Not surprisingly, learners who are generally high achievers or who are knowledgeable about an area of study can benefit from a high degree of learner control (Borsook, 1991; Gay, 1986; Hannafin & Colamaio, 1987), or that naive or uninformed learners require structure, interaction, and feedback to perform optimally (Borsook, 1991; Carrier & Jonassen, 1988; Higginbotham-Wheat, 1988, 1990; Kinzie, Sullivan, & Berdel, 1988; Schloss, Wisniewski, & Cartwright, 1988). Multimedia instruction should be designed to include opportunities for learners to acquire strategies for using the instruction optimally, perhaps in the form of elaborate help sequences, "strategy" modules within the program, or on-line advisement. The main point is that in multimedia instruction, individual learners will require different amounts of guidance, and systems can be built that provide tactical, instructional, and procedural assistance (Park & Hannafin, 1993). Instructional cues can be used productively, even with passive learners, to promote exposure to elaborations and consequently increase time-on-task and achievement (Lee & Lehman, 1993). Learner control with advisement seems to be superior to unstructured learner control for enhancing achievement and curiosity, promoting time-on-task, and stimulating self-challenge (Arnone & Grabowski, 1991; Hannafin, 1984; Mattoon, Klein, & Thurman, 1991; Milheim & Azbell, 1988; Ross, 1984; Santiago & Okey, 1990). Further, the amount of control available to a learner at any particular time in a program should not necessarily be fixed. Courseware should be adaptive. It should be able to alter instruction dynamically, based on learner idiosyncrasies (Borsook, 1991; Carrier & Jonassen, 1988).

Feedback

In any instructional system, and especially interactive multimedia learning systems, feedback supports learning by providing information to learners about their performance—either confirming successful performance or providing corrective information about unsuccessful performance. Learners maintain or change their own cognitive operations based on how new information about their performance matches their expectations about performance (Bangert-Drowns, Kulik, Kulik, & Morgan, 1991; Mory, 1992).

The nature of feedback in multimedia systems will vary, depending on the environment in which it is used. Generally, an instructional designer views feedback as an opportunity to reinforce, elaborate, clarify, or even magnify learning (Park & Hannafin, 1993). In prescriptive environments, feedback will often take the form of error detection and correction. Because instructional learning outcomes are explicit in prescriptive environments, it is possible (and probably desirable) to funnel the feedback about learner performance toward the intended outcome. In democratic multimedia environments, feedback will often take the form of advisement, that is, informing learners about the consequences of choices and patterns of choices, or providing recommendations about productive avenues of study. Because learners are defining specific learning outcomes in democratic environments, feedback will attempt to help learners articulate their own goals and help them follow productive paths through the learning system. In mutual environments, feedback can be characterized as negotiation. Learners set directions and make choices, and the learning system "learns" from patterns that emerge how to respond to the learner or provide new challenges. Feedback will often provide a "metacognitive viewpoint" for the learner, responding intelligently to learner actions, identifying intentions, and establishing levels of challenge for the learner.

An obvious, yet often-overlooked aspect of feedback in multimedia systems is that it can take the form of audio, graphic, or motion images, not merely text. Although it may not matter which type or combinations of images are used in most cases, it makes sense to use a variety of modes to promote interest.

Mory (1992) extracted principles from the literature on feedback, several of which have direct application to designing feedback in interactive multimedia. She observed that feedback acts to correct errors and that the effect is more powerful if the learner feels confident that the incorrect response is correct; yet in verbal information tasks, correct response feedback is better than no feedback. The primary implication for multimedia design would be to ensure that corrective feedback is provided in cases where learners make mistakes where they exhibit a high degree of certitude. One strategy might be to have learners declare their level of confidence at key points during instruction and then tailor feedback to acknowledge the professed level of confidence. Instruction utilizing response certitude estimates is less efficient, probably due to the time taken by the learner to make estimates, but efficiency is seldom a major consideration in interactive multimedia instruction.

Feedback effects also tend to be stronger when no other instructional text is present, thus increasing the feedback's informational effect. The obvious response to this discovery for multimedia design would be to erase screens prior to providing feedback, or otherwise isolate the feedback from its instructional context.

Should feedback in multimedia instruction be provided immediately or delayed? The answer is not clear, but it seems delayed feedback may be more effective for higher cognitive tasks than immediate feedback. It is possible that delaying feedback allows additional time for reflection, which may in turn facilitate learning challenging material.

Collaborative/Cooperative Learning Strategies

One prevailing criticism of multimedia learning is that it is isolationist and therefore contrary to the social goals of schooling. Recently, attention has been given to the application of cooperative learning strategies to environments typically designed for independent learning, with benefits reported for student satisfaction and time-on-task (Klien & Pridemore, 1992). Hooper (1992a) described approaches to extending cooperative learning strategies to computer-based learning environments. He emphasized that cooperative learning is only one approach to small group instruction and that it is characterized by a high degree of equality (equity among group members) and mutuality (engagement among members). In order to take advantage of cooperative learning strategies in multimedia designs, the following notions (adapted from Hooper, 1992a) are important.

Interdependence and Accountability: The performance of each member of a cooperative group must contribute to the group's achievement, and the reward structure must account for this requirement. The group's rewards should be based on the performance of all group members; if one member "coasts," it should cost the group. Intrinsic rewards should be emphasized. Multimedia materials should promote individual accountability coupled with group rewards.

Promotive Interaction: An individual's effort to bolster the efforts of other group members is promoted through heterogeneous grouping. Homogeneous grouping by ability can benefit high-ability and average-ability learners (Hooper, Temiyakarn, & Williams, 1993) but may be ineffective for low-ability learners (Hooper & Hannafin, 1988, 1991; Hooper, 1992b). Heterogeneous grouping, however, may benefit both high- and low-ability learners (Larson, Dansereau, O'Donnell, Hythecker, Lambiotte, & Rocklin, 1984; Yager, Johnson, & Johnson, 1985; Yager, Johnson, Johnson, & Snider, 1986). Generally speaking, cooperative multimedia learning groups should be heterogeneous generally, and only homogeneous if the group members are all high- or average-ability learners.

Training for Collaboration: Learners can be trained to use interactive strategies effectively (McDonald, Larson, Dansereau, & Spurlin, 1985), and training should be both content-specific and content-independent (Hooper, 1992a). Multimedia materials may need to include an independent module for developing global collaborative skills. Learners should be prompted periodically during the delivery of multimedia content to apply the skills in order to promote content-specific collaboration.

Group Development and Maintenance: Debriefing sessions following group processes should allow group members to reflect on effective and ineffective strategies they used. Multimedia designs can encourage learners to engage in this type of activity following instruction, but, in order for it to be successful, teachers should routinely guide reflective activities and promote group development.

Metacognition

Metacognition can be thought of as cognitive awareness; learners practicing metacognitive strategies are aware of their own knowledge levels and approaches to learning and are able to exercise control over their own cognitive processes. Metacognition is multidimensional, several components of which were outlined by Osman and Hannafin (1992). "Metamemory" includes skill with different memory strategies and an awareness of how to choose which is appropriate for a given task. "Metacomprehension" includes a range of skills that include being able to detect when one fails to comprehend something and is able to take appropriate remedial action. "Self-regulation" is an individual's ability to make fine adjustments to errors detected when the instruction provides no feedback. "Schema training" has to do with getting the learner to generate personally relevant structures for understanding material and becoming less dependent on structures provided by the instruction. "Transfer" is the ability of the learner to apply a strategy to an unfamiliar and dissimilar learning task.

What are some implications for designing interactive multimedia?

As multimedia environments are designed that respect the independence and initiative of learners, their responsibility for learning increases. The instructional designer's position in a prescriptive environment is, "I will assess the relevant needs and characteristics of learners and make design decisions that will optimize their learning opportunities." Failures to learn are seen as structural failures in the instructional edifice—failures that the instructional designer must repair. In more liberated multimedia environments, the shift of responsibility to the learner requires the focus to become, "Does the learner possess strategies for exploiting this material successfully?" In designing democratic multimedia learning environments, the issue becomes not leaving the learner adrift in a sea of content without the tools to be successful, and recognizing that the metacognitive demands placed on the learner increase in less structured learning environments (Park & Hannafin, 1993).

One method of helping learners respond to greater metacognitive demands is to provide opportunities for checking their own progress and to provide learner advisement about metacognitive strategies. Learners can be reminded about ways to approach materials (e.g., "Have you thought about trying this approach? It worked for you the last time you tried it."). Such strategies should focus on providing metacognitive prompts and promoting self-generated strategies, while weaning the learner from prompts as quickly as possible. Osman and Hannafin (1992) warn against designs in which the training in metacognitive strategies require more energy than the content to be learned. Beware of metacognitive overhead costs.

In cybernetic environments, systems "tune" themselves to the metacognitive strategies employed by learners, adjust to them, and advise the learner of trends that emerge. This environment assumes that programs are sufficiently sophisticated to extrapolate meaningful trends from patterns of learner responses, a type of cybernetic metacognition not currently widely available in desktop systems.

Tracking Navigation in Multimedia

A particularly difficult issue hovering around multimedia learning environments is assessing the trail taken by individuals through instruction. How does one track the performance of an individual traversing multimedia learning systems in which the learners may follow a seemingly endless number of paths through instruction? Audit trails (records of all responses a learner makes while engaged in interactive or hypermediated instruction) offer several approaches to data collection. The difficulty presented by audit trails is twofold: How should data be collected, and how can one make sense of the data?

The first difficulty has been addressed successfully in the literature. Data can be collected and represented in various statistical and graphic forms (Beasley, 1992; Misanchuk & Schwier, 1992; Williams & Dodge, 1993), and hypermedia routines are available that can be used to automate data collection (*cf.* Beasley, 1992; Williams & Dodge, 1993).

Once collected, audit trail data can be put to at least four uses: formative evaluation; basic research in instructional design; determining patterns of usage in public displays; and counselling or advising learners (Misanchuk & Schwier, 1992). These uses reveal the second, more difficult problem—making sense of the mountain of information audit trails produce. Tools, such as *Response Checker*, are emerging that provide embedded information management, intelligent tutoring, and database analysis (Shore, 1993), and these hold promise of providing approaches to analyzing audit trail data.

Screen Design

Hannafin and Hooper (1989) identified five functions of screen design: focusing attention, developing and maintaining interest, promoting deep processing, promoting engagement, and facilitating navigation through the lesson.

Screen displays give your product its distinctive "look" but may also influence how effectively individuals can learn. Most of the effort expended on screen design to produce aesthetically pleasing and instructionally effective multimedia appears to be based as much on art as on science; however, significant and growing attention has been paid to screen design in the literature of computer-based learning and multimedia design. Park and Hannafin advise designers to use "screen design and procedural conventions that require minimal cognitive resources, are familiar or can be readily understood, and are consonant with learning environments" (1993, p. 81). It is beyond the scope of this chapter to confront the myriad issues surrounding screen design; for a treatment of the topic, you can refer to Schwier and Misanchuk (1993). One issue that has not been addressed, and that represents a productive avenue of research in interactive multimedia, is the question of how to combine different media on a single screen to facilitate learning. How can motion video, audio, text, graphics, and animation support learning in a multimedia setting—and on a single screen?

Print Support

It is important to remember that print materials compose a significant part of most multimedia learning systems. Well-designed print materials can make the difference between successful and unsuccessful design. A great deal of technical support and instructional design knowledge is available. The best single source of advice I have found on this topic is Earl Misanchuk's recent book, *Preparing Instructional Text: Document Design Using Desktop Publishing*. It extracts design principles that support learning (in preference to aesthetics where the two clash), and bases recommendations on research, tradition, and common sense—in that order of priority.

TECHNICAL ISSUES IN
INTERACTIVE MULTIMEDIA

Multimedia computer systems are now available that combine digital video, audio, graphics, animation, and text in a single delivery system. If excellent quality video is required, a videodisc player is also required. In most cases, however, compressed digital video images are sufficient. In addition, compression technology is improving to the point that we can anticipate compressed digital video that is equivalent to analog formats in the very near future.

Digital Compression

In order be used effectively by multimedia computers, audio and video recordings need to be changed from their common analog formats (as they exist on videotapes and audiotapes) to digital formats (computer files). Compression software allows producers to digitize analog audio and video with their own computers and make the files small enough to use in computer programs. Programs essentially "pack" and "unpack" compressed files rapidly as they are used. Another approach to digitizing audio is called Musical Instrument Digital Interface (MIDI). MIDI is essentially a common protocol for communication between electronic musical instruments, such as synthesizers, and computers manufactured by various companies. Sounds originating from a synthesizer are converted by a MIDI interface and stored on a computer by using a specialized program called a sequencer. The numbers, like other digital data, can be edited or composed on a computer.

Compression software currently produces images and sounds that are noticeably inferior to the originals from which they were drawn. These problems will be short lived, however, as software and hardware improve. Of interest to instructional designers is when compressed audio and video images are sufficient to use in a learning product.

Interfaces

The trend in interfaces is toward "transparency," or attempting to provide natural and unimpeded interactions with learning materials. Transparency is beneficial for all users of interactive media, but particularly for individuals often ill-served by technology—those with physical and intellectual disabilities and individuals from an aging population. There are many exciting developments occurring in interface technology, the most interesting of which include voice recognition, speech synthesis, and virtual reality.

Voice recognition interfaces permit the user to give verbal instructions, commands, and responses to programs. Voice recognition is a desirable (almost transparent) interface; the user does not need to learn how to operate any external device or even make the effort to point. Voice recognition is growing in significance, most noticeably for learners with physical disabilities that hamper the fine motor activity necessary to manipulate a keyboard or mouse efficiently (Shuping, 1991).

Interface speech synthesis is the flip side of voice recognition and benefits individuals who have difficulty communicating verbally. A computer containing an internal voice synthesizer permits a user to type a message and the computer "speaks" the phrases. In effect, the software provides an audio interpretation of anything on the computer screen, including prerecorded text. This feature allows learners to listen to printed material or individuals who have difficulty typing to select phrases from pretyped menus of material to construct speech.

Virtual reality is a complete environment that is assembled and managed by a computer program, one in which the user "enters" and interacts with the program. Instead of sitting at a keyboard and viewing the "playing field," you wear a special interface that puts you on the playing field and makes you a player. The interface to accomplish this type of interaction is specialized and usually specific to a particular treatment, although most interfaces include some combination of goggles and gloves or data suits. The interfaces can give the user the sensation of touch and the ability to pick up virtual objects, move, and manipulate them. A great deal has been written in popular, electronic, and computer publications about prototypes and visions of virtual reality, but commercial applications are only beginning to emerge.

Multitask Multimedia Systems

An exciting development in multimedia is the seamless incorporation of "live" communication (television or telephone or both) with produced multimedia resources. Multimedia stations with two-way live interactive video make it feasible to link individuals and their computers in several locations to an instructor, each other, or an array of multimedia resources in real time. A typical multitask system includes desktop videoconferencing via a camera mounted atop your computer and other computers; screen sharing, in which groups of individuals on a networked system can simultaneously alter common screen data; data transfer, among stations or from central resource stations; and desktop control of telephone and electronic voice mail functions. Multitask multimedia systems do indeed offer exciting possibilities for interactive multimedia learning, particularly because they promote the social interaction and community learning features so often missing from traditional instructional designs.

SUMMARY

Many of the limitations commonly attributed to interactive multimedia may be minimized by careful instructional systems design. Rather than consider the advantages and limitations associated with specific media, we should concentrate on developing a tapestry of powerful instructional systems that together contribute to the development of productive learning environments. For example, although multimedia instruction is often criticized for inhibiting group interaction, it can be designed to promote social goals of learning; successful multimedia learning systems can be used to nurture a community of learners.

The maturation of research and development in multimedia learning, coupled with technological advancement, offers exciting opportunities to instructional designers. At the same time there appears to be a persistent philosophical shift away from prescriptive instructional design and toward generative approaches that encourage learners to engage resources to derive their own, unique constructions of learning. Despite considerable rhetoric, one philosophy will not "win out" over the other in practice. Objectivist and constructivist approaches will coexist. I suspect that there will be a persistent need for objective-driven instruction, particularly for training environments.

If philosophical and technological developments in education are to flourish, the educational marketplace will have to be tolerant of stumbles, because educators will make some unproductive decisions about the implementation of technology. Educators cannot wait for developments in technology to stabilize before adopting innovations, which will inevitably lead to problems. At the same time, market pressure will continue to increase for manufacturers to develop compatible products, and until interactive multimedia can be moved smoothly from one system to another, its adoption will be seriously inhibited.

Acknowledgment: The author would like to thank Todd Zazelenchuk for his critical reading of an earlier draft of this material.

REFERENCES

Arnone, M. P., & Grabowski, B. L. (1991). Effect of variations in learner control on children's curiosity and learning from interactive video. In M. R. Simonson and C. Hargrave (Eds.), *Proceedings of the 1991 Convention of the Association for Educational Communications and Technology*. Orlando, FL: Association for Educational Communications and Technology, 45-67.

Bangert-Drowns, R., Kulik, C., Kulik, J., & Morgan, M. (1991). The instructional effect of feedback in test-like events. *Review of Educational Research, 61*(2), 213-238.

Beasley, R. E. (1992). A methodology for collecting navigation data using IBM's *LinkWay:* A hypermedia authoring language. *Journal of Educational Multimedia and Hypermedia, 1*(4), 465-470.

Borsook, T. (1991). Harnessing the power of interactivity for instruction. In M. R. Simonson and C. Hargrave (Eds.), *Proceedings of the 1991 Convention of the Association for Educational Communications and Technology*. Orlando, FL: Association for Educational Communications and Technology, 103-117.

Carrier, C. A., & Jonassen, D. H. (1988). Adapting courseware to accommodate individual differences. In D. H. Jonassen (Ed.), *Instructional designs for microcomputer courseware*. Hillsdale, NJ: Lawrence Erlbaum.

Coldevin, G., Tovar, M., & Brauer, A. (1993). Influence of instructional control and learner characteristics on factual recall and procedural learning from interactive video. *Canadian Journal of Educational Communication, 22*(1), 113-130.

Gay, G. (1986). Interaction of learner control and prior understanding in computer-assisted video instruction. *Journal of Educational Psychology, 78,* 225-227.

Hannafin, M. J. (1984). Guidelines for determining locus of instructional control in the design of computer-assisted instruction. *Journal of Instructional Development, 7*(3), 6-10.

————. (1992). Emerging technologies, ISD, and learning environments: Critical perspectives, *Educational Technology Research and Development, 40*(1), 49-63.

Hannafin, M. J., & Colamaio, M. E. (1987). The effects of variations in lesson control and practice on learning from interactive video. *Educational Communications and Technology Journal, 35*(4), 203-212.

Hannafin, M. J., & Hooper, S. (1989). An integrated framework for CBI screen design and layout. *Computers in Human Behavior, 5,* 155-165.

Harvey, D. A., & Corbett, J. (1991). Unlimited desktop storage: Optical drives that blow away the competition. *Computer Shopper, 11*(11), 230ff.

Higginbotham-Wheat, N. (1988, November). *Perspectives on implementation of learner control in CBI*. Paper presented at the Annual Meeting of the Mid-South Educational Research Association, Lexington, KY. (ERIC Document Reproduction Service No. ED 305 898).

————. (1990). Learner control: When does it work? In M. R. Simonson and C. Hargrave (Eds.), *Proceedings of the 1990 Convention of the Association for Educational Communications and Technology*. Anaheim, CA: Association for Educational Communications and Technology. (ERIC Document Reproduction Service No. ED 323 930).

Hooper, S. (1992a). Cooperative learning and computer-based instruction. *Educational Technology Research and Development, 40*(3), 21-38.

————. (1992b). The effects of peer interaction on learning during computer-based mathematics instruction. *Journal of Educational Research, 85,* 180-189.

Hooper, S., & Hannafin, M. J. (1988). Cooperative CBI: The effects of heterogeneous versus homogeneous grouping on the learning of progressively complex concepts. *Journal of Educational Computing Research, 4,* 413-424.

―――. (1991). The effects of group composition on achievement, interaction and learning efficiency during computer-based cooperative instruction. *Educational Technology Research and Development, 39*(3), 27-40.

Hooper, S., Temiyakarn, C., & Williams, M. D. (1993). The effects of cooperative learning and learner control on high- and average-ability students. *Educational Technology Research and Development, 41*(2), 5-18.

Jih, H. J., & Reeves, T. C. (1992). Mental models: A research focus for interactive learning systems. *Educational Technology Research and Development, 40*(3), 39-53.

Jonassen, D. H. (1991). Objectivism versus constructivism: Do we need a new philosophical paradigm? *Educational Technology Research and Development, 39*(3), 5-14.

Kinzie, M. B., Sullivan, H. J., & Berdel, R. L. (1988). Learner control and achievement in science computer-assisted instruction. *Journal of Educational Psychology, 80*(3), 299-303.

Klein, J. D., & Pridemore, D. R. (1992). Effects of cooperative learning and need for affiliation on performance, time on task, and satisfaction. *Educational Technology Research and Development, 40*(4), 39-47.

Larson, C., Dansereau, D., O'Donnell, A., Hythecker, V., Lambiotte, J., & Rocklin, T. (1984). Verbal ability and cooperative learning: Transfer of effects. *Journal of Reading Behavior, 16,* 289-295.

Lee, Y. B., & Lehman, J. D. (1993). Instructional cuing in hypermedia: A study with active and passive learners. *Journal of Educational Multimedia and Hypermedia, 2*(1), 25-37.

Mattoon, J. S., Klein, J. D., & Thurman, R. A. (1991). Learner control versus computer control in instructional simulation. In M. R. Simonson and C. Hargrave (Eds.), *Proceedings of the 1991 Convention of the Association for Educational Communications and Technology.* Orlando, FL: Association for Educational Communications and Technology, 481-498.

McDonald, B., Larson, C., Dansereau, D., & Spurlin, J. (1985). Cooperative dyads: Impact on text learning and transfer. *Contemporary Educational Psychology, 10,* 369-377.

Merrill, M. D. (1991). Constructivism and instructional design. *Educational Technology, 31*(5), 45-53.

Milheim, W. D., & Azbell, J. W. (1988). How past research on learner control can aid in the design of interactive video materials. In M. R. Simonson and J. K. Frederick (Eds.), *Proceedings of the 1988 Convention of the Association for Educational Communications and Technology.* New Orleans, LA: Association for Educational Communications and Technology, 459-472. (ERIC Document Reproduction Service No. ED 295 652).

Misanchuk, E. R. (1992). *Preparing instructional text: Document design using desktop publishing.* Englewood Cliffs, NJ: Educational Technology Publications.

Misanchuk, E. R., & Schwier, R. A. (1992). Representing interactive multimedia and hypermedia audit trails. *Journal of Educational Multimedia and Hypermedia, 1*(4), 355-372.

Mory, E. H. (1992). The use of informational feedback in instruction: Implications for future research. *Educational Technology Research and Development, 40*(3), 5-20.

Osman, M., & Hannafin, M. J. (1992). Metacognition research and theory: Analysis and implications for instructional design. *Educational Technology Research and Development, 40*(2), 83-99.

Park I., & Hannafin, M. J. (1993). Empirically-based guidelines for the design of interactive multimedia. *Educational Technology Research and Development, 41*(3), 63-85.

Rieber, L. P. (1992). Computer-based microworlds: A bridge between constructivism and direct instruction. *Educational Technology Research and Development, 40*(1), 93-106.

Ross, S. M. (1984). Matching the lesson to the student: Alternative adaptive designs for individualized learning systems. *Journal of Computer-Based Instruction, 11*(2), 42-48.

Ross, S., Sullivan, H., & Tennyson, R. (1992). Educational technology: Four decades of research and theory. *Educational Technology Research and Development, 40*(2), 5-7.

Salisbury, D. F., Richards, B. F., & Klein, J. D. (1985). Designing practice: A review of prescriptions and recommendations from instructional design theories. *Journal of Instructional Development, 8*(4), 9-19.

Santiago, R. S., & Okey, J. R. (1990, February). *Sorting out learner control research: Implications for instructional design and development.* Paper presented at the Annual Conference of the Association for Educational Communications and Technology, Anaheim, CA.

Schloss, P. J., Wisniewski, L. A., & Cartwright, G. P. (1988). The differential effect of learner control and feedback in college students' performance on CAI modules. *Journal of Educational Computing Research, 4*(2), 141-149.

Schott, F. (1992). The contributions of cognitive science and educational technology to the advancement of instructional design theory. *Educational Technology Research and Development, 40*(2), 55-57.

Schwartz, E. (1987). *The educators' handbook to interactive videodisc* (2nd ed.). Washington, DC: Association for Educational Communications and Technology.

Schwier, R. A. (1993a). Classifying interaction for emerging technologies and implications for learner control. In M. R. Simonson and K. Abu-Omar (Eds.), *Proceedings of 1993 AECT Convention.* Ames, IA: Association for Educational Communications and Technology, 881-894.

———. (1993b). Learning environments and interaction for emerging technologies: Implications for learner control and practice. *Canadian Journal of Educational Communication, 22*(3).

Schwier, R. A., & Misanchuk, E. R. (1993). *Interactive multimedia instruction.* Englewood Cliffs, NJ: Educational Technology Publications.

Shank, G. (1993). Qualitative research? Quantitative research? What's the problem? Resolving the dilemma via a postconstructivist approach. In M. R. Simonson and K. Abu-Omar (Eds.), *Proceedings of 1993 AECT Convention.* Ames, IA: Association for Educational Communications and Technology, 903-930.

Shore, A. (1993, April). *Interactive multimedia and student assessment.* Paper presented at the annual meeting of the American Educational Research Association. Atlanta, GA.

Shuping, M. B. (1991). Assistive and adaptive instructional technologies. In G. J. Anglin (Ed.), *Instructional technology: Past, present, and future,* pp. 292-301. Englewood, CO: Libraries Unlimited.

Spector, J. M., Muraida, D., & Marlino, M. (1992). Cognitively-based models of courseware development. *Educational Technology Research and Development, 40*(2), 45-54.

Steinberg, E. R. (1977). Review of student control in computer-assisted instruction. *Journal of Computer-Based Instruction, 3*(3), 84-90.

Tennyson, R., Elmore, R., & Snyder, L. (1992). Advancements in instructional design theory: Contextual module analysis and integrated instructional strategies. *Educational Technology Research and Development, 40*(2), 9-22.

Williams, M. D., & Dodge, B. J. (1993). Tracking and analyzing learner-computer interaction. In M. R. Simonson and K. Abu-Omar (Eds.), *Proceedings of 1993 AECT Convention*. Ames, IA: Association for Educational Communications and Technology, 1115-1130.

Wilson, B. G. (1993). Constructivism and instructional design: Some personal reflections. In M. R. Simonson and K. Abu-Omar (Eds.), *Proceedings of 1993 AECT Convention*. Ames, IA: Association for Educational Communications and Technology, 1131-1149.

Yager, S., Johnson, D. W., & Johnson, R. T. (1985). Oral discussion, group-to-individual transfer, and achievement in cooperative learning groups. *Journal of Educational Psychology, 77,* 60-66.

Yager, S., Johnson, D. W., Johnson, R. T., & Snider, B. (1986). The impact of group processing on achievement in cooperative learning groups. *Journal of Social Psychology, 126*, 389-397.

11

Instructional Systems Design
Five Views of the Field

Shirl S. Schiffman
School of Education, University of Virginia
Charlottesville, Virginia

INTRODUCTION

Ambiguity seems to shroud the field of instructional systems design (ISD). Consider these facts: The number of academic programs in ISD in the United States has steadily grown to more than 200 (Miller, 1985). Graduates of these programs are in high demand in the job market (Morgan, 1986). Linkages with business and industry are strong and expanding (Carrier, 1986). Technology provides a steady stream of exciting tools for communication and instruction and ISD professionals are recognized as skilled in knowing how and when to use them.

Despite these indications of vitality and growth, an undertone of criticism depicts ISD as:

- concerned primarily with the use of hardware,

- concerned primarily with the production of materials,

- not really a field, but a simple step-by-step method that almost anybody can teach and *anybody* can learn in a short period of time,

- blind to any solutions other than training,

- a rigid, mechanistic, linear, and/or antihumanistic approach to educational planning,

- a synonym for behaviorism.

Most ISD professionals have heard these statements at some time in their careers. The question is, can they be dismissed as reflecting only an individual speaker's bias, or do they in any way accurately reflect the field as a whole?

Academic fields can be stereotyped by people with a limited knowledge base. ISD, a blend of psychology, education, communications, management, systems theory, and social science, may be more open than most fields to "authoritative" comments from outsiders who, seeing one part of the picture, think they see it all. Still, it may be advantageous to examine the source of the criticism to be certain the profession itself does not add fuel to the fire.

Toward that end, five views of instructional systems design are presented in this paper. Each is held by some segment of the population as a true representation of the field; each of the previously mentioned criticisms can be traced to one or more of these views. By classifying what should and should not be considered an accurate representation of the field, the paper ultimately affirms what ISD stands for in theory and practice.

The Media View

People with the media view of instructional systems design see the field primarily as a process of media selection (figure 11.1). They consider ISD professionals audiovisual specialists who know about the characteristics and effects of different kinds of media (as well as how to dry mount and laminate). ISD professionals are expected to be the first and loudest proponents of whatever new technology comes along and are valued for their technological expertise. Those holding this view are baffled by a designer who knows or cares little about the technical aspects of equipment operation; such a thing seems impossible given this perception of the field. The media view is particularly prevalent in higher education because ISD evolved from audiovisual education in many colleges and universities.

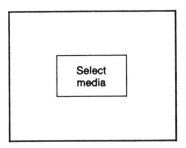

Fig. 11.1. Media view of instructional systems design.

Comments. Of course, designers *should* be knowledgeable of all potentially valuable technologies. However, the basic premise of this view—that a dichotomy exists between the use of media/technology and the teaching/learning process—is a perennial plague on the field. Although Gerlach and Ely (1980), among others, have made a strong case against the media view, it lingers.

The Embryonic Systems View

The embryonic systems view (figure 11.2) is similar to the media view, but emphasizes media production. Storyboarding, set design, graphic layout, photography, videotaping, editing, screen design, programming, and so on are assumed to be of paramount importance. Instructional planning is more a function of creative and artistic product development than of any systematic decision making.

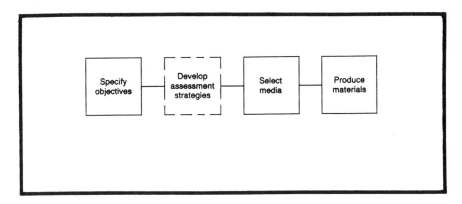

Fig. 11.2. Embryonic systems view of instructional systems design.

This view is common where materials are produced on demand for clients in higher education, government agencies, or the private sector. Consultation between clients and designers is largely the transmission of client-generated objectives for the development of a treatment in the chosen medium (also very likely predetermined by the client). According to this view, the development of assessment strategies to document learning outcomes is rare, but when undertaken is usually the task of the client. In fact, there is only one activity where the client must depend on the expertise of the design staff: production.

Comments. It is inexcusable for designers to use or produce low quality materials (unreadable transparencies, shabbily edited videotapes, etc.). Learning theory as well as aesthetics dictate well-crafted and attractive materials. On the other hand, professionals in the field must guard against putting disproportionate emphasis on production standards if they represent themselves as instructional systems designers. Suppose, for example, an instructor contracts with a commercial television production studio for the creation of a simple videotape of a laboratory procedure and is told that, from planning to scripting to postproduction, the process will take six months. An emphasis on broadcast quality perfection might be expected from these professionals. If, however, the instructor contracts with the ISD center in his own institution, is given the same timeline, and finds the suggested treatment more "artistic" than he feels necessary, several things may happen: (a) He may decide the project is not worth the time commitment, or (b) He may eventually invest in portable videotaping equipment and create his own materials in the future. In any event, whether or not he feels a six month timeline excessive for a simple project, his view of ISD will resemble figure 11.2.

The Narrow Systems View

This view (figure 11.3) begins to look more like a real systems approach. Additional steps that call for refinement and sequencing of the subject matter prior to production seem to legitimize the process although the steps of needs assessment and formative evaluation are noticeably absent. It is no secret that real-world design work is sometimes a reactive approach to immediate or "trendy" problems rather than a result of systematic analysis of organizational needs and priorities (Bernhard & DiPaolo, 1982). Likewise, formative evaluation may be shortchanged or ignored because of lack of time or resources (Dick, 1981) or because it is an unfamiliar or undervalued process.

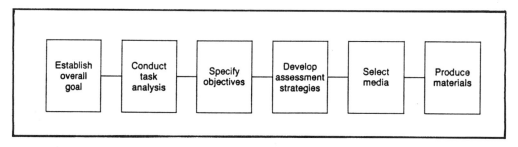

Fig. 11.3. Narrow systems view of instructional systems design.

The narrow systems view is common among those who consider instructional systems design a simple method that can be quickly taught "cookbook" style. It is the "in-two-weeks-you-too-can-be-an-instructional-designer" view so prevalent in the Human Resource Development (HRD) seminar circuit. Writing behavioral objectives and test items and conducting task analyses are seen as the primary hurdles to overcome.

Comments. Academics and practitioners should argue strenuously against any representation of ISD that excludes needs assessment and formative evaluation. There are two reasons why students, newly employed designers, clients, and observers of the field must see these processes as essential parts of the whole and not add-ons. First, as Dick (1981) has stated, formative evaluation "has anchored the instructional design process in an empirical tradition" (p. 31). The same could be said for truly data-based needs assessment that establishes the criteria by which formative evaluation measures the success of a project. These processes provide accountability for an often difficult, time consuming, expensive process that may affect many individuals.

Second, a view of ISD without these processes triggers the criticism that the field has "training blinders" since it implies that all needs/goals are instructional ones. A well-designed needs assessment first identifies the true needs of an organization and then determines which needs require the development of training and which require nontraining alternatives. The accuracy of these data will then be determined during formative evaluation. Even if time and resources are limited, the questions raised by needs assessment and formative evaluation must be addressed in any ISD project.

The Standard Systems View

The standard systems view (figure 11.4) is named for its resemblance to what is widely considered a fair representation of instructional systems design. The major processes usually associated with ISD are included. Needs assessment is at the head, formative evaluation brings up the rear. Summative evaluation appears as a means of producing empirical product evaluation/marketing data. Figure 11.4 is a clear schematic of a complex, multi-step process that would serve well as a working design model. Note the distinction, however, between a *model*, which serves as a type of shorthand for designers familiar with its theoretical underpinnings, and a perception or view of the field. What conclusions would someone draw from figure 11.4 assuming it to be representative of the totality of ISD?

First, consider merely the appearance of the graphic. It *is* linear. It looks rigid and mechanistic because of the step-by-step arrangement and the flowchart convention. As Chan (1984) points out, the lockstep sequence certainly does not appear "warm, humanistic, and artistic." He goes on to say that the jargon and maze of boxes and arrows associated with ISD lead many to believe that the field has "missed the mark, by failing to attend to global, holistic, and humanistic goals of education" (p. 8).

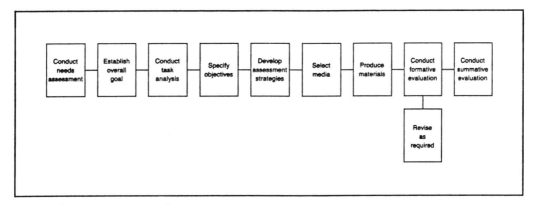

Fig. 11.4. Standard systems view of instructional systems design.

Figure 11.4 can also engender the belief that instructional systems design is a strictly behavioral approach to learning and instruction. The input-output structure and the emphasis on task analysis, objectives, and assessment of learning outcomes conjures up visions of machine-gradable (translation: low-level) training or, as Silberman (1970) puts it "the almost irresistible temptation to go after the things that can be measured" (p. 198).

Comments. Next to hardware, flowcharts like figure 11.4 are the most visible accouterments of the field. Designers may use models for organizational and communication devices, but others, unaware of the theoretical/research context from which they are derived and upon which they are dependent for enlightened and insightful implementation, often take them as graphic representations of the entire field. Hence, it is not uncommon to find that those who criticize ISD for being mechanical, antihumanistic, and/or behavioristic have a standard systems view of the field in mind.

Academics and practitioners must counter this view whenever possible by educating clients, students, and others about what is required to successfully implement the steps shown on figure 11.4. For example, it must be consistently stressed that the best needs assessment, task analysis, test items, and media selection in the world may be meaningless unless a designer simultaneously attends to matters of diffusion. Likewise, ISD professionals must be aggressive about linking the practice of the steps on figure 11.4 with relevant (and current) learning theory and research. Failure to make these connections consistently feeds directly into many criticisms of the field.

The Instructional Systems Design View

Figure 11.5 shows instructional systems design to be a synthesis of theory and research related to (a) how humans perceive and give meaning to the stimuli in their environments, (b) the nature of information and how it is composed and transmitted, (c) the concept of systems and the interrelationships among factors promoting or deterring efficient and effective accomplishment of the desired outcomes (Torkelson, 1977), and (d) the consulting and managerial skills necessary to meld points *a* through *c* into a coherent whole. The well known systems model functions as a series of gates that allow information to flow through at appropriate times. The gates facilitate systematic thinking in the midst of an often staggering number of variables designers attempt to control.

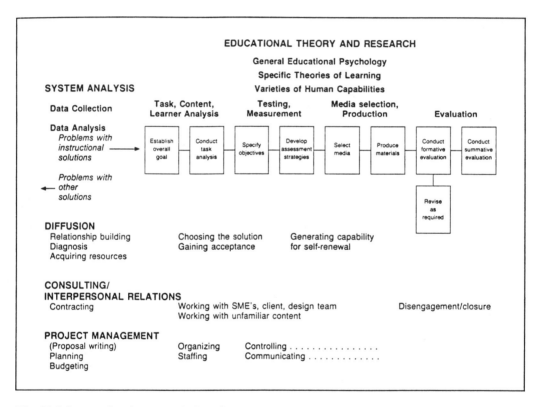

Fig. 11.5. Instructional systems design view.

A single designer is usually not expected to have all of the knowledge and skills shown on figure 11.5, although the smaller the design team, the more skills each person must have. However, whenever instruction is being designed, all five of the major categories (shown in capital letters on figure 11.5), are called into play. For example, when it is time to write instructional sequences and design page or graphic layout, all designers—with or without a knowledge of learning theory and message design (Fleming & Levie, 1978)—will make decisions on these issues. Designers lacking familiarity with relevant research and theory substitute instincts and a good eye when making these decisions. Ideally, theory, research, instincts, *and* a good eye all are at a designer's disposal.

Similarly, a designer unfamiliar with the research and strategies of diffusion will eventually be faced with the task of trying to assure successful adoption of whatever product or program has been produced. While luck, persuasiveness, and managerial mandate may aid the "diffusion-less" designer, the history of innovation would suggest these as highly unreliable techniques.

In short, the proper practice of ISD brings all the skills, knowledge, and attitudes shown on figure 11.5 to bear on the problems of a particular system in an orderly and precise manner. Furthermore, there is (or should be) a symbiotic relationship between the major categories. Designers' knowledge and skill in one area supports their work in other areas, as will be seen in the following description of the instructional systems design view.

EDUCATIONAL THEORY AND RESEARCH

General Educational Psychology

Designers should have an understanding of the principles of human physical, emotional, social, and mental growth and development. A knowledge of how socioeconomic status, IQ, sex differences, cognitive styles, creativity, and motivation may affect learning is also important. This background provides valuable insight into the characteristics of different target populations.

Specific Theories of Learning

A solid foundation in learning theory is undoubtedly the most essential element in the preparation of ISD professionals because it permeates all other dimensions shown on figure 11.5. Designers must be familiar with the theory and research on learning and must be able to apply them to actual practice. For example, a designer working on an early childhood education project will find insight into children's behavior and the value of a rich learning environment in the work of Piaget (1954). Ausubel (1968) and Rothkopf (1970) are valuable resources when producing textual materials. Designers familiar with social learning theory (Bandura, 1986) will not ignore environmental factors that significantly affect instructional programs, nor overlook the power of informal learning channels (e.g., observational learning). Bruner's (1973) rich philosophical insight into discovery learning and problem solving, Keller's (1983) work on motivation, Knowles' (1984) emphasis on factors that facilitate adult learning, and the work of others contribute to a designer's overall understanding of the learning process and skill in designing instructional strategies.

Cognitive science (Klatzky, 1980; Anderson, 1980; Gagne, E., 1985; Wildman & Burton, 1981) is making a major contribution to our understanding of how humans perceive, process, store, and retrieve information. Schema theory, elaboration, metacognition, automaticity, expert/novice studies, and transfer are only a few of the constructs studied by cognitive psychologists that have important implications for the design of instruction.

Without a broad-based foundation in learning theory the practice of ISD becomes narrowly focused on means (the steps in the systems model) rather than on the rightful end (learning). Academics must provide students with a solid background in the relevant literature; practitioners must be sure on-the-job exigencies do not preclude the influsion of learning theory into design and production procedures.

Varieties of Human Capabilities

ISD professionals must be able to distinguish between psychomotor skills and intellectual skills; attitudes and cognitive strategies; and skills requiring memorization of information and those requiring the application of previously learned information to problem situations (Gagne, R., 1985). This knowledge enables them to take advantage of research on the particular conditions under which each type of human capability is most likely to be learned. Thus, a unit intended to formulate or change attitudes will use entirely different instructional strategies than one composed primarily of verbal information.

Knowledge of human capabilities also enables a designer to be certain that the objectives of an instructional unit truly reflect the needs of the system. Training journals complain that classroom instruction does not transfer to on-the-job competence (Broad, 1982). One explanation for this is that the objectives of classroom instruction often do not match on-the-job requirements (e.g., a class presents and tests only verbal information when job requirements call for application of the information to novel situations). A thorough understanding of the attributes of each type of learning is insurance against such errors.

Finally, this knowledge guards against the trivialization or unnecessary simplification of instruction that occurs when (a) the objectives for a unit require only low-level learning, and/or (b) objectives are written only for skills that can be easily evaluated (e.g., by machine). ISD professionals must be alert to these issues. In relation to the former, they know that objectives can and should be written for higher intellectual skills: analysis, synthesis, problem solving, problem finding, etc. In relation to the latter they know that the problem is one of measurement (there *are* ways to measure achievement in problem solving, after all) and professional integrity (should a unit be designed that does not truly provide the skills required by the system?).

Task, Content, Learner Analysis

Task analysis has always been viewed as a critical and difficult step in the design of instruction. A traditional, behavioral orientation calls for breaking a goal into subgoals, thereby identifying essential prerequisites and mapping a logical sequence for presenting the content.

Cognitive science has broadened the concept of task analysis to include an analysis of the content itself. Such an analysis aims at determining the relationship between, and relative importance of, individual concepts within a body of content. One value of this relates to the presentation of material:

> What happens as readers try to progress through text material, for example, is that single ideas, concepts, rules, and other elements must be eventually integrated into some holistic structures organized around a few powerful ideas. The learner's task in this case is greatly facilitated when the content in question is well organized (Wildman, 1981, p. 17).

Another use for this information is to provide organizational and conceptual strategies such as advance organizers (Ausubel, 1968) or frames (Armbruster & Anderson, 1985) that learners can use to aid their own comprehension and retention of information.

A second cognitive perspective emphasizes the need to be aware of how students will process a particular body of content. Shulman (1986), for example, asserts that "pedagogical content knowledge also includes an understanding of what makes the learning of specific topics easy or hard" (p. 9). This idea considers how students' prior learning (or lack thereof)—both of content-specific information and cognitive strategies—may affect their success with a particular instructional unit.

The behavioral and cognitive orientations combine to suggest a challenging three-fold approach to task analysis: analysis of (a) the task, (b) the structure of the content, and (c) the learner. A grounding in learning theory and knowledge of the types of human capabilities will prove valuable during this complex process.

Testing, Measurement

On a large ISD staff, evaluation/measurement specialists may design the instruments and evaluation procedures. However, without a solid background in testing and measurement (Gronlund, 1981), designers are ill-prepared to (a) establish appropriate criterion levels for objectives (Thorman, 1982), (b) select appropriate assessment strategies for a particular target population, system and learning environment constraints, or type of human capability (Gagne & Beard, 1978), or (c) design instruments when necessary. They should be able to develop valid and reliable needs assessment instruments, various kinds of paper/pencil tests, attitude surveys, and observational checklists.

Media Selection, Production

Designers use their knowledge of learning theory and the varieties of human capabilities to make media selection decisions (Reiser & Gagne, 1983), as well as their knowledge of the extensive research on media (Schramm, 1977; Levie & Dickie, 1973). For example, pictures may be used to facilitate long-term memory, realistic, dramatic presentations for encouraging attitude change, print or graphic advance organizers before presenting a large amount of verbal information, video segments for teaching motor skills, etc. Cost, time, and logistical factors also play a major role in making media selection decisions (Clark & Salomon, 1986) as do the resources and constraints of a particular system. Production specialists (graphic artists, video production personnel, computer programmers, photographers) are often engaged once design specifications have been formulated. However, designers must know the capabilities of all forms of media and technology (including the most recent advances in interactive video and telecommunications) so that they know when and how each can be used appropriately. Knowledge about production techniques also improves the designer's ability to communicate with technical specialists working on a project.

Evaluation

The last subcategory under educational theory and research deals with the evaluation of instructional products and programs. Knowledge of evaluation theory and techniques, both formative (Dick & Carey, 1985) and summative (Tuckman, 1979) is essential since on this rests the ability to assess the effectiveness of the entire ISD process. Designers will benefit from a knowledge of quantitative and qualitative (Cook & Reichardt, 1979) methodologies.

SYSTEM ANALYSIS

System analysis is divided into two subcategories in figure 11.5: data collection, and data analysis. First, designers must know the goals, functions, resources, constraints, chain-of-command, and culture (Schein, 1986) of the organization in which they are working. Data must be gathered on the specific target populations within an organization to determine their general characteristics, motivation, sophistication as learners, and performance levels. (This information will be useful again during the task analysis phase.) Typical learning environments in the organization (formal, small group interaction, grapevine, on-the-job training, etc.) must also be studied. A designer's background in general educational psychology, learning theory, and the varieties of human capabilities provide excellent insight during this process.

When all relevant data are collected, they are analyzed to determine whether there are any gaps between what is and what should be (Kaufman & English, 1979). It is here that a designer separates those needs for which training is the appropriate solution from those with motivational or environmental solutions. Hence costly instructional programs are undertaken only when the system analysis deems a project worthy, appropriate, practicable, and likely to succeed. Because of their analysis, consulting, and managerial skills, designers often are qualified to recommend noninstructional solutions (e.g., changes in office information flow or managerial styles) as well as instructional ones.

DIFFUSION

Havelock (1973) lists six steps (shown on figure 11.5) necessary to bring about change in an organization. It should be noted that a well designed system analysis incorporates four of these steps: (a) a good relationship with the client is built and the designer's credibility established; (b) the problem(s) of the system are diagnosed; (c) all relevant resources are acquired; and (d) members of the system potentially affected by the innovation view the idea favorably because they (or at least key personnel) have been involved in the system analysis phase in some way. Once the solution for the project is chosen, the designer must see that the new instructional product or program can be maintained easily by the system. An understanding of the process of change, resistance to change, and categories of adopters (Rogers, 1983) prepares the designer to work sensitively and persuasively with different members of the client group while working through the steps of diffusion.

CONSULTING/INTERPERSONAL RELATIONS

Bell and Nadler (1979) list the phases of a consultancy as entry, diagnosis, response, disengagement, and closure. These parallel the diffusion steps, yet emphasize the professional (and possibly contractual) relationship between the designer and the client. Writing contracts (Walter & Earle, 1981-82), determining the appropriate style of consultancy for a particular client, and knowing how to disengage from and conclude a consulting agreement (Davis, 1975) are among the consulting skills designers should possess. Interpersonal and small group interaction skills (Tubbs, 1978) prepare designers to work successfully with subject matter experts (Coldeway & Rasmussen, 1984), clients, and other designers. The ability to work with unfamiliar content (Bratton, 1981) is another essential skill for designers.

PROJECT MANAGEMENT

Knirk and Gustafson (1986) list six stages of project management (shown on figure 11.5): planning, organizing, staffing, budgeting, controlling, and communicating. Craig (1976) offers specific guidelines for many of these functions. In some cases, designers must also be able to write proposals for project funding. Cost-benefit analysis (Head & Buchanan, 1981), general writing skills (Booher, 1982), and platform skills (Schleger, 1984) round out an array of organizational, managerial, and communication competencies for successful project management.

SUMMARY

A summary of the instructional system design view serves as a rebuttal to much of the criticism of the field:

- The main emphasis of instructional systems design is not the use of hardware. Although very important, hardware is but one of the tools designers may use to address the problems of a given system.

- The main emphasis of instructional systems design is not production. Production styles and technical superiority are viewed as aids to instructional effectiveness and not ends in themselves.

- Designers do not assume that training is the solution to every problem. They use system analysis procedures to determine where training is justified and where it is not.

- ISD is more than a simple method. It is a field requiring a wide range of psychological, sociological, interpersonal, and managerial skills if it is to be skillfully and creatively practiced. This is not to say that classroom teachers and others cannot master and benefit from basic ISD procedures. However, professional instructional systems designers must be prepared to design for different system constraints, populations, content areas (often unfamiliar ones), and forms of media and technology.

- Instructional systems design is rigid, mechanistic, and linear only in its insistence on systematic planning. It does not, for example, allow for inadequate, haphazard planning when the costs of production are so high and the stakes (individual and organizational development) even higher. Charges that ISD is antihumanistic are groundless. Designers with a background in educational psychology, learning theory, human capabilities, system analysis, and diffusion are fixed on the development of human potential and organizational health as primary goals.

- Although ISD clearly has roots in behavioral science, it is not in itself a learning theory—behavioral or otherwise. A designer may draw upon any number of psychological orientations depending on a given task and target population.

RECOMMENDATIONS

Although the preceding discussion has answered the common criticisms of the field, a concluding list of recommendations will be presented for consideration by ISD professionals.

1. The literature of the field sometimes promulgates distinctions between terms like instructional design and instructional development, instructional technology and educational technology—often with only the difference of a word or two. Not only are such fine discriminations confusing, but they tend to semantically chop the field into pieces. Should development really be thought of as in any way *separate* from design? The development of products and programs is inextricably intertwined with the instructional planning that draws upon learning and diffusion theory and system analysis data. Even if the staffing of ISD activities is differentiated, the process is a complex and *unified* one and should be consistently portrayed that way.

2. System analysis, consulting/interpersonal relations, diffusion, and project management skills are often presented as peripheral or even optional to ISD skills. This is unfortunate because the field is made to appear less than it is unless the mutually dependent interaction of these areas is emphasized. Admittedly, each category in

figure 11.5 has its own literature. Some diffusion literature, for example, even comes from sources outside education. Yet concern for diffusion is (or should be) prominent in a designer's mind long before an instructional goal is ever written. This is the only insurance against design projects that are immediately or eventually rejected by the target population—an unfortunate and unpleasant experience for both client and design team. Hence, diffusion—far from a peripheral skill—must be considered an essential part of the practice of design. The same is true for educational theory and research and the other categories in figure 11.5.

3. There is a bewildering array of titles for academic programs in the field: educational technology, instructional technology, instructional systems, instructional design, instructional development, educational media, educational communications, instructional science, instructional psychology, training, etc. Observers must wonder if titles are synonyms or if each is pregnant with idiosyncratic meaning! Although the situation is unlikely to change, there may be a need to insist on some standards regarding the naming of academic programs. Imagine the development of a new masters program specializing only in the production of interactive video. Can such a program rightfully be titled "instructional technology"? It seems reasonable that programs using the most common titles of the field (the first five on the list above)—even the ones that seem to emphasize the use of technology rather than design—have a corresponding obligation to be sure their curriculum reflects the scope of the field and not a single specialization.

CONCLUSION

The purpose of this paper has been to delineate aspects of instructional systems design that must be considered nonnegotiable items. Briggs (1977) defines ISD as:

A systematic approach to the planning and development of a means to meet instructional needs and goals; all components of the system are considered in relation to each other in an orderly but flexible sequence of processes; the resulting delivery system is tried out and improved before widespread use is encouraged (p. xxi).

Whether in schools or universities, business, industrial, health related, or military training, whenever ISD professionals are at work, they are translating this definition into practice. If they are skillful, they are juggling many sources of information and many kinds of skills with the needs and characteristics of their client. It is an important, fascinating, sometimes exhausting job.

REFERENCES

Anderson, J. (1980). *Cognitive psychology and its implications*. San Francisco: W. H. Freeman.

Armbruster, B., & Anderson, T. (1985). Frames: Structures for informative text. In D. H. Jonassen (Ed.), *The technology of text. Vol. 2*. Englewood Cliffs, NJ: Educational Technology.

Ausubel, D. (1968). *Educational psychology: A cognitive view*. New York: Holt, Rinehart & Winston.

Bandura, A. (1986). *Social foundations of thought and action: A social cognitive theory*. Englewood Cliffs, NJ: Prentice-Hall.

Bell, C., & Nadler, L. (Eds.) (1979). *The client-consultant handbook*. Houston: Gulf.

Bernhard, K., & DiPaolo, A. (1982). Profiling and targeting training and development needs. *NSPI Journal, 21*(10), 12-14.

Booher, E. (1982). Eleven myths about writing—and how trainers can debunk them. *Training, 19*(4), 40-43.

Bratton, B. (1981). Training the instructional development specialist to work in unfamiliar content areas. *Journal of Instructional Development, 4*(3), 21-23.

Briggs, L. (Ed.). (1977). *Instructional design: principles and applications.* Englewood Cliffs, NJ: Educational Technology.

Broad, M. L. (1982). Management actions to support transfer of training. *Training and Development Journal, 36*(5), 124-130.

Bruner, J. (1973). *The relevance of education.* New York: Norton.

Carrier, C. (1986). A first meeting of professors of educational technology: A summary of issues. *Journal of Instructional Development, 8*(3), 15-19.

Chan, T. (1984). In search of the artistry in educational technology. *Educational Technology, 24*(4), 7-12.

Clark, R., & Salomon, G. (1986). Media in teaching. In M. Wittrock (Ed.), *Handbook of research on teaching* (3rd ed.). New York: Macmillan.

Coldeway, D., & Rasmussen, R. (1984). Instructional development: A consideration of the interpersonal variables. *Journal of Instructional Development, 7*(1), 23-27.

Cook, T., & Reichardt, C. (Eds.). (1979). *Qualitative and quantitative methods in evaluation and research.* Beverly Hills, CA: Sage.

Craig, R. (Ed.) (1976). *Training and development handbook* (2nd ed.). New York: McGraw-Hill.

Davis, I. (1975). Some aspects of a theory of advice: The management of an instructional-developer, evaluator-client relationship. *Instructional Science, 3*, 351-373.

Dick, W. (1981). Instructional design models: Future trends and issues. *Educational Technology, 21*(7), 29-32.

Dick, W., & Carey, L. (1985). *The systematic design of instruction* (2nd ed.). Glenview, IL: Scott, Foresman.

Fleming, M., & Levie, H. (1978). *Instructional message design: Principles from the behavioral sciences.* Englewood Cliffs, NJ: Educational Technology.

Gagne, E. (1985). *The cognitive psychology of school learning.* Boston: Little, Brown.

Gagne, R. (1985). *The conditions of learning* (4th ed.). New York: Holt, Rinehart & Winston.

Gagne, R., & Beard, J. (1978). Assessment of learning outcomes. In R. Glaser (Ed.), *Advances in instructional psychology.* Hillsdale, NJ: Lawrence Erlbaum.

Gerlach, L., & Ely, D. (1980). *Teaching and media: A systematic approach* (2nd ed.). Englewood Cliffs, NJ: Prentice-Hall.

Gronlund, N. (1981). *Measurement and evaluation in teaching.* New York: Macmillan.

Havelock, R. (1973). *The change agent's guide to innovation in education.* Englewood Cliffs, NJ: Educational Technology.

Head, G., & Buchanan, C. (1981). Cost/benefit analysis of training: A foundation for change. *NSPI Journal, 20*(9), 25-27.

Kaufman, R., & English, F. (1979). *Needs assessment: Concept and application.* Englewood Cliffs, NJ: Educational Technology.

Keller, J. (1983). Motivational design of instruction. In C. Reigeluth (Ed.), *Instructional-design theories and models: An overview of their current status.* Hillsdale, NJ: Lawrence Erlbaum.

Klatzky, R. (1980). *Human memory: Structures and processes* (2nd ed.). San Francisco: W. H. Freeman.

Knirk, F., & Gustafson, K. (1986). *Instructional technology: A systematic approach to education.* New York: Holt, Rinehart & Winston.

Knowles, M. (1984). *Andragogy in action.* San Francisco: Jossey-Bass.

Levie, W., & Dickie, K. (1973). The analysis and application of media. In M. Travers (Ed.), *Second handbook of research on teaching.* Chicago: Rand McNally.

Miller, E. (Ed.). (1985). *The educational media and technology yearbook.* Littleton, CO: Libraries Unlimited.

Morgan, R. (1986). Foreword. *Journal of Instructional Development, 8*(3), 2.

Piaget, J. (1954). *The construction of reality in the child.* New York: Basic Books.

Reiser, R., & Gagne, R. (1983). *Selecting media for instruction.* Englewood Cliffs, NJ: Educational Technology.

Rogers, E. (1983). *Diffusion of innovations* (3rd ed.). New York: Free Press.

Rothkopf, E. (1970). The concept of mathemagenic activities. *Review of Educational Research, 40,* 325-336.

Schein, E. (1986). What you need to know about organizational culture. *Training and Development Journal, 40*(1), 30-33.

Schleger, P. (1984). Accentuate the positive, eliminate the negative. *Training and Development Journal, 38*(4), 97-101.

Schramm, W. (1977). *Big media, little media: Tools and technologies for instruction.* Beverly Hills, CA: Sage.

Shulman, L. (1986). Those who understand: Knowledge growth in teaching. *Educational Researcher, 15*(2), 4-14.

Silberman, C. (1970). *Crisis in the classroom.* New York: Random House.

Thorman, J. (1982). Criterion referenced evaluation and its effect on achievement and attitude. *NSPI Journal, 21*(10), 15-18.

Torkelson, G. (1977). AVCR—One quarter of a century: Evolution of theory and research. *AV-CR, 25*(4), 317-358.

Tubbs, S. (1978). *A systems approach to small group interaction.* Reading, MA: Addison-Wesley.

Tuckman, B. (1979). *Evaluating instructional programs.* Boston: Allyn & Bacon.

Walter, S., & Earle R. (1981-82). Contracting for instructional development: A follow-up. *Journal of Instructional Development, 5*(2), 26-31.

Wildman, T. (1981). Cognitive theory and the design of instruction. *Educational Technology, 21*(7), 14-20.

Wildman, T., & Burton, J. (1981). Integrating learning theory with instructional design. *Journal of Instructional Development, 4*(3), 5-14.

12

Instructional Plans and Situated Learning

The Challenge of Suchman's Theory of Situated Action for Instructional Designers and Instructional Systems

Michael J. Streibel

School of Education, The University of Wisconsin
Madison, Wisconsin

Lucy Suchman is a researcher at Xerox PARC (Palo Alto Research Center) who studies how ordinary folks use Xerox machines that have built-in help and diagnosis programs. She distinguishes between *plans* (such as the hierarchy of subprocedures for how Xerox machines should be used) and *situated actions* (i.e., the actual sense that specific users make out of specific Xeroxing events) and concludes that a theory of situated action is more true to the lived experience of Xerox users than a cognitive account of the user's plans (Suchman, 1987). Her distinction has profound implications for the discipline of cognitive science because cognitive scientists assume that plans are the essence of human actions. This assumption will be described throughout this essay as part of the cognitivist paradigm.

Suchman's distinction also poses a challenge for cognitive science based instructional design, because it leads to the following question; Do human beings, such as teachers and learners, follow plans (no matter how tentative or incomplete those plans might be) when they solve real-world problems or do human beings develop embodied skills that are only prospectively or retrospectively represented by plans? Suchman argues for the latter formulation. The question then becomes; Should instructional plans (e.g., drill-and-practice or expert tutoring instructional strategies) be designed into instructional systems in order to control instructional interactions when users of such systems learn in a situated action manner and not in a plan based manner? Furthermore, should any theory (i.e., instructional or learning theory) be used to guide the actions of teachers or learners?

The remainder of this essay will discuss Suchman's ideas about plans and situated actions as well as the implications of these ideas for the design and use of instructional systems. The essay will end with a brief discussion of John Seely Brown's extension of Suchman's ideas and a general set of recommendations for instructional designers who want to remain sensitive to the epistemology of situated learning.

This paper is reprinted with permission from the Fall 1989 issue of the *Journal of Visual Literacy, 9*(2). An earlier version of the paper was presented at the annual meeting of the Association for Educational Communications and Technology, Dallas, Texas, February 1-5, 1989.

PLANS AND INSTRUCTIONAL SYSTEMS

Cognitive science is an emerging specialty within educational psychology that merges ideas from information processing theory with disciplinary knowledge from computer science and artificial intelligence. Cognitive scientists make a number of assumptions about the world in order to conduct "normal science" in the Kuhnian sense of the term (Kuhn, 1970). For example, cognitive scientists treat mind as "neither substantial nor insubstantial, but as an abstractable structure implementable in any number of possible physical substrates" (Suchman, 1987, p. 8). Furthermore, cognitive scientists treat the human mind as nothing but mental operations that mediate environmental stimuli and transform mental representations into other cognitive structures called plans which, in turn, produce behavioral responses (Suchman, 1987, p. 9). Figure 12.1 provides a brief summary of the cognitivist model of mind.

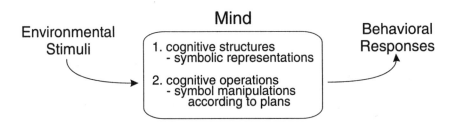

Fig. 12.1. Cognitivist paradigm.

The cognitivist paradigm also permits cognitive scientists to define learning as a change in cognitive structure and to study various lawful ways in which environmental stimuli can be manipulated in order to establish new cognitive structures (i.e., symbolic mental representations) and new cognitive operations (i.e., cognitive information processing). At the heart of the cognitivist paradigm, therefore, is the belief that the mind is a formal symbol manipulator that transforms symbolic representations into plan-based behavioral responses.

Cognition and Change

Several things are worth noting about the cognitivist paradigm. First, the cognitivist paradigm goes beyond the behaviorist paradigm since it claims learning to be *more than* changes in external behavior. Learning is defined as changes in cognitive structures as evidenced by changes in external behavior. R. M. Gagne expresses this cognitivist orientation when he uses the concept of learned capabilities in instructional design (Gagne, 1987; Gagne, Briggs, & Wager, 1988). Second, cognitive structures or plans are treated as the *causes* of behavioral responses. Environmental stimuli still play a role, but more as information and triggering stimuli, than as causes of behavior. The computer is the root metaphor for this point of view because computer programs are the clearest expression of how plans can use input data to control external actions (Pylyshyn, 1984). Finally, the cognitivist paradigm opens the door for conceptualizing teaching and learning in information processing terms (Streibel, 1986).

Instructional design theories, such as Gagne's theory, take the cognitivist paradigm one logical step further by claiming that an instructional plan can generate both appropriate environmental stimuli and instructional interactions, and thereby bring about a change in the cognitive structures and operations of the learner (Gagne, 1987; Gagne, Briggs, & Wager, 1988). Changes in cognitive structures and operations are inferred from the appearance of new but prespecified behavioral responses. C. M. Reigeluth articulates this next logical step when he describes the *prescriptive* use of descriptive instructional theories (Reigeluth, 1983; 1987). Figure 12.2 shows a brief schematic of these ideas.

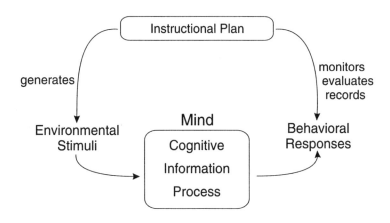

Fig. 12.2. Instructional system—prescriptive use of descriptive theories.

The cognitivist paradigm in instructional design also has a unified conception of the teacher and the learner. When instructional strategies are embodied in an instructional system, instruction is viewed as an information process that is coupled with the learner's cognitive processes via environmental stimuli. The essential aspect of the teacher, therefore, resides in the knowledge structures and instructional plans that they (i.e., instructional system) contain. The essential aspect of the learner resides in the new cognitive knowledge structures and operations that he, she, or it (i.e., machine learning system) constructs. Instructional plans in the teacher and cognitive operations in the learner here are both conceptualized in information-processing terms. Figure 12.3 spells out this reconceptualization.

The logical extension of the cognitivist paradigm described above does not imply the instructional plan in the instructional system *causes* the changes in the learner's behavior. The learner is not a *tabula rasa* as in the behaviorist paradigm (Mackenzie, 1977). Rather, the *interaction* of the learner's cognitive operations within the entire process of the instructional system leads the learner to *construct* new cognitive structures and operations. The cognitivist paradigm remains fundamentally constructivist and individualistic as J. Piaget has shown in several of his writings (Piaget, 1968).

Finally, the cognitivist paradigm permits one to posit that behavioral responses and cognitive structures and operations can be prespecified, because both the teacher, the learner, and their interaction are theoretically described in identical information processing terms. Suchman's discussion about plans and situated actions will question the whole cognitivist paradigm on this very point: Can the cognitivist paradigm provide an adequate conceptualization of human teaching and learning when these activities are fundamentally context-bound, situational activities and not context-free, plan-based activities? What is the problematic component of the cognitivist paradigm?

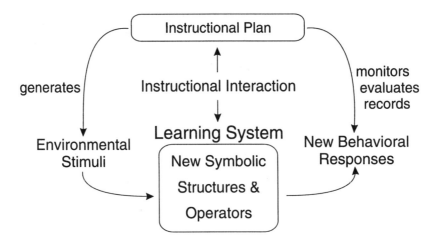

Fig. 12.3. Instructional system, in information-processing terms.

THE PROBLEMATIC ASPECT OF PLANS
AND INSTRUCTIONAL PRACTICE

The problematic aspect of the cognitivist scheme of things resides in the relationship between plans and situated actions *when human beings are involved.* The pivotal point of this problematic aspect centers on the notion of interaction. According to Suchman, the traditional notion of interaction revolves around the concept of "communication between persons" (Suchman, 1987, p. 6). However, in the cognitivist paradigm, interaction is restricted to the physical science concept of "reciprocal action or influence." Human learners who want to work within an instructional system, therefore, have to assume the ontology of a machine for themselves in order to "learn" from the machine (Streibel, 1986). That is, a learner has to act as an information processor in order to "interact" with an instructional system. This result is a direct consequence of the cognitivist view of mind which separates meaning, imagination, and reason from a bodily basis (Johnson, 1987). This result, however, also places the human learner in a bind: Plans are generic and apply to typical situations, whereas purposeful actions such as learning are unique and interpreted in the context of specific interactions. Figure 12.4 shows the generic dimensions *of* instructional systems.

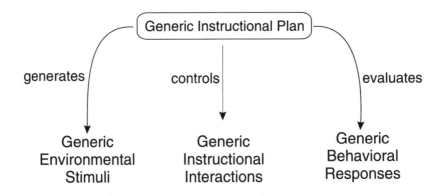

Fig. 12.4. Instructional system—generic dimensions.

Put simply, the assumptions of the cognitivist paradigm conflict with the "life world" of the human learner, because each learner brings a unique biography and history to each new learning experience and because each new learning interaction entails a unique, context-bound, sense-making process. Whereas, a cognitive model of human learning is a rational reconstruction of minimally situated actions, the "life-world" of human learning is phenomenologically and contextually bound. Whereas, a cognitive model of the processes of human learning is mechanical, the actual processes of human learning are experiential. And finally, whereas plans determine the meaning of actions in the cognitive model of human learning, the *in situ* interpretations of lived experiences by the participants determine the meanings of actions in the "life-world" of situated actions. A generic instructional plan in an instructional system can control a cognitive model of human learning but it cannot control the "life-world" of situated learning. Figure 12.5 summarizes the dimensions of the dilemma.

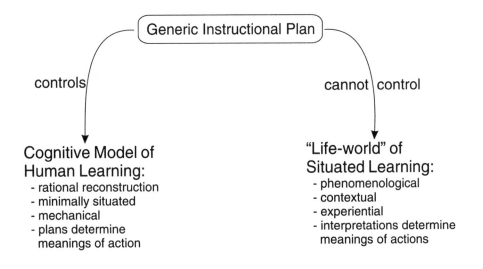

Fig. 12.5. Instructional system—cognitive model/"life-world" dilemma.

The problematic aspect of the cognitivist paradigm described above can be formulated as a question: Can human beings reason and learn in a situation where they have to deny the contextual nature of their thinking and knowing? Lucy Suchman provides a provocative answer: All real-world thinking and knowing (and learning) entails a form of context-bound and embodied, situational action and not plan-based interaction. Let's look at her arguments more closely.

"All activity, even the most analytic," claims Suchman, "is fundamentally concrete and embodied" (Suchman, 1987, p. viii). Furthermore, all "purposeful actions are inevitably *situated actions* ... [and] primarily *ad hoc*." By "situated actions," Suchman means simply "actions taken in the context of particular, concrete circumstances." This being the case, "plans as such neither determine the actual course of situated actions nor adequately reconstruct it" (Suchman, 1987, p. 3).

Everyday Instructional Design

I first encountered the problematic relationship between plans and situated actions when, after years of trying to follow Gagne's theory of instructional design, I repeatedly found myself, as an instructional designer, making *ad hoc* decisions throughout the design and development process. At first, I attributed this discrepancy to my own inexperience as an instructional designer. Later, when I became more experienced, I attributed it to the incompleteness of instructional design theories. Theories were, after all, only robust and mature at the end of a long developmental process, and instructional design theories had a very short history. Lately, however, I have begun to believe that the discrepancy between instructional design theories and instructional design practice will *never* be resolved because instructional design practice will always be a form of situated activity (i.e., depend on the specific, concrete, and unique circumstances of the project I am working on). Furthermore, I now believe instructional design theories will never specify my design practice at other than the most general level.

My experience as an instructional designer raises a deeper question. Does the problematic relationship, which exists between instructional design theory and practice, also hold for instructional theories and practice? That is, is there a problematic relationship between an instructional strategy or plan embedded in an instructional system and the resulting instructional practice? Furthermore, is there a problematic relationship between learning theories and learning practice? I have no doubt that instructional theories and learning theories are legitimate abstractions from, and rational reconstructions of, instructional and learning actions. However, I am beginning to question whether instructional theories or learning theories should be used to develop plans to prescribe instructional and learning actions. This dilemma is particularly poignant because I have been professionally trained to believe that:

- an instructional strategy can and should be designed into an instructional system,

- an instructional strategy or plan in an instructional system is the best (and some would say only) hope for guaranteeing a change in the cognitive structures and operations of the learner (Heinich, 1988).

Lucy Suchman's ideas help clarify the problematic aspect of the cognitivist paradigm as well as help reframe the problem.

PLANS AND SITUATED ACTIONS

Suchman first analyzes how plans are conceptualized in the cognitivist paradigm and then describes an alternative paradigm for how plans actually operate in human beings. In the cognitivist paradigm, plans are believed to be "prerequisite to and prescribe action, at every level of detail," because the "organization and significance of human action [resides] in [the] underlying plans" (Suchman, 1987, p. 27). Furthermore, in the cognitivist paradigm, mutual intelligibility between human beings reduces to

a matter of the reciprocal recognizability of our plans, enabled by common conventions for the expression of intent, and shared knowledge about typical situations and appropriate actions (Suchman, 1987, p. 27).

Shared knowledge structures, typical situations, and appropriate actions are, therefore, external and prior to the same things in other people. Furthermore, two people can only understand each other when they share the same symbolic representations about typical situations and appropriate actions. Intent here is tied to the plan of action for typical, and therefore context-free, situations. Figure 12.6 sketches out these ideas.

Cognitive Learning Paradigm

Plans:

1. prerequisite to action
or
prescription of action

2. at the heart of:
- the organization of action
- the significance of action

3. strong link to intention

Situated Learning Paradigm

Plans:

1. imaginative projection of action
or
rational reconstruction of action

2. at the heart of:
- reasoning about action
- communication about action

3. weak link to intention

Fig. 12.6. Cognitive and situated learning paradigms.

The problematic aspect of the cognitivist point-of-view arises, because the lived experience of two persons are not made up of identical representations. Suchman's argument here is ultimately based on an appeal to experience, because human beings have no privileged way of knowing whether an identity relationship exists between the cognitive representations of different people. Our phenomenological experience, on the other hand, tells us that our knowledge entails specific, contextual experience, and our actions proceed on the basis of context sensitive, embodied skills and not rationally constructed plans.

Suchman clarifies the problematic between plans and situated actions by claiming that:

> While the course of action can always be projected or reconstructed in terms of prior intentions or typical situations, the prescriptive significance of intentions for situated actions is inherently vague ... because we can state our intentions without having to describe the actual course that our actions will take (Suchman, 1987, pp. 27, 38).

Plans, in other words, say more about our reasoning about action than about the actual course of events. Suchman, therefore, claims that:

> The coherence of situated actions is tied in essential ways not to individual predispositions or conventional rules but to local interactions contingent on the actor's particular circumstances (Suchman, 1987, pp. 27-28).

Let us use our example of a learner interacting with an instructional system. Extrapolating from Suchman's arguments, the coherence of the learner's experience in this situation is not tied in essential ways to the instructional designer's intent (no matter how detailed or explicit these intentions are spelled-out as instructional objectives) nor to the instructional plan built into the instructional system. Rather, the coherence of the learner's instructional experience is tied to the sense that such a learner constructs out of the actual situation (of which the instructional system is just a part). Hence, the sense that *this* learner at *this* point in time and in *this* situation will make out of the learning situation cannot be predicted or even assumed to be understood by an instructional designer who is not part of the actual situation. The best an instructional designer can do is create an instructional environment where the learner's processes of situational sense-making are enhanced. What does this mean for an instructional designer? Suchman again provides a tentative answer.

Face-to-Face Interaction

Suchman considers face-to-face human interaction to be the "paradigm case of a system for communication ... because it is organized for maximum context sensitivity" (Suchman, 1987, p. 18). Furthermore, face-to-face communication "brings that context-sensitivity to bear on problems of skill acquisition ... for just [those] recipients on just [those] occasion[s]" (Suchman, 1987, p. 18). Face-to-face human communication, therefore, becomes the means through which actions in a unique situation for a unique learner are connected to larger personal and interpersonal interactions and, thereby, made mutually intelligible. In her own research on how novices learn to use Xerox machines, Suchman has users team up and engage in a conversation with each other about the concrete situation. Meanings are constructed and negotiated in an ongoing dialogue, and the plans that the Xerox machine happens to contain are only treated as resources. Furthermore, sense making is intimately tied to the resolution of emergent dilemmas by each group of users. Suchman therefore concludes that the "conversation" between the users gave coherence to their situation rather than the plans built into the Xerox machines. John Seely Brown has taken Suchman's ideas and generalized them to encompass everyday cognition (Brown, 1988). See figure 12.7 for a brief outline of these ideas.

Aspects of Everyday Cognition
John Seely Brown

1. act on situations
2. make sense out of concrete situations
3. resolve emergent dilemmas
4. negotiate the meaning of terms
5. use plans as resources
6. socially-construct physical and social reality

"conversation" with a situation

Fig. 12.7. Aspects of everyday cognition.

What roles *should* plans play in the context of situated actions? For our purposes, what role should instructional plans play in the actual operation of instructional systems? Based on our discussion so far, we can begin to draw some tentative conclusions. First, we should stop treating plans as mechanisms that bring about subsequent actions:

- in the case of human beings, plans should not be treated as "psychological mechanisms" that control and give meaning to subsequent behavior. Rather, plans should be treated as "artifact[s] of our *reasoning about* actions" (Suchman, 1987, p. 39).

- in the case of instructional systems, instructional plans should not be used to control instructional interactions. Rather, plans should be used for:

  a. communicating about situated actions with other human beings,

  b. reflecting on and reconceptualizing situational actions.

In short, *instructional plans should be used* by both instructional designers and instructional users *as resources for future situated actions.*

What do these tentative conclusions imply? How can one design instructional systems where instructional plans operate as resources for the learners and not as controlling mechanisms? Suchman's situated-action paradigm again helps clarify the relationship between plans and situated learning.

PLANS AND SITUATED LEARNING

What has Suchman concluded so far? First, she has claimed that "every course of action depends in essential ways upon its material and social circumstances" (Suchman, 1987, p. 50). Second, she has claimed that face-to-face communication and collaborative action are essential for sense-making in any situation. Finally, she has claimed that our knowledge of the physical and social worlds is inter-subjectively constructed by us. On the most general level, therefore, we can no longer view instructional systems as mechanisms that transmit knowledge or train skills in an information-processing sense of the term. Plans can play a communicative role but not a constitutive role in instructional interactions. To understand this more deeply, we have to examine Suchman's main propositions about plans.

Plans as Representations

First, Suchman admits that plans are representations of situated actions. However, these representations always come "before or after the fact, in the form of imagined projections or recollected reconstructions" rather than as controlling procedures during situated actions (Suchman, 1987, p. 51). Hence, plans orient us in situated actions rather than prescribe the sequence of actions. Instructional strategies should, therefore, only be used to orient future teachers or learners for situated learning and not prescribe how to teach or how to learn. The actual embodied skills of teaching or learning still have to be worked out by the teacher or learner. In the case of instructional designers, instructional plans should only be used as general *resources* for the design and development of instructional systems. In the case of the operation of instructional systems, the instructional strategy should not control the actual instructional interaction. Finally, in the case of the human learner, the instructional strategy should be used to orient the human learner towards the material rather than controlling and evaluating each behavior. The instructional system in this scenario would act more like a coach than an instructor or tutor, and the human learner's role would be more that of a self-teacher than of a student. Figure 12.8, page 154, summarizes this point.

Is the foregoing suggestion about instructional systems a romantic ideal? Is it unrealistic? No, because the actual reality of designing an instructional system will always turn out to be a form of situational action. "When it really comes down to the details," writes Suchman, "you effectively abandon the plan and fall back on whatever embodied skills are available to you" (Suchman, 1987, p. 52). The same can be said for instruction and learning. When an instructor or a learner gets down to the details of teaching or learning, the respective theories of instruction or learning are abandoned and the instructor or learner falls back onto his or her embodied skills in the situation. An instructional designer would, therefore, do well to provide the learner, using an instructional system, with the appropriate resources to develop the learner's embodied self-teaching skills.

Situation-Learning-Based Instructional Systems

1. use plans as resources to orient the learner towards action
2. include face-to-face dialogue to develop embodied skills
3. help learners problematize a situation & resolve emergent dilemmas
4. help learners develop situated discourse-practices
5. use collaborative learning structures
6. use language to construct physical and social reality

learners as "self-teachers" and "ethnographers"

Fig. 12.8. Situation-learning-based instructional systems.

The suggestion that instructional systems should help learners develop embodied learning strategy skills sounds remarkably like the rhetoric about learning strategies design (O'Neil, 1978; O'Neil & Spielberger, 1979). However, one cannot design plans to instruct learning-strategy skills either. Suchman clarifies this point by saying:

> It is frequently by only on acting in a present situation that its possibilities become clear.... In many cases, it is only *after* [my emphasis] we encounter some state of affairs that we find to be desirable [e.g., a 'teachable moment' in a classroom for a teacher] that we identify that state as the goal towards which our previous actions, in retrospect, were directed 'all along' or 'after all' (Suchman, 1987, p. 52).

An instructional designer cannot, therefore, predict which aspect of the instructional plan or which feature of the instructional system will be interpreted by the learner as a learning event, and so cannot design a plan for developing learning strategies. An instructional designer can, however, create a learning environment where learning strategies are used as resources by the learner. In a computer-based reactive learning environment called MENDEL, which I and my colleagues are developing at the University of Wisconsin, a computer program helps students compare their intermediate hypotheses about genetics experiments against the data that the computer generates (Streibel, et al., 1987). The program does not tutor students about problem-solving procedures or solve the problems for them. Rather, it offers students advice on how to check their ideas. The program does this, in spite of the fact that it contains an expert systems component which can solve the problem the student faces. The distinction between a plan as an instructional algorithm and a plan as an instructional resource is a very subtle one, but it definitely runs counter to Richard Clark's suggestion that the instructional design component of instructional systems is the most efficacious component as far as learning is concerned (Clark & Salomon, 1986).

Plans as Social Constructs

Suchman also argues that situated actions are "essentially transparent to use ... when action is proceeding smoothly" (Suchman, 1987, p. 53). Furthermore, plans and representations are only constructed by people when there is a breakdown in situated action. Hence:

> When situated action becomes in some way problematized, rules and procedures are explicated for purposes of deliberation [and communication] and the action, which is otherwise neither rule-bound nor procedural, is then made accountable to them (Suchman, 1987, p. 54).

Note that representations here do not stand in an essential relationship to actions. Rather, plans and representations are social and rational reconstructions of problematized situated actions.

Teachers in the critical pedagogy and experiential learning traditions have long known how to problematize learning situations and use reflection to turn experience into further action (Shor, 1980; Kolb, 1984; Boud, et al., 1985; Livingston, et al., 1987). In each of these traditions, teachers use face-to-face dialogue in order to problematize some part of the world and then use reflection as a way to get beyond the immediate situation. Furthermore, in each of these cases, teachers develop a dilemma language with the learners in order to foster mindful action (Berlak & Berlak, 1981). The key elements in the critical pedagogy and experiential learning traditions that develop embodied skills are, therefore, context bound discourse practices, negotiation of the very language used to characterize and resolve dilemmas, and reflective action. Both discourse practices and reflective actions go beyond any rules and procedures.

Instructional designers face a serious challenge from the critical pedagogy tradition because instructional designers are neither part of the actual instructional interaction that they create, nor are they able to articulate a plan to help students problematize, analyze, and reconceptualize the "life-world" of the learning situation. At best, instructional designers can only create simplified reactive learning environments where students work collaboratively to resolve artificial dilemmas.

Objectivity and Interpersonal Construction

Suchman's third proposition about plans deal with how the objectivity of situated actions is interpersonally constructed rather than given. Suchman writes:

> Objectivity is a product of systematic practices, or members' methods for rendering our unique experience and relative circumstances mutually intelligible. The source of mutual intelligibility is not a received conceptual scheme or a set of coercive rules or norms, but those common practices that produce the typifications of which schemes and rules are made (Suchman, 1987, p. 57).

An instructional system that operates according to a plan made prior to face-to-face interaction, therefore, undermines the very processes by which the objectivity of the physical and social worlds is apprehended by new learners. In the place of interpersonal construction of reality, such instructional systems offer a *coercive* rather than a *constructive* interaction. What can an instructional designer do about this? How can an instructional system avoid coercive interactions?

George Herbert Mead argued, as early as 1934, that the physical and social worlds are "constructed by us through language" (Suchman, 1987, p. 57). It is, therefore, through the medium of language, that a learner will construct and construe the objectivity of some part of the physical and social worlds. However, language is not a set of symbols communicated through a medium. Language itself is constructed out of social discourse practices. It is, therefore, *not* enough for an instructional designer to simply communicate messages about the physical and social worlds to the learner via the instructional system. Such a point of view would still legitimize coercive communication. What can an instructional designer do?

The best way to help learners make sense out of their learning situations is to help them approach the learning situation as ethnographers. A learning situation is, after all, a kind of social practice, and learners are, in effect, in the position of field workers who want to get into the disciplinary subculture's lore of knowledge. Ethnomethodologies are useful for learners because they deal with how members of a group make sense and how the "mutual intelligibility and objectivity of the social world is achieved" (Suchman, 1987, p. 58). An instructional designer who wants to address the constraints of situational learning will, therefore, have to find ways of creating instructional systems that give learners a chance to act as ethnographers.

Plans and Language

Suchman's final proposition about plans and situated actions deals with how "language is a form of situated action" because

> the significance of an expression always exceeds the meaning of what actually gets said ... the interpretation of an expression turns not only on its conventional or definitional meanings, not on that plus some body of proposition, but on the unspoken situation of its use (Suchman, 1987, pp. 59-60).

Hence, plans which try "to guarantee a particular interpretation" by providing "exhaustive action descriptions" are bound to fail because

> there [are] no fixed set of assumptions that underlie a given statement ... [and because] an instruction's significance with respect to action does not inhere in the instruction, but must be found by the instruction-follower with reference to the situation of its use (Suchman, 1987, p. 61).

Suchman continues by claiming that "interpreting the significance of action is an essentially collaborative achievement" (Suchman, 1987, p. 69). Mutual intelligibility, in fact, requires *constant* collaborative conversation. The reasons for this are simple. Our everyday interactions contain inevitable uncertainties and our language entails inevitable miscommunications. The only way to catch these uncertainties and repair these miscommunications is to conduct constant and *in situ* conversations. Interactive instructional systems, even those that use artificial intelligence technologies to model the communications process, are of no help here because

> there is a profound and persisting asymmetry in [the] interaction between people and machines, due to a disparity in their relative access to the moment-by-moment contingencies that constitute the conditions of situated interactions (Suchman, 1987, p. 185).

Human teaching and learning, therefore, require the presence of face-to-face linguistic engagement. Suchman's conclusion is all the more significant because she applies it to the acquisition of a simple procedural skill (i.e., how to use a Xerox machine).

JOHN SEELY BROWN'S EPISTEMOLOGY OF SITUATED LEARNING

So far, I have described Lucy Suchman's theory of plans and situated actions, and applied her ideas to the design and use of instructional systems. I would now like to end with a brief discussion of the epistemology of situated learning, in order to give some direction for further work in this area. My task is made easier by John Seely Brown because he has generalized Lucy Suchman's ideas and extended Jean Lave's earlier work on everyday learning and cognition (Brown, 1988; Brown, Collins, & Duguid, 1989; Rogoff & Lave, 1984; Lave, 1988).

John Seely Brown is a colleague of Lucy Suchman at Xerox PARC and one of the founders of the field of Intelligent Tutoring Systems. Intelligent Tutoring Systems are the most sophisticated forms of instructional systems and incorporate ideas from cognitive science, computer science, and artificial intelligence.

John Seely Brown also studied how human beings actually learn in the presence of intelligent tutoring systems and concluded that Suchman's theory of situated action was a more adequate account of the phenomena than a cognitive theory of plans. He, therefore, began to formulate an epistemology of situational learning that is sensitive to the nature of situational action.

Brown first spells out how ordinary folks think about real-world problems. Ordinary folks, says Brown (1988):

- act on concrete situations,

- resolve emerging dilemmas,

- negotiate the meanings of terms used to describe new situations,

- and ultimately use socially-constructed plans as resources for each new situation.

Figure 12.9 summarizes some of these conclusions.

Aspects of Cognition
John Seely Brown

Everyday Cognition:
1. act on situations
2. contextual sense-making
3. resolve emergent dilemmas
4. negotiate meanings
5. use plans as resources
6. socially-construct physical
   and social reality

Expert Cognition:
1. see through symbols
2. contextual sense-making
3. resolve ill-defined dilemmas
4. negotiate meanings
5. use plans as resources
6. socially-construct physical
   and social reality

Fig. 12.9. Aspects of cognition.

Experts and Novices

Brown then compares everyday cognition with expert cognition. Experts, according to Brown, are persons who have acquired a disciplinary subculture of knowledge and discourse-practice. The most interesting aspect of Brown's comparison is that everyday and expert cognition have very much in common. According to the cognitivist paradigm, however, expert plans and procedures are the very thing that distinguish experts from ordinary people. According to Brown, on the other hand, the only difference between expert and ordinary people is that experts have a set of models *through which* they act on situations; whereas, just plain folks act on situations with partial, and often incorrect, models. Both experts and everyday folks mix knowledge with use and belief in real-world situations and both socially-construct the objectivity of knowledge. Furthermore, everyday folks become experts through a socialization process of acquiring effective discourse practices in situated actions, just as experts do. Everyday folks do not become experts by acquiring expert knowledge or following expert rules (Dreyfus & Dreyfus, 1986).

Brown then spells out the epistemological shifts that take place when we move from a cognitivist paradigm to a situated learning paradigm. Figure 12.10 summarizes these shifts. Highlighted are those aspects of the paradigm shift that have a direct bearing on the design of instructional systems.

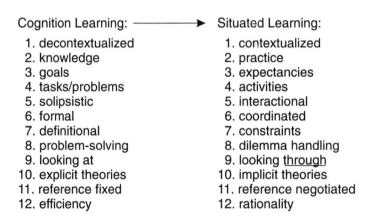

Epistemological Paradigm Shift
John Seely Brown

Cognition Learning: ⟶	Situated Learning:
1. decontextualized	1. contextualized
2. knowledge	2. practice
3. goals	3. expectancies
4. tasks/problems	4. activities
5. solipsistic	5. interactional
6. formal	6. coordinated
7. definitional	7. constraints
8. problem-solving	8. dilemma handling
9. looking at	9. looking <u>through</u>
10. explicit theories	10. implicit theories
11. reference fixed	11. reference negotiated
12. efficiency	12. rationality

Fig. 12.10. Epistemological paradigm shift.

The most obvious epistemological shift is from knowledge to practice. Learning is no longer a matter of ingesting externally-defined, decontextualized objects, but a matter of developing context-bound discourse-practices. This means the objectives of an instructional system can no longer be seen as a pre-defined end point for learning, nor instructional tasks as a *sine qua non* of instructional interaction. Rather, objectives can only be seen as expectations that constrain the direction the learner is going, and instructional tasks can only be seen as one of many activities the learner might choose to pursue.

The second epistemological shift is from problem-solving to dilemma-handling. This means that learning can no longer be viewed as a form of cognitive problem solving, but rather as a form of posing problems; a form of formulating hypotheses and terms to handle the problem; a form of negotiating criteria to evaluate the problem; and finally, a form of interpersonally resolving the problem. In some ways, the very word "problem" is inadequate in the situated learning paradigm because it reduces real-world dilemmas to cognitive puzzles that have explicit solutions built into them. Hence, the word "dilemma-handling" is a more adequate term.

The final shift that I want to mention involves the move from efficiency to rationality. Cognitive-science-based instructional systems, as I have shown in an earlier paper, are ultimately shaped by the economic criteria of systems efficiency rather than the qualitative criteria of excellence and substantive understanding (Streibel, 1986). Cognitive-science-based instructional systems, therefore, serve the "human interests" of someone other than the learner (Apple, 1975; Wolcott, 1977; Nunan, 1983; Bullough, Goldstein, & Holt, 1984). In the situated learning paradigm, however, the learner is at the center of negotiating the meaning of their [sic] actions, and therefore, at the center of negotiating what is rational to them [sic]. An instructional system that is sensitive to the situated learning paradigm, has to respect and encourage the very social-linguistic processes by which rationality is constructed. This is a tall order for instructional systems, even those as advanced as intelligent tutoring systems, because such systems have a very limited access to the "moment-by-moment contingencies that constitute the conditions of situated actions" (Suchman, 1987, p. 185). It is, however, a challenge that we, as instructional designers, will have to meet if we are to respect the way human beings actually learn.

REFERENCES

Apple, M. W. (1975). The adequacy of systems management procedures in education. In R. H. Smith (Ed.), *Regaining educational leadership*. New York: John Wiley.

Berlak, H., & Berlak, A. (1981). *Dilemmas of schooling: Teaching and social change*. New York: Methuen.

Boud, D., Keogh, R., & Walker, D. (Eds.). (1985). *Reflection: Turning experience into learning*. New York: Nichols.

Brown, J. S. (1988). Steps toward a new epistemology of situated learning. *Proceedings of the ITS-88. International Conference on Intelligent Tutoring Systems*. University of Montreal. Montreal, Canada. June 1-3.

Brown, J. S., Collins, A., & Duguid, P. (1989). Situated cognition and the culture of learning. *Educational Researcher, 18*(1), 32-42.

Bullough, R. V., Goldstein, S. L., & Holt, L. (1984). *Human interests in the curriculum: Teaching and learning in a technological society*. New York: Teachers College Press.

Clark, R. E., & Salomon, G. (1986). Media in teaching. In M. C. Wittrock (Ed.), *Handbook of research on teaching*. (3rd edition). New York: Macmillan.

Dreyfus, H. L., & Dreyfus, S. E. (1986). *Mind over machine: The power of human intuition and expertise in the era of the computer*. New York: Free Press.

Gagne, R. M. (Ed.). (1987). *Instructional technology: Foundations*. Hillsdale, NJ: Lawrence Erlbaum.

Gagne, R. M., Briggs, L. J., & Wager, W. W. (1988). *Principles of instructional design*. (3rd edition). New York: Holt, Rinehart & Winston.

Heinich, R. (1988). The use of computers in education: A response to Streibel. *Educational Communication and Technology Journal, 36*(3), 147-152.

Johnson, M. (1987). *The body in the mind: The bodily basis of meaning, imagination, and reason.* Chicago: University of Chicago Press.

Kolb, D. A. (1984). *Experiential learning: Experience as the source of learning and development.* Englewood Cliffs, NJ: Prentice-Hall.

Kuhn, T. S. (1970). *The structure of scientific revolutions.* (2nd edition). Chicago: University of Chicago Press.

Lave, J. (1988). *Cognition in practice.* Boston: Cambridge University Press.

Livingston, D. W., & Contributors. (Eds.). (1987). *Critical pedagogy & cultural power.* South Hadley, MA: Bergin & Garvey.

Mackenzie, B. D. (1977). *Behaviorism and the limits of scientific method.* London: Routledge Kegan Paul.

Nunan, T. (1983). *Countering educational design.* New York: Nichols.

O'Neil, H. F. (Ed.). (1978). *Learning strategies.* New York: Academic Press.

O'Neil, H. F., & Spielberger, C. D. (Eds.). (1979). *Cognitive and affective learning strategies.* New York: Academic Press.

Piaget, J. (1968). *Structuralism.* New York: Harper & Row.

Pylyshyn, Z. W. (1984). *Computing and cognition: Toward a foundation for cognitive science.* Cambridge, MA: MIT Press.

Reigeluth, C. M. (Ed.). (1983). *Instructional-design theories and models.* Hillsdale, NJ: Lawrence Erlbaum.

———. (Ed.). (1987). *Instructional theories in action.* Hillsdale, NJ: Lawrence Erlbaum.

Rogoff, B., & Lave, J. (Eds.). (1984). *Everyday cognition: Its development in social context.* Cambridge, MA: Harvard University Press.

Shor, I. (1980). *Critical teaching and everyday life.* Boston: South End Press.

Streibel, M. J. (1986). A critical analysis of the use of computers in education. *Educational Communications and Technology Journal, 34*(3), 137-161.

Streibel, M. J., Stewart, J. H., Koedinger, K., Collins, A., & Jungck, J. (1987). MENDEL: An intelligent computer tutoring system for genetics problem solving, conjecturing, and understanding. *Machine-Mediated Learning, 2*(1&2), 129-159.

Suchman, L. A. (1987). *Plans and situated actions: The problem of human/machine communication.* New York: Cambridge University Press.

Wolcott, H. F. (1977). *Teachers versus technocrats.* Eugene: University of Oregon.

13

A Comparative Analysis of Models of Instructional Design

Dee H. Andrews

Psychologist, Naval Training Equipment Center
Orlando, Florida

and

Ludwika A. Goodson

Instructional Designer, L. R. O'Neall and Associates, Ltd.
Tallahassee, Florida

INTRODUCTION

According to Friesen (1973, p. 1), instructional materials can be designed and created in two ways. The first way requires a master teacher, working alone to create an inspired work of art. The second requires the application of a system of logic in order to accomplish specified learning objectives. Although the "tried and true" master teacher method has a long history, it often is unaccompanied by empirical verification of effectiveness. By contrast, the scientific method requires the acquisition of learning data to provide feedback for the revision process. That is, a systemic or systematic approach is characterized by an input-output-feedback-revision cycle similar to the cybernetic model shown in figure 13.1, page 162.

The purpose of this chapter is to list and describe a representative sample of the instructional design models that have evolved from this basic systematic approach.

Instructional design models come from industry, education, the military branches, and a variety of other sources. They are often viewed, therefore, as valid only for vocational education. To make an effective choice the educator may want to know where the model comes from; why it was developed; how it relates to the educator's specific goals and setting; and what kind of documentation, application, and/or validation the model has undergone.

Reprinted from the *Journal of Instructional Development* by permission of the Association for Educational Communications and Technology. Copyright 1980 by AECT.

Author's Note. The authors acknowledge the critical review of an earlier draft of this paper provided by Leslie J. Briggs, Walter Dick, Ronald C. Laugen, and Robert J. Stakenas, and the editorial review provided by Melissa Wheeler, all faculty members of Florida State University. In addition, they appreciate the inspiration and thoughts on model construction provided by the late Robert J. Kibler of Florida State University and by Robert C. Roberts, Florida Developmental Services Program, Department of Health and Rehabilitative Services. This paper was presented at the 1979 AERA Convention, San Francisco, CA.

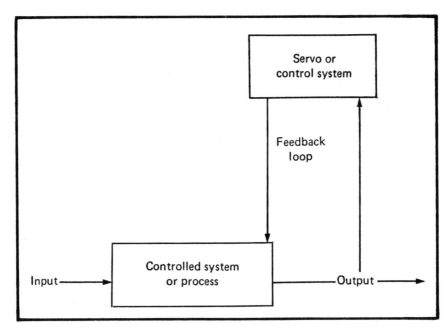

Fig. 13.1. Basic cybernetic model (Pratt, 1978, p. 5).

Past experience has shown that models of instructional design are important in education and that the systematic approach is both logical and useful. However, educators are often confused about which model to use because of the bewildering array reported and because of the omission of some basic component from the literature that describes the model or reports on how the model has been used. Another reason for the less than satisfactory acceptance of the systematic approach is the apparent absence of validation for many models. (In this paper, validation refers to confirmation of the degree of fit among objectives, form of instruction, and context of learning.) Other reasons seem to be the weak or nonexistent theory base for many models and the visible cost of design—a cost which may seem high because many educators fail to balance the cost of applying the model against the quality or utility of its outcome. Finally, there is the problem of how to interpret the concept *systematic*. For some, the components of the model are *systemic*, each affecting the others so that a change in one requires a change in other components. But for others, the components of the model are only *procedural*, a plan of separate steps, each proceeding in a sequence that is more linear than systemic.

To provide a more comprehensive idea of what constitutes a model of instructional design, this study will accomplish the following objectives:

1. Examine several possible definitions of models of instructional design.

2. Present the purposes for having and using models of instructional design.

3. Propose two categorical schemata for 40 existing models according to origin, theoretical underpinnings, purpose and use, and degree of documentation.

4. Offer an explanation for the existence of the large number of models of instructional design.

5. Suggest guidelines for use by instructional designers and educators to facilitate their choice of an appropriate model.

DEFINITIONS OF MODELS OF SYSTEMATIC INSTRUCTIONAL DESIGN

A model is usually considered to be an abstraction and simplification of a defined referent system, presumably having some noticeable fidelity to the referent system (Hayman, 1974, p. 4; Logan, 1976, p. 3). This fidelity is expected whether the model is intended to describe, prescribe, predict, or explain elements of the referent system, and whether the model is based on a set of implemented procedures or theoretical constructs. One of the problems in the literature on models of instructional design is associated with the basic definition of any model. That is, the fidelity of the model to the actual processes it represents will diminish as the specificity of the model diminishes.

Silvern defines a model (cited in AECT, 1977) as a "graphic analog representing a real-life situation either as it is or as it should be" (p. 168). The person who defines what "should be" in an instructional design model may be the model's developer. Some models, however, expect the client to determine the needs to be met by the use of the model. The educator who ultimately uses an instructional design model should know how and why the developer arrived at the model so the designer can determine the suitability of the model for the desired goals. Although a developer may initially intend only to describe what is being used on an individual project, the procedures described may become a prescriptive model if they are selected for use in another project or setting.

Models of instructional design have descriptive, prescriptive, predictive, and/or explanatory elements in varying degrees. That is, some models *describe* the components or activities of instructional design, but they are used as if they *prescribe* the necessary activities, and sometimes are presented as prescriptions. Implicit in the presentation of many models of instructional design (and explicit in some) is the prediction of effective instruction, that is, that intended learning will occur when the activities outlined in the model are followed. Finally, some models have such a strong basis in learning theory that they tend to *explain* instructional design in terms of the events of learning.

The systematic approach in the design of instruction is a problem-solving process known as instructional development, which requires the identification of instructional problems or needs and corresponding solutions by means of effective and efficient teaching-learning activities based on relevant objectives (Waldron, 1973, p. 2). But if the educator is not also informed of the processes and use of the appropriate theory base interpreting the model, the skills required to apply the systematic (systemic) approach may remain undeveloped, a problem expressed well by Hayman (1974).

It should be clear, however, that a model is not the same as a theory. Rather, a model might incorporate a number of theories. For instance, Joyce and Weil (1972) list a number of different models of teaching (including inductive teaching, jurisprudential teaching, nondirective teaching, operant conditioning, and others). These models incorporate theories about motivation, reinforcement, personality, and creativity.

While models may help to form an initial investigation into factors of instructional design, theories may allow for a better understanding and control of the learning environment. As we increase our understanding of the processes required for effective instructional design and development, we should explicitly state the constructs and propositions that evolve and, therefore, change the assumptions upon which a model rests.

LaGow (1977) contends that a theory, like a model of instructional design, should express the interrelationships (sequence and criteria) among the components.

An instructional design theory should be able to explain the sequence used in the design of instruction and provide a basis for criteria to judge the usefulness of tasks that are included in this activity. (p. 3)

The requirement for the model follows from the requirement for the theory: to prescribe the sequence of events and functions for the tasks that lead to effective instruction.

Some models of instructional design explicitly incorporate specific constructs related to effective instruction and learning, a characteristic that lends credibility to the use of the term *design*. Pye (1964) notes that while a painter or sculptor can choose any imaginable shape, a designer is limited by the function of the thing being designed (p. 7). Likewise, Simon (1969) notes that a complete design can be broken down into functional components (p. 73). Like other designers, an instructional designer cannot choose any imaginable shape for instruction. The limitations that arise stem from the function of instruction and, therefore, from the context of learning—a context that includes external as well as internal environments.

PURPOSES OF MODELS OF SYSTEMATIC INSTRUCTIONAL DESIGN

Instructional design models serve four purposes:

1. Improving learning and instruction by means of the problem-solving and feedback characteristics of the systematic approach.

2. Improving management of instructional design and development by means of the monitoring and control functions of the systematic approach.

3. Improving evaluation processes by means of the designated components and sequence of events, including the feedback and revision events, inherent in models of systematic instructional design.

4. Testing or building learning or instructional theory by means of theory-based design within a model of systematic instructional design.

As suggested in the review by Smith and Murray (1975), the procedures in models may be based more on the monitoring and control functions associated with general systems than with any clearly stated instructional purpose. Lowe and Schwen (1975) note that most instructional development is "a systematic process focused on improving the effectiveness and efficiency of learning and instruction in various educational environments" (p. 43). Vance (1976) and Waldron (1973) present a similar purpose statement, while Davis and McCallon (1974) modify this purpose in stating their intent to "translate *social science learning theory* for practical use in a variety of instructional settings" (p. xi) to serve as a guide "to the theory and practice of adult education" (p. 6). Even (1977) does not refer to theory, but retains the purpose statement presented by Lowe and Schwen (1975), focusing on classroom activities as the specific environmental context.

According to Gagne and Briggs (1974), the purpose of the systematic approach (or a statement of its usefulness) is that "it encourages the setting of a design objective, and it provides a way to know when that objective has been met" (p. 228). In view of this purpose, Gagne and Briggs observe that the systematic approach is useful in designing lessons and modules as well as instructional systems (p. 227). Other developers and reviewers have referred to the value of the systematic approach as a planning, organizational, and/or managerial tool for effective design and development (Branson, 1978; Kelly, 1976; Shoemaker & Parks, 1976; Smith & Murray, 1975; Teague & Faulkner, 1978).

Educators generally and instructional designers specifically often use a model of instructional design as a kind of game plan for their development efforts. This plan assures the educator that every piece of instruction that is used will, regardless of content, have recognizable elements. This sameness aids educators in a variety of ways: Formative evaluations and revisions are more systematic and congruent; the sequence of developmental and evaluation events is planned in a procedural context; media development is more efficient; and evaluation systems can be developed with quality as a key criterion. This sameness also allows standardization of a project's design efforts so that design becomes task specific. This enables increased communication and coordination among the members of a development project. For instance, the phrase "assessing learner needs" should be defined similarly by all project members. Major misunderstandings usually can be resolved by consulting the definitions and explanations provided with a model. The sequencing of events in a model also provides a management framework conducive to use of PERT techniques and other management strategies for ensuring the availability of human and material resources at required times. In this way project events can be scheduled to make efficient use of time, materials, and other resources (cf. Briggs, 1977).

Another useful purpose of a model of instructional design is to allow testing of the theory from which the model was constructed. Adair and Foster (1972, p. 2.31) suggest this purpose for pedagogical models when the specific theoretical constructs can be identified. However, a model of instructional design may also be the result of a component-testing or theory-building process, in which case the construction of the model is built on weak theory or no theory at all, as suggested by Roberts (1978, p. 7) in his review of program planning models. The difficulty in deciding which theory-related purpose is being used is expressed by Kaplan (1964), who warns that propositions may be tautologically presented so that they become "mistaken for genuine theory, and a program is accepted for its own fulfillment" (p. 273). Most models, however, as noted by Smith and Murray (1975), seem to be "exemplars of desirable or commendable operating procedures" (p. 13) instead of theory-based models (cf. Barson, 1965). That is, the assumptions and the interrelationship of factors are not revealed by the model. Instead, the model may be a frame of reference for only one setting in which it has been used.

The various purposes and advantages cited here are consistent with Banathy's (1968) preface statement about a major advantage of the systematic (systems) approach, which is that it enables us "to develop and manage complex entities" (p. iii). Throughout his book, Banathy also stresses that the defined outcomes determine the particular system purpose.

The use of a model will not ensure that any or all of the four suggested purposes are accomplished. There is, for example, the effect of human variation in interpreting and implementing available models. Also, Lowe and Schwen (1975) found that the documentation of instructional design models often omits detailed accounts of how the development process works in various settings. (An exception to this generalization is the detailed explication provided by Teague and Faulkner, 1978.) Nonetheless, the documentation serving as the basis for this report has provided a means by which the origins, purposes, and uses of instructional design models can be described and analyzed. The next section presents two categorization schemas for fulfilling this purpose.

CATEGORIZATION AND ANALYSIS

The categorization of components of models is a difficult task. Some references explicate theoretical considerations directly; others require inferences of theory. This study is not intended as a definitive statement about the status of any model. Instead, it is an analytical review of models as they are represented in available literature.

Models Reviewed

As the result of an extensive examination of books, journal articles, bibliographies, ERIC documents, and procedural manuals, over 60 possible target models were identified. To provide comprehensive (although nonrandom) sampling, the authors deliberately selected models applied in nonformal as well as formal settings and models applied for modular or course development as well as for large-scale curriculum or program development. To appropriately represent nonformal settings and large-scale development in this review, it was necessary to include program development as well as instructional development models, some of which represent the application of a prior model to a particular setting and purpose rather than a new model. Some of the models often cited in the literature are not reported here due to unavailability of the necessary references. A few models are reported because they are familiar to the authors through local use. However, the authors intend to provide representativeness in this study for the purpose of analytical organization, review, and synthesis, and in no way intend to suggest any inadequacy in those models not contained in this review. In fact, the models cited in this review represent an unevenness in amount and quality of information reported in the references.

Description of the First Schema

All of the models reviewed are compared to Gropper's (1977) list of 10 common tasks (table 13.1). This list is used as a referent in this paper because, although Gropper does not state which models provide the basis for his list, he does indicate that the list represents a synthesis of the best models. Also, it is a more recent source than others presenting "generally agreed upon" steps. For example, Merrill and Boutwell (1973) offer 5 basic components; Atkins (1975) offers 12; Gagne and Briggs (1974, p. 213) offer another 12.

During the review of the models, the authors found four additional components addressed separately by a number of models. These additional components are also shown in table 13.2, which is coded according to the list in table 13.1, with Tasks 1 to 10 representing Gropper's (1977) list and Tasks 11 to 14 representing the tasks often cited separately by other references.

Although Gropper only alludes to some of these last four tasks (11 to 14), they are listed separately to emphasize the importance of their consideration. Kaufman (1972) describes in detail the requirements for systematic needs assessment processes (Task 11) and provides a springboard for the work of Roberts (1978) among others. Tasks 12, 13, and 14 are inherent in the process of needs assessment but are listed separately because many people consider them separately. Banathy (1968), Churchman (1968), Hayman (1974), and von Bertalanffy (1968), who describe the systematic approach in terms of general systems theory, specify the requirements for thorough system analysis to identify complex interactions and environmental constraints, determination of alternative solutions to the identified problem, and thorough system synthesis to maximize efficiency and minimize cost—all following the identification of desired outcomes. Any model that does not account for these last four tasks is probably doomed to inefficiency, negligible impact, or total failure.

Many of the references shown in table 13.2 do give separate consideration to these issues. When designing instruction, it is critical, however, to consider these issues from two perspectives: (a) the internal conditions of learning (cf. Gagne, 1977; Gagne & Briggs, 1974; and Briggs, 1975), and (b) the environment (or the external conditions) in which the learning will occur. This second perspective is embellished partly by reference to formal versus nonformal settings and partly by particular constraints. As implied by Roberts (1978), a model with a high degree of fidelity to the internal conditions of learning may be "overly costly, time consuming, and distracting to the task at hand" (p. 52).

In recognizing the nature of needs assessment, it is important to realize that the analysis of the learner population (Task 5) is the type of needs assessment that identifies gaps between "current and prerequisite goals" (Gropper, 1977, p. 8) for the learner (cf. Maher, 1978, p. 26) based on the analysis conducted in Task 3—a task sometimes omitted in the design process. The needs assessment represented by Task 11 is more global, focusing on such issues as problem identification or occupational analysis, which provide the basis for the goal statements in Task 1.

(Text continues on page 170.)

Table 13.1.
Fourteen Common Tasks in Model Development

Task Number	Definition
1	Formulation of broad goals and detailed subgoals stated in observable terms
2	Development of pretest and posttest matching goals and subgoals
3	Analysis of goals and subgoals for types of skills/learning required
4	Sequencing of goals and subgoals to facilitate learning
5	Characterization of learner population "as to age, grade level, past learning history, special aptitudes or disabilities, and, not least, estimated attainment of current and prerequisite goals" (Gropper, 1977, p. 8)
6	Formulation of instructional strategy to match subject-matter and learner requirements
7	Selection of media to implement strategies
8	Development of courseware based on strategies
9	Empirical tryout of courseware with learner population, diagnosis of learning and courseware failures, and revision of courseware based on diagnosis
10	Development of materials and procedures for installing, maintaining, and periodically repairing the instructional program
11	Assessment of need, problem identification, occupational analysis, competence, or training requirements
12	Consideration of alternative solutions to instruction
13	Formulation of system and environmental descriptions and identification of constraints
14	Costing instructional programs

Table 13.2.
Tasks Included in Instructional Design Models

Reference for Model	Outcomes	Tests	Analysis	Sequencing	Learner attributes	Strategy	Media	Development	Tryout/revision	Install/maintain	Need	Alternatives	Constraints	Cost	Total
1. Army Security Agency, Legere, et al. (1966)	●	●	●	●	●	●	●	●	●		●				10
2. Atkins (1975)	●	●		●		●		●	●	●	●		●		9
3. Banathy (1968)	●	●	●	●	●	●	●		●	●		●	●	●	12
4. Bishop (1976)	●	●	●	●	●	●	●	●	●	●	●		●	●	13
5. Briggs & Wager (1979)	●	●	●	●	●	●	●	●	●	●	●	●	●	●	14
6. Brooks, et al. (1973)	●		●		●	●	●	●	●	●			●		9
7. Burkman (1976-1978); Laugen (1979)	●	●	●	●	●	●	●	●	●	●	●		●	●	13
8. Crittendon & Massey (1978)	●	●	●		●	●		●	●	●			●	●	10
9. Davis (1977)	●		●	●	●			●	●				●		7
10. Davis & McCallon (1974)	●		●	●	●	●	●	●	●	●			●	●	11
11. Dederick & Sturge (1975)	●	●	●	●		●		●	●	●	●				9
12. Dick & Carey (1978)	●	●	●		●	●	●	●	●		●	●			10
13. Even (1977)	●		●	●	●	●		●			●		●	●	9
14. Friesen (1973)	●	●	●	●	●	●	●	●	●	●	●		●	●	13
15. Gagne & Briggs (1974); Briggs (1975)	●	●	●	●	●	●	●	●	●	●	●	●	●	●	14
16. Glaser (1966)	●	●	●		●	●		●	●						7
17. Gropper (1973)	●	●	●	●	●	●	●	●	●	●					10
18. Hayman (1974)	●			●				●	●	●	●	●	●	●	9
19. Interservice Procedures (1975); Branson (1978)	●	●	●	●			●	●	●	●	●	●	●	●	12
20. Kaufman (1972)	●	●		●	●			●	●	●	●	●	●	●	11

Reference for Model	Outcomes	Tests	Analysis	Sequencing	Learner attributes	Strategy	Media	Development	Tryout/revision	Install/maintain	Need	Alternatives	Constraints	Cost	Total
21. Ledford (1973)	•		•		•	•	•	•	•	•					8
22. Lee (1975)	•	•	•	•		•	•	•	•	•	•	•	•	•	13
23. Mager & Pipe (1978)	•	•	•	•	•		•	•	•	•		•	•		11
24. Maher (1978)	•			•		•	•	•	•	•			•		8
25. Merrill (1973); Merrill & Boutwell (1973)	•	•	•	•		•	•	•	•						8
26. Michigan State University; Barson (1965)	•	•				•	•	•	•						6
27. Pennington & Green (1976)	•			•	•	•			•		•		•		7
28. Penta (1973)	•	•		•			•	•	•		•	•			8
29. Roberts (1978)	•	•	•	•	•	•	•	•	•	•	•	•	•	•	14
30. Scanland (1974)	•	•	•	•	•	•	•	•	•	•	•	•	•		13
31. Sherman (1978)	•		•	•	•			•			•	•	•		8
32. Shoemaker & Parks (1976)	•	•	•	•		•		•			•		•		8
33. Teague & Faulkner (1978)	•	•	•	•	•	•	•	•	•	•	•				11
34. Tennyson & Boutwell (1971)	•	•	•	•		•		•	•						7
35. Tosti & Ball (1969)	•			•		•		•		•					5
36. Tuckman & Edwards (1973) (cf. Davis, 1977)	•	•				•		•	•	•	•		•		8
37. Vance (1976)	•		•	•	•	•	•	•	•	•	•		•		11
38. Waldron (1973)	•	•	•			•	•	•	•	•			•	•	10
39. Wallen (1973)	•	•	•					•	•	•	•				7
40. Waters, et al. (1978)	•	•	•			•	•	•			•		•		8
Frequency	40	28	29	23	27	34	24	34	38	28	27	14	25	14	
Percentage	100	70	73	58	68	85	60	85	95	70	68	35	63	35	

Note: The models are listed alphabetically, because a chronological sequence reveals no definite evolutionary patterns for those models contained in this review. When examining the models chronologically, it appears only that tasks 3 to 4 and 10 to 14 are reported somewhat more frequently after 1972, but not consistently. A bullet (•) is used to denote the presence of a task in the particular model reviewed, as indicated by the reference for the model.

Some authors, instead of completing a needs assessment, proceed from the assumption that a broadly defined or stated learner need has been identified and therefore consider no other alternatives apart from the creation of an instructional solution. Others proceed as if the nature of the problem may require an alternative other than the acquisition of learning capabilities or the development of an instructional product. Some recognize that even when the problem pivots on learning capabilities of some sort, the solution may be another alternative such as management of a system or management of resources instead of creation of a new product or program. Briggs and Wager (1979) present a systems schematic of a model for the design of instruction (p. 10) which starts with stating the objectives and performance standards. But their explication of the model starts with determining needs, goals, and priorities (pp. 19-40) and resources, constraints, and delivery systems (pp. 41-59).

Although table 13.2 shows that the tasks outlined by Gropper are included in the models in this review, the inferences made in analyzing models according to the first matrix were sometimes generous in light of the amount of information or the outline of model components presented in the reference. The reader should refer to the results of the second categorization schema for information about the origin, theoretical basis, purposes and uses, and documentation associated with these models.

Description of the Second Schema

Table 13.3 defines the coding dimensions. Table 13.4, pages 172-173, is coded according to the numbers and letters assigned to the set of dimensions in table 13.3. For example, 1.1a means that there appears to be a theoretical basis for the total model, while 1.1b means that there appears to be a theoretical basis for only part of the model. Each of these dimensions is explained later in more detail. Figure 13.2, page 174, summarizes the results of table 13.4.

Origin. Knowledge of the origin of a model can help the educator use a particular model in the most appropriate manner. There are two main discernible sources of origin: theoretical and empirical. Of course, logical inference and combinations of theory and experience also are used to create or modify models of instructional design.

Theoretical models have as their origin a particular theory-based rationale, such as Banathy's (1968) approach based on general systems theory or Gagne's (1977) approach to the conditions of learning. As this paper is based on a sampling of systematic approaches to instructional design, it is not surprising that most models reflect this source.

In order to qualify as having an origin in general systems theory, the description of a model should contain specific reference to general systems theory or describe the systemic approach with emphasis on interaction of the components of the model as they relate to accomplishment of the intended outcomes in the intended environment. For example, Bishop (1976), Kaufman (1972), and Roberts (1978) reference in detail the ways of identifying and describing the total system objectives, the performance measures for the whole system, the effect of constraints and resources of the target system, and the management of the system, as well as specific interactive processes for accomplishing the defined outcomes through checking and rechecking in the feedback and revision processes.

Merrill and Boutwell (1973), however, refer to some of the same components as found in Bishop and Roberts, but stress learning theory and give no explanation of the system components that they briefly list. Similarly, Even's (1977) and Vance's (1976) approach to instructional design strongly emphasizes learning theory, as does the approach of Davis and McCallon (1974), who stress adult learning theory in particular. Thus, when learning theory, such as that constructed by Bruner (1966), Gagne (1977), or Houle (1972) provides the main basis for a model, with little or no reference to general systems theory, the model is judged to have a theoretical basis for only some of the components. This is the nature of the systematic approach, which logically makes use of learning theories in the direct design of instruction after outcomes

(Text continues on page 173.)

Table 13.3.
Dimensions Used in Model Schemata

Code	Dimension
1.0	Origin
1.1	Theoretical
1.1a	Total model (includes general systems theory or other total approach)
1.1b	One or some of the components (includes adult learning theory and other learning theories)
1.2	Empirical (includes reports of experience or research of viable processes)
2.0	Theoretical underpinnings
2.1	Emphasis on learning or instructional theory (includes constructs about adult learning requirements)
2.2	Emphasis on control/management/monitoring functions of systems theory
2.3	Emphasis on analysis function (includes content, task, and learning analysis of systems theory)
3.0	Purposes and uses
3.1	Teach instructional design
3.2	Produce viable instructional product(s) or activity(ies)
3.2a	Nonformal (includes military, industrial, governmental, vocational, nonformal adult education)
3.2b	Formal (includes public, higher, and professional education)
3.2c	Small-scale lesson/course/module development
3.2d	Large-scale curriculum/system/program development
3.3	Reduce costs of training/education
4.0	Documentation
4.1	Documentation, application, or validation data relating to use of the total model
4.2	Documentation, application, or validation data relating to part of the model (the mere outline and description of a model being insufficient to qualify as documentation)

Table 13.4.
Categorization by Origins, Theoretical Underpinnings, Purposes and Uses, and Documentation

Reference for Model	Origins			Underpinnings			Purposes and Uses					Documentation	
	1.1	1.1	1.2	2.1	2.2	2.3	3.1	3.2	3.2	3.2	3.3	4.1	4.2
	a	b					a	b	c	d			
1. Army Security Agency, Legere, et al. (1966)		●			●		●		●				●
2. Atkins (1975)								●		●			
3. Banathy (1968)	●		●	●	●	●	●	●	●			●	
4. Bishop (1976)	●		●	●	●	●	●	●	●	●			●
5. Briggs & Wager (1979)	●		●	●	●	●	●	●	●	●	●	●	
6. Brooks (1974)	●						●		●			●	
7. Burkman (1976-1978); Laugen (1979)		●						●	●	●		●	
8. Crittendon & Massey (1978)	●				●			●	●	●	●	●	
9. Davis (1977)	●							●	●	●			
10. Davis & McCallon (1974)		●	●	●			●	●	●				●
11. Dederick & Sturge (1975)		●					●			●	●	●	
12. Dick & Carey (1978)		●	●			●	●	●	●	●		●	
13. Even (1977)		●		●				●	●				●
14. Friesen (1973)	●			●	●	●	●	●	●	●			●
15. Gagne & Briggs (1974); Briggs (1975)	●		●	●	●	●	●	●	●	●	●		●
16. Glaser (1966)	●			●			●	●	●	●			
17. Gropper (1973)		●			●		●						
18. Hayman (1974)	●				●	●	●						●
19. Interservice Procedures (1975); Branson (1978)		●		●	●	●		●		●	●		●
20. Kaufman (1972)	●	●		●	●	●	●	●	●	●	●	●	
21. Ledford (1976)	●			●			●					●	
22. Lee (1975)		●						●	●				
23. Mager & Pipe (1974)	●			●			●	●	●	●	●		●
24. Maher (1978)						●			●			●	
25. Merrill & Boutwell (1973)					●	●	●		●	●			
26. Michigan State University; Barson (1965)		●	●					●	●			●	
27. Pennington & Green (1976)		●			●			●	●				●
28. Penta (1973)		●			●			●	●				●

Reference for Model	Origins		Underpinnings			Purposes and Uses						Documentation	
	1.1	1.2	2.1	2.2	2.3	3.1	3.2				3.3	4.1	4.2
	a	b					a	b	c	d			
29. Roberts (1978)	●	●		●	●	●			●			●	
30. Scanland (1974)							●		●				
31. Sherman (1978)		●		●		●						●	
32. Shoemaker & Parks (1976)	●	●		●	●	●	●	●	●			●	
33. Teague & Faulkner (1978)		●		●	●	●			●	●		●	
34. Tennyson & Boutwell (1971)	●			●	●			●	●			●	
35. Tosti & Ball (1969)	●		●	●			●	●		●		●	
36. Tuckman & Edwards (1973); (cf. Davis, 1977)		●	●		●		●		●			●	
37. Vance (1976)	●		●		●			●	●			●	
38. Waldron (1973)				●			●		●				●
39. Wallen (1973)	●			●	●		●		●				●
40. Waters (1978)	●	●	●				●		●			●	

are specified and before evaluation occurs. An exception to this generalization is Glaser's (1966) model, which is wholly grounded in learning theory. Although Glaser mentions feedback and revision along with psychological activities, the origin of the total model is clearly learning theory rather than general systems theory.

It would seem that theories related to organizational development might have a place in the classification of some models. That is, the strategies, targets, tactics, and management activities required to effectively implement an instructional project based on any model selected would also have impact on the workability of some models in different settings. Such concepts are not included in this particular review, though it would probably benefit the user to consider theories of organizational development when selecting a model to use. (Some models have no discernible theory base.)

Many models have their origin in the developer's or user's particular experiences with instructional design, as in the case of the Individualized Science Instructional System (ISIS) model, described by Burkman (1976-1978) and Laugen (1979), and in the Center for Studies in Vocational Education (CSVE) model described by Crittendon and Massey (1978). The descriptive model of a certain set of procedures in these cases produced good results and is an example of a description that may become a prescription for other users.

Developers may also borrow heavily from a previously existing model and add their own special modifications. For example, J. Davis (1977) presents a model adapted from Tuckman and Edwards (1973) (cited in Davis, p. 36; cf. Tuckman, 1969). Sherman (1978) bases his model on Hayman (1974), but lays out the type of learning capabilities and conditions required to master each of the systems process components in order to teach the systems approach. Brien and Towle (1977) did not present their own model, but instead referred their readers to Boutwell and Tennyson, Tuckman and Edwards, and Briggs. In this instance a more recent model described by Gagne and Briggs (1974) and Briggs (1975) is listed in place of the 1970 reference

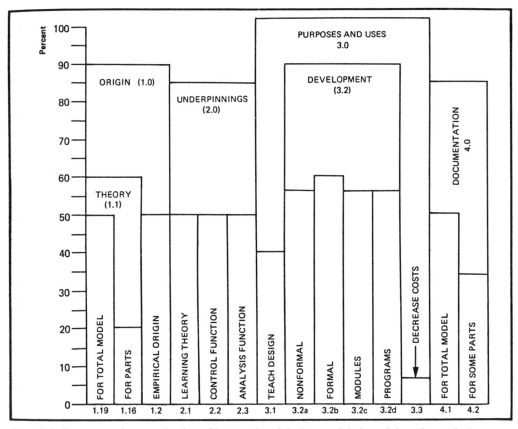

Fig. 13.2. Summary of categorization of instructional design models by origins, theoretical underpinnings, purposes and uses, and documentation.

to Briggs given by Brien and Towle. (Also see Briggs & Wager, 1979.) Of course, some models appear to be based on other models, but without specific reference to the particular source of origin.

Finally, a few models have either stated or implied origins that are both theoretical and empirical. This would seem to be the ideal set of origins, but few models fall into both categories.

Of the models reviewed, about 65 percent reported some source of theoretical origin, about 50 percent for the total model (such as general systems theory) and about 20 percent for only some of the components of the model. About 50 percent reported an empirical origin. (The reader is cautioned to remember that the categories are not mutually exclusive. Subsequently, the sums across dimensions of a category may equal more than 100 percent.)

Theoretical Underpinnings. This portion of the categorization schema displays three main divisions to show which models emphasize learning or instructional theory and which emphasize subdivisions (functions) of general systems theory.

Those models based on learning theory usually indicate this status early in the model's description and/or in the discussion about the model's purposes and uses. In a few instances, the authors of this paper made inferences about the probable theoretical basis for a given model. Sometimes this was done by analyzing the reference section of the source to identify the probable foundation of the model.

The two subdivisions of the general systems approach are: (a) the control/management/ monitoring function, and (b) the analysis function. The first function allows the educator to make sure that all portions of the instructional system behave in the prescribed manner. This is sometimes very difficult to accomplish with a large curriculum project. Special steps are often added to the model to assure the developer that every component will flow smoothly.

The second function allows the systems user to have confidence that the analysis of a task will proceed in a logical, orderly manner. Most of the models use this analysis function in order to simplify the complex concepts involved in a learning process.

Finally, some models seem to have no discernible theoretical basis as reported in the reference citation. These models usually appear to be based on one or more previous models and are concerned more with the addition of a new component or application than with building on the theoretical basis of the original model.

About 50 percent of the models emphasized an underpinning in learning theory, 50 percent in the control/management/monitoring function of general systems theory (either explicitly or implicitly), and about 50 percent in the analysis function. Together about 70 percent emphasized either the control or analysis function of the general systems model. This means that about 30 percent of the references reported in table 13.2 focused no discernible attention on two of the basic functional advantages of general systems theory. Of those who focused on learning theory, about 70 percent (11 of 15) also cited the general systems theory advantages. (About 30 percent did not do so.) Of those who focused on the general systems theory advantages, only about 40 percent (11 of 27) also cited a learning theory basis.

Purposes and Uses. The purposes and uses of a model center around one of three main categories: (a) teaching of the instructional design process, (b) production of viable instructional products, and (c) reduction in cost of education. Although almost every model could be used to teach the instructional design process, models placed in this category were limited to those expressly stating this as their purpose. The production of an effective product tends to take second place for models having this classification.

Many models are constructed to yield instructional products for the purpose of improving the training or education function of an organization. Two main settings are conceived within this category: (a) formal, and (b) nonformal education. A distinction between these settings is offered by Ingle (cited in Roberts, 1978, p. 4), who defines nonformal education as "any organized activity, outside of the established framework of the formal school and university system, which aims to communicate specific ideas, knowledge, skills, attitudes and practices in response to a predetermined need." Thus, the nonformal setting includes military, industrial, governmental, vocational, and other nonformal adult education activities. The formal setting is primarily limited to public, higher, and professional education activities. Except for activities unique to a specific setting, such as occupational analysis, many of the models could be used in either setting, although the reference may have named one type of organization as the focus of the model.

The models reviewed have two main uses: (a) the development of instruction on a small scale (lessons and modules), and (b) the development of instruction on a large scale (courses, curriculums, and programs). Generally, the source for the models cited herein indicates the intended use, although some inferences are made about uses based upon the particular products associated with the model, such as a module versus a program plan.

Few of the reviewed models mention any costs associated with the model. Those that do, however, make the point that economy of scale would enable educators using a particular model to reduce the per unit expenditure in their special setting. However, while Glasgow (1976) observes that the cost effectiveness of systematic development has no empirical basis, Carey and Briggs (1977) discuss cost-benefit approaches to the use of a system approach to instruction. Goodson and Roberts (1979) also present a two-by-two matrix of instructional quality versus product impact (p. 25) as an evaluation schema that can be used for cost-benefit analysis of instructional products within the staff training program of a human services agency.

Of the models reviewed in this study, about 40 percent reported the teaching of instructional design (or equivalent) as the primary purpose, 90 percent emphasized the production of an instructional product, and less than 10 percent reported cost reduction as a basic purpose. The setting category (nonformal and formal) was evenly split as was the scale of production (large and small).

Documentation. Unless an educator knows whether or not a particular model has been tried out in an actual instructional setting, it will be difficult to make a decision about that model's chance of success in the planned setting. Few of the models reviewed supply any data concerning their effectiveness. Some assert that the particular model works well, although no supporting data or descriptions of applications are provided. Since most of the models' sources are journal articles, it may be argued that too little space is available for the reporting of this type of data or information. However, the longer sources that were reviewed (books and ERIC documents) would seem to have little excuse for not revealing this data. (A pertinent question might be raised about the usefulness of publishing a model without having its efficacy established beforehand by means of a firm theory base and/or empirical base.)

An analysis of table 13.4 shows that even at the grossest categorization level, there was not one model which addressed all of the categories. In addition, only the "purposes and uses" category was addressed by all of the models. As the categorization became more specific, the percentages of models matched to categories continued to decrease.

Of the models reviewed in this study, about 50 percent reported documentation of some sort on the application of the total model, and about 35 percent offered some limited documentation. Finally, of those reporting some theoretical origin, about 70 percent (19 of 27) cited some form of documentation; but of those citing documentation, only 55 percent (19 of 34) cited any theoretical origin.

Analysis of Models. The analysis of the 40 models selected for this study using the two schemata described above is presented in tables 13.2 and 13.4. Table 13.2 shows the *tasks* included in instructional design models according to the first schema. Table 13.4 shows the categorization of ID models by origin, theoretical underpinnings, purposes and uses, and documentation (second schema).

POSSIBLE REASONS
FOR MODEL PROLIFERATION

There are a number of possible reasons for the large variety of models of instructional design. One of the most obvious reasons seems to be that many educational endeavors are afflicted with the "not-invented-here" syndrome. Much effort seems to be duplicated because educators do not seek out existing models of instructional design or available materials before they endeavor to develop their own. The symptoms of this malady usually take the form of an attitude that says, in effect, "We have our own special circumstances and problems here and any innovation (design model) which comes from outside our organization boundaries will very likely fail in our unique situation." This attitude is certainly not restricted to the educational field; industry, military, government, and many other types of organizations seem to fall prey to it just as easily. Molnar (1971) points out the tremendous inefficiency resulting from such an attitude.

> The large amount of uncoordinated research activities and the lack of preplanned linkages between research and practice has led to the existence of an expensive cottage industry in educational technology which tends to retool every academic year. Researchers and educators frequently demonstrate a strong resistance to the use of someone else's innovation. It has been said that if there was a Nobel prize for educational research, we would nominate an entire generation of researchers for their co-discovery of the wheel. (p. 7)

Another reason for the great number of models seems to be related to the degree of documentation that the models have. As stated by Logan (1976):

> Instructional systems development assumes more or less the previous reputations of other innovations. This delays acceptance of ISD, for as with other innovations, promised performance could not be met and, if met, could not be maintained. Developers of innovations often left the customers with inadequate supporting documentation if they left any at all. (p. 17)

Since many models are never tried out, educators may be skeptical about the model being reviewed and thus decide to develop their own.

Merely examining a model tells one very little about its efficacy. Unless performance data are available from tryout situations, the educator interested in choosing a model will have few objective criteria on which to base a decision. Because few available models actually exhibit tryout data, it is little wonder that designers are reticent about adopting or adapting even a well-known model. The risk of sinking a project's resources into a model which is, in effect, an unknown quantity must be disconcerting to a project director.

Yet another reason is linked to Alexander's (1964) observation about the nature of design: "What does make design a problem in real world cases is that we are trying to make a diagram for forces whose field we do not understand" (p. 21). This effort appears to be a problem within the context of learning within a particular educational environment as well as within the context of learning in general.

The major learning theorists, including Ausubel (1968), Bruner (1966), Gagne (1977), Piaget (1954), Skinner (1954), and others, present different propositions regarding the conditions for learning. These differences may have the greatest impact on the development of materials, but they may also cause individual educators to reject certain steps in available system approach models. For example, a strong advocate of discovery learning might reject the specification of objectives and corresponding direct match of instructional events to these objectives.

More often, however, the major steps of models are adapted to particular differences in the learning environment, whether it be nonformal or formal education, education for academic settings or for other institutional, business, or community settings. This type of difference is fairly obvious when we compare and contrast various models. When, for instance, we contrast the Davis-McCallon (1974) or Bishop (1976) models to the Dick-Carey (1978) or Gagne-Briggs (1974) models, this distinction becomes apparent. The major differences in these kinds of models appear to stem from variations in carrying out the major steps by means of specific events and activities.

At least three factors have forced educational researchers to develop and apply their own unique methods to such things as job analysis, test generation, construction of behavioral objectives, and implementation, evaluation, and revision of instruction.

1. Many educators feel very strongly that instruction should have a local, indigenous quality (Demerath & Daniels cited in Logan, 1976).

2. There is a lack of information on available authoring tools and procedures and a lack of clearinghouses for existing course materials (Logan, 1976).

3. Instructional development efforts are usually driven by a "raw empiricism" so that:
    Instructional materials are prepared on the basis of intuition, folklore, or experience and administered to members of the target population. If the students pass the test, the product is considered appropriate; if not, the materials are revised and tried again. This tryout revision cycle is repeated until the product works or the developers run out of resources or time (Merrill & Boutwell cited in Logan, 1976).

CONCLUSIONS

The review of models reported here provides an approximation of the state of the art regarding models of instructional design. Categorizing the models as shown in tables 13.2 and 13.4 may do injustice to some models and give undue credit to others. Even with these possible inequities, however, several substantial generalizations can be made with some confidence.

1. The components of the general systems approach applied to instruction have proliferated in varied forms with varied origins, purposes, uses, and documentation.

2. Learning theory bases are not explicitly prescribed in many of the models using a systematic approach to instructional design.

3. Documentation of the systematic application of the models for specific purposes and uses is generally inadequate for assessing the effectiveness of particular models.

4. Although the *systemic* approach is "an inquiry and a discipline, complete with theoretical underpinnings and a developed methodology" (Hayman, 1974, p. 495), many of the *systematic* instructional design models, as described in the literature, represent a series of mechanical or linear steps rather than the complex and rigorous analytical and cybernetic process required for effective application to instructional design.

5. The general tasks constituting a model of instructional design, though differing in sequence, are generic in that they may be applied across differing purposes, emphases, origins, uses, and settings. This attests to the robust quality of the systemic or systematic approach to instructional design.

6. Little concern or documentation is reported to demonstrate the cost-utility of using different models of instructional design.

7. Models such as those reported by Bishop (1976), Briggs (1975), Briggs and Wager (1979), Gagne and Briggs (1974), Roberts (1978), Scanland (1974), and Teague and Faulkner (1978), appear to provide enough explication to enable users to apply the reported models as intended. The reader is advised, however, to consider a model that matches the dimensions of the user's context and to make judgments about the adequacy of documentation and theory base before selecting a model to use. To begin patterning instruction after the first model encountered might very well be a mistake for two reasons: (a) the model may have been developed for a completely different setting for a completely different purpose, and (b) the model may not have been validated. A model may work well when finally used, but not many educators or project directors can afford the luxury of trying the model out with their own resources.

8. A few of the models reported are not models at all in that they fail to describe, explain, or predict elements in their referent system. Instead, they represent the use of jargon in a nearly tautological manner and possibly mechanical prescriptions inappropriate to the intended users. These models will be unnamed but the buyer should beware.

9. Instead of model proliferation, it would be more useful to engage in model evolution. That is, by examining, the two schemata presented in this paper, it should be possible not only to select the most appropriate model for given purposes and uses but also to identify at least the general type of theory basis for a given model. The results of the categorization and analysis schemata presented here indicate gaps in documentation or validation of models as well as in the theoretical bases of some models. Based on these results, the educator should consider describing particular theoretical bases and providing thorough documentation of the implementation of a given model. In this way, there could be more theory development and testing by means of model implementation.

In view of these generalizations and the comparisons provided in this analytic review of models of instructional design, it would be ill advised to recommend that one, and only one, grand pattern be used for all design efforts. However, a strong argument can be made that the large number of extant models is not only confusing, but also often wasteful of the resources over which educators and project directors have command.

REFERENCES

Adair, C. H., & Foster, J. T. (1972). *A guide for simulation design*. Tallahassee, FL: Instructional Simulation Design.

AECT. (1977). *Educational technology: Definition and glossary* (Vol. 1). Washington, DC: Association for Educational Communications and Technology.

Alexander, C. (1964). *Notes on the synthesis of form*. Cambridge, MA: Harvard University Press.

Atkins, W. A., Jr. (1975, December). What is instructional systems development? *Educational Technology*, pp. 17-21.

Ausubel, D. P. (1968). *Educational psychology: A cognitive view*. New York: Holt, Rinehart & Winston.

Banathy, B. H. (1968). *Instructional systems*. Belmont, CA: Lear Sieglar/Fearon.

Barson, J. (1965). *Instructional systems development: A demonstration and evaluation project*. U.S. Office of Education, Title VII-B, Project OE-3-16-025.

Bishop, L. J. (1976). *Staff development and instructional improvement: Plans and procedures*. Boston: Allyn & Bacon.

Branson, R. K. (1978, March). The interservice procedures for instructional systems development. *Educational Technology*, pp. 11-14.

Brien, R. L., & Towle, N. J. (1977, February). Instructional design and development: Accelerating the process. *Educational Technology*, pp. 12-17.

Briggs, L. J. (1975). *An overview of instructional systems design*. Tallahassee: Florida State University.

———. (Ed.). (1977). *Instructional design: Principles and applications*. Englewood Cliffs, NJ: Educational Technology Publications.

Briggs, L. J., & Wager, W. (1979). *Handbook of procedures for the design of instruction* (2nd ed.). Draft of second edition printed by Florida State University.

Brooks, R. D., Whitehead, J., & Miller, F. W. (1973, April). Application of a three-stage systems approach model for producing career awareness materials. *Audiovisual Instruction*, pp. 17-20.

Bruner, J. S. (1966). *Toward a theory of instruction*. New York: W. W. Norton.

Burkman, E. (1976-1978). *Individualized science instructional system (ISIS) project proposal*. Unpublished manuscript. (Available from Department of Educational Research, Development, and Foundations, Education Building, Florida State University, Tallahassee, Florida 32306.)

Carey, J., and Briggs, L. J. (1977). Teams as designers. In L. J. Briggs (Ed.), *Instructional design*. Englewood Cliffs, NJ: Educational Technology Publications.

Churchman, C. W. (1968). *The systems approach*. New York: Dell.

Crittendon, J. F., & Massey, R. (1978, March). *Florida's vocational curriculum system: Issues in statewide curriculum development*. Paper presented at the meeting of the American Educational Research Association, Toronto, Ontario.

Davis, J. J. (1977, December). Design and implementation of an individualized instruction program. *Educational Technology*, pp. 36-41.

Davis, L. N., & McCallon, E. (1974). *Planning, conducting, and evaluating workshops*. Austin, TX: Learning Concepts.

Dederick, W. E., & Sturge, H. H. (1975, June). An operational instructional systems model: U.S. Naval training. *Educational Technology*, pp. 28-32.

Dick, W., & Carey, L. (1978). *The systematic design of instruction*. Chicago: Scott, Foresman.

Even, M. J. (1977). *A new instructional design and development process for instructors of adults*. Lincoln: University of Nebraska. (ERIC Document Reproduction Service No. ED 146 366).

Friesen, P. A. (1973). *Designing instruction: A systematic or "systems" approach using programmed instruction as a model*. Santa Monica, CA: Miller.

Gagne, R. M. (1977). *The conditions of learning* (3rd ed.). New York: Holt, Rinehart & Winston.

Gagne, R. M., & Briggs, L. J. (1974). *Principles of instructional design*. New York: Holt, Rinehart & Winston.

Glaser, R. (1966). Psychological bases for instructional design. *AV Communication Review, 14*(4), 433-448.

Glasgow, Z. (1976, July). *Learning systems research, development, testing and evaluation*. Paper presented at the meeting of the International Learning Technology Congress and Exposition on Applied Learning Technology for Human Resource Development, Washington, DC. (ERIC Document Reproduction Service No. ED 126 854).

Goodson, L. A., & Roberts, R. C. (1979). *Competency-based staff training for retardation services personnel: A train-the-trainer requirement*. Paper presented at the meeting of the Florida Educational Research Association, Daytona Beach, Florida, January 1979, and of the American Educational Research Association, April 1979.

Gropper, G. L. (1973, May). *Development of course content and instructional materials/aids for the training of educational research, development, diffusion, and evaluation personnel*. Supplementary Final Report. (ERIC Document Reproduction Service No. ED 085 349).

———. (1977, December). On gaining acceptance for instructional design in a university setting. *Educational Technology*, pp. 7-12.

Hayman, J. L., Jr. (1974, May). The systems approach and education. *The Educational Forum*, pp. 491-501.

Houle, C. O. (1972). *The design of education*. San Francisco: Jossey-Bass.

Joyce, B., & Weil, M. (1972). *Models of teaching.* Englewood Cliffs, NJ: Prentice-Hall.

Kaplan, A. (1964). *The conduct of inquiry.* New York: Harper & Row.

Kaufman, R. A. (1972). *Educational system planning.* Englewood Cliffs, NJ: Prentice-Hall.

Kelly, R. E. (1976, March). *A systems approach to teaching.* Paper presented at the meeting of the Association for Educational Communications and Technology, Annual Conference, Anaheim, California. (ERIC Document Reproduction Service No. ED 124 184).

LaGow, R. L. (1977, April). *The utilization of grounded theory to identify instructional development elements in adult education programs.* Paper presented at the meeting of the Adult Education Research Conference, Minneapolis. (ERIC Document Reproduction Service No. ED 145 074).

Laugen, R. (1979, February 7). Personal communication.

Ledford, B. R. (1976). A panacea? *International Journal of Instructional Media, 4*(1), 53-56.

Lee, B. N. (1975). Instructional system development (ISD)—an Air Force way of life. *Journal of Educational Technology Systems, 4*(1), 33-41.

Logan, R. (1976, August). *Instructional systems development and learning strategies.* Paper presented at the meeting of the Midwestern Psychological Association, Detroit.

Lowe, A. J., & Schwen, T. M. (1975, June). The documentation of instructional development. *Educational Technology,* pp. 42-47.

Mager, R. F., & Pipe, P. (1974). *Criterion-referenced instruction: Analysis, design, and implementation.* Los Altos Hills, CA: Mager.

Maher, C. A. (1978, December). A system approach for delivering supplemental instruction to handicapped children. *Educational Technology,* pp. 25-29.

Merrill, M. D. (1973). Content and instructional analysis for cognitive transfer tasks. *AV Communication Review, 21*(1), 109-125.

Merrill, M. D., & Boutwell, R. C. (1973). Instructional development: Methodology and research. In F. N. Kerlinger (Ed.), *Review of research in education* (Vol. 1), Itasca, IL: Peacock.

Molnar, A. R. (1971). *The future of educational technology research and development.* Washington, DC: National Science Foundation. (ERIC Document Reproduction Service No. ED 054 642).

Pennington, F., & Green, J. (1976). Comparative analysis of program development processes in six professions. *Adult Education, 27*(1).

Penta, F. B. (1973, July). A systems model for the development of instructional materials. *Educational Technology,* pp. 12-15.

Piaget, J. (1954). *The construction of reality in the child.* New York: Basic Books.

Pratt, D. (1978, March). *Cybernetic principles in the design of instruction.* Paper presented at the Annual Meeting of the American Educational Research Association, Toronto. (ERIC Document Reproduction Service No. ED 154 799).

Pye, D. (1964). *The nature of design.* New York: Van Nostrand Reinhold.

Roberts, R. C. (1978). *The construction and field-testing of a program planning model for non-formal adult education in human service agencies.* Unpublished doctoral dissertation, Florida State University.

Scanland, W. (1974, April). *The instructional systems development function—How to get it done.* Paper presented at the National Society for Performance and Instruction Annual Conference, Miami, Florida. (ERIC Document Reproduction Service No. ED 095 839).

Sherman, T. M. (1978, September). Teaching educators to use the systems approach: An instructional analysis. *Educational Technology*, pp. 40-47.

Shoemaker, B. R., & Parks, D. L. (Eds.). (1976, June). *An instructional system design for vocational education.* Columbus: Division of Vocational Education, Instructional Materials Laboratory, The Ohio State University. (ERIC Document Reproduction Service No. ED 143 888).

Simon, H. A. (1969). *Sciences of the artificial.* Cambridge, MA: MIT Press.

Skinner, B. F. (1954). The science of learning and the art of teaching. *Harvard Educational Review, 24*(232), 86-97.

Smith, N. L., & Murray, S. L. (1975, March). The status of research on models of product development and evaluation. *Educational Technology*, pp. 13-17.

Teague, W., & Faulkner, T. L. (1978). *Developing performance objectives and criterion-referenced measures for performance-based instruction in vocational education.* Montgomery, AL: Division of Vocational Education, Alabama State Department of Education. (ERIC Document Reproduction Service No. ED 154 799).

Tennyson, R. D., & Boutwell, R. C. (1971). A quality control design for validating hierarchical sequencing of programmed instruction. *NSPI Journal, 4*, 5-10.

Tosti, D. T., & Ball, J. R. (1969). A behavioral approach to instructional design and media selection. *AV Communication Review, 17*, 5-25.

Tuckman, B. W. (1969, October). The student-centered curriculum: A concept in curriculum innovation. *Educational Technology*, pp. 26-29.

Tuckman, B., and Edwards, K. (1973). *A systems model for instructional design and management. An introduction to the systems approach.* Englewood Cliffs, NJ: Educational Technology Publications.

U.S. Army Combat Arms Training Board. (1975). *Interservice procedures for instructional systems development.* Ft. Benning, GA: Author.

Vance, B. (1976, May). *Applying an instructional psychology model to analysis of the reading task.* Paper presented at the Annual Meeting of the International Reading Association, Anaheim, California. (ERIC Document Reproduction Service No. ED 126 426).

von Bertalanffy, L. (1968). *General system theory: Foundations, development, applications.* New York: George Braziller.

Waldron, J. S. (1973). *Instructional development unit: A guide to organizing an instructional development unit in health science educational institutions.* Atlanta: Office of Audiovisual Educational Development, Bureau of Health Manpower Education and the National Medical Audiovisual Center, National Library of Medicine. (ERIC Document Reproduction Service No. ED 125 625).

Wallen, C. J. (1973, July). SATE: A systems approach to developing instructional programs in teacher education. *Educational Technology*, pp. 27-31.

Waters, B. K., Edwards, B. J., & Smith, B. A. (1978, March). Multimedia cognitive pretraining of Air Force pilots. *Educational Technology*, pp. 50-57.

14

Needs Assessment

Allison Rossett

College of Education, San Diego State University
San Diego, California

INTRODUCTION

Everyone acknowledges the importance of studying a situation before launching solutions to it. Everyone applauds the value of *analysis prior to action*. In the world of training and development, whether in a school district, a corporation, a government, or a social service agency, that initial pursuit of information about the situation is often called *needs assessment*. But what is needs assessment? What activities, concerns, or purposes? How can an instructional technologist think about needs assessment in order to plan and execute a useful one?

The literature is full of case studies for problems at banks, schools, recreation parks, and computer companies. Case studies and exhortations are augmented by gestalt suggestions about needs assessment:

1. Contact relevant managers and first line supervisors,

2. Inform them that you will be assessing lathe operators,

3. Write needs assessment instrument,

4. Obtain approvals from training director and managers,

5. Administer assessment,

6. Analyze data,

7. Recommend action based on results.

There is nothing wrong with the conclusions of this general and abbreviated example of the literature. The problem is with what is left unsaid. Little assistance is provided for the instructional technologist. Consider the positions of the following colleagues:

- Walt is an instructional technologist for one of America's largest insurance agencies. His corporation decides that sales agents need to use portable personal computers in their interactions with clients. The company is about to make this enormous investment in computers, and they wisely involve Walt and the others in the training group. In fact, the boss, having just attended an excellent training seminar, tells Walt she expects him to do a needs assessment before he launches any training programs.

- Bart is the manager of training for a company that sells fast food and fast food stores as franchises. He is informed that the complaints about quality of french fries have doubled in the past quarter. Upper management prides itself on the quality of these fries and fears the effect of lesser fries on corporate profits. They turn the problem over to Bart and his people, stressing the urgency of the situation. There is no time for study, they tell him, only solutions.

- Like clockwork, every year or so, the manager of staff development for the school district receives a mandate: Provide training for staff at all levels in improved race/ human relations. As Mindy sits there, she thinks back to last year, when she was asked to do exactly the same thing. Whatever shall she do?

Most instructional technology professionals agree that it is important to conduct needs assessments. But how? Where does needs assessment fit into everything else that needs to be done? Why do we do these assessments? What questions are asked? What sources are used? What tools do we use? These are the questions this chapter addresses.

THE PLACE FOR
NEEDS ASSESSMENT

Needs assessments are done when the instructional technologist is trying to respond to a request for assistance. Needs assessments gather information to assist professionals in making data-driven and responsive recommendations about how to solve the problem or introduce the new technology. While needs assessment may lead to the development of instruction, it does not always do so. The important role that needs assessment plays is to give us information, at the beginning of the effort, about what is needed to improve performance.

Figure 14.1 presents a simplified version of where assessment (analysis) fits into a systematic approach to the development of instructional interventions. Notice that needs assessment drives the system, shaping design, development, implementation, and evaluation decisions. In this figure, analysis is taking on a broad range of functions that include continuous examination of the effort in light of the assessed needs.

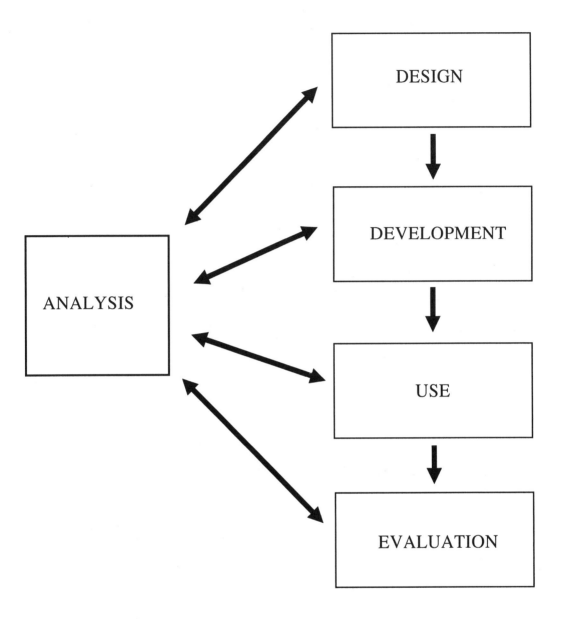

Fig. 14.1. Instructional systems development.

WHY WE DO NEEDS ASSESSMENT

There are five purposes for needs assessment. When we conduct needs assessments, we are seeking detailed information about the following factors.

Optimal Performance

What is it that the exemplary performer knows and does that exemplifies success? How should an insurance salesperson use a computer in home sales? What is it that a fourth grader must know about California history? What is involved in producing a delicious and crisp french fry? Instructional technologists turn to experts, documentation, standards, practices, texts, tests, and specifications for information about optimals.

Actual Performance

What are they doing to those french fries that makes them limp? Why are the supposedly repaired disk drives bouncing back from the field like souped up baseballs? What do the children already know about history or about California? Why does an upper level manager think there is a need for race/human relations training? What are employees doing or failing to do that prompts that interest? Records of employee performance, observations, and employee self-reports provide information about actuals.

Feelings

Instructional technologists want to know how learners or job incumbents feel about:

- The topic (e.g., the computer as a sales tool? race/human relations?),

- Training about the topic (e.g., class on safe manufacturing? modules on CA history?),

- The topic as a priority (e.g., product training for sales people or a course on the computer as a sales tool?), and

- Confidence surrounding the topic (e.g., do employees feel that they are capable of assembling more frangs? of operating a computer in the sale of insurance? of being more sensitive to ethnic and racial diversity?).

Cause(s)

Gilbert (1978), Mager & Pipe (1970), and Harless (1975) focused our attention on the *cause(s) of performance problems.* Why aren't managers turning in performance appraisals? Why are the ones they turn in incorrectly completed? Why are the french fries limp and the sales down? While my esteemed colleagues highlight *three* causes of performance problems, I find it useful to incorporate the more cognitively oriented work of Bandura (1977) and Killer (1979, 1983) into a system that recognizes *four* kinds of causes:

1. *They lack the skill or knowledge.* Even if they wanted to, they just couldn't do it. They lack the knowledge essential to writing behavioral statements on performance appraisals or securing data in the computer.

2. *The environment is in the way.* They don't have the tools, forms, or work space necessary to perform. The classic example is the computer that "keeps going down" or the purchase of a new and inferior lard for french fry production.

3. *There are no, few, or improper incentives.* What are the consequences of doing the job badly or not doing it at all? Perhaps the production of crisp fries has been ignored in the past, or the failure to respond to customer needs likewise has been ignored? Do star performers get loaded down with additional and nasty work assignments?

4. *The employees are unmotivated.* Traditionally we sought employee motivation in the external circumstances, the consequences, surrounding employees. But what about the *internal* state of the individuals involved? What is going on inside sales staff as they confront that new computer? Two factors contribute to motivation:

   a. value: how much and whether the topic (e.g., producing crisp fries, computerized insurance sales) is valued; and

   b. confidence: the amount of confidence the employee has that he or she can master the skills or knowledge (e.g., Am I the kind of person who is going to be able to learn how to use this computer? Will I be able to teach a class with children with 11 different countries of origin and 9 different languages and dialects?)

The relationship between value, confidence, and motivation works like this:

$$Value \times Confidence = Motivation$$

Which would you rather teach: a group of students who are required to take a class or a group of students who have volunteered? Of course, nearly all instructors or designers of instruction prefer volunteer students. They are *motivated*. What that means is that they attach high value to the content and believe they can grasp it, given good instruction. If you want to increase student motivation, build value and/or confidence.

Let us examine the *cause* of a performance problem. A restaurant has a problem with unpalatable coffee. This problem could have a variety of causes. We start our investigation with a quick tour of the kitchen. As we examine the coffee pot, we determine that the coffee filter device is broken. In this case the problem is environmental, and the solution is a new coffee filter device. This is not a problem that can be solved through training. Instead, fix the filter.

If the environment was all in order, we might next examine the incentives offered for making good coffee. Here we find that those who repeatedly make unpalatable coffee are relieved of that onerous duty, while the person who does it well is expected to do it repeatedly. The solution in this case is to change the incentive, and provide some sort of reward for making good coffee or a punishment for making bad coffee. This is not a problem that can be solved through training. Change the policy.

If the environment and the incentives are adequate, examine motivation. How do the waitresses feel about making good coffee? If they don't value making good coffee, then training or information is necessary to inform them of the value of coffee-making skills. Do they believe they are capable of making good coffee, that they have the capacity? If they aren't confident that they can handle it, you may have to build their confidence through training that provides successful models and provides early experiences with success.

If the environment, incentives, and motivation are operating properly, then the problem may be a skill or knowledge deficiency. Perhaps the waitresses do not know how to disassemble and clean the coffee pot, or perhaps they do not know the advantages and disadvantages of different types of cleansers. If this is the case, training is necessary.

Solutions

The quest for cause(s) of performance problems is urgent because recommendations about solutions must be based on the identified cause or causes. Figure 14.2 expresses the relationship between causes and solutions. Note the *range of solutions* that instructional technologists must be willing to consider and recommend.

CAUSES ⟶ SOLUTIONS

I.   Lack Skill/Knowledge

Training
Job aids
Selection

II.   Flawed Environment

Improved tools
Improved forms
Workplace and workstation re-design
Job re-design

III.   Improper Incentives

Improved policies
Better supervision
Improved incentives

IV.   Unmotivated Employees

Training
Information
Coaching
Better supervision

Fig. 14.2. Causes and solutions.

The impact of the mildly heretical splitting of incentive and motivation can be seen in the figure. Training can be extended to enhance motivation as well as to increase skills and knowledge. Problems caused by improper environments and incentives must be reported to management so that jobs can be redesigned and incentive programs put in place. For additional discussion of this topic and the general expansion of the role of the instructional technologist, see Rossett (1987, 1989).

HOW WE CONDUCT
NEEDS ASSESSMENT

Step One: Determine Purposes Based on Initiators

There are three kinds of initiating situations, each of which is represented by Walt, Bart, and Mindy in the following examples.

Performance Problems

These situations are handled neatly in the work of Harless (1975) and Mager & Pipe (1970). "They oughta know how. We taught them. They used to do it. What is going on? Why are they having this problem?"

Bart is engaged in solving a performance problem. Therefore, he must seek the *cause*(s) of the deteriorating french fries. He has a clear picture of optimals. That was done when the french fries were launched years ago, and it has been updated to match the new technologies for fry production. He also has a reasonably good grasp of the actuals through detailed reports by managers, customer complaints, and sales figures. His initial needs assessment narrows the problem to sogginess and limpness caused by improper fry timing in steps 7 and 8 in the cooking procedure. Possessing a clear picture of the gap between *optimals* and *actuals*, he now has to find out why there are inadequacies in the execution of these steps.

New Stuff

This is the prevailing situation in many corporations today, where new technologies, systems, and approaches are being added at a rapid rate. Most customer training falls in this category. So do the efforts to introduce employees to new technologies, software, and policies.

Walt is introducing a new system and must concentrate on the search for *optimals* and *feelings*. If computers (mainframes, minis, or other micros) are already in place, then he will also need to look at actual skills and knowledge. Cause is not an issue. There are four possible causes of any performance problem (absent skills or knowledge, messed up environment, improper incentives, poor motivation). If the system is new to the employees, we can presume the cause of a failure to operate it is that they don't know how.

Mandates

Examples of mandates are the annual telephone, EEO, safety, and leadership training programs. The reason for offering this training is sometimes political, sometimes a personal priority, and sometimes a case of a real and pressing need. Often, the training occurs because it always has or because it is mandated by an authority. There might be specific performance problems; then again, there might not be. There might be new content; then again, there might not be.

Mindy is facing two challenges: satisfying a murky mandate and finding the details of the problems being confronted in the area of race and human relations. This project is the personal priority of a new vice president, someone who is intensely concerned about the topic and wants a course up and running immediately. The judge is also watching. What is Mindy to do?

Mindy may either handle her project as *new stuff* or as a *performance problem*. If she decides to conduct her needs assessment as if it were new information or approaches, she will seek out the details of *optimal* race/human relations activity and the *feelings* surrounding such efforts. If (as I would recommend) she identifies particular gaps in performance, then she will seek the *cause* of those detailed problems. Treating this as a performance problem is the more politically risky approach; it is also the one that will lead to a lean and more targeted intervention. Figure 14.3 presents the relationship between the three kinds of initiators and the needs assessment purposes.

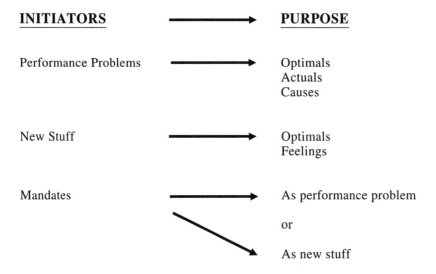

Fig. 14.3. Initiators and purposes.

Step Two: Identify Sources

Now that you have identified the kind of initiator and the kind of purposes, it is time to determine who has the information that you need. Where is it located? What are the constraints on getting the data? Who needs to know that you are involved with this innovation, problem or priority setting? Mindy's sources are different from Bart's. Remember that pre-training activity has the potential for extending the training function into every aspect of the corporation. What is the impression that the effort will make? How do you reconcile competing interests and priorities? How do you market your department and conduct needs assessment simultaneously?

What sources would Walt tap during his needs assessment? He should follow these steps:

1. Walt is confronting a situation in which a new technology is being introduced. Therefore, he will be seeking information on optimals and feelings. Because he suspects there is some expertise in computers in the sales force, he will attempt to determine actual/current skill levels as well.

2. Sources for optimals are vendor subject matter experts, sales agents and managers from the region in the company that was used as a test site for PC's, sales managers, and the upper level managers who launched this project. Sources for feelings are sales agents, sales managers, and families (customers). The source for actuals is a study that was done in 1988 on computer literacy in the company.

Step Three: Select Tools

Different purposes and sources require different tools. The factor that separates effective from ineffective tool use is planning. Do you know why you are contacting the source? Is your purpose clear? Have you established an agenda or an interview schedule to structure your time? Following are the options for tools.

Interviewing

The interview is the most prevalent needs assessment tool. It is appropriate for gathering data related to all purposes. One issue you will confront is whether to conduct the needs assessment in person or on the telephone.

It would be nice if I could provide a flowchart of variables that tell whether to use the telephone or meet in person. As I tried to work one out, I kept coming up with *it depends....* Figure 14.4, page 192, lists factors to take into account when deciding whether to meet in person or on the telephone.

Observing Employee Performance

While observation is a highly touted front end tool, it is not used that often. Why? I speculate that the main reason for its diminished popularity is the belief that observers alter employee performance. Thus, observation is a less effective tool for gathering information about *actuals*, unless you are working incognito. Observation is, however, a very effective tool for seeking *optimals*. If employees know that you are observing, then their efforts will more closely approximate *optimal* performance.

Another reason that observation has fallen out of favor is that we are much more interested in cognitive processes. Finally, after decades of a behavioral orientation to education and training, professionals are now interested in what it is that an employee thinks about and knows as the work is being done. Interviews, not observations, get at that kind of information.

Observations, however, are a very useful tool for finding out what is really happening at work. It is useful to use two levels of observation. The first seeks a broad *gestalt*. In general, what goes on? What are the major components of the job? What are the most frequently recurring challenges? In what order do things usually happen? What kind of information is shared? What kinds of references or tools are relied upon?

In the second level of observation, the instructional technologist is seeking details. What separates effective performance from ineffective performance? What kinds of responses close the sale? What are all the ways that insurance agents allay the concerns of clients about the computer? Which ways work best? How are bodies positioned, work areas arranged? Is there anything that supervisors are doing that appears to be influencing the quality of performance?

If You Want	Use
to inform someone about the project	telephone
to gather in-depth information	meeting
to discuss difficult, complex, or controversial subject matter	meeting
to check out a point or two	telephone
to enlist support from a colleague	meeting
to look at content that must be illustrated	meeting
to save money	telephone
to form a working relationship	meeting
to periodically nurture a working relationship	telephone
to get an "initial take" on something	telephone
to get information from many people	telephone
to get information from a few key individuals	meeting

Fig. 14.4. Variables affecting interviewing method.

Examining Records and Outcomes

This tool focuses on the outcomes of employee performance. Training professionals seek printouts, records, accident reports, and sales figures to capture the details of what employees are doing from the results of their actions. We can use examination to generate the details of *optimal* and *actual performance.*

The examination of extant data is a wonderful needs assessment tool because it is inexpensive. This tool takes the instructional technologist across the organization in search of the natural outcomes of effective and ineffective performance. It involves asking colleagues for the data that automatically flow from their work. The only challenge is to convince colleagues that they ought to release that information to you.

If you want to make a convincing argument, present your request in light of the needs assessment purpose it will fulfill. For example, "Bank tellers say they already know about the Funny Money Account and that they don't need training. Sales and marketing wants us to bring them in again and repeat the seminar. I want to take a look at the results of the work of the secret shoppers that your group did last month. Did tellers know the features? Could they explain the benefits? Could they make market comparisons? Did they fill out the proper forms? If we can look at your records, then we'll know whether or not they possess those skills and will be able to do something about it." This instructional technologist is seeking *actuals* and *cause* in regard to a performance problem.

Facilitating Groups

One way of getting and disseminating information during a needs assessment is through group meetings. Groups are commonly used to assemble an organization-wide accord on *optimals*. Walt, for example, must be certain that his course reflects a broad vision of optimal use of the computer in insurance sales. If it doesn't, his training might be avoided by segments of the company. Groups may also be used to seek information on all four other purposes, although the public nature of the forum may stifle honest discussion of actual performance, feelings, and causes.

The key to assuring a successful needs assessment meeting is to develop an agenda that includes:

- participants and roles;

- purposes of the meeting;

- process rules which have been or need to be established; and

- time, place, and length of the proceedings.

Discussion of the agenda with the group must focus on the crucial difference between the content or purposes of the meeting and the processes that will be used to achieve those purposes. Everyone at the meeting must be able to distinguish between why they are there and how they are going to operate.

Surveying Through Questionnaires

The survey is a usually anonymous device for soliciting opinions from large numbers of respondents. If you want the opinions of many, and/or statistical significance, and/or to impress the company with the democracy of the training group, surveys are an excellent tool. Surveys, because of the potential for anonymity, are particularly effective for gathering information on *cause, feelings*, and *solutions*. Hesitation in providing great detail in responses makes them less useful for gathering information on optimals and actuals.

A typology solves the problem of what to ask (Rossett, 1982, 1987). When an instructional technologist pounds a stack of survey returns and says, "I still don't know ..." or "I didn't get what I needed," or "Now what do I do with all this?" he probably is suffering from having asked the wrong questions. Problems of content can be addressed through the item typology, since the item typology is based on the reasons for this stage of assessment.

Type 1 items ask what need.

Type 2 items ask for details of the need.

Type 3 items provide proof.

Type 4 items ask for feelings and motivation.

Type 5 items ask for cause(s) of the problem.

Type 6 items ask about the respondent.

The two basic question types are structured items and open-ended items. Structured choice items are far better in surveys than are open questions. A forced choice item will say "which" or "what one of the following" or "rank this list" or "rate these according to...." You provide respondents with a fixed set of options to which they respond in a predetermined fashion. For numerous examples of each of the item and format types, see Rossett (1987). Below is an example of a type 5 question in a forced choice format:

Which of these has caused problems when you make pizza? Check *all* those that have been a problem. Place an asterisk (*) next to the one that you consider the biggest obstacle to the preparation of good pizzas.

    ____ maintaining the equipment

    ____ temperature control

    ____ judging texture

    ____ doing more than 12 pies at a time

    ____ cleaning the sensors

    ____ cleaning surfaces

    ____ interpreting the controls

Step Four: Conduct the Needs Assessment in Stages

Needs assessment shouldn't be a single act. One big survey will *not* get the job done. It is far wiser to use brief stages of assessment in which the trainer or designer makes several short forays in search of information related to purposes. What you learn in the first stage then enlightens your activities in later stages. The stages might look like this for Bart's staff as they contend with the soggy and limp fries:

Stage 1: Meet with randomly selected store managers to ask why there is a recent problem with the fries.

Stage 2: Meet with subject matter expert (nutritionist) to seek his opinion on the cause(s) of the problem. Relate what was learned in the meeting with the managers.

Stage 3: Observe the steps (6 and 7) in the cooking cycle, identified as the culprits. Randomly select cooks and ask them to do it. What do they think is the cause of the problem?

Stage 4: Meet with training management and the person who initiated the request for training to see if your findings are congruent with their hunches.

Step Five: Use Findings for Decision Making

The instructional technologist has completed needs assessment when the result is a clear picture of where different sources stand on the five purposes and how these interests relate to each other. Now, in addition to the benefits of having involved stakeholders in the process, instructional technologists are able to make decisions, based on facts, about:

- Whether or not training is appropriate;

- What kind of training is favored, for whom, and by whom;

- What other supportive interventions (like job aids, training for supervisors, expert systems, workstation redesign, or incentives) will solve the problem, introduce the new system, or respond to the mandate;

- Strategies for involving other related professionals in the effort;

- The content of courses, if training is judged appropriate; and

- How training and other interventions will be received by trainees, supervisors, customers, and others.

CONCLUSION

The role of needs assessment is to point the instructional technologist and the project in the right direction. What do you do first, next, next, next? How do you know when you know enough to move forward into the design and development of solutions? When the five purposes of needs assessment guide action, answers to these questions are obvious. First, determine the type of initiating situation. Then determine the appropriate purposes and identify the sources who can shed light on those purposes. Then plan stages and tools to gather information. Continuously report findings to management, keeping careful records of the data in light of the purposes of the needs assessment.

Deciding whether to observe, interview, or survey isn't the hard part. The challenge is to determine sources, plan stages of assessment, and frame questions that will enable a professional to move crisply from a general problem with limp french fries to a series of actions and recommendations that will guarantee yummy ones. Needs assessment is an essential ingredient in any instructional technology recipe.

REFERENCES

Bandura, A. (1977). Self-efficacy: Toward a unifying theory of behavior change. *Psychological Review, 84*, 191-215.

Carlisle, K. (1986). *Analyzing jobs and tasks*. Englewood Cliffs, NJ: Educational Technology Publications.

Dick, W., & Carey, L. (1985). *The systematic design of instruction* (2nd ed.). Glenview, IL: Scott, Foresman.

Gilbert, T. F. (1978). *Human competence: Engineering worthy performance*. New York: McGraw-Hill.

Harless, J. (1975). *An ounce of analysis is worth a pound of objectives*. Newnan, GA: Harless Performance Guild.

Keller, J. (1979). Motivation and instructional design: A theoretical perspective. *Journal of Instructional Development, 2*(4), 26-34.

———. (1983). Motivational design of instruction. In C. M. Reigeluth (Ed.), *Instructional-design theories and models*. Hillsdale, NJ: Lawrence Erlbaum.

Landa, L. (1974). *Algorithmization in learning and instruction*. Englewood Cliffs, NJ: Educational Technology Publications.

Mager, R. F. (1972). *Goal analysis*. Belmont, CA: Fearon Press.

Mager, R. F., & Pipe, P. (1970). *Analyzing performance problems, or you really oughta wanna*. Belmont, CA: Fearon Press.

Rossett, A. (1982). A typology for generating needs assessments. *Journal of Instructional Development, 6*(1), 28-33.

———. (1987). *Training needs assessment.* Englewood Cliffs, NJ: Educational Technology Publications.

———. (1989, May). Assess for success. *Training and Development, 43*(5), 55-59.

Zemke, R., & Kramlinger, T. (1982). *Figuring things out: A trainer's guide to needs and task analysis.* Reading, MA: Addison-Wesley.

15

Analysis of Task Analysis Procedures

David H. Jonassen
College of Education, Pennsylvania State University
University Park, Pennsylvania

and

Wallace H. Hannum
University of North Carolina at Chapel Hill
Chapel Hill, North Carolina

INTRODUCTION

This article is predicated on three assumptions:

1. Task analysis, regardless of how it is defined, is an integral part, probably the most integral part, of the instructional development process. All instructional development models to date include some task analysis procedures (Andrews & Goodson, 1980). Most developers indicate that a poorly executed task analysis will jeopardize the entire development process.

2. Task analysis may be the most ambiguous process in the development process. Task analysis represents one or more steps in the instructional development process, which purports to be a science; however, it contains uncertain knowledge and multiple interpretations. We contend that the ambiguity results from the diversity of procedures and definitions of the process. Definitions of task analysis range from the "breakdown of performance into detailed levels of specificity" to "front-end Analysis, description of mastery performance and criteria, breakdown of job tasks into steps, and the consideration of the potential worth of solving performance problems" (Harless, 1980, p. 7). This chapter evolved from the confusion experienced by an instructional design class trying to conceptualize the task analysis process. Trying to reconcile the myriad task analysis procedures performed at different levels in different situations can be exasperating. The option, too often practiced, is to use a single procedure that makes sense to the developer and apply it uniformly, thus overgeneralizing it to every instructional situation. Experienced instructional developers may

know intuitively which procedures to apply in various settings. However, the neo-phyte's semantic network of task analysis constructs is not sufficiently developed to allow him to know "intuitively" when to apply different task analysis "scripts" (i.e., procedures). So clarification should help the beginning developer.

3. Recent reviews of task analysis (Foshay, 1983; Kennedy, Esquire, & Novak, 1983) have been useful in identifying the various task analysis procedures and their functions. However, simply knowing what tools are available will not rectify the confusion encountered by inexperienced developers. The confusion results from not knowing which task analysis procedures to use in various situations. Foshay (1983) made some useful recommendations about when to apply which model, but he reviewed only three out of a long list of potential task analysis procedures. What design students need is guidance on when and where to apply the various task analysis procedures.

This article is dedicated to that purpose. We do not intend to review each procedure comprehensively. Nor can we claim a foolproof algorithm for recommending which procedures to apply in all circumstances. Task analysis remains too inexact a science to accomplish that goal. In order to make suggestions about when to apply the various task analysis procedures, we first must clarify what functions are integral to the process. Then, we will briefly discuss some situational variables that affect the task analysis process. From those variables, we shall derive a quasi-algorithm for suggesting alternative task analysis procedures that may be used to accomplish each task analysis function. Those procedures are annotated in the Appendix. Our purpose is to provide a framework for selecting and understanding task analysis procedures and applying them to the task analysis process.

TASK ANALYSIS FUNCTIONS

Much of the confusion about task analysis that frustrates inexperienced instructional developers results from a lack of agreement about what the process of task analysis involves. What exactly do designers do when they conduct a task analysis? That varies greatly among developers.

In some contexts, task analysis is limited to developing an inventory of steps routinely performed on a job. In others, task analysis is functionally synonymous with front-end analysis, including all instructional development procedures prior to determining instructional strategies. According to Romiszowski (1981), task analysis procedures pervade the four levels of instructional design. At the course level (Level 1), overall objectives are defined. At the lesson level (Level 2), objectives are refined and sequenced, and entry level requirements are specified. At the instructional event level (Level 3), the detailed behaviors are classified. At the learning step level (Level 4), task statements are elaborated on, as individual steps in the task are identified. Each step of this top-down, macro-to-micro instructional design process is heavily dependent on task analysis.

Kennedy, Esquire, and Novak (1983) recently identified the different components of task analysis as occurring in two separate phases. The task description phase consists of identifying, refining and ordering tasks. According to their survey, the instructional phase consists of the processes of: (1) specifying goals, needs, and objectives; (b) developing analysis tools (such as taxonomies and learning hierarchies); and finally (c) identifying outcome specifications (such as product descriptions and training considerations). They found considerable disparity among instructional development models in terms of the components each included as part of the task analysis process. One model included two of the ten, while another included only eight. This disparity creates even more confusion for instructional developers and particularly for students. Just what does the task analysis process involve?

We contend that the task analysis process consists of five distinct functions: (a) Inventorying tasks, (b) Describing tasks, (c) Selecting tasks, (d) Sequencing tasks and task components, and (e) Analyzing tasks and content level. These are functional descriptions of what is included in the task analysis process. The task analysis process, as performed in different settings, may involve some or all of these functions. The combination of functions that are performed depends upon situational design variables to be discussed later. Each function may be accomplished by using different procedures (see Appendix). Yet each different procedure imposes constraints on that function. So care must be exercised in selecting a procedure for accomplishing each of the task analysis functions. The purpose of this article is to provide some selection criteria to assist the beginning developer in deciding which procedures can be used to accomplish each of the task analysis functions. Deciding which functions must be accomplished depends upon the nature of the task, the instructional situation, the outcomes required, and the experience of the developer.

Inventorying Tasks

Task inventory is the process of identifying the relevant tasks that may be considered for further instructional development. This inventory may result from a variety of processes, such as job analysis, concept hierarchy analysis, and needs assessment procedures. How we arrive at the list of topics or tasks to be included in our system depends on the instructional context, the socio-cultural context, the learners being instructed, the management context, and the goal orientation of the educational or training system.

Describing Tasks

Task description is the process of elaborating the tasks, goals, or objectives identified in the inventory. Task descriptions may include listing (a) the tasks included in performing a job, (b) the steps in performing a task, or (c) enabling objectives for a terminal objective. The procedures for performing the task description function depend upon the nature of the information provided in the inventory. Task description always involves an elaboration of the tasks/goals stated in the inventory to a greater degree of specificity or detail. The emphasis here is thoroughness—ensuring that important instructional components are not excluded.

Selecting Tasks

Some instructional development models, especially those in the military, include a separate procedure for selecting from the task inventory those tasks for which training *should* be provided. Since it is impossible to train every person on every task to a level of proficiency that might be required by the job, developers often must select certain tasks for training. According to Tracey, Flynn, and Legere (1970), tasks that are feasible and appropriate for on-the-job, school, and follow-up training should be selected. This selection process may also result from a consideration of various system constraints, such as available time and resources (Davis, Alexander, & Yelon, 1974). In order to select tasks for training, developers need to rank or assign priorities to their training objectives. Task selection is also performed to avoid instructing or training students on material they already know. Thus, those tasks that have already been acquired are eliminated from the list of training objectives. While a task description elaborates the task into its component parts, task selection asks which of these tasks or components are entry level or prerequisite and which tasks are feasible to train. The result of this operation is the final list of training objectives. In many design models, selection is an implicit function, not one that is performed systematically.

Sequencing Tasks and Task Components

The task sequence is often implied by the nature of the tasks in the inventory or the components in the task description. However, the task sequence is more than simply a description of the sequence in which the task is performed. It indicates the sequence in which the instruction occurs. The sequence for performing the task implies an appropriate instructional sequence. For example, the training of employees to perform certain jobs implies a temporal sequence of tasks that models the job. This may not always be the most efficient sequence. Instructional sequencing may also be determined by the content/task analysis process or by the design model being used. For instance, elaboration theory (Reigeluth & Stein, 1983) prescribes a specific top-down, general-to-specific conceptual sequence for presenting material, where learning hierarchy analysis suggests a bottom-up, simple-to-complex sequence. According to taxonomies of learning, different content and different tasks suggest different sequences of instruction. So, sequencing varies according to the theory or model on which it is based.

Analyzing Task and Content Levels

Analyzing task and content levels is the function in the task analysis process in which the mental or behavioral performance required to acquire the task or knowledge is described. That is, designers describe the type of mental behavior, physical performance, or affective response required by the task. This usually takes the form of classifying the task statement according to various learning taxonomies.

Table 15.1 compares a number of these taxonomies, which describe learning in terms of hierarchies of content. Beginning with the lowest level or most fundamental forms of behavior (reflexes), they describe increasingly more complex mental responses or behavior (evaluation, problem solving, or strategies). The purpose of classifying tasks varies with different models. Normally, however, taxonomic classification of objectives and test items ensures consistency between the goals, the test items, and the instructional procedures. Exact instructional procedures for sequences are implied by some models and hierarchies, such as the component display theory (Merrill, 1983).

Objectives

Another component of the task analysis process that could arguably be included in the list of functions is the instructional or behavioral objectives. They are the most common component of all instructional development models (Andrews & Goodson, 1980). However, objectives are not a *process*. Rather, objectives are a *product*, resulting from task analysis or some other process. Objectives represent specific statements of the tasks being analyzed. Sometimes, objectives are an input to the task analysis process. That is, objectives are often determined by some process (needs assessment, curriculum guide, fiat) prior to the instructional developer being consulted. So the developer begins by inventorying the tasks limited by the objectives. More commonly, however, objectives and enabling objectives are the product of the task analysis process. They are an essential tool of all of the task analysis functions—inventory, description, selection, sequencing, and analysis—but do not constitute a separate function in the process. While they are essential to the process, for our purposes, they are not part of it.

Table 15.1.
Comparison of Taxonomies of Learning

Bloom, 1956	Gagne, 1966, 1977	Leith, 1970	Merrill, 1983*	Mager & Breach, 1967
		Stimulus discrimination		
Knowledge	Information	Response learning	Facts	Memorization
		Response integration		
			Procedures	Procedural
Comprehension	Concrete concepts	Learning set formation		Comprehension
	Defined concepts	Concept learning	Concepts	
Application			Rules	
Analysis	Principles		Principles	
		Hypothetico-deductive inference		
		Learning schemata		
Synthesis	Problem solving			
	Cognitive strategies			
Evaluation				
Affective domain	Attitudes			Attitude development
Psychomotor domain	Motor skills			

*At task level: remember, use, and find.

Needs Assessment

The distinction between task analysis and needs assessment is especially ambiguous, since they are complementary, contributory, and often overlapping processes. Needs assessment, like task analysis, is a process. It is a process that entails three or more functions depending upon definition. It is a formal process for determining the present capability of prospective learners, the desired outcomes, and the discrepancies between the two (Kaufman, 1972). It also frequently entails the ranking of those discrepancies in order of priority. In many respects, needs assessment mirrors task analysis. The sequence is often similar, and there is a variety of procedures available for performing needs assessment functions, some of which are often used to conduct task analysis functions. Yet, when it is performed, needs assessment nearly always precedes task analysis, so that it is usually contributory to task analysis. Needs assessment frequently comprises the task inventory and, with less frequency, the task selection functions of the task analysis process. Therefore, they overlap and complement each other. However, task analysis is a larger process that does not always depend on needs assessment.

Functions Included in the Task Analysis Process

Task analysis, as performed in various instructional development models, may include some or all of the previously described functions. The task analysis process varies, so the procedures used during the task analysis process may include only one or all of these functions. However, all task analysis procedures performed using various design models can be described by one or more of these functions. That is, these functions, as represented by most task analysis procedures, are usually distinct enough to be identified. Some procedures may perform two or more functions simultaneously. There is no universal temporal sequence in which these phases are performed. As mentioned earlier, Romiszowski (1981) recommends a top-down sequence of inventory, sequencing, analysis, and description. Most designers perform the inventory first, followed by a description. The analysis frequently precedes the sequencing. The functions and procedures used by the developer depend to a large extent on a group of variables to be described next.

TASK ANALYSIS VARIABLES

The variability in the procedures used to accomplish the task analysis functions results from: (a) the diversity of tasks being analyzed (from psychomotor tasks to complex problem-solving tasks); (b) the instructional situation (from assembly line to experimental laboratory); (c) the characteristics of the learners; (d) the designer's experience and training, and other project constraints; and (e) the instructional development model being applied. The problem is to determine which task analysis procedures are appropriate for accomplishing the task analysis functions. In order to do that, we need to identify the variables that affect the task analysis process and the different functions performed as part of it. These variables can then be used along with the functions as a method for determining the appropriate procedures to be used. A quasi-algorithm is needed for selecting from among available task analysis procedures. In order to do this, we need easily classifiable variables. Some important variables affecting the task analysis process which also lend themselves to classification are described below.

Micro-Macro

Task analysis procedures are used in different levels of instructional planning. Micro-level procedures are those that pertain to a relatively small portion of instruction, usually an individual objective, a single idea, or a single task. Procedures like Component Display Theory (Merrill,

1983) describe how to classify, test, and present instruction for an individual objective. Many traditional behaviorally oriented task analysis procedures, such as behavioral analysis (Mechner, 1967), mathetics (Gilbert, 1961), and learning contingency analysis (Gropper, 1974), analyze each objective for the discriminations, generalizations, and chains of behavior required to accomplish it. Even more contemporary task analysis procedures, such as information processing analysis (Merrill, 1978; 1980), analyze individual performances for their information processing requirements. At the micro-level, it is sometimes difficult to see how a single objective or task fits into the entire course. Micro-level analysis is important for determining task requirements and instructional procedures. However, when sequencing tasks, it is important to analyze the tasks from a macro-level to see how the task requirements fit together.

Macro-analysis usually implies unit or course level analysis. Knowing how to integrate and summarize more than one idea, task, or objective and synthesize them into a meaningful sequence is also an important task analysis function. Procedures such as elaboration theory (Reigeluth & Stein, 1983) provide specific guidelines based upon cognitive instructional theory for organizing and sequencing the components of a course. Concept hierarchy analysis (Tieman & Markle, 1983) is a process for analyzing the conceptual components of subject matter. The most prominent task analysis procedure, learning hierarchy analysis (Gagne & Briggs, 1979), also operates at a macro-level, although not always at a course level. Rather, it is used to identify and sequence the prerequisite skills or performances that lead to course goals. In order to design instruction successfully, it is necessary to develop this larger picture on how content is organized. The procedures used to do that are different from micro-level procedures.

Top-Down Bottom-Up

Task analysis procedures vary also in terms of their overall approach to analyzing tasks. Those procedures that are more concerned with content or concept analysis take a *top-down approach*. That is, they begin at the most general or abstract level of content or with the most general task description and proceed to break it down into its component concepts or tasks. Top-down analysis then is an elaborative process, seeking more detail and specificity. Learning hierarchy analysis (Gagne & Briggs, 1979), for instance, begins with a generic task and analyzes it for its prerequisite tasks, and those for their prerequisites and so on. Information processing analysis (Merrill, 1978; 1980) starts with a task and looks on a micro-level at the specific mental process that produces that performance. Top-down task analysis procedures proceed from the general to the specific in a hypothetico-deductive fashion.

Bottom-up task analysis procedures, on the other hand, start at the specific level and build up an instructional sequence. They proceed from the single task or steps in a task and proceed to construct a task sequence from it. This type of analysis is most common in job task analysis (Mager & Beach, 1967) where a designer starts by observing a sequence of steps involved in performing a task. The critical incident technique (Flannigan, 1954; Zemke, 1981) is also a bottom-up process, where analysis begins with describing the critical incidents in job performance. Bottom-up analysis procedures are specific-to-general, inductive types of analysis processes. In most industrial settings, they are helpful in analyzing job task requirements.

Job Task Analysis vs. Learning Task Analysis

An important distinction to task analysis is the source of the task and the orientation of the agency developing the tasks. Is the task being analyzed a job task or a learning goal or objective? That is, is it a job task analysis or learning task analysis? Is the agency developing training or educational sequences? Job task analysis occurs more commonly in business and industry, while learning task analysis is practiced more commonly in educational institutions.

Job task analysis is normally undertaken to solve a performance problem. Learning task analysis, on the other hand, is undertaken to develop a curriculum. The reasons for conducting task analysis will affect the nature of the process. While the curriculum resulting from a learning task analysis may prepare learners to perform the same jobs or roles for which job task analysis is used to develop training, the goal-orientation of the agencies conducting the analysis is different. Developers who design training sequences seek to develop mastery of specific tasks, whereas developers who design learning sequences usually are more concerned with mastery of subject matter knowledge. These orientations are reflected in processes normally referred to as job task analysis and learning task analysis. Educators foster knowledge acquisition; this approach is proactive. Trainers, on the other hand, are more reactive, engaged in an ad hoc attempt to rectify problems. Educators design pre-service instruction, whereas the trainer/ developer tends to design in-service training. The focus, orientation, and purpose of these two entities are usually disparate.

This difference in orientation is also reflected in the nature of the knowledge and tasks being analyzed. The job trainer is more concerned with procedural knowledge—how to do something or perform some task. The educator is more concerned with conceptual knowledge— the ideas, concepts, and principles and their interrelationships that constitute a field of study. The former usually results in near transfer of training, while the conceptual approach more often produces far transfer (Clark & Voogel, 1985). Job training is not as concerned with getting trainees to apply or transfer their skills to similar problems in different settings. Since educators do not know the specific settings into which their students will go, they must be more concerned with far transfer, that is, the ability of their students to apply knowledge in a broad range of settings. Trainers, therefore, tend to use more behavioral training methods, while educators stress cognitive processes. Behavioral methods promote near transfer; cognitive methods promote far transfer (Clark & Voogel, 1985). While industry and the military rely more on training, there are many educators in their ranks, just as a lot of training is conducted in traditional educational institutions.

These three variables are somewhat global classifications of task analysis procedures. However, when combined with the task analysis functions, they can be used to make recommendations for the task analysis procedures that should be employed. In the next section, these variables are combined to form a quasi-algorithm for making general recommendations regarding selection of appropriate task analysis procedures.

SELECTING TASK
ANALYSIS PROCEDURES

So far, we have described the ambiguity in the task analysis process and provided a scheme for describing and classifying task analysis procedures. The problem of which procedure to use to accomplish each task analysis function remains. We know that the ability to make informed judgments depends on experience. Experienced developers recommend task analysis procedures for use in different situations based upon their better developed "scripts" for the instructional development process. The purpose of this chapter then is to use our organizational scheme to make suggestions about which task analysis procedures may be used for each function. Based upon his review of three task analysis technologies, Foshay (1983) made some informed recommendations about which task analysis procedures would be appropriate under different conditions. For instance, he recommended learning hierarchy analysis for macro-level sequencing, concept hierarchy analysis for discriminating among concepts, and so on. However, his review considered only three of the many task analysis procedures available to developers.

In figure 15.1 we present a quasi-algorithm for selecting alternative task analysis methodologies. It is our belief that selecting from the many available procedures is best done through a sequence of decisions. The divisions in this algorithm are based upon the classifications of task analysis procedures previously discussed: (a) functions (inventorying, describing, selecting, sequencing, and analyzing) and (b) variables (micro-macro, top-down/bottom-up, and job vs. learning task analysis). In order to use the algorithm, first decide whether you are conducting a job analysis or an instructional analysis. That is, are you designing training for a specific job or are you developing a general unit of instruction? Next, consider the scope of learning. Are you developing instruction for a single task or objective or a set of course objectives? Are you operating at a macro-level or micro-level? Finally, decide which of the task analysis functions you are performing—inventory, description, selection, sequencing, or analysis. As you make this sequence of decisions and follow the appropriate paths, you are led to one or more numbers, which are keyed to the task analysis procedures listed and annotated in the Appendix. The numbered procedures shown at the bottom of each decision path in figure 15.1 are the appropriate procedures that may be used to accomplish the task analysis function in the setting implied by the decisions. The choice of which procedure to use depends upon the experience and/or preferences of the designer or some organizational decision by a design team.

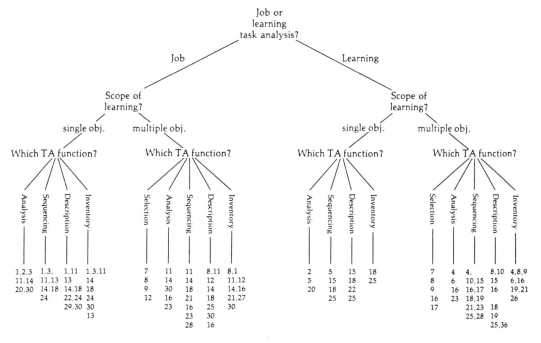

*The suggestions shown here are based on the normal, intended purposes for each method. So, they are not exhaustive. It is possible to innovatively apply each method to a variety of functions.

Fig. 15.1. Algorithm for selecting task analysis methodologies.

CONCLUSION

It is not our intention to offer a definitive prescription about which specific task analysis procedure should be used for every function in every setting. The knowledge about the task analysis process is too uncertain for us to make specific recommendations about which procedures to use to solve all design problems. Rather, we have tried to impose some organization on the task analysis process. In doing so, we hope to provide some guidance to the beginning developer in selecting the procedures that *could* be used to accomplish the various task analysis functions in different settings. Once you have used the algorithm to narrow your choices to a given category, you must familiarize yourself with the alternative procedures in order to make the final selection of task analysis procedures to be used.

REFERENCES

Andrews, D. H., & Goodson, L. A. (1980). A comparative analysis of models of instructional design. *Journal of Instructional Development, 3*(4), 2-16.

Bloom, B. S., Krathwohl, D. R., & Masia, B. B. (1956). *Taxonomy of educational objectives: The classification of educational goals. Handbook I: Cognitive domain.* New York: David McKay.

Buzan, T. (1974). *Use both sides of your brain.* New York: E. P. Dutton.

Clark, R. E., & Voogel, A. (1985). Transfer of training principles for instructional design. *Educational Communication and Technology Journal, 33*(2), 113-123.

Dalkey, N. C., & Helmer, O. (1963). An experimental application of the Delphi Method to the use of experts. *Management Science, 9*, 458-467.

Davies, I. K. (1976). *Objectives in curriculum design.* New York: McGraw-Hill.

Davis, R. H., Alexander, L. T., & Yelon, S. L. (1974). *Learning system design: An approach to the improvement of instruction.* New York: McGraw-Hill.

Design of courses of instruction. (1972). (Report No. MCOP11510 23A). Washington, DC: U.S. Marine Corps.

Diekhoff, G. M., & Diekhoff, K. B. (1982). Cognitive maps as a tool in communicating structural knowledge. *Educational Technology, 22*(4), 28-30.

Evans, J. L., Glaser, R., & Homme, L. E. (1962). The RULEG system for the construction of programmed verbal learning sequences. *Journal of Educational Research, 55*, 513-518.

Fields, A. (1982). Getting started: Pattern notes and perspectives. In D. H. Jonassen (Ed.), *The technology of text: Principles for structuring, designing, and displaying text.* (Vol. 1). Englewood Cliffs, NJ: Educational Technology Publications.

Fine, S. A., & Wiley, W. W. (1971). *An introduction to functional job analysis.* Kalamazoo, MI: Upjohn.

Flannigan, J. C. (1954). The critical incident technique. *Psychological Bulletin, 51*, 327-358.

Foshay, W. R. (1983). Alternative methods of task analysis: A comparison of three methods. *Journal of Instructional Development, 6*(4), 2-9.

Fussell, J. B., Powers, G. J., & Bennett, R. (1974). Fault trees: A state of the art discussion. *IEEE Transactions on Reliability, R-23*, 5-55.

Gagne, R. M. (1965). *The conditions of learning* (1st ed.). New York: Holt, Rinehart & Winston.

———. (1974). Task analysis—Its relation to content analysis. *Educational Psychology, 11*(1), 11-18.

———. (1975). *Essentials of learning for instruction.* Hinsdale, IL: Dryden Press.

———. (1977). *The conditions of learning* (3rd ed.). New York: Holt, Rinehart & Winston.

———. (1985). *The conditions of learning* (4th ed.). New York: Holt, Rinehart & Winston.

Gagne, R. M., & Briggs, L. J. (1979). *Principles of instructional design* (2nd ed.). New York: Holt, Rinehart & Winston.

Gentry, C. (1985, January). *Needs analysis: Rationale and technique*. Paper presented at the annual meeting of the Association for Educational Communications and Technology, New Orleans.

Gilbert, T. F. (1961). Mathetics: The technology of education (Special issues). *Journal of Mathetics, 1* and 2.

———. (1982a). A question of performance—Part I: The PROBE model. *Training and Development Journal, 36*, 21-30.

———. (1982b). A question of performance—Part II: Applying the PROBE model. *Training and Development Journal, 36*, 85-89.

Gropper, G. L. (1974). *Instructional strategies*. Englewood Cliffs, NJ: Educational Technology Publications.

Harless, J. H. (1980). Task analysis—A clarification of the term. *NSPI Journal, 19*(2), 4-5.

Harrow, A. J. (1972). *A taxonomy of psychomotor domain*. New York: David McKay.

Hershbach, D. R. (1976). Deriving instructional content through task analysis. *Journal of Industrial Teacher Education, 13*(3), 63-73.

Hoffman, C. K., & Medsker, K. L. (1983). Instructional analysis: The missing link between task analysis and objectives. *Journal of Instructional Development, 6*(4), 17-23.

Job task analysis manual. (1973). San Diego, CA: Naval Training Center—Service Schools Command, Industrialized Learning Development Group.

Jonassen, D. H. (1984). Developing a learning strategy using pattern notes: A new technology. *Programmed Learning and Educational Technology, 21*(3), 163-175.

———. (1987). Assessing cognitive structure: Verifying a method for using pattern notes. *Journal of Research and Development in Education, 20*(3), 1-4.

Kaufman, R. (1972). *Educational system planning*. Englewood Cliffs, NJ: Prentice-Hall.

Kennedy, P., Esquire, T., & Novak, J. (1983). A functional analysis of task analysis procedures for instructional design. *Journal of Instructional Development, 6*(4), 10-16.

Krathwohl, D. L., Bloom, B. S., & Masia, B. B. (1964). *Taxonomy of educational objectives, the classification of educational goals. Handbook II: The affective domain*. New York: David McKay.

Leith, G. O. M. (1970). The acquisition of knowledge and mental development of students. *(British) Journal of Educational Technology, 1*, 116-128.

Mager, R. F., & Beach, K. M. (1967). *Developing vocational instruction*. Belmont, CA: Fearon.

Martin, M. C., & Brodt, D. E. (1973). Task analysis for training and curriculum design. *Improving Human Performance Quarterly, 2*, 113-120.

McCormick, E. J. (1979). *Job analysis: Methods and applications*. New York: American Management Association.

McDermott, F. M. (1982). Try brainstorming—a quick route to job analysis. *Training/HRD, 19*(3), 38-40.

Mechner, F. (1967). Behavioral analysis and instructional sequencing. In P. C. Lange (Ed.), *Programmed instruction*. Yearbook of the National Society for the Study of Education. Chicago: Rand McNally.

Merrill, M. D. (1975). Learner control: Beyond aptitude—treatment interactions. *A Communication Review, 23*, 217-226.

———. (1983). Component display theory. In C. M. Reigeluth (Ed.), *Instructional design theories and models: An overview of their current status.* Hillsdale, NJ: Lawrence Erlbaum.

———. (1978). Hierarchical and information processing task analysis: A comparison. *Journal of Instructional Development, 1*, 35-40.

———. (1980). Analysis of a procedural task. *NSPI Journal, 19*(2), 11-15, 26.

Miller, R. B. (1962). Task description and analysis. In R. M. Gagne & A. W. Melton (Eds.), *Psychological principles in system development.* New York: Holt, Rinehart & Winston.

Reigeluth, C. M., Merrill, M. D., Branson, R. K., Begland, R., & Tarr, R. (1980). *Extended task analysis procedure (ETAP): User's manual.* Final Report, Army Training Development Institute. (NTIS No. AD-A098351)

Reigeluth, C. M., Merrill, M. D., & Bunderson, C. V. (1978). The structure of subject matter content and its instructional design implications. *Instructional Science, 7*(2), 107-126.

Reigeluth, C. M., & Rogers, C. A. (1980). The elaboration theory of instruction: Prescriptions for task analysis and design. *NSPI Journal, 19*(1), 16-26.

Reigeluth, C. M., & Stein, F. S. (1983). The elaboration theory of instruction. In C. M. Reigeluth (Ed.), *Instructional design theories and models: An overview of their current status.* Hillsdale, NJ: Lawrence Erlbaum.

Resnick, L. B. (1976). Task analysis in instructional design. Some cases from mathematics. In D. Klahr (Ed.), *Cognition and instruction.* Hillsdale, NJ: Lawrence Erlbaum.

Resnick, L. B., & Ford, W. W. (1982). The analysis of tasks for instruction: An information processing approach. In T. A. Brigham & A. C. Catania (Eds.), *Handbook of applied behavior analysis: Social and instructional processes.* New York: Irvington.

Romiszowski, A. J. (1981). *Designing instructional systems.* London: Kogan Page.

Stone, P. J., Dunphy, D. C., Smith, M. J., & Ogilvie, D. M. (1966). *The general inquiries: A computer approach to content analysis.* Cambridge, MA: MIT Press.

Thomas, C. A., Davies, I. K., Openshaw, D., & Bird, J. B. (1963). *Programmed learning in perspective: A guide to program writing.* Chicago: Educational Methods.

Tieman, P., & Markle, S. (1983). *Analyzing instructional context: A guide to instruction and evaluation* (2nd ed.). Champaign, IL: Stipes.

Tracey, W. R., Flynn, E. B., & Legere, C. L. J. (1970). *The development of instructional systems.* Fort Devens, MA: U.S. Army Security Agency Training Center.

Zemke, R. (1981). The critical incident method of analysis. In R. Zemke, L. Standke, & P. Jones (Eds.), *Designing and delivering cost effective training and measuring the results.* Minneapolis, MN: Lakewood.

APPENDIX

Task Analysis Methodologies

1. **Behavioral Analysis**. Like many other task analysis procedures, behavioral analysis (Mechner, 1967) grew out of programmed learning. In an attempt to develop systematic methods for sequencing frames of programs, Mechner suggested analyzing the components of each objective. Like Gilbert (1961) and Gropper (1974), he classified these components as discrimination, generalizations, or chains. He developed a set of rules for sequencing chains (procedures) and concepts, such as "never teach a discrimination without simultaneously teaching a generalization" (p. 94). The instructional developer can perform a behavioral analysis by merging the types of questions students might ask about discriminations, generalizations, and chains, such as "What are the steps at arriving at this conclusion?", "Where is all this leading?", or "What are some examples of concepts?" To the extent that we feel comfortable in generalizing programmed learning procedures, behavioral analysis provides a useful means for micro-level task analysis and sequencing of instruction.

2. **Bloom's Taxonomy**. Bloom and his colleagues (Bloom, Krathwohl, & Masia, 1956; Krathwohl, Bloom, & Masia, 1964) spent several years developing a taxonomic classification of cognitive and affective behaviors for purposes of test design. A taxonomy of psychomotor domain was added later (Harrow, 1972). These taxonomies later became the primary means for analyzing learning tasks. They describe in detail increasingly complex forms of cognitive behaviors (from knowledge to evaluation), affective behaviors (from receiving to articulation of a value concept), and psychomotor behaviors (from imitation to naturalization). These remain the most detailed descriptions of learning behaviors, still popular with many educators (see table 15.1).

3. **Brainstorming**. Brainstorming provides a quick route to job analysis (McDermott, 1982). The developer assembles skilled job performers in order to determine the model job performance. All steps and functions are posted on index cards on a large, clear wall. Using different color cards, all contingencies are posted for each step. Then the developer tries to get consensus on the most realistic alternatives to each of the listed contingencies. Finally, the knowledge and skill requirements for each step are stated. This brainstorming procedure is a quick and easy method for analyzing jobs. Its strength lies in the elaboration of contingent behaviors necessary for performing the job.

4. **Cognitive Mapping**. Understanding concepts is necessary but insufficient for understanding content. Learners must also understand the structural relationships between related concepts. So if we use content or concept analysis procedures for identifying concepts, we will need a method to derive the type and degree of relatedness among those concepts. Cognitive mapping provides a tool for this (Diekhoff & Diekhoff, 1982). Once the key concepts are selected, designers or subject matter experts should form all possible pairs of those concepts and rate each pair for degree of relatedness using a 1-9 scale. The relatedness matrix is treated as an intercorrelation matrix and analyzed using principal components analysis or multi-dimensional scaling. The output of the analysis is a map that spatially relates the inter-concept distances. This process could aid both the sequencing and analysis phases. Sequencing is aided because the clusters that are formed indicate content groups. While not a traditional form of taxonomic analysis, the meaning of concepts is enhanced by knowing relationships among concepts. Further analysis of these relationships adds another dimension of meaning (Jonassen, 1984).

5. **Component Display Theory**. The component display theory (Merrill, 1983) is a micro-level design strategy for organizing instruction for a single idea or objective in the cognitive domain. The designer begins by classifying each objective to be taught in terms of the nature of the task and the content, a distinction missing from most analysis schemes. An objective can require the learner to remember, use, or find either facts, concepts, procedures, or principles (see table 15.1). Component display theory recommends the use of four primary presentation forms (tell or ask generalities or instances) and six types of elaboration (context, prerequisite, mnemonic, mathemagenic help, representation, feedback). It then provides rules that state the required primary presentation forms and elaborators for different types of tasks and content. While component display theory is an instructional design system, much of which is used after task analysis, the task/content matrix is very useful for the analysis phase because of its explicitness.

6. **Conceptual Hierarchy Analysis** (Tieman & Markle, 1983; Reigeluth, Merrill, & Bunderson, 1978). The sequencing of instruction, according to concept hierarchy analysis, is implied by the structure of the content. Various content structures (description, comparison/contrast, temporal sequence, explanation, definition/examples, problem/solution, cause/effect) may suggest different sequences for different tasks. Concept hierarchy analysis is a macro-level task analysis procedure for identifying, organizing, and arranging instructional content in the absence of a specific procedure. It requires identifying and analyzing the network of concepts used in any content area.

7. **Criteria for Task Selection**. Most of the military task analysis processes include an explicit procedure for selecting from among tasks or objectives those in which training should be provided (*Design of courses of instruction*, 1972; *Job task analysis manual*, 1973; Tracey, Flynn, & Legere, 1970). The criteria for determining feasibility and appropriateness include: universality (transferability), difficulty of acquisition, cruciality to the mission, frequency of performance, practicability, achievability by trainees, quality of skill, deficiencies resulting from training, retainability, and need for follow-up training. With limited training resources, a broad range of skills to cover, and a large number of trainees, the military is obviously pressed to develop comprehensive training. These task selection criteria help to rank the importance of each task in order to provide training for the most important tasks first. While these criteria are seldom applied to educational (learning) problems, they could be.

8. **Critical Incident Technique**. Determining the tasks to be included in instruction is often accomplished by using critical incident analysis (Flannigan, 1954; Zemke, 1981). In this technique, experts identify the critical job incidents and their products. Incidents are edited for redundance, grouped into similar tasks, and then classified as positive or negative incidents. The incidents are summarized and then validated by the experts for completeness. This is a useful means for obtaining a list of relevant, real-world tasks to be included in instruction. It is a job-related technique, however, and is most useful for converting job descriptions into instructional inventories.

9. **Delphi Technique**. In selecting the tasks/content to be taught, it is often necessary to place the inventory in priority order. This often requires the informed judgments of subject matter experts. One of the most popular techniques for generating that data is the Delphi technique (Dalkey & Helmer, 1963), in which sets of comments/beliefs/questions are submitted to an anonymous group of subject matter experts for their judgments. Their responses are analyzed and summarized, and then become the questions for the next round of judgments. This iterative judgment-feedback cycle is continued until the panel reaches consensus. The result represents the convergent thinking of a group of experts. It can be a tedious process, but it is one of the most systematic for collecting judgments.

10. **Elaboration Theory**. The elaboration theory (Reigeluth & Rogers, 1980; Reigeluth & Stein, 1983) provides a simple-to-complex approach to organizing instruction in which concepts, procedures, or principles are iteratively detailed and epitomized. It is a macro-level strategy for organizing multiple objectives. For each single objective, component display theory is used to organize instruction. That is, instruction starts at a general level with an epitome (i.e., the organizing of content ideas). These general ideas are then elaborated in progressively more detailed steps. Each level of elaboration has its own epitome (overview), which indicates the content structure of that elaboration, a summarizer (e.g., statement, example, or self-test), and a synthesizer to integrate that level of elaboration to all higher level elaborations. In addition, elaboration theory employs strategy components, such as analogies, cognitive strategies, and learner control. Elaboration theory views task analysis as a form of content analysis; from that point of view it supports the task inventory, description, and sequencing functions. The analysis steps include selecting the operations to be taught, deciding which to teach first, sequencing the remaining operations, creating the epitomes, and designing instruction on each operation (Reigeluth & Rogers, 1980). Performed in the context of elaboration theory, these represent a comprehensive and systematic top-down approach to learning analysis that is seldom ever used to organize job-related training.

11. **Extended Task Analysis Procedure**. The extended task analysis procedure (ETAP) (Reigeluth, Merrill, Branson, Begland, & Tarr, 1980) is a 12-step process for analyzing procedural tasks that combines hierarchical and information processing analysis procedures. It was developed for the military specifically to support job training. The three phases of the process include process analysis (identifying each step using information processing analysis), sub-step analysis (identifying the sub-steps for each step), and knowledge analysis (identifying the knowledge required to perform the task). The result is a multi-dimensional representation of the learning task including a flowchart, a list of sub-steps, and a list of component facts and principles. What is unique to ETAP is the factor-transfer and principle-transfer analysis. In complex

transfer tasks that include a large number of conditions or factors, ETAP identifies all the factors and creates decision rules and more general common rules for dealing with those factors in a transfer situation. Where those factors cannot be identified easily, ETAP identifies and sequences into instruction the necessary principles for properly executing the transfer task. Attention to this transfer of training is often absent in instructional design models, especially in the task analysis process.

12. **Fault Tree Analysis**. Another method for selecting the tasks to be taught focuses on avoiding errors or faults. Fault tree analysis (Fussell, Powers, & Bennett, 1974) predicts undesired events that may affect the operation of a system and provides the basis for redesigning it to prevent those occurrences. It can be used to select those tasks necessary for preventing undesired events. The result of such an application of fault tree analysis is a priority list of training needs. Working backward from a statement of an undesired event (previously identified), fault tree analysis represents all antecedent conditions that could have caused the event. The same process is repeated for each of those events, with each causal condition represented by an AND or OR logic gate. This process produces a tree of causal events, which shows each of the critical paths that produce the undesired event and the probability of the occurrence of each. Working with this information the designer could select those paths with the highest probability of occurrence as the most important training needs. This is a technical procedure that also requires a thorough knowledge of the operation system by the developer in order for it to be successful (Gentry, 1985).

13. **Functional Job Analysis**. Functional job analysis conceptually defines worker activity and defines methods for measuring worker output (Fine & Wiley, 1971). All jobs require workers to relate to data, people, and things (machines). Each job can be defined in terms of the workers' interactions with these three elements. Those interactions are actually limited. That is, there are only a few ways the workers can interact with certain types of machines. The job functions related to these three elements are sequential and hierarchical, proceeding from simple to complex. In that sense, it is much like learning hierarchy analysis, which specifies all of the prerequisite tasks to each goal. So analysis of any job task describes how the worker relates to data, people, and things as well as the relative amount of involvement he/she has with each element. This comprehensive analysis of job tasks has been adopted by several private and governmental organizations as their job analysis procedure.

14. **Job Task Analysis** (Mager & Beach, 1967). In the context of developing vocational instruction, the task analysis procedures focus on job description—what a worker does under the conditions that the job is normally performed, rather than what you would like him/her to do. The procedure requires the designer to list all of the tasks in a job and the steps included in each task; i.e., what a person does when performing the step, the type of performance involved (see table 15.1), and the expected difficulty in learning it. From the task analysis, the designer derives course objectives after first determining what the learners already know. Course objectives, then, describe those things that learners should be able to do at the end of the course. Except for the determination of the type of performance required by each step, this is a vocational, behavioral analysis technique that focuses on the inventory function.

15. **Information Processing Analysis** (Merrill, 1978; 1980; Resnick, 1976; Resnick & Ford, 1982). Similar to learning hierarchy analysis, information processing analysis describes the sequence of cognitive operations required for solving a class of problems. Such analysis usually represents the information processing sequence in algorithmic form. The goal of such analysis is to model the covert mental operations of a learner while performing a task, rather than modelling the overt behavior exhibited by the learner. While it is normally applied to problem solving, information processing analysis may be used to describe other tasks. Such analysis must be generic so that it may be applied to a range of problems (tasks). It may imply a forward or a backward sequence of development, depending upon the problem-solving technique employed. (See also Path Analysis, 25.)

16. **Instructional Analysis**. Instructional analysis is a comprehensive set of task analysis procedures intended as a critical link between task analysis and writing instructional objectives (Hoffman & Medsker, 1983). By analyzing the component skills, instructional analysis seeks to identify "New learning," excluding those skills already known from a list of "instructional" objectives. So, after identifying and sequencing component skills and eliminating extraneous ones, the instructional analyst identifies the type of learning required by the remaining skills using a hybrid taxonomy. This taxonomy includes complex procedures that are pre-defined, interrelated sequences of operations that can be considered a unit. So, starting with a task analysis, the instructional analyst analyzes the type of learning and conducts a traditional hierarchical analysis, a procedure analysis, or a combination analysis that combines the complex procedures. After identifying support skills not integral to the task, a learning map that combines all of the

previous analyses is constructed. Instructional analysis is a super-procedure that adds to task analysis. It represents one of the most comprehensive task analysis processes available.

17. **Learner Control of Instruction** (Merrill, 1975). Learner control describes an instructional strategy rather than a procedure for designing instruction. Essentially, it argues for allowing the learner some degree of self-determination of the content and strategies of instruction (Merrill, 1983). The content may consist of the objectives, lesson, or module selected by the learner. It has the most significant implications for task analysis in the sequencing and selection functions. Giving students the opportunity to select what they will learn as well as the order in which they will complete instruction can preclude some of the sequencing operations normally performed by the designer. To responsibly select instructional content requires some metacognitive skills, which many learners do not possess. Because of this, the research findings related to learner control have been mixed, at best.

18. **Learning Contingency Analysis**. A task inventory or description provides a set of tasks, or steps in a task, and the ordering of these. Usually performance of one task/step is contingent on another, which is contingent on a prior skill. Since these contingencies have implications for instructional sequences, designers can develop a corresponding progression of steps to be taught. The progression or sequence is dependent on the relationships among tasks/steps. A learning contingency may be necessary, facilitative, or nonexistent depending upon four types of relationships: superordinate/subordinate, coordinate input/ output, shared elements, or no relationship (Gropper, 1974). The sequence in which behavioral components should be learned in turn depends upon the nature of the relationship. For instance, Gropper (1974) suggests that an output that becomes an input for another performance should be taught first. This type of task analysis describes the behavioral components of an objective, rather than the traditional taxonomies that are used to describe the terminal performance depicted by the objective.

19. **Learning Hierarchy Analysis** (Gagne, 1965, 1974, 1975, 1977, 1985; Gagne & Briggs, 1979). Learning hierarchy analysis has become so universal that many equate it with task analysis. Based on his own taxonomies of learning (Gagne, 1965, 1977, 1985), Gagne has described a method for developing a hierarchy of learning skills (see table 15.1) for organizing learning tasks. While it could be used to organize instruction for job tasks, it is commonly associated with learning analysis. This is a backward chaining technique for elaborating the prerequisite skills for accomplishing an instructional objective. Learning hierarchy analysis has evolved from a behavioral analysis method for describing the structure of a task and the essential prerequisite skills that comprise that task. For any objective, learning hierarchy analysis describes the prerequisite concepts, principles, and strategies necessary for acquiring the skill implied by the terminal objective. The optimal sequence of instruction can be inferred from such learning hierarchies.

20. **Learning Taxonomy** (Leith, 1970). While structurally similar to Gagne's taxonomy, Leith's (1970) taxonomy (see table 15.1) provides specific instructional suggestions in the form of conditions. Leith devoted as much of his hierarchy to associative processes as Gagne did in his earlier work. The primary difference is at the higher end of the taxonomy, where Leith included problem solving and schemata development. Schemata are general networks of ideas and operations. This reference to schemata reflects the shift in the sixties toward a more cognitive orientation in the psychology of learning.

21. **Master Design Chart**. One means for using objectives to plan curriculum is to develop a master design chart (Davies, 1976). A master design chart is a matrix, with one axis listing content areas and the other listing specific behaviors (objectives). In designing such a chart, the designer first identifies the objectives along the behavioral axis. Second, the content of subject matter is broken down and displayed along the content axis. Third, each cell in the matrix should be evaluated for the emphasis on each type of behavior that should be manifest for each area of content. The resulting matrix reflects the emphasis of the curriculum and could be used to sequence the tasks in a course. It could also be used in a more top-down way at the front end to inventory the tasks to be included in an instructional unit. The master design chart is an alternative method of matrix analysis.

22. **Mathetics**. Emerging from the programmed instruction movement, mathetics was promoted by Gilbert (1961) as the technology of education, a complete system for task analysis and instructional design. This behavioral approach diagrammatically represented the task sequence that was established by observing and analyzing a master performer. The task analysis classified behavior as consisting of chains, multiple discriminations, and generalizations. Rather than classifying objectives, this taxonomy describes the processes that comprise an objective (Gropper, 1974). Gilbert's concern with the stimulus portion of the

S-R association resulted in a specific set of instructional procedures based on the task analysis. These procedures include demonstrating, prompting, or releasing the learner. Gilbert also suggested rules for deciding what content to include and the sequence in which it should be presented. While mathetics has not lived up to his prediction as the technology of education, it represents one of the most comprehensive behavioral task analysis systems available.

23. **Matrix Analysis.** Like many task analysis procedures, matrix analysis (Evans, Glaser, & Homme, 1962; Thomas, Davies, Openshaw, & Bird, 1963) emerged from the programmed instruction literature as a means for sequencing program frames. In designing programs (or other forms of instruction), designers first identify the important concepts and convert those into a set of specific rules. The rules should then be sequenced in some order. In order to adequately communicate knowledge, the interrelationships among rules need to be understood and taught. In order to identify all of the pertinent interrelationships, a matrix is created. The matrix, which shows all possible interrelationships, requires that the designer do a pairwise or cell-by-cell assessment of the relatedness between each possible pair of rules. Each pair is classified as an association (the rules are related and similar) or discrimination (the rules are related but different). The sequence of instruction is reflected in the matrix, so that by observing the matrix, the designer can quickly discern omissions, inverted or misplaced rules, or any other sequencing problem. From the matrix, a flow diagram describing the different types of frames is developed, showing the final sequence of instruction. Matrix analysis could be used to help sequence any form of instruction.

24. **Methods Analysis.** Methods analysis is a micromotion analysis of any job based on detailed motion studies (McCormick, 1979). These often use operation charts that describe in detail the actions of workers at a single location, using standardized symbols to depict each motion of the worker. Micromotion studies analyze videotapes of workers performing jobs in terms of basic motions and develop a simultaneous motion cycle chart that describes the motions of each hand and the body. This type of micro-level analysis is useful for deriving the description phase for psychomotor tasks.

25. **Path Analysis** (Merrill, 1978; 1980). Path analysis is the second phase of information processing analysis. In conducting a path analysis, the designer identifies the unique paths through an information processing flow chart. This is especially important when a process contains iterative subprocesses. Paths are depicted by listing the numbers of all the operations on a flow chart that the learner executes going from start to stop. Comparing the sequence and inclusiveness of different paths provides a metalevel analysis of the information processing that occurs. This analysis shows the superordinate/subordinate relationships among various paths. That is, some paths may be embedded hierarchically in other paths. Those paths (representing skills) that are subordinate to others are also prerequisite to them, so that learning hierarchy analysis (Gagne, 1965, 1977, 1985) can then be used to analyze the skills. These hierarchical paths are then converted into task sequences for orienting instruction. (See also Information Processing Analysis, 15.)

26. **Pattern Noting.** Pattern notes were originally conceived as a notetaking method (Buzan, 1974; Fields, 1982) for summarizing the content of notes in a network map form. To construct a pattern note, you box the key issue or item in the center of a clean sheet of paper. You begin to free associate related topics and write those on lines connected to the box. Sub-issues are written on lines linked to the initial lines. You continue to elaborate the lines until the related topics are complete, and then interconnect any related topics on the maps with lines. Pattern notes are excellent organizational and retrieval strategies (Jonassen, 1984) that reflect a person's cognitive structure (Jonassen, 1987). They can assist the task analysis process most in terms of the inventory and description functions when the content of instruction is being identified. They are conceptual in nature, so they could support concept hierarchy analysis. Pattern noting, as a measure of cognitive structure, is also a useful measure of prior learning. Pattern noting can depict interrelatedness of prior knowledge, rather than a unidimensional, single score on a pretest. It is similar to, though distinctly different from, concept mapping (4).

27. **PROBE Model.** The PROBE model (Gilbert, 1982a, 1982b) is a performance analysis procedure that consists of eight sets of questions that analyze the capabilities of workers and the environments in which they work. These individual differences and environmental questions concern the inspiration and instrumentation available to employees as well as the motivational contingencies that result in performance. The questions are used to analyze any performance problem situation in terms of employee skills and motives, knowledge and training, adequate information and feedback, proper tools and responses, and appropriate incentives. The PROBE model is a conceptually sound and practical performance analysis process. It was not designed as a task analysis procedure; it is broader in scope. It could, however, yield useful information to anyone performing a task analysis. The questions related to knowledge and training

function as a needs assessment procedure that would supply the basis for task analysis. So, the PROBE model is a useful strategy supporting the task analysis procedure.

28. **Syntactic Analysis** (Stone, Dunphy, Smith, & Ogilivie, 1966). One of the most difficult parts of task analysis is organizing a large number of tasks that have been inventoried. Syntactic analysis reviews each task statement syntactically (i.e., looks for statements with similar terms, performing the same syntactic function). For instance, task statements can be analyzed for common direct objects. Those with common direct objects, indicating various performances on the same object, cluster together (Martin & Brodt, 1973). Syntactic analysis can also search for synonyms of objects or other syntactic elements. It is used primarily to order task statements.

29. **Task Description** (Miller, 1962). A task description specifies the sequence of stimulus-response associations required to complete a task (Miller, 1962). This includes specification of the cues or indicators perceived by the performer, the task activities, and the conditions surrounding each performance required for accomplishing each task. Task analysis further clarifies the behavioral requirements of the task where the designer looks for some behavioral structure in the task. The task description and analysis process, according to Miller (1962), is a molecular process concentrating only on the behavioral aspects of performance.

30. **Vocational Task Analysis**. Hershbach (1976) proposed a three-step task analysis model that includes a task inventory, a task description, and a task analysis. In the task inventory, the designer identifies the steps, or task elements and sub-elements, using observation and interview techniques. Analysis of tasks qualifies the task description and analyzes the behavior using learning hierarchy analysis (Gagne, 1965, 1977, 1985) or Bloom's taxonomy (Bloom, Krathwohl, & Masia, 1956). No explicit technique is described for sequencing tasks, except those implied by the task analysis step. Hershbach essentially applies classic task analysis procedures to industrial education.

16

Applications of Research to the Design of Computer-Based Instruction

Gary R. Morrison
College of Education, University of Memphis
Memphis, Tennessee

Steven M. Ross
College of Education, University of Memphis
Memphis, Tennessee

Jacqueline K. O'Dell
College of Education, University of Arkansas
Fayetteville, Arkansas

The enthusiasm and predictions of the advocates of computer-based instruction today are reminiscent of the zeal of the advocates of programmed instruction. In the early 1960s, Skinner predicted how teaching machines would revolutionize the schools (Department of Education, 1960). Two decades later, Bork (1987) and Papert (1980) predicted that computers would revolutionize education and the way we learn. Research on computer-based instruction (CBI) has been supportive of its effectiveness (Kulik, Bangert, & Williams, 1983), yet it is unlikely that CBI or any other computer-based delivery system will produce results necessary to proclaim it "better" than traditional methods. Tomorrow's students are no more likely to see a revolutionary change caused by computers than the students of the 1970s saw from programmed instruction. A more likely scenario is one in which the unique characteristics of the computer are exploited to deliver instruction in an effective and efficient manner. The future of computer-based delivery systems appears to belong to the designer of the instructional strategy as opposed to the computer hardware.

In this chapter we examine instructional strategies that take advantage of the computer's attributes to create an efficient and effective learning environment. Specifically, we review three major areas of research and instructional design related to CBI, and conclude by discussing recent developments and their potential impact on instructional technology.

215

SCREEN DESIGN

One of the first concerns of a designer is to design effective, user-friendly screens. Many of the heuristics for designing CBI displays are based on prior research in printed text (Hartley, 1987), and they basically recommend the use of liberal white space, double spacing, and left-justified text. Heines (1984) identified five functional areas of a screen, although all five might not be used in a single screen. First, a screen should have *orienting* information (e.g., how many more frames or questions remain). Second, the screen should display directions for the learner in a consistent location. Third, the program should echo or display the students' responses. Fourth, a display area for informative error messages should be provided. Fifth, the options available to the student (e.g., quit, review, go to previous screen) should be displayed in a consistent area. Heines's approach provides the designer with guidelines for developing a consistent user interface that increases the user friendliness of the software. The ROPES model developed by Hannafin and Hooper (1989) suggests screen design techniques for improving retrieval, orienting, presenting, encoding, and sequencing of lesson content. Heuristics are provided for enhancing each of these tasks.

Much of the research on CBI screen design has paralleled the research on printed materials, as exemplified by studies on reading speed (Fish & Feldman, 1987), line length, and leading (e.g., Grabinger, 1983). An area that has received less research attention is screen density (Morrison, Ross, Schultz, & O'Dell, 1989). The number of words, sentences, or ideas presented in a single frame on a computer is generally limited to 960 (40-column) or 1,920 (80-column) characters as compared to the much greater number (approximately 3,600 characters) on a typical printed page. Using nonrealistic stimulus materials, Grabinger (1983) supported the general literature design recommendation by finding that subjects preferred designs with adequate white space and openness. In asking whether the same results would be obtained if realistic materials (a lesson on statistics) were used, Morrison, Ross, Schultz, and O'Dell (1989) varied screen density by presenting the same content on either one, two, three, or four different screens. Using these materials, results from two studies indicated greater preferences for higher-density over lower-density designs. These results suggest that subjects may apply different perspectives when evaluating screens with realistic content because of the need to process the information so that it can be recalled or applied at a later time.

ADAPTIVE CBI

A second question designers must answer is who will control the lesson, the student or the program (i.e., the designer). One of the major advantages of CBI over other instructional delivery systems is the ease of implementing learner control options. These options allow individual learners to determine the sequence of the lesson, the number of problems to work, when to review the content, and the type and amount of feedback received. However, research suggests that learner control options may not always be a feasible method for individualizing instruction (e.g., Carrier, Davidson, & Williams, 1985; Tennyson, 1980). As Ross and Morrison (1989) suggest, "Many students, especially low achievers, lack the knowledge and motivation to make appropriate decisions regarding such conditions as pacing,... sequencing content,... use of learning aids,... and amount of practice" (p. 28).

The concerns about learner control decisions provided a rationale for implementing an advisement function to guide learners in their choices. Ross and Rakow (1982) used varied incentive levels as a source of information on which lessons were likely to require the selection of extra instructional support (greater difficulty = greater incentive level). This strategy resulted in increased learning gains. Tennyson and his associates (e.g., Johansen & Tennyson, 1983) provided explicit advisement about how many examples to select before and during the lesson using an intelligent CBI system. The results indicated that the advisement groups had higher learning gains than the control groups.

In contrast to learner control strategies that vary instructional support, studies by Morrison, Ross, and O'Dell (1988) and Ross, Morrison, and O'Dell (1988) allowed learners to select either high-density (elaborated) or low-density textual contexts on a statistics lesson. While there were no significant effects on achievement, results suggested the learner control option was used effectively by the students in adapting the density variations to their reading levels. Specifically, less skilled readers were more likely to select the high-density version, while more skilled readers were more likely to select the low-density version. In a third study by Ross, Morrison, and O'Dell (1988) learners selected preferred thematic contexts (sports, education, business, or abstract) of the examples. Again, there were no achievement effects; learners appeared to vary their selections adaptively by switching from familiar (preferred) contexts to less familiar ones as the lesson progressed. Most important, learners who were allowed to choose preferred contexts also elected to study a greater number of examples. These findings and others (e.g., Hannafin, 1984) suggest that "learner control is not a unitary construct, but rather a collection of strategies that function in different ways depending on what is being controlled by whom" (Ross & Morrison, 1989, p. 29).

Contextual adaptation can also be effective when controlled by the program rather than the learner. Anand and Ross (1987) and Ross and Anand (1987) personalized mathematics problems by substituting personal data about the student for standard referents (e.g., citing friends' names, favorite food, etc.). Students who received the personalized examples performed better and reacted more positively to the lesson than did control subjects.

FEEDBACK

A third question that designers need to consider is the amount and type of feedback provided the learner. Feedback has been the focus of several studies (cf. Schimmel, 1988 and Kulik & Kulik, 1988) since Pressey's (1927) early work. Concerns about the use of feedback in CBI have generated a renewed interest in its application (e.g., Dempsey & Driscoll, 1989). Of particular interest are the timing and type of feedback used in the instruction.

Feedback given immediately (or as soon as practical) after the learner makes a response is described as *immediate feedback*. A definition of *delayed feedback* is more difficult because of differing conceptions by researchers of what constitutes a delay. Van Dyke and Newton (1972) define delayed feedback as four to eight seconds, while others have extended the time to one or more weeks (Kulik & Kulik, 1988). Peeck and Tillema (1978) have defined immediate feedback as feedback given after each item or response, and delayed feedback, regardless of time delay, as given at the end of a series of items or at the end of the test.

Prior research has identified four types of feedback. First is knowledge of response (KR), in which the program simply tells the learners if their answers are "right" or "wrong." Second is knowledge of correct response (KCR), in which the learner typically receives a message such as "no, the correct answer is...." Third is answer until correct (AUC) feedback, which may tell the learner the response is incorrect and to try again. The fourth type of feedback is elaborative feedback or "anticipated-wrong-answer" (AWA), which tells the learner that the response was incorrect and provides information about the nature of the error (e.g., "You added rather than multiplied").

Results from the feedback studies suggest that immediate feedback is more effective than delayed feedback (Kulik & Kulik, 1988), and that most forms of feedback are more effective than no feedback (Smith, 1988). Schimmel (1988), however, found the research to be inconsistent in establishing one of the four types of feedback as more effective. Dempsey and Driscoll (1989) combined and compared different forms of feedback in a CBI lesson and found no differences between the strategies. Their results suggested that the more complex forms of feedback (e.g., KCR and AWA), aside from taking more time to develop and implement, might interfere with learning because of the additional elaboration.

Computer-based instruction provides a more efficient means of implementing and testing different forms of feedback than print-based materials. Future research should investigate optimum conditions for the different types of feedback as well as possibilities for adapting feedback to individual differences.

This review has identified three areas to address when designing CBI. First, the screen(s) need to be designed in a consistent manner, with the appropriate amount of content displayed in each frame. Second, the designer must determine what properties of the instruction can be adapted to students (e.g., whether instructional support and/or context will be manipulated) and whether the adaptation can be achieved more effectively through learner or program control. Third, the type, frequency, and timing of the feedback must be determined. Each of these decisions will necessarily be dependent on the characteristics of the learners and the nature of the content.

IMPACT OF ADVANCES IN COMPUTER TECHNOLOGY

Although the strategies reviewed above are not unique to CBI, their form and efficiency are directly influenced by CBI's unique attributes (online adaptation, immediate knowledge of results, etc.). Thus advances in computer technology have the potential to affect not only instructional strategies, but the instructional design process as well. There are four immediately identifiable areas that will influence the field of instructional technology: multi-media systems, intelligent CBI, expert systems, and automated development tools.

Multi-Media Systems

Improvements in digital storage devices such as videodiscs and CD-ROM (compact disk-read only memory) disks offer new possibilities for integrating motion, graphics, still pictures, and digitized sound CBI. Using multi-media (e.g., multi-image slide/tape or interactive video) presentations until now has typically involved a major effort that was only cost justified for instruction delivered to a large number of students. The compactness and lower cost of the newer storage devices and enhanced technology now make it practical to offer multi-media presentations to smaller groups on an individualized basis. Advances in screen resolution, digitization of images, and speech synthesis create new possibilities for CBI lessons with realistic pictures, motion, animation, and sound at costs far below those of producing an interactive videodisc. One can easily imagine a sophisticated computer system that includes the attributes of all existing media. Designers would no longer need to justify the selection of an individual medium. Rather, they will need a model for determining which attributes to use with a particular instructional strategy. Such a model might focus on the motivational value of the attributes, the perceived difficulty of learning from material presented with a set of attributes, and the cost of producing or manipulating a set of attributes.

Intelligent CBI

The increasing availability and sophistication of artificial intelligence tools has the potential to help us create new models and instructional strategies for CBI. Future CBI materials are likely to include a model of a novice's schema and an expert's schema for use in instructional decision making. For example, Tennyson (1984) described an intelligent adaptive system that used a Bayesian probability model for determining when the student has mastered the content. Future courseware may include response-sensitive systems that will determine when a student has failed to understand the content, by accepting and processing natural language input in response to open-ended questions or generative strategies.

Expert Systems

An expert system in a database of knowledge that is sorted and selected by an algorithm programmed with a set of rules derived from an expert (Welsh, 1987). One current use of expert systems is the development of intelligent job aids. Harmon (1986) describes Campbell Soup Company's expert job aid that diagnoses equipment problems based on observations entered into the system. Future possibilities include the development of expert systems to aid in making instructional design decisions based on the current database of instructional research. Such a system would recommend an optimum instructional strategy for implementation based on student, environmental, and content data.

Automated Development Tools

Another area in which we are likely to see a significant impact on instructional design is the development of automated development tools. These tools can vary from CBI authoring systems to systems that help a subject matter expert complete a task analysis, write objectives, and structure an instructional strategy (e.g., Cantor, 1988).

SUMMARY

Computer technology provides the designer with more efficient options than are available in most other media for implementing a variety of instructional strategies. Of concern, however, is the effectiveness of these strategies when implemented in CBI. For example, the screen limitations imposed on the presentation of content in CBI poses new problems concerning the chunking of content that have not been adequately addressed in prior research. The increased efficiency and reduced concern about the physical length of the lesson with CBI offers opportunities for implementing alternative presentations and different forms of feedback.

This increased efficiency for implementing a variety of strategies should not encourage designers to create alternative strategies on a wholesale basis. Rather, consideration of the research literature and careful logic should be used to determine the optimum approach for the objectives. In addition, researchers should investigate not only the effectiveness of these new designs, but the efficiency in terms of learning and development.

REFERENCES

Anand, P., & Ross, S. M. (1987). Using computer-assisted instruction to personalize math learning materials for elementary school children. *Journal of Educational Psychology, 79*, 245-252.

Bork, A. (1987). *Learning with personal computers*. New York: Harper & Row.

Cantor, J. A. (1988). An automated curriculum development process for Navy technical training. *Journal of Instructional Development, 11*, 3-11.

Carrier, C., Davidson, G., & Williams, M. (1985). The selection of instructional options in a computer-based coordinate concept lesson. *Educational Communication and Technology Journal, 33*, 199-212.

Dempsey, J. V., & Driscoll, M. P. (1989). *The effects of four methods of immediate corrective feedback on retention, discrimination error, and feedback study time in computer-based instruction*. Paper presented at the Annual Meeting of the American Educational Research Association, San Francisco, California.

Department of Education [producer]. (1960). *Teaching machines and programmed learning* [film]. New York: Duart.

Fish, M. C., & Feldman, S. C. (1987). A comparison of reading comprehension using print and microcomputer presentation. *Journal of Computer-Based Instruction, 14*, 57-61.

Grabinger, R. S. (1983). *CRT text design: Psychological attributes underlying the evaluation of models of CRT text displays.* Unpublished doctoral dissertation, Indiana University.

Hannafin, M. J. (1984). Guidelines for using locus of instructional control in the design of computer-assisted instruction. *Journal of Instructional Development, 7*(3), 6-10.

Hannafin, M. J., & Hooper, S. (1989). *An integrated framework for CBI screen design and layout.* Paper presented at the Annual Meeting of the Association for Educational Communications and Technology, Dallas, Texas.

Harmon, P. (1986). Expert systems, job aids, and the future of instructional technology. *Performance and Instruction, 25*, 26-28.

Hartley, J. (1987). Designing electronic text: The role of print-based research. *Educational Communication and Technology Journal, 35*, 3-17.

Heines, J. M. (1984). *Screen design strategies for computer-assisted instruction.* Bedford, MA: Digital Press.

Johansen, K. J., & Tennyson, R. D. (1984). Effect of adaptive advisement on perception in learner controlled, computer-based instruction using a rule-learning task. *Educational Communication and Technology Journal, 31*, 226-236.

Kulik, J. A., & Kulik, C. (1988). Timing of feedback and verbal learning. *Review of Educational Research, 58*, 79-97.

Kulik, J. A., Bangert, R. L., & Williams, G. W. (1983). Effects of computer based teaching on secondary school students. *Journal of Educational Psychology, 75*, 19-26.

Morrison, G. R., Ross, S. M., & O'Dell, J. K. (1988). Text density level as a design variable in instructional displays. *Educational Communication and Technology Journal, 36*, 103-115.

Morrison, G. R., Ross, S. M., Schultz, C. E., & O'Dell, J. K. (1989). Learner preferences for varying screen densities using realistic stimulus materials with single and multiple frame designs. *Educational Technology Research and Development, 37*, 53-60.

Papert, S. (1980). *Mindstorms: Children, computers, and powerful ideas.* New York: Basic Books.

Peeck, J., & Tillema, H. H. (1978). Delay of feedback and retention of correct and incorrect responses. *Journal of Experimental Psychology, 38*, 139-145.

Pressey, S. (1927). A machine for automatic teaching of drill material. *School and Society, 25*, 549-552.

Ross, S. M., & Anand, P. (1987). A computer-based strategy for personalizing verbal problems in teaching mathematics. *Educational Communication and Technology Journal, 35*, 151-162.

Ross, S. M., & Morrison, G. R. (1989). In search of a happy medium in instructional technology research: Issues concerning external validity, media replications, and learner control. *Educational Technology Research and Development, 37*(1), 19-33.

Ross, S. M., & Rakow, E. A. (1981). Adaptive instructional strategies for teaching rules in mathematics. *Educational Communication and Technology Journal, 30*, 67-84.

Ross, S. M., Morrison, G. R., & O'Dell, J. K. (1989). Uses and effects of learner control of context and instructional support in computer-based instruction. *Educational Technology Research and Development, 37*, 29-39.

————. (1988). Obtaining more out of less text in CBI: Effects of varied text density levels as a function of learner characteristics and control strategy. *Educational Communication and Technology Journal, 36*, 131-142.

Schimmel, B. J. (1988). Providing meaningful feedback. In D. H. Jonassen (Ed.), *Instructional designs for microcomputer courseware* (pp. 183-195). Hillsdale, NJ: Lawrence Erlbaum.

Smith, P. L. (1988, January). *Toward a taxonomy of feedback: Content and scheduling.* Paper presented at the Annual Meeting of the Association for Educational Communications and Technology, New Orleans, Louisiana.

Tennyson, R. D. (1980). Instructional control strategies and content structure as design variables in concept acquisition using computer-based instruction. *Journal of Educational Psychology, 72*, 525-532.

————. (1984). Artificial intelligence methods in computer-based instructional design. *Journal of Instructional Development, 7*, 17-22.

Van Dyke, B. F., & Newton, J. M. (1972). Computer-assisted instruction: Performance and attitudes. *Journal of Educational Research, 65*, 291-293.

Welsh, J. R. (1987). Expert system shells: Tools to aid human performance. *Journal of Instructional Development, 10, 15-19.*

17

Message Design
Issues and Trends

Barbara L. Grabowski
College of Education, Pennsylvania State University
University Park, Pennsylvania

Message design within the context of the field of instructional technology has three main thrusts: message design for instruction, message design for learning, and general principles that span both. Each thrust is exemplified and supported by a body of literature that includes a theoretical foundation, research support, and a synthesis into principles or specific design strategies.

The purpose of this chapter is first to define four key concepts whose definitions have helped chart the course for each thrust, then to provide an overview of each major thrust by identifying key researchers and key findings. This is not an exhaustive review, but rather shows related trends and their impact on instructional design.

KEY CONCEPTS

A discussion of message design issues can take several directions because of the many possible interpretations of the term. It seems appropriate, therefore, to define key concepts before discussing the various ways it can affect what instructional designers do to create an environment where learning can occur. Four concepts emerge as key to the topic: message, learning and instruction, media, and message design. Each is defined here to create a foundation for interpreting the principles of message design that have evolved in the field.

Message

Messages, from a traditional perspective, include any pattern of signs used for communication between sender and a receiver. Fleming and Levie (1978) narrow this definition to limit "messages" to those patterns of signs or symbols that modify behavior in any one of the three *instructional* domains: cognitive, affective, or psychomotor.

To appreciate the impact of message on the design of instruction requires the recognition that "sign" is an all-important contributing attribute depicting the *form* the message takes. Anderson and Meyer (1988, p. 15) define "sign" as a "general term used to describe anything that cognitively comes to stand for something else, whether a thing or an idea." This "thing or idea" includes all of the standard patterns of visual and audio signs, as well as "textures, odors, gestures, melodies" (Anderson & Meyer, 1988, p. 15). The purpose of sign is to activate any combination of the five senses that function as the receptors of information. At the initial stages of information processing, the physical form of the message will affect what information is actually attended to and perceived by the learner.

Although this definition of sign may appear to limit message design to issues of physical form, it is important to understand its impact beyond this interpretation. A sign as physical form, while extremely important, is too circumscribed in its interpretation. The actual inductive composition of the message, to use Rothkopf's (1976) term, may indeed make as much of a difference in learning as its external composition. Once information is attended to and perceived, it is actively processed in working memory for later storage in long-term memory (Osborne & Wittrock, 1983; Gagne, 1985). This is important because "memory depends far more on the stimulus-as-encoded than stimulus-as-presented" (Eysenck, 1984, p. 103). Inductive strategies used within a message, therefore, should evoke coding, organization, integration, and translation activities necessary for further comprehension, retention, and future retrieval (Rothkopf, 1970; Barry, 1974; Sutliff, 1986). This relationship is shown in figure 17.1. After a macro instructional design has been performed, attention to message design from the physical organization as well as its inductive composition is needed. This chapter deals with "message" from both perspectives.

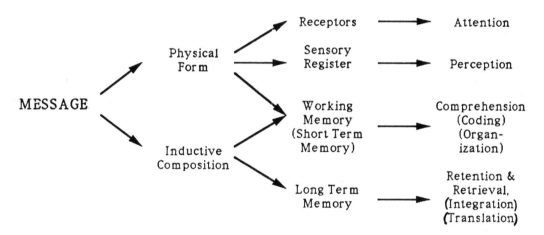

Fig. 17.1. Types of message design affecting stages and levels of processing.

Learning and Instruction

The second concept important to understanding message design interrelates information, instruction, and learning. These terms denote the purpose of the message. Because of their interrelationship, message design serves overlapping as well as unique functions. Only their unique functions are addressed below.

Information has commonly come to be known as "bits and pieces of discrete (content), fragmented and particular" (Wilson, 1983, p. 83). On the other hand, the difference between *instruction* and *learning* has been classified by Fleming and Levie (1978) according to the locus of the activity; that is, *instruction* occurs outside the learner, while *learning* is the result of internal cognitive processes within the learner. *Instruction*, therefore, may be defined as a way of organizing and sequencing information for the learner which may include any or all of a number of essential elements, such as presentation of information and provision of examples, practice, and feedback (Reigeluth, 1983). *Learning*, on the other hand, results from effective coding, organization, integration, and translation of information. While instruction and learning always require information, information is not always instructional, nor does simply viewing information always result in learning. Also, instruction does not always cause learning, nor does learning always require instruction (Grabowski & Curtis, 1990).

Message design related to an informational message attempts to affect attention, perception, and hopefully, but not necessarily, comprehension. As a result, informational message designers would be most concerned with its physical form. As shown in figure 17.2, message design for instruction deals with attention, perception, and comprehension, as well as, but not necessarily, retention and retrieval. This also places most of the design emphasis and effort on the physical form of the message. Message design for learning directly addresses the cognitive processes required of retention and retrieval and therefore would be most concerned with the inductive composition of the message. The concepts presented in this chapter are limited to those with a purpose of instruction and/or learning, rather than the simple presentation of information.

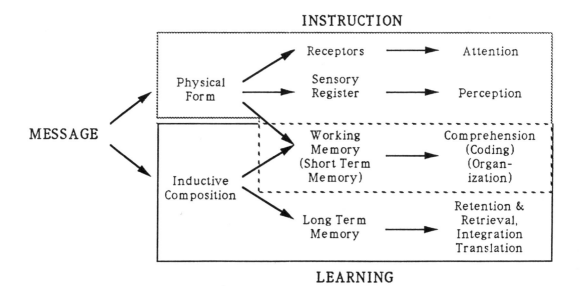

Fig. 17.2. Relationship of message design to instruction and learning.

Media

The third important concept to define and relate to message design is media. Media have been defined as the "carrier(s) of the message from the transmitting source ... to the receiver of the message" (Romiszowski, 1988, p. 8). Fleming's (1987, p. 234) definition broadens the concept to "mediator," which elevates its importance from being a mere delivery vehicle to "something that intervenes between parties at variance to reconcile them."

Adopting one definition over the other will determine the level of importance one gives to the medium in the final design of the message. Regarding the medium as a mere vehicle would imply that message design principles are generic to all media and that any medium can deliver a message equally as effectively. This argument seems to have the greatest plausibility for designing the inductive composition of a message that is not as limited to the physical limitations of a specific medium. One limitation to this interpretation, however, is the medium's ability to accept various forms of user input.

Conversely, while one cannot deny the importance of Clark's (1983) argument for the position that the effectiveness of instruction is inextricably related to its instructional design, one also cannot ignore the fact that when designing the physical form of a message, media attributes play an important role in media *selection*. In other words, they may inherently determine how message design strategies are ultimately implemented, especially in terms of specific attributes facilitating or detracting from the message. Romiszowski (1988) and Fleming (1987) support the position that while more than one medium should be able to deliver the message with equal effectiveness, not all media will be able to present the required learning stimuli nor the options for student responses.

This chapter deals with general principles that are media independent, as well as giving special consideration to text and electronically transmitted video.

Message Design

The last concept combines the elements of the first three into "message design" itself. In general, design is the "analysis of a communication problem" for the purpose of developing a plan for the deliberate manipulation of the symbols conveyed (Fleming & Levie, 1978). Message design is one step in the instructional development process which carries out the specifications of the instructional design blueprint in greater detail. Like blueprints from a house which do not specify the finishing touches of color, furniture, placement, etc., instructional blueprints do not specify the "form" the message should take. Within the structure of the specified instructional design, message design takes shape. These designs are planned for the physical form (instruction) and the inductive composition (learning) of a message. Message design for instruction deals with those external factors out of the control of the learner which can facilitate learning, while message design for learning deals with those strategies which activate internal factors to have learning actually occur.

KEY CONTRIBUTORS

Message Design for Instruction and Learning

Major contributions to the field have been made by several key researchers and research teams for both message design for instruction and message design for learning. These contributions come in two forms: synthesis of basic research into applied principles, and development of specific messaging techniques. Several major contributors through books and edited books are summarized in table 17.1. This list is by no means exhaustive, but rather, it should serve as a starting point for studying the concepts in more depth. It must also be noted that these works were compilations of research conducted by hundreds of others who conducted the basic research.

Table 17.1.
Major Contributions to Message Design

Message Design	Synthesis	Specific Medium	Specific Technique
Instruction (physical form)	Hartley (1978, 1985) Chu & Schramm (1968) Heines (1984) Willows & Houghton (1987) Houghton & Willows (1987)	Text/Computer Television Computer Text Text	Horn (1973, 1974) Structured Writing
Both Instruction and Learning	Fleming & Levie (1978) Jonassen (1982, 1985)	None Text/ Computer	
Learning, Inductive Composition	Wittrock (1974a,b)		Hodgson (1968, 1972, 1974) Structural Communication

KEY PRINCIPLES

Message Design for Instruction

Message design for instruction involves planning for the manipulation of the physical form of the message. Herein is where typographical principles come into play, especially those related to specific media, including text design, screen design, and video design. Only text and computer-based message design are presented here. For a summary of each of the other areas, the reader is directed to those works noted in table 17.1.

Text Design

Several different factors which need to be considered when designing text messages have been identified by key text designers. These factors include proportion, sequence, emphasis, unity, and balance (Reilly & Roach, 1986); page size, consistency, typefaces, sizes, and spacing, organizers, cueing, and writing clarity (Hartley, 1985); repetition, novelty, reward, sensory experiences, outlining, and spacing (Hand, 1982); interpolation, delineation, serialization, and stylization (Waller, 1982); labeling, highlighting, and illustrating (Duchastel, 1982); semantic distance, sequential and directional relationships for diagrams and charts (Winn & Holliday, 1982; Winn, 1987); content, writing style, words-print, graphs and diagrams, and pictures (Romiszowski, 1988); and redundancy, decision structure, functional groupings, and organizational use of white space (Wright, 1982).

From these factors, some general principles can be derived:

- Select page size based on other physical features to be used in the text design (Hartley, 1985).

- Use consistent spacing and reference areas so as not to confuse the learner (Hartley, 1985; Reilly & Roach, 1986; Hand, 1982).

- Use spatial layout and white spacing to organize the display (Hartley, 1985; Hand, 1982; Reilly & Roach, 1986; Wright, 1982).

- For typefaces, type sizes, and spacing, consider "sensible phrasing" and line length as one factor in their selection (Hartley, 1985).

- Beware of nonstandard typefaces, capitals, italics, and underlining that impair reading flow (Hartley, 1985).

- Be cautious with the use of color since it can have both an enhancing and a detracting effect on learning (Hartley, 1985).

- Use summaries, headings, questions, and lists to help organize and sequence text (Hartley, 1985; Duchastel, 1982).

- Short sentences and simple vocabulary will enhance comprehension (Hartley, 1985).

- Use illustrations when they contribute to a message, but be aware that they may also detract from it because of complexity or conflicting information (Hartley, 1985; Levin, Anglin, & Carney, 1987; Dwyer, 1978; Duchastel, 1982).

- Cartoons may enhance motivation, but not necessarily comprehension (Hartley, 1985).

- For graphs and charts, make semantic distance, sequential relationships reflect reality, and directional relationships follow natural flow for reading (Winn & Holliday, 1982; Winn, 1987).

- Keep tables and graphs simple, especially for low-ability learners (Winn & Holliday, 1982).

- Use signaling strategies since both the content and the signaling strategy are stored in memory (Meyer, 1985; Duchastel, 1982).

This list includes only a representative sample of principles, and therefore does not intend to be exhaustive. For further guidelines, the reader is directed to the original authors.

Computer Display

Hartley (1985) also provides us with guidelines for message design for computer-based/assisted learning. He states that much of what we have learned with text-based research can be applied to electronic screen design: consistent use of spacing, good use of white space, logical organizations, etc. However, there are important limitations that will affect message design. These limitations present problems of legibility, search and retrieval, and "writing text to match this medium." Unlike text, computer displays are limited to the amount of information that can be displayed on the screen at one time, and do not contain the same visual navigational cues. Special attention must be given to carefully crafting displays that are not confusing, yet provide a gestalt, as well as help readers know where they are in the lesson. Hints are provided for writing, signaling text, presentation speed, and the use of color.

Heines (1984) also contributes significantly to this body of principles. Besides reiterating Hartley's points, he expands his recommendations to include three important additions. The first is consistent use of space on the screen (functional areas) for orienting information, directions, student responses, error messages, and student options. Second, he recommends strategies for using the dynamics of the display to direct attention (through pop erases or wipes, for example). Finally, his discussion of navigational issues as they relate to menu design provides the CBT designer with useful guidelines.

Merrill (1982) presents a list of recommendations about designing for computer-based instruction. He organizes these principles around format, paging, ease of use, interaction, and the importance of formative feedback. He makes several recommendations not mentioned by the other two authors: avoid scrolling, require a minimum of keystrokes, minimize the time to generate title pages, mask pauses, and avoid sarcastic feedback.

Structured Writing

One specific technique that plans for the deliberate manipulation of the physical form of the message is structured writing, advanced by Robert Horn (1976; 1982). The reader is directed to these works for further detail.

Message Design for Learning

DiVesta (1989, p. 56) states that "elaboration and organization of text material have powerful effects on learning ... but it is not mere elaboration—the making of an idea more complex—that facilitates learning and memory ... [it is] elaboration that meaningfully relates new target information to old that makes the new information understandable." Message design for learning involves the planning for the inductive composition of the message which induces the learner to meaningfully relate the target information to the old. Guidance for designing for learning comes from Wittrock's (1974a; 1974b; 1985) generative model of learning. This model is described next.

Generative Learning Strategies

A very important current body of research is examining inductive messages that evoke active cognitive processing. The most promising model is the generative learning model proposed by Wittrock (1974a; 1974b). A basic assumption behind his model is that the learner is not a passive recipient of information, but rather an active participant in the learning process, with integration and translation as the desired outcome. The conscious construction of meaning occurs in short-term or working memory where information is being drawn both from long-term memory and the environment (Osborne & Wittrock, 1983).

This model can provide guidance for designing messages that are mentally engaging. DiVesta (1989) states that what is important is that instruction can influence the learner's achievement and understanding. This is especially important as a main assumption underlying instructional technology. In this model, the goal is to "determine the effects of instruction, based on what it causes the learner to do." In general, research results have shown increased gains in learning when the learner is an active rather than a passive participant in the learning process (see, for example, Peper & Mayer, 1986; Bull & Wittrock, 1973; Carnine & Kinder, 1985).

Examples of strategies learners use to generate meaning include paraphrases, analogies, explanations, inferences, outlines, summaries, creative interpretations, images, cognitive maps, diagrams, relevant examples, titles and headings, questions, mnemonics, questioning, clarifying, and predicting (Goetz, 1983; Jonassen, 1985; DiVesta, 1989).

Structural Communication

One very promising technique that evokes active mental processing is structural communications, advocated by Hodgson (1968; 1971; 1974). This method is perhaps one of the most powerful ways of structuring automated, conversational dialogues to achieve higher-order learning objectives. It has proved itself in many varied educational contexts (Egan, 1976; Romiszowski, 1976; 1986), including high-level management decision making (Hodgson & Dill, 1970; Hodgson, 1971), and holds great untapped potential for improving current interactive instructional systems design (Romiszowski & Grabowski, 1987; 1989).

To promote reflective thinking, stimulating initial learning materials are presented and then followed by a highly personalized and interactive dialogue which challenges the learner to solve new and multifaceted problems. The structure includes several key features: initial learning materials, problem sets, random array of response components in a response matrix, and discussion guides with comments linked to the learner's inclusion or exclusion of items in the response set. This guided dialogue was simulated in printed texts, which after presenting a basic reading assignment would pose a number of open-ended discussion problems. To respond, the learner would construct a sort of essay outline by selecting the factors that make up the "best case" or solution for a long list of usually 20 to 30 candidate statements (Hodgson, 1968; 1971; 1974). The learner then analyzes the information presented, synthesizes a personal viewpoint, and selects the items from the response matrix that support this viewpoint. The structural communication methodology handles this dialogue by means of a diagnostic tool called the discussion guide. The discussion guide then identifies specific comments that the author has written to clear up certain misconceptions or compare contrasting viewpoints.

Message Design for Both Instruction and Learning

Fleming and Levie in 1978, and in two later works (Fleming, 1987; Levie, 1987) addressed message design from both an instructional and a learning perspective by tying their recommended principles to levels of information processing. Their later organizing framework includes attention, perception, learning, and concept formation with a learner model with four learning needs: a learner who actively seeks stimulation, is "attentive to order," uses a "strategy for dealing with that stimulation and order," and "derives meaning from the environment" (p. 256). Like message design principles for physical form, their attention and perception principles deal with selectivity, novelty, organization, similarity, and proximity-contiguity, expectancy, uncertainty. Like message design for learning, they group their principles of concreteness, prior knowledge, and salient criterial attributes, limited capacity, similarity, and primacy-recency, activity, strategy, mental imagery, and elaboration, and finally, meaningfulness and feedback.

REFERENCES

Anderson, J. A., & Meyer, T. P. (1988). *Mediated communications*. Newbury Park, CA: Sage.

Barry, R. J. (1974). The concept of mathemagenic behaviors: An analysis of its heuristic value. *Perceptual and Motor Skills, 38*, 311-321.

Bull, B. L., & Wittrock, M. C. (1973). Imagery in the learning of verbal definitions. *British Journal of Educational Psychology, 43*(3), 289-293.

Carnine, D., & Kinder, C. (1985). Teaching low-performing students to apply generative and schema strategies to narrative and expository materials. *Remedial and Special Education, 6*(1), 20-30.

Chu, G., & Schramm, W. (1967). *Learning from television: What the research says.* Washington, DC: National Association of Educational Broadcasters.

Clark, R. E. (1983). Reconsidering research on learning from media. *Review of Educational Research, 53*(4), 445-460.

DiVesta, F. (1989). Applying cognitive psychology to education. In M. C. Wittrock & F. Farley (Eds.), *The future of educational psychology.* Hillsdale, NJ: Lawrence Erlbaum.

Duchastel, P. (1982). Textual display techniques. In D. H. Jonassen (Ed.), *The technology of text, vol. 1.* Englewood Cliffs, NJ: Educational Technology Publications.

Dwyer, F. (1978). *Strategies for improving visual learning.* State College, PA: Learning Services.

Egan, K. (1976). *Structural communication.* Belmont, CA: Fearon Press.

Eysenck, M. W. (1984). *Handbook of cognitive psychology.* Hillsdale, NJ: Lawrence Erlbaum.

Fleming, M. (1987). Displays that communicate. In R. M. Gagne (Ed.), *Instructional technology foundations.* Hillsdale, NJ: Lawrence Erlbaum.

Fleming, M., & Levie, H. (1978). *Instructional message design.* Englewood Cliffs, NJ: Educational Technology Publications.

Gagne, E. (1985). *The cognitive psychology of school learning.* Boston: Little, Brown.

Goetz, E. (1983). *Elaborative strategies: Promises and dilemmas for instruction in large classes.* (ERIC Document Reproduction Service No. ED 243 073).

Grabowski, B., & Curtis, R. (1990). *Information, instruction and learning.* (IDDE Working Paper). Syracuse, NY: Syracuse University.

Hand, J. D. (1982). Brain functions during learning: Implications for text design. In D. H. Jonassen (Ed.), *The technology of text, vol. 1.* Englewood Cliffs, NJ: Educational Technology Publications.

Hartley, J. (1978). *Designing instructional text.* New York: Nichols.

———. (1982). Designing instructional text. In D. H. Jonassen (Ed.), *The technology of text, vol. 1.* Englewood Cliffs, NJ: Educational Technology Publications.

———. (1985). *Designing instructional text.* New York: Nichols.

Heines, J. (1984). *Screen design strategies for computer-assisted instruction.* Bedford, MA: Digital Press.

Hodgson, A. M. (1968). A communication technique for the future. *Ideas, 7.* Curriculum Laboratory, Goldsmith College, University of London.

———. (1971). An experiment in computer-guided correspondence seminars for management. In D. Packham (Ed.), *Aspects of educational technology, volume V.* London: Pitman.

———. (1974). Structural communication in practice. In A. J. Romiszowski (Ed.), *APLET yearbook of educational and instructional technology, 1974/5.* London: Kogan Page.

Hodgson, A. M., & Dill, R. (1970, December). Sequel to the misfired missive. *Harvard Business Review, 48*(6), 105-110.

Horn, R. E. (1976). *How to write information mapping*. Lexington, MA: Information Resource.

———. (1982). Structured writing and text design. In D. H. Jonassen (Ed.), *The technology of text, vol. 1*. Englewood Cliffs, NJ: Educational Technology Publications.

Houghton, H. A., & Willows, D. M. (1987). *The psychology of illustration: Instructional issues*. New York: Springer-Verlag.

Jonassen, D. H. (1982). *The technology of text, vol. 1*. Englewood Cliffs, NJ: Educational Technology Publications.

———. (1985). *The technology of text, vol. 2*. Englewood Cliffs, NJ: Educational Technology Publications.

Levie, W. H. (1987). Research on pictures: A guide to the literature. In D. M. Willows & H. A. Houghton (Eds.), *The psychology of illustration: Basic research*. New York: Springer-Verlag.

Levin, J. R., Anglin, G., & Carney, R. N. (1987). On empirically validating functions of pictures in prose. In D. M. Willows & H. A. Houghton (Eds.), *The psychology of illustration: Basic research*. New York: Springer-Verlag.

Merrill, P. F. (1982). Displaying text on microcomputer. In D. H. Jonassen (Ed.), *The technology of text, vol. 1*. Englewood Cliffs, NJ: Educational Technology Publications.

Meyer, B. J. (1985). Signaling the structure of content: Introduction. In D. H. Jonassen (Ed.), *The technology of text, vol. 2*. Englewood Cliffs, NJ: Educational Technology Publications.

Osborne, R. J., & Wittrock, M. C. (1983). Learning science: A generative process. *Science Education, 67*(4), 489-508.

Peper, R. J., & Mayer, R. E. (1986). Generative effects of notetaking during science lectures. *Journal of Educational Psychology, 78*(1), 34-38.

Reigeluth, C. (1983). *Instructional design theories and models: An overview of their current status*. Hillsdale, NJ: Lawrence Erlbaum.

Reilly, S. S., & Roach, J. W. (1986). Designing human/computer interfaces: A comparison of human factors and graphic arts principles. *Educational Technology, 26*(1), 38-40.

Romiszowski, A. J. (1976). *A study of individualized systems of mathematics instruction at the post secondary levels*. Unpublished doctoral thesis, University of Loughborough, England.

———. (1986). *Developing auto-instructional materials*. New York: Nichols.

———. (1988). *The selection and use of instructional media*. New York: Nichols.

Romiszowski, A. J., & Grabowski, B. (1987). *Some neglected CAL methodologies and their potential for new interactive systems of instruction*. Paper presented at the 1987 SALT Conference on Developments in the Design of Interactive Instruction Systems.

———. (1989). Interactive video and cognitive structures: A technique for enhancing the effectiveness of interactive simulations and games. *Proceedings for Interactive Instruction Delivery*. Warrenton, VA: Society for Applied Learning Technology.

Rothkopf, E. Z. (1970). The concept of mathemagenic activities. *Review of Educational Research, 40*(3), 325-336.

———. (1976). Writing to teach and reading to learn: A perspective on the psychology of written instruction. In N. L. Gage, (Ed.), *The psychology of teaching methods*. Chicago: University of Chicago Press.

Sutliff, R. (1986). Effect of adjunct postquestions on achievement. *Journal of Industrial Teacher Education, 23*(3), 45-54.

Waller, R. (1982). Text as diagram: Using typography to improve access and understanding. In D. H. Jonassen (Ed.), *The technology of text.* Englewood Cliffs, NJ: Educational Technology Publications.

Willows, D. M., & Houghton, H. A. (1987). *The psychology of illustration: Basic research.* New York: Springer-Verlag.

Wilson, P. (1983). Mission and information: What business are we in? *The Journal of Academic Librarianship, 14*(2), 82-86.

Winn, W. (1987). Charts, graphs, and diagrams in educational materials. In D. M. Willows & H. A. Houghton (Eds.), *The psychology of illustration: Basic research.* New York: Springer-Verlag.

Winn, W., & Holliday, W. (1982). Design principles for diagrams and charts. In D. M. Jonassen (Ed.), *The technology of text, vol. 1.* Englewood Cliffs, NJ: Educational Technology Publications.

Wittrock, M. C. (1974a). Learning as a generative process. *Educational Psychologist, 11*(2), 87-95.

———. (1974b). A generative model of mathematics education. *Journal for Research in Mathematics Education, 5*(4), 181-196.

———. (1985). Teaching learners generative strategies for enhancing reading comprehension. *Theory into Practice, 24*(2), 123-126.

Wright, P. (1982). A user-oriented approach to the design of tables and flowcharts. In D. H. Jonassen (Ed.), *The technology of text, vol. 1.* Englewood Cliffs, NJ: Educational Technology Publications.

18

"Flawless" Consulting for the External Consultant

William Coscarelli

Curriculum and Instruction, Southern Illinois University
Carbondale, Illinois

The theory of consulting has been thoroughly covered in two books: Edgar Schein's classic, *Process Consultation: Its Role in Organizational Development*, and Peter Block's *Flawless Consulting: A Guide to Getting Your Expertise Used*. This chapter elaborates on Block's approach to consulting, especially as it applies to a consultant working outside the client's organization.

THE TAO OF FLAWLESS CONSULTING

Block (1981) summarizes his approach to consulting in the final paragraphs of his book:

> The focus here on skills, requirements, and techniques is really just a vehicle for expressing support to the belief that your real task as a consultant is to be constantly noticing what you are experiencing and to behave as authentically as possible.... There is a paradox in this. We all want to have influence. We all want our expertise used. We want to have a feeling of control, perhaps power. The way to gain this control is, in a way, to give it up. Being authentic is to reduce the amount you control and censor your own experience. To censor your own experience is to give other people tremendous power over you. You are letting their reactions determine how you function. The way to have leverage is not to give it away. The way to avoid giving leverage away is to reduce the extent you restrain yourself from acting on your own instincts and perceptions. Acting without restraint is being authentic. Being authentic and attending to the task requirements of each phase [of the consulting process] is consulting flawlessly (p. 195).

All of this is somewhat esoteric unless you happen to have a few years of practice under your belt, when it begins to make sense. However, if you are just beginning to work in a consultant's role you are probably at a stage where this makes little sense. Following is my interpretation.

Setting the Stage

Block does adopt the classic distinctions among types of consultancies that Schein proposed: product consultation, medical consultation, and process consultation. However, Block uses different labels, with some variation in philosophy. Essentially, product = pair-of-hands, medical = expert, and process = collaboration. Block also feels that any consultant brings three sets of skills to a project: (1) the technical skills related to the discipline, whether they are instructional design skills, electrical engineering, etc.; (2) the interpersonal skills that apply to all interactions, such as listening, confrontation, group management, etc.; and (3) consulting skills that follow five major stages: entry/contracting, problem diagnosis, feedback to the client, implementation of the intervention, and a final decision to recycle, terminate, or extend the relationship. Progress through these stages can take a very short time (one hour) or quite a long time (one year), but they must be completed fully and in sequence for one to consult "flawlessly."

Some Assumptions

There are perhaps two major themes to Block's writing that I have identified and that the reader should consider when applying his work in a given project: (1) in each stage of the consultation you and the client must share responsibility equally to consult flawlessly, and (2) putting into words what you are experiencing "is the most powerful thing you can do to have the leverage you are looking for and to build client commitment" (Block, 1981, p. 31). These themes make the most sense if you accept the view that your world is populated with Theory Y types: people motivated by intrinsic desires to improve. The themes don't work well if you are in a Theory X or related kind of environment, where people are viewed as needing extrinsic motivators to keep working. (The Marine boot camp at Paris Island is a good model case Theory X environment.)

Block is addressing primarily the internal consultant (see p. 107), the one who has a salaried position in an organization. A consultant outside the organization is more likely to find that the balance of responsibility has shifted to the consultant and not the client. The trick is to keep the balance under control and not end up, like a small child, stuck at the top of the seesaw at the mercy of another. The trick to finding this balance probably does lie in Block's assertions that one attend to each of the stages and that putting into words what you are feeling is the best strategy to gaining the leverage you need to build client commitment.

MATURING AS AN
EXTERNAL CONSULTANT

As an external consultant, you probably are trying to provide a professional service. You can take an aggressive marketing approach that befits a new business, or a more reactive one that typically characterizes academics who consult. (For guidance on the logistics and daily practice of the business side of being a consultant, see Robert Kelley's *Consulting: The Complete Guide to a Profitable Career*.) Whether they are proactive or reactive in building a consulting career, people go through certain stages on their way to enlightenment as a consultant. I have found that a developmental sequence exists for those who do *not* have a salaried position in an organization where they can serve as an internal consultant. One can operate flawlessly as an external consultant, but it is necessary to adapt the themes just discussed. Following is a description of the developmental sequence.

Stage I: I Should Pay You

When you begin to contemplate your first consultancy, you first encounter your own insecurity as a professional. After all, you wonder, I'll probably learn more from this job than I give back to them. What if I miss the deadlines? How much should I charge? Maybe I can solve this dilemma by offering to do the job for a fee to be paid only if my solution works. No, if I do that maybe they will think I don't have confidence in my services. From this conundrum, a resolution evolves that leads to stage II.

Stage II: You Pay Me Something (Please?)

At this point in your career you have decided you really can ask for the money, but you aren't too sure it is fully justified. As a neophyte in the business you feel that you can, in a sense, be honest with your clients about your weaknesses by offering them a reduced fee compared to that of the marketplace in general. You figure that if you get the job, you will learn a great deal from it; if you mess up, the client will think it's still a reasonable service for the cost. The words "paying my dues" come often to your lips as you describe your life to friends and colleagues.

Stage III: You Pay Me Something (Gulp!)

After having "paid your dues" for a while you begin to think that maybe you do have a saleable skill. In fact, you probably begin to think you might actually be pretty good. You probably are, if you have been working in the area for a while. Then one day you are asked to bid on a contract that you think you could do, but you are beginning to realize that anything you do takes a lot of time, and you really aren't making any money on your contracts. So it is with no small degree of trepidation that you respond to client inquiries with a fee that starts to look about what everyone else in the field is charging. You hope that your client doesn't push too hard about the fee, but expect you probably will lower it if push comes to shove and you might lose the contract. Luckily for you, the client accepts your offer. You redouble your energies to prove you are as good as expected and turn in a better than average product. After some success at this stage you begin to believe that your services are worthwhile, and you are about ready to enter stage IV.

Stage IV: I Need "X!"

Looking back on your career, you now realize you have come a long way. Looking toward your future, you begin to wonder how you will pay the mortgage, fund your retirement, why taxes are so high for people who work as hard as you do, and in general adopt a more Republican view of life. With the dual realization that you can compete and that the local grocery store doesn't have a special line in it for "those who work hard but don't have as much money," you now become more confident and less tentative. You view a professional relationship as one in which you are a fully equal partner with needs and wants that have to be addressed. Not only do you expect, and ask for without flinching, fair market value for your services, but you begin to realize that you don't have to fly excursion rate to see the client; you can travel on a full-fare ticket enabling you to switch flight times if you get out early or need to stay later. You are more likely to assert that a deadline is impossible and suggest an alternative that allows you to maintain an outwardly normal lifestyle during the project.

Stage V: This Is Getting Me Nowhere

Up to now you have been taking just about any project that makes it to your door, and more recently, those that met your needs. You've been good and the word is starting to get out that you are a competent vendor. People begin to call you and ask you to take on a project, but you realize for the first time that if you keep this up you will nickel and dime your lifestyle to death with piecemeal projects. You realize you can't reinvent the wheel with each client and come to understand the value in specialization and recognition of your product. You know this stage has arrived when you turn down your first project, for example, because it means writing more instruction (which you can do but are tired of doing) instead of boilerplating something you have already done or providing an off-the-shelf service. If you are successful at this level, and continue to work at it, you may then reach the final state. Manic swings between highs and lows continue to exist and make you wonder if this is really the business for you.

Stage VI: I'm Busy, But If It's Worth My Time

For the first time, you see time as money. If the government is going to take one-third to one-half of everything you earn, if you have to go out and hire people to handle a large project, if you have to ride herd on the help to keep quality stable.... If I'm going to go through all this, you think, then I might as well get paid for it. I'm busy with my current services and I can pay the rent now, so if a client wants something we really need to talk because I know I probably won't do it myself, I have a staff for this. (Though in the back of your mind is the thought that all of this could come apart at any moment.) The highs and lows are still there, but with a more stable and less extreme emotional cycle.

Alternatively, you may be consulting part time (the traditional academic model). Your current university job pays the health insurance and you won't starve. You really want to do your classes justice, so you can't take everything that comes your way. Maybe two projects a year, those that have intrinsic value for your professional development, or the more profane aspect of remuneration—or maybe even both.

ADAPTING THE ASSUMPTIONS OF FLAWLESS CONSULTING

Block's flawless consultant is quite aggressive in asserting the need for equality in the relationship. From a theoretical stance, this makes sense. What one is trying to do is establish a situation in which all parties can operate freely and openly. From a communicology perspective, you are trying to establish a communication pattern with the largest possible open Johari window (see Schein, 1988, 32). From a counseling perspective, you are trying to establish what Carl Rogers would call psychological safety and psychological freedom. When these conditions are met, the theory goes, people can bring all of their energies to solving the problem so it stays solved, the goal of a process consultation model.

The Contract

As you begin your consultation, in any stage of your career and with any model, you will first need to reach a common understanding of your roles. Block provides a nine-point outline for defining roles and expectations:

1. The boundaries of your analysis.

2. Objectives of the project.

3. The kind of information you seek.

4. Your role in the project.

5. The product you will deliver.

6. What support and involvement you need from the client.

7. Time schedule.

8. Confidentiality.

9. Feedback to you.

He refers to this as a contract. He is quite explicit that the contract should be "brief, direct, and almost conversational" and that the purpose of the contract is "to communicate, not to protect yourself in court" (Block, 1981, p. 46). However, and I feel this is a big however, referring to this document as a contract sets you up for some real problems. The most significant problem is that a written contract has little meaning in your life. Let's face it, even the charges of a small corporate legal staff can overwhelm your life and bank account if you decide to contest some aspect of the project, not to mention the damage to your good name among company members who will remember you at the time of the next request for bids. No, Block is aggressive in asserting that the word *contract* conveys an important statement of personal roles and responsibilities during the project, but because his focus is on internal consultants, the legal overtones of the term *contract* are obviated.

All consulting experiences have an underlying psychological contract (Block calls it a social contract) that includes the unstated assumptions of what will happen in the project. The psychological contract is your best single point of leverage in your project because it operates at a tacit level that recognizes human wants and needs.

At any given critical juncture of the project, you will find that a little goodwill goes a long way. A professional acquaintance of mine summarized it all when he said, "People buy from people. And people buy from people they like." My friend wasn't just referring to the exchange of money, he also sensed that people will respond positively when their needs and wants are recognized. I use a simple compromise to deal with the tension between formal contracts and psychological contracts. I call the statement about the project, using a term preferred by a large accounting firm, a *letter of understanding*. I find this term has the effect of causing people to react at a level that more closely approximates the psychological contract. I also agree with Block that it should be short and conversational, and I rarely need more than two pages to summarize any project. After I have worked with someone and we have established a relationship, I rarely need a contract of any kind beyond an oral statement should there be a new project or a modification to a current one.

One last point about Block's contract. He continues the push to recognize the equality of the relationship by including a specific requirement that the client provide feedback about the results of the consultant's intervention at a specified time after the project (step 9). This is a natural need, but one that most clients will find somewhat foreign to their normal way of doing business. I prefer not to make a point of it, but in fact to consider it part of my ongoing relationship with the client. I want this person to be able to talk to me about the intervention six months after I'm gone. I have enjoyed knowing nearly all the people I have worked with, and communicate with them about once a year just to talk and see what's new. Inevitably, they will tell me about the politics of the project, the shifting priorities of their company or their life, and

I inevitably learn more through this informal discussion about my successes and failures than through any formal feedback system.

On the other hand, if you have to deal with large equipment purchases, regular payments to employees, etc., you will probably want to bolster your letter with a more formal contract. In the end, though, my advice is to be guided by the spirit of the law (the psychological contract), not the letter of the law (the formal contract).

The Language You Use

The preference Block has for the word *contract* highlights another position that I would caution you to review. Block (1981, pp. 24-29) provides a number of short scenarios that are designed to illustrate the conversation surrounding implementation of each stage of the consulting contract (letter of understanding). His examples tend to begin with words such as "I will need," "I will begin," "I would like," or [you] "Spend three days with me." This use of language tends to reflect a direct expression of needs and wants, but it can create an atmosphere of unbalance in roles. The use of "I" so strongly and often can suggest a measure of certainty on the part of the consultant (read, "I know the answers") that detracts from the desired collaborative process (read, "What's the best way for us to go now?"). More tentative language that reflects this latter position, such as "Maybe we should," or "How about," will accurately communicate your needs and wants in most settings without giving the impression that you feel superior to the client. (The quality of what you say after "Maybe we should" will determine whether the client feels superior to you.)

Who Is the Client?

One of the most difficult questions you will have to answer may be: Who is my client? If things go well, there will be no problem. Your client is the person with whom you negotiated a letter of understanding. (Don't forget Block's point that you can't write your letter with a client who isn't in the room. Make sure all parties are in agreement with your understanding of the project; it will make life easier later if things get sticky.)

In general, an internal consultant has less vested interest in a project than the external consultant. An external consultant in the later stages of life as a consultant is less likely to be tempted by the dilemma of accepting an inappropriate solution to a problem; for example, with interactive video instruction when the problem is personnel selection, in return for a large contract and a continued relationship. The external consultant may also find that while he or she has established a letter of understanding with one person, perhaps that client is the problem being investigated. Should confidentiality be breached and the data sent to higher levels of the organization under the assumption that the organization is the real client and not the person in the room? After all, it is the organization that pays the salaries of its employees; don't supervisors have a right to data that can fix a problem? The Theory Y assumption of the flawless consultant may lead you to believe that everything will work out if you "put into words what you are experiencing." But it may not work out, economically or otherwise. You may choose to terminate the relationship (or find yourself terminated) as you reassess your decision of who the client is. In the end, doing the right thing is being flawless. And doing it when you have reached a later stage of your career is easier than when you begin, for reasons of economics and experience.

THANK YOU SIR,
MAY I HAVE ANOTHER?

"Being a consultant can be a lonely business," one independent consultant friend of mine once said. She is right. The image of the well-dressed consultant moving around the nation or the planet, making hundreds of thousands of dollars a year while exploring fascinating problems, is probably a reality for a few stars in the world. But for most of us, things are more pedestrian. A number of independent consultants I know expect to spend at least three days a week marketing themselves for every day or two of work; punctuated by an occasional large project that lets them think they will make the next mortgage payment. As an external consultant you will be paid at a much higher salary than your project officer, but you have none of the security, benefits, etc., that make life in a stable organization less manic. You should understand that in many instances the outside consultant is a disposable commodity to be blamed for failure and ignored for success. You need to understand your expendability, but you should never accept being treated in a manner that forces you to sublimate your wants and needs. Block has an interesting viewpoint on the folly of working "bent-over":

> Being very compliant with a client, not making our wants known, going along with something we don't have confidence in—all makes us feel bent-over. So we work bent-over. The client notices our bent-over position and, after a short while, begins to think this is the way we normally work—bent over. As a result, when the client needs someone who works standing up straight, someone else gets called in (p. 76).

This point was driven home to me recently when my partner and I noticed that the written feedback we were getting from one part of an organization we were working with was less than professional. The language was very much that of a parent to a child. We absorbed it for a while, since after all "being a consultant can be a lonely business, and we are being paid for our time," but it finally reached a point where we knew nobody in the organization itself would ever write notes to other employees using this tone. At a following meeting we took the project officer aside and indicated that we felt the tone was inappropriate: "Even consultants have feelings," my partner said. Things haven't been the same since, which is good news. The feedback language improved and our clients' interpersonal interactions moved from professional to professional and friendly.

As you enter an organization early in your career as a consultant, it is easy to forget that they may need you just as much as you need them. Keep in mind that someone has made a decision to hire you, and has thus put his or her judgment on the line for the boss and peers to view. Your client probably shares your interest in having you do well. However, don't confuse assertiveness with aggression in your confrontations.

THE TAO REVISITED

I hope that you see flawless consulting as a means to getting your expertise used. Constantly noticing what you are experiencing and acting on these observations and feelings doesn't mean doing therapy or continual confrontation with the client. What it means is watching the environment and identifying the forces that help or hinder both the organization and yourself. When you are in touch with these, and you act on them in an open and honest manner in each stage of the consultation process, then you are acting flawlessly. Being flawless may be harder when you begin your career as a consultant because of professional insecurity or economic problems, but it is important to maintain your integrity and not work "bent-over." Don't expect everyone you work with to respond positively to your efforts, but by and large they will. If they don't then consider what they ask of you, and decide for yourself if your response is flawless.

REFERENCES

Block, P. (1981). *Flawless consulting: A guide to getting your expertise used.* Austin, TX: Learning Concepts.

Kelley, R. E. (1986). *Consulting: The complete guide to a profitable career.* New York: Charles Scribner's Sons.

Schein, E. (1988). *Process consultation, volume I: Its role in organizational development.* New York: Addison-Wesley.

19

"Murphy's Law Strikes Again and Again and Again and ..."

Harold Scharlatt
President, Training and Development Associates, Inc.
Lexington, Kentucky

I have been doing instructional design work for over 20 years. Most of that time the work has been in connection with management development workshops and projects for a wide variety of major corporations. I have been an internal consultant for a Fortune 50 company, a partner in a growing consulting firm, and, for the past 12 years, an independent consultant, trainer, and designer. Over the years, I have been quite lucky and quite successful. However, on occasion, even the most beautiful, perfectly developed piece of design work—a virtual instructional design masterpiece—FLOPS! What I would like to share with you in this chapter is a brief look at a few of my "flops." These anecdotes may provide you with a little insight into some of the potential problems that we instructional designers have to prepare for when our oh-so-perfect designs come face to face with the "real world."

KNOW WHICH AUDIENCE IS GOING TO SHOW UP

I had designed a workshop on managerial negotiations for a chemical company. The point of the workshop was to take some of the fundamental skills and techniques that professional labor relations negotiators use and modify them for the every day job of a manager. Managers negotiate all the time as part of their continuing managerial activities. They negotiate to acquire scarce resources, they negotiate to establish corporate priorities, they negotiate with their customers, and so on. If we could instruct relatively new managers in some tried and true face-to-face influencing skills, it would surely add to their professional productivity for many years to come.

The specific course objectives were clarified, the content was determined, the materials were gathered, the design was created, and a pilot was set up. Unfortunately, the client, who was responsible for setting up the pilot session, did not populate the workshop with the intended heterogeneous group of new managers. Rather than have a group of participants who would mirror the target population, the pilot group consisted of highly experienced labor negotiators. They came because they wanted to test the new "negotiations course" against their many years of expertise. They hated the workshop. As you might imagine, they thought it was much too simplistic and that the cases used were much too generic. The workshop was never presented again.

The cause of the problem: The client fails to monitor the attendees to ensure that they represent the population for whom the training was actually designed.

YOU CAN'T EXPECT A "GAME PLAN" TO WORK WHEN THEY CHANGE THE "GAME"

A one-day workshop on effective delegation had been presented a few times to groups of middle managers in a computer company. As is typically done in many organizations, this computer company would give the course participants an evaluation form at the end of each session and they would rate their satisfaction with the course. This evaluation would then be the key factor in deciding whether or not to repeat the workshop. The evaluations on the first few sessions were promising, and the new course had begun to look as if it would be viewed as a worthwhile opportunity to learn some methods for fine-tuning an important, basic set of skills. This response could result in it being offered as part of the regular training curriculum.

Thirty minutes before the next scheduled session, the instructor was informed that an important series of mini-meetings was taking place throughout the plant site all day and that some participants might have to miss a small part of the session. Well, as the day was beginning, the instructor asked which of these people were going to have to miss a few moments of the day. The answer: all the participants in the class were going to be out, probably from one to two hours and at different times throughout the day.

Taking a step backward, the instructor reminded the participants of the original set of objectives, briefly previewed the outline that was to have been followed during the day and the type of activities that were to take place within that outline. They then decided which activities could be done within the anticipated abbreviated and disjointed schedule, what possible activities could be done individually with the instructor's guidance, what resources the participants could follow up on later on their own, and what handout materials might be detailed enough to just take away and use. The day proceeded as a cross between an instructional smorgasbord and a fire drill that left the instructor a bit frazzled but feeling that a reasonable amount had been accomplished under these conditions. Unfortunately though, some of the participants on their evaluation forms rated the class as just average in such areas as meeting all the objectives, the value of its activities, and the instructor's training ability. It became another class that was not quite able "to make the cut" on to the standard curriculum.

The cause of the problem: Training is seen as a low priority and any other event takes precedence.

KNOW JUST HOW "SOPHISTICATED" THE GROUP REALLY IS

I had done a great deal of work with senior-level managers to help them deal more effectively with rapid organizational change. So when I was asked to develop a customized seminar for a service-oriented company going through just such a change, it seemed like a fairly straightforward assignment. One of the design parameters that the client insisted upon was that we build into the design an opportunity for the participants to view a number of "change models" put forth by various experts so that the participants would be exposed to a myriad of perspectives. I could put forth my own "model" as part of this assortment, but she wanted the participants to be able to compare and contrast, synthesize and distill these various approaches; I was not to oversimplify the issues or the concepts.

I agreed that the issues surrounding organizational change should not be oversimplified, but that in a one-day workshop, it would help to provide more focus. That would allow me—and the participants—to get further into discussions of the applicability of these models to the real situation these people faced back on the job. The client disagreed. She said the managers were a highly sophisticated group that needed to be exposed to a high-level set of ideas that would allow them to determine their own application next-steps.

As you're reading this, I'm sure you've already figured out the outcome of this particular flop of mine. The participants all felt that the workshop would have been a lot more helpful if we could have focused on the applicability of a single, simple model.

The cause of the problem: The client projects their level of understanding of the subject matter (in this case high) on to the intended participants.

SOMETIMES THE DESIGNER'S PERSPECTIVE IS DIFFERENT THAN THE GROUP'S

At a steel mill, I was working with a group of second-level supervisors to develop a plant-specific program on providing constructive criticism to hourly employees. The workshop was to be built around a large number of mini-cases depicting various realistic situations that could take place throughout the plant site. These situations would have great face validity because locations, equipment, and events would come directly from the experiences that the supervisors would share with me. The cases would be imbedded throughout a 16-hour workshop that would be presented in four half-day sessions. Each session would focus on a few key learning points, and the accompanying cases would demonstrate the correct and incorrect applications of those learning points. Session participants were to be first-line supervisors who would discuss each case and apply it to their everyday situations.

One of the long-term benefits of developing the cases with the assistance of the second-level supervisors was that after they had helped me pilot the sessions, a few "chosen volunteers" would take over the facilitation of the sessions. The participants would then be getting their instruction from their own bosses and their bosses' peers.

After a number of pilots were run and minor modifications were made, all the mini-cases were audiotaped. The audiotape was helpful in a few ways: 1) it provided variety in a class built around discussion; 2) it made the cases more realistic and interesting; and 3) it overcame the concern we had with some of the reading skills of the future participants.

The project was about to be wrapped up and I had a final meeting with the "facilitator-supervisors" and the plant manager. I said that everything was ready to go, and the supervisors said that was almost true but that they still had one modification to make. I couldn't imagine what it was. To my astonishment, they said they had to remake all the tapes! They were going to do them more "realistically." They were going to add all those four-letter words that we had left out.

The cause of the problem: The eventual user of the product had a different work environment than any of the designers.

FIND OUT WHAT THE CLIENT REALLY WANTS— AND WHY THEY WANT IT

I was asked by an internal human resources consultant at a large high-tech firm to present a workshop on "advanced" team facilitation techniques. The company had recently begun to move in the direction of creating self-managed work teams. The internal consultant was charged with the task of finding someone to customize a proven workshop and train a number of team leaders in a two- or three-day format. A number of trainers were being looked at as the possible choice by each of us putting on one "sample session."

I had great reservations about presenting a "generic sample session" but was assured that the human resource person would sit in on each session and would, of course, realize that the workshop would later be designed around a more specific and focused set of objectives—for a more specific target participant population. (At this point, you're probably one step ahead of me. You're probably guessing that this potential work "flopped" because the human resource person thought it was too generic. That would have been a likely "Catch 22," but it was not the one that happened on this particular fiasco.)

Because I had not had the opportunity to learn very much about the particular participants in this pilot-type session, I thought I'd take a little longer with introductions, finding out about their individual experiences in team facilitation. As an "advanced" team facilitators workshop, the training was to be especially flexible with the learnings and activities—to meet the appropriate level of need.

I asked the first participant to describe his team and his experience with them. He said that he really had just been recently told that he was a team leader and wasn't yet sure who was going to be on his team. Well, I figured he was one poor guy who had gotten in this program by mistake but we'd help keep him up the best way we could. The second participant said that she knew who was on her team, so I didn't have to worry about that, but that she could use a lot of help since this was the first week of the team's existence and she had absolutely no idea how to begin her new role. In response to what must have been a very perplexed look on my face, a participant on the other side of the room said, "If you think she has a problem figuring how to lead her team, what about me? I'm the new team leader and I'm a temporary part-time employee." This participant had gotten to be the team leader and attend this session by having his name pulled out of a hat two days ago. I took a few additional random comments from around the room and realized that all the participants were in about the same situation. In fact, they commented on how surprised they were when they saw the title of the session.

I took a giant step backwards and came up with a series of questions around teams, facilitation, needs, experience, expectations, etc., for extemporaneously created triads to answer on chart paper while I walked to the back of the room to talk with my client. I asked him how this group was ever assembled to come to an "advanced" team facilitator workshop. He said that the company's new vision and culture called for everyone to be customer-driven. His customer—the manager of the section where these people worked—had asked for an advanced course, so that's what he was going to give him. I explained to the client my opinions on why I thought he had entirely missed the concept of "customer-driven," and why I did not appreciate having the totally wrong set of participants for the workshop.

I managed to put together some good, solid activities in beginning facilitation skills throughout the first day. That night I, of course, redesigned what was now going to take place on the second day, and the class went quite well. However, that internal consultant decided not to use me for the series of workshops. I imagine he felt that I just wasn't customer-driven.

The cause of the problem: An intermediary fails to challenge a client to help clarify their true needs and objectives.

IT CAN HAPPEN—YOU (OR SOMEONE ELSE) JUST MAKES A MISTAKE

This little story is really not so much about a design that failed as it is about a mistake that in about five seconds negated the potential benefits of a perfectly good instructional design for a two-day program.

I had designed and presented the same two-day workshop on decision making to managers from a steel company about six times before. Each time, my presentation came after a rather dry half-day presentation about company benefits. The person presenting the topic was a well-liked and knowledgeable person, but the presentation content was informational and, by its nature, not very exciting. I would therefore try to kick off my session as enthusiastically as possible.

On this particular day, I began as usual by telling the group how active and challenging the next two days would be and how they really needed to participate and be part of the learning equation. This was, thankfully, not going to be two days of lecture because we were about to delve into a topic that called for active skill practice and experimentation. To emphasize the new instructional format, I took the portable podium that the previous speaker had used and gave it a dramatic shove toward the side of the room. I'm afraid my enthusiasm got the best of me, and I shoved the podium much too strongly. It crashed into the wall right behind where my colleague, the previous speaker, was standing and just shattered! It made a tremendous noise and sent pieces flying everywhere. I did my best to meekly apologize and just move on. Luckily, no one was hurt, but neither did anyone forget what a "jerk" this new guy in the front of the room was. The resulting lack of credibility led to two very negative, unsatisfying days for the participants and myself.

The cause of the problem: A piece of bad luck (but it does highlight the importance of having a positive opening segment built into your design).

IF YOU HAVE TO, FORGET THE DESIGN
AND TEACH-TO-NEED

During a three-day workshop for an electronics company on how to successfully apply the organization's performance appraisal system, we had an opportunity that I thought would really be the coincidental "icing on the cake." The new vice president for this division was going to pay a visit to this site on the afternoon of the second day.

The goal of the workshop was to teach managers to view the appraisal system in a positive light. To see it not as a burden, not as unnecessary paperwork, and not as a way to threaten or punish people. The system, when used as a proper, constructive developmental tool, could motivate employees, not intimidate them. We had spent one and a half days discussing the concepts, techniques, and attitudes that were needed to implement the system as it was intended.

After lunch, along with the rest of the population at the site, we all headed into the auditorium to hear the vice president's initial inspirational speech to the "troops." To make a very long story mercifully short—he spent the first 45 minutes showing slides that reviewed and analyzed the past year's financial results and production statistics. He then spent 15 minutes berating the workforce for its lack of motivation in achieving what he considered to be unacceptable results. His final line sticks with me to this day—over 12 years later: "Remember, that if you can't get the job done, there's a line of people at the gate who can!"

Presentation over, we head back to class. As you might imagine, no one wanted to discuss anything but the new vice president's message and his attitude. I let the gripe session run for a few minutes, then suggested that we forget the planned outline for the rest of the day. Instead, we listed our concerns about the substance and style of the presentation, identified the various accountable groups and managerial levels responsible for addressing the concerns, and discussed ways in which we could honestly handle reactions by our subordinates.

It would have been foolish to think that when we left that auditorium we could have simply put aside what had transpired and gotten back on track in our session. Instead, we used the energy around the presentation in the most productive manner we could. Also, of course, that evening I worked on 1) how we could integrate the fallout caused by the vice president into the theme of the program and 2) what activities could be deleted from the outline to balance the time spent on a tangent that day.

Maybe, in some odd way, the discouraging presentation led the program's discussion into areas that were even more meaningful than could have been expected. However, it certainly caused a rethinking of our workshop's objectives and the necessary design changes.

The cause of the problem: An external event or person has such a tremendous impact on the program that the planned activities lose importance.

A DESIGN IS SOMETIMES NO LONGER
YOURS TO CONTROL

Often you design a course in an area of content in which you have no expertise. I did this for a doctor who wanted to present a series of workshops on dealing with substance abuse in the workplace. Although he was an expert in that field, he had no background in either instructional design or management training. I contracted to help him gain sufficient expertise in both.

He spent a great deal of time sharing his expertise, content sources, and proposed course materials with me before I began to get a feel for what might be the best design for these workshops. The initial design was built around his stated objectives and desired content pieces and was ready to test. We decided to first test the instructional segments in small pilot sessions, then, after modifications were made, to pilot the full course. These pilots were different in one respect than most pilots. The participants in these sessions were well aware that the doctor was not a trainer and was really seeking their critique on the content and design of the workshops. Preparing him to make professional-level presentations was to come over time. At the end of each of these pilots, not only would we review the participants' critiques, but I would coach the doctor on his presentation skills; he improved with each session. After a reasonable amount of time, the workshop and his training ability were both in good shape and I wished him well and closed out my involvement in the project—satisfied that it was a job well done.

A number of months later, I learned that someone had suggested me for another design project but that the potential client declined to consider me for the task. When my friend inquired about the reason for the declination, she was informed that the person had seen a course I designed on substance abuse and felt it was an inferior workshop. I managed to "catch up" with my workshop again soon thereafter and learned that it no longer resembled the one I had designed. The doctor had modified the workshop as he went along and turned it into something that was much more his than mine. Well, that makes sense—but I didn't want the "credit" for it.

The cause of the problem: The client owns this product and can alter it in any way that he sees fit.

As I've tried to point out by recalling some of my less-than-successful projects, it is often the project that fails—in spite of a good design. As the old saying goes, "The operation was a success but the patient died." There are a plethora of intervening variables that cause a designer to be no longer in full control of their own design effort. Although no one can completely predict or prevent these types of unfortunate situations, I would like to propose a few general principles that my experience has shown to be helpful in somewhat lessening the probability of having to face a flop.

SOME GUIDING PRINCIPLES

1. Talk directly with the client (and as little with intermediaries) as early—and as often—in the design process as possible.

2. Talk with as many of the expected participants (and their supervisors) as possible.

3. At the outset of the workshop, clarify the participants' expectations.

4. If necessary, modify (usually lower) the group's expectations.

5. Keep the participants' learning as your first priority and modify your outline on a teach-to-need or -interest basis.

6. Break expectations and objectives into more realistic time frames and be prepared to extend the length of the full project.

7. If a design of yours is going to be "handed-off" to someone else, overtly distance yourself from it.

8. Try to alter the unacceptable but learn to accept the unalterable.

9. Don't assume anything!

10. Be prepared to cancel a project that you know is not going to be able to be done at your level of excellence.

Fortunately, none of these flops were disastrous, and I've had the good fortune to have them well counterbalanced by successes. However, it doesn't hurt to think about these incidents once in a while. They remind me not to assume things, not to take things for granted, and not to get too complacent in my instructional design efforts. They also remind me that after I create the oh-so-perfect design and set it in concrete—I need to carry a big sledgehammer along "just in case Murphy shows up."

20

The School Library Media Specialist's Role in Instructional Design
Past, Present, and Future

Donna J. Baumbach
Department of Educational Services
University of Central Florida, Orlando, Florida

As we approach the beginning of the twenty-first century, we find ourselves faced with increased pressures to bring about reform in public education. Educators as well as the public are calling for a reassessment of the goals of education, for change in curricula, change in teaching methods, and changes in assessment and evaluation.

Looking back over this century, however, we find little in education that has changed. Principals, superintendents, teachers, and even students have the same tasks, roles, and responsibilities as they had 10, 50, or even 100 years ago. I have heard it said that if Benjamin Franklin were to return to life, he would find little in these United States that he could recognize except, perhaps, for our classrooms. How then can we expect any change to take place in our educational system?

There is one role in education that has been forced to keep pace with changes brought about by the information age and the computer age and which may well exert considerable influence on education in the coming years. Changes in the role of the school library media specialist coupled with changes in society and changes in technology point to a bright future for education.

THE PAST

Kathleen Craver (1988) has written an extensive review of the standards for the library media field, the literature related to the instructional role of the school library media specialist, and relevant research related to that literature. In brief, she finds that theory is not always reflected in practice. In the first half of this century, school libraries, if they existed, served simply as depositories for materials and, perhaps, as study halls. It was not until the middle of the century that the role of the school library media specialist (or *school librarian* at that time) as a key element of the instructional process began to develop.

The 1950s

As late as 1953-1954, only 37 percent of U.S. secondary schools reported receiving the services of a centralized library (Craver, 1988). With the launching of *Sputnik* in 1957, a renewed interest in education and a call for educational reform, accompanied by a heavy infusion of federal funds for instructional materials in all formats, began the move toward the resource center concept and away from the library as a central depository of books. The role of the school librarian began to change. Several articles appeared urging school librarians to become involved in curriculum committees (Henne, 1951; Davis, 1953). But school librarians, with formal training in print materials, were busy adjusting to acquiring, processing, housing, and utilizing materials in nonprint formats. For the most part, their role in instruction was limited to getting teachers to use a wide variety of materials. Nevertheless, "selecting appropriate materials for instruction" is an instructional design competency with which school library media specialists have long been acquainted.

The 1960s

During this decade, National Defense Education Act (NDEA), Library Services and Construction Act (LSCA), and Elementary and Secondary Education Act (ESEA) funds allowed schools to purchase large quantities of nonprint materials. Craver (1988) reports that the words *analyst designer,* and *preparer,* describing the role of the media specialist, began to enter the literature. The 1969 AASL/DAVI standards for school library media programs made some references to the instructional role of the media specialist. Practice reflected the media specialist's role as supplying materials in a variety of formats to meet instructional needs and in instructing students in library skills.

The 1970s

In the 1970s, Craver (1988, p. 53) states, "the school library finally received assurances that its educational goals and objectives, which in many cases were ahead of the times, were now appropriate." A new proactive role was described by Hug (1975) and Wehmeyer (1976), among others, which included media specialists as an integral part of the instructional process; they were to assist teachers in designing instructional strategies and in producing materials. Chisholm and Ely (1979) published one of the first books to focus on the instructional design process and the media specialist's role in that process. The 1975 AASL/AECT standards *Media Programs: District and School* described functions related to the instructional design process. Craver (1988, p. 55) states that "by the end of the seventies, the school media specialist's instructional role had evolved in the literature to one of prominence." But research studies tended to indicate that the role had not actually evolved in practice.

The 1980s

The 1980s saw the school media specialist faced with the microcomputer revolution in schools. As computers came into the school, media specialists usually added installation, maintenance, the teaching of computer literacy, and inservice for teachers to their responsibilities. In addition, because of their training in the selection of instructional materials, they became responsible for reviewing and selecting instructional software. During this decade, the media specialist discovered that the microcomputer could be used to manage inventory, circulation, overdue notices, correspondence, and other management and clerical functions, but while time was saved eventually, there was a steep learning curve for the media specialist who tried to implement such automated functions.

The early 1980s also provided in the literature a definition of the instructional roles of the media specialist (Thomason, 1981; Wehmeyer, 1984). But in addition to adding to the philosophical base, practical ideas for implementation were presented. Instructional design models specific to the school and the school library media center were introduced (Turner & Naumer,

1983; Cleaver & Taylor, 1983; Johnson, 1981). Inservice activities for school library media specialists often focused on this instructional role. Two taxonomies were developed that presented graduated levels of involvement in instructional development for school library media specialists (Turner, 1985; Loertscher, 1988). Both encouraged media specialists to become involved in the instructional development process at *any* level and to work toward higher levels of the taxonomy. Finally, *Information Power* (1988), the long-awaited AASL/AECT national standards, formalized the involvement of the library media specialist in the school program as having three distinct roles: teacher, information specialist, and instructional consultant (see figure 20.1).

Two Taxonomies of Instructional Design for School Library Media Specialists

Turner (1985)

4. **Action Education**—Library media specialist works as part of a team, implementing a number of the steps in the instructional design process. Often the purpose of involvement at this level is to increase the teacher's ability to perform one or more of the steps.

3. **Reaction**—Informal response to random request for assistance from a teacher.

2. **Passive Participation**—Involves little or no interaction between the library media specialist and the faculty member. The library media specialist selects and maintains materials, equipment, and facilities which assist the faculty member in implementing a particular step.

1. **No Involvement**—No intervention is required, the teacher has not requested involvement by the center, or the library media specialist is unwilling or unable to intervene.

Loertscher (1988)

11. **Curriculum Development**—Along with other educators, the library media specialist contributes to the planning and structure of what will actually be taught in the school or district.

10. **Instructional Design, Level II**—The library media center staff participates in resource-based teaching units where the entire unit content depends on the resources and activities of the LMC program.

9. **Instructional Design, Level I**—The library media specialist participates in every step of the development, execution, and evaluation of an instructional unit. LMC involvement is considered enrichment or supplementary.

8. **Scheduled Planning in Support Role**—Formal planning with a teacher or group of students to supply materials or activities for a previously planned resource-based teaching unit or project.

7. **Evangelistic Outreach**—A concerted effort is made to promote the philosophy of the LMC program.

6. **Planned Gathering**—Gathering of materials is done in advance of class project upon teacher request.

5. **Cursory Planning**—Informal and brief planning with teachers and students for library media center involvement.

4. **Spontaneous Interaction and Gathering**—Spur-of-the-moment activities and gathering of materials occur with no advance notice.

3. **Individual Reference Assistance**—Students or teachers retrieve requested information or materials for specific needs.

2. **Self-Help Warehouse**—Facilities and materials are available for the self-starter.

1. **No Involvement**—The library media center is bypassed entirely.

Fig. 20.1. Taxonomies of instructional design for school library media specialists.

THE PRESENT

The actual practice of instructional consultation or instructional design by the school library media specialist still lags far behind the literature, and the attitude toward such practice ranges from full endorsement to extremely critical (Turner & Zsiray, 1989). But we are beginning to understand the reasons for such a disparity between theory and practice, and we also are beginning to understand the elements that support the instructional design role of the media specialist in the school environment. Turner's (1982) survey of ALA-accredited preparation programs indicated few course offerings devoted to instructional design. Few competencies in instructional design were required by many library schools, and several schools required none. Many adapted skills learned in courses designed to meet the needs of instructional designers preparing for careers in business, industry, and the military. Royal (1981) found that while library media specialists felt competent in instructional design, they felt the sources of their competency were their undergraduate education programs, not their library education.

In addition to preparation, several other factors have been researched that affect the instructional design consultation practice by school library media specialists. Based on an extensive review of the literature, Turner and Zsiray (1989) concluded that a knowledgeable and outgoing media specialist who works in a supportive environment, that is, an environment in which the principal encourages the media specialist to work with teachers, where there are rewards for improved instruction, and where the teachers recognize the role of the media specialist as an instructional consultant who works cooperatively to improve teaching, will be successful. In addition, the more formal courses in educational media/school library media a teacher has, the more sophisticated will be the level of use. The final keys to success, according to the literature, are solid clerical support, adequate budget, and time to carry out consultative activities.

Media specialists have found support in *Information Power* (1988) for establishing a solid, proactive library media program that establishes partnerships with teachers, administrators, and the public. State professional organizations and the national professional associations, AASL and AECT, are working to implement these guidelines. While media specialists may be moving toward full implementation of *Information Power*, many are caught up in the technological revolution. As they were called upon to integrate computers into the media program in the early 1980s, media specialists now are faced with learning about, acquiring, processing, utilizing, and integrating CD-ROM databases, interactive video, videodisc, hypermedia, and other new and emerging technologies. In addition, many school media specialists, having recently completed automation of their circulation systems, are now faced with converting library media center records to full MARC format to establish electronic catalogs and regional and statewide databases. While no media specialist can argue against the importance of this step toward access to information for their teachers and students, a heavy burden has been placed upon already busy school library media specialists.

THE FUTURE

Schiffman (1987) predicted the role that school library media specialists could play in influencing public education and pointed out several factors that make it appropriate for them to do so:

> First, it is the only part of a school that cuts across all discipline areas. School library media specialists have contact with all teachers and administrators, unlike most others in instructional roles. The SLMC is already the repository and distributor of instructional media for the schools. Nation-wide, they are also increasingly becoming the centers for computer technology, as administrators and teachers realize the difficulty in maintaining the hardware and software originally placed in classrooms.

This factor has begun to give the school library media specialist more "power," for in the schools, as in other institutions, the person who controls the computers is considered an influential figure (pp. 42-43).

The school library media specialist is becoming increasingly involved with technology. Computer networks within the school and beyond often are based in and contain library media center resources made possible by the media specialist's early work with automation in the school library media center. State and regional networks for resource sharing are being established in which school library media specialists will be the primary contacts for interlibrary loan to serve the needs of both teachers and students. Media specialists are implementing online databases, CD-ROM resources, and teleconferencing. They are faxing documents to neighboring schools. Automation of clerical functions has become routine, and this coupled with flexible access policies is providing time for media specialists to focus on the consultation and instructional design roles. The role of the school library media specialist as an information specialist and a technology resource is becoming increasingly evident as it becomes increasingly important.

School library media specialists are about to close the gap between theory and practice. *Information Power* (1988) continues to build the base of support from other educators through publications in education journals and periodicals outside of the school library media field and through presentations at education conferences relating the school library media program to administration, curriculum development, and content areas such as science, social studies, mathematics, and English. School library media specialists are receiving leadership training through state and national professional associations and are encouraged to use those skills to bring their programs to the forefront. School library media preparation programs are undergoing dramatic changes as they, too, seek to implement *Information Power*. The Association for Educational Communications and Technology and the American Association of School Librarians' formal association with the National Council for Accreditation of Teacher Education (NCATE) accrediting process will formalize the teaching of competencies in instructional design and development. As of 1992, programs seeking NCATE accreditation will need to provide evidence of providing specific competencies in coursework, including skills in instructional design, consultation, and leadership.

Before this decade ends, school library media specialists will have the skills, the support, and the power to make changes happen in education. The best, as they say, is yet to come.

REFERENCES

Chisholm, M., & Ely, D. (1979). *Instructional design and the library media specialist*. Chicago: American Library Association.

Cleaver, B., & Taylor, W. (1983). *Involving the school library media specialist in curriculum development*. Chicago: American Library Association.

Craver, K. (1988). The changing instructional role of the high school library media specialist: 1950-1984. In F. McDonald (Ed.), *The emerging school library media program: Readings*. Englewood, CO: Libraries Unlimited.

Davis, W. (1953, February). A new look at school library service. *School Activities and the Library*, 1-8.

Henne, F. (1951). *A planning guide for the high school library*. Chicago: American Library Association.

Hug, W. (1975). *Instructional design and the media program*. Chicago: American Library Association.

Information power: Guidelines for school library media programs. (1988). Chicago: American Library Association and Washington, DC: Association for Educational Communications and Technology.

Johnson, K. (1981). Instructional development in schools: A proposed model. *School Media Quarterly, 9*(4), 256-271.

Loertscher, D. (1988). *Taxonomies of the school library media program.* Englewood, CO: Libraries Unlimited.

Media programs: District and school. (1975). Chicago: American Library Association and Washington, DC: Association for Educational Communications and Technology.

Royal, S. (1981). Instructional design: Are school library media specialists really changing? (Part I). *Arkansas Libraries, 40*(1), 8-18.

Schiffman, S. (1987). Influencing public education: A "window of opportunity" through school library media centers. *Journal of Instructional Development, 10*(4), 41-44.

Thomason, N. (1981). *The library specialist in curriculum development.* Metuchen, NJ: Scarecrow Press.

Turner, P. (1982). Instructional design competencies taught at library schools. *Journal of Education for Librarianship, 22*(4), 276-282.

———. (1985). *Helping teachers teach.* Littleton, CO: Libraries Unlimited.

Turner, P., & Naumer, J. (1983). Mapping the way toward instructional design consultation by the school library media specialist. *School Library Media Quarterly, 22*(4), 276-282.

Turner, P., & Zsiray, S. (1990). The consulting role of the library media specialist: A review of the literature. In *Papers for the Treasure Mountain Research Retreat.* Englewood, CO: Hi Willow Research and Publishing.

Wehmeyer, L. (1976). *The school librarian as educator.* Littleton, CO: Libraries Unlimited.

———. (1984). *The school librarian as educator.* (2nd edition). Littleton, CO: Libraries Unlimited.

21

Instructional Technology and Public Education in the United States

The Next Decade

Robert A. Reiser
College of Education, Florida State University
Tallahassee, Florida

and

David F. Salisbury
College of Education, Florida State University
Tallahassee, Florida

> Instructional technology is today largely supplementary to the two primary media of instruction: the textbook and the teacher.... Eliminate all of the technology, and education would go on with hardly a missed lesson. (Kurland, cited in Commission on Instructional Technology, 1970)

> It has been less than a decade since the first personal computers appeared on the education scene. Schools have acquired computers rapidly since then, but most elements of the instructional process remain the same. (Office of Technology Assessment, 1988)

These two statements make similar points regarding the effects of instructional technology on public education in the United States, yet the second statement was made nearly two decades after the first. What sort of statement will we be able to make about instructional technology and public education a decade from now? Will instructional technology play a significant role in the public schools? Before we try to answer these questions, let us define what we mean by instructional technology.

DEFINITION

Most educators equate instructional technology with media, the physical means (other than the teacher, printed material, and chalkboard) that teachers use to help them deliver instruction to students. Instructional hardware (machines and equipment) and software (the programs and materials presented via the hardware) are included in this definition. We believe that this definition of instructional technology is seriously flawed, for several reasons. First, although the teacher, printed material, and the chalkboard are themselves a means for presenting instruction, they are typically viewed as being in a different category than other media; indeed, they are rarely referred to as media. Second, under this definition, media are viewed strictly as aids or supplements to the teacher, they are not considered as a primary means for delivering instruction. Third, and most important, this definition focuses on technology as products, whereas we believe technology should be viewed as a process.

Rather than equating instructional technology with media, we prefer to think of it as a systematic means of identifying instructional problems and designing, implementing, evaluating, and revising solutions to those problems. This "systems approach" definition and others like it (e.g., Commission on Instructional Technology, 1970) have become the standard view of many professionals who claim instructional technology as their field of endeavor. Yet there are many others in the profession who adhere to the "media" definition of the field. In this chapter we examine instructional technology from both perspectives, viewing it as media and as a systematic process for solving instructional problems.

Regardless of the definition used, most would generally agree that instructional technology has not had a major impact on public education in the United States. A recent survey of the use of media in the public schools revealed that although the number of videocassette recorders and computers in the schools has increased dramatically during the past decade, these media have had relatively little effect on the instructional practices that are employed (Office of Technology Assessment, 1988). And, as far as the systems approach is concerned, there have been very few wide-scale efforts to use this methodology to help improve schools in the United States (Branson & Grow, 1987; Burkman, 1987b; Rossett & Grabowsky, 1987), even though the approach has been used successfully in other settings (Mager, 1977; Morgan, 1989).

Is it likely that the role instructional technology plays in the public schools will change during the next decade? We believe that the answer to this question hinges, in large part, on the issue of whether the structure of schools will change. If, as is quite likely, schools continue to be structured as they are today, then the role instructional technology plays within the schools is unlikely to change very much. On the other hand, if schools are restructured, we believe instructional technology is likely to play a major role within that restructured environment. We examine both scenarios below.

MAINTAINING THE CURRENT
SCHOOL STRUCTURE

Those who have studied the history of innovation in public schools have noted how difficult it is to bring about substantive change in that environment (Popkewitz, 1979; Cuban, 1988). During the past century, public schools in this country have withstood numerous onslaughts and have continued to rely on the same basic approach to the delivery of instruction. In light of the difficulties school reformers have faced in the past, we believe it is unlikely that major restructuring will take place on a large scale within the next decade. Furthermore, we believe that if schools are not restructured, the role technology will play will continue to be a minor one. This prediction applies to the use of media as well as to the application of a systems approach.

Use of Media Under Current Conditions

Why do we think it unlikely that the use of media in public schools will increase dramatically during the next decade? Because, without restructuring, the factors that have previously inhibited the use of media in schools will still be in place. Cuban (1986) describes a number of such factors, including limited accessibility of hardware and software, lack of suitable software, poor instructional quality of software, faulty implementation procedures, and the "tradition of teaching." Each of these factors is discussed in greater detail below.

Limited Accessibility of Hardware and Software

Oftentimes, hardware breaks down or becomes obsolete, or the software that a teacher would like to use is not readily available. In addition, because the amount of hardware in a school is usually quite limited, media are often housed in a single location in the school. Teachers must then schedule their students to visit that location, or must request that the media be brought to their classroom at a specified time. Either situation is often viewed as troublesome by the teacher. Furthermore, although the cost of some of the newer technologies, such as the computer, has dramatically decreased, the cost of purchasing sufficient equipment is often cited as a major problem by educational administrators (Office of Technology Assessment, 1988). Thus, the problem of media accessibility still exists and, in our opinion, is likely to persist over the next decade.

Software Suitability and Quality

Up to now, much of the software that has been produced has focused on a few content areas and has not met the wide range of instructional needs of educators. Furthermore, most software has not been adequately field-tested (Komoski, 1984; Office of Technology Assessment, 1988). Thus, it is not surprising to find educators often indicating that the quality of educational software must be improved. Until such time as private enterprise decides to devote more effort to field-testing, or until the government is willing to help fund the costs of instructional materials development, the quality of software is likely to remain a concern and is likely to inhibit the use of media in the schools.

Faculty Implementation Procedures

In the past, decisions to adopt an instructional innovation, such as a new piece of media hardware, have been made by administrators who have then mandated or encouraged classroom teachers to use this innovation. Unfortunately, as many authors have pointed out (Burkman, 1987a; Cuban, 1986; Popkewitz, 1979), these decisions are often made with little or no teacher input. As a result, teachers often reject the innovation, or rarely use it. Furthermore, in most cases, little consideration is given to how these innovations will be integrated into the ongoing instructional program. Without such consideration, these innovations are unlikely to be used successfully (Glaser & Cooley, 1973; Popkewitz, 1979). As long as administrators continue to make adoption decisions with little or no teacher input, and with little thought as to how a new innovation will fit in with existing practices, it is likely that most instructional innovations will not be successfully implemented in the schools.

"Tradition of Teaching"

Finally, as Cuban (1986) clearly indicates, the "tradition of teaching" mitigates against the use of technology in classrooms. Those who enter teaching have spent many years as students, sitting in classrooms in which instruction was presented primarily, if not exclusively, by the teacher. Few of those entering the teaching profession have experienced situations in which technology played a major role in the delivery of instruction. This situation was most likely true throughout the new teacher's career as a student, including the years the new teacher spent in a teacher training program. Thus, the predominant model of instruction the new teacher is likely to have been exposed to is the traditional lecture/discussion model. And, while it may be the case that the new teacher decided to join the profession in order to reform it, the decision is more likely to have been based, in part, on some positive attitudes toward the traditional instructional model. Thus, in many cases, the new teacher is likely to be predisposed toward using traditional techniques, rather than toward adopting new instructional innovations.

The new teacher's predisposition toward using traditional methods is likely to be reinforced once that individual is thrust into the classroom. In order to cope with the many difficulties a new teacher faces, such individuals are likely to rely on many of the traditional methods they were exposed to for so many years. Furthermore, in seeking help from their more experienced peers, new teachers are likely to receive advice that emphasizes the value of traditional techniques. Thus, the "tradition of teaching" is likely to have a powerful influence on teachers, and they will usually be reluctant to abandon that tradition in order to try something new.

In summary, we believe that unless the fundamental structure and operating practices of schooling are altered, the factors described above will continue to inhibit the use of instructional media in the public schools. Will the use of the systems approach in public education be inhibited as well? The next section examines this issue.

Use of the Systems Approach Under Current Conditions

Assuming that schools are not restructured, is it likely that the use of the systems approach in public education will increase over the next decade? Before we answer that question, let us describe what "employing the systems approach" means to us. In our view, using the systems approach in public education means (1) clearly specifying instructional goals and objectives, (2) carefully selecting instructional materials and planning instructional activities that would enable students to meet those objectives, (3) designing assessment instruments that would adequately assess student attainment of the objectives, (4) implementing the instructional program that was created in this fashion, (5) analyzing student performance under such a system, and (6) continually attempting to improve the system based on the results that were obtained.

To what extent do these activities already take place within public schools? Certainly some teachers already do some of these things. However, the use of systems approach procedures in the schools certainly is not widespread (Branson & Grow, 1987; Burkman, 1987b; Rossett & Grabowsky, 1987).

Given the current structure of public education in the United States, what is the likelihood that the systems approach will be used to a much greater extent than it has been? Let us examine this question by looking at the various levels at which a decision to implement the systems approach might be made. We will start at the national and state level, and work our way down to the individual classroom.

As Burkman (1987b) points out, there are over 17,000 school districts in the United States, each of which is run by a group of administrators who have a great deal of autonomy in deciding the educational policies and instructional practices their school district will adopt. This decentralized arrangement makes it highly unlikely that a decision to adopt an instructional innovation will be made at the national or state level. The likelihood of this occurrence is further diminished when such an innovation has received as little publicity as the systems approach has.

Is it likely that a decision to adopt the systems approach will be made at the local school district level? Let's answer this question by pointing to several facts. One is that many of us who are proponents of the systems approach have failed to become involved in trying to solve the problems facing the public schools (Schiffman & Gansneder, 1987). School administrators are unlikely to accept a solution offered by people who have not been helping them fight their problems. Of course, if the solution has received a good deal of favorable publicity, administrators often adopt a different point of view. However, the systems approach has not received that sort of publicity, which leads us to another fact: many administrators at the district level are unaware of systems approach concepts or do not see those concepts as relevant to solving the major problems facing their districts. Furthermore, most school districts do not have staff positions for instructional systems designers. Without a place at the planning table, systems people are unlikely to have much influence on the decisions that are made there. For these reasons, it is unlikely that a decision to adopt a systems approach to instruction will be made at the district level.

The factors that are likely to inhibit the acceptance of the systems approach at the district level are also likely to work against the adoption of this approach at the school level. That is, inasmuch as most systems advocates have not become involved in trying to solve the problems facing the schools, have not done much to make principals aware of the systems approach, and have failed to adequately promote the systems approach as a potential solution to the problems facing public education, it is unlikely that many principals or other school-level administrators will be strong advocates of the approach.

Is it likely that many inservice teachers will change their practices and start using the systems approach to help them plan their instruction? For several reasons, we do not think so. First of all, the systems approach is not part of the "tradition of teaching." As indicated earlier, it is very difficult for innovative practices to become part of that tradition. Making the task even more difficult is the fact that some of the concepts associated with the systems approach, particularly developing behavioral objectives and objectives-based tests, have received mixed reviews from teachers (Shrock & Byrd, 1987). The negative reactions some teachers have to these concepts will make it even more difficult to get them to buy into the systems approach as a whole. Furthermore, when student discipline, rather than instructional planning, is the primary concern of many teachers, it is unlikely that those teachers will want to spend much time employing a technique that focuses on the latter.

Given this state of affairs, and barring a major restructuring of the schools, is there any hope that the systems approach will become more widely used in public education? We believe the answer is yes, and we base our hope on preservice teachers. Why preservice teachers? Because these "teachers-to-be" are not as yet set in their ways regarding instructional planning and thus are more likely than inservice personnel to be receptive to the systems approach view to instructional planning.

Equally as important, there appears to be a growing trend towards exposing preservice teachers to systems approach concepts. For example, many educational psychology textbooks now devote considerable attention to many of the steps in the systems approach process (Snellbecker, 1987). And in the past few years we have witnessed the publication of several textbooks for preservice teachers that focus on employing the systems approach in the public schools (e.g., Dick & Reiser, 1989; Gagne & Driscoll, 1988; Sullivan & Higgins, 1983).

Of course, exposing preservice teachers to systems approach concepts does not ensure that they will use those concepts once they get into the "real world" of public education. Indeed, once these individuals are put into the schools, it is quite likely that they will adopt the prevailing practices in that environment, rather than employ the methods they were exposed to as part of their teacher training program. However, we are hopeful that if systems approach practices are taught *and modeled* in such a program (even if such practices are employed in only a single course), many preservice teachers are likely to see the value of employing such an approach, and are likely to try to use it when they become teachers. Whether they will persist in their efforts will depend on a variety of factors, not the least of which is how well those of us involved in teacher education have trained them to adapt their use of the systems approach to the reality of public education.

There are those who indicate that it is futile to pin our hopes on teacher training as a means of substantially improving the quality of instruction in the public schools (e.g., Branson, 1987). These critics may indeed be correct, but unless public schools are radically restructured, we believe that one of our best bets for improvement lies with training preservice teachers in using the systems approach to improve their instructional practices.

In summary, we believe that if schools are not restructured, then instructional technology, whether it is viewed as media or the systems approach, will continue to play a rather small role in public education during the next decade. However, we are hopeful that preservice teachers who are trained during the next decade will be better prepared to use the systems approach as a means of improving the quality of instruction in the public schools.

RADICAL RESTRUCTURING

We have discussed the potential contribution of instructional technology if one assumes the continuation of the current structure and operating practices of schools. At this point, we want to discuss the viewpoint that instructional technology will not and cannot make any significant improvement without radical redesign of schools.

Under the current structure of schools, decision-making practices are diverse and decentralized, educational goals are fuzzy, instruction is usually group-based and delivered by a teacher, and student progression is usually automatic from one grade to the next. In addition, the system is highly personnel-intensive, with the bulk of the budget going to teacher and administrator salaries, leaving little money for instructional innovations. This structure is antithetical to a technology-based system in which educational goals and objectives are clear, instruction is often individualized and delivered by media other than the teacher, and progression is based on mastery of skills. Can we modify the current structure so as to make it more amenable to the infusion of technology? Probably not.

Why is it so difficult to change the current system? Part of the reason is that the current model of schooling was never designed. Rather, it grew out of the oral tradition and has remained essentially unchanged since about the mid-1800s (Cuban, 1988; Hoetker & Ahlbrand, 1967). Even though the system has gradually adapted to changes in the environment, the basic structure of teacher presentation, seat-work, homework, and group instruction has persisted since the early nineteenth century.

Any system that has evolved over as many decades as has our public education system builds up complex social and administrative mechanisms that serve to maintain and support it. These mechanisms usually exist in the form of administrative structures, organizational and cultural norms, and legislative policies. This is why, when instructional innovators attempt to change one part of the system, the system almost always works to change itself back again. The innovations either are adapted to fit the existing system or else they are sloughed off, allowing the system to remain essentially untouched. We straighten the deck chairs, but the structure of the ship we are traveling on remains the same.

Literature on innovation has shown that it is difficult, if not impossible, to make important and lasting improvements in a system through gradual, piecemeal approaches (Heuston, 1977). Rather, important improvements generally have come about through "quantum-leap" changes followed by gradual fine-tuning until desired results are reached. This is why radical restructuring of the system may be necessary in order for any improvements to have a positive and *lasting* effect.

It is important to point out the distinction between restructure and reform. Reform means making adjustments to improve the existing system, doing the same but more of it, or doing the same but better. Restructuring, on the other hand, fundamentally alters organizations through a design process. Restructuring involves looking at what you want to achieve and then designing an organizational structure and approach that will allow you to achieve these results. Reform is analogous to remodeling a building; restructuring is analogous to designing and constructing a new building based on specifications and needs.

Almost all of the numerous reports and recommendations from national and state commissions on educational reform have focused on "fine-tuning" the current model. They have called for longer school days, a longer school year, increased pay for teachers, or increased standards. Yet none of these recommendations would alter the fundamental operating practices of schooling that we have described above. A majority restructuring of the current model may be necessary in order to achieve significant improvements in education.

Research has demonstrated that a variety of instructional strategies can be used in order to achieve significant improvements in student learning (Cohen, Kulik, & Kulik, 1982; Kulik, Kulik, & Cohen, 1979, 1980; Walberg, 1984, 1986). These strategies include:

- increasing time-on-task (the actual proportion of time that students are thoughtfully engaged in learning);

- increasing the amount and relevance of individual feedback to each student;

- adopting a performance-based progression system, rather than a system where all students spend the same amount of time studying instructional material;

- pacing instruction to the capabilities of the individual student, rather than to the class average; and

- utilizing cooperative learning strategies, peer tutoring, and diagnostic-prescriptive methods.

Unfortunately, most of these strategies are difficult, if not impossible, to implement under the current group-based, time-based, teacher-as-primary-source-of-instruction model of education. In order to put these strategies in place, a major restructuring of the current system is essential.

In our view, the systems approach and a variety of instructional media will play a key role in the design and implementation of a restructured school system. The systems approach can be used to analyze current instructional problems and design solutions to those problems, making best use of the human and non-human instructional resources that are available. If this approach is used properly, it is likely that much of the instruction that is now delivered by teachers will be presented by other media. Teachers will then be able to spend more time on such tasks as planning instruction and guiding and motivating students.

Under these circumstances, many instructional activities are likely to be presented by computers, video, CD-ROM, and interactive videodisc. In most cases, these devices would be part of a networked system so that individual students could access the instructional materials at any time at individual learning stations. These systems, if well designed, could diagnose individual student needs, present appropriate sequences of instructional activities, require students to demonstrate mastery of one set of skills before moving on to the next set, and provide continuous progress reports on individual students.

Computers can also be used to provide basic administrative functions. For example, computer systems currently exist that can efficiently keep track of class attendance; handle scheduling of students, classrooms, and resources; keep inventory of instructional materials; and provide grade reporting. By using computers to perform these functions, teachers and other school personnel should be more free to perform their uniquely human roles, and have greater opportunities for more personal interaction with students.

Attempts to develop schools that incorporate many of the features we have described are currently under way. For example, a group at Indiana University has designed a "third-wave educational system" (Reigeluth, 1987) and is working on plans to implement it. And a group at Florida State University is currently developing a "Schoolyear 2000" model for education, which utilizes new technologies in a totally designed environment (Center for Educational Technology, 1989). Those who are involved in these efforts have acknowledged that the task they are undertaking is a difficult one, but they see it as the best means for making significant improvements in public education in the United States.

CONCLUSION

In conclusion, we believe that during the next decade instructional technology is not likely to have a significant impact on public education. What can we do to make it more likely that instructional technology will play a major role in the schools? We can do a good job of teaching preservice teachers about the systems approach, and thus, perhaps, influence the instructional practices they employ when they become teachers. Or, if we are really ambitious, we can work toward radical restructuring of the public schools. Regardless of the tack we take, we believe it will take a lot of very hard work to change the role instructional technology plays in the schools. But if we are willing to work at it, perhaps the quotations at the beginning of this chapter will not be applicable 10 years from now.

REFERENCES

Branson, R. K. (1987). Why the schools can't improve: The upper-limit hypothesis. *Journal of Instructional Development, 10*(4), 15-26.

Branson, R. K., & Grow, G. (1987). Instructional systems development. In R. M. Gagne (Ed.), *Instructional technology: Foundations* (pp. 397-428). Hillsdale, NJ: Lawrence Erlbaum.

Burkman, E. (1987a). Factors affecting utilization. In R. M. Gagne (Ed.), *Instructional technology: Foundations* (pp. 429-456). Hillsdale, NJ: Lawrence Erlbaum.

————. (1987b). Prospects for instructional systems design in the public schools. *Journal of Instructional Development, 10*(4), 27-32.

Center for Educational Technology. (1989). *Schoolyear 2000: Models for excellence.* Tallahassee, FL: Center for Educational Technology, Florida State University.

Cohen, P. A., Kulik, J. A., & Kulik, C. C. (1982). Educational outcomes of tutoring. *American Educational Research Journal, 19*, 237-247.

Commission on Instructional Technology. (1970). *To improve learning: An evaluation of instructional technology.* New York: R. R. Bowker.

Cuban, L. (1986). *Teachers and machines: The classroom use of technology since 1920.* New York: Teachers College Press.

————. (1988). A fundamental puzzle of school reform. *Phi Delta Kappan, 69*, 341-344.

Dick, W., & Reiser, R. A. (1989). *Planning effective instruction.* Englewood Cliffs, NJ: Prentice-Hall.

Gagne, R. M., & Driscoll, M. P. (1988). *Essentials of learning for instruction* (2nd ed.). Englewood Cliffs, NJ: Prentice-Hall.

Glaser, R., & Cooley, W. W. (1973). Instrumentation for teaching and instructional management. In R. M. W. Travers (Ed.), *Second handbook of research on teaching* (pp. 832-857). Chicago: Rand McNally.

Heuston, D. (1977). *The promise and inevitability of videodisc in education.* Paper submitted to the National Institute of Education, WICAT, New York and Orem, Utah. (ERIC Document Reproduction Service No. ED 153 646).

Hoetker, J., & Ahlbrand, W. P., Jr. (1967). The persistence of the recitation. *American Educational Research Journal, 6,* 145-167.

Komoski, P. K. (1984). Educational computing: The burden of insuring quality. *Phi Delta Kappan, 65,* 244-248.

Kulik, J. A., Kulik, C. C., & Cohen, P. A. (1979). A meta-analysis of outcome studies of Keller's Personalized System of Instruction. *American Psychologist, 34,* 307-318.

———. (1980). Effectiveness of computer-based college teaching. *Review of Educational Research, 52,* 31-60.

Mager, R. F. (1977). The "winds of change." *Training and Development Journal, 31*(10), 12-17.

Morgan, R. M. (1989). Instructional systems development in third world countries. *Educational Technology Research and Development, 37,* 47-56.

Office of Technology Assessment. (1988). *Power on!: New tools for teaching and learning* (GPO No. 052-003-01125-5). Washington, DC: U.S. Government Printing Office.

Popkewitz, T. S. (1979). Educational reform and the problem of institutional life. *Educational Researcher, 8*(3), 3-8.

Reigeluth, C. M. (1987). The search for meaningful reform: A third-wave educational system. *Journal of Instructional Development, 10*(4), 3-14.

Rossett, A., & Grabowsky, J. (1987). The use, mis-use, and non-use of educational technologists in public education. *Educational Technology, 27*(9), 37-42.

Schiffman, S. S., & Gansneder, B. M. (1987). Graduate programs in instructional technology: Their characteristics and involvement in public education. *Journal of Instructional Development, 10*(3), 22-28.

Schrock, S. A., & Byrd, D. M. (1987). An instructional development look at staff development in the public schools. *Journal of Instructional Development, 10*(4), 45-53.

Snellbecker, G. E. (1987). Instructional design skills for classroom teachers. *Journal of Instructional Development, 10*(4), 33-40.

Sullivan, H. J., & Higgins, N. (1983). *Teaching for competence.* New York: Teachers College Press.

Walberg, H. J. (1984). Improving the productivity of America's schools. *Educational Leadership, 41*(8), 19-30.

———. (1986). Syntheses of research on teaching. In M. C. Wittrock (Ed.), *Third handbook of research on teaching* (pp. 214-229). New York: Macmillan.

22

The Internet in Higher Education

David M. Crossman
School of Education, University of Pittsburgh
Pittsburgh, Pennsylvania

INTRODUCTION

"Are you connected?" "Who, me?" "Yeah, you!" "Well, I think so." "Actually, doesn't Al Gore take care of that?" "You mean you think your government will do it for you?" "I know it seems silly, but ... , I just supposed we were all connected to the Information Superhighway."

It is difficult to pick up any periodical, popular or professional, that does not refer, often in a feature article, to the Information Superhighway. To many, the Information Superhighway, or Infobahn, or more currently, the I-Way, is an electronic state of mind that exists somewhere out in the distant future, to be dealt with at a later time after cellular telephone companies, Warner, Bell Atlantic, and TCI finally agree on their relationships.

For many of us in higher education, however, a large chunk of the I-Way is already here. It is, of course, the Internet, the largest and fastest growing complex of computer networks in history. Known only to a relatively few military and government specialists just a few years ago, the Internet now comprises over 6,000 networks and is growing at the rate of 10 percent a month! Each day 10 million people use the Internet to send and receive e-mail around the globe (Gibbs & Smith, 1993).

Some have argued that the Internet represents the most significant step in refining human communications since the introduction of television in 1939. It certainly has the potential to change the way all of us get and share information. The Internet is already larger than the largest library and permits the sharing of files as easily with a colleague in Australia as one down the hall. The prospect of downloading complete text files in a few minutes from a computer 17,000 miles away whets the appetite of any educator who remembers the weeks of waiting for a book from library loan. To be able, in less than an hour, to exchange e-mail with a colleague in Brazil puts international communications on an entirely new and different basis.

The Merit Network Information Center (gopher nic.merit.edu), through the efforts of Larry Landweber at the University of Wisconsin, lists 62 nations that currently have Internet accessibility, with more being added every day. I have a doctoral student who is beginning his research on the ways in which Malaysian educators communicate research information with each other via the Internet.

The Internet provides one of the richest and most democratic information tools ever developed. Electronic bulletin boards exist by the thousands. Chat lines permit schoolchildren and their teachers to talk with children and teachers throughout the world. Listservs provide information forums on virtually every topic. One of the fastest growing dimensions of the Internet is the publication of electronic journals, hundreds of which are already available. One of my students published an article last year in a refereed electronic journal. The time from the electronic submission of the manuscript to its reading by referees and subsequent electronic publication was one month—contrasted with the year or more that is often consumed through conventional publication procedures.

The Internet promises to change the way we get information and the way we do our work. It provides easy access with colleagues throughout the world. For the first time, it matters not at all what type of computer you have. All can be seamlessly interconnected with the use of the TCP/IP (Transmission Control Protocol/Internet Protocol). From the simplest Mac to the most complex workstation, TCP/IP provides the key to complete interconnectivity.

Recently, I was visited by a colleague and former student, now on the faculty of Chulalongkorn University in Bangkok. We were discussing the advantages of the new series of AERA listservs. I mentioned that I am a subscriber to Division C, Learning and Instruction, and have found it very useful to me. She asked how to subscribe. From my office, we telnetted to her account in Bangkok and sent a subscription message to Arizona State University. In less than 20 minutes she had a confirmation. I asked her if she wanted to read her e-mail. "Why not?" she answered. She found a long message to her in Bangkok, from a former student in Texas. I printed her message for her and we went to lunch. Thai food.

On a dark, foggy night last summer, in my little retreat on the coast of Maine, visibility outside was about 10 feet. My wife needed to use our computer to process a few words. I agreed, reluctantly. It took me five minutes to extract myself, seven menus deep, from the specimen library of the Australian National Botanic Gardens in Canberra. The extraordinary power of the Internet struck me that evening. I had been effortlessly wandering about in a library 15,000 miles away, but could not even see my car at the end of the driveway.

THE INTERNET

The Internet is a collection of interconnected computer networks all sharing the TCP/IP protocol. Although many of the participating networks are tightly controlled by a variety of institutions and businesses, the Internet itself is scarcely controlled at all. It is almost organic and has a virtual life of its own. It is owned by no one. To the extent that it is managed at all, it is managed by the Internet Society, a loose confederation of individual members and others representing a variety of computer-related groups, such as Educom. In 1994, nominees to the board of trustees of the Internet Society were drawn from the United States, Australia, Japan, Mexico, the Netherlands, and South Africa—a widely international group. Their concerns are primarily with the establishment of access standards ensuring interconnectivity.

According to Mitchell Kapor, the chairman of the Electronic Frontier Foundation, "Getting information from the Internet is like taking a drink from a fire hydrant" (Cooke & Lehrer, 1993).

I recently learned about a former student of mine who had met her future husband on a Usenet chat line. They were swept off their feet reading each other's text, arranged to meet, fell in love, were married, and now live in California.

The power of the Internet is formidable. In Richard Smith and Mark Gibbs' excellent book, *Navigating the Internet,* Smith, a doctoral student at the University of Pittsburgh at the time, describes how, as a result of some workshops given about the Internet, he decided to give a course about the Internet over the Internet in the summer of 1992. He expected 30 or 40 people to participate but was astonished when 864 people registered. A second workshop overwhelmed him with 15,000 participants from over 50 countries (Gibbs & Smith, 1993). Few of us have taught 15,000 students in an entire academic career!

Unlike the complexities and often substantial costs of distance education based on telecommunications, computer network-based distance education is fairly inexpensive. Most, but not all, Internet communications can be transacted in plain black and white, using text, supported by a computer of modest size and cost. If home access is desired, and that certainly is a great convenience, a modem is necessary, ranging in cost from $100 to $400 depending upon the speed required. I use an antique, outmoded, obsolete, slow Macintosh SE, coupled with an equally lethargic 2400 baud modem. With these two antique tools, I reach to the corners of the earth every night. The excitement never stops.

In the April 27, 1994, issue of the *Chronicle of Higher Education,* Robert L. Jacobson, in an article entitled "The Coming Revolution," describes the promise that, unlike technological disappointments of the past, such as programmed instruction, educational technology of the 1990s will have a profound effect on the way students learn and the way teachers teach. So much so, that Stanford, Carnegie Mellon University, MIT, and other institutions have formed high-powered committees to try to manage the process.

At CMU, for example, there is a "fantasy" committee, examining what they have called the "AAAA Initiative." The four A's refer to a speculation about what might happen if a technology were developed that permitted *anyone* to send or receive *anything* electronically to or from *any* place at *any* time. The Internet comes very close to realizing that inquiry right now. Although most of us send and receive black and white text, sophisticated Internet users are downloading and uploading QuickTime movies, complex graphics, and sound of CD quality.

This semester, I began my Professional Issues course (consisting entirely of professional adults) by insisting that all students get computer accounts and communicate with me by e-mail before the second class meeting. Not all rose to the occasion. However, by the third class meeting, I had heard from all 17 students. I urged them to e-mail me and to tell me what was on their minds. And they did. Some went on. And on. And on. It was fascinating to see how students used this new communications medium. I confess that whereas my early responses were long and elaborate, my style led to shorter messages as the term matured. By the end of the term, I was very creative with the one-liner. Regardless, I found that students were writing to me in a very new way.

Where Did the Internet Come From?

In order to facilitate Department of Defense-funded research efforts, the ARPANET (Advanced Research Projects Agency Network) was formed in 1969 to interconnect four computers: one at the University of Utah, a second at the University of California at Santa Barbara, a third at the University of California at Los Angeles, and a fourth at the Stanford Research Institute (SRI).

In 1981, CSNET (Computer Science Network) tied into the NSFNET (National Science Foundation Network) and ARPANET, forming the basis of what was to become the Internet backbone. In 1983, the Internet was formed as ARPANET combined with MILNET (Military Network). In March 1990 ARPANET was dismantled; in 1991 CSNET was disbanded and the Internet emerged (Gibbs & Smith, 1993, p. 5).

What Is the Internet Now?

Some say it is a state of mind. Others claim that it is the most democratic communications process ever invented. Some say it is the world's first real global forum. Some say it is the "Cyberspace" that William Gibson conceived in his book, *Neuromancer* (Gibson, 1984). Harley Hahn and Rick Stout, in their book *The Internet Complete Reference*, call the Internet the most significant achievement in the history of mankind (Hahn & Stout, 1994a). Well, their enthusiasm may have carried them a bit far. However, for the first time, anyone with access to an Internet node, with a modem and computer, however modest, can connect to the most astonishing communications network ever developed.

It may very well be that the Internet is enjoying its finest hour right now. However, concern lurks on the horizon. For most institutional users, the Internet is free. One can send and receive e-mail anywhere in the globe to any place that is connected. Files can be sent and received almost anywhere. Databases of the most obscure nature can be searched from the comfort of one's office or home. There is a pioneer spirit on the "net." There is a spirit of cooperation based in novelty and experimentation. Recently, a teaching assistant at my university mistakenly inquired to an entire listserv population about how she should go about subscribing to the list, rather than e-mailing the moderator. Instead of being verbally disciplined, she received 35 offers of assistance.

Like any new technology, the Internet is undergoing great change. Developed during the days when the only users were computer scientists and hackers, access to many features of the Internet involves the use of arcane commands that are not at all intuitive. Certainly not very complicated, these commands must simply be memorized in order to navigate this extraordinary resource. Access to the Internet is a classic case of the COIK formula (clear only if known).

James Gleick (1994) reports that the information future is out of control. He suggests, correctly, that virtually every communication provider is jockeying for a piece of the Internet action—and that monumental confusion is the result. He is certainly right. Every large corporation in America, and thousands of small ones, have their eyes on the Internet as a new way of doing business. This is a major issue, since NSF guidelines now all but exclude commercial activity on the Internet.

Herbert Schiller (1993) discusses this emerging debate, suggesting that if the structure of the Internet is taken over by private business, it will become an "almost exclusively privatized social landscape. The public and the public's interest will at best be given marginal attention, if not entirely excluded." This struggle, going on in corporate board rooms and in Congress, may well determine the direction that the Internet will take.

INTERNET ACCESS TOOLS

The Internet is owned by no one, controlled by no one, and grows very much like the organism it resembles—a piece of protoplasm that moves into every corner of our communications consciousness. Its resources are unimaginably large and certainly provide a sense of reality to Marshall McLuhan's famous "Global Village."

The Internet is changing, some would say maturing, faster and in more ways than can be followed by any one individual. What was available a month ago is no longer available, but something newer, better, larger, more comprehensive has invariably taken its place. So, "cyberspace" is a frustrating world.

My early efforts involved accessing detailed weather forecasts in Alaska, zip codes for Kansas, and, from the University of Minnesota's gopher, access to the CIA World Fact Book, a cornucopia of international geographic facts for more countries than I had heard of, including the number of communists in each. Oman has "none." However, getting information that is really useful requires much more work. The key to the use of the Internet is in the development of navigation skills. Imagine the Library of Congress without a catalog, on-line or otherwise. The collection would be almost useless. So it was on the Internet, until just a few years ago—a huge collection of information without a catalog. Fortunately, much of that is beginning to change.

The Virtues of E-mail

Certainly the most widely used feature of the Internet is e-mail. Every day millions of people from all walks of life send and receive e-mail, to every corner of the globe. As more people obtain e-mail accounts, it becomes more useful all the time and, for many, has already become a real alternative to the U.S. Postal Service (snail mail!).

This morning, at home, I turned on my computer and modem and read a message from a newly admitted Taiwanese student writing to me from Taipei, inquiring about which books he might read to prepare for his first work at my university. I responded immediately. He probably had my message within the hour. How is this different from the telephone, you might ask? First, it is free (at least for many institutional users). Second, both the sender and receiver of the message do so at a time convenient to each, eliminating the traditional game of "telephone tag." Third, when the message is written, it can be easily and electronically stored for later use, if necessary. Finally, and this is a personal judgment, e-mail can be, and often is, more thoughtfully constructed than a telephone call.

This semester, I urged all of my students to obtain e-mail accounts and to communicate with me about our courses together, subject matter, ideas, and issues that seemed important to them. I received the most extraordinary variety of responses, most of them thoughtful, carefully constructed, and serious minded—a kind of communication very different from the telephone call or the personal interview.

For day-to-day correspondence, e-mail is a spectacular time-saver. Contrasted with the conventional writing or dictating of a letter to a colleague, having it processed, spell-checked, proofread, printed, and finally mailed, sometimes several days later, an e-mail message can be prepared in a matter of minutes and sent and received and read by the recipient, often in less than an hour. Further, the message can be sent from any location with a computer and access to the network. My computer and modem at home permit me to read and respond to correspondence on a schedule convenient to me. In addition, when traveling, I can telnet to my university from any location accessible to the Internet and read my e-mail as if I were in my office.

Finding Out Who's Who—And Where They Are

One of the frustrations of using e-mail is obtaining the e-mail address of an individual. There is no comprehensive directory of users yet, but the finger command and the whois server are often helpful. In many local systems, it is possible to type finger at the system prompt and then enter the last name of the individual being searched. This search strategy will often yield a list of everyone in the system with that last name. One often learns, in addition, the person's e-mail address, the last time he or she logged onto the system, and how many e-mail messages remain unread. Individuals can, if they wish, place additional information in this "plan file." Such information often includes planned trips away from the institution, vacation schedules, or other trivia you feel compelled to share with the world.

The finger command by itself is useful for the local system only. If the name of a distant computer system is being sought, one alternative is to inquire at the Internet Information Center, which is accessed by the telnet command rs.internic.net. Once connected to the Network Information Center, one enters the whois command. At the "whois" prompt, it is a simple matter to inquire about the address of a distant computer. For example, at the "whois" prompt, one might inquire about the University of Pittsburgh. One learns that there are over 20 networks at the University of Pittsburgh, but that the main domain is pitt.edu. Then, by combining the finger command with the results of the "whois" inquiry, one can locate an individual address. Thus, the command finger crossman@pitt.edu yields the address dmc+@pitt.edu. The addresses of most individuals that have e-mail accounts can be identified in this way.

Listservs

One of the most interesting information sources on the Internet is the listserv. Separate from the newsgroups and bulletin boards, which will be described in the next section, listservs arrive along with the rest of your e-mail.

Listservs are actually mailing lists, and are of two types: moderated and unmoderated. The moderated list is filtered through an individual who ensures that the subject of each message posted to the list is appropriate to that list. The unmoderated list accepts postings without editorial intervention. There are hundreds of lists on virtually every topic, ranging from the academic to the bizarre. One of the most popular and useful published list of lists is *INTERNET: Mailing Lists* (Hardie & Neou, 1994).

One can also obtain an on-line academic list-of-lists from Kent State University. You can obtain this list through anonymous ftp from ksuvxa.kent.edu in the *library* directory. The files are named acadlist.file1, acadlist.file2, etc.

Many of these lists generate a great deal of traffic, which can easily clog up your e-mail. Twenty messages a day is common on many moderately active lists. Therefore, it is important to choose with care. It is very easy to find that you are getting much more information than you can read or utilize. Regular deletion of read or unusable messages is important to keep your e-mail software running quickly.

One of the interesting features of the mailing list is the variety of responses that emerge as new issues are raised. A single posting on a new topic may yield dozens of responses, from Hong Kong, from Scotland, from Australia, from Europe, as well as throughout this country. Interested professionals emerge from institutions large and small, well known and obscure. The debate is hot and heavy and sometimes goes on for days. Then, another issue is raised and the discussion shifts to the new topic. It is a seductive process. Intense interest in one of these groups can consume all of your time. Beware!

Usenet

A second way to read and participate in specialized discussions is through the Usenet. Not really a network at all, Usenet is a vast collection of discussion groups on virtually every conceivable topic. Although nearly every institution that utilizes Usenet maintains a series of discussion groups of unique interest to the local region, over 2,500 discussion groups are of general interest and are found in most institutions using the Usenet software.

Unlike the mailing list, which arrives and is read as e-mail, Usenet groups, commonly called "newsgroups," are available through software separate from e-mail. One of the most common is the rn newsreader. Most newsreaders perform similar functions; it is wise to choose one, learn its operating commands, and stick with it for the sake of simplicity.

A newsreader permits the user to choose newsgroups or "subscribe" to selected groups. Once "subscribed" to, the newsgroup title appears when the rn opens Usenet. Actually, the process of subscribing to a newsgroup is simply a way to select those groups that you want to read on a regular basis. These subscriptions are a practical necessity because there are frequently 5,000 or more newsgroups from which to choose. As with most research libraries, casual browsing is usually not an efficient way to get information, although it certainly can be fun. Of course, it is possible to scan all newsgroups that are carried by a particular institution—a long process. Many Internet reference books, such as *The Internet Complete Reference* (Hahn & Stout, 1994a), carry a list of most of the major groups. Regional groups, however, are rarely listed or accessible outside of the region. The actual newsgroups that are carried in a specific institution are determined by a systems administrator in that institution.

Once the operating commands for your selected newsreader have been mastered, it is then possible to "subscribe" and "unsubscribe" to any newsgroup, to read the articles contained within any group, and to place an article of your own or "post" an article to the group. Through an elaborate system of interconnected servers, your local posting, if you wish, is carried regionally, nationally, and finally to all the international Usenet servers. Thus, you need to be certain that what you have to say is what you want hundreds of thousands of strangers to read. And answer!

One of the most interesting and certainly democratic dimensions of Usenet is the extraordinary variety of information available. It ranges from the academic, serious, and sometimes profound, to the frivolous, erotic, bizarre, and, sometimes, plain stupid. Just like life.

Telnet

One of the most useful features of the Internet is the ability to connect from your computer to a remote computer in order to access information on that remote machine. The Telnet program, for example, permits the user to access the Internet Information Center as described above. At the system prompt one types the command telnet, then the address of the distant machine housing the Internet Information Center: rs.internic.net. Thus, the entire command line becomes telnet rs.internic.net. Once connected to a remote host computer, you will be asked to provide an ID and a password. If you have an account on that remote machine, you simply provide your ID and password. If not, many remote hosts will permit you to log on anonymously and then permit you to access publicly available files. In such situations, you enter anonymous in place of your ID and then supply your ID when asked for your password.

For example, I maintain a courtesy account at the University of Maine for use in the summer. Located over 100 miles from the university, I utilize a packet switch circuit (using an 800 number) to connect to the University of Maine. From there I can then telnet to remote host computers. One convenience of this arrangement is the ability to connect to the University of Maine via the packet network, and then telnet to the University of Pittsburgh and be able to open and read e-mail as if physically located in Pittsburgh. Looked at from a broader point of view, it is possible then, for anyone with access to a local Internet node, to telnet to his or her home institution, for the purpose of reading e-mail or utilizing other resources of the home machine. This process, with only slight variations, is the way to reach distant machines for access to gopher and ftp purposes, to be discussed next.

Gopher

Developed at the University of Minnesota, the term "gopher" appears to be a mixed pastiche of the Minnesota mascot and the little cyberdroid that scurries about getting us whatever we need—the "go-fer." The gopher client-server system is certainly the most easily understood and most easily used Internet tool. Requiring relatively few, simple commands, the gopher is intuitive and satisfying to use. There are hundreds of gopher servers available on the Internet. Most large universities maintain their own. In addition, by using the telnet command, one can reach other computers and access their gopher servers directly.

Last year, in response to an international student who had complained that his classmates did not understand his country and culture (which was absolutely true), an American student, demonstrating the capabilities of gopher in class, connected to the University of Minnesota Gopher, then connected to "Libraries," then connected to "On-line books," then connected to the CIA World Fact Book, then searched the fact book for the country in question. More data about the country were put on the screen than any reasonable person would want to know.

Gopher servers are organized in a branching tree structure, presenting ever more specific information as one descends deeper into the menus available. Each of the several thousand gopher servers available provides local information as well as access to gopher servers else-where. One of the most exotic Internet trips that one can take is to the menu item entitled, "All the Gopher Servers in the World." This exciting menu lists hundreds of gopher locations around the world, including the names of dozens of unfamiliar universities whose curriculum, pro-grams, faculty, and structure are available to any interested cyberspace visitor.

Once the "root" gopher page opens, the items in the menu are listed by number. Navigating gopher is simplicity itself. By using the return key or the right arrow key, one can move down this menu to make a selection. A similar process is followed for each succeeding menu page, until the desired document is located. A stroke of the u key will display each of the preceding menu pages until the root gopher page is reached. The quit command will close the gopher connection and return the viewer to the system prompt.

Unlike the file transfer protocol (ftp) discussed below, a gopher file is received and then disconnected from the host computer. Then, it is reconnected when another file is requested. Thus, the connection is made and broken as files are retrieved and used. This process sometimes causes sudden and inexplicable connection failures. So, although gopher is certainly the most user-friendly Internet access tool, it often requires a great deal of patience.

Veronica and Jughead

Because the Internet contains the largest collection of information ever assembled, there is a very great need for bibliographic tools. Veronica provides a searching tool for hundreds of gopher servers that are available. Frustrated by the difficulty of finding information in the many gopher servers available, Steven Foster and Fred Barrie of the University of Nevada at Reno developed the first version of Veronica in 1992. Similar to Archie, which searches ftp sites, Veronica is based on keyword search strategies and displays search results in the same format as gopher itself. Therefore, the same commands can be used to access the fruits of the Veronica search.

Whereas Veronica searches all of gopherspace, Jughead, developed by Rhett (Jonzy) Jones at the University of Utah Computer Center and released in March of 1993, searches only a limited area of gopherspace, often a single university gopher menu structure.

File Transfer Protocol

The File Transfer Protocol (ftp) is magic. And frustrating. It is magic because it permits the transfer of any of thousands of documents to one's own computer. And frustrating because of the variety of arcane UNIX commands required to make it work. The completion of a successful ftp is, however, one of life's most satisfying experiences. The idea of being able to transfer a document on almost any topic to one's own computer and then to read it on the screen, modify it, or print it, makes one light-headed with excitement!

A great program called Fetch, written by Jim Matthews of Dartmouth College, simplifies the ftp process for the Macintosh and permits the use of standard Macintosh conventions, which, in turn, initiate ftp commands. Fetch is useful when connected directly to the Internet through an Ethernet line or from a Serial Line Internet Protocol (SLIP) connection, but cannot be used through a modem alone (Fraase, 1993).

Although the availability of ftp sites and files is almost endless, Scott Yanoff of the University of Wisconsin at Milwaukee provides what is probably the most useful short list of Internet sources, including ftp sites. Updated on a regular basis, the list, approximately 16 pages, contains Internet addresses on subjects ranging from the weather to the American Philosophical Society. The list is available by anonymous ftp at the following address: csd4.csd.uwm.edu. The access path is /pub/inet.services.txt. That is, once connected by anonymous ftp to the csd4.csd.uwm.edu computer (University of Wisconsin at Milwaukee), the Yanoff List entitled inet.services.txt is in the pub directory. Perhaps the most comprehensive published list of Internet addresses is *The Internet Yellow Pages* (Hahn & Stout, 1994b).

Archie

Archie, so named because it sounds like "archive," was developed at McGill University as a student project. As in the cartoon, VERONICA and Jughead are simple characters, whereas Archie is more complicated. He serves as a search mechanism for ftp servers and provides a bibliographic searching tool for the millions of files available through the File Transfer Protocol. It is one thing to know that there is a lot out there in cyberspace, but it is something else again to know how and where to look for this information.

Archie is really a collection of servers that draw information from more than a thousand ftp sites on a regular basis, thus providing current index information on more than 2.5 million files, all available by ftp. Scott Yanoff currently lists 18 publicly accessible Archie sites, including sites in Australia, Austria, Finland, Germany, Japan, Korea, New Zealand, Portugal, Sweden, Taiwan, and Ireland, as well as a number in the United States (Yanoff, 1994). Like a huge card catalog, Archie provides keyword searching for all anonymous ftp locations.

Wide Area Information Server (WAIS)

Developed by Thinking Machines Corporation, Apple Computer, and Dow Jones, WAIS provides a keyword search mechanism that connects to over 400 sources throughout the world. WAIS can be accessed through some local clients, through some gopher servers, and directly by several public clients in the United States and one in Finland located at info.funet.fi. WAIS is unique among search mechanisms in that it provides a score of the number of times the keyword is found for each document identified. Although that does not necessarily make the document with the highest score the most useful, it is often helpful in making a decision about which documents to read.

World Wide Web (WWW)

Developed in Switzerland by Tim Berners-Lee of the European Particle Physics Laboratory (CERN) as a way to share scientific information, the World Wide Web has become one of the most sophisticated and seamless ways of accessing information on the Internet. WWW has the capability of linking a variety of information and communication formats, such as gopher, Usenet, ftp, WAIS, and telnet sessions. What is unique and different about the interface of WWW is that it is based in hypertext. Each displayed WWW document contains a linking mechanism similar to the button metaphor used in Apple's HyperCard. The document may highlight a word or provide a number after a word or idea to which another resource is linked. By responding to the number or other signal within the document, related issues can be called up directly. Similarly, through the use of appropriate commands, the user can back up to his point of entry into the Web.

As this chapter was being written, there were WWW servers in the Netherlands, Australia, Switzerland, Israel, Slovakia, Taiwan, and many more in the United States. Some WWW servers tend to specialize. For example, one American server is located at the Cornell University Law School: telnet fatty.law.cornell.edu. Not surprisingly, that server is rich with legal documents. The original Swiss server at CERN is accessed by the following Telnet address: telnet info.cern.ch. Each server site provides its own browser and each is slightly different, although all are intuitive and easy to use. However, because WWW is hypertext based, it is very different from other access tools and requires practice to use it skillfully (Hahn & Stout, 1994a).

Mosaic

Certainly the most sophisticated Internet browser now available is Mosaic. It was developed by Marc Andreessen at the National Center for Supercomputing Applications at the University of Illinois. Mosaic is the newest derivative of the World Wide Web. It is available in color with special versions available for XWindows, for Microsoft Windows, and for Macintosh. Mosaic requires substantially more computing power than other access tools. For the Macintosh, for example, it requires System 7 or later; MacTCP 2.0.2 or later; 2.0.4 or later recommended, and 4 megabytes of RAM. Mosaic itself occupies 2 megabytes of RAM. Finally, it requires at least 5 megabytes of hard disc space. Mosaic can be downloaded by ftp from the University of Illinois at ncsa.uiuc.edu.

Mosaic is colorful, seamless, and extraordinarily powerful. Through WWW, it can access gopher servers, WAIS servers, any ftp site, anything on Usenet, anything accessible on telnet, and all hypertext documents. Largely because of the availability of Mosaic, new WWW servers are sprouting up almost daily. In April of 1994, NCSA announced that there were 1,200 web servers now in operation (NCSA, 1994).

Mosaic was first released in April 1993 for the X platform. In December 1993, version 2.0 was released along with version 1.0 for Apple Macintosh and Microsoft Windows platforms. The Mosaic client utilizes the HyperText Transfer Protocol (HTTP) of the World Wide Web (NCSA, 1994). In addition to text, Mosaic supports video, pictorial information, graphics, and sound in an integrated multimedia environment.

Clearly, Mosaic is a step in the direction of clarity and simplicity. It permits seamless movement throughout the Internet and has the potential for becoming the standard user interface.

SUMMARY

By any standard, the Internet is the most comprehensive information resource ever developed. Almost 25 years since its inception as a military network, the new Internet has been discovered by millions as an efficient way of communicating and exchanging information, particularly in written form.

For some, and especially those in academic life who enjoy Internet access provided by their institutions, e-mail has become a new and practical way to interact with colleagues and students. One of the great pleasures of using e-mail is the capability of writing mail on your own schedule and receiving mail the same way. Many are discovering unique ways in which e-mail can contribute to the educational experience and increase productivity. The ready availability of inexpensive modems and computers has made the home and the office equally productive work areas.

On-line access to information has also changed the way many academics live their lives and pursue their careers. Regular visits to the library were a standard way of life for many faculty and students. Now, the catalogs of hundreds of libraries are only a few keystrokes away. However, the availability of full text is only beginning to be addressed. At the same time, ephemeral material of all kinds, government documents, and countless other databases, are all available through ftp, gopher, Usenet, telnet, WAIS, and the World Wide Web. Although much of the Internet still suggests a frontier mentality with shared skills and frustrations, access tools such as Veronica, Jughead, and Archie have made the Internet usable and accessible to those with the time and patience to learn how to use them.

The Internet has, without question, changed the way that many look at the rest of the world. In a single morning, it is not uncommon for an academic listserv to receive inquiries and responses from individuals in a dozen different countries—all collaborating on a single issue as if they were assembled around a single table.

The Internet is both sophisticated and primitive. It is certainly sophisticated in the extraordinary technologies that have made possible such a complex information exchange. To be able to search a data file in Taiwan and transfer that file to one's office in a matter of a few minutes is amazing. However, the arcane commands required to do it are reminiscent of Morse code or naval signal flags. That obscurity, of course, is changing and will continue to change. The incredible growth of user-friendly Mosaic is ample evidence of movement in that direction.

The financing of the I-Way is another major area in flux. Who will ultimately pay for the Internet and related communication technologies? Every large and many small businesses want a piece of the Information Superhighway. Still more or less under the wing of the National Science Foundation, the Internet may ultimately become a commercial creature. Never before have so many communication and entertainment companies been angling so fiercely to get a piece of the action.

One of the great frustrations among those without institutional affiliations is how to get wired. America Online, CompuServe, Delphi, GEnie, MCI Mail, and hundreds of other commercial firms are offering Internet access, for a price. For many, the price is too high. The battle will be fought in front of us in the next few years. The debate will be coming soon to a computer near you.

Regardless, the Internet is the most exciting communication development of our time. "Are you connected?" I hope so.

I would like to express my thanks to Dr. Sandi Behrens of the Software Engineering Institute at Carnegie Mellon University, Pittsburgh, for her many helpful suggestions and careful reading of this chapter as it was being prepared.

REFERENCES

Cooke, Kevin, & Lehrer, Dan. (1993). The whole world is talking. *The Nation, 257*(2), 60-64.

Fraase, Michael. (1993). *The Mac Internet tour guide: Cruising the Internet the easy way.* Chapel Hill, NC: Ventana.

Gibbs, Mark, & Smith, Richard. (1993). *Navigating the Internet.* Carmel, IN: Sams.

Gibson, William. (1984). *Neuromancer.* New York: Ace Books.

Gleick, James. (1994). The information future: Out of control (and it's a good thing too). *The New York Times Magazine.* May 1, 54-57.

Hahn, Harley, & Stout, Rick. (1994a). *The Internet complete reference.* Berkeley: Osborne, McGraw-Hill.

———. (1994b). *The Internet yellow pages.* Berkeley: Osborne, McGraw-Hill.

Hardie, E. T. L., & Neou, V. (1994). *INTERNET: Mailing lists.* Englewood Cliffs, NJ: PTR Prentice-Hall.

Jacobson, Robert L. (1994). The coming revolution. *The Chronicle of Higher Education*, A26-29.

Merit Network Information Center. (1994, February). *Internet Gopher*, nic.merit.edu.

National Center for Supercomputing Applications (NCSA). (1994). *MOSAIC Announcements,* March 22. mosaic@ncsa.uiuc.edu.

Schiller, Herbert I. (1993). The "information highway": Public way or private road. *The Nation, 257*(2), 64-66.

Wired. San Francisco, CA: editor@wired.com.

Yanoff, Scott. (1994). *Special Internet connections.* yanoff@csd4.csd.uwm.edu.

23

Applications of Educational Technology
The International Perspective

Alexander J. Romiszowski
School of Education, Syracuse University
Syracuse, New York

INTRODUCTION: PERSPECTIVES
AND VANTAGE POINTS

At the end of World War II, the Soviet Union, having effectively annexed Poland, made a goodwill gesture by building, in the center of devastated Warsaw, a "Palace of Culture." This enormous building, which houses dozens of theaters and cinemas, as well as restaurants, convention centers, and offices, stands amid several acres of empty space, which previously were occupied by hundreds of residential and commercial buildings. Its design is intriguing to say the least, being some Soviet architect's interpretation of a Chicago 1920s skyscraper, transported from a crowded downtown environment and adapted to "fill" the wide open space where it stands. Having, in addition, been "easternized" by the addition of minarets and other Kremlin-like embellishments, it rises from a broad base, in ever narrower layers, like some gigantic, overdecorated wedding cake, and culminates in a tall central spike of a tower.

A visitor to Warsaw asked a resident where to go to get the best panoramic view of the city. He was told to go to the top of the Palace of Culture. "Is that because it is the highest building in Warsaw?" he asked. The reply came back like a shot. "No, it's because it is the only vantage point from which you cannot see the Palace of Culture."

Although the links between this story and educational technology may not be very obvious (though I assure you they do exist), it does serve to illustrate the importance of "vantage points" and how they influence the view, or perspective, that one forms. One problem in planning this chapter was to decide what vantage point to adopt. Should I paint the perspective from the position of someone in the United States, looking out at the world, or of someone "out there" looking at this peculiarly U.S. export called instructional technology? In less nationalistic terms, should I adopt the vantage point of an instructional technologist, looking out at the world's educational problems, or of an educator in any nation with its fair share of educational problems, looking at what instructional technology can offer in the way of solutions?

American Export or International Phenomenon?

Without a doubt, educational technology as a discipline owes more to American research and development efforts than to any other source. The field and its terminology were invented in the United States. Most well known researchers in the field have been Americans. In quantitative terms, there are more educational technology-related graduate programs, and more graduates are produced in the United States, than in the rest of the world put together. In a recent book setting out the "foundations of instructional technology" (Gagne, 1987), well under one percent of all references quoted are of non-U.S. origin, and indeed, most of the foreign references are concentrated in one chapter dealing with large-scale educational technology projects in developing nations, executed with the assistance of U.S. educational technologists. There is a strong tendency to view educational technology (and particularly "instructional" technology) as a peculiarly American contribution to educational methodology.

This is not a very healthy viewpoint. When Americans take this viewpoint, significant contributions to the technology by foreign researchers and developers may go unnoticed for a long time. For foreign educators to take this viewpoint may result in resistance to educational technology based more on nationalistic fears of "American cultural imperialism" than on educational grounds.

The truth is that educational technology, though born and bred in the United States, is now a well-established international phenomenon, flourishing in all parts of the world. Indeed, it is playing a more significant role in developing or changing educational practices in many countries throughout the world than in the United States itself.

DISSEMINATION OF EDUCATIONAL TECHNOLOGY THROUGHOUT THE WORLD

The Association of Educational and Training Technology in the United Kingdom has for over 20 years published an *International Yearbook of Educational and Training Technology*. As past editor of this yearbook, I originated a database of "centers of activity" in our field. The present editor, Chris Osborne, has continued to update this database, using the latest computer-based tools in an attempt to make the data as comprehensive and as up-to-date as possible. The latest edition of this yearbook (AETT, 1989) lists information on 1,166 centers of activity in educational technology-related fields. Figure 23.1, page 276, shows the regional breakdown of the database. These figures do not have any great scientific value. They are somewhat slanted to favor those countries and regions with which it is easier to maintain communication in the English language. They are not consistent in defining the degree or extent of activity and of course are a compilation of what the centers reported, rather than the result of an independent investigation. In particular, because they were compiled for a primarily British readership by British editors, they report a much greater number of centers, in more detail, for the United Kingdom than for elsewhere. However, they are reasonably representative for the rest of the world. For example, the figure of 121 U.S. universities is quite close to the figures compiled by the Association for Educational Communications and Technology (AECT, 1985) in its recent surveys of graduate studies in our field. If anything it is likely that as one moves further from Europe and the English-speaking world, into Africa, Asia, and Latin America, the numbers presented underestimate actual levels of dissemination and use.

	Total
INTERNATIONAL/REGIONAL CENTERS	
International agencies, organizations, etc. 34	
Regional multinational organizations, etc. 51	
	85
CENTERS IN THE UNITED KINGDOM	
Universities/higher education institutions 90	
Other research/development/use centers 150	
	240
CENTERS IN THE UNITED STATES OF AMERICA	
Universities/higher education institutions 121	
Other research/development/use centers 109	
	230
CENTERS IN THE REST OF THE WORLD (by region)	
Europe (not including UK) 210	
Asia/Australasia 189	
Latin America and Caribbean 90	
Africa 64	
Canada 41	
Middle East 17	
	611
TOTAL NUMBER OF CENTERS LISTED IN 1989 YEARBOOK	1166

Fig. 23.1. Centers of activity in instructional technology.

We are left with the conclusion that there is much educational technology activity throughout the world. What is the nature of this activity? What is its contribution to education locally, and to the field of educational technology in general? Space constraints preclude the exhaustive analysis of cases from all parts of the world. Therefore, I will examine one particular phenomenon, open learning, which has originated largely outside the United States (mainly in Great Britain) and which is having a very significant impact on world education and training.

OPEN LEARNING IN GREAT BRITAIN:
A MINI CASE STUDY

The Open University: Its Birth and Impact

The Open University was initially conceived for political reasons. It was the postwar Labor government's vision of a higher education system accessible to all sectors of society, free from geographical, social, economic, or other barriers. Originally conceived of as the "university of the air," it was to be a mass-mediated, culturally oriented alternative university, open to all. As plans developed throughout the 1960s, the educational technology movement was also growing in power and influence, so that as planning passed from the political to the strategic stages, several prominent educational technologists became involved. The results have been significant for the success of the Open University as an institution and for its impact on the rest of higher education, in Great Britain and worldwide.

The strategic planning for the Open University, performed by a task force that included some of the most prominent educational technologists of the time, was probably one of the first large-scale and systematic attempts to use the systems approach as a design methodology for a whole institution (Neil, 1970). One of the planning decisions taken was the adoption of a "course team approach" (a multidisciplinary team of subject experts, media experts, and educational technologists) as the basis for all course and material development. This decision had important implications well beyond its technical "good sense." It was perhaps the first successful inroad on the traditional university concept of "academic freedom." Although the professor was still the chief source of decisions on *what* to teach, these decisions had to pass the test of difficult-to-satisfy educational technologists who delighted in asking *why*. Once the "what and why" questions were hammered out, the heat would really turn up as all three of the parties on the course team would argue out just *how* the content should be taught. In the first five years of operation, some 20 percent of the academic faculty resigned because of an inability to adapt to this method of course design. On several occasions the university was close to abandoning the course team approach. However, the Institute of Educational Technology won the day and the course team approach continued to be used, slowly developing into a most effective methodology for the generation of high-quality educational materials (Lewis, 1979).

Another fortuitous early decision was to distribute the Open University's learning materials through established systems. The bulk (some 80 percent) of instruction is through the print medium. These materials are distributed through existing bookstores. The radio and television programs are carried by the BBC. This means that all basic materials are readily available to all, whether registered for a course at the university or not. It is not surprising, therefore, that many other institutions have adopted Open University course materials for their own courses (Bates, 1975).

It is probable that the widespread availability of the relatively cheap and exceptionally well designed Open University course materials had a greater impact on both the content and the methods of teaching in British universities than have all the government legislation and incentives since World War II aimed at reforming and modernizing higher education (Perry, 1976). In the process, the Open University became Great Britain's largest educational publisher. This, more than any other single factor, enabled the university to survive the drastic educational cuts perpetrated by successive governments through the late 1970s and early 1980s. Not only did it survive better than most other institutions, but it also continued to extend its influence worldwide, acting both as a consultant to many nations on the design and operation of distance learning and as a supplier of course materials.

The Spread of Open Learning in Great Britain

Perhaps the most important spin-off from the Open University experience has been the popularization and wide-scale adoption of "open learning." This is not necessarily distance learning (though it may be). It does, however, embody the principles of open access to learner-directed learning from modularized learning resources (Hodgson et al., 1987). It is not limited to higher education, nor indeed to formal education. The "Open Tech" projects in Great Britain are examples of how the approach can be used to revolutionize vocational training (Partridge, 1986).

THE OPEN LEARNING
PHENOMENON WORLDWIDE

Open learning is now not only a growth phenomenon in education and training inside Great Britain, but is also a significant British "export" to the rest of the world. There are now hundreds of open learning projects and institutions worldwide. Of course, not all have been the direct result of events in Great Britain. Some are in fact much older in origin than the Open University. But many of those set up in the last 20 years have been strongly influenced by the open learning philosophy and methodology developed largely in Great Britain. To illustrate the extent of this movement, one might mention the Commonwealth of Learning, an information exchange organization set up in 1987 by some of the nations in the British Commonwealth. The group's objective is to make available to all Commonwealth nations the open learning courses that are already in existence in other member nations (Commonwealth Secretariat, 1987). A database of existing courses is being created and maintained. At the time of writing, there are upward of 10,000 different course offerings listed (Maraj, 1990).

The numbers of students involved worldwide in distance and open learning is difficult to estimate with accuracy, but a few examples of specific countries and institutions may serve to give an impression of the extent and importance of this trend. Many Asian countries now rely on distance education systems as key elements in their national educational efforts. In China there are over one million students currently registered in open learning higher education systems. Thailand and Indonesia use distance education intensively, with about half a million students in each country. The Korea Correspondence University enrolls a quarter of a million. In the Soviet Union, some 1.5 million, or 30 percent of all higher education students, study through distance education (Daniel, 1988).

In Latin America, the numbers per institution are more modest, but there are many more institutions—over 50 in the latest *Yearbook* count—that currently operate distance education projects. Not all of these may embody the principles of open learning, as distance education in Latin America was already well established on a large scale long before the open learning movement got up to speed. Some projects do, however, exhibit the essential characteristics of the open learning philosophy. Many of these are not in higher education institutions, but offer vocational training, or even basic elementary and secondary education on an open learning basis. In Chile, for example, remedial mathematics and language skills training have for many years been offered by the technical college system on an open access basis, which involves the distribution of the basic study materials as a free supplement to one of the Sunday papers. These are supported by distance-mediated tutorial help using a variety of delivery systems. In Brazil, a similar project is now under way to impart basic computer literacy skills to the population as a whole. Another Brazilian project is operated by one of the major television and media networks, Rede Globo, as a national, for-profit undertaking (but with federal government support). This network offers several hours daily of high-quality instructional television, geared towards adults who failed or missed their elementary or secondary education. In addition, there are weekly self-study magazines and backup texts, published to a reasonably high quality (in terms of instructional design and printing standards), available at all newspaper stands. It is estimated that over a million students participate regularly in the program, although a somewhat smaller number avail themselves of the opportunity to take the final school-leaving examinations. Current plans involve an agreement between this network and the biggest private bank, Bradesco, to use available excess capacity of their electronic banking network as a medium for rapid interactive tutorial support to students. Every town will have a study center at the bank, open to anyone who has problems with the self-study units.

Australia is another heavy user of open learning for technical and vocational education. Having had successful early experiences in backing up the outback's "flying doctor" service by basic first aid instructions over radio, many projects now exist that combine self-study materials with radio-telephone-based tutorials and conferencing. Much nurse and teacher training is performed in this way. In the Pacific Islands, open learning systems are used by the

University of the South Pacific (from Fiji) and by Micronesia (from Guam). In Africa, Nigeria is prominent in the use of open learning, and other countries such as Kenya and Zambia are following its example (IEC/CET, 1987).

In the so-called old world, open learning is also a growing trend, illustrating that it is not just applicable to the problems created by poor basic educational provision or geographical barriers to "place-based" learning. Even a small country such as the Netherlands, where any point can be reached from any other in a few hours, has a thriving Open University. So have Germany and Spain. Just about every European country has some form of institutionalized open learning system operating at some level of education or vocational training. In the "new" world, Canada is one of the world's more intensive users of distance education, both for higher education (e.g., at the University of Athabasca) and for other levels (e.g., the Vancouver-based Open Learning Agency).

THE VIEW FROM THE TOWER

What about the United States? Where does it fit into this scenario? From the vantage point of their ivory towers, the inventors of instructional technology may be tempted to gaze out over this world scene with satisfaction, in the belief that all those years of research and development have had significant impact. Closer scrutiny of the details of many of these projects and their parent institutions reveals that their daily practices diverge from the more rigorous principles of the profession as laid out in the standard literature. Materials are of course systematically designed, developed, revised, and improved. But the process is guided much more by a pragmatic eclecticism than by some model of instructional design that spells out the design steps in detail. Delivery media are selected, but the criteria are derived from economic, practical, and availability factors, rather than from some research-based prescription. Control and evaluation systems are developed and implemented, but they owe more to local customs, culture, and traditions than to a general evaluation model (Race, 1989).

Yet overall the systems work, often very well indeed. How can this be? Are our theories and the research base upon which they are founded faulty? Or are some other factors in play here? Maybe such questions were in the minds of the instructional technology program at Indiana University when it organized its 1989 Summer Institute around the theme: "The Role of Educational Technology in Distance Education." At the time I found this a little amusing, as just 20 years earlier I had participated in a conference on the theme: "The Role of Distance Education in Educational Technology." How times change!

The fact is that the open learning movement, starting with the open universities and followed by the proliferation of projects and institutions at all levels of education and training, has been so successful largely because it has sprung up as a no-nonsense answer to real educational needs, and has generally been backed as a general approach at government or other political decision-making levels. It has generally spread in a "top-down" manner, from organizational structure and policy, to strategic planning, to the tactics and logistics of course development and delivery. This is in contrast to many, perhaps most, instructional design and development projects, which have worked from the "bottom-upwards," trying to influence the excellence of educational institutions, or even whole national systems, by working on the effectiveness of individual components, without prior organizational commitment to support this work from inception to wholesale dissemination and use.

The successful open learning systems of the past couple of decades are very much "each one a product of its own environment," well adapted to local realities in terms of political and cultural factors, as well as the more technical aspects that spring from needs analysis, content analysis, task analysis, etc. In the detail of their execution, some of them may not be exemplary cases of the technology of instructional design. But they are good enough to make a difference in the context in which they exist.

THE VIEW OF THE TOWER

This does not necessarily discredit the value of sophisticated instructional design theory. No doubt the devotion of more systematic and more theory-based effort to the details of the design would result in some improvements in the product beyond what is currently obtained. But sometimes such detail may cost more than the improvements are worth, or at least may be perceived that way by the project's sponsors. And even if such a perception is incorrect, it is foolish to insist on technical perfection if it leads to support for the whole project being cut off. I have written more extensively elsewhere on the anatomy of failure of educational technology projects, and how to avoid failure for reasons not related at all to technical incompetence of the project team (Romiszowski, 1981; 1989). It is sufficient to say here that pragmatic compromises tend to win over technical rigidity.

In conclusion, let us remind ourselves that a technology is never value-free. Unlike the pure scientist, who can defend his study of any phenomenon (say nuclear fission) on the grounds of a value-free search for new knowledge, the technologist, or applied scientist, having accepted the challenge to apply the new-found knowledge to a practical purpose, has often unconsciously taken a moral standpoint, or accepted a set of values, that justify the aim of the endeavor. Educational technology as taught and practiced in the United States has grown up in a context of local values, which have influenced the viewpoints of science and the decisions on how to apply it and to what purpose. The result is a brand of "instructional technology" which is particularly well suited to the context of American culture and American education. It should not be surprising that the same general principles may result in somewhat different practical procedures when applied in different cultural contexts.

Many writers have alerted us to the dangers of exporting our home-grown methodologies as prepackaged solutions to the educational problems of other countries. We are exhorted that, as consultants, we should be ever sensitive to the local cultural differences that may make our proposals inoperative or unwelcome. But little is done to teach us how to take that objective, analytical viewpoint. Perhaps the comparative study of the relative success of alternative approaches to similar problems in different sociocultural contexts is an important missing facet of our educational technology master's and doctoral programs? Perhaps the study of the open learning movement, on a worldwide basis, may be a way to develop this aspect? There is an immense and growing literature base to study, including some existing analyses (e.g., MacKenzie et al., 1975; Paine, 1988).

POSTSCRIPT

In July 1988, I participated in the World Congress of Comparative Education, which was held in Rio de Janeiro. One of the subsections of this congress was concerned with the theme of new technologies of education. Two "technologies" were discussed: distance education and computers. Let us overlook for the moment that these are not strictly technologies, in the "process" sense of the word, but rather specific technological solutions to some (in this context, unspecified) problems. It was interesting to compare the discussions on these two topics.

When the predominantly Latin American participants engaged in group discussions on distance education, they were seen to be speaking about "their" systems, with national characteristics and identity and with which the speakers identified. It was quite obvious that although radio, television, or print were not invented in Latin America, the way to use these media in their projects had at least in part been locally developed in response to local needs, and the systems, however effective or ineffective in their detail, were at least acceptable in their totality. When the discussions moved to the use of computers in education, the atmosphere changed dramatically. These systems were seen as imported foreign bodies. Accusations of U.S. cultural imperialism abounded. The more convincing the presenter's argument for the effectiveness of computer-assisted instruction, the greater was the perceived danger of the innovation. The perception that most Latin American educators seemed to have of computer-based education was not dissimilar to the Warsaw resident's perception of the Palace of Culture.

The true transfer of technology involves helping the receiving culture to perceive what is relevant in another culture's practices, so as to adopt or adapt only what is potentially useful to the local reality. Let's not go around leaving expensive technological "palaces" as goodwill gifts, which because of their local inappropriateness, only serve to create bad will towards both us and the technology we profess, but do not always practice!

REFERENCES

AECT. (1985). *Masters curricula in educational communications and technology.* J. K. Johnson (Ed.). Washington, DC: Association for Educational Communications and Technology.

AETT. (1989). *International yearbook of educational and training technology.* C. Osborne (Ed.). London: Kogan Page.

Bates, A. (1975). *Non-O.U. use of O.U. materials.* (Research Report). Milton Keynes: Open University Press.

Commonwealth Secretariat. (1987, October). *Report of the heads of government meeting.* Vancouver, BC: Commonwealth Secretariat.

Daniel, J. (1988). *The worlds of open learning.* In N. Paine (Ed.), *Open learning in transition.* London: Kogan Page.

Gagne, R. M. (Ed.). (1987). *Instructional technology: Foundations.* Hillsdale, NJ: Lawrence Erlbaum.

Hodgson, V., et al. (1987). *Beyond distance teaching: Towards open learning.* Milton Keynes: Open University Press.

IEC/CET. (1987). *Commonwealth co-operation in open learning.* London: Commonwealth Secretariat.

Lewis, B. N. (1979). Course production at the Open University 1: Some basic problems. *British Journal of Educational Technology, 2*(1), 4-13.

MacKenzie, N., Postgate, R., & Scupham, J. (1975). *Open learning: Systems and problems in postsecondary education.* Paris: UNESCO Press.

Maraj, J. A. (1990, January). *The telecommunications challenges of distance education.* Proceedings of the PTC90 Annual Conference of the Pacific Telecommunications Council, Honolulu, Hawaii.

Neil, M. W. (1970). A systems approach to course planning in the open university. In A. J. Romiszowski (Ed.), *A systems approach to education and training.* London: Kogan Page.

Paine, N. (Ed.). (1988). *Open learning in transition.* London: Kogan Page.

Partridge, L. (Ed.). (1986). *Open tech directory.* London: NEC/Manpower Services Commission.

Perry, W. (1976). *Open university: A personal account.* Milton Keynes: Open University Press.

Race, P. (1989). *The open university handbook.* London: Kogan Page.

Romiszowski, A. J. (1981). *Designing instructional systems.* (Chapter 20: Why projects fail?) London: Kogan Page.

————. (1989, November). Avoiding failure through better project planning and analysis: Case studies of avoidable failure in instructional systems design and development projects. *Educational and Training Technology International, 26*(2), 95-112.

24

Diffusion and Adoption of Instructional Technology

Keith P. Garland

Professional Education Division, Technology Services Group
The Arthur Andersen Worldwide Organization
St. Charles, Illinois

> It must be remembered that there is nothing more difficult to plan, more doubtful of success, nor more dangerous to manage than the creation of a new system. For the initiator has the enmity of all who would profit by the preservation of the old institution and merely lukewarm defenders in those who would gain by the new ones.
>
> *Machiavelli, 1513*

This advice sits over my desk and serves as a constant reminder of the task that faces the instructional technologist who promotes the use of new technologies and methods of instruction, not for the sake of using the new just because it's there, but for the benefit of the hundreds and thousands who will be affected by its adoption.

This quotation is also found in the now classic *Diffusion of Innovations*, by Everett Rogers (1983). For anyone responsible for the diffusion of new technologies, such as CD-ROM, multimedia, video conferencing; and new techniques, such as minimalist design, this book is a great source of ideas. Rogers provides sound guidance, and his ideas are especially applicable to problems encountered by the instructional technologist acting as a change agent. Instructional technology benefits, barriers faced by the instructional technologist, and some ways for overcoming such barriers are covered in this chapter.

Instructional technology for some people means the hardware and software or "technology used in education." To others it is the techniques and methods of instruction or "technology of education" (Percival & Ellington, 1984). For this discussion, instructional technology will be considered to be part of the broader view of technology described by Jacques Ellul in *The Technological Society* (1964). This view includes machines, techniques, and the whole fabric of society. I believe this broader view must be taken by the instructional technologist if new technologies are to be introduced, diffused, and successfully adopted.

BENEFITS

Instructional technology in its broadest sense—i.e., needs assessment, instructional design, computer use, media selection, and evaluation—can reduce training costs and improve performance. In my organization, for example, significant benefits have been realized by using a systems approach to developing training programs. The systems approach, coupled with sophisticated course development techniques and hardware/software technology, yields consistent, high-quality training programs. For years we have relied on well-designed, paper-based, self-study, and centralized instructor-led training approaches. Now, after investigating and evaluating new approaches, there is a gradual shift toward alternative delivery strategies that will allow quality improvement and/or reduction of training costs. Benefits arise from savings of travel costs, reduced or eliminated instructor costs, and conservation of learner time and cost by avoiding already mastered knowledge/skill areas through the use of computer-based testing. Since most employers pay salaries while employees are being trained, each hour of unneeded training avoided can amount to substantial savings when one considers the volume of personnel being trained. In addition, on-demand delivery ensures that learners receive training in time for actual use on the job where the knowledge or skill is relevant.

In schools, colleges, and universities, students are not usually paid to learn; however, technology can be used to individualize lessons, thus improving the quality of learning and for some students increasing the amount of education available in a given time frame. This is important when it is recognized that people have multiple intelligences (Gardner, 1989) or multiple aspects of intelligence and styles of learning (Sternberg, 1988). It is extremely difficult for an instructor of a class with 30 or more students to keep up with all this complexity, with the variety of intellectual levels, and with different learning styles. New techniques and technologies, such as collaborative learning or computer-based tutorials and simulations, must be adopted to enhance the skills of the teacher if the goal is to improve the quality of education.

Given that technology, appropriately used, can provide significant benefits to the learner, what are some barriers to adopting new education and training technologies? How can instructional technologists help organizations and institutions change and adopt new technologies?

BARRIERS

Major factors to be considered by the instructional technologist are people issues, including cultural traditions, risk aversion, lack of knowledge, and user acceptance. Cost and infrastructure issues must also be considered.

People Issues

The culture developed within an institution or within an organization can act as a barrier to change. The difficulty encountered with transplanting the open classroom approach from Great Britain to the United States during the 1960s (Garner, 1989) is a good example of this. Another example of a cultural barrier is the tradition found in most business organizations of relegating computer work to subordinates. As a result of this tradition, many executives do not regularly use computers and may even be reluctant to use them for training.

Change becomes an issue when it creates uncertainty. Under normal circumstances people are reluctant to change if things are working well. Consequently, new ideas about how to develop and conduct training may not be accepted simply because the untried seems too risky. For example, there may be concern that converting from traditional instructor-led to alternate strategies, such as computer-based delivery, would reduce effectiveness because personal contact for networking or group discussion during the process is lost.

Knowing who and where your clients are and what they want is also important. "A change agent ... influences client's innovation decisions" (Rogers, 1983). For an instructional technologist to be effective as a change agent, he or she must understand that such clients are spread throughout an organization. There are many varieties of clients or "buyers" (Porter, 1985) who can make or break the adoption of a new technology. These include, but are not necessarily limited to, management, information systems technologists, subject experts, instructional designers (other than the instructional technologist acting as the change agent), and most important, learners. The instructional technologist must understand the concept of "buyer value" (Porter, 1985). Buyer value, according to Porter, involves lowering buyer costs or raising buyer performance. This includes meeting buyers' desires and expectations of the new product or technique.

Some characteristics of buyers of instructional technology follow:

- *Management*—Typically authorize and approve spending for new technology. They represent the organization or institution and are primarily interested in costs and benefits, although they may have biases about educational practices that could present barriers to adopting innovative techniques. They expect the product or technique to improve performance and to do so in a cost-effective manner.

- *Information systems technologists*—Concerned with hardware and software standards that support compatibility, connectivity, and interoperability. Experience has shown them that the introduction of technologies different from standards can raise the cost of such items as programming, training, and technical support. They will need to be shown that the benefits of using new technologies outweigh costs and that such technologies can be successfully integrated with the current installed base.

- *Subject experts*—Primarily interested in protecting the integrity of their material. They frequently believe that, since they are the experts, they know how best to teach their subjects. They will need to be won over and convinced by the instructional technologist that their material will be easier to learn using new delivery techniques and technology.

- *Instructional designers*—Specifically interested in instructionally sound approaches and may or may not have worked with new technologies of delivery such as advanced computer-based or video conferencing techniques. This group needs to be convinced that the use of new technology will be effective as a delivery strategy.

- *Learners*—As end users, learners must find the new technology acceptable if it is to be successfully adopted. Material must be interesting and motivating; technical environments must be easy to use and easily accessible. Learners may also require training in skills, such as keyboarding, to make use of computer-based training applications.

Cost Issues

Cost can arise as a barrier to the acceptance of any new technology. This includes development as well as delivery cost. What is frequently not understood, however, is the cost of not adopting new approaches. For example, if one hour of paid student time can be saved in a course and that hour, multiplied over hundreds or thousands of students, exceeds the cost of the technology needed to save the hour, then the use of the technology may be justified.

Infrastructure Issues

Availability of or access to equipment and software can be a big factor in adopting new technology. People's schedules may not permit them to use new technology unless it is readily available.

Another major barrier is the technology that is in place and working. It includes such items as standards, operating system software, and the base of machines to be used for training delivery. A new technology that relies on new software and equipment will have to overcome the inertia of maintaining existing systems, and it may be possible to introduce it only at the rate that new hardware and software replace old systems. This is not a barrier that one can directly attribute to people, although some decision makers may have the power to change the situation.

OVERCOMING BARRIERS

The instructional technologist striving to overcome these barriers and improve the chances for successful diffusion of beneficial instructional technologies can try a number of strategies and approaches. These approaches involve people at all levels of the organization, since any group can help or hinder diffusion depending on its perception of the value of the new technology. Approaches that address cost and infrastructure concerns should also be considered. The instructional technologist acting as a change agent should develop a plan that targets a variety of audiences and includes more than one strategy for diffusion. The plan could be considered analogous to marketing strategies used for commercial products.

Overcoming People Issues

Management presentations can be used to gain acceptance at the top of an organization and are important in getting strategic support for diffusion. Management is most interested in performance improvement and cost-effectiveness. In a business situation, this should lead to competitive advantage. Management wants courses to be well received by the learner, but if the first two criteria are not met, acceptance matters little from management's perspective.

The instructional technologist can present facts and figures from external and internal sources where the new technology, such as interactive video, has been successfully applied. Testimonials of favorable experience by groups within the organization can be presented to management to gain backing for further diffusion.

Demonstrations can be effective in generating interest at all levels of an organization, from learners to top management. Functions and features of the product shown in a real-life setting provide potential buyers with an opportunity to try a tangible product; the product is no longer just a description in a brochure.

Prototypes specifically designed to meet end users' needs can be effective. The buyer is heavily involved with the instructional technologist in the definition, design, and development of the prototype product. This approach helps gain commitment while minimizing risk. If the prototype proves to be successful with learners, then further development of the approach is justified. If the prototype is found to be defective, the buyer has avoided a major investment. He or she still has the option of trying another approach that may be successful.

A successful pilot test can be used to gain the confidence of a larger audience with similar needs. A pilot is the tryout of a finished training product early in its life cycle with the expectation that it will be adopted by a large number of users over time. The instructional technologist will want to have any training product formally evaluated in terms of user acceptance, performance improvement, and cost-effectiveness as compared to alternative methods. Defects detected during pilot are repaired to ensure that users will accept the product. Favorable report results can be used to promote usage among other groups.

Not all innovation is diffused top-down (Rogers, 1983). In some cases instructional technologists will find themselves acting as technology transfer agents between groups. Someone interested in computer-based multimedia may want to see what other groups are doing. In this situation, the instructional technologist serves as a conduit and puts one group in contact with another to further the diffusion of the innovation.

The instructional technologist who is an expert in a given technology, such as computer-based training, can also spread that expertise to others through formal training programs or through participation as a member of a project team. The more people are familiar with a new instructional technology, the more likely is its use in an organization.

Publicity and promotion channels can be used by the instructional technologist to disseminate the advantages and benefits of the innovation. Channels include in-house meetings, newsletters, reports, or circulating files. One-on-one selling is important too. The instructional technologist should take advantage of informal personal contacts and establish relationships with others to spread the word about innovations.

External recognition from professional societies is important, too, because it comes back to influence decision makers within one's own organization.

Overcoming Cost Issues

To overcome cost barriers the instructional technologist should take a life cycle cost-benefit approach to training development and delivery and compare alternative strategies. While development and capital cost may be higher for technology-based instruction, it may yield substantial delivery savings over the volume and life of the training (i.e., annual audience size times shelf-life in years) far in excess of initial costs. Such savings typically arise from elimination of travel and instructor time, reduction of learner time, and/or improved job performance. The instructional technologist is more likely to gain support for new technologies when such savings and performance improvement are well documented and presented to key decision makers.

Overcoming Infrastructure Issues

The preceding discussion of cost-benefit can be a major factor in overcoming infrastructure issues. Showing the benefits of adding equipment or upgrading existing systems can help gain support for new technologies. If cost savings and performance improvement do not justify major changes in the infrastructure, there may still be justification for introducing new technologies on an incremental basis. Courseware could be built to take advantage of planned migration to new delivery systems, or there may be ways to introduce less sophisticated versions of new technology on existing systems with plans to upgrade in the future. Once a beachhead is established, further diffusion of new technology is made easier.

SUMMARY

The instructional technologist, as a change agent, has to deal with a variety of potential barriers in promoting the diffusion of innovations used in the learning process. These barriers include cultures, individuals, cost issues, and infrastructure.

To overcome these barriers, the instructional technologist must think more like an entrepreneur, work on many fronts, and be armed with a variety of alternative strategies. In the complexity of today's and tomorrow's world, going beyond a single approach to diffusion or promotion of new technology with just one group will increase chances for its successful adoption by other groups.

REFERENCES

Ellul, J. (1964). *The technological society*. New York: Vintage Books.

Gardner, H. (1989). *To open minds: Chinese clues to the dilemma of contemporary education*. New York: Basic Books.

Percival, T., & Ellington, H. (1984). *A handbook of educational technology*. London: Kogan Page.

Porter, M. E. (1985). *Competitive advantage: Creating and sustaining superior performance*. New York: Free Press.

Rogers, E. M. (1983). *Diffusion of innovations* (3rd edition). New York: Free Press.

Sternberg, R. J. (1988). *The triarchic mind: A new theory of human intelligence*. New York: Viking.

25

Distance Education in the Next Decade

Robert E. Holloway

Center for Excellence in Education, Northern Arizona University
Flagstaff, Arizona

and

Jason Ohler

Educational Technology Program, University of Alaska Southeast,
Juneau, Alaska

Our effort, in this compilation of forecasts, is to help educators make decisions about careers, funding, advocacy, policy, and learning. Any forecast is beneficial, not because of its accuracy, but because it makes us think about what might happen and why. Once that process is underway we become sensitive to "noises in the night," such as federal funding priorities, new technologies, and public interest. This sensitivity makes us more likely to review our action plans, make corrections, and by using this feedback increase our probability for success.

A FORECAST

The next decade and century will see increasingly intensive use of various modes of distance education. (The catch in that statement is "various modes.") The reasons for such an increase are clear: There are new technologies seeking new markets, important political agendas, especially at the international level, sufficient novelty to intrigue anyone, empires to be built, and compelling need for access justifiable on moral grounds. In short, there is something for everyone's agenda. Just think how many disenfranchised groups might want to use such a service: minorities, women, native peoples, the handicapped, the religious, the easily intimidated, people with scheduling difficulties, etc. The potential audience for distance education is much more varied and much larger than we suspect. It is the size of this audience which, once recognized, will give business the impetus it needs to develop distance education on a large scale. Beyond equity, imagine the sparks flying as school administrators, school boards, parent groups, and the National Education Association battle over entirely new issues, such as the impact of electronic education on tenured teaching, balancing the budget with potentially low-cost electronic learning options, how to define what it means "to have a teacher present in the classroom," revising teacher certification requirements to accommodate those teachers who electronically cross-service area boundaries, etc. All of this new territory is emotionally charged. It promises to be a lively debate. In the end, "school" will be a different place.

Resources

The state of the art and projections for the future are best summed up in *Linking for Learning: A New Course for Education*, produced by the Office of Technological Assessment (OTA), a service group for the U.S. Congress (1989). The document does more than reflect practice. OTA reports such as this recommend policy and funding and, since Congress authorizes the reports, the recommendations have high visibility. Other helpful summaries are Clark's (1989) commentary on distance education in U.S. schools, and George et al. (1989) because of the emphasis on communication rather than engineering.

If you need current information, there are several major conferences on distance education and one major journal. Some of the sponsors of major conferences are (1) Oklahoma State University; (2) Continuing and Vocational Education at the University of Wisconsin—Madison; (3) the National ITFS Association; (4) National Technological University; and (5) the TeleCon conventions sponsored by Applied Business TeleCommunication, San Ramon, California. There are also international conferences and very tentative plans for a North American conference at the beginning of this decade. For a more scholarly update, start with the *American Journal of Distance Education*.

The thesis of the rest of this forecast is that the context of economics, adopting individuals, policy, and other large-scale concerns determines what happens in distance education more than what goes on within distance education as an applied subspeciality of technology. If we are to do more than be on the right bandwagon, we must take a role in shaping that context: we must lead the parade.

DEFINITIONS

Distance education is more than a distribution technology. While landlines using networks, satellite-delivered interactive television, and local storage of information are equally important for different reasons, they are not at all important in terms of learning. It is important that we remember we are in the business of education and that the disseminating techniques are a means to an end, not the end itself. One definition of *learning* is *change*. We can use a variety of delivery techniques to bring about change. The foci must be that change and what brings it about, not the engineers of delivery, the production mavens, or the cost-efficiency bureaucrats. We must be clear in our purpose and effective in communicating that purpose: education and change.

What we have called *education* for the past century has consisted of a learning dynamic in which students attend local schools to receive group-based, face-to-face instruction. In contrast, distance education occurs when the student is in one place and the teacher, peer learners, or resources are in another. Course delivery and maintenance are carried out using a broad range of technologies, from conventional mailed cassettes and printed material to exotic two-way transcontinental interactive video. Regardless of how the learning relationship is maintained, distance education is significant because of its divergence from the common, centralized school model toward a more decentralized, flexible model. Distance education reverses the social dynamics of "schooling" by bringing school to students, initiating the first serious reconsideration of the local school as our only educational delivery option.

Distance education is not new. It developed in earnest on a number of fronts in this country about a century ago. It only seems new because it has picked up so much momentum in the past two decades. Two primary forces have converged to create the momentum, forming a gestalt favoring distance education's growth. First, the affordability of today's powerful information technologies (such as microcomputers, videocassette recorders (VCRs), dependable reception and transmission technology) enable widespread modern distance education to occur. The trend of technology towards increasing power and decreasing cost promises to continue, proportionately increasing distance education's technical viability.

Second, powerful currents in rapidly evolving American culture have produced new kinds of students. The mobility of today's work force; the need for frequent skill upgrading of workers in geographically dispersed workplaces; the demand for equity of educational access for all citizens; the need for an educated public to sustain the processes of commerce and democracy; and the overwhelming desire by highly individualistic Americans for flexibility, options, and control of one's (and one's family's) life make distance education a predictable development. For an enlightening discussion of the many forms of distance education, see Giltrow (1989) for definitions and, especially, the international context of distance education.

CAUTIONS

Our resources are always limited. Some years ago a mentor patiently explained that every good idea did not necessarily need to be acted on. We may not have followed this advice very well, but do appreciate its truth. Most of us have scattered energy among many projects, often seeing our effects fade away because projects are many and resources are scarce. Among the most scarce resources is time. That is, the task is one that can be done but the follow through for maintenance is even greater than the initiation cost. This is somewhat of a truism, but still significant because distance education is expensive in both time and resources. The many early efforts by World Bank and others (whole national systems) that have failed make this an important fact. Saying yes to distance education is similar to saying yes to development of computer-assisted instruction. Hundreds of hours are on the line, and once they are committed the money involved cannot be used for something else. Assuming one says "Yes, let's do it!" what can be expected?

In the near term, many distance education services promise to be expensive. Thus, inequities that already exist between poor and better off school districts will just be amplified, widening the gap between those who have access to opportunity and those who do not. A new and exciting approach to education does not necessarily mean that it is based on new and exciting thinking. We should be vigilant in this regard.

From a very practical point of view, major errors are going to be made in terms of institutional adjustment to the demands of distance education. Distance education is not, as some mistakenly think, the simple translation of content from one delivery medium to another. Distance education touches every facet of an educational organization, not just teaching. Counseling, administration, student registration—all have to make adjustments. And distance education brings with it new pedagogical demands not anticipated in the face-to-face model. For instance, most evaluation in K-12, and in many cases postsecondary as well, goes in one direction, from teacher to student. It is an evaluation model without a feedback loop. This makes the establishment of community in any real sense impossible. For distance education to be truly successful, there has to be feedback to make up for the lack of face-to-face give and take. And this feedback is as necessary for convenience store satellite instruction as it is for schools.

Most applications of technology in education are quiet failures, from language labs to television relay balloons over Korea. The success rate is, at best, that one out of ten new applications finds a place in the classroom. This rate of success does not differ a great deal from innovations in other areas, including the private sector. Public education does not have the money to risk for research and development that is found in other segments of the government such as the military, or in entrepreneur efforts such as digital storage for cable. We must be sensitive to larger social and economic movements, influence them where we can, and be proactive in adapting new technologies.

Distance education is frequently described as an innovation. Innovation and change have occurred before, and we can benefit from looking at the forces that are likely to shape distance education. There is an extensive body of research on how ideas and practices spread. Rogers (1983) is the most readable proponent of this line of research. He includes education and technology among the several disciplines that have an important research tradition in studying change. An important development in educational administration has been management of change. The explanatory power of this change paradigm is greater than simple economics and far exceeds any justification based on learning. (Educators frequently fall into the trap of explaining changes based on improved learning. While it may be justification, it is not a demonstrated fact in such movements as consolidated schools, adult education, or even training.)

Instructional developers need applied, practical knowledge. The technology and knowledge are transferred to us. "Transfer" is one segment of the "Knowledge Cycle" model (Rich, 1981). For definitional purposes, this cycle can be described as a linear process of invention, demonstration, commercial development, dissemination, and transfer.

The first phase is invention, when conception occurs. The next phase, demonstration, requires supporting engineering. Sometimes, as with computing, the concept precedes the demonstration by hundreds of years. The next phase, commercial development, is to a great extent determined by production-selling price ratios. Education is a hard market with a low unit price ceiling. Even in industry the training department has a relatively small budget, so the technology is disseminated to other markets.

After invention, demonstration, commercial development, and dissemination have taken place, transfer to education finally occurs. Distance education, again, serves as an identifiable example of the process. The tools of distance education were initially developed commercially for entertainment, especially television, and for data processing in business and government, especially computing, and finally were transferred for education and instructional use. Certainly there have been significant adaptations made in technological products as a result of instructional use, but most technologies are not invented, developed, or initially targeted for education.

Transfer, what we are trying to do with the technology of distance education, is not simply moving technology from one place to another. It is adapting the technology, the knowledge, to a different setting. Our most important strategy in planning for distance education is building in the time and resources for adaptation needed in the transfer. Many proposals are written with promises to be up and running as soon as the equipment is installed. Assuming the time allowed for the equipment includes enough slack to allow for problems and still stay on schedule, the people skills and commitment require at least twice the resources to get started and keep going, and must be scheduled so that there is time to build a trust level, rehearse, develop formative evaluation, and discuss and get commitment on compensation issues. Implementation of distance education is resource intensive. We need to deliver what we promise and allow ourselves time and money to do so. If money is short, extend the time. But do not underestimate the commitment.

Educators are not in the forefront of those asking for technology. It has been pushed to the top of political and public agendas, mostly by journalistic hype and engineering marvels, but also by compelling demonstrations of effectiveness and efficiency, often in applications that are possible only with the new technologies. What we ought to do in response is less clear. Most of us believe major changes are or will be taking place and we don't want to miss opportunities. But we are less sure in which opportunities to invest our limited resources or what may be the consequences. We are not alone in our confusion, nor is the need for more informed decision making limited to technology and education.

DISSEMINATION STRATEGY

How to translate the engineering marvels to applications requires as much invention as the initial engineering. One cannot just "plug it in." Bok, the president of Harvard, sets a high priority for solving the problems of translating inventions into usable products. The usable products may be marketed, but even then they are not developed for education. (Of all the technologies, from blackboard to computer, *none*, with the possible exception of the overhead projector, was developed for teaching.) Further, the manufacturers and vendors have little motivation to adapt commercial applications to new uses for learning. Adoption does not require retooling and increases profits.

Educators are an important link in *how*, not *if*, technological change comes about. How rapidly and how effective this technological change happens depends to a large extent on the perceptions of educators. How much does it help me do my job? Does it really make my job easier or the results observably better? Such decisions are more likely to be right if there is some basis, such as experience, for decisions. The important thing is for us to get as much experience in technologies as we can so that we can decide whether to put more or less effort into adapting specific distance learning technologies for instruction. We need to find out how the several stakeholders perceive the proposal. (See, e.g., Simonson, et al., 1989.)

A widely accepted technology is most often defined by a single characteristic: its use makes a task rewarding for the user. The user includes the student first, and the faculty second. The reward to the agency is too remote to be a concern in day-to-day operation. If the practice does not make performance of a task rewarding, then there is little motivation to accept the technology. If the practice simplifies or expedites accomplishment of a goal, the probability of acceptance is high. A distasteful task, such as driving over a hundred miles after a night class, is simplified by using a videotape and guide. The other leading characteristic is an increase in reward. For a farmer, the reward is a greater yield. In education, since faculty and teachers do not benefit from greater enrollment or even increased learning, the rewards must be carefully identified and agreed upon and potent enough to motivate participation.

RECOMMENDATIONS FOR
THE PROFESSIONAL

To improve your knowledge base there are basically four things to do: find out what governmental, educational, commercial agencies (particularly state and local) are doing to promote distance education; keep your eye on the literature; talk to people in the business; and get online.

Your state government or school board may already have compiled information about relevant distance education services or have assigned someone to such a task. For instance, several states already have long-range plans for the entire state. See, for instance, Levinson's report on planning in Texas (1989). If you are a high school educator, find out what the university nearest you is doing in distance education; there may be ways to share technology and resources. More and more businesses are using distance education to train geographically dispersed work forces—is there a way to work with them, perhaps? The point is not to reinvent the wheel. Where you can work cooperatively, do so. And this begins with just finding out what is going on right around you.

By far the best way to come up the learning curve is to talk directly to local people in the business, those who are pioneering the use of distance delivery in their own small but exciting ways. They know the lay of the land, and in most cases they are right under our noses. Distance education has all the indications of evolving in the same way educational computing did: from the ground up, based on initiatives by a small number of teachers with vision. If it is the experience of distance learning that you are after, there is nothing like taking a course by distance delivery to get your feet wet.

Technology publications and articles on technology are not difficult to find. Most of us find it easier to stack up the publications, propping them with good intentions. Take the time to do two things. First, skim periodicals, especially ubiquitous publications, such as *T.H.E. Journal*. Such publications pride themselves on current news and their references are short. People noted are usually happy to be contacted. Second, search ERIC and PsycLIT CD-ROM for topics similar to yours. The last ten years of ERIC list 1,295 records under "distance education" with 140 in 1989. Using "television," 9,290 records are listed, 2,736 are in journals, and 170 of those were published in 1989. PsycLIT indexes 1,300 journals from 50 countries.

Articles will be more research oriented. "Distance education" showed only ten entries for the last seven years. At the least, bibliographies will provide leads to other literature.

Using one of the electronic mail systems and subscribing to the Distance Education Newsletter or a free bulletin board, such as an EDTECH (on BITNET or CREN, EDTECH@OASTVMA), you can identify hot issues and often know what is going to happen before there is a public announcement. As with identification of experts through the literature, any contributor can be contacted separate from the electronic bulletin board and you can get information fast and free.

In terms of what to do on a small budget, if you are a teacher who wants to incorporate distance education into the classroom, computer and audio conferencing offer very cost-effective distance delivery options and can be a great place to start. They are very adaptive, ideal for the creative teacher. Simple activities, such as audio-conferencing with the author of a book you have had your class read, or computer conferencing with students from other countries to discuss cultural differences, can provide powerful learning opportunities that can be obtained relatively cheaply. However, little happens of any magnitude without administration buy-in, and the best way to achieve that is to succeed on a small level first.

Put most of your effort into finding the right people, rather than the most exciting technology: that sounds obvious but it is a commonsense rule that is violated rather frequently. Some teachers work well on camera, behind a microphone, or running a computer conference, and others do not. Find teachers who feel comfortable and work well with the media, then give them all of the technical support you can afford. Their job is to teach, not splice cords together or figure out why their conferencing software is misbehaving. The more transparent the media are to them, the better service they will deliver. This has a financial payoff too: the better a teacher works with media, the less necessary the expensive elements of distance delivery course work (like graphics and sophisticated editing) become to the creation of a quality product.

RECOMMENDATIONS FOR THE PROFESSION

Market forces and media reporting are going to result in new legislative programs for underwriting technology in schools and training. The media try to interpret and appraise events and trends. The policy makers try to interpret what the public wants from the media and formulate policy that benefits their constituents. If you agree that this process accounts for a significant portion of legislative initiative, then the actions we need to take are clear. We have opportunity to influence both media and policy makers by publicly stating our recommendations. To be successful our statements must be timely, eloquent, persuasive, and frequent. Keep the focus on learning and change.

No one has the option of holding back the increased use of technology in society at large, and gradually in education. We do have the option of influencing how the technology is used, and it is essential that we exercise that option. Kennedy's Star Schools legislation was expanded by a few partisans left out of the initial proposal. That was successful mainly in causing many people to talk to each other and plan. Dole's $6 million grant to Kansas, however, did not benefit from open competition. This is not an indictment of these programs; it is intended as a description of how things are and where our energies must be focused to be effective. The long term success of tight control of decisions is unlikely. Studies of the process of decision making consistently find little evidence of the conscious and purposeful use of policy analysis in reaching a policy decision. We must change this.

An analysis of the communications policy review process shows that the standards we live with are established by a process that has been doing little more than seeking a means for negotiating the needs of the major industrial interests already in control of most aspects of American communications. Far from actually encouraging new or pluralistic approaches to owning, controlling, and developing the next generation of U.S. telecommunications, the policy review effort has actually tended to make more concrete the major characteristics of the prior conditions. This is not a complaint so much as an observed fact that we must include in our planning.

The communications industries are the cornerstone of the infrastructure of economic systems. Their impact and influence are spread throughout the economy. The deficiencies in communications public policy are attributable to the fact that neither policy planning nor advocacy has been viewed as part of the permanent regulatory responsibility, ensuring that the social costs of technological opportunities delayed, neglected, misdirected, and foregone will be great. For the larger perspective, see Bieber, et al. (1989) for a discussion of issues across national boundaries.

Policy to facilitate cooperation can help us avoid learning the hard and expensive way that we should be creating multipurpose, cooperatively designed networks rather than a series of stand-alone networks to separately serve education, government, and business. The benefits of creating multipurpose networks, sharing of intra- and interstate and even international resources, and consulting a cross-section of people (teachers, students, administrators) to help design them will, in many cases, only be appreciated in hindsight.

It is interesting to imagine what the future might look like. Besides providing access to equipment that is not affordable on an individual basis, such as chemistry labs and gymnasiums, schools may become institutions whose most cherished aim is to deliver all of those services now considered of secondary importance: sports, art, choir, socialization, and individual attention. Information may be presented in a number of formats and administered in a number of ways. Some school boards could start by not filling positions vacated by less popular teachers, and turning to other delivery options to meet teaching needs. Or parents might take education into their own hands, developing study groups for their children using television teachers or powerful computer systems as primary information resources. We may well be deciding in the future how much of our tax dollar will go to the local school system and how much is retained to purchase access to information systems or other educational experiences. School as we know it may become *an* option, not the only choice.

REFERENCES

Barker, Bruce O., et al. (1989). Broadening the definition of distance education in light of the new telecommunications technologies. *American Journal of Distance Education, 3*(1), 20-29.

Bieber, Jacques, et al. (1989). Common issues in distance education. *European Journal of Education, 24*(1), 47-78.

Clark, G. Christopher. (1989). Distance education in United States schools. *Computing Teacher, 16*(6), 7-11.

George, Donald, et al. (1989). A communication process: Electronic media in distance education—A review. *International Journal of University Adult Education, 28*(2), 1-23. (ERIC Document Reproduction Service No. ED 308 858).

Giltrow, David. (1989). *Distance education.* (Association for Educational Communications and Technology Presidents' Library Brief). Washington, DC: AECT.

Holloway, R. E. (1984). *Instructional technology: A critical perspective.* Syracuse, NY: Educational Resources Information Center (ERIC).

———. (1989). Interview with Jason Ohler. *TechTrends, 34*(5), 62-67.

Levinson, Cynthia Y. (1989). *Research in planning and practice for technology in Texas.* 26p. (ERIC Document Reproduction Service No. ED 307 858).

Rich, R. F. (1981). *The knowledge cycle.* Beverly Hills, CA: Sage.

Rogers, E. M. (1983). *Diffusion of innovations*. (3rd ed.). New York: Free Press.

Simonson, Michael R., et al. (1989). *Satellite communications and high school education: Perceptions of students, teachers, and administrators*. 32p. (ERIC Document Reproduction Service No. ED 308 841).

U.S. Congress. Office of Technology Assessment. (1989, November). *Linking for learning: A new course for education*. (OTA-SET-430). Washington, DC: U.S. Government Printing Office.

26

The State of the Art of Instructional Television

Marjorie A. Cambre
College of Education, Department of Educational Policy and Leadership
The Ohio State University, Columbus, Ohio

Instructional television (ITV) plays a unique and somewhat contradictory role in the annals of instructional technology. Several scholars currently prominent in the field have written off instructional television as a failed medium. On the other hand, utilization data from many areas establish that hundreds of thousands of teachers are using instructional television each year. What is the true story of ITV, and what appears to be the future of this medium? These and other questions are addressed in this chapter.

WHAT IS INSTRUCTIONAL TELEVISION?

One of the problems plaguing instructional television is that it shares part of its name with a medium that is as ubiquitous in our homes as the telephone. Because commercial, cable, and public (sometimes called educational) television are so familiar and accessible, most people assume they know what instructional television is also, and they prejudge the medium without really experiencing it. The definitions below provide important distinctions in the kinds of television available for educational purposes, and the particular and unique focus of instructional television.

Instructional television (ITV) has traditionally been defined as television designed and produced specifically for elementary and secondary grade students with the expectation that it would help those students to achieve "identified, specific learning goals under the administration and supervision of professional educators in a formally structured learning environment" (Sikes, 1980, p. 19). Because of its clear curriculum orientation, ITV is sometimes called "school television." Examples of instructional television series in current use include "Newscasts from the Past," "Global Geography," and "Community of Living Things." These and many other ITV programs are usually broadcast on Public Broadcasting System (PBS) stations

This chapter is an adaptation of work published in Cambre, M. A. (1987). *A reappraisal of instructional television*. Syracuse, NY: ERIC Information Analysis Products; and Cambre, M. A. (1988). Instructional television: An update and assessment. In D. P. Ely (Ed.), *Educational media and technology yearbook 1988*. Englewood, CO: Libraries Unlimited, Inc.

296

during the school day, or distributed by national vendors or by local ITV agencies. Unless videocassette recorders (VCRs) are liberally used, people working outside of home or school settings and/or who are not involved with ITV on a daily basis have little opportunity to be exposed to ITV in its current expressions.

The more familiar type of programming is "educational television," now called "public television," which has the broader mission of conveying information and culture to audiences of all ages. Many of these programs are now used in schools or assigned for home viewing, and are broadcast on PBS stations from late afternoon through prime time. Examples of these programs include "Nova," "Nature," and "Masterpiece Theatre." Also in this category are the Children's Television Workshop's series, most notably "Sesame Street," "3-2-1 Contact!" and the mathematics series, "Square One TV." Several of these series are available in ITV schedules as well as after-school PBS lineups.

There are a host of other uses of television in school that do not technically fall under the definition of ITV but are frequently included under its name. These include college credit telecourses, distance learning (with one-way or two-way television), critical viewing skills, and classroom productions. The newest addition to this list is the controversial Whittle plan, *Channel One.* This commercial venture proposes to provide junior and senior high schools with a 12-minute daily news program produced especially for the high school audience, including two minutes of commercials. In exchange for airing this daily program schools would receive a generous grant of equipment. At this writing, *Channel One* has just undergone pilot testing and controversy is raging among educators about the advisability of mixing the educational process with commercial interests.

With so many possible variations, it is no wonder that there are some misunderstandings about what ITV really is. The confusion is exacerbated by the multitude of delivery systems available to disseminate the television picture. The most common and cost-effective transmission of the ITV signal is by satellite to the PBS stations, or to local cable companies or ITFS (Instructional Television Fixed Services) systems. Some school systems or regional media centers have invested in satellite dishes to receive the ITV signal directly through Direct Broadcast Satellite (DBS). Few today expect that signal to be used live in the classroom. On the contrary, videotape has become the medium of choice for using ITV programming. Tapes may be recorded from the satellite signal or from intermediate distribution signals, or they may be purchased directly from distributors.

There is a recent movement afoot within the ITV community away from the use of the word *television*. The Agency for Instructional Television (AIT), the oldest and largest producer/distributor of ITV materials, recently changed its name to the Agency for Instructional Technology. In their recent publications they refer to "video technology" when describing instructional television. The new names represent a shift in emphasis precipitated primarily by the infusion of the videotape recorder, the computer, and (by anticipation) videodisc into the schools. A serendipitous side effect is the shedding of negative associations with commercial television, and with the image of ITV as a failed medium. For purposes of this chapter, the traditional definition of ITV presented above, as well as the name, will be used.

ORGANIZATIONAL STRUCTURE

In the 30 or more years of its existence, instructional television has assumed continuously evolving forms and structures as a profession within the general field of educational communications and technology. If there is a common theme to the evolution it is creative tension between centralization and decentralization.

This tension is exemplified in the history of ITV production in this country. In the late 1950s and early 1960s, when school television began to take shape, productions were locally produced to meet local school needs. A combination of federal and private funding spurred the formation of instructional television libraries; as collections grew, it became evident that mediocre to poor low-budget productions were duplicating themselves across the country. It was clear that if instructional television were going to survive, the quality of the product had to be improved. The Agency for Instructional Technology assumed the leadership and set the standard for quality control through cooperative productions. Middleton (1979) traces the development of cooperatively produced, high-quality school television that began in the late 1960s and continues to this day. One indicator of the imperative to cooperate is the continuously rising costs of production. Local productions in 1962 cost in the neighborhood of $165 per 15-minute program. Today, the estimate for high-quality ITV productions is approximately $3,000 per minute.

While some local production still takes place with varying degrees of success, the bulk of instructional television products today are designed and produced for national distribution. An elaborate structure within the industry provides a forum for voicing local interests and needs, so that these may be taken into account when productions are planned.

At the present time there are over 150 local ITV agencies in the United States. Headed up by an ITV director, these agencies are often divisions of state departments of education or of public broadcasting stations. Some are independent organizations or functions under the aegis of state boards of regents, local school boards, or other educational governing groups. These local agencies serve as brokers of ITV programming to school districts and schools in their viewing areas. Their primary contacts are district- and school-level ITV coordinators, or where these don't exist, media center directors, librarians, teachers, and school administrators themselves. In 1982-1983, the date of the last national survey of instructional television use in the United States, approximately 55 percent of the schools with ITV available had building-level ITV coordinators. Approximately half of the districts with ITV available had district-level ITV coordinators (Riccobono, 1985, p. 6).

The main contact between the ITV agencies and the schools is ITV utilization specialists, of which there are approximately 380 today. These are typically ex-teachers who have been hired by the agencies because of their interest and skills in using ITV and their ability to train other teachers to do so. Through workshops, mailings, and school visits, the utilization specialists encourage the use of instructional television in schools.

The expense and expertise involved in typical ITV programming, coupled with the complexities of distribution and the legalities of leasing rights, have necessitated support structures at several levels. Three regional agencies support ITV at the present time: Pacific Mountain Network (PMN), Central Educational Network (CEN), and Southern Educational Communications Association (SECA). These agencies coordinate and administer group buys of ITV products; arrange satellite and broadcast feeds; encourage local productions; and above all provide forums for professional exchange, both intra- and interregional. In addition, each has a responsibility within the national ITV community.

PMN is responsible for FirstView, a yearly gathering at which all new ITV materials are screened. This gives potential purchasers an opportunity to learn about new programming, and producers a chance to assess needs for the coming years. CEN conducts SatScreen, a companion gathering to FirstView, which allows a broader viewing audience to see new programming via satellite broadcast. Teachers and curriculum specialists are encouraged to take advantage of this national screening and, through their respective ITV agency, vote on which programs they would like to see in their school television schedules for the coming year. Once new programming has been selected and added to the schedule, SECA administers the transmission via National Instructional Satellite Schedule (NISS). In total they transmit approximately 1,250 hours of ITV programming throughout the school year.

Through the years PBS has been especially interested in the marketing and promotion of ITV. Instructional television programming is made available across the United States on PBS stations. The Corporation for Public Broadcasting (CPB) also represents the national picture in ITV circles, and plays the important role of administering federal funding.

Producing, distributing, and using instructional television is a labor-intensive, expensive, and complex endeavor. It has become an industry with hundreds of professionals working to sustain it. There is a concerted effort by those professionals to meet local needs while at the same time pooling their resources to maintain high-quality programming that can be shared by all.

IMAGES OF ITV

As the production and support structure for ITV has grown and changed through the years, so has its on-screen image. The best of today's ITV productions are tightly designed, cleverly scripted, and professionally produced visual lessons. There is a sophistication and a demand for quality governing ITV today that distinguish it markedly from its predecessors. Unfortunately not all ITV programs that appear on local schedules enjoy the same high quality, but on the whole the image of ITV is good. Instructional television has gone through several interesting stages to arrive at its current "look."

Television as Master Teacher

In the late 1950s and early 1960s, with television production technology largely confined to studios and live broadcasts, instructional television was promoted as a vehicle for disseminating exemplary teaching. The master teacher idea spawned studio classrooms in which "talented" teachers conducted classes that were broadcast widely. The use of television was said to fill two needs: (1) overcoming the shortage of qualified teachers (particularly in science, math, and languages), and (2) eliminating classroom overcrowding. Some television enthusiasts went so far as to suggest a restructuring of schooling. The Educational Media Study Panel, a group of educators and broadcasters assembled in 1960 to advise the commissioner and the U.S. Office of Education, published the following:

> Television can share the best teaching and the best demonstrations; self-instructional materials can conduct drill expertly and give the student a new freedom to work at his own best rate. A teacher who has these devices working for him may not have exactly the same duties as before, but his duties will be no less important. The student who has these devices working for him will not spend his day exactly as before, but his learning opportunities will be no less, and probably considerably more.
> A school where these new devices are in use may find itself bursting out of old patterns. Instead of classes of 35 alternately being lectured to, studying, and reciting, it may assemble groups of several hundred to watch the television lecture or demonstration, but devote a greater proportion of its teacher time to individualized instruction. Instead of waiting his turn for class drill, a student may follow his own drill schedule with self instructional materials or language laboratory. (*Educational Television*, 1962, p. 5)

Adding insult to injury, proponents of the master teacher idea suggested that while being replaced by the television teacher, the classroom teacher could use the opportunity to watch the master teacher for purposes of improving his or her teaching skills! In 1965 Costello and Gordon (p. 13) wrote: "After about 15 years of research into educational television by teachers and administrators, one conclusion is clear. Television is a *means* by which good teaching can be spread to more people than ever before in the history of the world, probably at less cost per student than present instruction."

In retrospect it is clear that talented teachers were not necessarily the best television talent. It is also evident that production values are important for holding audience interest. The master television teacher concept did more to threaten classroom teachers and bore students than it did to promote the use of television for instruction or to solve the problems of education. In fact, the situation was so bad in instructional television in the late 1960s that this statement appeared in the report of the Carnegie Commission on Educational Television: "With minor exceptions, the total disappearance of instructional television would leave the educational system fundamentally unchanged (*Public Television*, 1967, p. 81).

As practitioners began to realize that the "talking head" format resulting from the master teacher concept was not the best use of the medium (and even perhaps that a talking head was not the best method of teaching), arguments for using television were put forth that were diametrically opposed to those of earlier years. The basis of the new arguments was that television should be used to do what teachers could *not* do in their own classrooms.

"You Are There"

In its next phase, instructional television was promoted for its ability to bring, not master teachers, but *the world* to the classrooms of America. In Wilbur Schramm's popular book, *Quality in Instructional Television* (1972, pp. 13-14), the point is made that instructional television is often at its best when it does not instruct; that the job of television is to take children out of the classroom, and to convey the *human* aspects of situations rather than factual information. Aided by the availability of videotape and portable equipment (film, of course, was always available), production crews could indeed get out of the world of the studio and into the world of real people and living things. The "look" of ITV changed dramatically for the better; its uses did also, but with more mixed results. At about the same time, a similar yet slightly different argument was being made for using live commercial television in the classroom; that is, that allowing children to witness special live news events would give them a sense of belonging to the world, a sense of sharing in the making of history.

These arguments were more palatable to teachers, who would much rather be usurped by a news event or an educational "tour" than by another teacher, and to administrators, who could buy one or two television sets for the auditorium rather than one for each classroom. Unfortunately, the "you are there" phenomenon had the negative effect of relegating television to the position of enrichment, from which it has never really recovered. First, it conveyed the notion that television was interruptive, in that however infrequently important news events were broadcast during the day, everything else stopped when they were aired so that students and teachers might watch television. Second, it suggested that television was an occasional special activity much like assemblies, field trips, and sporting events; that it was used in larger gatherings, rather than in the regular classroom; and that it was not *really* related to school work.

A third and more subtle effect of this kind of school television promotion was the perpetration of the notion that television is a unidimensional reality. Because we use the word with an occasional qualifier to mean everything from "60 Minutes" to "Dallas," from "Nova" to "MathWorks," we invite predispositions depending on a person's background and customary use of the medium.

Curriculum Extension

Throughout much of the 1970s ITV proponents had to fight the prejudices they had inherited from earlier times: that television was a boring replacement of the teacher on the one hand, or that it was merely incidental on the other. They did so mainly by creating high-quality, curriculum-related school television series that used the conventions and formats of the medium in an entertaining, "softly" instructional way. The prevailing argument at this time was that television should be used in schools to *broaden* the curriculum by introducing new subject matter that was not currently being taught, such as economics, art, critical thinking, and social and emotional growth. In contrast to the "deadly dull" productions of earlier decades, school television of the 1970s took on a much more polished and entertaining look to present curriculum-related subject matter that teachers might not ordinarily deal with in a way that could not be replicated in the classroom. School television was now promoted not as a replacement, but as an extension of the teacher; not as enrichment, but as an important complement to the classroom curriculum.

Basic Curriculum

By the late 1970s the pendulum had swung from the new and nonstandard curriculum areas back to the basics in response to yet another of the "back to basics" movements that occur with regularity in public education. The Skills Essential to Learning projects from AIT were products of this movement, as were "The Write Channel" from Mississippi ETV, "Counterplot" from Maryland ITV, and a host of others. The result was a respectable body of ITV materials designed to assist teachers in teaching not only the basic skills but their application to life situations.

The present trend seems to include an emphasis on the humanities and world affairs. "Newscasts from the Past" is an award-winning history series produced in 1986, and "Global Geography" was released in 1988. AIT is currently developing "Geography in American History" in response to the growing demand for more and better geography instruction in this country.

WHAT THE RESEARCH SAYS

Although some researchers have expressed disappointment in the quality of ITV research, we have learned quite a bit about ITV and about learning from television in general through the 30 or so years of ITV research. We have learned, unequivocally and irrevocably, that a well-designed and produced television program can and does teach. This is especially verifiable when the potentials of the medium are exploited and content visualization is maximized. It is most especially true in the hands of a skilled teacher. ITV has been shown to be most effective when previewing and postviewing activities are used by the teacher.

Another significant thing we have established once and for all is that media comparison studies, as exemplified by the question "Does it teach better than...," are generally uninformative and inappropriate. We know this because, as Salomon and Gardner (1986, p. 14) put it, "stripping the medium down to its bare bones (the experiment wouldn't be perfect otherwise) affects nothing in and of itself." The classic example of this type of controlled comparative study is the comparison of the live teacher to the video-transmitted image of that teacher, with all other things held constant. This, of course, is an appropriately controlled experiment, but it is not a test of the effectiveness of instructional television. Happily this point no longer needs to be labored.

Three productive types of inquiry activities have been employed to date in studying educational and instructional television: basic and applied research, formative evaluation, and impact studies. Basic research is exemplified by studies of the effects of television and the attributes of television on children, with effects usually being measured in the areas of knowledge, attitudes, and behavior. This line of research has provided among other things the taxonomies of formal features or conventions of the medium and the systematic exploration of the effects of these features. Dorr (1986), Howe (1983), Meyer (1983), and Bryant and Anderson (1983) provide excellent overviews of basic research. While it is impossible to summarize the results of basic research here, it is important to note that the numerous investigations in this category have produced information useful to producers and users of television for learning alike.

By its very nature formative evaluation is a private activity, conducted within and for the development team to determine the effectiveness of a particular product. It has a long tradition in educational and instructional television (Cambre, 1981) and continues to be an important component of most funded ITV projects. Most formative evaluation reports are in-house documents meant only for those in a position to improve the product. Some formative evaluation summaries, notably those conducted by the Children's Television Workshop and the Agency for Instructional Technology, are shared with the public for the insights they provide about programming variables as well as about formative evaluation methodology. These reports can be obtained from the respective agencies.

Numerous studies have been conducted to determine the impact of ITV series once they are in use, or to describe the circumstances of use. These studies are sometimes carried out as summative evaluations or field tests during the first or second years of release. Many of these studies are conducted for the purpose of persuading funders to continue contributing to a worthy cause. Some are motivated by research interests sparked by a hunch that something important is happening. Some, as Johnston (1987) points out, are conducted as the result of pressure from the very people who wanted the series created.

ITV impact studies run a wide gamut of rigor from in-house surveys of teacher users requesting their perceptions of how a series is working to carefully controlled, third-party experimental research. In some instances multiple studies are conducted and the results synthesized in a style resembling but not equivalent to meta-analysis. This approach is extremely useful, as it yields data from many sites collected under different conditions. The most notable examples of a multi-study approach to measuring a series' impact are those surrounding the economics series produced by AIT in cooperation with the Joint Councils for Economic Education (Shea, 1980).

Throughout the years of television availability in schools, researchers have consistently found that it can and does teach, both intended and incidental content, both skills and behaviors, both facts and fictions. It has also been established that instructional television can motivate, can stimulate an interest in what children need and ought to learn. Finally, research suggests that the better designed and produced the television lessons are, the better students will learn from them.

Some questions seem to be neglected in television research, among them those relating to when and how to visualize instruction. Educators and researchers pay lip service to the importance of meeting the needs of all types of learners, and the capability of instructional media to facilitate this; yet they fail to show in a specific or convincing way through research with instructional television how visualizing abstract concepts or complex phenomena enables this goal to be reached. There is much work to be done in this regard.

WHO IS USING ITV?

The last attempt to obtain reliable data about ITV use at the national level was the School Utilization Study (SUS) conducted by the Corporation for Public Broadcasting during the 1982-1983 school year. The researchers employed a stratified, multistage probability sample representative of approximately 11,500 public school districts and Catholic dioceses, 81,000 school buildings, and 2,137,000 classroom teachers (Riccobono, 1985). Among numerous other findings, the survey revealed that 54 percent of the teachers (791,000) reported using ITV (defined in the broadest sense, that is, any school use of television for instruction), and that better than half of the teachers at every level of K-12 schooling reported some use. However, 58 percent of those reporting use indicated that they did not use entire series. This is an interesting finding, and perhaps suggests that ITV producers should reconceptualize the form in which ITV is produced and disseminated.

Were this type of survey to be repeated today, an increase in ITV use figures would not be surprising, given rather dramatic increases in VCR availability in schools in recent years. Quality Education Data (QED) report that VCR availability increased from 31 percent in 1983 to an estimated 80 percent in 1987 (Hayes, 1986).

Carlisle (1987) employed a journalistic research methodology to gather qualitative data about actual cases of ITV use from 158 subjects in 12 states and 70 communities in the United States. There were 83 teachers in the sample averaging 16 years' experience, 45 administrators, and 30 media coordinators. While this study was commissioned by the Agency for Instructional Technology, thereby carrying the stigma of self-interest, it does provide a fascinating account of how ITV is being used to best advantage by many who see its value. *Video at Work in American Schools* is a rich collection of anecdotes and observations and, in the telling, provides hundreds of ideas for using instructional television in the classroom.

SUMMARY AND CONCLUSIONS

Instructional television has survived in American education. Despite ups and downs and criticisms from many quarters, it is stronger and better than it has ever been. The lessons learned through the years are reflected in the best of the ITV series available today. There are continuous efforts to improve the amount and quality of available programming, and more recently to look into newer technologies such as interactive video. New insights into the ways people learn will continue to demand visualization of the curriculum through television and videobased technologies.

REFERENCES

Bryant, J., & Anderson, D. R. (Eds.). (1983). *Children's understanding of television: Research on attention and comprehension*. New York: Academic Press, 1983.

Cambre, M. A. (1981). Historical overview of formative evaluation of instructional media products. *Educational Communication and Technology Journal, 29*(1), 3-25.

Carlisle, Robert D. B. (1987). *Video at work in American schools*. Bloomington, IN: Agency for Instructional Technology.

Costello, L. F., & Gordon, G. N. (1965). *Teach with television: A guide to instructional TV* (2nd edition). New York: Hastings House.

Dorr, A. (1986). *Television and children: A special medium for a special audience*. Beverly Hills, CA: Sage.

Educational television: The next ten years. (1962). (A report and summary of major studies on the problems and potentials of educational television, conducted under the auspices of the United States Office of Education). Stanford, CA: The Institute for Communication Research.

Hayes, J. (Ed.) (1986). *Microcomputer and VCR usage in schools*. Denver, CO: Quality Education Data.

Howe, M. J. A. (Ed.) (1983). *Learning from television: Psychological and educational research*. New York: Academic Press.

Johnston, J. (1987). *Electronic learning: From audiotape to videodisc*. Hillsdale, NJ: Lawrence Erlbaum.

Meyer, M. (Ed.) (1983). *Children and the formal features of television*. New York: K. G. Saur.

Middleton, J. (1979). *Cooperative school television and educational change: The consortium development process of the Agency for Instructional Television*. Bloomington, IN: Agency for Instructional Television. (ERIC Document Reproduction Service No. ED 201 303).

Public television: A program for action. (1967). (The report and recommendations of the Carnegie Commission on Educational Television). New York: Bantam Books.

Riccobono, John A. (1985). *School utilization study: Availability, use, and support of instructional media. 1982-83 final report*. Washington, DC: Corporation for Public Broadcasting. (ERIC Document Reproduction Service No. ED 256 292).

Salomon, G., & Gardner, H. (1986). The computer as educator: Lessons from television research. *Educational Researcher, 15*(1), 13-19.

Schramm, W. (Ed.) (1972). *Quality in instructional television.* Honolulu: University Press of Hawaii.

Shea, J. (1980). *Trade-offs: What the research is saying.* (A research report of the Agency for Instructional Television, No. 82). (ERIC Document Reproduction Service No. ED 249 968).

Sikes, R. G. (1980). Programs for children: Public television in the 1970s. *Public Telecommunications Review, 8(5), 7-26.*

27

Instructional Media Production

Dennis Pett
School of Education, Indiana University
Bloomington, Indiana

and

Scott Grabinger
School of Education, University of Colorado at Denver
Denver, Colorado

INTRODUCTION

As the concept of instructional technology progressed from audiovisual education to educational media to the present, the process of designing and producing instructional media paralleled its growth. The time periods for these stages can be classified roughly as follows: 1940s and 1950s—audiovisual, 1960s and 1970s—educational media, 1980s and the near future—instructional technology. These are not definitive periods, and the models, technologies, and techniques overlap to a considerable extent. For example, computers have provided methods that were unavailable in the 1940s for creating high-quality graphs, but many graphs for instructional purposes are still being produced by the older methods. However, these time periods are a convenient way of describing the changes that have taken place in the design/production process during the past half-century.

Production of instructional materials prior to the 1940s was largely focused on commercial materials such as films and lantern slides and teacher- or instructor-made "simple" materials such as bulletin boards and charts. The production of these was seldom related to a larger construct, so this chapter deals only with post-1940 aspects of instructional media production. Emphasis is on production in educational institutions and in-house production units, not on materials produced by commercial production houses.

1940s AND 1950s

As a result of instructional needs of the military forces during World War II, the demand for audiovisual materials took a big step forward, a step that affected the methods of instruction in public education, colleges and universities, government agencies, and business and industry. Excellent instructional media required excellent production. By 1950 several schools had introduced courses in audiovisual production. These dealt with the most used media of the time: still pictures, charts and posters, bulletin boards and displays, slides, overhead transparencies, tape recordings, and in some places, filmstrips and motion pictures. Although these are familiar media today, the form and the production techniques have changed greatly in many cases. Lantern slide projectors used 3¼-by-4-inch slides, and 35mm slides were usually mounted in glass and used in projectors that had no automatic features. Overhead transparencies used the lantern slide or a 5-by-5-inch format. Tape recording was limited to ¼-inch tape used on rather bulky recorders, and motion picture production was limited to the slow (ASA 16) reversal films of that time.

The models used to guide the production process were simple. They were teacher based and included the elements of planning, production, utilization, and, to a limited extent, evaluation. The research base for designing and producing instructional media was limited. The Penn State Studies were among the few research-based guides available (Hoban & Van Ormer, 1950).

Techniques

Illustrations for instructional materials were often created by skilled artists. When these skills were not available, a picture file was frequently the basis for illustrations. Pictures from magazines, advertisements, or other sources were manipulated by techniques such as projection tracing, squaring, or photosketching. Black-and-white photography was commonly used for original photos and copying drawings and pictures for slides, filmstrips, overhead transparencies, or display prints. Color slides (35mm) were gaining in popularity as new, easy to use cameras came on the market.

Most methods of lettering were slow and required a great deal of skill. Hand lettering, pens and guides such as the Wrico systems, and mechanical systems such as LeRoy or Letterguide were commonly used. Rubber stamps, stencils, and cutout letters were employed for such things as posters and displays. Standard typewriters were used for 3¼-by-4-inch slides and primary typewriters were used for overheads.

The most common ways of mounting artwork during this period were rubber cement and dry mounting using a hot press. The addition of color to artwork was accomplished by the use of colored pencils, paints, or inks. The primary copy/duplication processes used were spirit duplication and screen duplication, known more familiarly by the brand names "Ditto" and "Mimeo." Diazo processes and dual-spectrum copiers were used to make overhead transparencies, and a wide variety of silver-based photographic materials were used for copying.

Audio production moved into the magnetic tape era in the late 1940s. One-quarter-inch and 16mm sprocketed tapes required bulky, heavy equipment. Motion picture production for instructional purposes moved from 35mm black-and-white to 16mm color during this period and, like audio equipment, cameras and lights were bulky and heavy.

1960s AND 1970s

The period between 1960 and 1979 was a time of growth and transition that led to the dynamic changes of the 1980s. Changes in technology modified or replaced the instructional media used in schools or training settings.

Lantern slides virtually ceased to exist, and 35mm slides assumed increased importance as automatic projectors using the "carousel" principle became available and as high-quality, easily used 35mm cameras and faster slide films were introduced. The development of multi-image programming equipment increased the use of slides as it changed from punched tape, to tone, to digital control.

With the introduction of the thermal process, and later the electrostatic process, it became easy and relatively inexpensive to make 8-by-10-inch transparencies from a typed page, and the old small-format overhead projectors were replaced by 8-by-10-inch models. (This was not always a beneficial change: a transparency from a typed page is far more legible on a 3¼-by-4-inch or on a 5-by-5 transparency than on an 8-by-10-inch transparency.)

The models for guiding production became increasingly detailed, paralleling the increased emphases on the instructional development process. Typical models included:

- Analyzing the educational or training needs.

- Knowing the physical, socio-economic, educational, and psychological characteristics of the audience.

- Delineating the content to be communicated.

- Deciding the most appropriate learning and teaching strategies.

- Evaluating each step of the process.

During this period numerous research studies relating to perception, memory, concept learning, and attitude change principles were conducted. These were summarized by Fleming and Levie (1978). In addition, many research studies were carried out that dealt with practical considerations such as legibility of projected materials, the use of color, and typographic variables, and a set of practical strategies for improving visual learning that was based on research results was developed by Dwyer (1978).

Techniques

Many of the production techniques of the 1940s and 1950s continued to be used through the 1970s, and some continue to be used in the 1980s. A summary of methods used for graphic, photographic, and reprographic production can be found in *The International Encyclopedia of Education* (Burbank & Pett, 1985; Dayton, 1985). Details of production techniques can be found in *Techniques for Producing Visual Instructional Media* (Minor & Frye, 1970) and in *Planning and Producing Instructional Media* (Kemp & Dayton, 1985).

Illustration continued to be done by skilled artists, and there was a significant increase in the availability of high-quality, copyright-free clip art. In the late 1970s graphic programs for computers became available that allowed artists to create quality materials in less time than traditional methods. Photography made great strides in this period. Black-and-white films improved in quality and color slides became technically easy to create as cameras were automated and fast color films became available.

Lettering by hand methods gave way to dry transfer "rubdown" letters and machines that used pressure to transfer letters to film or paper backings. For large-scale production, photo-typesetting equipment became available at reasonable cost. Rubber cement continued in use and a variety of mounting materials for use in a dry mount press were introduced. Pressure-sensitive mounting materials for use in a dry mount press were introduced. Pressure-sensitive mounting materials and waxing machines for paste-up work were also in common use. Traditional methods of adding color were augmented by the use of transparent rubdown sheets.

Copying and duplicating processes underwent major changes. Although spirit and screen processes were still used during this period, electrostatic copiers took over the bulk of paper copying jobs, and rivaled offset duplication for many quantity jobs. Color electrostatic copiers were introduced that provided full-color paper prints or transparencies from colored artwork or slides. Thermal processes largely replaced diazo for making transparencies as the quality of thermal transparencies increased and as a wide variety of negative and positive thermal materials became available.

For classroom and training purposes small, lightweight audiocassette recorders replaced the $\frac{1}{4}$-inch format, although the latter continued to be used for recording master tapes. Three-quarter-inch and one-half-inch video formats largely replaced 16mm film for motion media production in educational and in-house production settings.

The changes of this period were largely doing better or faster the things that production specialists had been doing for many years. They were small developments compared with what was to come in the next decade.

1980s AND BEYOND

Say good-bye to Wrico and LeRoy and hello to laser printers, videodiscs, hypermedia, and computers. The 1980s marked a period of transition from hand art skills to computer skills. Personal computers; graphic workstations; and dot matrix, color, and laser printers have changed radically the way graphic artists and instructional production specialists perform their work. Inexpensive computer chips are in almost all new production equipment: flatbed scanners, computer graphics workstations, video and sound digitizers, camcorders, video cameras, still cameras, videodisc and CD-ROM players, and video editors.

The revolution in computing power began in the late 1970s and early 1980s. The Apple II+ computer was the first to bring an unbelievable amount of computing power—48K of random access memory (RAM) and an 8-bit microprocessor—to anyone who could afford the $3,000+ purchase price. IBM followed shortly after Apple with their first personal computer in early 1982 (16K of RAM with a 16-bit processor). Initially both computers gained acceptance and credibility in the workplace with the use of word processors and spreadsheets, but graphics programs followed quickly. At the same time, personal computers were appearing in schools, homes, and offices; smaller chips were being used literally by the bushel in toys, home appliances, tools, cars, planes, and consumer electronics. We moved from a situation in which the computer was at first a useful tool for specialized, large-scale applications to one in which a computer is necessary in an increasingly competitive world. In other words, that the computer has had an effect on the production of instructional materials should come as no surprise; it is a logical reflection of what has happened in the rest of society.

The overall effect of the computer on instructional production is not minor. It has changed how artists and producers work and it has also altered (or will) their roles in the production process. Production specialists have had to learn new ways to produce old materials—new ways that increase productivity and save time. They have also had to learn to use new forms of media such as CD-ROM, interactive videodisc, and hypermedia. This section of the chapter focuses on some of the most significant changes in production techniques and in the role of the production specialist.

Production

Though a personal computer that is both inexpensive (such as less than $1,500) and powerful (32-bit processors, multi-tasking) is rather elusive, the computers and workstations available today offer features of power and functionality for independent production specialists that were considered impossible just five short years ago. In fact, thanks to the computer, most production specialists have available more production tools than ever before. Individual production specialists can produce camera-ready color graphics in a matter of minutes instead of days, with an ever-growing array of graphics software.

Early graphics programs were primitive and rudimentary, giving users minimal capabilities. This early software usually supported only the drawing of lines and boxes. Text was available, but with crude and limited font selections. The programs worked slowly on the computer and were rather cumbersome to use. However, even these early programs showed artists that the computer was on the scene to stay, for despite the disadvantages it was possible with simple, inexpensive graphics programs (e.g., Beagle Bros. programs) to use the slow Apple II computer to produce overhead transparency masters in a fraction of the time it took with pen and ink or pressure-sensitive letters. Today, a variety of powerful graphics software are available for use and almost every conceivable need.

The computer graphics workstation alone is not responsible for all the new developments in production in the 1980s. There have also been significant developments in the use of video (thanks again to miniaturization and computer chips). At the beginning of the 1980s color video cameras cost about $5,000 and were only portable on a heavy duty tripod with wheels. Now, high-quality, affordable (less than $1,000) VHS and 8mm cameras and camcorders are routinely carried on family excursions, vacations, and camping trips. Just as with the advances in computers, portability and affordability have placed the use of video in the hands of more people.

Even more significant and exciting is the development of new forms of media. Consumer models of digitized still cameras are available, though at a high price. These cameras record still images on a disk for later playback through a television set—no film, no processing. The combination of laser disks and computers is producing new types of interactive technologies, such as CD-ROM disks, videodisc, and digital video-ROM disks. These combinations of technologies will have the most lasting impact on production. Producers will spend less time learning production techniques and will spend more time learning instructional design principles and new ways to create interactive presentations using hypermedia, computer databases, read only memory (ROM) technologies, and videodisc.

Computer Graphics

The use of computer graphics on personal computers has produced the single greatest change in production methods of the 1980s. Graphics software has evolved into a family of software programs that help in the development of instructional presentations, publishing, and illustration. There are five classes of software used in preparing productions: paint, draw, image enhancement, presentation, and desktop publishing programs. (This list does not include CAD/CAM programs, which fall more within the realm of engineering programs.)

Paint Programs

Paint programs are the direct descendants of the early line/box/text programs. One of the first of great note was MacPaint, introduced with the first Macintosh computers. The tools available in paint programs simulate familiar tools used by graphic artists: paint brushes, air brush, eraser, resizable geometric objects, a wide range of font styles and sizes, and patterns for shading and emphasis. These programs are generally easy to learn and give both experts and novices the chance to produce high-quality graphics after just a few hours of training. These programs are called "paint" because they work by turning pixels on and off on the screen—painting the screen. Printouts are made by "dumping" the screen to a printer, which prints a black mark for each pixel that is black on the screen. Newer versions also print in color.

Draw Programs

With the advent of laser printers, a new type of graphics program was needed. The resolution of paint programs does not match the quality of resolution a laser printer is capable of producing. Draw programs (e.g., Illustrator 88 by Adobe or FreeHand by Aldus) produce artwork through calculations rather than pixels, and are therefore capable of producing smooth, high-quality output on any printer capable of reading the calculations—from 300-dot-per-inch laser printers to 3,000-dot-per-inch photo quality machines. Draw programs do not use the customary tools, but rather lines, curves, circles, and polygons—geometric objects that can be replicated by formulae. It takes longer to produce an image with a draw program, but the quality of printed output is significantly higher than from paint programs. Production specialists often begin with an illustration produced on a paint program and trace it with a draw program to enhance the ultimate output quality.

Image Enhancement Programs

To help graphic artists who use draw programs, a relatively new addition to the graphic genre is image enhancement. Some of these programs (e.g., Super 3-D by Silicon Beach) take images that are created in two-dimensional draw programs and create a three-dimensional image. Other programs are designed to enhance images scanned from flatbed scanners or created in draw and paint programs by adding shading, shadow, detail, or perspective (e.g., Darkroom by Silicon Beach). These programs are extremely complex and take a lot of time to learn to use. They are intended primarily for those who create graphic images professionally.

Presentation Programs

Draw and image enhancement programs are intended primarily for graphic artists. People whose job it is to produce presentations such as slide/tapes or overhead transparencies do not need the sophistication of these programs for text- and line-art-based presentations. Presentation programs (e.g., PowerPoint by Microsoft) produce masters for slides and overheads in black-and-white or in color using simple line and box tools with a variety of text fonts and styles. If more sophisticated images are necessary, they can be imported from draw or paint programs.

For production of the images, conventional dot matrix or laser printers may be used. However, presentation programs are also set up to communicate with illustration reproduction companies (e.g., Genigraphics) for high-quality slides and transparencies. Files can be sent over the telephone lines via modem to a sophisticated, high-resolution color camera. The camera produces a picture and the company returns the slide or transparency the next day (via U.S. mail or an express mail service). These large companies use cameras and color printers that cost tens of thousands of dollars; however, smaller cameras (less than $10,000) are available that permit production specialists to produce slides on-site.

Finally, presentation programs offer one other service to users: presentations. The images created for production may also be put together to run a presentation while individuals are watching the screen. Most of the programs also automatically put together notes and handouts for speaker and audience. In other words, the presentation program can serve as both a production tool and a presentation medium. With the use of a liquid crystal overhead display or large screen projector, the images may be shown to groups.

Desktop Publishing

The last class in the graphics genre is the most well known. Desktop publishing programs combine text from word processors, and illustrations from paint or draw programs, and add graphics such as lines, boxes, and shading to create layouts for publications. Desktop publishing created a productivity revolution in the production of books, magazines, newsletters, posters, and flyers. These programs (e.g., PageMaker by Aldus, QuarkXPress by Quark) have eliminated the need for hard copy paste-ups. With the aid of scanners or video digitizers, it is possible to create a book or magazine in which the first paper seen or felt is the final copy distributed to the readers. Text and graphics that used to take days to lay out now take only a few hours.

Ancillary Programs

There are other programs that are intended primarily to enhance the previously described programs. There are hundreds of fonts available. Other programs provide templates for forms, schedules, and newsletters. Some permit users to develop their own fonts. Finally, even the clip art publishers of the past have gotten into the act by providing hundreds of disks of files of clip art that can be used in the draw and paint programs.

Duplication and Distribution

Duplication has also seen radical changes. The use of mimeograph and spirit duplication machines has declined greatly in favor of the more expensive, but more convenient, electrostatic (photocopy) process. Many electrostatic machines provide multiple color capabilities (color toner cartridges) and size adjustments. Four-color electrostatic machines first made a showing in the early 1980s, but were prohibitively expensive to operate. By the late 1980s color machines were common production aids, especially in large printing and graphic shops, with small color laser printers priced at less than $10,000.

However, nothing has had an impact on duplication comparable to the document facsimile machine. The use of facsimile (FAX) machines doubled between 1987 and 1988. FAX machines in the $500 range make this technology affordable for individuals as well as business. With FAX, a person in Los Angeles can order a logo from an artist in Denver, Colorado. The artist in Denver can send draft copies to Los Angeles via FAX for checking as quickly or quicker than walking to an office next door. Although quality of the low-end machines prevents their use for production-ready copy, they are useful for checking both graphics and text and for disseminating information.

Video

Advances in video production are characterized primarily by enhancements in portability and quality. VHS is the de facto standard, especially since Sony stopped producing the higher quality Beta machines. The latest VHS equipment is capable of recording via the light of a single candle and weighs little more than three pounds. Video equipment keeps getting smaller and better, with 8mm tape the newest format for portable equipment. U-Matic (¾-inch pro video equipment), still the choice for broadcast quality productions, is disappearing from the instructional scene. Cameras have on-board titling ability and sound synchronization. High-end cameras and videocassette recorders offer minor editing capabilities, though even editing equipment is now affordable (about $4,000) for instructional production purposes. All of these developments have put video production in the hands of almost anyone.

New Media Formats

In the area of new media, the development of greatest impact is the spread of videodisc and CD-ROM and its variations. Initially a popular independent study device in business and the military, use of laser videodisc players is increasing in the classroom for group presentations, lab simulations, and independent study (Phillipo, 1988). The videodisc player provides concrete illustrations by presenting slides in any order, illustrates motion and speed in any direction and speed, and offers the advantage of high-quality stereo sound or dual-language soundtracks. When combined with a computer, the videodisc provides sophisticated branching and response characteristics. Again, because of the tie-in with the computer, the production specialist of the future must be prepared to develop or write the software to execute these implementations.

The Role: Planning and Design

It is easy to see how the computer is responsible for most of the changes in the way production of video, publications, and graphics is done. However, changes in production techniques and production tools are evolutionary. The greatest influence of the microprocessor is not the change in *how* things are produced but in *what* the production specialist does at several different levels of the production process.

On the production level, because of the abundance of new tools available to just about everyone through the computer, designers must place a greater emphasis on basic elements of design. This is especially important for schools that train producers of instructional materials who must wear many hats in the instructional design process. Producers must be trained more thoroughly in basic layout and design principles—principles that deal with white space, type fonts, kerning, leading, margins, contrast, and color combinations. They must learn to use those text elements to enhance perception, attention, reading, and learning.

On the instructional level, the basics of any instructional problem will always exist and must be considered in detail. A process must be used to develop instructional materials for a specific audience and specific objectives. However, with the advent of interactive media, that planning and design process is more complicated. Production designers need to consider the nature of the interaction between the medium and the student when designing some of the new materials.

There is yet another level, the combination of both production and instruction principles in the same production task. With interactive media, specialists must also learn to design for CRT screen displays, computer overlays on video screens, and the presentation of hypermedia. The computer display screen poses unique and as yet unanswered questions. Unlike the printed page, which is a discrete piece of information, computer screens can change and move. There really is no such thing as a "single screen." A computer can add and subtract, position and reposition information on the screen. It can add multiple windows and change colors. In conventional CBT applications, the appearance of most screens can be anticipated. However, with the advent of hypermedia displays and intelligent computer-assisted instruction, it may not be possible to anticipate the appearance of every screen, so guidelines will have to be built into the program to govern the display of legible screens.

In addition to displays, production specialists must learn principles for interactive presentations. Re-purposing videodiscs and CD-ROM is a new production skill. In the past, the production specialist was responsible for producing the materials necessary for a presentation. Videodisc and CD-ROM and other compact disk technologies present a collection of images (still and moving) that the production specialist may be called upon to "produce" for a presentation. However, in this case the production skills needed will be the programming necessary to link those media with a computer so they may be presented when the presenter or learner needs them. Hypermedia presents special problems for the producer. Images and text must be combined from a variety of sources, often in ways that were not anticipated. Instructional producers need to be part of the entire planning process for hypermedia systems. They have to establish basic production parameters within which a system will work.

CONCLUSION

The changes in instructional production provide a number of significant productivity benefits for users. But they also mean that production specialists must change their approach to the development of instructional materials. Emphasis on old hand art skills such as lettering, mounting, and preparation of slide flats is reduced. Thanks to the computer, anyone can draw a straight line, as well as curves, circles, ellipses, polygons, etc. The old emphasis on sketching, mockups, and models is also reduced because of the ease of changing things in a computer. The weight of the line, the size of a box, the style of a headline can be changed with a few key strokes. Of course, with the new benefits come new problems, particularly in the area of design. The flexibility in production fosters "sloppy" thinking and execution. And just because people have the capability to do something does not mean they have the "taste" to execute it properly.

Overall, in the past several decades, the field of instructional production has moved from an emphasis on the production of concrete images to an emphasis on interactivity. In the past, producers and educational programs concentrated on techniques to create images and materials. Now interactive media place an emphasis on design processes and principles. Production of materials takes much less time to learn and to do. With laser discs, it is even conceivable that a producer will produce nothing; instead, the "production" process will focus on the linking of those images to achieve a specific instructional goal. The focus of instructional production is rapidly changing to be on learners and learning as opposed to chemicals, inks, pens, and mounting processes.

REFERENCES

Alton, S. (1981). *Audio in media*. Belmont, CA: Wadsworth.

Burbank, L., & Pett, D. (1985). Photographic production and photographic services. In *The international encyclopedia of education*. Oxford: Pergamon Press.

Burbank, L., & Pett, D. (1985). Reprography. In *The international encyclopedia of education*. Oxford: Pergamon Press.

———. (1989). Designing instructional materials: Some guidelines. In R. A. Braden, D. G. Beauchamp, L. W. Miller, & D. M. Moore (Eds.), *About visuals: Research, teaching and applications, readings from the 20th annual conference of The International Visual Literacy Association, Inc*. Blacksburg, VA: Virginia Tech University.

Dayton, D. (1985). Graphics production. In *The international encyclopedia of education*. Oxford: Pergamon Press.

Dwyer, F. (1978). *Strategies for improving visual learning*. State College: Learning Services.

Fleming, M., & Levie, W. (1978). *Instructional message design*. Englewood Cliffs, NJ: Educational Technology Publications.

Hoban, C., & Van Ormer, E. (1950). *Instructional film research 1918-1950*. State College: The Pennsylvania State College.

Kemp, J., & Dayton, D. (1985). *Planning and producing instructional media*. New York: Harper & Row.

Minor, E., & Frye, H. (1970). *Techniques for producing visual instructional media*. New York: McGraw-Hill.

Pett, D. (1989). Visual design for projected still materials. *Educational Technology, 29*, 1.

Phillipo, J. (1988). Videodisc players: A multi purpose audiovisual tool. *Electronic Learning, 8*, 3.

28

The Status and Future of Research in Instructional Design and Technology Revisited

Michael J. Hannafin
Center for Instructional Development and Services, Florida State University
Tallahassee, Florida

and

Kathleen McDermott Hannafin
Center for Educational Technology, Florida State University
Tallahassee, Florida

In 1985, an examination of the factors influencing research productivity in the instructional technology (IT) field was written (Hannafin, 1985). The article reflected the views of a wide range of IT professionals and scholars, and the admittedly biased views of disciplined inquiry as a foundation to both the credibility and the survivability of the IT field. The ideas were molded in large measure by attendees at the inaugural meeting of the Professors of Instructional Design and Technology (PIDT), held in Bloomington, Indiana, earlier in the year. In this chapter, the issues and biases reflected in that article are reexamined given the developments of the past five years.

STATUS OF IT RESEARCH: 1985

Three major forces influenced the development of IT research prior to 1985: behavioral science research traditions, diffuse research identity, and attitudes of the field toward research.

Behavioral Science Research Traditions

The behavioral sciences evolved a set of research traditions and standards within which disciplined inquiry was conducted, implemented, and disseminated. Since the IT field was rooted, in large part, in the behavioral sciences, the same standards for research were tacitly adopted. To many both within and outside the field, research in the field was often measured by experimental research yardsticks. Thus the influence of these research traditions was strengthened. Many IT faculty were perceived by their institutions as behavioral scientists; research expectations evolved accordingly. The absence of a distinct intellectual identity intensified, while the proportion of research produced by IT scholars declined.

During IT's infancy, the absence of a distinct intellectual identity was to be expected. The behavioral sciences, psychology in particular, provided a sturdy base from which a strong theoretical foundation might emerge with distinct, but related, research problems, issues, and methodologies, but this never happened. Although competing research models were encouraged by IT leadership (Clark & Snow, 1975; Guba, 1981; Heinich, 1984), the field continued to be dominated by experimental research. Driscoll (1984), for example, presented 13 alternative paradigms for research in instructional systems including ethnography, technique development, and cost-effectiveness models. As of 1985, few had been exploited.

Despite encouragement from leadership and suggestions for implementing alternative research methods, the field remained dominated by research conducted by researchers in related fields. As a consequence, fewer IT faculty produced research and the field became increasingly shaped by the research and development (R&D) generated by researchers outside the field.

Diffuse Research Identity

In the absence of competing research priorities and proven alternative paradigms, the IT field's research identity weakened. Sachs (1984) studied the citation patterns in the *Journal of Instructional Development* and *Performance and Instruction*—two primary journals in the instructional design and technology field—to identify both common themes in the instructional design literature and the most productive scholars in the IT field. Sachs identified only a couple of distinctive themes, and comparatively few influential scholars. Even among the influential scholars, several were among the ranks of educational psychologists, with strong, but neither primary nor exclusive, interests in instructional technology (e.g., David Ausubel, Robert Gagne, Robert Tennyson, Jerome Bruner, etc.). He reported that few scholars had multiple citation patterns across IT periodicals literature, and concluded that R&D was only loosely based on the previous works of IT scholars. Few researchers used previously published works in the framework for their own ideas; authors often published in isolation from existing research.

Sachs provided a snapshot of the field prior to 1985. His findings underscored both the often haphazard development of IT research and the poor internal R&D linkages within the field. Sach's findings, consistent with our original paper, suggested that IT researchers were unlikely to advance their own field appreciably, and portended a significant problem for the 1990s.

Attitudes Toward Research

The pre-1985 IT academic faculty were most accurately characterized as consumers rather than producers of research. The lack of research may have been a consequence of indifference toward or lack of familiarity with available methods, competing demands, or simple lack of interest in research. Whatever the cause, the evidence was compelling. Few IT faculty were producing scholarly R&D; fewer still appeared prepared to do so.

The problem was attributed to a number of factors. Many stated that research was not well supported in their institutions. Several noted that teaching loads were excessive, and that service demands for IT programs were disproportionate to other academic programs. Others suggested that they lacked the expertise to plan and publish original R&D. Still others pointed to the economic disincentives for publishing compared with the more lucrative payoffs garnered through consulting. A few questioned the necessity for research given the highly applied nature of most programs. There were significant ideas about how faculty can productively spend their time; clearly, research was not a priority to most.

Barriers to IT Research

The next task was to objectively isolate true barriers to research. Assuming barriers could be objectively identified, steps could be taken to remove them. Three major barriers to IT research were isolated: implicit publication standards, the vastly expanded role of IT programs, and the lack of commitment to research.

Implicit Publication Standards

Faculty across disciplines have cited editorial gatekeeping and other implicit standards of acceptability as deterrents to publishing original research (Boice & Jones, 1984). Likewise, PIDT participants argued that the editorial review process was governed by implicit standards of acceptability and entrenchment in traditional behavioral science research models. Many argued that "editorial gatekeepers" responded most favorably to familiar methods, experimental research methods in particular, thus encouraging old research traditions and inhibiting new methods. Participants felt that editors and reviewers were disinclined to consider alternative research approaches for publication. Many also voiced special frustration with the perceived widespread editorial bias against qualitative research.

A number of potential solutions were proposed. Solutions included increasing editorial latitude in the range of work and types of methodologies considered for publication. Participants were cautioned that "alternative" was not simply a euphemism for "sloppy," and that a high degree of competence and rigor was needed for any disciplined inquiry. Writers could not and should not expect that scholarly journals will simply acquiesce to the demand for "different" when the case cannot be made for "better." Further, it was necessary to identify which problems required study before methods could be selected. It made little sense to endorse one methodology over another independent of the problems to be investigated. The basic relationship between problem identification and methodology was reaffirmed. The call was for greater awareness of different problems confronting the IT field, and the importance of varied methods, sometimes quite different from traditional experimental methodologies, required for study.

Expanded Role of IT

Two major concerns were identified: (1) the rapid expansion of the field and the programs that support growth, and (2) the consequence of expanded roles on the field's research identity. Participants agreed that, from an R&D perspective, expansion has been a double-edged sword: As the mass of the field increased, research identity decreased. Expansion has opened new employment markets, in turn increasing the enrollment in IT programs. Yet, expansion has also spread our resources, both physical and intellectual, thinly over a growing range of roles and settings.

Perhaps the most negative effect of rapid growth through 1985 was the further divergence of interest, expertise, and effort within the field. IT had evolved a dubious intellectual identity, attributable in part to the progressive diffusion of research focus across programs. We had no common "lore." Our few productive researchers' interests were often quite dissimilar, doing little to collectively establish or advance a common identity. Instead, competing roles, often focusing on service to the myriad of problems and settings associated with our expanded field, had been cultivated. For example, in response to the expanded number of needed graduates and programs, considerable attention had been focused on professional certification of instructional designers (Bratton, 1984). One consequence had been a declining effort in the preparation of future researchers in our graduate programs. Our faculty modeled other behaviors, and students were simply raised and weaned in nonresearch environments. Even in cases where successful research programs were in place, there was little collective correspondence across programs to evolve unifying empirical foundations for the field.

Few solutions were offered and fewer were unanimously endorsed by participants. Because expanded, successful programs and roles were already operational, it was difficult to justify refocusing to establish and strengthen a unified research agenda. In retrospect, it was probably naive to assume that wholesale shifts in priorities could happen. Faculty autonomy is the cornerstone of academic life. Those committed to effecting such a change were already engaged in scholarly research that had done little to unify IT constituents. Those not yet committed were already committed elsewhere and had garnered considerable momentum in their chosen roles. In academe, there can be no coercion. Diversity proved to be the greatest strength in expanding our programs, but our most persistent obstacle to advancing a research agenda for the IT field.

Commitment to Research

Although highly valued in university settings, few institutions adequately supported research with needed time, resources, or students. Yet individual research productivity varied widely under nearly identical institutional conditions. The key factor appeared to be an evolved indifference, a highly individualized indifference, to becoming a productive scholar. Individuals had "other things to do," and thus lacked a researcher's motivation. Indeed, many programs appeared to be relatively immune from the "publish or perish" standards of higher education. Without commitment, it mattered little how circumstances conspired to make research difficult to conduct. Increased support may make it easier, but not necessarily more likely, for research to increase.

The aforementioned barriers and issues could be readily distilled into one relatively simple point: Faculty chose to spend time elsewhere doing other things. The debate over research was lively. The participants were appropriately indignant over the demise of disciplined inquiry among the ranks. Why, then, has there been no appropriate response? Repeatedly, participants asked, "Why isn't someone doing research in...?" The question need never have been asked. The answer was simple but painful: As a field we were more satisfied with debating than actually conducting and publishing research.

STATUS OF IT RESEARCH ENTERING THE 1990s

Have the status or future of research in IT changed much recently? As we enter the 1990s, evidence suggests that both the program and research identities of the field remain as diverse as ever. Schiffman and Gansneder (1987) illustrated the diversity of IT by noting numerous and varied missions across IT graduate programs. Miller and Mosley (1987) listed 62 doctoral and more than 200 master's degree IT programs, and an additional 41 educational computing graduate programs, in the *Educational Technology and Media Yearbook*. These numbers have grown steadily during the past decade. Department affiliations range from curriculum and instruction, to educational psychology, to personnel and management, to library and information science, to vocational education; programs are located in independent university centers and interdepartmental units, schools and colleges of education, colleges of business, schools of communication, and so on. It is clear that "diverse" remains the single best description of the IT field.

The basic problems noted in 1985 remain, but several important issues must be addressed. In this section, several recurring issues are reconsidered. Several of the assumptions raised initially are re-analyzed, and a number of somewhat different conclusions are drawn.

Is Diversity an Asset or a Liability?

Diversity is not inherently problematic. Often, diversity helps to expand the perspectives taken on a problem, yielding solutions not possible from single perspectives. One could argue persuasively that diversity is the primary strength of credible disciplines. Indeed, in 1985, we viewed our diversity as a potential strength for future research.

But diversity also places many limits on our capacity to emerge as a discipline. We tend to advance wholly different, often conflicting, images of the field. We have yet to articulate the collective core knowledge of IT, tacitly contributing to the image of IT as "everything and nothing." Our resources are often spread thinly across a broad array of priorities, none of which receives sufficient support to make significant, visible gains. Clearly, there is a cost associated with diversity. Much of this cost is evident in the weakened research and theoretical foundations of the IT field.

Does IT Need a Unifying Research Agenda?

Little significant progress has been made in either establishing or systematically pursuing a research agenda. New ideas have been advanced for guiding research (Clark, 1989) and the acceptance of alternative research methods, but as a field we have emphasized other nonresearch priorities.

Our diversity, again, has influenced the viability of establishing a common research agenda. Within IT diversity has engendered conflicting priorities. We are not so much a collection of diverse scholars with complementary views on consensus problems as a group unable to identify which problems to pursue. The diversity of the IT field has diluted our research focus and inhibited the emergence of unifying research agendas. The varied perspectives and interests of the IT field make the creation of a unifying research agenda highly unlikely (Clark, 1978; Clark & Snow, 1975).

Perhaps it is unrealistic to strive for a unifying IT research agenda. Perhaps we are more like engineers than scientists after all. The field is no longer "new" in the same sense described by Schuller (1985); our window of opportunity may already have closed. Given the nature of the evolution of the field, it may be more fruitful to identify those root disciplines (Clark, 1989) where the foundations of IT can be strengthened. Those within the field with R&D interests might align their interests more clearly with those of the root disciplines. IT may never attain the status of other scientific disciplines, but this may be more an academic than a practical issue. Efforts to translate relevant R&D from allied disciplines will likely prove more fruitful than attempting to establish a unifying agenda among the diverse interests represented in the IT field.

Is There Interest in Research?

There is evidence to suggest that, as a group, we neither produce nor read much IT-related research. Higgins et al. (1989) reported that AECT members expressed considerable interest in reading about program development and new technologies, but very little interest in reading either basic or theoretical research. Carrier and Dick (1988) note that although many professors expressed interest in pursuing research, few were allocated time to pursue these interests. Hannafin (1989) reported that IT faculty published comparatively little research in refereed journals, and that very few IT scholars published research indexed in the 1987 *Social Science Citation Index*.

Based upon data cited in the 1985 article, as well as recent evidence, research interest remains weak. Where productivity is apparent, it tends to be highly localized both in terms of who publishes the research and the ultimate impact of published work. This is a pattern that has persisted for some time, with little evidence of a significant change in attitude. We must conclude, therefore, that our field has demonstrated little interest in either publishing original research or reading basic or theoretical research.

Where Do We Focus Our Research Efforts?

In an effort to classify research published in IT journals, Dick and Dick (1989) compared the contents of the *Journal of Instructional Development (JID)* and *Educational Communication and Technology Journal (ECTJ)*. The authors analyzed both the topic and focus of articles published over a period of seven years, as well as the influence of academic rank and affiliation of authors. The findings indicated that comparatively little basic or theoretical research was published by a handful of university faculty. Not surprisingly, practitioners were more inclined to publish applied than basic research.

Hannafin (1989) reported that faculty were far more likely to publish in applied versus basic research journals. Among the outlets in which faculty publications appeared were 912 separate periodicals, the overwhelming majority of which were highly applied in nature. Publication focus typically emphasizes program development and instructional methods over empiricism. This pattern seems likely to continue.

Has Research Productivity Increased?

Clark (1989) reported that significant increases in the number of IT-related articles can be seen over the past decade. This is an encouraging sign for those concerned with the meager output of IT scholars in the past. Yet, during the same decade, the number of IT programs and faculty has grown significantly as well. The increases observed by Clark, therefore, may be attributable to increased mass versus individual productivity.

The overall figures on "meaningful" contributions to the literature are not encouraging. Hannafin (1989) estimated that fewer than 5 percent of the university faculty wrote the applied and basic research published in the 10 top periodicals (according to IT faculty). Top-rated basic periodicals include the likes of *Educational Communication and Technology Journal* and *Journal of Computer-Based Instruction*; top-rated applied journals include the aforementioned *Educational Technology, Journal of Instructional Development*, and *Performance and Instruction*. This implies that a full 95 percent of faculty members in the academic programs contribute little to either the theoretical or applied scholarship of their field. Research productivity remains distressingly low.

Have We Made a Commitment to Research?

Previously, it was suggested that "The ID field is not lacking fuel—only fire" (Hannafin, 1985, p. 29). Little has changed in this regard. While opportunities for research continue to emerge in areas such as distance learning, technology in teacher education, utilization of emerging technologies, and so forth, the issue of commitment remains. There is little evidence that the IT field has demonstrated the needed commitment in the past; there is no reason to expect that significant commitments will be forthcoming in the future. Yet, the IT field continues to grow, raising the question of whether empirical research is really necessary. We have obviously been successful, if not unified, in many of our undertakings. It is an issue of priorities, and thus far research and scholarship have not been high on the list.

Yet this does not imply that neither research nor commitment are needed. Commitment has many manifestations, each of which has its own supporting rationale. Clearly, there is much to learn about how we have implemented our craft in the past, and how we will evolve given future developments in technology, psychology, and so forth. Some have suggested that IT may be better served by formalizing methods for interpreting the implications of related R&D generated elsewhere than by attempting to produce its own. Perhaps we have evolved to precisely this point. We need a commitment not to chart our own IT research future, but to identify a stronger sense of "fit" with allied, root disciplines, and emphasize important translations and interpretations for the IT field.

SUMMARY AND CONCLUSIONS

It is difficult to be both realistic and optimistic regarding the future of IT research. If we continue on our present course, the field will be plagued by lack of direction, definition, and focus. IT will continue its emphasis on training practitioners, but will be unable to forge its own destiny and advance its own research. The field will continue to grow, becoming more diffuse, moving current IT researchers into disciplines where research is nourished.

Perhaps it is time to accept that IT is a subset of other varied disciplines, and not a discipline by itself. Our destiny, in effect, is shaped through the various disciplines in which we are represented. Our focus should be to assess how instruction and technology are conditionally appropriate within each discipline, not on the portability of the process across often diverse fields. Some research cross-fertilization now possible would be lost; there is little evidence that we have properly exploited this opportunity to date. Although this option may meet with much resistance in the IT community, the potential payoffs may be the greatest.

This chapter is an indictment of neither the IT field nor the academic programs that train IT professionals. Instead, we have attempted to place the issues related to research and the IT field, discussed initially in 1985, in a somewhat different perspective. It should be apparent that we view research as central to the long-term prosperity of any field, but we have come to accept that there are varied ways in which that research can be advanced. The IT field needs a strong research foundation, but it may no longer be viable to strengthen it from within. This is not a eulogy for research and IT; it is what our field does best—a pragmatic assessment of needs, means, and ends.

REFERENCES

Boice, R., & Jones, F. (1984). Why academicians don't write. *Journal of Higher Education, 55*(5), 567-582.

Bratton, B. (1984). Professional certification: Will it become a reality? *Performance and Instructional Journal, 23*(1), 4-7.

Carrier, C. A. (1986). A first meeting of professors of education technology: A summary of issues. *Journal of Instructional Development, 8*(3), 15-19.

Carrier, C. A., & Dick, W. (1988, May). *Research activities of professors of instructional design and technology.* Paper presented at the PIDT Conference, Bloomington, Indiana.

Clark, R. (1978). Doctoral research in educational technology. *Educational Communication and Technology Journal, 26,* 165-173.

———. (1983). Reconsidering research on learning from media. *Review of Educational Research, 53,* 445-459.

————. (1989). Current progress and future directions for research in instructional technology. *Educational Technology Research and Development, 37,* 57-66.

Clark, R., & Snow, R. (1975). Alternative designs for instructional technology research. *AV Communication Review, 23,* 373-394.

Dick, W., & Dick, D. (1989). Analytical and empirical comparisons of the *Journal of Instructional Development* and *Educational Communication and Technology Journal. Educational Technology Research and Development, 37,* 81-87.

Driscoll, M. (1984). Alternative paradigms for research in instructional systems. *Journal of Instructional Development, 7*(4), 2-10.

Guba, E. (1981). Criteria for assessing the trustworthiness of naturalistic inquiries. *Educational Communication and Technology Journal, 29,* 75-92.

Hannafin, K. M. (1989). *An analysis of the scholarly production of instructional systems faculty.* Unpublished doctoral dissertation, The Pennsylvania State University.

Hannafin, M. J. (1985). The status and future of research in instructional design and technology. *Journal of Instructional Development, 8*(3), 24-30.

Heinich, R. (1984). The proper study of instructional technology. *Educational Communication and Technology Journal, 32*(2), 67-87.

Higgins, N., et al. (1989). Perspectives on educational technology research and development. *Educational Technology Research and Development, 37,* 7-18.

Miller, E. E., & Mosley, M. L., eds. (1987). *Educational media and technology yearbook*, Vol. 13. Littleton, CO: Libraries Unlimited.

Sachs, S. (1984). Citation patterns in instructional development literature. *Journal of Instructional Development, 7*(2), 8-13.

Salomon, G., & Clark, R. (1977). Reexamining the methodology of research on media and technology in education. *Review of Educational Research, 47,* 99-120.

Schiffman, S. S. (1986). Instructional systems design: Five views of the field. *Journal of Instructional Development, 9*(4), 14-21.

Schiffman, S. S., & Gansneder, B. M. (1987). Graduate programs in instruction technology: Their characteristics and involvement in public education. *Journal of Instructional Development, 10*(3), 22-28.

Schuller, C. F. (1985). Some historical perspectives on the instructional technology field. *Journal of Instructional Development, 8*(3), 3-6.

29

Paradigms for Research in Instructional Systems

Marcy P. Driscoll

Department of Educational Research, Florida State University
Tallahassee, Florida

INTRODUCTION

According to Kuhn (1970), no paradigm for research ever solves all the problems it defines, nor do two competing paradigms leave the same problems unsolved. When planning research and deciding among paradigms, then, the question is: Which problems most urgently require solutions? It is important to answer this question because adherence to particular research paradigms may affect which problems we are ultimately able to solve.

According to Kuhn, the paradigm that guides our research necessarily delimits our problems, theoretical assumptions, and methodologies. In a mature science, one paradigm typically dominates. Progress occurs when this dominant paradigm, unable to account for a growing number of anomalies discovered in the course of normal scientific inquiry, is replaced or "overthrown" by a competing paradigm (Kuhn, 1970). In a developing science, by contrast, numerous paradigms may vie for acceptability and dominance.

Instructional systems *is* such a developing science. It draws from the research and theory of several fields, including psychology and information systems, to establish a basis for its own theory development and research. As it does so, it will also reflect shifts in theoretical or research paradigms that these fields may undergo. Heinich (1970), for example, documents the theoretical shift from behavioral to cognitive that has occurred in psychology and discusses the impact of that shift on theory development and research in instructional technology. New research paradigms are also finding their way into educational research (e.g., naturalistic inquiry in evaluation, Lincoln & Guba, 1985; semiotic inquiry, Cunningham, 1987, and Shank, 1987; qualitative inquiry, Erickson, 1985), and many of these hold promise for research in instructional systems. The point is that because of the developing nature of instructional systems, the field should embrace a wide variety of research paradigms and not yield to the dominance of any one. Moreover, identifying underlying assumptions of any given research paradigm and examining the implications of changing those assumptions can lead researchers to increasingly creative solutions to research problems (Cunningham, 1987).

This paper represents an updated, revised, and expanded version of a previously published paper by the same author (1984). Alternative paradigms for research in instructional systems, *Journal of Instructional Development, 7*(4), 2-5.

The traditional experimental paradigm plays an important role in our search for functional laws and cause-effect relationships. Since it is perhaps the most familiar and dominant mode of inquiry, it serves as a useful starting point for the discussion of research paradigms available to instructional systems researchers. When maintaining experimental control becomes difficult in an instructional investigation, researchers may choose from among a variety of quasi-experimental designs to permit them to make valid causal inferences even in the absence of rigid experimental control (Cook & Campbell, 1979). These are discussed next. Finally, a variety of alternatives to experimental inquiry is presented. These are useful for investigating the many interesting and important questions facing us in instructional systems that are noncausal in nature.

The research paradigms included in this chapter are discussed in relation to the types of instructional systems research problems they may enable us to investigate. To the extent possible, reference is made to resources, describing in more detail their assumptions and critical features. Then, specific examples are presented of these paradigms as they have been implemented in instructional systems research.

PARADIGMS FOR RESEARCH IN INSTRUCTIONAL SYSTEMS

Summarized in table 29.1, page 324, are a variety of paradigms for research and specific examples of research studies in instructional systems that have employed these paradigms. Each is discussed below, both in terms of how it might generally apply to the field and how at least one researcher has employed it.

Experiment

Experimental research designs offer the most effective means of establishing causal influences on a phenomenon of interest. They provide tests of hypotheses that have been generated through previous research, observation, or theory. An essential characteristic of experimental designs is that they seek to eliminate or minimize sources of error or bias so that the effects of interest can be unequivocally attributed to the researcher's manipulations. Thus, laboratory settings are frequently chosen to maintain control over extraneous variables, subjects are randomly selected and assigned to experimental treatments, and treatments are often of short duration to minimize effects of maturation or attrition (Tuckman, 1988).

Experimental designs are useful to instructional systems researchers for isolating and examining the effects on learning of single or interacting instructional variables. Salisbury and Klein (1988), for example, conducted an experimental study to compare the effects on performance and attitude of students using a computer-based drill strategy—the progressive state drill—vs. their own strategy with flashcards to learn 100 word-number pairs. Effects in question concerned which drill strategy was superior for learning verbal information and what influence either would have on student attitude toward learning.

Quasi-Experiment

Quasi-experimental designs for research represent a step between strictly experimental and nonexperimental paradigms. They deserve attention because they solve some of the problems raised with respect to experimental control in instructional research. For example, it is not always possible or desirable in instructional research to randomly assign individual students to treatment conditions or to assign some students to receive a particular treatment which others will not get.

Table 29.1.
Examples of Research Paradigms Employed in Instructional Systems Research

Research Paradigm	Study Utilizing the Paradigm
Experiment	1. Salisbury & Klein (1988)—a study to compare the differential effects on verbal learning and attitude of two drill strategies.
Quasi-Experiment	2. Hannafin (1983)—a study of the performance effectiveness of an empirically verified instructional system vs. traditional instruction over an 8-month span.
Meta-Analysis	3. Bangert, Kulik, & Kulik (1983)—a meta-analysis of mastery-based approaches to instruction.
	4. Kulik & Kulik (1988)—a meta-analysis of the timing of feedback in studies of verbal learning.
	5. Klauer (1984)—a meta-analysis of the effects of pre-instructional acts, such as behavioral objectives, questions, and learning directions, on intentional and incidental learning.
Case Study/Ethnography	6. Baird & White (1982)—a case study in which the process of learning genetics with understanding is investigated.
	7. Allen (1986)—an ethnographic study of classroom management from the perspective of students.
Systems-Based Evaluation	8. Hanson & Schutz (1978)—a research and development effort to install, evaluate, and improve a new, research-based instructional program.
Cost-Effectiveness	9. Klein & Doughty (1980)—a study of cost-effectiveness evaluation applied to an innovative program in higher education.
	10. Tsang (1988)—a review of cost studies in education conducted in developing nations.
Model Development	11. Keller (1987)—the development of a model of motivational design.
Technique Development	12. Driscoll & Tessmer (1985)—the development and testing of a rational set generator for teaching and testing defined concepts.
	13. Smith & Wedman (1988)—the use of a new means for collecting formative evaluation data from students: read/think-aloud protocols.

Other problems stem from the myriad of uncontrolled factors present in classroom settings that can nullify the application of laboratory findings to these settings. Effects found in short-term experimental studies may also fail to hold up in the long term because of these mitigating classroom influences. But studies conducted directly in these settings will face problems with experimental control. Cook and Campbell (1979) present numerous designs for field settings in which all the controls of the laboratory cannot be maintained. They discuss statistical as well as design strategies for use in these settings that will permit valid causal inference despite the lack of controls.

A specific example of a quasi-experimental study in instructional systems is Hannafin (1983), who investigated achievement differences in mathematics between Anglo and Hispanic students assigned to either traditional instruction or an empirically verified instructional system. The study took place over a period of eight months, and is one of few studies to examine performance effectiveness of instructional systems over an extended period (see also Ebmeier & Good, 1979; Grabe & Latta, 1981).

Meta-Analysis

A nonexperimental technique that uses previously reported research findings as its "subjects," meta-analysis (Hedges & Olkin, 1985; Abrami, Cohen, & d'Appollonia, 1988) can serve an increasingly important function in instructional systems research. It provides a statistical means for synthesizing research findings, a task that typically precedes the planning of a "next step" in any line of research. It can help us come to global conclusions as to whether a previously researched instructional technology has an effect on learning and how large the effect is. This is particularly important when controversies exist in the literature over the effectiveness of a particular technology.

Kulik and his associates have been responsible for a number of recent meta-analyses of research on mastery-based approaches to high school instruction (Bangert, Kulik, & Kulik, 1983) and the timing of feedback in studies of verbal learning (Kulik & Kulik, 1988). In addition, Klauer (1984) synthesized effects of such pre-instructional activities as behavioral objectives, questions, and learning directions on intentional and incidental learning.

Case Study and Ethnography

While quasi-experimental designs help us to control for contextual influences on learning variables, these influences become an integral part of the investigation in case studies (Yin, 1984) and ethnography (Goetz & LeCompte, 1984). Both assume that context in part determines and defines any phenomenon in question. Thus, for example, different contextual influences may operate in different settings, mediating the effects of any particular learning variable or technology. Explanation of effects must therefore directly consider what contextual factors were operating and how they affected results. Case studies and ethnographies are especially suited to answering "how" and "why" questions, such as "How are textbooks actually used in schools?" and "Why do cooperative groups seem to enhance motivation to learn?"

Baird and White (1982) use case study to investigate the individual's involvement in learning. They assume that general learning principles will be so masked by context and individual differences that they should not be specified *a priori* but rather allowed to emerge as an investigation proceeds. In a study examining how several adults learn and retain genetics concepts and skills, Baird and White identified and described two different learning styles and specific recurring learning deficiencies that led to inadequate learning.

A type of case study, ethnography draws from the assumptions and methodologies of anthropology and sociology. Those applying ethnography to education seek to study the "culture" of a teaching-learning environment, and employ such techniques as observation, interviewing, and content analysis of human artifacts. True ethnographies are hard to find in the research literature, largely because they take extensive time to conduct and typically voluminous pages to report. Allen (1986), however, demonstrates in a limited fashion the nature of an ethnographic investigation. He spent weeks as a participant observer in a high school in order to understand student culture in relation to the management of the classroom.

Systems-Based Evaluation

Factors stemming from the context in which a new technology or instructional system is implemented can greatly affect its success or effectiveness in the setting. Social, political, or economic problems can impair technology effectiveness to as great or greater degree than some inherent problem with the technology itself. To monitor these types of influences, then, systems-based (Cooley & Lohnes, 1976; Borich & Jemelka, 1982) or naturalistic (Guba & Lincoln, 1981) approaches to evaluation offer a great deal. Systems-based designs will enable us to determine what makes technologies effective in some settings and not others, so that we will be less likely to discount a technology simply because it was not the solution to a particular problem.

Hanson and Schutz (1978) followed a systems-based, developmental approach to install, evaluate, and then improve a new, empirically based instructional program. The point of their project was not to compare the new program to some competing one, but to use data on a continual basis to make adjustments in the new program so that it would be effective for that setting.

Cost-Effectiveness and Cost Analysis

Questions of cost-effectiveness and cost benefit increasingly arise in a tight economy where ways of cutting costs while maintaining effectiveness are welcomed. Cost analyses can help to reveal one technique or set of procedures to be more or less expensive than a competing technique. As for questions of effectiveness, criteria by which a technique or program is judged beneficial despite its cost should be defined, taking into consideration situational variables.

In a series of articles on cost-effectiveness analysis and its use to evaluate educational programs, Doughty (1979), Lent (1979), Beilby (1980), and Klein and Doughty (1980) discuss conceptual and practical criteria for judging cost-effectiveness, presented models for applying cost analysis to decisions about educational technology applications, and provide a case study of these analysis techniques applied to an innovative program in higher education. Klein and Doughty (1980) also reflect on their experience of conducting a cost-effectiveness study and presented both benefits and problems that resulted from it.

While cost analyses of instructional systems have not appeared in great numbers on a national level, they have often been an important part of studies on education in other countries. Tsang (1988) reviews cost studies in education conducted in developing nations, and concludes with recommendations well worth the attention of instructional systems researchers anywhere.

Technique and Model Development

Briggs (1982) suggests that future research in instructional systems include both model and technique development and validation. As learning environments grow more diverse and learners participate more in determining what they will learn, new models of instructional design or substantial revisions to old ones may be warranted. Similarly, as content to be learned grows more problematic, new techniques for analyzing and presenting it may be required. It has also been a fond hope that instructional systems may one day have an impact on public school education. Perhaps a new model that takes account of teachers' as well as students' needs will make this possible.

Technique development was the object of Driscoll and Tessmer (1985) and Smith and Wedman (1988). Driscoll and Tessmer devised a new method for systematically creating examples for teaching concepts and testing student acquisition of them. The method produces examples that cover a full range of concept discrimination and generalization. Smith and Wedman employed a new means for collecting useful formative evaluation data from students: read/think-aloud protocols. As for model development, Keller (1987) represents an excellent example of meeting an increasingly critical need in instructional systems with his ARCS model of motivational design.

SUMMARY

The examples described above are by no means exhaustive of what has been or could be done in instructional systems research. It is also worth noting that research paradigms need not be applied singly to answer questions of interest. Rather, it may be to our advantage to combine them, as in, for example, a hypothetical quasi-experimental study investigating differential effects of two instructional strategies that also include measures of development time and cost.

CONCLUSION

We will miss asking and investigating important questions concerning our instructional design models, their implementations, and their applications if we hold to a narrow view regarding research. Experimental designs have predominated on our research scene, and they do answer some of our questions, particularly with reference to single and interacting learning variables. But, lest we become myopic, let us permit our view to embrace a range of inquiry paradigms for research in instructional systems. Our field can only gain from this approach.

REFERENCES

Abrami, P. C., Cohen, P. A., & d'Appollonia, S. (1988). Implementation problems in meta-analysis. *Review of Educational Research, 58*(2), 151-180.

Allen, J. D. (1986). Classroom management: Students' perspectives, goals, and strategies. *American Educational Research Journal, 23*(3), 437-459.

Baird, J. R., & White, R. T. (1982). A case study of learning styles in biology. *European Journal of Science Education, 4*(3), 325-337.

Bangert, R. L., Kulik, J. A., & Kulik, C. C. (1983). Individualized systems of instruction in secondary schools. *Review of Educational Research, 53*, 143-158.

Beilby, A. (1980). Determining instructional costs through functional cost analysis. *Journal of Instructional Development, 3*(2), 29-34.

Borich, G. D., & Jemelka, R. P. (1982). *Programs and systems: An evaluation perspective.* New York: Academic Press.

Briggs, L. J. (1982). Instructional design: Present strengths and limitations, and a view of the future. *Educational Technology, 22*(10), 18-23.

Cook, T. D., & Campbell, D. T. (1979). *Quasi-experimentation: Design and analysis issues for field settings*. Boston: Houghton Mifflin.

Cooley, W. W., & Lohnes, P. R. (1976). *Evaluation research in education: Theory, principles and practice*. New York: Irvington.

Cunningham, D. J. (1987). Outline of an education semiotic. *American Journal of Semiotics, 5*(2), 201-216.

Doughty, P. (1979). Cost-effectiveness analysis trade-offs and pitfalls for planning and evaluation of instructional programs. *Journal of Instructional Development, 2*(4), 17, 23-25.

Driscoll, M. P., & Tessmer, M. (1985). The rational set generator: A method for creating concept examples for teaching and testing. *Educational Technology, 25*(2), 29-32.

Ebmeier, H., & Good, T. L. (1979). The effects of instructing teachers about good teaching on the mathematics achievement of fourth grade students. *American Educational Research Journal, 16*(1), 1-16.

Erickson, F. (1985). Qualitative methods in research on teaching. In M. C. Wittrock (Ed.), *Handbook of research on teaching* (3rd ed., pp. 119-161). New York: Macmillan.

Goetz, J. P., & LeCompte, M. D. (1984). *Ethnography and qualitative design in educational research*. Orlando, FL: Academic Press.

Grabe, M., & Latta, R. M. (1981). Cumulative achievement in a mastery instructional system: The impact of differences in resultant achievement motivation and persistence. *American Educational Research Journal, 18*(1), 7-14.

Guba, E. G., & Lincoln, Y. S. (1981). *Effective evaluation*. San Francisco: Jossey-Bass.

Hannafin, M. J. (1983). Fruits and fallacies of instructional systems: Effects of an instructional systems approach on the concept attainment of Anglo and Hispanic students. *American Educational Research Journal, 20*(2), 237-250.

Hanson, R. A., & Schutz, R. E. (1978). A new look at schooling effects from programmatic research and development. In D. Mann (Ed.), *Making change happen*. New York: Teachers College Press.

Hedges, L. V., & Olkin, I. (1985). *Statistical methods for meta-analysis*. Orlando, FL: Academic Press.

Heinich, R. (1970). *Technology and the management of learning*. Washington, DC: Association for Educational Communications and Technology.

Keller, J. M. (1987). Development and use of the ARCS model of motivational design. *Journal of Instructional Development, 10*(3), 2-10.

Klauer, K. J. (1984). Intentional and incidental learning with instructional texts: A meta-analysis for 1970-1980. *American Educational Research Journal, 21*(2), 323-339.

Klein, J., & Doughty, P. (1980). Cost-effectiveness evaluation: A case study of an innovative program in higher education. *Journal of Instructional Development, 3*(3), 19-24.

Kuhn, T. S. (1970). *The structure of scientific revolutions*. Chicago: University of Chicago Press.

Kulik, J. A., & Kulik, C. C. (1988). Timing of feedback and verbal learning. *Review of Educational Research, 58*(1), 79-97.

Lent, R. (1979). A model for applying cost-effectiveness analysis to decisions involving the use of instructional technology. *Journal of Instructional Development, 3*(1), 26-33.

Lincoln, Y. S., & Guba, E. G. (1985). *Naturalistic inquiry.* Beverly Hills, CA: Sage.

Salisbury, D. F., & Klein, J. D. (1988). A comparison of a microcomputer progressive state drill and flashcards for learning paired associates. *Journal of Computer-Based Instruction, 15*(4), 136-143.

Shank, G. (1987). Abductive strategies in educational research. *American Journal of Semiotics, 5*(2), 270-290.

Smith, P. L., & Wedman, J. F. (1988). Read/think-aloud protocols: A new data source for formative evaluation. *Performance Improvement Quarterly, 1*(2), 13-22.

Tsang, M. C. (1988). Cost analysis for educational policymaking: A review of cost studies in education in developing countries. *Review of Educational Research, 58*(2), 181-230.

Tuckman, B. W. (1988). *Conducting educational research.* (3rd ed.). San Diego, CA: Harcourt Brace Jovanovich.

Yin, R. K. (1984). *Case study research.* Beverly Hills, CA: Sage.

30

Qualitative Research— A Case for Case Studies

Rhonda S. Robinson
Northern Illinois University

A grounded theory examination of the visual aspects of interactive televised instruction in a distance learning setting ... (Oliver, 1992)

A one teacher case study of the connection between pedagogy and practice in a technologically advanced first grade class room ... (Dana, 1993)

An ethnographic examination of one school's use of *Channel One* ... (Robinson, 1994)

An in-depth description of what instructional designers *really* do "on the job" ... (Pitlik, unpublished)

A critical analysis of educational film, its hidden assumptions and messages ... (Trudell, 1990)

A close reading of educational television and its underlying structure ... (DeVaney, 1994)

A study which developed alternate methods for conducting formative evaluation of interactive video ... (Savenye, 1992)

A participant-observer study of one school's use of video production instruction as part of a new form of literacy, combining print, video and computer technologies ... (Reilly, 1994)

All these recent studies were conducted by educational technology scholars using qualitative methods. The ways of knowing from which they were designed are nonpredictive ones. The types of questions they address are noncomparative, noncausative, and nondirectional. In other words, they are all qualitative studies, using a variety of methods and designs to approach interesting question areas and types of data collection.

What is qualitative research? How does it differ in intent or results from the more common quantitative research in educational technology? What is the paradigm shift that has resulted in qualitative methods becoming more important to our field in the past few years? And what methods should a researcher study prior to proposing a qualitative study?

Short portions of this chapter have appeared previously in the *Journal of Thought*, 25, 1&2, Spring 1990, and in the 1987 *Proceedings* of the Association of Educational Communications and Technology national convention. Both publications have given permission for use.

This chapter introduces the background and history of qualitative research in educational technology, explains the paradigm quandary, and suggests issues important to the future of qualitative research in our field. A variety of references are listed for further investigation of the topic.

BACKGROUND

Emerging as a separate field in the 1940s, educational technology drew upon theory bases from psychology, learning, and perception. The field was derived primarily from behavioral and cognitive psychology, and consequently based its seminal research on strict experimental models appropriate to the early questions and hypotheses developed. Media was tested experimentally and found (at the time) to be effective.

In the 40 years of research that followed, the same positivist paradigm predominated. New media were tested against old, characteristics of learners and specific media were compared, and relationships between learners and media were explored, all using various accepted experimental designs.

More recently, the field has broadened its definition to include instructional design, media analysis, and learner attitudes, among other topics. Researchers are asking a variety of new questions, many of which would be difficult to examine using traditional experimental methods. Currently, most of the published scholarship in educational technology has been based upon experimental and descriptive studies. The leading researchers, those who train future scholars in research methods, have only recently begun to accept a full range of research methodologies for educational technology. Consequently, educational technology journals publish few reports based upon nonexperimental designs. Because reports of alternate methodologies are few, researchers in educational technology have only the models of research reports in other fields to assist them in research design and reporting.

The experimental "bias" in educational technology has been questioned by many researchers seeking to expand the areas of scholarship in the field. Becker (1977) recommended alternate methodologies to approaching educational technology research. Cochrane et al. suggested that researchers base new areas of inquiry on "the ethnography of situations in which people use visual materials (an anthropological approach)" (1980, p. 247). They stressed the importance of recognizing that visual learning is a cultural phenomenon and should be studied with techniques and analyses appropriate to cultural processes. Heinich (1984), in his N.I.E.-funded 10-year review paper, encouraged researchers to engage in more "naturalistic" inquiry. "Through the use of naturalistic inquiry, I am sure we will discover important factors ... that have been ignored too long ..." (p. 84). Heinich also argued that such research should be encouraged in dissertation work and should be more disciplined and more perceptive than experimental studies.

Alternative methodologies would lead the field of educational technology to new questions and to often ignored areas, such as the impact of educational technologies on social relationships and educational institutions. Kerr suggested that methods drawn from sociology, policy sciences, and anthropology could "shed new light on problems that have traditionally been approached using psychological research methods" (1985, p. 4). Kerr felt that asking new questions in less traditional ways was critical to the future of education.

This growing need for studies that do not appear to fit the traditional experimental paradigm has been recognized. Yet training of researchers continues in the traditional vein. Coursework provides extensive knowledge and experience primarily in experimental research studies (of the traditional, single variable, hypothesis-testing variety).

THE PARADIGM DEBATE

Recently, much debate in educational technology has emerged around the "paradigm shift" that many scholars are noting if not applauding. There seem to be three basic approaches to this debate. First, the "died-in-the-wool" empirical researchers, whose training and practice have long been accepted, see questions for research that require quantitative methods for inquiry. When these researchers discuss the "paradigms" of educational technology, they are generally discussing the variety of technologies and design techniques needing further investigations. Some of these researchers have not yet acknowledged that meaningful results can be derived from any other way of knowing the world. Their view is often called a positivistic approach to knowing.

Second, some researchers and scholars report that they appreciate both perspectives: the positivist and the more "naturalistic." Often, however, these researchers have confused methods of inquiry with actual paradigms of knowing. They will report that they have accepted qualitative methods, but those methods are merely one more data-gathering technique in an empirical study. There is a large difference between recommending surveys or interviews or even observation and recommending that the field consider a paradigm other than the scientific paradigm now guiding our research.

Third are the researchers whose ideas encompass a more critical theory perspective, like those represented in the February 1994 *Educational Technology*, edited by Yeaman, Koetting, and Nichols. Many in this group have explored, discovered, and integrated new paradigms for knowing into their own approaches to educational technology. They have acknowledged that "knowing" can take on many meanings and that our field has been limited by its past sense of the "known." They question the prevailing paradigm under which our research is conducted. The nonscientific paradigm can be productively used to develop new areas and methods of research in instructional technology. Such methods as linguistic analysis, phenomenology, case study, grounded theory, action, participation, observation, and simulation can all be "borrowed" from other well-defined and -developed disciplines and applied to our field. These methods have as their advantage the development of breadth and depth of research not possible in the experimental methods.

This awkward paradigm debate has misserved the progress of our field. Instead of arguing which side we face, or belittling the contributions of the other side, we should be debating how to best improve and enhance the progress of our field. With such acceptance of a duality of perspectives would come great growth and some much-needed refocusing of directions.

Our field has been criticizing itself long enough. For 10 years valued scholars have gently (or not so gently) indicated that we need new questions, new fields of inquiry, and new horizons for innovation. We have read and discussed these recommendations—but where is the debate leading us? The educational world still has a fairly limited and skewed idea of what kind of contributions educational technologies can make to the improvement of education. We have yet to be embraced, or even approached, as part of the solution to the crisis in education or the answer to the challenge of the next century.

The paradigm debate should be declared a draw. If we would just accept that there are many ways of knowing and many questions left unanswered, we could proceed. Those scholars interested in perfecting experimental techniques to investigate the effectiveness of specific design, production, or utilization of technologies could proceed to do so, but with the understanding that they are asking only part of the question, that they are focusing on external reports and not the whole learner.

Conversely, those involved in "alternate" paradigms should drop that term from their vocabularies. All ways of knowing and all social constructs should be equally accepted and represented in our literature. Not just methodologies but approaches to understanding should be accepted and incorporated into the teaching and practice of research in our field. Individuals should be encouraged to question and consider how they approach the world, how they understand learning, and how they believe knowledge is achieved. If these kinds of questions were encouraged from the outset, we could all have more confidence in the results of research conducted from any perspective. It is time for our field to move ahead, to accept the dual perspectives of our paradigm debate, if we are to meet the challenges of the future and be at all helpful in shaping the educational success of the next century.

QUALITATIVE METHODOLOGY

As to how we actually learn to approach new problems and to conduct research in new ways, our field has few answers. In 1986-87 I surveyed program chairpersons to ask them to describe ways in which research skills were taught in their programs (Robinson & Ong, 1987). Many reported that the courses in research methodology were housed in educational psychology programs. Others mentioned that their program had a research planning course in which students learned to pose appropriate questions and design effective methods of inquiry. Most acknowledged that they encouraged students to "use appropriate methods to investigate their questions when designing research studies." However, very few programs included any coursework that introduced the paradigm shift that was just starting to emerge, and even fewer had any organized way in which all approaches to research-question generation were introduced. In other words, although students learning research methods were being "encouraged to design studies to appropriately answer their questions," few students were given help in posing nonexperimental questions.

In universities where both quantitative and qualitative methods are introduced, students are provided the range of possibilities for questions and issues that raise researchable problems. Although the balance is still in favor of quantitative research, several noted programs are introducing students to a variety of research methods and to the paradigm shift as earlier discussed. What seems necessary is not just the availability of coursework, but the encouragement of faculty to help students develop a research agenda that expands beyond the traditional.

As a person possibly fairly new to the field, how does all this affect you? You may not yet see how the research agenda of the field is changing, or how it has affected what we know and study, or how we define ourselves. However, you should recognize that it is the research of our field that defines what the field considers important, what areas of inquiry approach the important issues. (Refer to several other chapters in this text for examples.)

With new methods and critical perspectives emerging as both acceptable and valued additions to our research, how is one to proceed? Any student reviewing a topic of interest will find primarily quantitative research reports from which to discover the "stuff" of our field. Only recently have qualitative studies been published in our major journals and as chapters in research-related books. When reviewing literature to understand content, to discover the "rules" that govern our design, development, and our utilization of technology, that literature which is most helpful is either quantitative or anecdotal. That is, the information is either drawn from experimental treatments or from experience. However, a great deal of information is left out when the literature does not also include any case study or ethnographic looks at the content areas in question. Our field, as has been established, has suffered somewhat from this drive for *how-to* information at the expense of *why* and *how-come* inquiry.

A common topic for a research project in education technology is any new innovation involving technology. As you know, film, radio, television, and programmed instruction were all researched innovations of their time. More recently, computer-assisted instruction and various instructional design components have been the focus of much research. So it seems natural that when a new application of technology is initiated researchers will follow the models of the past and begin to investigate its use and value using comparative questions, such as "How effective is this technology?" or "How well do students learn using this?"

The rest of this section presents an example of using qualitative research. Whittle Communications offered an innovative project to help schools deal with geographic and current events illiteracy in presenting their *Channel One* program to junior and senior high schools throughout the country. By offering school districts equipment and wiring in exchange for commercial minutes, Whittle created quite a bit of interest in this link between business and education interests. One group of scholars were attracted to the diversity of issues presented by this project and saw it as a perfect laboratory for a variety of problems, questions, and research.

Using traditional methods, the questions that would be appropriate would include: How well do students learn? How effective is the program in conveying information about world geography and current events? How does the program affect students' knowledge of these topics? How do students using *Channel One* compare to those learning in more traditional ways? Who tests better on current events tests, students using *Channel One* or students without it?

Considering the types of questions appropriate to a qualitative perspective, a different set of research issues would emerge. Qualitative researchers ask *how?* and *why?* and *with what effect?* The impact of the program, the description of the classrooms, the policy makers' and decision makers' thought processes, and the students' reactions and preferences all become important. A series of studies, published as *Watching Channel One* (1994, ed. DeVaney), includes both quantitative and qualitative studies, and shows the differences in problem areas, question formation, data collection, and analysis that help define both types of research methods. The book is also an excellent example of applying structural and poststructural theories to research projects, and has several chapters that analyze media as text. Researchers seeking models of research reports using qualitative methods would do well to seek out these and others cited within that text. Other sources for information about specific methods and research examples are listed in the references.

QUALITATIVE RESEARCH DEFINITIONS

One of the confusions around qualitative research is the variety of definitions and terms used and misused in the literature. Although the following list is not exhaustive, it should help in giving meaning to the discussion. We must keep in mind that "the need to label our studies or identify ourselves as working within particular scholarly traditions is partly self-imposed, partly the result of institutional requirements and academic posturing" (Wolcott, 1990, p. 45). Wolcott also reminds us that we should not fault a study incorrectly labeled, but consider its worth as determined by whether or not the report is "thorough, informative, and insightful" (p. 45).

Qualitative research is a very complex entity with definitions that change over time. In tracing this development through five historical moments, Denzin and Lincoln offer a current definitions "summary" statement, which declares that

> Qualitative research is multimethod in focus, involving an interpretive, naturalistic approach to its subject matter. This means that qualitative researchers study things in their natural settings, attempting to make sense of, or interpret, phenomena in terms of the meanings people bring to them ... [using a] variety of empirical materials— case study, personal experience, introspective, life story, interview, observational, historical, interactional, and visual texts—that describe routine and problematic moments and meanings in individuals' lives (Denzin & Lincoln, 1994, p. 2).

Naturalistic research helps to understand "the persons involved, their behavior and perceptions, and the influence of the physical, social, and psychological environment or content on them" (Smith & Glass, 1987, p. 257).

A *case study* is a research method that attempts to address questions of how or why, within a real-life situation over which the researcher has little control (Yin, 1989).

Ethnography has been defined as "the art and science of describing a group or culture" (Fetterman, 1989, p. 11), and involves detailed investigation of a small number of cases, even one, with unstructured data. *Participant observation* is research carried out by a person "playing an established role in the scene studied" (Denzin and Lincoln, 1994, p. 248). "Both ethnography and participant observation have claimed to represent a uniquely humanistic, interpretive approach, as opposed to supposedly 'scientific' and 'positivist' positions" (Denzin & Lincoln, 1994, p. 249).

Phenomenology is a process used to "understand the meaning of events and interactions to ordinary people in particular situations.... Phenomenologists believe that multiple ways of interpreting experiences are available to each of us through interacting with others, and that it is the meaning of our experiences that constitutes reality" (Bogdan & Biklin, 1992, p. 34). *Grounded theory* seeks to discover new questions by the "discovery of theory from data ..." which provides us with "relevant predictions, explanations, interpretations and applications" (Glaser & Strauss, 1967, p. 1).

Critical inquiry is a view derived from the arts and humanities and focuses on defining, expounding, and evaluating creative works or products and processes. Critical inquiry can include approaches such as semiotic, postmodern and deconstructionist, critical theory, and criticism and connoisseurship (Hlynka & Belland,1991).

Locating examples of each type of method is a difficult task. Several such reports were cited at the opening of the chapter. However, keep in mind that these methods are not mutually exclusive, but that some of them utilize differing theoretical constructs which make them incompatible.

In addition to the examples already noted in the *Channel One* text, the next best source for qualitative research reports is recent dissertations. Even though dissertation research is often the first such project undertaken by a student, it is students who are conducting and reporting much of the qualitative research in educational technology areas of interest. The studies mentioned at the opening of this chapter were conducted primarily by students or the professors at the institutions who have a longer history of encouraging qualitative work. The reference information is included for further review.

If this discussion and your own experience have convinced you to consider qualitative research methods or critical approaches to our research problems, how should you proceed?

1. Ask questions of the previous research reported in the topic area of your interest.

2. Consider knowledge as contextual and personal.

3. Read resources on qualitative research; take research courses; develop skills by doing exercises and practicing such techniques as interviewing, observing, and analyzing in natural settings.

4. Read other qualitative dissertations and research reports.

5. Find human resources on campus to help discuss and review your work.

6. Enlist in QUALRS-L or other electronic listservers available to help you keep involved in the dialogue about qualitative research.

7. Review the computer software, such as Ethnograph, available to help with data organization and analysis.

8. Believe in your questions and your approach; live with ambiguity and uncertainty while you work!

9. Enjoy your project!

10. Consider publishing sources only once you have finished; such journals as the *Journal of Visual Literacy*, the research section of *Educational Technology Journal*, and *ETR&D* publicize their interest in all methods, but you need to investigate publishing patterns to find an outlet for your work beyond conference presentations.

FUTURE CONSIDERATIONS

With these many methods and new ways of thinking becoming more accepted, there are several issues about qualitative research in our field that will need addressing. Answers may come from the social sciences or from further involvement of critical perspectives, but the questions will need to be faced. The first involves the reporting of qualitative research. Getting published is still very difficult because many qualitative studies are too long to condense to journal length, but scholarly publication in a refereed journal is still the "requirement" of untenured researchers. Also, the methods of reporting qualitative research projects, including essays, narrative reports, stories, novels, and (auto)biographical reports are still unaccepted as scholarly work in many of our research journals.

The second issue revolves around conducting research, because there seem to be fluid lines between methods and techniques. Some studies use visuals as data or as text to be analyzed. Others involve a substantial review of the literature done after the categories of the data have emerged from the study itself, rather than much literature being reviewed prior to the data collection. Issues about the participants are still worrisome as well; gaining confidentiality, getting institutional approval, involving participants in the research reports and data presentation, and maintaining anonymity when promised are all important.

A third issue is one that seems never to go away: the question of reliability and validity of qualitative research. Although many of the texts recommended for reviewing this topic deal with these two items, qualitative research still gets challenged by other researchers along these lines. Qualitative researchers have resolved the issue for themselves, but they still face the challenge from the quantitative side of the field.

Qualitative research in educational technology is needed. It is well-documented that the information derived qualitatively is interesting, vital, and necessary to the growth of our field. Qualitative methods are rigorous, complex, and learnable, if you take the time. Certainly, encouraging qualitative research projects will change our field in its direction, issues, and possibly even in our understanding of how we learn and perceive ourselves, our work, our world. Perhaps this introduction has encouraged you to begin the journey to understanding our field in that new way.

REFERENCES CITED

Becker, A. D. (1977). Alternative methodologies for instructional media research. *AV Communication Review, 25,* 181-194.

Cochrane, L. M., Younghouse, P. C., Sorflaten, J. W., & Molek, R. A. (1980). Exploring approaches to researching visual literacy. *Educational Communications and Technology Journal, 28,* 243-265.

Dana, A. S. (1993). Integrating technology into the classroom: Description of a successful first grade teacher. Unpublished doctoral dissertation, Northern Illinois University, DeKalb.

Denzin, N. K., & Lincoln, Y. S. (1994). *Handbook of qualitative research.* Thousand Oaks, CA: Sage.

DeVaney, A. (1994). Reading the ads: The Bacchanalian adolescence. In A. DeVaney (Ed.), *Watching Channel One.* Albany: SUNY Press.

Fetterman, D. M. (1989). *Ethnography: Step by step.* Newbury Park, CA: Sage.

Glaser. B. G., & Strauss, A. L. (1967). *The discovery of grounded theory: Strategies for qualitative research.* New York: Aldine.

Heinich, R. (1984). The proper study of instructional technology. *Educational Communication and Technology Journal, 32,* 67-88.

Hlynka, D., & Belland, J. C. (1991). *Paradigms regained.* Englewood Cliffs, NJ: Educational Technology Publications.

Kerr, S. T. (1985). Asking new questions about technology and the social world of education. *Educational Communications and Technology Journal, 33,* 3-8.

Oliver, E. L. (1992). Interaction at a distance: Mediated communication in televised courses. Unpublished dissertation, Northern Illinois University, DeKalb.

Pitlik, D. (1994). Habits of professionalism: An ethnographic investigation of the human enterprise of instructional design. Unpublished dissertation, Northern Illinois University, DeKalb.

Reilly, Brian. (1994). Composing with images: A study of high school video producers. *Proceedings of ED—MEDIA 94, Educational multimedia and hypermedia.* Charlottesville, VA: Association for the Advancement of Computing in Education.

Robinson, R. S. (1994). Investigating *Channel One*: A case study report. In A. DeVaney (Ed.), *Watching Channel One.* Albany: SUNY Press.

Robinson, R. S., & Ong, L. D. (1987). Naturalistic inquiry in educational technology. In Simonson & Jurasek (Eds.), *Proceedings* (of selected research and development presentations at the 1987 national convention of the Association of Educational Communications and Technology). Washington, DC: AECT.

Savenye, W. C. (1992). Alternate methods for conduction formative evaluations of interactive instructional technologies. *Proceedings* (of selected research and development presentations at the 1987 national convention of the Association of Educational Communications and Technology). Washington, DC: AECT.

Smith, M., & Glass, G. (1987). *Research and evaluation in education and the social sciences.* New York: Prentice-Hall.

Trudell, B. K. (1990). Selection, presentation, and student interpretation of an educational film on teenage pregnancy: A critical ethnographic investigation. In E. Ellsworth & M. H. Whatley (Eds.), *The ideology of images in educational media.* New York: Teacher's College Press.

Wolcott, H. F. (1990). Making a study more ethnographic. *Journal of Contemporary Ethnography, 12*(1), 44-72.

Yeaman, A. R., Koetting, J. R., & Nichols, R. G. (Eds.). (1994). Special issue: The ethical position of educational technology in society. *Educational Technology, 34*(2), 5-72.

Yin, R. K. (1989). *Case study research*, 2nd ed. Beverly Hills, CA: Sage.

ADDITIONAL SUGGESTED REFERENCES

Apple, M., & Jungck, S. (1990). "You don't have to be a teacher to teach this unit": Teaching, technology, and gender in the classroom. *AERJ, 27*(2), 227-251.

Belland, J., Duncan, J. K., & Beckman, M. (1991). Criticism as methodology for research in educational technology. In D. Hlynka & J. Belland (Eds.), *Paradigms regained.* Englewood Cliffs, NJ: Educational Technology Publications.

Bogdan, R. C., & Biklen, S. K. (1992). *Qualitative research for education: An introduction to theory and methods.* Boston: Allyn & Bacon.

Connelly, F. M., & Clandinin, D. J. (1990). Stories of experience and narrative inquiry. *Educational Researcher, 19*(5), 2-14.

Cruickshank, D. R. (1990). *Research that informs teachers and teacher educators*. Bloomington, IN: Phi Delta Kappa Educational Foundation.

Denzin, N. K., & Lincoln, Y .S. (1994). *Handbook of qualitative research*. Thousand Oaks, CA: Sage.

Driscoll, M. P. (1989, July). Alternate views: On nonexperimental inquiry in instructional systems. *Educational Technology*, 33-34.

Eisner, E. W. (1991). *The enlightened eye: Qualitative inquiry and the enhancement of educational practice*. New York: Macmillan.

Ellsworth, E., & Whatley, M. H. (Eds.). (1990). *The ideology of images in educational media*. New York: Teachers College Press.

Fletcher, J. D., Hawley, D. E., & Piele, P. K. (1990). Costs, effects and utility of microcomputer assisted instruction in the classroom. *AERJ, 27*(4), 783-806.

Gage, N. L. (1989). The paradigm wars and their aftermath: A "historical" sketch of research on teaching since 1989. *Teachers College Record, 91*(2), 135-149.

Goetz, J. & LeCompte, M. (1984). *Ethnography and qualitative design in educational research*. San Diego: Academic Press.

Guba, E. & Lincoln, Y. (1981). *Effective evaluation: Improving the usefulness of evaluation results through responsive and naturalistic approaches*. San Francisco: Jossey-Bass.

———. (1982). Epistemological and methodological bases of naturalistic inquiry. *Educational Communication and Technology Journal, 30,* 233-252.

Higgins, N., & Igoe, A. (1989). An analysis of intuitive and model-directed media-selection decisions. *ETR&D, 37*(4), 55-64.

Howe, K., & Eisenhart, M. (1990). Standards for qualitative (and quantitative) research: A prolegomenon. *Educational Researcher, 19*(4), 2-9.

Jacobs, E. (1987). Qualitative research traditions: A review. *Review of Educational Research, 57*(1), 1-50.

Knuth, R. A., & Goodrum, D. A. (1991, April). *Roundtable: A collaborative process tool to support the negotiation of meaning*. Paper presented at the Annual Meeting of the American Educational Research Association, Chicago, IL.

Lampert, M. (1990). When the problem is not the question and the solution is not the answer: *Mathematical Knowing and Teaching. AERJ, 27*(1), 29-64.

LeCompte, W. L. M., & Preissle, J., with Tesch, R. (1993). *Ethnography and qualitative design in educational research* (2nd edition). New York: Academic Press.

———. (Eds.). (1992). *The handbook of qualitative research in education*. New York: Academic Press.

Lincoln, Y. S., & Guba, E. G. (1985). *Naturalistic inquiry*. Beverly Hills, CA: Sage.

Marshall, C., & Rossman, G. B. (1989). *Designing qualitative research*. Newbury Park, CA: Sage.

Mathison, S. (1988). Why triangulate? *Educational Researcher, 17*(2), 13-17.

Merriam, S. B. (1988). *Case study research in education: A qualitative approach*. San Francisco: Jossey-Bass.

Merriam, S. B., & Simpson, E. L. (1984). *A guide to research for educators and trainers of adults*. Malabar, FL: Robert E. Krieger.

Miller, S. I., & Fredericks, M. (1991). Post-positivistic assumptions and educational research. *Educational Researcher, 20*(4), 2-8.

Munbe, H. (1986). Metaphor in the thinking of teachers. *Journal of Curriculum Studies, 18*(2), 197-209.

Rankin, R. O. (1989). The development of an illustration design model. *ETR&D, 37*(2), 25-46.

Sherman, R. R., & Webb, R. B. (1988). *Qualitative research in education: Focus and methods.* London, New York, Philadelphia: Falmer Press.

Spindler. (1988). *Doing ethnography of schooling.* Prospect Heights, IL: Waveland.

Strauss, A. L. (1987). *Qualitative analysis for social scientists.* New York: Cambridge.

Strauss, A. L., & Corbin, J. (1990). *Basics of qualitative research.* Newbury Park, CA: Sage.

Wolcott, H. F. (1990). *Writing up qualitative research.* Newbury Park, CA: Sage.

31

Inquiry in Instructional Design and Technology
Getting Started

Gary J. Anglin
College of Education, University of Kentucky
Lexington, Kentucky

Steven M. Ross
College of Education, University of Memphis
Memphis, Tennessee

Gary R. Morrison
College of Education, University of Memphis
Memphis, Tennessee

A requirement of some master's degree programs and virtually all doctoral programs in instructional design and technology is that students do original research. Practicing professionals in various work settings also find themselves involved in research projects of various types. Clark (1978, p. 166) suggests that "one of the foremost goals of all doctoral programs is to produce graduates who are both capable of and motivated toward scholarship regardless of the professional roles they assume." What is research? How do we distinguish between research and other forms of discourse? One definition listed in the *Oxford English Dictionary* is that research is a "course of critical or scientific inquiry." For our purpose we will define research as disciplined inquiry which involves the use of established research methodologies.

There are several excellent books that discuss research methodologies for the social and behavioral sciences. Many of these books focus on specific aspects of doing research such as methods, design, and analysis (e.g., Bogdan & Biklen, 1982; Kirk, 1982; Shulman, 1988). Shulman (1988) lists various methods that help to define and are used in educational research. Shulman's listing includes historical studies, philosophical, case studies, ethnographic field studies, experiments, quasi-experiments, and surveys. In chapter 28 Marcy Driscoll discusses various research methods or paradigms for research in instructional systems. Why then should we write a chapter on doing inquiry in instructional design and technology?

First, we feel that graduate students, and for that matter anyone planning to do disciplined inquiry, should consider a number of points long before beginning a specific research project. We will discuss some of these considerations. Second, it is our belief that a most critical part of the process is selecting an area and topic. Thus we provide a framework for selecting a topic which we believe can be used regardless of the specific methodology used.

In the first section of the chapter general advice is offered to those who plan to make disciplined inquiry a part of their career and life. In the second section a specific approach is presented that we hope will help individuals select a specific topic for investigation. Some of our advice will be more appropriate for graduate students, but we think that much of it is appropriate for anyone who will do disciplined inquiry.

ADVICE

Reading

Are you just beginning a graduate program? Begin a regular program of reading now. You will be required to read a number of books and articles in the courses you complete. While this reading would certainly be part of your reading program, the approach we suggest encompasses much more than course reading. Become familiar with the library at your university. One way to get started is to make a list of the journals in the library that might include articles of interest in your field. Then produce an action plan for each semester or year that includes the dates and times you will view the table of contents of the journals on your list. Read the abstracts of the articles you have identified as potentially interesting. Then, read the articles you selected based on the content of the abstract. Also, keep an idea book. For each article you read, record *your* reactions to the article for future reference. Since many journals are quarterly you might plan to look at the journals on your list four or five times a year. Finally, select two or three significant journals in your field and review the table of contents of each journal for the last 10 years. Again, read the abstracts and selected articles; record your reactions to each author in your idea notebook. The intent at this stage is to *expand* your horizons, not *select* a specific research topic.

In addition to reading primary sources in journals we suggest that you also identify and read "significant" books in your area of specialization as well as in related disciplines. A number of these "must" readings will be identified for you in courses and in books and articles. For example, Reigeluth (1983) provides a list of significant contributors to instructional design theory. This list could provide a point of departure for your background reading in instructional design and technology. There are many other books in psychology, philosophy, communication, and organizational behavior which should be on your required reading list (e.g., Bowers, 1988; Flanagan, 1984; Gardner, 1985). In your idea notebook include a section titled "books to read." Remember, at first you are trying to broaden your perspective, both in your areas of specialization and in related disciplines.

Organization and Planning

The organization of daily life is also an important consideration for the intellectual worker. In a typical doctoral program students are required to complete a sequence of prescribed courses, written and oral examinations, a dissertation proposal, and a defense of the dissertation. Many students also work full- or part-time. With so many external requirements, obligations, and deadlines, organization and time allocation become essential. What are the requirements for intellectual work? How will you organize your days and use your time? Sertillanges (1960, p. 42) suggests that, "If you want to entertain knowledge as your guest, you do not need rare furniture, nor numerous servants. Much peace, a little beauty, certain conveniences that save time, are all that is necessary." We suggest that you consider the following goals when you plan and allocate your time:

1. Master your area of specialization,

2. Develop knowledge and skill with at least two research methods (Shulman, 1988),

3. Interact with students and faculty outside of formal classes, seminars, and work settings,

4. Become involved in research projects, and

5. Include some time for inspiration and renewal.

You will spend a significant portion of time mastering your discipline and developing knowledge and skill concerning research methods. Coursework and related reading, practica, and internships are the primary means used to help students master their area of specialization and develop mastery of research methods. Doctoral program requirements will usually emphasize goals one and two.

We believe that informal interaction with other students and faculty is a critical component of intellectual growth. Many questions are asked in an informal setting that would not surface in a class or work setting. Also, a sense of group cohesiveness is usually developed. One approach is to organize an informal group that meets for dinner on a regular basis. In some instances faculty initiate such gatherings. However, do not wait for someone else to be the organizer; take the initiative yourself.

Professional meetings also provide a means for you to interact with other individuals who are doing research. You can get involved by presenting a paper, attending graduate student programs, or volunteering to serve on a committee. Some professional organizations offer conference internships for graduate students. There are many professional organizations that you may want to consider joining, including the Association for Educational Communications and Technology, the American Educational Research Association, and the National Society for Performance and Instruction.

A significant goal to set for yourself is to become involved in a research project early in your graduate student years. Identify a faculty member whose research interests appear interesting to you and volunteer to help collect and evaluate articles, collect and code data, or assist with the development of stimulus materials. Depending on your level of involvement, you could end up being a co-author when the results are published. There is much to learn from classes and related readings about doing research. But there are also many things you will learn only if you become involved in doing research.

The organization of your life should also include time for inspiration and renewal. There are a number of activities you could consider, depending on your preferences and interests. Involvement with the arts, general reading, and camping are a few. Identify activities that inspire you and make sure to include them in your plan. Guitton (1964, p. 47) states that "it is a serious misunderstanding of the mind's nature to think of it only in terms of activity."

We have offered advice on getting started with inquiry in a doctoral or master's program. It was suggested that two critical areas are development of a plan for reading and the organization of daily life. Assuming you have followed our advice in "Reading" above, you have implemented a regular reading plan and are in the process of achieving the five goals we identified. How might you get started doing primary research?

PLANNING RESEARCH

How do you get started in planning a research study? The main problem for many beginning researchers is putting the cart before the horse, which in research parlance translates into selecting methods, a design, or worse, a statistical analysis procedure (as in "Won't I need to use analysis of variance to get my dissertation approved?") before clearly deciding what questions they want to investigate. The usual result of such "backward planning" is a collection of methods that lack a unifying purpose of direction. To help you avoid this error, the following pages present a seven-part model that will guide you through a logical sequence of planning steps.

Selecting a Topic

What general topic area interests you? Is it adaptive instruction, learner control, computer programming, or some other focus? A research study should be thought of as something that you will live with for awhile, perhaps a year and probably more (not too much more, we hope, for your thesis or dissertation!). A "shot-gun" marriage with a topic area that doesn't interest you, but is imposed by your advisor or suggested by a best friend, is almost certain to be an unpleasant experience. Research can be fun and involving when you have a natural curiosity about the subject; it can be drudgery when you don't.

Identifying the Research Problem

The next step is to determine what problem or concern to investigate within your topic area. Sometimes the problem will be immediately identifiable based on your present knowledge and interests. In other instances, it may be only a general idea that needs to be more carefully considered and sharpened. For example, a few years ago, one of us became interested in children's solving of math word problems. The particular idea was making word problems more interesting to students to increase motivation and learning. The basis for a research problem was thus established, but some library time was needed to sharpen the premises and specific focus. Through a review of the literature, the problem evolved into one concerning whether meaningful learning could be enhanced by using a microcomputer to personalize problems for each student. Regardless of your focus, a thorough literature search will be essential here and/or at various other places in the planning process.

Conducting a Literature Search

Although there are several approaches to doing a literature review, a few key ideas and techniques can help you improve your efficiency. A starting point for a search is the journal indexes, such as *Psychological Abstracts*, *Current Index to Journals in Education* (*CIJE*), or *Research in Education* (*RIE*). To gain the most efficiency in using these indexes, you must start with two or three key terms. These terms are listed in the respective thesauri for each index. Thus, a few minutes spent locating key terms can make your search time more efficient. A second approach is to find the citation in one of the indexes for a key article you have read and note the terms used to classify the article. These terms are your starting point for the literature review and may need to be revised as you make progress.

There are two approaches to searching these indexes. First is year by year through the bound volumes. Although this approach is laborious and you might not find every article, it does allow you to browse. You may also find other articles of interest in the process. Second is a computerized search that uses an electronic database stored on a main frame or CD-ROM. The electronic search is very fast and thorough for the key terms *entered*. Unfortunately, you cannot browse through articles stored before or after the one the computer selected. While it is easy to generate a list of 100 articles, computer-based searches provide a false sense of security that all the related articles have been identified. Both of these approaches are just the beginning of the search.

The next step is to retrieve the articles your search identified. A trip to the library, however, requires some planning. First, write each of your references on a notecard. Second, sort the cards chronologically and then alphabetically by journal. Third, gather your supplies, which should include extra notecards, a pen and pencil, paper clips, and money for the copy machines. Fourth, read through your index cards and classify the articles by their relevance to your study (e.g., critical, probable, or "long shot").

When you arrive at the library, ask a librarian where information is kept concerning the location of journals. For example, current journals are probably located in one place, bound journals in another location, and microfilmed journals in another room. Organize your research according to the importance of the articles ("critical" ones first). You might want to make a photocopy of important articles and only make notes on others.

Your initial search will probably identify one or more key articles. One way to expand the search is to read the references cited in those articles. This approach, however, only provides you with older articles. Another option is to search through the *Social Sciences Citation Index* to see if your key articles are cited elsewhere. This method provides more recent articles on your topic. To broaden your search, a third strategy is to examine indexes of journals in related fields and of related international journals.

Problem Articles

There may be times when you cannot locate a particular journal or ERIC paper. There are six strategies for obtaining these elusive papers. First, check with your librarian to see if another library in the area has the journal. Many libraries have such a list and exchange agreements with other libraries. Second, order a copy through interlibrary loan. This process may take a few days and possibly cost a few dollars, but it is quite reasonable. Third, write to the author and request a copy. Current addresses are available through association directories. Most authors are pleased to know that someone is reading their research and may even include additional articles. Fourth, try to order the article through University Microfilms as either a microfilm or paper copy. Fifth, ask your librarian to help you locate the journal published and then call and request to purchase a single back issue. Sixth, if you are searching for a paper in ERIC, check *Psychological Abstracts* and *CIJE* for a three-year period after the paper was presented to see if it was published in a journal.

Stating the Research Questions

We have now reached what is probably the most critical step in the planning process. Once defined, research questions provide the basis for planning all other parts of the study: design, materials, and data analysis. Unfortunately, it is sometimes difficult to convince beginning researchers of this. As stated earlier, a common tendency is to focus much too early on which treatments to compare or what design (e.g., experimental or correlational) to use. These decisions are obviously important, but they cannot be reasonably addressed until you know exactly what you want to find out. Research questions convey those goals.

At this point you have identified a problem (step 2) and are familiar with the literature (step 3). Based on this background, what specific questions do you want your study to answer? As you think of questions, write them down in a list. Don't worry about their exact phrasing, whether others will like them, or having too many. Before you actually begin the study, there will be many opportunities (perhaps a lot more than you want!) to present your ideas to others and obtain reactions. Chances are that you will also revisit the library to read more about a specific theory or prior study. Thus, this initial list will probably not be the final one, but will serve as a useful starting point for planning how the study will be performed. As an example, table 31.1 lists the questions used in the personalization study referred to earlier. In the following pages, we return to this table to illustrate how research questions directly guide subsequent planning steps.

Table 31.1.
Example of Research Questions and Procedural Planning for an Actual Study

Questions	Design	Instrumentation	Statistical Analysis
1. Will personalizing contexts improve problem solving relative to using concrete or abstract contexts?	Experimental: Three Groups	a. Achievement tests	One-way Analysis of Variance
2. Will personalizing contexts improve attitudes toward the lesson?	Experimental: Three Groups	b. Attitude survey	One-way Analysis of Variance
3. Are attitudes and problem solving performance related?	Correlational	a and b	Pearson Correlation
4. What are the logistics of personalizing problems?	Descriptive	c. Experimenter journal	Narrative report
5. What are teacher's reactions about the practicality and value of the personalized strategy?	Descriptive	d. Interview	Narrative report

Determining the Research Design

Your research design will be determined primarily by two factors: (1) what the research questions require (of course!), and (2) what is feasible given the resources or conditions at hand. Space restrictions limit how much can be said here about different design approaches, but, as a brief introduction, we'll note three general categories. *Experimental-type* designs are used to test hypotheses regarding causation; for example, that a particular instructional strategy leads to better student performance. Making causal inferences requires a high degree of experimental control, such that all conditions for the "treatment" group and the control group are identical except for the particular strategy being tested. A true experimental design, in which subjects are randomly assigned to treatments, is best able to achieve this control, but is oftentimes impractical. A quasi-experimental design, which uses intact groups (e.g., two existing classes), is less rigorous but generally easier to implement. Additional design categories are the *correlational* and *descriptive* approaches. Correlational studies examine how variables relate to one another (e.g., amount of computer experience and attitudes toward word processing) rather than whether one causes the other. Descriptive studies depict conditions as they exist in a particular setting (e.g., the number of teachers at different grade levels who use computer-based instruction).

Equipped with a basic knowledge of design approaches, the next task is to determine what is needed for each research question. Your study may therefore include several approaches; for example, an experimental part and a descriptive part. To illustrate, the second column of table 31.1 lists the designs used to address the research questions in the personalization study. Note that where treatment groups were compared on some dependent (outcome) measure, an experimental design was specified. Question 3, concerning a relationship between variables, naturally required correlation. Questions 4 and 5 were descriptive in nature, concerning the researcher's experiences in implementing the personalization strategy and the teachers' reactions to its instructional use. Keep in mind that as a beginning researcher you do not have to be a design expert; your advisor or committee are there to help you in this area.

Determining Methods

Methods of the study include (1) subjects (participants), (2) materials and instrumentation, and (3) procedures. What kind and how many participants does your research design require? For the present example (table 31.1), it was decided that to manipulate the three treatments (questions 1 and 2) we would need about 60 elementary school students. Two or three teachers would also be needed for the strategy evaluation (question 5).

Sometimes the specific resources needed will be obvious. When uncertainties exist, construct a list on a question-by-question basis. This procedure is illustrated in table 31.1 (column 3) for the identification of assessment instruments for the personalization study. Basic to all five research questions was obviously the need for a computer-based mathematics lesson that would convey the personalization and control strategies. A specific lesson idea and target grade level evolved through discussion with teachers and examination of curriculum materials. Because the lesson would be unique to our study, we were faced with designing our own achievement test (a common situation in educational research) and attitude survey to inquire about the particular materials used. As you plan your own research, a good rule to follow is to try to obtain existing validated instruments where you can; when existing measures provide a poor fit with your research questions, you will be better off developing your own using the guidelines described in most educational measurement texts.

The last step in planning the methodology is to develop a procedural plan. What logical sequence of steps will provide the information needed to answer the research questions? What materials will be used or information given to subjects at each step? You may find it helpful to begin by constructing a general outline. Once you become more confident about the basic procedures, the important task will be to describe them in narrative form (as required in a prospectus or proposal). Our best advice: Write the narrative so that another person could conduct the study for you just by reading it (this does not imply, however, that you'll ever find such a person). The more precise you are, the better basis you will have for conducting the study and your committee will have for evaluating it.

Identifying Statistical Analysis Procedures

Some beginning researchers can't wait to identify the statistics they will use, doing this (unfortunately) as the first rather than last step in the planning process. Others would be most happy if the statistical component somehow magically disappeared. For most types of research in instructional technology, some statistical analysis will be needed. The good news is that if you have gone through the preceding six steps, specifying an analysis plan is very straightforward and easy. If statistics aren't your strength, no need to worry. Show someone who knows statistics (usually there's such a person on your committee) a clear set of research questions and design descriptions, and that person will be able to identify readily what analyses are needed. Your task is then to learn from a practitioner's standpoint why those analyses are appropriate, what types of information they provide, and how to interpret those results. Interested readers can examine in table 31.1 (last column) a list of the analyses selected for the personalization study. Note that each is matched to a specific research question.

CONCLUSION

We hope that the suggestions and guidelines provided in the preceding sections will be helpful as you begin your involvement with research in your graduate program. Developing a plan of reading, taking appropriate courses in research methods and instructional technology applications, and assisting in faculty members' projects are important in establishing readiness to initiate your own research study. Using a systematic planning approach, such as the present seven-step model, will help you to identify and investigate problems that interest you and are currently of interest in the field. More important, a systematic approach is likely to result in a higher quality study and a much more positive experience for you as a new researcher.

REFERENCES

Bogdan, Robert C., & Biklen, S. K. (1982). *Qualitative research for education*. Boston: Allyn & Bacon.

Bowers, C. A. (1988). *The cultural dimensions of educational computing: Understanding the non-neutrality of technology*. New York: Teachers College Press.

Clark, R. E. (1978). Doctoral research training in educational technology. *Educational Communication and Technology Journal, 26*, 165-185.

Flanagan, O. J., Jr. (1984). *The science of mind*. Cambridge, MA: MIT Press.

Gardner, H. (1985). *The mind's new science: A history of the cognitive revolution*. New York: Basic Books.

Guitton, J. (1964). *A student's guide to intellectual work* (A. Foulke, Trans.). Notre Dame, IN: The University of Notre Dame Press. (Original work published 1951).

Jaeger, R. M. (Ed.). (1988). *Complementary methods for research in education*. Washington, DC: American Educational Research Association.

Kirk, R. E. (1982). *Experimental design*. (Rev. ed.). Belmont, CA: Brooks/Cole.

Reigeluth, C. M. (1983). Instructional design: What is it and why is it? In C. M. Reigeluth (Ed.), *Instructional-design theories and models: An overview of their current status*. Hillsdale, NJ: Lawrence Erlbaum.

Sertillanges, A. G. (1960). *The intellectual life: Its spirit, conditions, methods* (M. Ryan, Trans.). Westminster, MD: The Newman Press. (Original work published 1920).

Shulman, L. S. (1988). Disciplines of inquiry in education: An overview. In R. M. Jaeger (Ed.), *Complementary methods for research in education*. Washington, DC: American Educational Research Association.

32

Research on Instructional Media, 1978-1988

Richard E. Clark
University of Southern California
Los Angeles, California

and

Brenda M. Sugrue
Information Systems Division, National Institute for Higher Education
Limerick, Ireland

INTRODUCTION

This is the first of a series of annual reviews that will identify trends, discuss the implications of findings, and propose directions for future research in the area of instructional media. Although the reader may not find all relevant media studies discussed in this review, we will attempt to describe all important trends in the literature, focusing on research that defines *media* as technological devices employed for the purposes of instruction. However, we will also consider the relevance of emerging trends in research on instructional media for the development of a technology of instruction. We will begin by noting the paradigm shift that has occurred in research on instructional media during the past decade, from a behavioral to a more cognitive approach. We will briefly describe the argument for applying the new cognitive approach to media research and then expand on it in the body of the discussion. Next, we will introduce an extensive framework for organizing past and present research in a way that distinguishes between behavioral, cognitive, attitudinal, and economic issues relating to the use of instructional media. Finally, we will identify the most promising areas for future research.

The research for this chapter was largely completed while Richard Clark was Distinguished Visiting Professor at the National Institute for Higher Education in Limerick, Ireland. The authors wish to acknowledge Mr. Patrick Kelly, Director of the Information Systems Division at NIHE Limerick, for his encouragement and support for this research. Reprinted from *Educational media and technology yearbook 1988*. Englewood, CO: Libraries Unlimited.

PARADIGM SHIFT

In their recent review of the past decade of research on the use of media in teaching, Clark and Salomon (1986) noted that there has been a paradigm shift from behavioral to cognitive theories and corresponding research questions in instructional media research. This shift follows the transition in psychology from behavioral to cognitive theories of learning. A behavioral theory of learning focuses on environmental causes of changes in behavior without reference to the mental processes mediating such changes. In contrast, a cognitive theory of learning views learning as a constructive process, with the learner actively engaged in the process of integrating new knowledge with old. Factors that determine whether learning results from instruction are students traits such as general ability, prior knowledge, and motivation; learning task differences such as their procedural and declarative characteristics; and instructional methods that place more or less cognitive burden on learners. Within the new cognitive paradigm, learning may be defined as the degree to which previously learned knowledge and skills can be transferred to new contexts and problems.

Instructional Media Research in the Behavioral Paradigm

Under the behavioral paradigm, research on instructional media centered on the means of instruction as independent variables and on learning outcomes in the form of knowledge or skill acquisition as dependent variables. Media comparison studies dominated the research journals. These studies emphasized comparisons of the learning impact of newer media such as television with more traditional media such as classroom instruction. Evidence from these studies usually favored newer media. Thus, during the early days of the motion picture, studies tended to favor movies over teachers. Later, similarly designed studies favored television over teachers, movies, or textbooks. Other studies, inspired by the behaviorist preoccupation with reinforcement, investigated the reinforcement value of various media. As a result of these studies, conducted largely in the quarter century between 1950 and 1975, the media movement grew and prospered. Sometime after the early 1970s, however, a change began in the media literature—a change that reflected the move to cognitivism in the psychological literature.

Instructional Media Research in the Cognitive Paradigm

The cognitive paradigm acknowledges the interaction between external stimuli (presented by any medium) and internal, cognitive processes that support learning. Under the cognitive paradigm, cognitive processing is studied as a dependent or outcome variable, and learner characteristics are studied as independent or mediator variables. The assumption is that learners often affect the way they experience the instructional stimulus through their previously acquired beliefs, values, expectations, general ability, and prior knowledge of the subject matter. The cognitive paradigm ascribes to the learner a far more active and less externally controlled role in learning from instruction than did the behaviorist paradigm. So, with the advent of cognitive theories of learning, media comparison questions were discarded because they assumed that media alone contributed to learning. In the cognitive approach to research on instructional media, more attention is devoted to the way various media attributes (such as the imagery-evoking properties of visual presentations in memory tasks) interact with cognitive processes to influence learning. Thus, researchers began to examine how specific elements of an instructional message might activate particular cognitions for certain learners under specific task conditions. Aptitude-treatment interaction (ATI) research has been welcomed by media researchers who expect it not only to suggest which specific media attributes are most effective for whom but also to indicate the kinds of cognitions that are or may become involved in the processing of different types of symbol systems (Salomon, 1979).

Unlike previous research concerned with the comparison of different media, the next generation of researchers has investigated the way different modes of information presentation are processed by the learner and how these processing capabilities develop. The results of some of these studies appear to yield important implications for instruction. For example, Anderson and Lorch (1983) have found that children attend to televised material that is comprehensible to them, implying that comprehensibility determines attention rather than the other way around. This finding suggests that instructional production techniques should be oriented to convey comprehensible information rather than to attract attention. Newer media literacy programs are attempting to draw on this research and apply it to instructing children on how to get more selective knowledge out of mediated instruction (e.g., Dorr, Graves, & Phelps, 1980).

Generally, it appears that media do not affect learning in and of themselves. Rather, some particular qualities of media may affect particular cognitive processes that are relevant for students with specific aptitude levels to learn particular knowledge or skills. However, these cognitive effects are not necessarily unique to any particular medium or attribute of a medium. Later in this review, we will describe evidence supporting the claim that the same cognitive effect may be obtained by many media and media attributes. This suggests that media are functionally equivalent. This fact, discussed in detail in the next section, has led a number of researchers to claim that media do not influence learning but that they do greatly influence the cost (time, expense) of learning.

The change in the basic paradigm for instructional media research is not from an instructionally centered (situational) approach to a learner-centered (personological) one. Rather, it is a shift from a unidirectional view to a reciprocal view. The new cognitive paradigm assumes that instructional powers do not reside solely in the media, for the way we perceive media influences what we learn from them. However, learners are not the sole power brokers, for their perceptions are founded on the kinds of information and instructional methods delivered by different media. This assumption of reciprocity is identical to the one underlying recent advances made in other related fields such as personality research (e.g., Kyllonen, Lohman, & Snow, 1984), spatial cognition (e.g., Olson & Bialystok, 1983), aptitude processes (Kyllonen, Lohman, & Snow, 1984), and person-environment interaction (Salomon, 1974b).

There have been at least two results of the shift to the reciprocal, cognitive paradigm for media research. First, researchers have been attempting to identify critical attributes of media that not only distinguish between media in meaningful ways but also affect learning relevant cognitions. This led to clearer distinctions between the means of information delivery and manipulation (e.g., radio, computers, television, books) and other components of media, notably their intrinsic modes of information presentation and the kinds of mental operations they afford. The second result of the shift in focus is the long-overdue development of theories of learning from media that could guide recommendations on the use of particular media for particular instructional objectives.

FRAMEWORK FOR ORGANIZING RESEARCH ON INSTRUCTIONAL MEDIA

Research on instructional media can be classified according to the main independent and dependent variables studied. There are four main types of dependent variables of interest to researchers in this area: performance outcomes, cognitive processing, efficiency/costs, and equity of access to instruction. Although there are many acceptable candidates for a list of media research variables, three main types of independent variables frequently arise in the existing research: media characteristics (including type of medium, specific attributes of a medium, symbol systems available within a medium), student characteristics (including general ability, attributions, preferences, and prior knowledge), and instructional method. Any combination of these dependent and independent variables may be investigated in a particular study.

The research of the past decade has included the following combinations, which relate to four distinct types of issues:

- Behavioral Issues: effects of type of medium on achievement

- Cognitive Issues: effects of media attributes on cognitive processing and on achievement

    effects of instructional method on cognitive processing and achievement

    interactive effects of student aptitudes and instructional method on cognitive processing and achievement

- Attitudinal issues: interactive effects of student attitudes/attributions/expectations and instructional method or medium on cognitive processing and achievement

- Economic Issues: effects of type of medium on cost of instruction

    effects of type of medium on time for instruction.

These four types of issues are used here as the framework for organizing the research of the past decade.

RESEARCH RELATING
TO BEHAVIORAL ISSUES

Media Comparison Studies

Until recently, a typical study in the area of instructional media compared the relative achievement of groups who received similar subject matter from different media. With the advent of each new instructional medium, a new crop of such studies emerges, comparing the new medium with an older one. During the past decade, television research has diminished considerably, being replaced by computer-assisted learning studies, which belong to the familiar but generally fruitless media comparison approach. Each new medium seems to attract its own set of advocates who make claims for improved learning and stimulate research questions that are similar to those asked about the previously popular medium. Most of the radio research approaches suggested in the 1950s were very similar to those employed by the television movement of the 1960s (e.g., Schramm, 1977) and to the more recent reports of the computer-assisted instruction studies of the 1970s and 1980s (e.g., Clark, 1985). It seems that similar research questions have resulted in similar and ambiguous data. Media comparison studies, regardless of the media employed, tend to result in "no significant difference" conclusions. These findings have been incorrectly offered as evidence that different media are equally effective as conventional means in promoting learning. No significant difference results simply suggest that changes in the outcome scores (e.g., learning) did not result from any systematic differences in the treatments compared. In these studies, media are mere conveyances for the treatments being examined. Although media often are not the focus of study, the results are erroneously interpreted as suggesting that learning benefits had been derived from various media. So, for example, when a booklet containing a version of programmed instruction resulted in more learning than a teacher's lecture (minus the programmed instruction feature) on the same topic, the results are often interpreted as favoring the medium of books. The active ingredient, in studies that find one medium superior to another, is usually some uncontrolled aspect of the instructional method (e.g., programmed instruction) rather than the medium. In the 1970s, skepticism about media comparison studies, still being conducted in apparently large numbers, began to grow. Levie and Dickie (1973) noted that most overall media comparison studies to date had been fruitless and suggested that most learning objectives could be attained through "instruction presented by any of a variety of different media" (p. 859). This observation was echoed by Schramm (1977), who says, "learning seems to be affected more by what is delivered than by the delivery system" (p. 273).

During the past decade, more effort has been made to analyze and refocus the results of existing comparison studies. The statistical technique called meta-analysis has proved to be a most useful approach to summarizing instructional media (and other kinds of educational) research. The current meta-analyses of media comparison studies provide evidence that any reported significant differences in performance have been due to confounding in the treatments employed in the studies. Because this claim is somewhat controversial and the use of meta-analysis is expected to increase in the next few years, the next section presents a discussion of the advantages and disadvantages of meta-analyses when applied to media comparison studies.

Reviews and Meta-Analysis of Media Studies

A comprehensive and often-cited review by Jamison, Suppes, and Wells (1974) surveyed comparisons of traditional instruction with instruction via computers, television, and radio. Their survey used a *box score* tally of existing studies, evaluations, and reviews of research. They concluded that a small number of studies reported advantages for media and others indicated more achievement with traditional instruction, but the most typical outcome was no significant difference between the two. As they explained, "when highly stringent controls are imposed on a study, the nature of the controls tends to force the methods of presentation into such similar formats that one can only expect the 'no significant differences' which are found" (p. 38).

However, there have been criticisms of the box score method of summarizing past media research (e.g., Clark & Snow, 1975). Many of these criticisms have been accommodated by newer meta-analytic methods of teasing generalizations from past research. A recent series of meta-analyses of media research was conducted by James Kulik and his colleagues at the University of Michigan (Clark, 1985, contains citations for these meta-analyses). Generally, meta-analyses allow for a more precise estimate of treatment effect sizes than was possible a few years ago. Meta-analytic procedures yield *effect size estimates* that are converted to percentage of standard deviation gains on final examination scores due to the more powerful treatment, if any. Most of the meta-analytic surveys of media research demonstrate a typical learning advantage for newer media of about one-half a standard deviation on final examination performance, compared with conventional (i.e., teacher-presented) treatments. In the case of computer-based instruction studies in college environments, for example, this advantage translates as an increase from the 50th to the 66th percentile on final examinations in a variety of courses. This is an impressive accomplishment if we accept it at face value. Closer inspection of these reviews, however, reveals that most of the large effect sizes attributed to computers in these studies are actually due to poorly designed studies and confounding (Clark, 1983, 1985).

According to Clark (1983), the most common sources of confounding in media research seem to be the uncontrolled effects of (a) instructional method or content differences between treatments that are compared, and (b) a novelty effect for newer media, which tends to disappear over time. Evidence for each of these controlled effects can be found in the meta-analyses and will now be considered.

Uncontrolled Method and Content Effects
in Meta-Analytic Studies of Media

In effect size analyses, only adequately designed studies are supposed to be included in the statistical analyses. Studies chosen for the Kulik analyses represent a great variety of design features, subject matter content, learning task types, and grade levels. The most common result of box score surveys is a small and positive advantage for newer media over more conventional instructional delivery devices. However, when studies are subjected to meta-analysis, our first source of rival hypotheses, medium and method confusion due to poor research design, becomes evident. The positive effect for newer media more or less disappears when the same instructor produces all treatments (Clark, 1985). Different teams of instructional designers or different teachers probably give different content and instructional methods to the treatments that are compared. If this is the case, we do not know whether to attribute the advantage to the medium or to the differences between content and method being compared. However, if the effect for media tends to disappear when the same instructor or team designs contrasting treatments, we have reason to believe that the lack of difference is due to greater control of nonmedium variables.

Clark and Salomon (1986) cited a number of researchers in the past who have reminded us that when examining the effects of different media, only the media being compared can be different. All other aspects of the mediated treatments, including the subject matter content and method of instruction, must be identical in the two or more media being compared. In meta-analyses of college level computerized versus conventional courses, an effect size of one-half a standard deviation results when different faculty teach the compared course. Clark (1983) found that this effect reduces to about one-tenth of a standard deviation advantage when considering only studies in which one instructor plans and teaches both experimental and control courses. Presumably, this very weak but positive effect for college use of computers over conventional media is due to systematic but uncontrolled differences in content and/or method, contributed unintentionally by different teachers or designers.

The evidence in these meta-analyses pointing to confounding is that it is the method of instruction rather than the choice of medium that leads directly and powerfully to learning. The conclusion that media do not influence learning directly can be summed up in an analogy: In instruction, media serve a function similar to the different forms in which prescription medicines are delivered. One would not claim that a tablet or a liquid suspension of a drug altered the effects of the drug on human biological functions (except to make it more or less efficient). Nor is it important, except for efficiency purposes, whether a drug is administered by the medium of injection or by oral ingestion. It is the prescription compound that influences biology, not the medium of delivery. Here, the drug medium (tablet or liquid suspension) is analogous to the instructional medium of computer or teacher in education. It is not the computer that alters learning any more than the tablet influences biological processes in a different way than the liquid form of a drug. Both the choice of drug medium and instructional medium influence the efficiency and the cost of delivering the active ingredient. In neither case is the essential biology or psychology of the target systems influenced. The active compound in a drug is a mixture, analogous to what most of us call a combination of instructional method and information. It is the method, not the medium that influences the psychological processes that produce learning.

Since the inception of cognitive theory, methods are defined as external representations of the cognitive processes that are required for learning. Examples and analogies are instances of instructional methods as is the structure imposed on information that is presented during instruction. An example provides external support for one variety of a cognitive process that has been called *connecting*. Examples encourage us to connect new information with relevant prior experience. Analogies support a different type of cognitive connecting process. The analogy allows us to connect a current problem with the solution to that problem, which, while it is in our experience, we do not notice as relevant. When we first encountered mathematics, many of us profited from the analogy that adding and subtracting fractions was similar to slicing pie. Familiar teaching methods such as giving examples and analogies may be delivered by any of a variety of media with the same learning effects.

Uncontrolled Novelty Effects with Newer Media

A second, though probably less important, source of confounding in media comparison studies is the increased effort and attention research subjects tend to give to media that are novel to them. The students' increased attention sometimes results in an increased effort or persistence, which yields achievement gains. If attentiveness is due to a novelty effect, these gains tend to diminish as students become more familiar with the new medium. This was the case in reviews of computer-assisted instruction at the secondary school level (grades 6 to 12). An average computer effect size of three-tenths of a standard deviation (i.e., a rise in examination scores from the 50th to the 63rd percentile) for computer courses tended to dissipate significantly in longer duration studies. In studies lasting four weeks or less, computer effects were one-half a standard deviation. This reduced to three-tenths of a standard deviation in studies lasting five to eight weeks and further reduced to the familiar and weak two-tenths of a standard deviation computer effect after eight weeks of data collection. Effects of two-tenths or less account for less than 1 percent of the variance in a comparison.

The Kuliks report a similar phenomenon in their review of visual-based instruction (e.g., film, television, pictures). Although the reduction in effect size for longer duration studies approached significance (about .065 alpha), there were a number of comparisons of methods mixed with different visual media, which makes interpretation difficult (cf. Clark & Salomon, 1986). In their review of computer use in college, the Kuliks did not find any evidence for this novelty effect. In their comparison of studies of one or two hours duration with those which held weekly sessions for an entire semester, the effect sizes were roughly the same. Is it possible that computers are less novel experiences for college subjects than for secondary school students?

Conclusions and Applications of Media Comparison Research

General media comparisons and studies investigating the relative learning effectiveness of different media have yielded little that warrants optimism. Even in the few cases where dramatic changes in achievement or ability were found to result from the introduction of a new medium such as television or computers, it was not the medium per se that caused the change but rather the curricular reform that accompanied the new medium. This in itself is an important observation. A new medium often seems to encourage the support of expensive instructional design, curriculum changes, and/or organizational changes in the educational establishment. This pattern seems to recur throughout history with the advent of each new medium. Such a pattern can be useful for reformers who wish to attract support for efforts to improve instruction, revise curriculum, and/or reshape ossified organizational structures: Wait for a new medium and then attach reform proposals to requests that the new medium be adopted.

However, media researchers are cautioned against arguing for newer media and accompanying reforms by promising (even implicitly) that the new medium can be expected to produce learning advantages. If government or education officials have historically been willing to support expensive instructional development and curriculum reform only when a new medium is adopted, we should be willing to encourage such reforms when needed. However, the research clearly indicates that any learning gain associated with a new medium cannot be said to be caused by the choice of medium.

RESEARCH RELATING TO
COGNITIVE ISSUES

Cognizant of the limitations of media comparison studies, researchers turned their attention to other types of questions. These newer approaches focused on a study of the attributes of media and their influence on the way that information is processed in learning. In this approach, many media were thought to possess attributes such as the capacity to slow the motion of objects or *zoom* into details of a stimulus field or to *unwrap* a three-dimensional object into its two-dimensional form. These attributes were thought to cultivate cognitive skills when modeled by learners, so that, for example, a child with low cue-attending ability might learn the cognitive skill of zooming into stimulus details (Salomon, 1974a), or novice chess players might increase their skills in recognizing potential moves and configurations of chess pieces through animated modeling of moves and patterns. Because this type of question dealt with the way that information is selected and transformed in the acquisition of generalizable cognitive skills, many believed that the possibility of a coherent theory dealing with media attributes was forthcoming. In addition, it was exciting to imagine that these media attributes might result in unique cognitive skills because they promised to teach mental transformations that had not heretofore been experienced.

The promise of the media attributes approach is based on at least three expectations: (a) that the attributes are an integral part of media and would provide a connection between instructional uses of media and learning; (b) that attributes would provide for the cultivation of cognitive skills for learners who needed them; and (c) that identified attributes would provide unique independent variables for instructional theories that specified causal relationships between attribute modeling and learning. The final point (c) is most important because it represents a renewed search for evidence of a connection between media (or media attributes in this instance) and learning. The discussion of media attributes that follows is an attempt to explore the evidence for each of the three expectations listed above.

Are Media Attributes the Psychologically
Relevant Aspects of Media?

The first expectation was that media attributes would somehow represent the psychologically relevant aspects of media. However, few of the originators of the media attribute construct (Salomon, 1974b) claimed that they were more than correlated with different media, that is, that any one media attribute was available from more than one (and often many) media. Because they are not exclusive to any specific media and were only associated with them by habit or convenience, media attributes are not media variables any more certainly than the specific subject matter content, format, organization, or layout of a book is part of the definition of a book. In fact, the early discussions of media attributes most often referred to symbol systems or symbolic elements of instruction. All instructional messages were coded in some symbolic representational system, the argument went, and symbols vary in the cognitive transformation they allow us to perform on the information we select from our environment. Some symbolic elements (animated arrows, zooming) permit us to cultivate cognitive skills. However, many different media can present a given attribute so there is no necessary correspondence between attributes and media. Media are mere vehicles for attributes so the term media attributes is misleading.

Do Media Attributes Cultivate Cognitive Skills?

The second expectation of the attribute approach was that attributes would provide for the cultivation of cognitive skills for learners who needed them. Salomon (1979) and more recently Greenfield (1984) have reviewed research where symbolic features of mediated experiences and instruction were shown to affect differentially the skills activated in the service of knowledge acquisition and the mastery of these skills. Such research was inspired, in part, by Jerome Bruner's (1964) argument that internal representations and operations partly depend on learning "precisely the techniques that serve to amplify our acts, perceptions and our ratiocinative activities" (p. 2). Such a view implies that unique coding or structural elements of the media (e.g., filmic causal sequences) or uniquely afforded activities (e.g., computer programming) may have unique effects on related mental skills. Thus, employing a coding element such as a close-up, or the allowing for students' manipulation of input data may activate specific mental operations that facilitate the acquisition of knowledge as well as improved mastery. In one study by Salomon (1974a), students who had difficulty attending to cues in a visual field learned the skill by seeing it modeled in a film where they saw a camera "zoom" from a wide field to close-up shots of many different details. An analysis of the task suggested that effective cue attending required an attention-directing strategy that began with a view of the entire stimulus and then narrowed the stimulus field until a single, identifiable cue remained. For those students with low cue-attending skill (the requisite cognitive skill to perform the task), Salomon (1974b) reasoned that the required instructional method would be modeling. In this case, the construction of the model followed an analysis of the symbol systems, which allowed this particular method to be coded for delivery to the students. Although the zooming treatment used was available in many media (e.g., film, television, videodisc), the students seemed to model the zooming and used it as a cognitive skill that allowed them to attend to cues.

However, in a partial replication of this study, Bovy (1983) found that a treatment that used an *irising* attribute to provide practice in cue-attending was as effective as Salomon's zooming in cultivating the skill during practice. Irising consisted of slowly enclosing cues in a circular, gradually enlarging, darkened border similar to the effect created by an iris which regulates the amount of light permitted through a camera lens. More important, however, was Bovy's finding that a treatment that merely isolated cues with a static close-up of successive details singled out by the zooming and irising was even more effective in cultivating cue-attending skill than either zooming or irising. It may be that only the efficient isolation of relevant cues is necessary for this task.

In a similar study, Black (cf. Clark, 1983) taught chess moves to high or low visual ability undergraduates through a standard narration and (a) still pictures, (b) animated arrows with the pictures, or (c) a motion film from which the still pictures were taken. While all three conditions worked for the higher ability students, low visualizers learned the chess moves equally well from the arrow and the motion treatments, which were significantly better for them than the static pictures. Here, as in the Salomon (1974a) study, we presume that the modeled chess moves compensated for the low-ability student's lack of spatial visualization. Unlike Salomon's, Blake's subject profited from two different operational definitions of the necessary model, animated arrows and moving chess pieces. Different stimulus arrangements resulted in similar performances but, as we might expect, led to nominally different cognitive processes being modeled. The necessary process for learning chess moves, the visualizing of the entire move allowed each piece, could therefore be operationalized in any of various sufficient conditions for successful performance. Therefore the recommendation is to exercise caution in future research on symbolic elements of media.

The possibility of skill activation and cultivation from specific media attributes raises new conceptual and empirical questions. If media's symbolic modes of information presentation can activate, even cultivate, mental operations and skills, are these skills unique? What is their utility? How far do they transfer, if at all? These questions are of particular interest with respect to the use of computers in instruction for many computer-afforded activities are rationalized in terms of their unique effects on transferable skills. One would need to distinguish between, say, the acquisition of a particular image or operation, on the one hand, and the cultivation of imagery ability or generalized skill, on the other. It is one thing if children learn from televiewing only how to become better televiewers or from programming in Logo how to be better Logo programmers; it is another if they show skill cultivation that transfers beyond the boundaries of that medium or activity.

Work by Scribner and Cole (1981) concerning the effects of acquiring basic literacy skills in nonschool settings serves as a warning against unwarranted optimism here. Contrary to earlier claims, they found no evidence to show that literacy acquired in nonformal education affected abstract thinking or, for that matter, any other generalizable ability. The subjects they studied were denied the opportunity to acquire and practice reading and writing in the variety of contexts that may amplify the effects of basic literacy into transferable skills regardless of the medium or symbol system used in the instruction. Varied and prolonged practice would presumably enable the literate individuals to apply the initially specific operations in a variety of complex tasks and situations, thus to allow the generalizability of these skills.

The road from possible to actual transfer is fraught with difficulties. It is certainly not a matter of one-shot, brief experiences and encounters, except in the unlikely event that considerable mental effort is expended in reaching transferable conclusions, formulating rules, or generating guiding metacognitions. In all, it appears that media's symbolic forms and computers' afforded activities may have skill-cultivating effects, but these are not necessarily unique nor easily transferable. Future research, particularly that concerned with computer-afforded learning activities, will do well to ask not just whether particular skills are acquired but also how else they could be developed, and under what instructional, contextual, and psychological conditions they can be made to transfer. The problem lies not in the fact that symbol systems can be made to cultivate skills but in whether these symbolic elements or attributes are *unique, exclusive to any particular medium, or necessary for learning*. If the attributes identified to date are useful in instruction, they are valuable. However, theory development depends on the discovery of basic or necessary processes of instruction and learning. It is to this point, the third expectation of media attribute theories, that the discussion turns next.

Unique Media Attributes and Theories of Instruction

From our discussion so far, it seems reasonable to assume that media are best conceptualized as delivery vehicles for instruction and not as variables that directly influence learning. Although certain elements of different media, such as animated motion or zooming, might serve as sufficient conditions to facilitate the learning of students who lack the skill being modeled, symbolic elements such as zooming are not media and merely allow us to create sufficient conditions to teach particular cognitive skills. All of the attributes investigated so far are only correlated with media (each attribute is available from a number of media) and no attributes have been found to produce unique cognitive effects. In science, sufficient conditions are those events that were adequate to produce some outcome in a past instance. There is no guarantee, however, that sufficient conditions will ever produce the outcome again because the variable that caused the outcome was merely correlated with the condition. For example, a computer might be sufficient to produce the desired level of achievement in one instance but might fail in another. The determination of necessary conditions is a fruitful approach when analyzing all instructional problems, and it the foundation of all instructional theories. Once described, the necessary cognitive operation is a specification, or recipe, for an instructional method. We can employ a great variety of media, and possibly, a similar variety of symbol systems to achieve the same type of learning. However, we cannot vary the requirement that the method somehow model the crucial cognitive process required for the successful performance of the task.

It is the identification of the critical features of necessary cognitive processes that underlies the construction of successful instructional methods and the development of instructional theory (Clark, 1983). The cognitive process features must be translated into a symbol system understandable to the learner and then delivered through a convenient medium. The cognitive feature in the chess study was the simulation of beginning and ending points of the moves of the various chess pieces. In the cue-attending studies by Salomon and Bovy, the cognitive features were probably the isolation of relevant cues. It is the external modeling of these features in any symbol system understood by the student that yields the required performance. When a chosen symbol system is shaped to represent the critical features of the task and other things are equal, learning will occur. When a medium delivers a symbol system containing this necessary arrangement of features, learning will occur also but will not be due to either the medium or the symbol system. This issue is related to the problem of external validity.

Although it is often useful instructionally to know about sufficient conditions for producing desirable levels of achievement, our theories seek necessary conditions. Without necessary conditions we run the risk of failing to replicate achievement gains when we change the context, times, or student clients for instruction. Instructional theory (Shuell, 1980) seeks generalizations concerning the necessary instructional methods required to foster cognitive processes. Instructional media attribute research to date has not led to such generalizations and does not promise to do so in the future. However, an area where there is a great deal of promise for applying past research and for new directions is in research on attitudes toward media.

RESEARCH ON ATTITUDES TOWARD MEDIA

In recent years there has been a great deal of interest in the effects of learner values, attitudes, and beliefs toward media. This section briefly reviews that research. Before presenting a model for understanding these studies however, we caution the reader to note that, in attitude studies, the independent variable is *not* media but our beliefs or values related to media. Therefore, if there are learning or motivation benefits uncovered in these studies, they may not be attributed to media. Attitude variables are learner variables and learning gains must be attributed to individual differences or learner traits.

Attitude research has a long history. Critics of the area have noted a number of serious flaws in study design and have disputed the utility of research results for the development of instructional prescriptions. Recently, however, there has been a promising series of developments that have resulted from the growth of cognitive theories of learning. Although space does not permit a detailed account of these developments; a brief summary of them follows.

In general, researchers believe that our attitudes, beliefs, and values influence our motivation to learn. Motivation is typically measured by either our willingness to engage in a task (i.e., to choose one task over a number of things that compete for our attention) and/or to invest effort in a task we have selected to perform. Effort investments can range from very shallow (i.e., when we perform automatically, mindlessly, and without much thought) to very deep (i.e., when we give all our attention and intelligence to a task). Motivation is one of the necessary components of learning. We may have all the necessary ability for learning without the motivation to invest effort. Similarly, we may have motivation and lack ability. The difference between motivation and intelligence is analogous to the difference between gasoline and the engine of an automobile. Although the analogy fails in a number of areas, the best engine will not run on an empty tank and the highest octane gas will not cause a car to run when the engine has a mechanical problem. If learning is enhanced when values, beliefs, or attitudes change, it is because the learner gains motivation to engage in a task or invest the required level of effort—the engine gets gas. If an increase in motivation does not increase learning, the problem may have been a lack of ability—the engine malfunctions.

Attitude research has resulted in some very confusing results. Although our expectation of a positive relationship between attitude and learning is generally borne out in the research literature, we find a number of studies where the reverse is true. There is a significant group of well-designed studies where more positive attitudes toward a medium result in less learning and other studies where negative attitudes result in more learning. Clark and Salomon (1986) reviewed a number of specific studies with these conflicting and counterintuitive results. The outcome of an analysis of these studies suggests that the relationship between attitude (and our resulting motivation to learn) on the one hand and learning on the other is not direct or monotonic.

A New Cognitive Theory of Motivation to Learn from Media

The most exciting new cognitive *self-efficacy* theory of motivation (Bandura, 1978; Salomon, 1981) suggests that the relationship between attitude toward media and learning is best conceptualized as an *inverted U*. This theory suggests that students invest effort on the basis of their beliefs about, or attitude toward, two factors: (1) the requirements of a task, and (2) the students' assessment of their own skills related to task requirements. Salomon calls these two factors *perceived demand characteristics* (PDC—for task requirements) and *perceived self-efficacy* (PSE—for self-assessment of required skills). Drawing on Bandura's theory, Salomon hypothesizes that as a student's perception of the difficulty of a medium increases from low to moderate, the effort he or she will invest in learning from that medium increases from very low to its maximum level. The same result occurs when a student's perception of his or her own skills increases from low to moderate. However, when a student's perception of the difficulty of a medium reaches a very high level or judgment about his or her own skills at learning from a medium is very high, the effort investment falls to very low levels. It is moderate levels of PDC and/or PSE that result in the greatest level of motivation. In addition, there may be large national and cultural differences in PDC and PSE judgments. Salomon (1984), for example, notes that North American students generally believe that television is an easy medium while books are difficult. Although there is nothing essentially more difficult about books, students will generally invest more effort in learning from them than from a televised presentation. Salomon notes that Israeli children, who have a different perception of the demands of televised instruction, do not make the same distinctions.

This new motivation theory may go some distance in explaining the often counterintuitive research findings in previous research on attitudes, values and beliefs about media such as those described by Salomon (1981, 1984) and Clark (1983). For example, studies that have shown increases in motivation (or learning) with decreases in attitude toward a specific medium are now predictable given the self-efficacy theory.

Research on Liking or Valuing Different Media

One of the areas not adequately addressed by attitude theory is the construct of *value*. We may value a medium and prefer to learn from it simply because we like it, not because it represents an easier way to learn or because the learner perceives him or herself as more or less capable with it. There is currently very little research on values for learning from one or another medium. There is a budding interest in values, however, in current cognitive theories of learning. Researchers interested in this area might consult studies by Dweck and Bernechat (1983) for direction. Generally, we suspect that a student's values will influence his or her decision to engage in learning from a specific medium (or a learning task) but not the amount of effort they invest (recall the distinction made earlier between engagement and effort in motivation theory). We may have ability and an attitude that would allow for effort to be spent at a medium but simply value some other medium so much more that we refuse to choose to learn from the medium employed for instruction. This may have been the case in attitude studies reported by Saracho (1982) and Machula (1978-79). These and other studies (Clark, 1983) suggest that student values for or against certain media may change radically over a brief span of time within the same instructional module. One indication of these changes is the extent to which student attention and engagement in tasks wanders on and off their tasks as they choose to think about things other than the instructional task. Indications that values change in a brief span of time suggest that the design of studies in this area contain measurement techniques that are sensitive to such changes.

Conclusions About Research on Attitudes Toward Media

Cognitive theories of motivation have brought a measure of clarity to research on attitudes, values, and beliefs about media. Previous research results that seemed conflicting and counter-intuitive are now more understandable. Generally, attitude research is better conceptualized as part of motivation theory, and media researchers interested in attitudes or values are urged to master the growing and vigorous literature on cognitive theories of motivation—particularly the work that has resulted from Bandura's self-efficacy theory and the extensions of that theory by Salomon (1981, 1984). Basically, the cognitive theories suggest that all motivation results from the answer to three largely implicit questions learners ask themselves: (1) Do I like this medium (or learning task)? (2) What skills are required to learn from this medium (or learning task)? and (3) Do I have the skills that it takes to learn from this medium (or learning task)? The answer to the first question leads learners to choose to learn from one or another valued medium. The answers to the second two questions influence the amount of effort they invest in learning from any given medium.

Researchers in this area are urged to focus on a careful measurement of engagement, level of effort, values and related constructs such as perceived demand characteristics, and perceived self-efficacy. In addition, researchers are urged to separate learning from motivational issues in studies. This can be accomplished by insuring that motivation studies are not confounded by ability or prior knowledge differences on the part of subjects. In this way, the motivational influences on achievement will be separated from the contribution of general and specific abilities.

One final suggestion is in order. We suspect that these new cognitive theories of motivation imply some changes in our understanding of research on feedback during instruction. This is particularly important in the design of research on the interactivity advantages of computer-based instruction (CBI). Many CBI studies are designed to investigate different forms of interaction between learner and computer courseware. The feedback given by the computer may be conceptualized in many ways, but if researchers think of it as answering one or more of the three motivation questions (in addition to other questions), the literature in this area may become more productive. In other words, feedback might be about values, media demands on the learner or the learner's capabilities to learn from one or more media—depending on whether the researcher wanted to manipulate engagement with a medium or the amount of effort invested in learning from a given medium.

ECONOMIC ISSUES IN MEDIA RESEARCH

One of the least obvious yet most compelling aspects of the media research conducted during the last decade is the large number of economic questions and the scarcity of economic studies. There is a growing consensus that past media comparison, media attribute, and motivation studies indicate that media do not influence whether someone learns from instruction. Learning seems to be due to factors such as task differences, instructional methods, and learner traits (including attitudes) but not the choice of media for instruction. Another way to state this conclusion is that media do not influence the psychological elements of learning and have no place as independent variables in attempts to predict learning outcomes. Yet, it seems that there is equally dramatic evidence that media do influence the economic elements of learning. That is, under certain conditions media can dramatically influence the cost of learning.

Here, *cost* can be defined in any of a variety of ways—as the amount of time it takes a learner to reach an achievement criterion or a development team to develop, revise and/or present instructional programs; as the cost in resources (such as dollars, committed facilities, or the drain on an organization); and/or as the cost of access to instruction by different types of learners (in dollars, effort, or time). For example, comparisons of computer and conventional instruction often show a 30 to 50 percent reduction in time to complete lessons for the computer groups (Clark & Salomon, 1986). Although some of this dramatic economic advantage of computers may be due to a novelty effect that disappears over time, not all time savings are attributable to research design errors. One of the reasons for exploring these cost of media issues is that they allow for additional analyses of the psychologically based effectiveness studies or what economists call cost-effectiveness research.

Cost-Effectiveness Studies of Computers in Primary and Secondary School Settings

A recent review of cost-effectiveness studies of media use (primarily devoted to computer-based instruction) has been conducted by Henry Levin (1986; Levin & Meister, 1985) at Stanford University. He has reanalyzed a number of recent, comprehensive, cost-effectiveness studies that were conducted in elementary and secondary schools. His conclusions note that computer-based instruction cost-effectiveness is relatively poor in most of the better evaluation studies. However, when sites made a determined effort to promote full utilization of the medium and software, the cost-effectiveness ratio increased by a factor of 50 percent. Levin also found evidence that there are dramatic cost-effectiveness differences for the same CBI program at different implementation sites. That is, when the same program is implemented at different schools or cities, the cost-effectiveness ratio changes significantly—by as much as 400 percent. This strongly suggests that different strategies for managing media systems and the implementation of mediated instruction can greatly influence the cost of achievement from computers (and perhaps other media as well). Because we would expect that the media courseware would produce the same level of achievement at different sites, management and organizational factors are most likely to influence cost and, in some cases, inhibit achievement.

Media Economics Research Design Suggestions

Levin cautions researchers in this area that a great number of flawed cost-effectiveness studies have been conducted. He located reports of about 80 studies but was only able to use 8 of them for his analysis. In his view, 72 of the studies were so seriously flawed that they could not be used. He also presents a very engaging discussion of the issues surrounding CBI implementation—a discussion that all media researchers interested in conducting studies in this area should read. He notes, for example, that elementary school computer systems tend to be more fully utilized than those in secondary or college settings, which may account for the typically larger achievement effect sizes found in the primary school meta-analyses by the Kuliks (Clark, 1985).

We strongly recommend increased research on the economics of instructional media in the next few years. Although school systems in the United States are not forced to rationalize their plans in terms of cost-effectiveness yet, we seem to be moving in that general direction. We may find that some media make certain instructional methods cheap enough for broad implementation. For example, computers and videodisc media may provide the constant interaction that individualized instruction requires but has only been previously available from expensive, live teachers. In this case it would not be necessary to claim that computers made a unique contribution to learning in order to rationalize their use in education. It would be sufficient to provide evidence that a medium made some necessary instructional method cheap enough to be affordable within current levels of support.

SUMMARY AND CONCLUSION

Since the mid-1970s there has been a movement away from research questions and studies inspired by a behavioral view of learning. The trend in the past decade has been toward scholarship that is rooted in the new cognitive theories of learning from instruction. The results of media comparison studies and, more recently, media attribute studies indicate that media are best conceptualized as delivery vehicles for instruction and not as variables that directly influence learning. In general, most previous research on instructional media has identified some sufficient conditions for learning and for the cultivation of cognitive learning skills. Future research should aim to determine necessary conditions for learning, i.e., the unique aspects of a medium or of the instruction delivered by the medium that models the cognitive processes required for successful performance on particular learning tasks. We might also adopt a broader definition of the outcomes of learning—one that includes levels of transfer of knowledge and skills desired.

Our reading of the past decade of media research strongly suggests that the learning that occurs from well-prepared media presentations is actually due to three factors or types of variables: (1) learning task type (e.g., more procedural or more declarative tasks); (2) individual learner traits (e.g., motivation, general ability, and prior knowledge); and (3) instructional method (e.g., the way that the instructional presentation compensates for deficits in learner traits that are required for learning). Instructional technology research in the next decade might profitably focus on interactions between these variables. In these studies, media should be employed as delivery devices that will aid the researcher's control of treatment duration, reliability, and quality.

The motivational effects and the cost-effectiveness of instructional media have remained largely unexplored. Attitudinal studies have been conducted in large numbers but with conflicting results and without the benefit of theory. Now that cognitive research has provided motivational theories such as Bandura's and Salomon's, future motivation research with media will be more fruitful. Researchers interested in motivation issues are urged to clarify some of the measurement problems in past research on variables such as *engagement, level of effort,* and *values* in relation to media presentations. In addition, motivational research should avoid direct measurement of learning outcomes. Current cognitive theory assumes that motivation influences either engagement in a task and/or the amount and quality of effort expended to learn. Therefore, research in this area should use engagement and effort expended as dependent variables that, in turn, are presumed to influence learning.

The limited research available on cost-effectiveness of instructional media indicates that, under certain conditions, media can dramatically influence the cost of achievement. There is a great need for research to identify and quantify the management, implementation, and organizational factors that influence the cost-effectiveness of various instructional media for various kinds of subject matter, instructional methods, and students. We strongly support and urge an increase in the amount of economic research on media. These are the studies that, in the long run, may prove to be the most fruitful for media researchers.

REFERENCES

Anderson, D. R., & Lorch, E. P. (1983). Looking at television: Action or reaction. In J. Bryant & D. R. Anderson (Eds.), *Watching TV, understanding TV.* New York: Academic Press.

Bandura, A. (1978). The self system in reciprocal determinism. *American Psychologist, 33,* 344-358.

Bovy, R. A. (1983). Defining the psychologically active features of instructional treatments designed to facilitate cue attendance. Paper presented at the annual meeting of the American Educational Research Association, Montreal, Quebec (April 1983).

Bruner, J. S. (1964). The course of cognitive growth. *American Psychologist, 19*, 1-15.

Clark, R. E. (1983). Reconsidering research on learning from media. *Review of Educational Research, 53*(4), 445-460.

————. (1985). Confounding in educational computing research. *Journal of Educational Computing Research, 1*(2), 28-42.

Clark, R. E., & Salomon, G. (1986). Media in teaching. In M. Wittrock (Ed.), *Handbook of research on teaching* (3rd edition). New York: Macmillan.

Clark, R. E., & Snow, R. E. (1975). Alternative designs for instructional technology research. *AV Communication Review, 23*(4), 373-394.

Dorr, A., Graves, S. B., & Phelps, E. (1980). Television literacy for young children. *Journal of Communication, 30*, 71-83.

Dweck, C. S., & Bernechat, J. (1983). Children's theories of intelligence: Consequences for learning. In S. G. Paris, G. M. Olson, & H. W. Stevenson (Eds.), *Learning and motivation in the classroom.* Hillsdale, NJ: Lawrence Erlbaum.

Greenfield, P. (1984). *Mind and media: The effects of television, video games and computers.* Cambridge, MA: Harvard University Press.

Jamison, D., Suppes, P., & Wells, S. (1974). The effectiveness of alternative instructional media: A survey. *Review of Educational Research, 44*, 1-68.

Kulik, J. A., Kulik, C.-L., & Bangert-Downs, R. (1985). Effectiveness of computer-based education in elementary schools. *Computers in Human Behavior, 1*, 59-74.

Kyllonen, P. C., Lohman, D. F., & Snow, R. E. (1984). Effects of aptitudes, strategy training and task facets on spatial task performance. *Journal of Educational Psychology, 76*(1), 130-145.

Levie, W. H., & Dickie, K. (1973). The analysis and application of media. In R. M. W. Travers (Ed.), *Second handbook of research on teaching.* Chicago: Rand McNally.

Levin, H. M. (1986). Cost-effectiveness of computer-assisted instruction: Some insights. Report No. 86-Septi-13. Stanford, CA: Stanford Education Policy Institute, School of Education, Stanford University.

Levin, H. M., & Meister, G. R. (1985). Educational technology and computers: Promises, promises, always promises. Report No. 85-A13. Stanford, CA: Center for Educational Research at Stanford, School of Education, Stanford University.

Machula, R. (1978-79). Media and affect: A comparison of video-tape, audiotape and print. *Journal of Educational Technology Systems, 7*(2), 167-185.

Mielke, K. W. (1968). Questioning the questions of ETV research. *Educational Broadcasting, 2*, 6-15.

Olson, D., & Bialystok, E. (1983). *Spatial cognition.* Hillsdale, NJ: Lawrence Erlbaum.

Salomon, G. (1974a). Internalization of filmic schematic operations in interaction with learners' aptitudes. *Journal of Educational Psychology, 66*, 499-511.

————. (1974b). What is learned and how is it taught: The interaction between media, message, task and learner. In D. Olson (Ed.), *Media and symbols: The form of expression, communication and education.* (The 73rd yearbook of the National Society for the Study of Education.) Chicago: University of Chicago Press.

————. (1979). *Interaction of media, cognition and learning.* San Francisco: Jossey-Bass.

————. (1981). *Communication and education, social and psychological interactions.* Beverly Hills, CA: Sage.

————. (1984). Television is easy and print is "tough": The differential investment of mental effort in learning as a function of perceptions and attributions. *Journal of Educational Psychology, 76*(4), 647-658.

Saracho, O. N. (1982). The effect of a computer-assisted instruction program on basic skills achievement and attitude toward instruction of Spanish speaking migrant children. *American Educational Research Journal, 19*(2), 201-219.

Schramm, W. (1977). *Big media, little media.* Beverly Hills, CA: Sage.

Scribner, S., & Cole, M. (1981). *The psychology of literacy.* Cambridge, MA: Harvard University Press.

Shuell, T. J. (1980). Learning theory, instructional theory and adaption. In R. E. Snow, P. Federico, & W. Montigue (Eds.), *Aptitude, learning and instruction* (Vol. 2). Hillsdale, NJ: Lawrence Erlbaum.

33

Instructional Technology and Attitude Change

Michael Simonson
College of Education, Iowa State University
Ames, Iowa

Attitudes are predispositions to respond. They have the potential to influence learning. Instructional technologies are often used to present messages designed to change attitudes. This chapter reviews the relationship between instructional technology and attitudes. First, instructional technology and attitude will be defined. Next, the importance of attitudes will be discussed. Finally, guidelines will be offered for developing instructional situations using technology when attitude changes are desired.

DEFINITIONS

Instructional technology is a complex, integrated process involving people, procedures, ideas, devices, and organization for analyzing problems and devising, implementing, evaluating, and managing solutions to those problems involved in all aspects of human learning (AECT, 1977). More recently, instructional technology has been redefined as the theory and practice of design, development, utilization, management, and evaluation of processes and resources for learning (AECT, 1994).

Attitudes and attitude change have been discussed at least since the beginning of this century (Thomas & Znaniecki, 1918). The study of attitudes has been an important area of interest to educational psychologists who often were also interested in such related concepts as propaganda. Educators have been concerned about attitudes because of their impact on learning, and although attitudes have not been convincingly linked to achievement, they have been long considered an important component of effective instruction.

Attitude has been a difficult concept to adequately define, primarily because it has been defined by so many, but also because of the word's differing lay uses and connotations. One of the earliest definitions of attitude was proposed by Thomas and Znaniecki (1918). They defined attitude as: "A mental and neural state of readiness, organized through experience, exerting a directive or dynamic influence upon the individual's response to all objects and situations with which it is related." More recently, Zimbardo and Leippe (1991) defined attitude as: "An evaluative disposition toward some object based upon cognitions, affective reactions, behavioral intentions, and past behaviors ... that can influence cognitions, affective responses, and future intentions and behaviors."

Attitudes are latent and not directly observable in themselves, but they act to organize, or to provide direction to, actions and behaviors that are observable. Attitudes are related to how people perceive the situations in which they find themselves. Also, attitudes vary in direction (either positive or negative), in degree (the amount of positiveness or negativeness), and in intensity (the amount of commitment with which a position is held; Smith, 1982).

Attitude positions are the summary aggregation of four components: (a) affective responses, (b) cognition, (c) behaviors, and (d) behavioral intentions (Zimbardo & Leippe, 1991). The affective component of attitude is said to consist of a person's evaluation of, liking of, or emotional response to some situation, object, or person. *Affective* responses reflect one's attitude with sensations of pleasure, sadness, or other levels of physical arousal. The *cognitive* component is conceptualized as a person's beliefs about, or factual knowledge of, the situation, object, or person. The *behavioral* component involves the person's overt behavior directed toward the situation, object, or person. The *behavioral intention* component involves the person's plans to perform in a certain way, even if sometimes these plans are never acted upon. These four components of attitude form an attitude system. The components are not isolated but are interrelated and produce an organizing framework or mental representation of the attitude object (Smith, 1982).

IMPORTANCE OF ATTITUDES

When educators design classroom situations, they normally have two categories of outcomes in mind: those directed toward cognitive goals and those related to the attitudes of the learner. There is little necessity to argue the importance of the acquisition of knowledge by a student as a result of instruction. Achievement is the paramount objective of most classroom activities. However, it may also be important to recognize the need for establishing attitudinal goals and for planning activities designed to facilitate attitudinal outcomes in learners as a consequence of an instructional situation. As a matter of fact, it has become increasingly apparent to those involved in educational technology research that one of the major, and possibly unique, consequences of instructional situations involving media is the likelihood of the development of positive attitudinal positions in students.

The most powerful rationale for the need to promote attitude positions in learners would be to demonstrate a direct relationship between attitudes and achievement, or liking and learning. Numerous researchers have identified such a relationship (Fenneman, 1974; Greenwald, 1965, 1966; Lamb, 1987; Perry & Kopperman, 1973; Simonson, 1977; and Simonson & Bullard, 1978). However, most educational researchers are reluctant to claim that there is any cause-and-effect linkage between these two learner variables (Zimbardo & Leippe, 1991). There are too many intervening forces likely to influence the relationship between how a person feels and how he or she acts.

The impact of attitude on learning is only one reason for interest in attitudes; other arguments convincingly explain why attitudes of learners are important. First, most educators would agree that at times it is legitimate and important for learners to accept the truth of certain ideas; in other words, to accept an attitudinal position. Second, although the strength of the relationship between attitudes and achievement is unclear, it seems logical that students are more likely to remember information, seek new ideas, and continue studying when they react favorably to an instructional situation or like a certain content area. Third, in some instances, influencing the attitudes of students is not desirable, so educators should be aware of which techniques affect attitudes. In this way, possible bias can be recognized and eliminated. Last, student attitudes toward an instructional situation can tell the teacher a great deal about the impact of that situation on the learning process.

DESIGN GUIDELINES

Researchers have attempted to evaluate the impact various instructional technology-based procedures have on attitude formation and change. Simonson (1979) developed guidelines for the planning, production, and use of instructional media to promote attitude formation and change, thus translating theoretical information into procedures applicable to the instructional design process. These recommendations have been tested a number of times by researchers desiring to change attitudes (Lamb, 1987; Simonson et al., 1987). Recently, research results were reviewed, and Simonson's guidelines were revised and reoriented to reflect current approaches in cognitive science.

Guideline #1: *Attitude change is likely because of, and learners react favorably to, situations involving the use of instructional technologies to present messages that are authentic, relevant, and technically stimulating.*

One practical technique for instruction using technology is based on the concept of anchored instruction. Anchored instruction, as described by the Vanderbilt Cognition and Technology Group (1990), uses technology to provide a realistic situation for learning. Technology presents real-world events that become the anchor for learning. Although the Vanderbilt Group's studies concentrate on the cognitive consequences of anchored instruction, there is ample anecdotal evidence that anchored instruction also influences attitudes.

Simonson et al. (1987) reported on a series of three studies that attempted to determine if situations that used media to deliver messages authentically were more effective in creating attitude change than mediated situations that presented situations less authentically. They found that authentic, mediated instruction could be designed to promote desired attitudinal change.

Dimond and Simonson (1988) studied filmmakers who produced persuasive films. These filmmakers indicated that presenting authentic situations in their films was a basic component of the films' persuasiveness. In other words, filmmakers indicated that presentations of authentic, real-world situations were critical ingredients of successful persuasive films. Filmmakers also indicated that when they produced persuasive films they almost always "believed" in the attitudinal positions advocated in these films. Dimond and Simonson hypothesized that the act of filmmaking was an authentic situation that acted to influence the filmmaker's attitudes.

Similar results have been reported in the literature for decades. Levonian (1960, 1962, 1963) described a landmark study that incorporated the use of a preproduction survey of the target audience to determine attitudinal positions towards India. The results of this survey were used as input in the production of a persuasive film on India. This approach made the resulting motion picture about India more authentic and realistic to the audience, which in turn contributed to desired attitude changes.

Authenticity and realism were examined further by Croft, Stimpson, Ross, Bray, and Breglio (1969) and Donaldson (1976). Both studies reported that authentically presented situations were most effective in producing attitude changes toward intercollegiate athletics and the disabled. Booth and Miller (1974) and Winn and Everett (1978) investigated the authenticity provided by pictures produced in color versus those only in black and white. They reported a relationship between the use of color, authenticity, and attitude formation.

Authentic instruction, typically instruction anchored in technically stimulating media, such as the Vanderbilt Group's Jasper series (Vanderbilt, 1990), has a positive attitudinal impact on learners. The assumption is that positive dispositions developed during participation in authentic situations encourage students to actively pursue additional learning.

Guideline #2: *Learners are persuaded, and react favorably, when mediated learning situations include the discovery of useful new information about a topic.*

Most students like to learn. They react positively when relevant new information is presented to them. Inert knowledge, knowledge that can be recalled but is not spontaneously used in problem solving (Whitehead, 1929), is often not perceived positively by learners. Sherwood, Kinzer, Hasselbring, and Bransford's (1987) interesting work on logarithms demonstrates this point. Many youngsters do not see the importance of learning logarithms, even though almost everyone remembers studying them. To many students, logarithms are inert knowledge. On the other hand, mathematicians, statisticians, and computer programmers do not feel this way. They use logarithms and realize their power as tools to solve problems. It is safe to say that those who use logarithms have a much more positive attitude about them than those who do not use them.

Levonian's (1960, 1962, 1963) landmark studies support this guideline. Levonian produced a film that presented useful and relevant information. The content of the film was selected so it would not be "inert," but so that it would be relevant. Jouko (1972) reported similar results. The study demonstrated that the less pre-instruction knowledge students had about a topic the more attitude change that was produced after an informational and persuasive lesson. There was a negative relationship between pre-instruction familiarity about a topic and attitude change as a result of participating in a relevant persuasive situation.

A similar conclusion was reported in a study by Knowlton and Hawes (1962). This study determined that knowledge about a topic was often necessary for a positive attitude position toward the idea. Stated another way, new knowledge may need to be discovered by learners when attitude changes are desired (e.g., Jouko, 1972), or knowledge may need to be present for a learner to have a favorable attitudinal position toward the situation in which they are involved (Knowlton & Hawes, 1962). The results of two additional studies using video reported similar findings (Thirion, 1992; Harkins & Petty, 1981).

Guideline #3: *Learners are positively affected when persuasive messages delivered by instructional technology are encountered in situations that are authentic and credible.*

A direct relationship exists between attitude about a situation and the individual's perception of the authenticity and relevance of the situation. Source credibility has been recognized as an important criterion for attitude change since the early 1950s. Mediated situations will often be valued positively, and will be influential, if persuasive messages are delivered by a credible source or discovered in a credible situation. Kishler's (1950) classic study found that when the actor in a persuasive film was cast as a member of a highly credible occupational group, it was likely that attitude changes advocated by the actor would occur. Viewers considered the message to be authentic, so it influenced them. A study by Carter (1990) also supported the relationship between source credibility and attitude change. Results indicated that when subjects were told that the message was prepared by an expert, attitude changes tended to be more positive.

Two studies reported that the use of social modeling was an effective means of promoting attitude change. The use of slide or tape and print materials using positive role models had a significant affect on student attitudes toward nontraditional careers (Savenye, 1990). Evans, Rozelle, Maxwell, Raines, Dill, Guthrie, Henderson, and Hill (1981) used students as real-world models in films created to deter smoking. Groups viewing films in this study considered the messages to be credible and authentic and exhibited less smoking behavior and indicated less intention to smoke.

Many studies have looked at human sources of information delivered by media. However, one study in the literature examined the effects of credible and noncredible computer sources of information. Gahm (1986) found persuasion increased as the perceived authenticity of a computer message increased.

The content of media-based instructional situations is a critical variable in determining attitude formation and change. If information is presented authentically and intelligently (i.e., credibly), it is likely that it will be favorably received and will be persuasive.

Guideline #4: *Learners who are involved in a situation requiring their participation in the planning, production, or delivery of mediated instruction are likely to react favorably to the situation and to the message delivered by the media.*

Involving learners in the planning, production, and delivery of media can be considered a form of apprenticeship—a cognitive apprenticeship. If students participate in a situation they feel is realistic and not fabricated, they will generally react by indicating they have a positive attitude about it. Simsek (1993) investigated the issue of audience involvement by studying the effects of learner control in computer-based cooperative learning. A comparison was made between students exercising control over pacing and sequence and students using software that controlled the pacing and sequence. The students with control over the lesson had a more positive attitude toward the delivery system and the subject matter. Learner control, as opposed to program control, was found to promote better attitudes.

Video is traditionally a very passive instructional medium. When merged with computer technology, interactive video allows the learner to become involved in instruction. Dalton and Hannafin (1986) found interactive video instruction produced significant improvements in learner attitudes when compared with computer-based instruction and video alone.

Active involvement in the learning situation has been examined in many research studies. In one, Erickson (1956) found that students who actually produced a film on science concepts reacted more favorably toward instruction and toward science than did students who only watched science films. Coldevin (1975) involved students in message delivery through the use of various review and summarization techniques that were a part of the instructional sequence. A short review after the television lesson subunits produced the most favorable attitude reports from students. Simonson (1977) conducted an experiment in which students were convinced to make counterattitudinal videotapes without realizing that attitude change was the primary purpose of the activity. The process of involving subjects in making these videotapes was found to be successful in producing significant attitude changes in college students. In all of these studies, learners thought they were solving real-world problems. They were learning by doing and often were apprentices to more knowledgeable mentors.

It would seem that in the affective domain the active learner perceives instruction and information more favorably than does the passive learner. Student involvement is an important technique for promoting desirable attitudinal outcomes.

Guideline #5: *Learners who participate in discussions in which technology-based instructional situations are openly critiqued are likely to develop favorable attitudes toward the situations and toward the messages.*

Follow-up discussions, a powerful technique for promoting positive attitudes, were evaluated by several researchers (Howard, 1990). Follow-ups usually involved learners in an analysis or critique of the instructional situation and message presented. Allison (1966) found that significant attitude changes occurred only when postviewing discussions were held. Fay (1974) reported similar findings in a study that used follow-ups to a film on the problems of the handicapped and the need for barrier-free buildings. Attitudes toward continuing education were significantly altered after classroom teachers saw a film and participated in a discussion on the subject (Burrichter, 1968). These studies demonstrated the importance of learner involvement in authentic discussion activities. The researchers carefully constructed the learning situation to make sure the students felt their opinions were important.

Lamb (1987) found that including social interaction in the form of a postinstruction discussion was an effective instructional technique that promoted changes in attitudes toward wearing seat belts. This study examined the effects of three learner involvement strategies incorporated into a persuasive, computer-based lesson. The situations that included postinstruction discussions were found to be the most effective in promoting attitude change. The study also found that the absence of emotional involvement by the learner toward the message was shown to be detrimental to attitude change. Students stated that they considered discussions to be real and that this authenticity was important to them.

Guideline #6: *Learners who experience purposeful emotional involvement or arousal during media-rich instructional situations are likely to change their attitudes in the direction advocated in the situation.*

Participating actively in an authentic event requires intellectual involvement that can elicit emotions in the learner. For this reason, the research seems to indicate that guideline #6 is extremely powerful. For example, the use of subliminal messages to arouse emotion and therefore affect attitude change was examined in two studies. Although the subliminal messages had no identifiable impact on weight loss, subjects who viewed the videotape with subliminal messages showed an improved attitude toward eating and exercise (Treimer & Simonson, 1986). Edwards (1990) reported on the results of a similar study.

Janis and Feshbach (1953) presented high school students a slide and audiotape program on the effects of poor dental hygiene. The intensity of a fear-arousing appeal were varied in three versions of the presentation to determine the most influential delivery technique. All three methods were successful in producing aroused, affective reactions in the students. However, a minimal fear-arousing appeal was most successful in modifying attitudes because the stronger versions left students in a state of tension that was not alleviated by the remedies offered during the slide show. Janis and Feshbach concluded that strong, fear-producing appeals were not as effective in changing attitudes as were more moderate appeals because the audience became motivated to ignore the importance of the threat to reduce the tension they felt. The more frightening message was not as authentic and, therefore, was not as effective. It was found that only fear-provoking messages that were considered to be authentic influenced attitudes. The more dramatic and fearsome presentations were not considered to be realistic or authentic and were less effective. In other words, if messages are too frightening, they are not considered authentic and do not affect attitudes.

Rogers (1973) reported on a study that supported this position. Public health films dealing with cigarette smoking, safe driving, and venereal disease were tested in three different studies. It was found that the more noxious a film was, the more fear that was aroused in viewers. However, it was also reported that these fear-arousing films were most effective in changing attitudes when preventatives or statements of probability of exposure to the malady discussed in the film were included as part of the motion picture.

Another study addressing the relationship between fear-arousing videos and attitude change was conducted by Berry and Simonson (1983). Subjects viewed either a fear-provoking persuasive video or a fear-provoking video with remedies. The message was concerned with smoking. Experimental treatments significantly influenced subjects' attitudes, as compared to attitude changes in the control group, and the more authentic situations presented by the videos were considered to be the most effective at changing attitudes.

The studies supporting guideline #6 indicate that viewers' participation in the learning process is important when attitudinal outcomes are desired. In these cases, involvement was emotional, rather than behavioral. It would seem that learner involvement in a situation is a powerful technique if attitudinal outcomes are to be important consequences of instruction.

CONCLUSION

Media are primarily carriers of information. There is no best medium. However, there probably are "best mediated situations" that will maximize the likelihood of developing specific desirable attitudes in learners. Critically applying the general guidelines listed above will promote the discovery of attitudinal positions for students that are likely to contribute to healthy, positive learning situations.

REFERENCES

Allison, R. W. (1966). The effect of three methods of treating motivational films upon attitudes of fourth, fifth, and sixth grade students toward science, scientists, and scientific careers (Doctoral dissertation, Pennsylvania State University, 1966). *Dissertation Abstracts, 28,* 994.

Association for Educational Communications and Technology. (1977). *Educational technology: Definition and glossary of terms, volume 1.* Washington, DC: Author.

———. (1993). *Instructional technology: The definition and domains of the discipline.* Washington, DC: Author.

Berry, T., & Simonson, M. R. (1983, January). *Use of fear in persuasive messages.* Paper presented at the 1983 Annual Convention of the Association for Educational Communication and Technology, New Orleans, LA.

Booth, G. D., & Miller, H. R. (1974). Effectiveness of monochrome and color presentations in facilitating affective learning. *AV Communication Review, 22,* 409-422.

Burrichter, A. W. (1968). A study of elementary public school personnel attitudes toward continuing education in selected communities in Wyoming: An experiment in changing adult attitudes and concepts. Unpublished doctoral dissertation, University of Wyoming.

Carter, R. W. (1990). Effects of expertise and issue involvement on rehabilitation counselors in the selection of computer technology for their clients. *Dissertation Abstracts International, 51,* 1545B.

Coldevin, G. O. (1975). Spaced, massed, and summary as review strategies for ITV production. *AV Communication Review, 23,* 289-303.

Croft, R. G., Stimpson, D. V., Ross, W. L., Bray, R. M., & Breglio, V. J. (1969). Comparison of attitude changes elicited by live and videotape classroom presentation. *AV Communication Review, 17,* 315-321.

Dalton, D., & Hannafin, M. J. (1986). The effects of video-only, CAI only, and interactive video instructional systems on learner performance and attitude: An exploratory study. In M. R. Simonson (Ed.), *Proceedings of the Annual Convention of the Association for Educational Communications and Technology,* 154-162.

Dimond, P., & Simonson, M. R. (1988). Film-makers and persuasive films: A study to determine how persuasive films are produced. In M. R. Simonson (Ed.), *Proceedings of the Annual Convention of the Association for Educational Communications and Technology,* 200-212.

Donaldson, J. (1976). Channel variations and effects on attitudes toward physically disabled individuals. *AV Communication Review, 24,* 135-144.

Edwards, K. (1990). The interplay of affect and cognition in attitude formation and change. *Journal of Personality and Social Psychology, 59*(2), 202-216.

Erickson, C. W. H. (1956). Teaching general science through film production. *AV Communication Review, 4*, 268-278.

Evans, R. I., Rozelle, R. M., Maxwell, S. E., Raines, B. E., Dill, C. A., Guthrie, T. J., Henderson, A. H., & Hill, P. C. (1981). Social modeling films to deter smoking in adolescents: Results of a three-year field investigation. *Journal of Applied Psychology, 66*(4), 399-414.

Fay, F. A. (1974). Effects of a film, a discussion group, and a role playing experience on architecture student's attitudes, behavioral intentions, and actual behavior toward barrier free design (Doctoral dissertation, University of Illinois, 1974). *Dissertation Abstracts International, 34*, 6445A.

Fenneman, G. C. (1974). The validity of previous experience, aptitude, and attitude toward mathematics as predictors of achievement in freshman mathematics at Wartburg College (Doctoral dissertation, University of Northern Colorado, 1973). *Dissertations Abstracts International, 34*, 7100A.

Greenwald, A. G. (1965). Behavior change following a persuasive communication. *Journal of Personality, 33*, 370-391.

———. (1966). Effects of prior commitment on behavior change after a persuasive communication. *Public Opinion Quarterly, 29*, 595-601.

Harkins, S. G., & Petty, R. E. (1981). Effects of source magnification of cognitive effort on attitudes: An information-processing view. *Journal of Personality and Social Psychology, 40*(3), 401-413.

Howard, D. J. (1990). Rhetorical question effects on message processing and persuasion: The role of information availability and the elicitation of judgment. *Journal of Experimental Social Psychology, 26*, 217-239.

Janis, I. L., & Feshbach, S. (1953). Effects of fear-arousing communications. *Journal of Abnormal and Social Psychology, 48*, 78-92.

Jouko, C. (1972). *The effect of directive teaching materials on the affective learning of pupils.* Jyvaskyla, Finland: Institute for Educational Research, Report Number 139.

Kishler, J. P. (1950). *The effects of prestige and identification factors on attitude restructuring and learning from sound films.* University Park, PA: The Pennsylvania State University. (ERIC Document Reproduction Service No. ED 053 568).

Knowlton, J., & Hawes, E. (1962). Attitude: Helpful predictor of audiovisual usage? *AV Communication Review, 10*, 147-157.

Lamb, A. S. (1987). Persuasion and computer-based instruction: The impact of various involvement strategies in a computer-based instruction lesson on the attitude change of college students toward the use of seat belts. *Dissertation Abstracts International, 49*, 238A.

Levonian, E. (1960). Development of an audience-tailored film. *AV Communication Review, 8*(1), 62-68.

———. (1962). The use of film in opinion measurement. *AV Communication Review, 10*(4), 250-254.

———. (1963). Opinion change as mediated by an audience-tailored film. *AV Communication Review, 11*(4), 104-113.

Perry, G. A., & Kopperman, N. (1973). *A better chance-evaluation of student attitudes and academic performance, 1964-1972.* Boston: A Better Chance.

Rogers, R. W. (1973). *An analysis of fear appeals and attitude change.* Final report, University of South Carolina, Grant No. 1 RO3 MH2215701 MSM, National Institute of Mental Health.

Savenye, W. C. (1990). Role models and student attitudes toward nontraditional careers. *Educational Technology, Research and Development, 38*(3), 5-13.

Sherwood, R., Kinzer, C., Hasselbring, T., & Bransford, J. (1987). Macro-contexts for learning: Initial findings and issues. *Journal of Applied Cognition, 1*, 93-108.

Simonson, M. (1977). Attitude change and achievement: Dissonance theory in education. *Journal of Educational Research, 70*(3), 163-169.

————. (1979). Media and attitudes: An annotated bibliography of selected research—Part II. *Educational Communication and Technology Journal, 28*(1), 47-61.

Simonson, M., Aegerter, R., Berry, T., Kloock, T., & Stone, R. (1987). Four studies dealing with mediated persuasive messages, attitude, and learning styles. *Educational Communication and Technology Journal, 35*(1), 31-41.

Simonson, M., & Bullard, J. (1978). Influence of student expectations and student sex on predicting academic success. Paper presented at the meeting of the Midwest Educational Research Association, Chicago. *Resources in Education,* ERIC Document Reproduction Service No. 114049.

Simsek, A. (1993). The effects of learner control and group composition in computer-based cooperative learning. In M. R. Simonson (Ed.), *Proceedings of the Annual Convention of the Association for Educational Communications and Technology*, 953-990.

Smith, M. J. (1982). *Persuasion and human action.* Belmont, CA: Wadsworth.

Thirion, E. M. (1992). Attitude and behavior change of a group of young masculine road-users. *Masters Abstracts, 31*, 440.

Thomas, W. I., & Znaniecki, F. (1918). *The Polish peasant in Europe and America.* Boston: Badger.

Treimer, M., & Simonson, M. R. (1986). Old wine in new bottles: Subliminal messages in instructional media. In M. R. Simonson (Ed.), *Proceedings of the Annual Convention of the Association for Educational Communications and Technology, 764-779.*

Vanderbilt Cognition and Technology Group. (1990, August-September). Anchored instruction and its relationship to situated learning. *Educational Researcher*, 2-10.

Whitehead, A. N. (1929). *The aims of education.* New York: Macmillan.

Winn, W., & Everett, R. (1978). *Differences in the affective meaning of color and black and white pictures.* Paper presented at the Annual Convention of the Association for Educational Communications and Technology.

Zimbardo, P., & Leippe, M. (1991). *The psychology of attitude change and social influence.* Philadelphia: Temple University Press.

34

What We Know (and What We Don't Know) About Training of Cognitive Strategies for Technical Problem-Solving

Wellesley R. Foshay
The Roach Organization, Inc.
Rolling Meadows, Illinois

Let us start by identifying a fundamental dilemma of any practicing instructional developer: the models by which we work have considerable practical utility, and they are generally well grounded in theory. But the business of translating theory into practice is always risky. As Cunningham (1986) points out,

> ...we must rid ourselves once and for all of the notion that science will produce "truth," fixed and immutable for all time. Our notion of generalizability must be radically altered. We must allow ourselves the discomfort that comes when we realize that we are less certain about things than we previously imagined.

In this view, theory in principle does not lead smoothly and unambiguously to generalizable prescriptions for practice. Instead, practitioners must use theory as a "point of view" or a means for forming expectations of how real-world problems will behave. These expectations help the practitioner understand the complexity of real-world problems, and they help structure decisions about what to do. While it is true that the map is not the territory, it is also true that to navigate in the territory, one must have a map: theories are only abstractions of reality, but reality can only be understood through the point of view provided by theory.

And so it is now, as instructional developers seek to incorporate the theory of information processing cognitive psychology into their practical models of instructional design. As always, the research is incomplete and in some cases contradictory. But even so, we must ask if there are models, modes of analysis, or prescriptive principles which are powerful enough to improve the practice of an instructional developer who uses them.

An earlier version of this chapter was presented to the American Educational Research Association, Washington, DC, April 1987. Reprinted with permission from the *Journal of Structural Learning*.

The helpful comments of professors R. M. Gagne and J. M. Scandura on an earlier draft of this paper are gratefully acknowledged.

The answer is a (heavily qualified) "yes," in the opinion of recent reviews, such as Fredericksen (1984) and André (1986). To evaluate these opinions, it is appropriate to examine how thinking about instructional design might change to incorporate cognitive theory. This examination also will help illuminate some unanswered theoretical questions and identify some tools which practitioners will need in order to effectively modify their design practice.

Let us take as the point of departure the topic of teaching troubleshooting, as one might find it in content areas such as electronic circuit fault detection, mechanical system repair, computer software debugging, or medical diagnosis. Troubleshooting has the advantage of being a common subject of training courses, and also a common topic of cognitive research. However, troubleshooting is generally well-structured compared to other kinds of problem solving (such as design tasks), so the degree of generalizability to other cognitive tasks must be questioned.

First, we will quickly review common (behaviorally-based) design practices for training in troubleshooting. Then, we will examine some of the cognitively-based recommendations for teaching problem solving which have been recently published, and see how they might be applied to design of troubleshooting training. Finally, we will identify some unanswered questions of importance to practitioners seeking to incorporate cognitive principles into their instructional designs. As part of the discussion, we will note certain key divergences between Scandura's Structural Learning Theory (SLT) and other cognitive theories.

BEHAVIORALLY-BASED DESIGN PRACTICES FOR TROUBLESHOOTING TRAINING

The behaviorally-based approach to teaching troubleshooting is essentially algorithmic. For example, popular treatments such as Mager's (1982) often include recommendations such as these:

1. Identify the system's most common faults.

2. Derive one or more algorithm(s) for troubleshooting each common fault, using a split-half strategy. A full analysis includes identification of conditions, actions, and feedback for each step.

3. Sequence instruction in each algorithm (or algorithm segment) using sequencing rules (e.g., teach prerequisite parts before wholes).

4. Teach each algorithm (or algorithm segment) separately, teaching the steps in retro-grade sequence. Structure practice of each step so it includes:

   - realistic stimuli (conditions)

   - realistic responses

   - immediate feedback on accuracy of the response, in detail

   Continue practice until the behavior is satisfactorily shaped.

Limitations of the Behavioral Approach. Instructional design strategies incorporating these features have been in use for over twenty years, and they have been shown repeatedly to be effective. However, the behavioral approach has not been without critics. For example, Duncan (1985) makes these points:

1. Detailed procedure analysis of the sort required is costly. Each system fault requires a separate algorithm, or algorithm segment.

2. Technicians resist using a fully algorithmic approach.

3. The algorithms are very situation-specific, and thus expensive to update.

4. Retention of algorithm details is a constant problem, because most of the faults (and their associated algorithms) are rarely encountered—and thus rarely practiced.

5. Transfer of troubleshooting skills to new systems or new faults is relatively low.

It may be that experiences with these limitations are at the root of the common practice of using job aids to record troubleshooting algorithms, wherever possible. When they can be used in the work situation, job aids effectively offset the problem of retention, and the need for transfer is greatly reduced. However, the cost of the analysis and the need for constant updating still remains.

Recent cognitive research suggests some ways of overcoming some of these limitations. To see how, let us next summarize some key findings from that research.

KEY COGNITIVE PRINCIPLES OF
RELEVANCE TO TROUBLESHOOTING

Of the various lines of cognitive research, two of perhaps greatest interest to instructional designers teaching problem solving deal with knowledge representation and with the things that expert problem solvers know. While these findings are familiar, we will review each to facilitate later discussion.

Knowledge Representation. In general, cognitive researchers have tended to draw distinctions between types of knowledge. For example, André's chapter on problem solving in a recent introductory text (André, 1986) distinguishes between:

*   Concepts, or schemata, which are stored as sets of multiple discrimination rules and as prototype examples; and

*   Production systems, including rules, principles and skills, which specify the conditional relationships between concepts.

In addition, André makes the familiar distinction between:

*   Declarative knowledge, which supports the ability to classify or define; and

*   Procedural knowledge, which supports the ability to perform.

An exception has been Scandura's Structural Learning Theory (Scandura, 1986). In SLT, both declarative and procedural knowledge are subsumed in a single rule structure. In the rule structure, higher-order rules subsume lower-order ones, and separate knowledge structures are not postulated.

Expert Knowledge. In studying differences between expert and novice problem solvers, André's review distinguishes two types of knowledge important for our purposes:

*   Heuristic knowledge. Heuristics, or generally applicable (but imprecise) production systems, are used by experts to control problem representation and selection of solution strategy.

- Domain-specific knowledge. Experts have mastered large arrays of knowledge specific to a particular domain. This knowledge probably includes:

  — the symbol system in use

  — the structure of the system

  — types of problems

  — problem solution algorithms

  — strategies for applying heuristic knowledge to domain specific knowledge.

Again, there is a contrast with SLT. SLT does not allow for extra-domain knowledge, other than a single "goal-switching" control mechanism, which is taken to be innate. What others call heuristics are taken within SLT to be higher-order rules, which may be applied to generate lower-order (content-specific) rules as required.

Another important phenomenon is automaticity, or the ability to process certain kinds of highly standardized algorithms rapidly and with minimal cognitive processing load (Schneider & Shiffrin, 1977). There is growing evidence that automaticity is important because it frees up attentional power for other, less standardized tasks. Elio (1986) suggests that this effect applies to production systems, but not to concepts. In other words, rapid recall of facts does not necessarily facilitate learning of advanced skills, but rapid performance of component subskills does.

Finally, the expert's reasoning process itself has been studied. Elstein, Schulman and Sprafka (1978) characterized physician's reasoning process as hypothetico-deductive, meaning that expert physicians usually formulated a small number of hypotheses early in the problem-solving process, then gathered the information with the greatest power in discriminating between competing hypotheses. This is essentially a refinement of earlier views (for example, Gagne, 1954) that activities such as fault identification are essentially tree-structured deductive tasks involving sequential discrimination of multiple cues. However, more recent work (Patel & Groen, 1986) suggests that this kind of backward reasoning may *not* be used universally. At least in the case of problems of moderate difficulty, a forward reasoning process seems to be more characteristic of experts.

With these basic concepts in mind, let us now turn to the problem of teaching troubleshooting by addressing it as a subset of the general issue of teaching problem solving.

HOW TO TEACH
TROUBLESHOOTING

If we approach the task of designing instruction for troubleshooting by using a standard instructional design model, it makes sense to first discuss the analysis of the task, and then to address the selection of appropriate instructional strategies.

Analyzing the Task. The theory reviewed above leads to some significant departures from conventional task/content analysis. The analysis procedure might look like this:

1. If experts use a symbol system to describe the system, identify it. Then analyze the characteristics of the symbol system through a conventional concept analysis.

   This recommendation is based on the finding that knowledge of an appropriate symbol system is the first level of an expert's domain-specific knowledge.

2. Using this symbol system, represent the system under study, identifying components within the system. The level of detail of analysis should be such that the smallest unit of analysis corresponds to the smallest component to be acted upon in troubleshooting. The analysis should include at least the name and function of each system component.

    This corresponds to the identification of concepts or schemata for an expert's domain-specific knowledge, or the lowest order of rules in an SLT rule structure.

3. For each component, identify the failure modes and the probabilities and costs associated with each failure. Then group the failure modes into categories.

    This corresponds to identification of the expert's knowledge of the types of problems which occur. The recommendation to attach probabilities and costs to the failures is consistent with Elstein, Schulman, and Sprafka (1978), and also with work done with some expert systems.

4. For each *category* of failure, identify the solution algorithm for isolating the problem. The algorithms are specific indicators or tests which isolate component failures. They are not complete algorithms for troubleshooting the entire system. It may also be worthwhile to identify the relative cost and reliability of each test.

    This corresponds to an expert's knowledge of problem solution algorithms for each problem type, or higher-order rules within SLT. There is some evidence from studies such as Elstein, Schulman, and Sprafka (1978) that experts also take into account the cost and reliability of each test when weighing the information value of each alternative.

5. For the system as a whole, derive heuristics which may be applied to guide linking of the detailed solution algorithms to find a particular fault.

    This corresponds to an expert's knowledge of problem solving strategies, or the highest-order rules within SLT.

Compared to conventional behavioral analysis, this task analysis is much more comprehensive, yet potentially simpler to perform. It shows the structure of the system when it works, and when it doesn't work; it also shows the production systems used by an expert when troubleshooting at a precise and a heuristic level. However, it does not do what a behavioral analysis would: it does not map the exact algorithms needed to troubleshoot every particular fault in a specific system. Instead, it assumes that detailed troubleshooting algorithms are constructed by experts as they are confronted with each malfunction. To do this, the experts draw on all five types of knowledge analyzed above. If all five types of knowledge are taught to learners in an effective way, the assumption is that they also will be able to construct the algorithms as experts do.

This approach to cognitive task analysis also differs from that proposed by Brien and Duchastel (1986). In their technique, discrete learner objectives are developed for reproduction competencies (for which the learner is expected to recall the algorithm), and production competencies (which the learner must generate). The production competencies correspond to the troubleshooting algorithms mentioned in point 4 above. However, Brien and Duchastel do not seem to make separate provisions for heuristic knowledge, as recommended in point 5 above. Furthermore, structural analysis of the relationships between the rules in the knowledge structure is not discussed.

With the task analysis complete, let us turn to the design of the instructional strategy.

Instructional Strategies. It would seem logical to teach each of the five types of knowledge with a separate instructional strategy. However, there is considerable controversy over whether this is really effective. For example, Duncan (1985) reported improvements in fault-finding efficiency, but not accuracy, when various problem representation strategies were taught. Improvements in accuracy came only with practice. An attempt to directly represent production systems to physics students by Hewson and Posner (1984) yielded mixed results. Others have concluded that greater transfer occurs when concepts and production systems are taught in an integrated fashion as a complete system representation. Scandura (1986) concurs from both theoretical and empirical evidence that use of separate instructional strategies is both less efficient and less effective.

While integrated teaching of concepts and production systems may be best for declarative knowledge, the opposite may be true of procedural knowledge such as the specific algorithms and general heuristics known by experts. Chaiklin (1984) has argued that verbal representation of procedural rules assists novices as they master the rules, even though the verbal representations drop out when experts use the procedures. Furthermore, Chaiklin argues that even experts may return to verbal representation of the rules when confronted by a difficult problem.

These recommendations are far from certain. Each of them could be challenged by citing conflicting research findings. However, it appears (at least to this author) that they represent the most persuasive positions among current work. Combining them with more widely recognized instructional strategy recommendations leads to this instructional strategy for teaching troubleshooting:

1. First, teach the symbol system used to represent the problem. The symbol system is essentially a system of declarative knowledge involving both terms and concepts. Procedures for teaching terms and concepts using sequences of definitions, positive and negative examples have been well documented, most recently by Tennyson and Cocchiarella (1986).

2. Then, teach the system under study, including both its components and their causal relationships (how the system works). This corresponds to the recommendation to teach concepts and production systems simultaneously. Procedures for teaching in this way are outlined by Tennyson and Cocchiarella (1986).

3. Continue teaching the system by identifying the failure modes of each type of system component and how each failure affects the system as a whole (how it works when it doesn't work). Again, this is an example of teaching both concepts and production systems at the same time, so the instructional procedures would be as in the previous step. However, in this case the content directly concerns system malfunctions.

   If the designer wishes to teach probabilities and costs for each class of failure, these would be two kinds of concept attribute to teach.

4. Teach algorithms for isolating each type of component failure. These would be specific algorithms that provide definitive tests to isolate each class of component failure. They would be taught using standard procedure teaching strategies, such as those outlines by Salisbury, Richards, and Klein (1985).

5. Teach heuristics for troubleshooting the system in general. Use a practice strategy which asks the learner to state the heuristics and use them by applying them to troubleshooting the system. In other words, practice of the heuristics would involve asking the learner to verbalize them as they generate and state specific algorithms for troubleshooting given problems in specific systems. This is an application of Chaiklin's (1984) recommendation and is also consistent with Gagne (1954).

A general consideration is whether, in each step, the learner should continue practice until automaticity is achieved. As previously noted, Elio's (1986) argument that automaticity facilitates learning of production systems but not concepts suggests that extended practice should be planned at least for steps 2 through 4, especially in exercises requiring the learner to apply the production systems by stating or predicting functional relations. Reasoning from Duncan's (1985) review, one would expect the extended practice to affect only accuracy and speed of solving such exercises.

It should also be noted that steps 2 through 5 would involve heavy use of simulation to teach the production systems and heuristics. The realism of such simulations should be carefully regulated. The simulations should provide only the practice of relevance for each step. Consequently, they are likely to be relatively unrealistic, allowing for considerable intrusion of instruction into the simulation. This is consistent with Munro, Fehling, and Towne's (1985) recommendation for computer-based simulations.

The strategy described above represents a plausible application of some current research. However, many of the recommendations may be open to challenge based on studies other than those cited. Furthermore, the author could identify no examples of actual instructional systems using all five of the recommended strategies. To illustrate some of the recommendations, the next section will briefly describe a commercial training product which applies some of them. Then, a final section will summarize some of the points of controversy surrounding the instructional strategy proposed above.

CICS MAINTENANCE:
A PRACTICAL APPLICATION OF
SELECTED PRINCIPLES

The CICS Maintenance product (Robbins & Connors, 1987) was developed by Advanced Systems, Inc. as the introductory course in its curriculum to teach IBM's CICS application programming system. The course was implemented in a combination of linear video with a printed text exercise manual (Video Assisted Instruction, or VAI), and level III interactive video, with a supplementary printed text component and a pocket reference job aid (Interactive Video Instruction, or IVI). The target audience for the course is proficient applications programmers and systems analysts who are learning CICS for the first time. Needs analysis showed that beginning CICS programmers are first assigned to maintenance tasks, such as fixing bugs or adding features to existing CICS programs. In spite of this, there are no reference manuals or training products which explicitly teach this skill. Instead, it is widely regarded by CICS experts as one which is hard to learn and not usually mastered until the programmer has had a number of years' experience with CICS.

The course thus represents a radical departure from conventional CICS entry-level training in at least two ways. First, it is an explicit attempt to teach novices a skill which experts widely believe "can be learned, but not taught." Second, the course is an explicit attempt to teach a high-level problem-solving skill.

The course is not a full implementation of the analysis and design strategy outline above. However, some of the principles identified were applied. These are described below.

Task Analysis
- Analysis of the symbol system was in this case analysis of the CICS programming language itself, using conventional methods of concept analysis.

- Representation of the system under study. The system under study was CICS programs, as implemented in typical programming structures. Analysis thus included identification of typical programming structures as executed in blocks of CICS code. Analogies to COBOL programming also were identified.

- Failure modes. The failure modes included both commonly occurring bugs and frequent maintenance requests. These were identified by expert CICS programmers and then grouped into categories. No attempt was made to exhaustively identify every possible bug or maintenance requirement. Instead, only the problems which were most commonly occurring and most typical of their category were analyzed.

- Solution algorithm. Specific solution algorithms, such as debugging tests or modification procedures, were not separately identified in task analysis.

- Heuristics. For each category of bug or maintenance request, "rules of thumb" were identified, in the form of small productions for "things to check" or "points to consider." These then were sequenced into a flowchart (a format chosen because of its familiarity to the audience), even though the result was not fully deterministic.

Instructional Strategies
- Teaching the symbol system was done early in the course, in linear video with text-based practice, using standard concept teaching sequences involving careful isolation and presentation of concept attributes, use of positive and negative example sequences, and spaced practice involving generation of simple code and discrimination of positive and negative examples of concepts.

- Teaching the system under study was done by introducing the basic programming structures through analysis of blocks of CICS code and through analogy to COBOL.

- Teaching the failure modes was done by introducing the heuristic flowchart in interactive video. At its highest level, the cells in the flowchart are a taxonomy of program update types. This taxonomy was taught using conventional coordinate concept teaching strategies.

- Teaching the heuristics was done by presentation of each of the production systems ("rules of thumb") shown in the flowchart to be relevant to each type of program update. Practice was two-level: first, in an on-line CBT format, learners were asked to analyze a typical CICS maintenance request and select the production systems which applied to that problem. Then, learners were given a "final exercise" involving handling of a simulated maintenance request and manual rewriting of CICS code.

The course is structured to facilitate self-paced mastery learning. However, practice is insufficient to lead to true automaticity for any of the skills taught.

While the course is a conscious attempt to apply some of the principles identified in this paper within the constraints of a practical, commercial development project, it is not without compromise. To complete the course within constraints of time and budget, a number of design decisions had to be made which are not fully supported by the research cited above. Thus, the project helped us identify a number of topics of interest to instructional designers which do not appear to be fully explored by research. These topics will be discussed in the next section.

WHAT WE DON'T KNOW ABOUT TEACHING TROUBLESHOOTING

The research cited above, and our experience with the CICS project, leads to articulation of a number of questions which are as yet not fully answered in the literature. These include:

1. How should knowledge be represented? In the CICS project, flowcharts were used to represent what was really a heuristic process. Concept hierarchies were used for the concept analysis. However, other authors have used a large variety of representation techniques, especially for production systems, heuristics, and rule structures. As yet there are no standard recommendations for the representation system to use in a cognitive task analysis. Scandura (1986) argues that the various representation systems have varying strengths, much as do different computer programming languages. If this is so, then what is needed are recommendations for when to use each representation system.

2. Should the strategy components of the skill be directly verbalized and taught, or should they be acquired inductively through practice? Chaiklin (1984) is typical of those who advocate direct verbal teaching of cognitive strategies. Other investigators argue for inductive modeling (discovery) of strategies through practice, with little or no verbalization of the strategy.

3. Do the principles of teaching procedures apply to cognitive strategies and heuristics? Principles of procedure teaching such as those summarized by Salisbury, Richards, and Klein (1985) may apply, but it may be that other techniques are more appropriate.

4. How should simulations be constructed for practicing the procedural knowledge components of troubleshooting skills? There are indications that carefully constructed by unrealistic simulations are more effective than realistic simulations, especially early in the learning process (see, for example, Munro, Fehling, & Towne, 1985). However, empirically validated guidelines for constructing such simulations are only fragmentary.

5. How can a designer predict when the benefits of achieving automaticity outweigh the development costs for the extended practice sequences? Authors such as Elio (1986) argue that automaticity is needed for low-level algorithmic components of problem solving, in order to manage attentional loading in higher-level components. If this is so, what decision rules can a developer use to identify *a priori* the component subskills truly requiring automaticity?

Many more questions could be derived, of course. But it should be clear that research on the learning psychology side of the cognitive field far outstrips the research on the instructional psychology side. In many ways, the situation is analogous to that over twenty years ago, when behavioral theories did a much better job of describing learning than of prescribing instruction. At that time, a behaviorally-based instructional psychology was developed. Perhaps it is time to do the same, using cognitive psychology as a basis.

REFERENCES

André, T. (1986). Problem solving and education. In G. D. Phye and T. André (Eds.), *Cognitive classroom learning: Understanding, thinking and problem solving*. New York: Academic Press.

Barsalou, L. W., & Bauer, G. H. (1984). Discrimination nets as psychological models. *Cognitive Science, 8*, 1-26.

Brien, R., & Duchastel, P. (1986, November). Cognitive task analysis underlying the specification of instructional objectives. *Programmed Learning and Educational Technology, 23*(4), 363-370.

Chaiklin, S. (1984). On the nature of verbal rules and their rules in problem solving. *Cognitive Science, 8*, 131-155.

Cunningham, D. J. (1986). Good guys and bad guys. *Educational Communication and Technology Journal, 34*(1), 3-7.

Duncan, K. D. (1985). Representations of fault-finding problems and development of fault-finding strategies. *Programmed Learning & Educational Technology, 22*(2), 125-139.

Elio, R. (1986). Representation of similar well-learned cognitive procedures. *Cognitive Science, 10*, 41-75.

Elstein, A. S., Schulman, L. S., & Sprafka, S. A. (1978). *Medical problem solving: An analysis of clinical reasoning*. Cambridge, MA: Harvard University Press.

Fredericksen, N. (1984). Implications of cognitive theory for instruction in problem solving. *Review of Educational Research, 54*(3), 363-407.

Gagne, R. M. (1954). An analysis of two problem-solving activities. Air Force Personnel & Training Research Center Research Bulletin AFPTRC-TR-54-77.

Hewson, P. W., & Posner, G. J. (1984). The use of schema theory in the design of instructional materials: A physics example. *Instructional Science, 13*, 119-139.

Mager, R. (1982). *Troubleshooting the troubleshooting course, or debug d'bugs*. Belmont, CA: Pitman Learning.

Munro, A., Fehling, M., & Towne, D. (1985). Instruction intrusiveness in dynamic simulation training. *Journal of Computer-Based Instruction, 12*(2), 50-53.

Patel, V., & Groen, G. (1986). Knowledge based solution strategies in medical reasoning. *Cognitive Science, 10*, 91-116.

Robbins, A., & Connors, M. (1987). *CICS maintenance*. Course #5055 (Interactive Video and Video Assisted Instruction). Arlington Heights, IL: Advanced Systems.

Salisbury, D., Richards, B., & Klein, J. (1985). Designing practice: A review of prescriptions from instructional design theories. *Journal of Instructional Development, 8*(4), 9-19.

Scandura, J. M. (1986). System issues in problem solving research. *Journal of Structural Learning, 9*, 1-13.

Schneider, W., & Shiffrin, R. (1977). Controlled and automatic human information processing: I. Detection, search and attention. *Psychological Review, 84*(1), 1-66.

Tennyson, R., & Cocchiarella, M. (1986). An empirically based instructional design theory for teaching concepts. *Review of Educational Research, 56*(1), 40-71.

35

Evaluation
A General View

Edward Kifer
Educational Policy Studies and Evaluation, University of Kentucky
Lexington, Kentucky

INTRODUCTION

My intent in this chapter is to propose a general perspective from which to view evaluation studies. The view, one hopes, will provide both a framework from which to judge evaluations and also a way to think about conducting them. Missing from the chapter is a discussion of areas requiring technical expertise. Things not included, among others, are questions of sampling designs, instrument construction, interviewing techniques, field notes, validity and reliability, and the analysis of educational objectives. Instead, the focus is on providing a framework into which can be fitted some or all of these technical matters.

The chapter ends with an example of the questions that might be raised and designs to answer them when conducting an evaluation of a new curriculum. Embedded in that example are some technical considerations. These are alluded to but not elucidated.

WHAT IS EVALUATION?

Evaluation can be defined as disciplined inquiry to determine the worth of things, where *things* may include programs, products, procedures, or objects. As a way to ask and answer questions, evaluation activities, aims, and methods can be distinguished from more traditional research, which is another type of inquiry. There are three dimensions on which research and evaluation can differ.

First, evaluation need not have as its objective the generation of new knowledge. Evaluation is applied; research is basic. Second, evaluation, presumably, produces information that is used to make decisions or form a basis for making decisions or determining policies. Evaluation yields information that has immediate use; research need not. Third, evaluation is a judgment of worth. Evaluations result in value judgments; research need not and some would say should not.

EVALUATION MODELS

There are a plethora of evaluation models. Each requires a skilled evaluator to implement and each focuses on slightly different issues in the course of conducting an evaluation. Each has its strengths and weaknesses; each may be more applicable to one setting than another.

Figure 35.1 provides a heuristic for evaluation studies. An evaluator chooses one or more of the existing evaluation models, applies his or her skills to a problem, and conducts a study within a set of constraints. An evaluation may contain aspects of each of these dimensions. Any one evaluation may not be a pure type, but one may be able to see some aspects of the models discussed below.

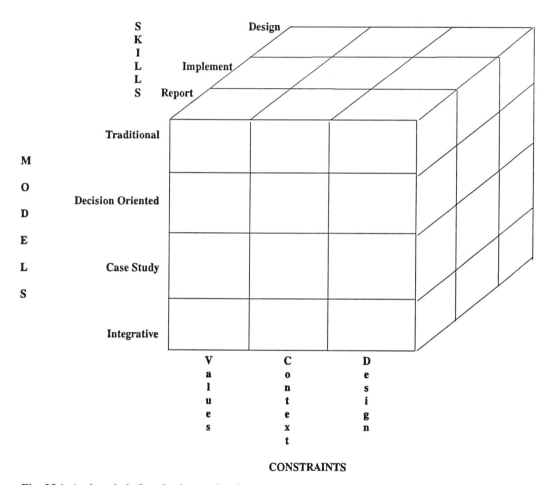

Fig. 35.1. An heuristic for viewing evaluations.

Traditional—Tyler Rationale

This is probably the first evaluation model in what could be called the "modern era" of evaluation. It is based on the work of Ralph Tyler (1949), who emphasized consistency between goals, experiences, and outcomes.

For Tyler, goals are to be made operational in terms of measurable (behavioral) objectives reflecting changes that will occur in participants when they have received appropriate instruction or have had appropriate experiences. Samples of the outcomes of instruction or experiences are collected both immediately after them and later as a follow-up. Baseline information (what the participants knew prior to the treatment) is crucial in order to assess changes, so pretest-posttest designs are called for. If the goals are not met, one looks for ways to change the instruction and the experiences. Tyler's is mainly a goal attainment model, with a heavy emphasis on a broad array of behavioral outcomes.

Decision-oriented—Stufflebeam

Stufflebeam (1983) emphasizes collecting information from a variety of sources to provide a basis for making better decisions. This model, often given the acronym CIPP (context, input, process, and product), distinguishes various phases of an evaluation study. A context evaluation focuses on needs of a particular group; provides a rationale for a set of goals and objectives; and provides a basis for planning a program, activity, or curriculum. An input evaluation provides information about how one can marshall resources to structure activities and experiences in order to increase the probability that one can meet specific objectives. This is an analysis of what a system is capable of doing and of which of a competing set of strategies might be most efficient given specific goals. Process evaluation is used to monitor programs and check the degree to which the planned programs or activities have been implemented. Product evaluation focuses on outcomes and decisions about whether goals have been reached. Process evaluation is a piece of the CIPP model that most closely resembles the Tyler rationale.

Case Study—Ethnographic—Stake

While the traditional or decision-oriented models are labeled by some as quantitative approaches to evaluation, case studies or ethnographic ones may be called qualitative (Stake, 1967). The emphasis is on understanding what is being evaluated; being responsive to various diverse interests and audiences, sometimes called stake holders, of the evaluation; and, more or less, using methods associated with anthropology to gather evidence about what is being evaluated. Characteristics of this approach include being a participant observer, asking key informants about what is happening, and providing information about whether or not a program has been implemented. While routine data collection may include administering traditional questionnaires and tests, the main thrust here is on the perceptions and experiences of the observer.

Goal Free and Integrative—Scriven

A goal free approach emphasizes determining all of the effects or outcomes and deciding whether the effects, either intended or not, are desirable (Scriven, 1967; 1983). A program should have a set of goals, but an evaluator should not restrict an inquiry into those preordained outcomes. Meeting trivial goals means a trivial program. Not meeting difficult but desirable goals might be the best a program could do. Unintended outcomes may be more powerful and compelling than the intended ones. One is interested not only in outcomes but also in what it costs to produce them. That is, part of an evaluation is to weigh costs versus benefits. Scriven (1983) has integrated his approach through a key evaluation checklist, part of which is used in the example part of this chapter.

Although I describe both "qualitative" and "quantitative" models in the above discussion, I do not believe that this is a useful way to distinguish between the models. Some questions are best answered using one approach; others need different ones. There is room within each of the basic models to conduct both "qualitative" and "quantitative" studies. As the example at the end of this chapter indicates, a thorough evaluation is likely to use diverse methods which fall in both the qualitative and quantitative camps. For a discussion of these differences, see Cook and Reichardt (1979).

There are, of course, other models of evaluation. I have chosen these because they cover a range of alternatives. For discussions of other models and perspectives, Popham (1975) and Madaus, Scriven, & Stufflebeam (1983) are excellent sources. It is important to recognize the variety of models and methods available to an evaluator. I also think it is important to recognize that no evaluation study need be a pure type. Any one study can be a hybrid depending on the questions being asked and the means used to obtain the results.

ADDITIONAL SPECIFICATIONS

Having chosen a model, an evaluator then applies a set of skills to design a particular study which operates within a set of powerful constraints. Some of the more important skills and salient constraints are elaborated upon in the next two sections.

Skills

Designing

An evaluator must ask appropriate questions and gather evidence that responds to those questions. Important questions are determined by the nature of what is to be evaluated. For example, a change in curriculum assumes that different types of learning outcomes are expected. A proper focus for an evaluation would be how much students advanced toward these new goals and what other (unintended) things they learned. A new product (software for a computer) might also be evaluated in terms of changes in students but would also include such computing-relevant dimensions as the speed of the program, how easily used and learned, whether the presentation was aesthetically pleasing, what kinds of feedback were provided, and how the program dealt with errors.

Implementing

When choosing a set of procedures and types of instrumentation, an evaluator seeks congruence between them and the proposed evaluation design. A common complaint about new programs is that they have not been implemented correctly. This is also true of evaluations. Often there is a knee-jerk reaction against using anything but questionnaires or tests to collect information. Such techniques as interviewing, videotaping, and merely talking with participants are shunned because they are too soft. But they are, in fact, powerful ways to collect important information about the product or process being studied.

Assessing

What data are collected and how they are analyzed should be consistent with the design and implementation of the evaluation. There is a tendency to collect too much of the wrong kind of data. For lack of a clear vision of what should be evaluated and how that evaluation should be conducted, loads of data are collected that are never used. Also, some types of data (existing records or a paper trail) are ignored at the expense of less relevant information. There is too much emphasis on questionnaires and too little collecting and archiving of well-focused data.

Reporting

Good evaluation reports are focused on an appropriate audience and report complex results in straightforward, understandable ways. While a research paper follows more or less well-known and accepted conventions, that is not true of an evaluation report. Most evaluations are done for several different audiences. Tailoring reports to those audiences is a major facet of producing an effective evaluation. Effective reporting can vary from a short one- or two-page summary to the more conventional, full-scale report.

Constraints

Values

Evaluations should include a judgment of worth, looking at value orientations and potential conflicts. Traditional research is reported in a "value free" context and uses neutral language as a vehicle for claiming objectivity. In virtually all evaluation settings a question of why this thing being evaluated is good should be at the center of inquiry. Evaluators should seek to raise values issues, not repress them.

Contexts

Context constraints include how the setting of an evaluation impinges on what can be done effectively. Politics influence what can be done in an evaluation. Stakeholders will differ in terms of what they believe should be done. Evaluators and evaluations should be responsive to many constituencies, but there will be avenues of inquiry and seemingly pertinent questions that will be difficult to pursue or ask. These conflicts, too, must be brought to light, not hidden from the various audiences.

Design

The constraint here is on how the design of an evaluation can affect the strength of conclusions that might be reached. In traditional research, experiments allow one to talk about cause and effect in powerful ways. In most evaluation contexts it is difficult to have experimental control over the relevant variables. However, thoughtful designs and appropriate methods can be used so that one can produce information and evaluations that are useful. Quality of information gathered during an evaluation is of greater importance than the power of the evaluation design.

THE FORMATIVE-SUMMATIVE DISTINCTION

Operating above or through this proposed view of evaluation activities is the distinction made by Scriven (1967) between the roles of formative and summative evaluation. While developing a product, one collects information about that process and its progress. If things are not going as planned—there were unforeseen obstacles, changes in personnel, a redirection of efforts—an evaluator should document and respond to those deviations. Putting the project back on track through evaluation activities during the process is formative evaluation.

At the end of the development phase, after some entity has been put in place, one wants to know what its effects are. This type of evaluation is summative. For summative evaluations one is interested in making statements about what works and what does not work, what changes and what does not change, and what is worthwhile and what is not worthwhile. A summative evaluation leads to final reports about the effectiveness of what is being evaluated.

One practical example of the distinction between formative and summative evaluation can be found in mastery learning (Bloom, 1968). Instructional units in this approach are assumed to be structured linearly. That is, learning a first unit is a necessary but not sufficient condition for learning a second. General topics subsume these instructional units. In the mastery paradigm one typically gives formative tests after each of the instructional units. Based on the results of those evaluations, students are given additional work or receive the next instructional unit. After having completed all of the units, where each has a formative evaluation and students have mastered each, an overall evaluation of the broader general topics is done. This final evaluation is summative and used to determine the extent to which students have accomplished what was expected in the general unit.

It is the case, of course, that this summative evaluation could be considered a formative one for the next general idea or issue to be addressed. These distinctions—formative versus summative—are based on two different notions. First, there is the question of whether the role of the evaluation is to intervene in a process to change it: That would be formative. If the role is to make statements about effectiveness, that is summative. But effectiveness statements can play a formative role as well. This happens when one changes the level at which an analysis is conducted. In the mastery example, the summative results for the general idea covered in the instruction could provide formative information for the next level of instruction. For example, one could use the summative evaluation of a first course in statistics as a formative evaluation for the second.

AN EXAMPLE EVALUATION

As an example of the kinds of questions that could be asked and the kinds of methods that might be used to evaluate a particular thing, I have chosen the Perseus project (Crane & Mylonas, 1988). I chose this for several reasons. (1) It is an ambitious attempt to provide an interactive database on classical Greek civilization. Because it is ambitious, one can have an ambitious evaluation scheme. (There are those who say that evaluation activities should be provided 20 percent of the budget allocated for the development of a project.) (2) It seeks to combine advanced computing technology with a view of learning that emphasizes inquiry. (3) Its possible educational roles are sufficiently diverse (it is a learning tool for students, a structuring tool for instructors, a reference for all interested in classical Greece, and an expandable database for future research publications and other related efforts), so a diverse set of evaluation questions and techniques is called for.

Crane & Mylonas (1988) suggest that some formative evaluation activities have already been completed. For example, there has been work done with students that suggests the Perseus approach is more fun for them. Instructors have reported that students are more confident and better informed using Perseus than they were prior to its implementation. Let us assume that Perseus is at a stage where it might be implemented in several settings and used in ways that were envisaged by the authors. What kinds of questions, methods and approaches might be used to evaluate Perseus?

While Scriven (1983) might advocate beginning with a needs assessment, I will assume that a program of this type can be justified intrinsically by how it can enhance knowledge of classical Greece. Instead of beginning with a needs assessment, I will start with one general and several basic questions that could (and I think should) be asked about a project of this magnitude. I do not claim that this is the most important question that can be asked about a complex program like this. Rather, I want it to be a good question. Without any great deal of difficulty I could have generated 10 or more questions of this sort.

The general question is: Does Perseus enhance learning about classical Greek civilization? The general question leads to more specific ones. The first question is: Does Perseus enhance learning? There are other questions involved in that one: (1) Do students learn more and better when using Perseus in a course on classical Greek civilization? (2) Can instructors in a Western civilization course use Perseus as a way to integrate information about classical Greece in their course? (3) Which components of Perseus are used most effectively by students in a classical Greek course? (4) Which components of Perseus are used most effectively by students in a related course? (5) Do the computing requirements of Perseus hinder its adaptation to existing courses? There are many others.

Creating a Design

The first question is a classic curriculum evaluation question, so one could start with Tyler and think of a pretest-posttest follow-up design. One could peruse a course syllabus of an existing Greek civilization course to see what content was covered and what was supposed to be learned by the participants. Based on those specifications, pretest information (it need not only be through objective tests but could include term projects or portfolios of what students had done during the course, and need not be limited to "cognitive" outcomes but could include an array of opinions, attitudes, and preferences) would be specified; a parallel set of information would be gathered immediately after the course; and, sometime later in the students' careers, this information would be collected again. If this were a typical course, this might be sufficient to assess the outcomes of learning with Perseus. Big gains would be attributed to the innovation and Perseus would be deemed successful.

But if there were no major gains, the design would not provide a means to assess what went wrong. For Perseus the intense computing that one must do is an obvious difficulty in integrating the material into the existing course. Hence, at least two variations are needed in order to institute a more powerful evaluation. First, one would build upon the existing design by making it a comparative study. Instead of a single location, one would choose multiple sites. For the multiple sites one would select two comparable courses: one receives Perseus and the other does not.

To respond to the issue of the intense computing demands, different ways would be used to show students and faculty how to master Perseus. Such planned variation might include for one site a two-week training session, for a second site a Perseus-trained expert who would be available to construct laboratory experiences and assist students and faculty in the use of the system, and for a third the training materials available with the product would be supplied. The net result of the first addition to the basic design is the need for at least three sites and two courses at each site. Obvious comparisons would be made between Perseus and non-Perseus and between the different training techniques.

However, without some knowledge of the extent to which either Perseus or the training sessions were implemented, one would not have a basis for forming conjectures about why a program worked in one site and not at another. Hence, one needs on site an observer or some proxy for an observer in order to be able to find out what happened at the different sites. The importance of such an observer has been well documented by Trend (1979).

For the second variation, I will add an observer to each of the sites. That observer's task is to describe as well as possible what happened at each site. That would include monitoring the training programs, talking with students and faculty who used Perseus, perhaps learning Perseus so as better to understand it, and describing the contexts in which the instruction took place.

Having chosen the design and implemented the evaluation schema, and having within the schema a way to talk about what kinds of constraints were imposed on the evaluation, I will assume that all has gone well (which, of course, will never be the case) and that, as the evaluator, I have received all of the information collected from my study. My problem now is to provide reports on the success, or lack of it, of Perseus. I have at my disposal the quantitative data gathered during pretest and posttest for each of the conditions. I have information about what went on in the training sessions. And I have a description of what occurred at each of the sites. My job is to make sense of this voluminous data set.

My first job is to determine my audiences. First there is the agency that funded my evaluation, then the producers of Perseus. Then there is an audience of potential users of the innovation. There is also a cohort of evaluators who are interested (presumably) in what I have done and a cohort of developers who wish to know more about Perseus and its implementation. There is a public that is interested in the educational effects of technology. (There may be others but that is enough for this discussion.)

First, I must report to the funding agency. That report would be the longest and most comprehensive. But rather than conceive of that as a single report, I view it as three separate ones. First is an eight- to ten-page summary of what was found. That summary is a kind of

"Reader's Digest" that highlights the most important findings, discusses the biggest obstacles faced by this program, and arrives at a conclusion of whether or not Perseus is a good thing. The second report is the typical final report. It contains a detailed description of Perseus, how it was implemented in the various sites, the major results of the evaluation, an interpretation of those results, and a judgment of the worth of Perseus. The appendix of the report contains the raw data and descriptive information gathered during the evaluation. The third report is the data archive. Data are structured so other persons can analyze results. The field notes are contained in files easily accessible to such software programs as the Ethnographer. This third report, a data archive, provides a basis for secondary analyses of this complex project.

To the developers I send a report that is formative in nature. It details what types of things might be changed in order to make Perseus more amenable to being exported. This report need not be long, but should be prescriptive.

Assuming that the project fared well, one should think of still another kind of report. That should be aimed at an audience of potential users. Its focus would be on those things necessary for adopting Perseus. It would include the kinds of training, the resources, and the general configuration of hardware and other computing essentials that are needed successfully to adopt the Perseus program.

Finally, one could produce a brief press release that would inform the public at large of what new and good things are available within academe.

CONCLUSION

I have, I hope, provided a sketch of what kinds of things can be done under the broad heading of an evaluation study. The sketch is a general one that encourages the potential evaluator to be eclectic in terms of models, to have questions drive a design, not to be greatly concerned with whether one is doing a qualitative or a quantitative study, and to report responsibly to a variety of audiences.

This is a broadly based curriculum example, but the approach is general. If an evaluator wished, for instance, to look at only the technical pieces of Perseus—things such as the appropriateness of content, the speed of the machine, the quality of the graphics, the extent to which the database was integrated so that text and appropriate graphics were easily accessible— such things as choosing defensible outcomes (what should a program like this be able to do), varying the setting (users with different needs and past experience), planning the variation (use in different courses and settings), and reporting to a variety of audiences would be germaine.

REFERENCES

Bloom, B. S. (1967). Learning for mastery. *Evaluation Comment, 1*(2), 1-12.

Bloom, B., et al. (1971). *Handbook of formative and summative evaluation of student learning.* New York: McGraw-Hill.

Cook, T. (Ed.). (1978). *Evaluation studies annual review, 3.* Beverly Hills, CA: Sage.

Cook, T. D., & Reichardt, C. I. (Eds.). (1979). *Qualitative and quantitative methods in evaluation on research.* Beverly Hills, CA: Sage.

Crane, G., & Mylonas, E. (1988). The Perseus project: An interactive curriculum of classical Greek civilization. *Educational Technology, 28*(11), 25-32.

Madaus, G. F., Scriven, M., & Stufflebeam, D. L. (Eds.). (1983). *Evaluation models.* Boston: Kluwer-Nijhoff.

Patton, Michael Quinn. (1980). *Qualitative evaluation methods.* Beverly Hills, CA: Sage.

Popham, W. J. (Ed.). (1975). *Educational evaluation.* Englewood Cliffs, NJ: Prentice-Hall.

Scriven, M. S. (1967). The methodology of evaluation. In *Perspectives of Curriculum Evaluation.* (AERA Monograph Series on Curriculum Evaluation, no. 1). Chicago: Rand McNally.

————. (1974). Pros and cons about goal-free evaluation. *Evaluation Comment, 3,* 1-4.

————. (1983). Evaluation ideologies. In G. F. Madaus, M. Scriven, & D. L. Stufflebeam (Eds.), *Evaluation models.* Boston: Kluwer-Nijhoff.

Stake, R. E. (1967). The countenance of educational evaluation. *Teachers College Record, 68,* 523-540.

Stufflebeam, D. L. (1983). The CIPP model for program evaluation. In G. F. Madaus, M. Scriven, & D. L. Stufflebeam (Eds.), *Evaluation models.* Boston: Kluwer-Nijhoff.

Trend, M. G. (1979). On the reconciliation of qualitative and quantitative analyses. In T. D. Cook & F. Reichardt (Eds.), *Qualitative and quantitative methods in evaluation research.* Beverly Hills, CA: Sage.

Tyler, R. W. (1949). *Basic principles of curriculum and instruction.* Chicago: University of Chicago Press.

36

Professional Competencies and Certification in the Instructional Technology Field

Barry Bratton
College of Education, University of Iowa
Iowa City, Iowa

CERTIFICATION DEFINED

Professional certification is the formal recognition individuals received from an independent body of peers who have examined their work and evaluated it against some published external standards. The standards vary among professionals, obviously, but the more common ones include membership in a professional association, successful completion of a program of study, and satisfactory performance on an examination. Achieving certification means recognition for possessing specific knowledge and skills at a specified level of competence. Individuals who do not wish to be certified are free to continue working in the same field, but they cannot promote themselves as "certified." Accreditation and licensure are sometimes mistakenly confused with certification. Accreditation recognizes school, college, and university programs that meet certain standards. Licensure, on the other hand, is a legal requirement to protect the public from incompetent practitioners.

Professional certification is not the same as teacher certification. The latter is a misnomer because, in reality, it is a form of licensure. State governments, for example, require that teachers hold a valid certificate in order to teach in public schools.

ESTABLISHING COMPETENCIES

Professional certification rests on the assumption that those people served (e.g., students, teachers, trainers, clients, administrators, etc.) by the members of another field are not always able to judge the quality of the work performed. One way to protect the consumer is for the members of the profession to decide whether their colleagues possess the necessary knowledge and skills to practice in a competent manner. The responsibility for establishing and maintaining the standards for competent performance, therefore, rests with each profession. In many cases the professional associations take on this task. In the instructional technology field two professional organizations have shown tentative interest in certification: the Association for Educational Communications and Technology (AECT) and the National Society for Performance and Instruction (NSPI). Task forces representing AECT and NSPI first worked cooperatively to investigate the viability of certification through a joint task force composed primarily of experts in instructional and training design. The joint task force concluded that a final decision on certification would be premature until it was clear that competencies could be identified. It also decided to use the instructional design area as the first case because this area was the most familiar to the task force members. After three years of research, debate, and formative evaluation, the joint task force produced a list of 16 skills in which instructional designers should be competent. Within each area are essential subcompetencies. Competent instructional designers are able to:

1. Determine projects that are appropriate for using instructional design methodologies.

2. Conduct needs assessments.

3. Assess the relevant characteristics of learner/trainees.

4. Analyze the characteristics (resources, constraints, values, etc.) of the organization's environment.

5. Perform task/content/job analyses.

6. Write statements of performance objectives.

7. Develop the performance measurements.

8. Sequence the performance objectives.

9. Specify the instructional strategies.

10. Design the instructional materials.

11. Evaluate the instructional/training.

12. Design the instructional management system.

13. Plan and monitor instructional design projects.

14. Communicate effectively in visual, oral, and written forms.

15. Interact effectively with other people.

16. Promote the use of instructional design.

Soon thereafter the joint task force elected to become an independent body and restructured itself into a not-for-profit corporation. This action was taken to ensure impartiality and to actively solicit financial support for the corporation's goals. The organization was named the International Board of Standards for Training, Performance and Instruction (IBSTPI). The persons who served on the first governing board of IBSTPI were Barry Bratton, president (University of Iowa), J. Robert Carleton (Vanguard Group), Maurice Coleman (Arthur Andersen & Company), William Coscarelli (Southern Illinois University), Rob Foshay (Advanced Systems, Inc.), Judith Hale, secretary (Hale Associates), Cathleen Hutchison (General Motors Corporation), Thomas Leavens (Leavens, Armiros, & Ross), Linda Robinson (The Contact Group), James Russell (Purdue University), Charline Seyfer (Mountain Bell), Sharon Shrock (Southern Illinois University), Kenneth Silber, vice president (AT&T Communications), Sivasailam Thiagarajan (Institute for International Research), and Odin Westgaard (Hale Associates). The variety of organizations and settings in which these individuals worked, the education they had received, and their professional experiences helped ensure that the competencies represented the state of the art.

The board was helped also by input from the NSPI Standards Committee and the AECT Certification Committee as well as suggestions from individuals throughout the country. The board adopted the agenda of the joint task force and initiated the task of identifying the competencies of a competent trainer/teacher. Competent instructors are able to:

1. Analyze course materials and learner information.

2. Assure preparation of the instructional site.

3. Establish and maintain instructor credibility.

4. Manage the learning environment.

5. Demonstrate effective communication skills.

6. Demonstrate effective presentation skills.

7. Demonstrate effective questioning skills and techniques.

8. Respond appropriately to learners' needs for clarification or feedback.

9. Provide positive reinforcement and motivational incentives.

10. Use instructional methods effectively.

11. Use media effectively.

12. Evaluate learner performance.

13. Evaluate the instruction.

14. Report evaluation information.

Both the designer and the instructor competencies were developed with the following precepts in mind:

- The competencies would reflect the skills of a professional regardless of current job title, academic degree, or type of training.

- The competencies would be performance-based rather than academically oriented.

- While some employment situations might proscribe a designer or teacher/trainer from exhibiting every competency, all the competencies could be demonstrated if needed.

There are several ways in which these and future competency studies can be helpful to the instructional designer:

1. They are a source of information for persons seeking information about instructional technology.

2. They provide experienced designers and trainers/teachers with a tool for self-assessment and professional growth.

3. They provide a common set of concepts and vocabulary that will improve communication among the members of the instructional technology field.

4. They are a vehicle for communicating with employers and persons in other professions.

5. They provide the academic preparation programs with information to develop curricula, courses, internships, and standards.

6. They are a vehicle for communicating to other fields the professional applications of instructional technology.

7. They can be a model for identifying the competencies in other specialties in the instructional technology field.

8. They can be a basis for defining the parameters of the instructional technology field.

As difficult as the work may be, defining the competencies of specialized groups (such as instructional designers) appears to be easier than gaining support for setting standards and instituting a process by which the truly competent can be recognized. The International Board of Standards investigated the certification processes employed by a variety of credentialing agencies. The board took the philosophical position that the credential should reflect performance as opposed to the experience, education, or philosophy a person may have accumulated. This decision therefore ruled out typical paper-pencil tests, oral examinations, or portfolio reviews.

ASSESSMENT CENTER APPROACH

One potentially useful means of assessing on-the-job activities and decisions is the "assessment center." This is the name given to a series of assessments presented to persons who seek jobs or promotions that require high levels of judgment and interpersonal skills. During the assessment, a candidate may be asked to participate in a simulated meeting with a "client" for the purpose of constructing a needs assessment, or to review the objectives and the evaluation methodology for internal consistency, or to recommend the appropriate delivery medium for a specific project. Trainer observers monitor and evaluate candidates' responses and behaviors throughout a variety of experiences and then meet with them in a debriefing session, where each candidate is given the opportunity to explain or give a rationale for the decisions and actions that were taken.

The assessment center approach (or something comparable) is appealing because it (1) does not rely solely on paper-pencil tests, (2) does not focus on the recall of academic information exclusively, (3) has high face validity, and (4) is real-world performance oriented. However, this methodology is not without its drawbacks. Complex simulations and exercises must be created in such a way as to permit applicants to use many skills. The simulations must be reality based but with high fidelity. The observers must be well-trained for their roles as actors (to maintain fidelity) and as assessors (for realiability of the judgments). Only a limited number of candidates can be assessed at any one time.

Even if a perfect assessment process were available, certification would not become a fait accompli. The members of the field will decide if they wish to be certified; recall that it is a voluntary service. If they choose not to seek a certificate, the program will fail before it starts. Regardless of the future of certification, the act of self-examination that produced both the instructional designer and instructor competencies has provided a unique perspective on our roles in the education and training arenas.

REFERENCES

Bratton, B. (1984). Professional certification: Will it become a reality? *Performance and Instruction Journal, 23*(1), 4-7.

Bratton, B., & Hildebrand, M. (1984). Plain talk about professional certification. *Instructional Innovator, 25*(9), 22-24, 49.

Coscarelli, W. (1984). Arguments for certification. *Performance and Instruction Journal, 23*(1), 21-22.

Gilley, J., Geis, G., & Seyfer, C. (1986). Let's talk certification. *Performance and Instruction Journal, 26*(1), 7-17.

Lee, C. (1986). Certification for trainers. *Training, 23*(11), 56-64.

Mager, R., & Cram, D. (1985). The regulators are coming. *Training, 22*(9), 40-45.

Shrock, S., & Foshay, W. (1984). Measurement issues in certification. *Performance and Instruction Journal, 23*(1), 23-27.

37

Employment Profiles and Compensation for Educational Technologists, 1983-1986

Joseph A. Hutchinson

Division of Instructional Support & Development, Louisiana State University
Baton Rouge, Louisiana

and

Pauline M. Rankin

Division of Instructional Support & Development, Louisiana State University
Baton Rouge, Louisiana

Few topics pique our professional interests as much as salaries and employment information. Educational technologists are interested in the comparison of job descriptions and compensation plans for individuals who have backgrounds and responsibilities similar to theirs. Additionally, administrators of educational technology programs are concerned with employing and retaining persons who are appropriate for the positions. To accomplish that task, the administrators require information regarding educational/training experiences, salary levels which are commensurate with the responsibilities of the position, and other factors.

In 1983 the authors conducted a study of employment conditions and income levels of members of the Association for Educational Communications and Technology. A summary of that study was published in *Instructional Innovator* (April 1984). This article reports on a follow-up study designed to identify changes since 1983. It was undertaken as a result of membership requests for updated information. Factors such as the national economy, cutbacks of educational technology personnel and programs, the resulting mobility of AECT members, and the employers' requirements for selecting appropriate personnel contribute to the need for a comprehensive and current body of information regarding the employment and compensation profiles of educational technologists.

Reprinted from *Educational media and technology yearbook 1987*. Littleton, CO: Libraries Unlimited.

METHODOLOGY

A survey instrument similar to the one used in 1983 was mailed to 20 percent of the AECT membership in the spring of 1986. The sample was stratified according to the various types of work settings reported in the AECT membership database. The questionnaire was designed to collect data regarding the following aspects of employment:

- Work setting

- Job classification (description)

- Minimum education required for the position held

- Actual level of education attained by the individual

- Length of employment in the field

- Length of employment in current position

- Annual income

- Basis of employment (12-month, 9-month, length of project, other)

- Source(s) of funding for the individual's present position

- Demographic information (age, sex, ethnicity, geographic location)

A total of 440 (57 percent) usable questionnaires were returned. To provide commonality for job classifications, the brief descriptions found in table 37.1, page 400, were listed. Respondents were asked to indicate the description which most closely approximated their own responsibilities. Information regarding salary levels was solicited by means of a checklist item on the questionnaire. Increments of $2,000.00, ranging from "less than $10,000.00" to "greater than $60,000.00" were used.

Table 37.1.
Job Classification.

Audiovisual Specialist

Performs in a specialty function of the audiovisual field, such as the production and use of audiovisual materials, the utilization and maintenance of audiovisual equipment, or the design and specification of learning facilities.

Librarian/Information Specialist

Major responsibilities relate to selection, acquisition, classification, cataloging, and distribution of materials; locating curriculum, instructional, and research materials; and may include some supervisory and administrative duties.

Media Director/Administrator

Manages the organizational and personnel functions of an audiovisual, library, or media program.

Other Educational Administrator

Manages the organizational and personnel functions of an institution in areas other than audiovisual, library, or media programs.

Teacher/Professor

Instructs and develops courses or programs in an education or training program; subject matter may be in any area.

Curricula/Instructional Developer

Develops units, modules, or courses, and programs of instruction; specifies objectives, content scope and sequence, instructional strategies, and materials for particular learners; may have duties for inservice development of instructors or administrators.

Television Production Specialist/Director

Plans, installs, maintains, or uses television system; plans and produces televised instruction; evaluates television utilization in the education or training organization; may hire or train staff and participate in inservice development of instructors.

Educational Computing Specialist/Director

Plans, installs, maintains, or uses computer systems; plans or produces computer-assisted or computer-managed instruction; evaluates computer hardware and software; directs computer literacy programs.

Researcher/Consultant

Conducts basic or applied investigation and experimentation, and/or gives professional advice.

GENERAL FINDINGS

Demographics

The mean age of AECT members in 1986 was 45.4 years, with the range extending from 22.0 to 75.0 as compared to the 1983 study when the mean age was 44.5 years, with the range extending from 24.0 to 77.0. The 1986 mean age for men was 45.6 and the mean age for women was 45.1. In terms of job classification, members aged 60 and over tended to be media directors, library/information specialists, and audiovisual specialists while the younger members were fairly evenly represented in all job categories. Very few working members were below age 30.

The study indicated that 95.45 percent of the members were Caucasian, a statistic which was virtually the same as reported in the 1983 study. All other ethnic groups combined represented only 4.55 percent of the total usable responses. The breakdown of the ethnic minorities was as follows: black, 2.05 percent; native American, 0.23 percent; Hispanic, 0.91 percent; and Asian/Pacific Islander, 1.36 percent. A 1976 study of members conducted by Molenda and Cambre (1977) revealed that 11.4 percent were members of ethnic minority groups.

The male/female ratio of members remained virtually the same as in the prior study (64 percent male and 36 percent female).

Education

As in 1983, the level of education attained by AECT members somewhat exceeded requirements. The majority of respondents hold graduate degrees: 52.50 percent hold master's degrees, while 33.41 percent hold doctoral degrees. The level of education required for employment was reported as master's, 50.91 percent, and doctoral, 22.95 percent. Furthermore, 17.05 percent of the positions required a bachelor's degree, but only 5.23 percent of the respondents report that degree as the highest level of education attained. Likewise, 4.77 percent of the positions were reported as requiring an associate/technical degree or no specific education. Less than 2 percent of those surveyed indicated their highest level of education as a high school diploma or associate/technical degree. Men held advanced degrees in larger proportions than women (53.33 percent doctorates versus 27.22 percent doctorates). However, 46.67 percent of the men reported that the doctorate was required for their jobs compared to only 16.46 percent for women.

Length of Employment

How long do AECT members work in the field? The study indicated that 34.55 percent have been employed in the field for 10 years or less; 45.68 percent reported working from 11 to 20 years; 17.95 percent from 21 to 30 years, while not quite 4 percent indicated a period of 31 to 40 years.

Many individuals experience job mobility: 45.68 percent have been in their present position for 5 years or less, while 33.86 percent have had the same job for more than 10 years.

An examination of the number of years in the field by gender reveals that women's participation in the field in significant numbers is a relatively recent trend, beginning approximately 18 years ago. Men and women report employment as educational technologists in approximately equal numbers for the last 10 years. Individuals having 13 years or more in the field are predominately male. Males reported an average of 15.4 years of employment compared to 12.6 for females.

Work Basis

The majority of respondents are hired on a 12-month basis (59.32 percent), with employment on a 9-month basis being reported by 21.59 percent of the persons surveyed. Less than 1 percent (0.91) of the respondents reported that they were employed for the duration of a specific project. The remainder of the respondents reported being employed for terms which did not fall into any of the three categories mentioned above.

Sources of Funding

Respondents reported that funding sources for their positions were as follows: 64.58 percent from governmental appropriations (federal, state, or local); 27.05 percent from profits, tuition, or other income generated by the institution; 5.87 percent from other sources.

Work Setting

Table 37.2 provides the reported distribution of AECT members by work setting. Colleges and universities remain the single largest employer of members (42.14 percent), while school districts ranked second (16.63 percent). These were followed by individual secondary schools, junior/community colleges/technical institutes, commercial/business/industry, other, and regional media service centers. All other work settings were reported at statistically insignificant levels.

Table 37.2.
AECT Membership by Work Setting

	1983		1986		Change	
	N	%	N	%	N	%
Individual Elementary School	18	3.82	15	3.42	-3	-10.59
Individual Secondary School	43	9.13	40	9.11	-3	-0.20
School District	58	12.31	73	16.63	15	35.04
Commercial/Business/Industry	33	7.01	25	5.69	-8	-18.72
Military	3	0.64	3	0.68	0	7.29
Junior/Community College/ Technical Institute	45	9.55	35	7.97	-10	-16.55
Regional Media Service Center	20	4.25	24	5.47	4	28.75
College/University	197	41.83	185	42.14	-12	0.75
Government Department of Education	4	0.85	13	2.96	9	248.69
Nonprofit Organization	12	2.55	1	0.23	-11	-91.06
Other	38	8.07	25	5.69	-13	-29.41
TOTAL	471	100.00	439	100.00		

Approximately one-half (50.11 percent) of the survey respondents were employed in settings which could be collectively categorized as higher education. Slightly over 29 percent reported K-12 employment.

When compared with similar data from the 1983 study, increases were noted in the percentage of educational technologists employed by government departments of education, regional media service centers, and school districts. Employment in elementary schools, business/industry, junior/community colleges, and nonprofit organizations declined.

Table 37.3, page 404, provides data relative to gender and occupation as reported for each work setting. When compared with the overall gender distribution of AECT (male 64 percent, female 36 percent), the authors found a significantly higher proportion of females employed by elementary schools, government departments of education, and business/industry. A similar trend was reported for males employed by junior/community colleges and regional media service centers. The male/female distribution in other work settings was near that of the general membership.

Occupations

Librarian/information specialists and audiovisual specialists were most often employed in K-12 settings, while members employed by institutions of higher education tended to work as media directors and teachers/professors (table 37.3). Curricula/instructional developers and researchers/consultants were found principally in the commercial/business/industry sector.

The majority of individuals responding to the survey indicated having responsibilities in two or more of the occupations described on the questionnaire. The primary responsibilities given and their frequencies are listed in table 37.4, page 405.

The general membership of the association appears to be increasingly composed of individuals having administrative and/or teaching responsibilities. These categories comprised 58.64 percent of the membership in 1986, whereas they accounted for only 39.48 percent in 1983 (a composite increase of 48.53 percent). On the other hand, reported employment as television producer/director, researcher/consultant, and audiovisual specialist declined between 1983 and 1986 by 66.13 percent, 68.12 percent, and 28.18 percent, respectively. The authors suspect a correlation between lowered numbers of persons employed in those categories and a decline in the general membership during the same period.

Compensation

The general salary range reported for AECT members as a whole extended from less than $10,000.00 to greater than $60,999.00, with a mean of $34,736.00. The mean salary in the 1983 study was $29,672.00. When analyzed as a function of the work setting (table 37.5, page 405), the authors found that at $40,500.00, the average salary of individuals employed in regional media service centers exceeded the average salary of each of the other work settings. As in 1983, the work setting providing the lowest average annual salary was that of the individual elementary school. However, 80 percent of those members were employed on a 9-month basis. When extrapolated to 12 months, the yearly average would project to $37,244.00.

With the effect of inflation factored in, the authors found that most members realized modest gains in terms of "real dollars." Members working in business/industry lost ground, while those in regional media service centers, secondary schools, and nonprofit organizations made significant gains.

Table 37.3
Gender and Occupation Distribution by Work Setting (In Percengages)

	Male	Female	Occupation* A	B	C	D	E	F	G	H	I
Individual Elementary School	26.67	73.33	9.99	60.00	20.00	6.67	13.33	0.00	0.00	0.00	0.00
Individual Secondary School	60.00	40.00	30.00	30.00	20.00	0.00	0.00	0.00	0.00	0.00	0.00
School District	67.12	32.88	17.81	6.85	61.64	4.11	1.37	4.11	2.74	1.37	0.00
Commercial/Business/Industry	56.00	44.00	8.00	0.00	4.00	8.00	0.00	52.00	4.00	8.00	16.00
Military	66.66	33.34	0.00	0.00	33.33	33.33	0.00	33.33	0.00	0.00	0.00
Junior/Community College/ Technical Institute	80.00	20.00	8.57	11.43	57.14	8.57	11.43	0.00	0.00	2.86	0.00
Regional Media Service Center	79.17	20.83	0.00	8.33	87.50	0.00	0.00	0.00	0.00	4.17	0.00
College/University	68.11	31.89	7.03	3.24	36.76	7.03	34.05	5.41	4.32	1.62	0.54
Government Department of Education	38.46	61.54	15.38	0.00	46.15	15.38	0.00	7.69	0.00	0.00	15.38
Nonprofit Organization	100.00	0.00	0.00	0.00	0.00	0.00	0.00	0.00	0.00	100.00	0.00
Other	52.00	48.00	4.00	16.00	24.00	24.00	8.00	8.00	4.00	0.00	12.00

*Occupation

A, Audiovisual specialist
B, Library/information specialist
C, Media director
D, Other educational administrator
E, Teacher/professor

F, Curricula/instructional developer
G, Television producer/director
H, Educational computing specialist/director
I, Researcher/consultant

Tabler 37.4.
Primary Occupations

	1983 %	1986 %	Change %
Media Director	25.03	40.91	63.44
Audiovisual Specialist	14.55	10.45	-28.18
Teacher/Professor	14.45	17.73	22.70
Library/Information Specialist	10.58	9.55	-9.74
Curricula/Instructional Developer	9.42	7.05	-25.16
Television Producer/Director	8.06	2.73	-66.13
Researcher/Consultant	7.12	2.27	-68.12
Educational Computing Specialist/Director	5.76	2.05	-64.41
Other Educational Administrator	5.03	7.27	44.53

Table 37.5.
Compensation by Work Setting

Work Setting	1983 Average $	1986 Average $	Adjusted 1986 Average (CPI)* $	Income Gain/Loss $	Gain/Loss %
Commercial/Business/Industry	34,635	36,520	33,260	(1,375)	-3.97
Military	34,332	39,666	36,126	1,794	5.22
Government Department of Education	32,999	37,000	33,698	699	2.12
School District	31,982	37,054	33,747	1,765	5.52
Regional Media Service Center	31,899	40,500	36,885	4,986	15.63
Junior/Community College/ Technical Institute	29,488	33,971	30,939	1,451	4.92
College/University	29,455	33,281	30,311	856	2.90
Other	28,221	39,960	36,393	8,172	28.96
Nonprofit Organization	27,332	33,000	30,055	2,723	9.96
Individual Secondary School	26,208	31,800	28,962	2,754	10.51
Individual Elementary School	24,666	27,933	25,440	774	3.14

*Adjusted for 1983-86 rise in Consumer Price Index.

By examining salary as a function of occupation, the authors found that, as in 1983, individuals employed as other educational administrators received the greatest mean salary ($41,687.00). Educational computing specialists/directors dropped to the lowest position, reporting an average annual salary at $27,000.00. Library/information specialists realized the greatest gains over inflation, followed by media directors, and researchers/consultants. Educational computing specialists were the biggest losers to inflation, followed by teachers/professors, and television producers/directors. Other occupations showed modest gains (table 37.6).

Table 37.6.
Average Annual Salaries by Occupation

	1983 Average $	1986 Average $	Adjusted 1986 Average (CPI)* $	Income Gain/Loss $	Gain/Loss %
Other Educational Administrator	36,666	41,687	37,966	1,300	3.55
Media Director	31,119	37,882	34,446	3,327	10.69
Teacher/Professor	30,923	31,884	29,038	(1,885)	-6.09
Researcher/Consultant	30,500	37,100	33,789	3,289	10.78
Television Producer/Director	30,476	32,166	29,295	(1,181)	-3.87
Curricula/Instructional Developer	30,148	35,516	32,346	2,198	7.29
Educational Computing Specialist/ Director	28,500	27,000	24,590	(3,910)	-13.72
Audiovisual Specialist	24,346	27,434	24,985	639	2.63
Library/Information Specialist	23,983	30,761	28,015	4,032	16.81

*Adjusted for 1983-86 rise in Consumer Price Index.

There was a positive relationship between education achieved and salary. The average annual salary received by members reporting high school diplomas as their highest level of formal education was $25,000.00. Individuals holding doctorates received an average of $39,496.00 annually. Table 37.7 shows salaries relative to education achieved. As in the previous study, the greatest incremental difference between levels remains between the master's and doctoral degrees. Compensation for the bachelor's degree increased the most over the three-year period (9.90 percent).

The geographical area in which an individual is employed appears to have some influence upon income. Table 37.8 compares salary levels reported among AECT regions in the 1983 and 1986 studies. Although members in Region IX reported the highest average salary ($38,866.00), Region I realized the greatest net increase over the last three years (23.60 percent). Regions VI and VIII lost ground to inflation.

Table 37.7.
Average Income by Education Attained

	1983 Average $	1986 Average $	Adjusted 1986 Average (CPI)* $	Income Gain/Loss $	Gain/Loss %
High School Diploma	21,800	25,000	22,769	969	4.44
Associate/Technical Degree	24,333	27,800	25,319	986	4.05
Bachelor's Degree	25,041	30,217	27,520	2,479	9.90
Master's Degree	28,054	32,415	29,522	1,468	5.23
Doctorate	34,378	39,496	35,971	1,593	4.63

*Adjusted for 1983-86 rise in Consumer Price Index.

Table 37.8.
Income by AECT Region

AECT Region	1983 Average $	1986 Average $	Adjusted 1986 Average (CPI)* $	Income Gain/Loss $	Gain/Loss %
I	24,453	33,187	30,225	5,772	23.60
II	28,538	34,491	31,413	2,875	10.07
III	26,728	33,571	30,575	3,847	14.39
IV	24,577	32,357	29,469	4,892	19.90
V	31,094	34,578	31,492	398	1.28
VI	32,580	34,791	31,686	(894)	-2.74
VII	28,111	34,508	31,428	3,317	11.80
VIII	28,028	30,724	27,982	(46)	-0.16
IX	31,498	38,866	35,397	3,899	12.38

*Adjusted for 1983-86 rise in Consumer Price Index.

Table 37.9, page 408, presents the results of an analysis of salary levels as a function of the combined variables of work setting and occupation. As stated previously, many AECT members have diverse responsibilities, cutting across the occupational categories investigated. Therefore, the figures presented are from computations based upon the primary responsibility reported on each returned questionnaire.

Table 37.9.
Income by Work Setting and Occupation (In Dollars)

					Occupation*				
	A	B	C	D	E	F	G	H	I
Individual Elementary School	†	27,000	29,666	38,999	24,000	†	†	†	†
Individual Secondary School	30,333	32,666	33,500	35,000	28,000	31,000	†	†	†
School District	31,153	27,800	40,111	33,666	38,999	32,000	34,000	36,999	†
Commercial/Business/Industry	25,000	†	32,999	39,000	†	38,384	32,999	32,000	39,000
Military	†	†	26,999	56,999	†	34,999	†	†	†
Junior/Community College/ Technical Institute	22,333	30,500	37,600	39,000	28,500	†	†	16,999	†
Regional Media Service Center	†	26,000	42,904	†	†	†	†	18,999	†
College/University	23,461	32,333	34,882	44,384	32,920	32,200	29,250	24,333	†
Government Department of Education	20,000	†	39,000	47,000	†	32,999	†	†	40,000
Nonprofit Organization	†	†	†	†	†	†	†	32,999	†
Other	30,999	37,500	48,000	39,333	22,000	35,000	50,999	†	43,000

*Occupation   †None reported.

A, Audiovisual specialist
B, Library/information specialist
C, Media director
D, Other educational administrator
E, Teacher/professor

F, Curricula/instructional developer
G, Television producer/director
H, Educational computing specialist/director
I, Researcher/consultant

Finally, the possible existence of any significant differences between the incomes of men and women was examined. The average annual salary reported by AECT females was $6,659.00 less than their male counterparts ($30,468.00 versus $37,127.00). This is an increase over the $4,050.00 difference found in the 1983 study, and may in part be a result of the facts that, on the average, men had been employed in the field longer and held a higher proportion of advanced degrees than did women. When the employment variables of work setting, occupation, years in position, and education achieved were held constant, no significant differences in salaries were found.

HIGHLIGHTS OF THE SURVEY

1. The mean salary of the survey was $34,736.00.

2. Since 1983, most members realized some degree of gain in terms of real dollars.

3. AECT Region I members realized the greatest net increase since 1983; Region IX members report the highest salaries.

4. When variables of work setting, occupation, years in position, and education achieved were held constant, no significant differences existed between the salaries of men and women.

5. The gender composition is approximately two-thirds male and one-third female.

6. The level of education attained by AECT members frequently surpasses the requirements of the positions held.

7. Colleges and universities employ the largest group of members.

8. The majority of the association's members are employed in administrative or teaching positions.

9. The proportion of respondents who identified themselves as members of an ethnic minority group is small.

10. The mean age of AECT members is 45.5 years.

RECOMMENDATIONS

1. Follow-up studies should be conducted every five years with results reported to the membership.

2. Other organizations need to be made aware of the availability of the data in order that their members receive the information needed for decision making.

3. The association can exercise its leadership role by establishing other types of ongoing studies to report information needed by its members.

REFERENCES

Hutchinson, J. A., & Rankin, P. M. (1984). Survey of salaries, education, and funding in instructional technology. *Instructional Innovator, 29*(4), 14-35.

Molenda, M., & Cambre, M. (1977, April). The 1976 AECT member opinion survey. Income comparisons. *Audiovisual Instruction, 17*, 47-51.

38

Professional Publications and Organizations in Instructional Technology and Related Fields

Donna J. Baumbach
Instructional Technology Resource Center
University of Central Florida

Stephen J. Guynn
Bloomington, Indiana

Gary J. Anglin
Department of Curriculum and Instruction
University of Kentucky

There are many professional publications and organizations that focus on topics of interest to instructional design and technology professionals. In this chapter, some of these are identified. While we have attempted to be thorough in our listings, we have not been exhaustive. There are other excellent organizations and publications that may appeal to special interests of instructional technologists.

First, we present a list of publications of interest. For each journal listed, we have included the name and address of the professional association or the publisher affiliated with the journal. We have also included a brief annotation of the journal's scope and focus. Then, in the next section, we present a list of professional associations of interest to instructional technologists. We have also included the address of the organization and its publication(s).

We wish to thank Mark Yannie of the University of Central Florida for his assistance in providing the most current information available at press time especially for this edition.

PROFESSIONAL PUBLICATIONS

ADCIS News
> Association for the Development of Computer Based Instructional Systems
> International Headquarters
> 1601 W. 5th Avenue, Suite 111
> Columbus, OH 43212
>
> *AN* contains information about activities in the field of computer-based instruction.

Adult Education: A Journal of Research and Theory
> American Association for Adult and Continuing Education
> 2101 Wilson Boulevard, Suite 925
> Arlington, VA 22201
>
> *AE* publishes research literature about adult education issues.

AEDS Journal. See *Journal of Research on Computing in Education*

American Educational Research Journal: A Quarterly Publication of the American Educational Research Association
> American Educational Research Association
> 1230 17th Street, NW
> Washington, DC 20036
>
> *AERJ* reports articles based on controlled, quantitative educational research.

American Journal of Distance Education
> Office for Distance Education/College of Education
> The Pennsylvania State University
> 403 S. Allen Street, Suite 206
> University Park, PA 16801-5202
>
> *AJDE* presents writings on teaching that occurs where teachers and students are separated by distance.

American Psychologist
> American Psychological Association
> 750 1st Street, NE
> Washington, DC 20002-4242
>
> *AP* provides documentation about the American Psychological Association's research interests including recent scientific and practical developments.

Aspects of Educational Technology. Continues *Programmed Learning & Educational Technology*
> Association for Educational and Training Technology
> Centre for Continuing Education
> Northhampton Square
> London EC1V 0MB
> England
>
> *AET* presents articles related to educational and training technology.

Audiovisual Instruction. See *TechTrends*

AV Communications Review. See *Educational Communication and Technology*

British Journal of Educational Technology
    Council for Educational Technology for the United Kingdom
    Sir William Lyons Road
    University Science Park
    Coventry CV4 7EZ
    England

    BJET provides practical and research writings across a wide range of educational technology issues.

Canadian Journal of Educational Communication. Continues *Media Message*
    The Queensway, Suite 1318
    Etobicoke, Ontario M90 5H5
    Canada

    CJEC is the journal of the Association for Media and Technology in Education in Canada.

Computers and Education
    Elsevier Science Ltd.
    P. O. Box 880
    Kidlington, Oxford OX5 1DN
    England
        or
    Elsevier Science
    660 White Plains Road
    Tarrytown, NY 10591-5153

    CE features technical research project reports.

Education and Computing: The International Journal
    Elsevier Science Publishers B. V.
    Postbus 211
    100 AE Amsterdam
    The Netherlands

    EC is an international journal with articles about education and computing.

Educational Communication and Technology: A Journal of Theory, Research and Development.
    See *Educational Technology Research and Development*

Educational Researcher
    American Educational Research Association
    1230 17th Street, NW
    Washington, DC 20036

    ER is primarily devoted to discussing research methods and the ways research is reported and used.

Educational Technology
    Educational Technology Publications, Inc.
    700 Palisades Avenue
    Englewood Cliffs, NJ 07632

    ET articles include research reports, brief literature summaries, and opinion pieces.

Educational Technology Research and Development. Continues *Educational Communication and Technology Journal, AV Communication Review,* and *Journal of Instructional Development*
Association for Educational Communications and Technology
1025 Vermont Avenue, NW, Suite 820
Washington, DC 20005-3516

ETRD is a scholarly journal for educators interested in instructional technology and its applications to effective teaching and learning.

Evaluation and Program Planning
Elsevier Science Ltd.
P. O. Box 880
Kidlington, Oxford OX5 1DN
England
        or
Elsevier Science
660 White Plains Road
Tarrytown, NY 10591-5153

EPP reviews innovative means of data analysis, interpretation, and evaluation.

Instructional Innovator. See *TechTrends*

Instructional Science: An International Journal
Martinus Nijhoss Publishers
c/o Kluwer Academic Publishers
Distribution Center
101 Philip Drive
Norwell, MA 02061

IS is a communication forum for its readers in education, psychology, and the social sciences.

Journal of Computer Assisted Learning
Blackwell Scientific Publications, Ltd.
Osney Mead
Oxford OX2 0EL
England

JCAL publishes articles on topics of interest to computer-assisted learning advocates.

Journal of Computer-Based Instruction
Association for the Development of Computer Based Instructional Systems
International Headquarters
1601 W. 5th Avenue, Suite 111
Columbus, OH 43212

JCBI includes scholarly research and descriptions of practical computer-based instruction techniques.

Journal of Educational Computing Research
Baywood Publishing Co.
P. O. Box 337
26 Austin Avenue
Amityville, NY 11701

JECR includes articles concerning the pedagogical uses of computers.

Journal of Educational Psychology
American Psychological Association
750 1st Street, NE
Washington, DC 20002-4242

JEP publishes research articles in educational psychology.

Journal of Educational Technology Systems
(Society for Applied Learning Technology)
Baywood Publishing Co.
26 Austin Avenue
Amityville, NY 11701

JETS discusses applications and issues related to enhancing productivity through the appropriate utilization of technology in education, training, and job performance.

Journal of Educational Television
Educational Television Association (UK)
Carfax Publishing Co.
P. O. Box 25
Abington, Oxfordshire OX14 3UE
England

JET publishes articles about educational television and related educational applications.

Journal of Instructional Development. See *Educational Technology Research and Development*

Journal of Interactive Instruction Development
Communicative Technology Conference
Society for Applied Learning Technology
50 Culpepper Street
Warrenton, VA 22186

JIID is a scholarly journal that focuses on interactive delivery systems.

Journal of Research on Computing in Education
International Society for Technology in Education
University of Oregon
1787 Agate Street
Eugene, OR 97403

JRCE contains reports of research on the use of computers in instructional settings as well as theoretical pieces and book reviews.

Journal of Special Education Technology
Council for Exceptional Children
Technology and Media Division
P. O. Box 328
Peabody College
Nashville, TN 37203

JSET articles illustrate the use of computer-assisted instruction in special education situations.

Journal of Technology and Teacher Education
Society for Information Technology & Teacher Education
c/o Association for the Advancement of Computers in Education
P. O. Box 2966
Charlottesville, VA 22902

JTTE articles include research and projects related to technology and inservice and preservice teacher education.

Journal of Typographical Research. See *Visible Language*

Performance and Instruction. See *Performance & Instruction Journal*

Performance & Instruction Journal. Continues *Performance and Instruction*
National Society for Performance and Instruction
1300 L Street, NW, Suite 1250
Washington, DC 20005

PIJ contains articles of interest to instructional technologists.

Performance Improvement Quarterly
National Society for Performance and Instruction
1300 L Street, NW, Suite 1250
Washington, DC 20005

PIQ is a journal addressed to professionals in the practice of human performance technology and its related disciplines.

Programmed Learning & Educational Technology. See *Aspects of Educational Technology*

School Library Media Quarterly
American Association of School Librarians
50 E. Huron Street
Chicago, IL 60611

SLMQ presents practical and analytical articles useful to instructional technologists interested in school library media centers.

Simulation and Gaming: An International Journal of Theory, Design and Research
Association for Business Simulation and Experiential Learning
Sage Publications, Inc.
2455 Teller Road
Newbury Park, CA 91320

SG includes research, design, and theoretical articles on games and computer simulations.

Studies in Adult Education. See *Studies in the Education of Adults*

Studies in the Education of Adults. Continues *Studies in Adult Education*
National Institute of Adult Continuing Education
21 De Monfort Street
Leicester LE1 7GE London
England

SEA publishes adult and continuing education information focusing on the United Kingdom educational environment.

TechTrends: For Leaders in Education and Training. Continues *Audiovisual Instruction* and *Instructional Innovator*
Association for Educational Communications and Technology
1025 Vermont Avenue, NW, Suite 820
Washington, DC 20005-3516

TT includes articles on various instructional technology topics and issues.

Training: The Magazine of Human Resources Development
Lakewood Publications, Inc.
50 S. Ninth Street
Minneapolis, MN 55402

T contains training-related articles for training managers in business, government, and health-care settings.

Training and Development
American Society for Training and Development
P. O. Box 1443
1640 King Street
Alexandria, VA 22313

TD publishes articles supporting the professional interests of training managers and developers.

Visible Language: The Quarterly Concerned with All That Is Involved in Our Being Literate.
Continues *Journal of Typographic Research*
Rhode Island School of Design
2 College Street
Providence, RI 02903

VL presents research results and discussion concerning the role of written language.

PROFESSIONAL ORGANIZATIONS

American Association for Adult and Continuing Education
1101 Connecticut Avenue, NW, Suite 700
Washington, DC 20036

Publication: *Adult Education*

American Association of School Librarians
50 E. Huron Street
Chicago, IL 60611

Publication: *School Library Media Quarterly*

American Educational Research Association
1230 17th Street, NW
Washington, DC 20036

Publications: *American Educational Research Journal*; *Educational Researcher*

American Psychological Association
750 1st Street, NE
Washington, DC 20002-4242

Publications: *American Psychologist*; *Journal of Educational Psychology*

American Society for Training and Development
P. O. Box 1443
1640 King Street
Alexandria, VA 22313

Publication: *Training and Development*

Association for Business Simulation and Experiential Learning
Sage Publications, Inc.
2455 Teller Road
Newbury Park, CA 91320

Publication: *Simulations and Gaming*

Association for Educational Communications and Technology
1025 Vermont Avenue, NW, Suite 820
Washington, DC 20005-3516

Publications: *Educational Technology Research and Development*; *TechTrends*

Association for Educational and Training Technology
Centre for Continuing Education
Northhampton Square
London EC1V 0MB
England

Publication: *Aspects of Educational Technology*

Association for Media and Technology in Education in Canada
500 Victoria Road
North Guelph, Ontario N1E 6K2
Canada

Publication: *Canadian Journal of Educational Communication*

Association for the Development of Computer Based Instructional Systems
International Headquarters
1601 W. 5th Avenue, Suite 111
Columbus, OH 43212

Publications: *ADCIS News*; *Journal of Computer-Based Instruction*

Association of Special Education Technology
Council for Exceptional Children
Technology and Media Division
P. O. Box 328
Peabody College
Nashville, TN 37203

Publication: *Journal of Special Education Technology*

Council for Educational Technology for the United Kingdom
Sir William Lyons Road
University Science Park
Coventry CV4 7EZ
England

Publication: *British Journal of Educational Technology*

Educational Television Association (UK)
Carfax Publishing Co.
P. O. Box 25
Abington, Oxfordshire OX14 3UE
England

Publication: *Journal of Educational Television*

International Society for Technology in Education
University of Oregon
1787 Agate Street
Eugene, OR 97403

Publication: *Journal of Research on Computing in Education*

National Society for Performance and Instruction
1300 L Street, NW, Suite 1250
Washington, DC 20005

Publications: *Performance Improvement Quarterly*; *Performance & Instruction Journal*

Society for Applied Learning Technology
50 Culpepper Street
Warrenton, VA 22186

Publications: *Journal of Interactive Instructional Development*; *Journal of Instructional Delivery Systems*

Society for Information Technology & Teacher Education

c/o Association for the Advancement of Computers in Education
P. O. Box 2966
Charlottesville, VA 22902

Publication: *Journal of Technology and Teacher Education*

Index

Catalytic rationale (reason for computer use), 46
CD-ROM, 28, 260, 308, 309, 311, 312
Center for Scholarly Technology (University of
    Southern California), 45
Central Educational Network, 298
CERN. *See* European Particle Physics
    Laboratory
Certification
    assessment center approach, 397
    defined, 393
    and professional competencies, 394-96
Channel One, 48, 297, 333, 334
Child abuse, 89
Children's Television Act of 1990, 52
Children's Television Workshop, 297, 301
CICS Maintenance course, 380-81
*CIJE. See Current Index to Journals in
    Education*
Clark, Richard, 154
Clientele (of ISD), 91
Clients, needs of, 243-44
CNN Newsroom, 48
Coaxial cable technology, 43
Cognition, 366
Cognitive apprenticeship, 107-8
Cognitive mapping, 209
Cognitive science, 53, 57
    constructivist, 103-4
    constructivist approach applied to instruc-
        tional design, 104-9
    definition, 102
    everyday cognition, 152, 157fig.
    expert cognition, 157fig.
    and objectivism, 102-3
    plans. *See* Plans
    traditional, 102-3
Cognitivist, paradigm, 146-47
    and "life world" of learner, 149
    and situated learning paradigm, 151fig.,
        158-59
COIK formula (clear only if known), 266
Collaboration, training for, 123
Collaborative learning strategies, 122-23
Comenius, Johann, 96-97
Commission on Instructional Technology, 5, 6
Commtex, 53
Communication systems and social institutions,
    69-70
Compact discs. *See* CD-ROM
Component display theory, 209
Computer Curriculum Corporation, 49
Computer Science Network, 265
Computer-based instruction, 215, 281
    and artificial intelligence, 218-19
    and automated development tools, 219
    displays, 227-28
    and expert systems, 219
    feedback, 217-18
    and impact of computer technology advances,
        218-19

    learner control, 216-17
    and multi-media systems, 218
    screen design, 216
Computer-based technology, 43
Computers, 45-46, 55, 260-61. *See also*
    Computer-based instruction
    Apple II+, 308, 312
    cost-effectiveness in school settings, 361
    graphics programs, 308, 309-310
    IBM-PC, 308
    in instructional development, 17-18
    and instructional media, 308, 312
    and journalism, 75
    and legal profession, 74-75
    Macintosh, 309
    1980s, 308
    printers, 279
    reasons for use in schools, 46
Conant, Eaton H., 75
Conceptual hierarchy analysis, 210
Constructivism, 41, 53
Constructivist orientation, 119
Consulting
    Block's approach, 233-34
    contracts, 236-38
    defining who the client is, 238
    "flawless," 233-34, 236-38
    hazards of, 239
    language usage, 238
    stages of development, 234-35
    types of, 234
Control (in design), 246
Cooperative learning strategies, 88-89, 122-23
Corporation for Public Broadcasting, 49, 298,
    302
Covey, Stephen, 116
Craver, Kathleen, 248
Criterion-referenced measures, 16
Critical incident technique, 210
Critical inquiry, 335
Cross-age tutoring, 89
Crosscultural, 53
CSNET (Computer Science Network), 265
C-Span, 48
Current Index to Journals in Education (CIJE),
    53
Cybernetic multimedia environment, 120
Cyberspace, 265

Dalton Plan, 13
Definition of Educational Technology, The, 57
Delphi technique, 210
Democratic multimedia environment, 120
Derrida, Jacques, 116
Design guidelines, 367-70
Design theory, 85. *See also* Instructional design
Designers, perspective of, 243
Desktop publishing programs, 310
Dewey, John, 80-81